African polyphony and polyrhythm

This work is devoted to the subject of polyphony and polyrhythm in Central Africa. It is divided into six independent parts. The first is a general introduction to the *social* and *typological* aspects of traditional Central African music.

The second concerns the execution of polyphonic music throughout Sub-Saharan Africa. The first section of this part contains a *proposal for classification* of the various techniques employed. The second provides a chronological listing and a critical analysis of source materials on polyphony of the African continent (diverse reports and descriptions from 1497 to the 1920s).

The third part deals with the available *technological tools*, i.e., with how polyphonic music transmitted by oral tradition can be studied, the various ways of recording it, and a detailed description of the author's method, its theoretical basis and its anthropological validity.

The fourth part deals with the *conceptual tools*: the notion of relevance the question of transcription of orally transmitted music and the analytical procedures applied to it.

The fifth part is devoted to the *temporal structuring* of African music. This point is of capital importance for understanding Central African polyphony and polyrhythmics. A description of the principles underlying the temporal organisation of traditional Sub-Saharan music is here provided.

The sixth and last part deals with the diverse *polyphonic and polyrhythmic techniques* to be found in the Central African Republic. A typology is proposed, and separate chapters are then devoted to each of the four categories which are set up, and to their underlying principles. These chapters are illustrated with over 450 music examples.

Each part is intended to be self-contained so that it can be read independently. This is expressed by the division of the work into *Books*.

African polyphony and polyrhythm

Musical structure and methodology

SIMHA AROM

Translated from French by
MARTIN THOM, BARBARA TUCKETT and
RAYMOND BOYD

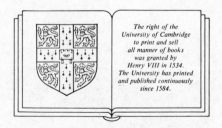

CAMBRIDGE UNIVERSITY PRESS
Cambridge   New York   Melbourne   Sydney

EDITIONS DE
LA MAISON DES SCIENCES DE L'HOMME
Paris

Published by the Press Syndicate of the University of Cambridge
The Pitt Building, Trumpington Street, Cambridge CB2 1RP
40 West 20th Street, New York, NY 10011, USA
10 Stamford Road, Oakleigh, Melbourne 3166, Australia
and Editions de la Maison des Sciences de l'Homme
54 Boulevard Raspail, 75270 Paris Cedex 06

First published in French as
*Polyphonies et polyrythmies
instrumentales d'Afrique Centrale*
by SELAF 1985

First published in English by
Cambridge University Press 1991, as
African Polyphony and Polyrhythm

Printed in Great Britain at the University Press, Cambridge

British Library cataloguing in publication data

Arom, Simha
African polyphony and polyrhythm: musical structure and
methodology.
1. African music
I. Title
781.76

Library of Congress cataloguing in publication data

Arom, Simha.
[Polyphonies et polyrythmies instrumentales d'Afrique centrale. English]
African polyphony and polyrhythm: musical structure and
methodology/Simha Arom; translated by Martin Thom, Barbara
Tuckett, and Raymond Boyd.
    p.   cm.
Translation of: Polyphonies et polyrythmies instrumentales d'Afrique centrale.
Includes bibliographical references and index.
ISBN 0-521-24160-X
1. Music–Africa, Central–History and criticism.
2. Counterpoint. 3. Musical meter and rhythm. I. Title.
ML350.A7613 1991
781.2′84′0967–dc20

ISBN 0 521 24160 X hardback
ISBN 2 7351 0378 1 hardback (France only)

ME

In memory of my parents Liba and David, who died in Auschwitz, as did so many other innocent victims of the worst consequences of racism.

Master: What do you think? Can people who play flutes or guitars or other instruments of the same kind be in any way compared to a nightingale?

Disciple: No.

M: What then makes them different?

D: I would say that the musicians have some sort of art, but the bird only sings by its own nature. . .

M: You believe that art is some kind of reasoned activity, and that those who make use of it make use of reason, do you not?

D: I do.

M: Whoever is unable to make use of reason cannot then make use of his artistic faculty.

D: Definitely not.   (Augustine, *De musica*, I, iv, 6)

There is no music in the proper sense *unless man imposes some kind of order.*
                                                                    (Chailley 1963: 295)

Theory is the moment of scientific revolution, a Sunday for science; the other six days are left for observing, experimenting, and classifying.   (Molino 1975: 56)

The proof of the analysis is in the synthesis.   (Lévi-Strauss 1960: 25)

None of the procedures or properties which we esteem characteristic of music endowed with a writing system cannot be found to some extent in music from oral traditions. In the final analysis, the difference between these two kinds of music may lie not so much in what one of them has and the other has not, as in what one of them still has and the other no longer has.   (Schaeffner 1936: 342)

Contents

BOOK VI STRUCTURAL PRINCIPLES AND THEIR APPLICATION

Illustrations

Foreword *by György Ligeti*

In autumn 1982 a former student of mine, the Puerto Rican composer Roberto Sierra, brought to my attention a collection of instrumental and vocal ensemble music of the Banda-Linda tribe from the Central African Republic, recorded by Simha Arom. The record 'Banda Polyphonies', then several years old, was no longer available so I re-recorded it on to a cassette and made a photocopy of Arom's introductory text. Having never before heard anything quite like it, I listened to it repeatedly and was then, as I still am, deeply impressed by this marvellous polyphonic, polyrhythmic music with its astonishing complexity.

For many years I have been fascinated by the musical epoch from Vitry and Machault to Ciconia, and since my acquaintance with his work in 1980, by the music of Conlon Nancarrow. Undoubtedly my interest in the music Arom has recorded stems also from the proximity I feel exists between it and my own way of thinking with regards to composition: that is, the creation of structures which are both remarkably simple and highly complex. The formal simplicity of sub-Saharan African music with its unchanging repetition of periods of equal length, like the uniform pearls of a necklace, is in sharp contrast to the inner structure of these periods which, because of simultaneous superpositioning of different rhythmic patterns, possesses an extraordinary degree of complexity. Gradually, through repeated listening, I became aware of this music's paradoxical nature: the patterns performed by the individual musicians are quite different from those which result from their combination. In fact, the ensemble's superpattern is in itself not played and exists only as an illusory outline. I also began to sense a strong inner tension between the relentlessness of the constant, never-changing pulse coupled with the absolute symmetry of the formal architecture on the one hand and the asymmetrical internal divisions of the patterns on the other. What we can witness in this music is a wonderful combination of order and disorder which in turn merges together producing a sense of order on a higher level.

Since my first introduction to the music of the Banda Linda, I have had the opportunity of listening to diverse recordings of sub-Saharan music collected by Simha Arom, Hugo Zemp, Gerhard Kubik, Alfons Dauer and many other ethnomusicologists. During the spring of 1984, while in Jerusalem, I met with Simha Arom, at which time he showed me his transcriptions in full score of this and other Central African music and explained to me their melodic and rhythmic structure.

Needless to say I was greatly impressed by his ingenuity at realising a notation of such complex music. The immense difficulty lies in the fact that the human ear and brain cannot distill the separate rhythmic patterns of the individual players from the intricate rhythmic labyrinth of the ensemble. Arom's method of extracting the individual parts is as efficient as it is simple: by recording separately each player, the score can then be reconstructed part for part. Unfortunately, as the parts function only in terms of the collective structure and have in themselves no autonomous 'meaning', the performers have neither learned nor practised their parts individually and are virtually unable to play them without hearing the complete ensemble. Arom elegantly circumvenes this problem by providing each musician in turn with headphones through which he hears a recording of the complete ensemble. This allows the musician to play his part 'alone' and for it to be separately recorded and later transcribed.

I consider Simha Arom's fundamental work to be of equal importance for both the scientific and the musical world. For the ethnological research of African culture, the technique of playback and subsequent recording provides the material essential to fruitful investigation and better understanding of the structure of this highly sophisticated music culture. For composition, it opens the door leading to a new way of thinking about polyphony, one which is completely different from the European metric structures, but equally rich, or maybe, considering the possibility of using a quick pulse as a 'common denominator' upon which various patterns can be polyrhythmically superimposed, even richer than the European tradition.

Preface

When I got off the plane in Bangui, the capital of the Central African Republic, on 30 November 1963, it was the first time I had ever set foot on the African continent. I had no idea that this date was to mark a turning point in my career.

The country was celebrating the anniversary of its independence on the following day, 1 December. Groups from several provinces were to put on shows of traditional music during the festivities. Within twenty-four hours, I was thus able to make myself acquainted with a variety of the types and techniques of the country's music.

At the time I was a performing musician and played the French horn in a symphony orchestra. For me, as for many Europeans in the 1960s, there was no 'real' music outside Western music. I was conditioned by a cultural background too narrow to allow easy comprehension of anything as different and as disconcerting (in the etymological sense of the word) as African music. I thus found myself suddenly plunged into a universe of sound which was as strange to me as it was unexpected: there were groups of percussion instruments playing tightly interlocked rhythms, orchestras of up to twenty wind instruments in which each musician would play only a single note in an extremely strict and precise polyphonic latticework, choirs singing incredibly complex and yet perfectly coherent contrapuntal music, and many other surprises. Everything was performed from memory with no conductor to provide coordination. The extent to which the performers were apparently unconstrained was equally bewildering.

The result of this first encounter was 'love at first sight'. I was struck by the diversity, colour, and vitality which flowed from this music, and found its complexity a challenge to myself as a musician. I was intrigued by the elusiveness of something 'always the same though never the same', and by the way the performing techniques appeared to ally constraint with freedom. My first intuitive impression (which time has confirmed) was nevertheless that, in all the types of music I had heard, there were principles of similarity hidden beneath countless variations. My initial reactions of shock and stimulation drew me gradually into the study of traditional Central African music.

My new career received a strong boost from a four-year stay in Bangui which allowed me to make many trips about the country, at times to very out-of-the-way places. This gave me the chance to make initial contact with several ethnic groups and obtain information about their music. At the same time, I became acquainted with the way in which their music was traditionally performed and got both overall and close-up views of the practices it involved. I noticed certain regularities and common principles, but also differences, for example in the use of instruments and compositional techniques. During this lengthy period in direct contact with the music, I was able to make many recordings and some first attempts at analysing some of the repertories.

While conventional field recording techniques might have sufficed for transcribing and analysing monodic music, polyphony and polyrhythmics were a different question. The interweaving of the vocal and instrumental parts was such that they could not be untangled, even by the most experienced ear. It was relatively easy to get each of the constituent parts alone, but proper transcription and analysis required more: the real problem was to find out *how they fitted together*.

It was only much later (in 1971) that I had the idea of trying to overcome this difficulty by adapting the *playback*, or *re-recording* technique, which is widely used in Western popular music, to field conditions. This meant starting with a conventional stereophonic recording of a polyphonic piece (used as the reference version), and reconstructing it part by part. The musicians play their parts, one after the other, while listening through headphones to the previously recorded part or parts. Only the first musician uses the full version of the piece as his guide for reproducing and synchronising his own part (see below, Book III).

This *experimental method* was tried out for the first time during field work in 1972. The results were fully satisfactory and opened the way for further research, which is presented in this work.

There are four different but complementary fields of ethnomusicological research:

(1)   the study of the social aspects of music
(2)   the study of the 'tools' that produce it (the voice and musical instruments)
(3)   the study of the way the users conceive of it and
(4)   the study of music as a system.

There is a certain ambiguity in the name of the discipline itself. This is clear from the meaning attached to it in different languages. In German, *Musikethnologie*, the ethnology of music, implies that the ethnological aspect takes priority. But the French *ethnomusicologie* (like the English 'ethnomusicology', the musicology of ethnic groups) suggests that the musicological aspect is primary.

This work firmly embraces the latter outlook: it is a *musicological* study of Central African polyphony and polyrhythmics. I take the view that musicology deals essentially with the study of *music* as a part of the sociocultural system which is native to its performers.

All ethnic music, whatever its social function, displays a systematic organisation. It has a grammar, just like a language, and is thus governed by rules which underlie a theory, even if the latter is almost always *implicit*.

Since music has no semantic density, it is evidently a purely *formal* system. To paraphrase Saussure's view of language, music 'is a system which refuses all ordering but its own' (1916: 43). This, of course, does not imply that certain languages or musical systems practised within a single geocultural area will not have a variety of common features attributable to their history, development, or cultural affinities.

The primary object of this work is to describe the principles underlying the musical system of traditional Central African polyphony and polyrhythm. In this context, a *description* should do four things:

(1)   it should list the procedures used in music of this kind, and classify them in a *typology*;
(2)   for each type of procedure observed, there must be an explanation of

how it is organised, both vertically (in terms of the 'con-sonance' and inter-weaving of the parts) and horizontally (the temporal organisation and syntax). In other words, its internal coherence must be displayed;

(3)   the description must include a detailed analysis of each piece, i.e. show how its parts are divided into segments (on the basis of the principles of recurrence and substitution), what variations are possible, and where the points of substitution are located;

(4)   finally, for each part, it must determine the ultimate reference used by the musician as a *model*; this is a condensed (in fact 'minimal') formula with respect to which all variations are produced, and which summarises all of the part's characteristic features, and *only these*. Modelisation thus allows us to apprehend the relations prevailing between the spontaneous production of a musical event and the idea it springs from. The synthetic model of the poly-phonic or polyrhythmic structure of any piece is, of course, obtained by placing the minimal formulae for each of its constituent parts one above the other.

When we have the models for a number of pieces from a homogeneous set (e.g., a musical category, or a repertory with a certain number of common features), we can define its style, if by style we mean (as Nettl does) 'the aggregate of characteristics which a composition has, and which it shares with others in its cultural complex' (1964: 169).

If our purpose is to describe music transmitted by oral tradition, we must obviously make the musical material itself and its structural principles the *centre* of our attention. Given this starting point, we should try to set up a hierarchical classification of all the kinds of data, both musical and extramusical, which will have to find a place in our description, for *together they constitute a network of multiple polyvalent relationships* (see Arom 1982). Assuming the music to have the central role, we must base our hierar-chy firstly on the *distance of each item in the data from the centre*, and secondly on the establishment of a threshold beyond which ethnological and cultural data are no longer directly related to this centre.

The relationship among the different kinds of data can be visualised as a set of concentric circles. Whether a given item is to be included in any circle will not depend on its belonging to the same type, but *rather on its distance from the elements in the central circle*.

The musical material (the investigator's corpus), and the structural principles he has been able to extract from this corpus and its constituent parts (scales, forms, technical procedures, stylistic features), are *always* in the central circle.

The second circle should contain the material tools and conceptual devices which allow us to substantiate some of the data in the central one. The material tools include the musical instruments and voices. The conceptual devices, which make up the *vernacular metalanguage referring to music*, include the terminology relating to instru-ments, to units into which musical discourse can be broken down, and to categories whose names reflect the differences a given ethnic group recognises in its own music.

The third circle will contain the sociocultural functions of the music in the corpus: how it is connected with rituals, ceremonies, dances and/or attendant circumstances of a social, family, or personal nature. Some of these data display a special relationship to data in the second circle. For example, the common function of all the pieces performed on the occasion of initiation rites is concordant with their inclusion in a category created by the existence of a single term in the language to designate them.

Other circles may be provided where necessary, e.g., a fourth circle may contain general symbolic elements such as myths associated with a given piece, instrument, or vocal/instrumental technique. The data contained in this circle are obviously only weakly relevant with respect to the central one, and lead us away from our main interest (even when there is a rather stronger relationship to data in the second circle). A myth explaining how a repertory was acquired will thus be important for understanding the *Weltanschauung* of a given group, but will not be relevant for our purposes if it has no effect on the musical principles of the repertory. If no *organic* connection can be established between the contents of the fourth and the central circle, we will want to exclude the former from the description as such. We may then rely only on the data in the first three circles in order to establish the coherence of our description.

The intrinsic nature of each circle's relation to the central one thus determines both its contents and its distance from the centre. The degree of 'intrinsicality' is thus stronger between neighbouring circles and weaker when the circles are further away. The outer circle may be relevant and provide support for the description in some cases, but not in others. Even in the latter case, however, its peripheral nature is helpful in enabling us to determine exactly where the outer limit of the field of description lies.

It should thus be clear that we will be limiting ethnological information concerning the sociocultural context for the performance of the music we study to the relevant minimum. The interested reader may consult the bibliography at the end of this work for references to the principal publications on these matters.

We will also treat subjects with a closer connection to ethnomusicology in the same way when they offer no particular enlightenment for our purposes. The reader should thus not expect detailed descriptions of how musical instruments are made, nor explanations of the symbolic elements which often surround such activities. Nor will we transcribe the words to certain songs supported by polyphonic and/or polyrhythmic music. All considerations of an aesthetic nature have been firmly set aside, particularly my own, of course, but also those of the people whose music is under study.

While the construction of musical instruments is not a matter for discussion here, the performing techniques used for melodic instruments (horns and flutes) and polyphonic ones (harps, sanzas, and xylophones) cannot be ignored, since the music they produce is intimately connected with the nature and interaction of their intrinsic capacities. It would, for example, be impossible to understand how the parts performed by each of the xylophone player's hands combine, without some knowledge of how the keys are laid out and assigned to his hands. A brief description will therefore be provided for each instrument studied, explaining its topology, how it is played, and what principles govern its use.

The only possible approach to the study of music from an oral tradition is *synchronic*. We are seeking to describe a *state of music*, something like the *state of a language* which, according to Saussure (1916: 142), 'is not a point, but rather a period of some given length during which the sum total of all modifications is minimal. It may be ten years, a generation, a century, or even longer.'

The synchronic study of music involves observing how it works and determining the laws imposed on it by its own structure at a given historical stage and in a specific cultural context, *independently of its prior evolution*. This is not because we are not interested in the history and development of the music, but rather because we have no way of observing this process. We are constrained by the absence of any written samples, and the paucity (and unreliability) of historical reports. We are thus usually deprived of 'indirect' knowledge of the past, i.e., further back than three or four generations. Under such circumstances, any hypotheses about how music has evolved would be mainly or completely unverifiable. That is why the synchronic approach provides the only sound methodological foundation for the study of the music of societies with no written tradition.

An approach of this kind must nevertheless be largely empirical, since the investigator must start with a *tabula rasa* and try to fill it up by collecting whatever kinds of information are available and seem relevant: recordings of the musical material itself and comments on performance, local classifications, the sociocultural functions of different repertories, and so on. It is as if we had to put together a puzzle with no prior knowledge of the model, the shape of the pieces, or even how many pieces there are. . .

Gradually, however, we begin to see an order, and the internal coherence of the system emerges. It becomes possible to define categories based on the use of identical sets of instruments and specific musical procedures. Vernacular concepts are elicited which, while often metaphorical, correspond to a certain musical reality. In this way, our approach leads us from the *observation of musical activity and its raison d'être to the discovery of an underlying theory.*

The preceding is a brief sketch of how I went about decoding Central African polyphonic and polyrhythmic music. From a strictly technical standpoint, three operations are involved:

(1)   the separation of the constituent parts of the piece under study
(2)   the determination of the way they fit together and
(3)   the ascertainment of the common temporal unit governing them.

If polyphonic parts are to be recorded in *succession* rather than simultaneously, the performers must be placed in an artificial, and to them quite unusual, situation. We should therefore recall that I am proposing an *experimental* method. Book III sets forth the theoretical presuppositions of this method and discusses its inherent drawbacks and advantages. It will therefore be useless to go into these questions at this point. I should only like to remark that many years of experience have convinced me that its benefits far outweigh any failings and, even more importantly, that it can be used without deforming either the musical activity of the voluntary participants or the structure of the music itself. On the contrary, in societies where there is practically no conceptualisation or abstract speculation about the *substance of the music*, the (in every sense of the word) *unheard-of* experience of listening to the parts of a polyphonic construction, first separately, then in combinations of increasing numbers of parts (in successive layers, as it were) provides a strong stimulus to the verbalisation of the musicians' reactions, i.e., to the emergence of the (often implicit) vernacular musical terminology, and thereby makes those who know the tradition aware of the individuality and the complexity of their musical heritage. I may add that the method involves *active* experimentation, insofar as the musicians themselves decide how it should be applied at all stages prior to transcription. The set of operations leading from performance to modelisation of a given piece, like the steps which allow the model to be checked by deriving new versions of the piece from it, are not speculative in nature; rather, they take the material form of recordings made by the traditional musicians themselves.

Another important feature of the re-recording method is that the synthetic reconstruction of musical entities by layers brings about the neutralisation of the classical antinomy opposing the notions of analysis and synthesis. This conflict can now be transformed into the *oscillation* of a permanent dialectical movement.

The corpus providing the ground-work for this study was collected in two stages, the first preparatory and the second operational. The preparatory stage covered the years 1964–7 when, while living in the Central African Republic, I was able to conduct a variety of surveys involving some sixty ethnic groups from various parts of the country. This yielded me recordings and explanatory data for about a thousand pieces of music representing a wide variety of types and categories, and displaying a range of musical principles as put into practise.

Those four years introduced me to the subtleties of Central African traditional music, allowing me to grow accustomed to it and begin to assimilate its principles. By the end of that time, it no longer seemed foreign to me.

The corpus which has yielded all the transcriptions and analyses included in this work was, however, itself collected during the second stage between 1971 and 1983, in the course of eight field trips lasting a total of fifteen months, sponsored by a research group under the aegis of the Centre National de la Recherche Scientifique (CNRS) in France. Since 1976, this group has been known as the Laboratoire de Langues et Civilisations à Tradition Orale (LACITO).

The first analytical recordings were made during a trip in 1972. From then on, all my efforts have been devoted to building up a set of recordings representative of all the types of polyphony and polyrhythm to be found in the Central African Republic. This corpus is comprised of the following material:

(1) conventional stereophonic and analytic (i.e., playback) recordings of over two hundred pieces covering the full range of polyphonic and polyrhythmic procedures

(2) some fifty cassette recordings of survey material, accompanied by explanatory documentation

(3) nearly five hundred colour slides and as many black and white photographs providing visual documentation

(4) some thirty super-8 films with sound track, showing how the musicians behave and react in experimental conditions.

Just as a corpus can have different levels, so can it have different *aspects*. Our recordings, which are intended to be representative of all the polyphonic and polyrhythmic procedures to be found in a geocultural area, can thus be distributed typologically into no more than four categories: strict polyrhythm, hocket polyrhythm, polyphony produced by melodic instruments, and vocal polyphony. None of these constitutes a level in the corpus; rather they are homogeneous elements within the same level (subcorpuses, so to speak). In the course of this work, we will have to establish their internal coherence or relevance and their mutual limits.

At this point, we may introduce the notion of *saturation*. We say that a set is saturated when no further additional item can in any way affect its essential properties. Observation of Central African polyphonic and polyrhythmic procedures shows that the basic principles of their horizontal and vertical organisation can be determined with no more (and usually less) than ten pieces for any type, whatever their ethnic origin. In other words, the internal coherence of each type or category is proven by the fact that no significant change of a systematic nature ever results from adding a new piece. This situation is effectively captured by Jakobson's metaphor: 'As painters used to say, *"un kilo de vert n'est pas plus vert qu'un demi kilo"*' (1960: 374).

Why then have I bothered to collect two hundred pieces? The answer is, to make sure I was right. This required submitting a large number of pieces in each category to the re-recording test. What was initially only an intuition, or at most a hypothesis, could thereby be corroborated.

The use of ethnic criteria would be inappropriate to a study devoted to the analysis of the musical techniques involved in Central African polyphonic and polyrhythmic procedures. Musicological criteria alone, i.e., the procedures themselves, are valid for our purpose, independently of which group uses them. That is why all the music described and analysed hereafter will be classified, not according to its origin or to whatever sociocultural circumstances may be connected with it, but according to the musical techniques it utilises. Although most of the procedures are used by nearly all Central African ethnic groups, music from only seven of these will be sufficiently representative for our descriptive purposes. These groups are: the Zande people who live on the eastern side of the Central African Republic, the Banda-Dakpa, Banda-Linda and Sabanga peoples who inhabit the centre, the Gbaya people in the west, and the Ngbaka people and Aka pygmies in the southwest.

This book is composed of six independent parts. The first is a general introduction to traditional Central African music dealing with its *social* aspects (functions, relationship of music to language and dance, learning processes) and *typological* features (vocal and instrumental music, formal structures, plurivocality, scalar systems, repertories, classification).

The second part looks at polyphonic music in the whole of sub-Saharan Africa. Its first section proposes a *classification* of polyphonic techniques (heterophony, overlapping, drone, parallelism, homophony, ostinato, imitation, hocket, counterpoint). The second contains a *state of the art*, i.e., a chronological presentation of the written sources concerning polyphony on the African continent (reports and descriptions by travellers, missionaries, and colonial administrators from 1497 to the 1920s, and specialised publications thereafter). All are subjected to critical examination.

The third part deals with the *technological tools*, i.e., the difficulties involved in studying polyphony in an oral tradition, the techniques used to record such music, a detailed description of the method on which this work is based and a discussion of its theoretical assumptions and anthropological validity.

The fourth part examines *conceptual devices*: the notion of relevance, the problems involved in transcribing orally transmitted music, and the analytical procedures and ways of substantiating them.

The fifth part is devoted to a subject which goes far beyond the limits of the Central African Republic, but is essential to understanding the country's polyphony and polyrhythm: the *temporal structuring* of African music. This part includes a critical discussion of Western terminology relating to metre and rhythm, a number of proposed definitions in this field, and a description of the principles underlying the temporal organisation of traditional sub-Saharan music.

The sixth and final part deals with the *polyphonic and polyrhythmic techniques* found in the Central African Republic. It begins by proposing a typology, and then devotes a separate chapter to each of four categories and their underlying principles. These are illustrated by numerous transcriptions and analyses of specific pieces. Finally, there is a discussion of the ways in which these different procedures can be found to combine in Central African musical practice.

The subject matter to be dealt with is so varied that, despite their many points of contact, the parts are so presented as to be self-contained, and can be read separately. This is the reason for calling them 'Books'.

PREFACE TO THE ENGLISH EDITION

This book was written between 1978 and 1980 and, after a brief interruption, between 1982 and 1984. Originally commissioned by Cambridge University Press, it was published in French in 1985 under the title *Polyphonies et polyrythmies instrumentales d'Afrique Centrale. Structure et méthodologie.*

The English translation follows the text and bibliography of the French edition. Since then, my research has become more and more focused on the field now termed the cognitive sciences. But it appears, retrospectively, that this cognitive orientation, without being explicitly developed, was already present to some extent in this work.

Acknowledgements

I must first express my gratitude to the government of the Central African Republic, which allowed me to travel throughout the country, assured me the support of local authorities, and made it easy for me to obtain permits to record, take photographs, and make films.

Under the auspices of the Centre National de la Recherche Scientifique, the LACITO (Laboratoire de Langues et Civilisations à Tradition Orale) furnished the necessary material, logistic, and financial support for my field work.

Several people have earned my deepest gratitude in diverse ways. First among these are Jacques Chailley, who supervised my research for many years; the musicians who have taken an active interest in my work, particularly Luciano Berio, Gary Bertini, Pierre Boulez, Alexander Goehr, and György Ligeti; musicologists and ethnomusicologists such as Israël Adler, David Epstein, Jean-Jacques Nattiez, and the members of Equipe de Recherche 165 (also a part of the Centre National de la Recherche Scientifique) directed by Gilbert Rouget; and other scholars such as Maurice Godelier, Abraham Moles and Jean Molino. I have benefited from discussion with all of them.

Jacqueline M.C. Thomas, Luc Bouquiaux (the director and former assistant director, respectively, of the Laboratoire de Langues et Civilisations à Tradition Orale), and France Cloarec-Heiss introduced me to the techniques of phonological description in linguistics, and thereby enabled me to follow new avenues of research into ways of adapting them to the analysis of music of oral tradition. Their encouragement has always been invaluable. They have also accompanied me on field trips and taken a close interest in the work of building up the corpus on which this work is based. I must also thank my young colleague, Vincent Dehoux, who greatly assisted me during my trips to the field. Yves Moñino was instrumental in introducing me to Gbaya musicians. Both he, Jacqueline M.C. Thomas, Luc Bouquiaux, France Cloarec-Heiss, and Raymond Boyd have checked the spelling and meaning of vernacular terms in the languages they have studied.

I am also indebted to those who have read parts of the manuscript and suggested corrections: Didier Alluard, Claude and Frank Alvarez-Pereyre, Jacques Meunier, and particularly Geneviève Dournon and Gilles Cantagrel who followed the preparation of this work from beginning to end.

Finally, I dedicate this book to those whose talent has made it possible: the Aka, Gbaya, Banda-Dakpa, Banda-Linda, Ngbaka, Sabanga, and Zande musicians who have worked with me. May this be the sign of my deep and enduring gratitude, first of all for their participation in the often tedious task of making the analytic recordings, but also for their goodwill, good humour, interest in the work we have done together and, particularly, patience.

Not to be forgotten are all those who have mediated between myself and the musicians by providing indispensable linguistic and psychological assistance. Theirs has been the particularly difficult and delicate task of acting as interpreters, in both senses of the word, for people from two widely differing cultural worlds. They have invariably acted with responsibility, dedication, and perseverance (often even indefatigability), but also with tact, and have given freely of their time, effort and, frequently, ingenuity. When the researcher becomes so close to the people who are customarily called his 'informants', lasting relationships are created. I want to offer particularly warm thanks at this time to my friends, Marcel Mavodé, who assisted me in my work with the Ngbaka people; Barnabé Endjékessé who guided me among the Banda people, and Joseph Ogalema who played the dual role of translator and organiser (or should I say impresario?) while I worked with the Aka pygmies. Severin Gourna accompanied me during my visits among several peoples. His good nature, sensibility, and personal commitment to my projects made my work not merely easier, but also much more enjoyable.

Finally, I offer grateful thanks to Raymond Boyd, Martin Thom and Barbara Tuckett for their translation of my French text and to Michael Black and Penny Souster for their careful editorial work.

May anyone I have overlooked at the end of this long list forgive the omission.

In conclusion, I would like to render hommage to all my predecessors, and particularly to the late Rev. A.M. Jones, who have spent some fifty years now trying to solve the riddles of the polyphony and polyrhythmics of black Africa, often with only the rudimentary technical means of years ago at their disposal. I hope that this book will prove a worthy continuation of their efforts.

Book I

The music of the Central African Republic

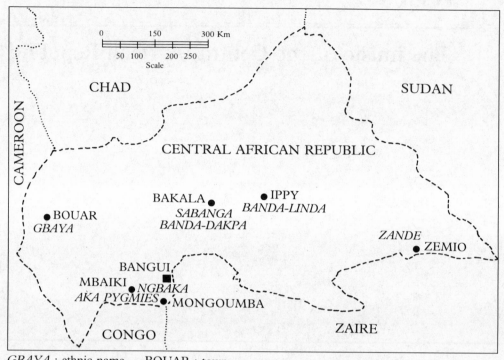

GBAYA : ethnic name   BOUAR : town

1 General introduction

1.1   GEOGRAPHICAL SURVEY

The area with which we are concerned is the former Oubangui-Chari, which became the Central African Republic in 1958. It is situated between the second and the eleventh degree of latitude north and between the fourteenth and twenty-eighth degree of longitude east. Neighbouring states include Chad to the north, Sudan (ex-English Sudan) to the east, Cameroon to the west, and the People's Republic of Congo and Zaïre to the south.

From east to west, the Central African Republic measures 1200 kilometres by 600 kilometres and occupies a quadrilateral of 617,000 square kilometres, a surface area roughly equal to that of France and of the three Benelux countries.

The course of the river Ubangi, joined by the Mbomu forms its Southern frontier. Together with the Congo, of which it is a tributary, the Ubangi (which is navigable as far as the capital, Bangui) connects the country to the Atlantic. Two mountain masses, to the east (Fertit, whose highest point is 1,400 metres) and to the west (Yade, 1,420 metres), frame a vast plateau, whose attitude averages 600 to 700 metres. Separating the two basins of the Congo to the south, and of the Chad to the north, this plateau is traversed by numerous important watercourses, which serve as channels of communication and, in former times, of migration.

It is usual to distinguish between four different geographical zones. From south to north, we find:

(1)   in the far south, a zone of equatorial forest
(2)   from the south to the centre, a zone of shrubby savannah, transected by strips of forest that follow the watercourses
(3)   from the centre to the north, a zone of savannah that becomes more and more arid
(4)   in the far north, a Sahellian zone.

Climatically, the year has two seasons, a dry season and a rainy one. The rainy season lasts the longest in the south, which is closest to the Equator, in fact for some nine months, i.e., for the whole year excepting winter (which lasts from December to February). In the centre of the country, the dry season lasts almost half the year (from November to March). The further north one goes, the less rain there is.

The country's equatorial zone contains the northern part of the Great Forest, becoming steadily less dense. The forested regions favour the cultivation of the coffee-shrub, whereas the savannah is better suited to the cotton plant. Cotton production is the major element in the country's agriculture.

3

1.2   SURVEY OF THE COUNTRY'S ETHNIC GROUPS

Official figures state that the Central African Republic contains some three million people, belonging to around a hundred different ethnic groups. Between 200,000 and 400,000 of them may be said to be 'urbanised'.

Central Africa has been, in the past, a kind of cross-roads for slave raids. Except for the Pygmies, for whom the Great Forest has served from time immemorial as a kind of refuge in the west and south-west, the present inhabitants settled relatively recently in the country, as a result of migrations in the eighteenth and nineteenth centuries.

The groups in the north of the country tend to be Islamicised; notably the Yulu, the Sara-Kaba, the Runga and the Kara. The others, who form the majority of the Central African population, were Animists until the time of the first European advance into their country, towards the end of the last century, but today are more or less Christianised, or on the way to becoming Christians. Of these latter, the main groups are the Banda, established in the centre and in the east of the country; the Manja and the Gbaya, in the centre and in the west; the Nzakara and the Azande, in the far east. Each of these groups may be subdivided into numerous smaller branches. Thus, for the Banda alone, fifty or so have already been recorded. Each sub-group has its own name but, in most cases, considers itself to belong to the wider category of the group.

In addition to these larger groups, mention should be made of those that live on the banks of the Ubangi, namely, the Patri, the Sango, the Yakoma, and the Gbanziri, and the forest peoples, namely, the Ngbaka, the Isongo, the Monzombo, the Mbimu or Mpyemo, the Kaka, and also the various Pygmy groups (the Aka, the Mbenzele, the Ngombe), who are very probably the oldest inhabitants of the country.

No matter how large it is, whether it is a small tribe or one of the sub-groups of a larger ethnic group, each population can be distinguished from all the others by a certain number of specific cultural features, of which the most obvious is speech, be it a language or a dialect, and (what most concerns us here) a particular musical idiom. This tends to take the form of a set of songs and rhythmical patterns, and manifests itself also by the use of particular scales, instruments or of specific instrumental ensembles. One can conceive of the remarkable richness and astonishing musical variety that a country with a hundred or so different tribal groups can offer, even if the populations of many of them have fallen in size.

However, from this apparent diversity emerges a real unity. It consists in the source and social function of these musics, in their mode of transmission, and also in certain structural principles upon which they are based. All of these aspects will be considered in detail in the following chapter.

1.3   ACCULTURATION AND THE VITALITY OF THE MUSIC

The first Europeans arrived in Central Africa at the end of the last century. Their arrival brought, among other things, the setting up of numerous evangelical missions in the small towns and bush villages, followed by a relatively widespread Christianisation. This produced a form of religious syncretism, in which traditional customs and newly acquired Christian rites were fused. But the missionaries' strictly musical contribution was a fairly limited one. They devised canticles, based, with varying degrees of success, on melodies and melodic phrases derived from local tradition, and by the introduction, in religious services, of some traditional instruments, especially percussion. This 'hybridisation' did not seriously damage an ancestral patrimony that was firmly established, and organically linked to the social life of the community.

Nevertheless, in the past few decades, various factors have together conspired to undermine the traditional musics, without at the same time replacing them with a specific 'modern' music. As is the case throughout Africa, the drift of villagers into the capital in search of work has produced an ethnic mixing; the educational system has tended to ignore ethnic musics in its programme of studies, and to prefer patriotic hymns based on European marching songs or French popular songs. In public places, and in night clubs in particular, the so-called 'Afro-Cuban' or 'Congolese' musics, and more recently 'pop' music are the fashion.

The traditional musics are firmly embedded in history. They have evolved and are still in evolution. In a society with an oral tradition music is perpetually being renewed, an organic and in some sense a self-perpetuating renewal reinforced by elements derived from the surrounding traditional world, and the influence of ethnic group on ethnic group.

In spite of the profound changes that have affected this country since the advent of the European, and in spite of the presence nowadays, even in the most remote regions, of transistor radios receiving so many different kinds of musics (European 'light' music, 'pop', jazz, and above all 'Afro-Cuban' or 'Congolese' rhythms), music in its traditional environment withstands all these encroachments and is still a living force. It seems impervious to all these blandishments and disdains to borrow. In the villages, the two forms of music co-exist without mixing.

However, musics that are tied to a function which, socially, economically or religiously, no longer has a ground or origin, are bound to wither away. Consider, for instance, a milieu in which hunting took place with snares, and which had a specific ritual. When technological changes, such as the appearance of the rifle, bring about the disappearance of this sort of hunting, the ritual falls into disuse, and with it the music that was tied to it, and naturally the instrument needed to play this music.

This disappearance is accomplished in two successive phases. At first, being no longer reserved for the performance of a specific function, the music is available for other purposes. Some pieces disappear at this stage. Others, the most liked, 'fall into the public domain': the music changes its status, and from being 'sacred' simply becomes the accompaniment to ordinary social dancing. Simultaneously, the words of the songs will also have lost their ritual function and, having become useless, conventional and mostly improvised words are substituted for them, usually on current topics of interest. As for the instruments, they suffer the same fate as the music. They may go on being used to accompany it in its final transformations but having lost their ritual standing they may even become musical toys for children. At the end of this first phase, some musics have disappeared, others are degraded, the words have been lost, the instruments may or may not survive.

With the second phase, the instruments themselves disappear for good. Indeed, if an instrument, not long before associated with a ritual function, is somewhat difficult to manufacture, once its *raison d'être* is gone, there will no longer be any incentive to try to replace it. A first stage will entail its desacralisation, but there will follow a second stage, when the last specimen is no longer in use, and it will then totally disappear. The men belonging to the generation immediately following the disappearance of the original function will preserve some memory of the ritual, of the music and the instrument associated with it, but with the second generation even this memory will have gone. The transmission of the music, being exclusively oral, will have ceased, whilst the instrument itself, being perishable, will no longer be a part of that tribe's organological heritage. So it is that a whole section of a musical tradition may disappear for good.

It is indeed fortunate that, in a very large number of African societies, authentic traditional musics are still vigorous, but it is important to remember, thinking in terms of the continent as a whole, that a significant part of this exceptionally rich heritage has already disappeared without trace. Since this is the case, and since the process is now accelerating, Erich von Hornbostel's warning given sixty years ago is more pertinent than ever: 'As yet we hardly know what African music is; if we do not hasten to collect it systematically and to record it by means of the phonograph, we shall not even learn what it was' (Hornbostel 1928).

2   The general features of traditional music

2.1   Introduction

Before presenting a sketch of the general characteristics of the musics to be found in Central Africa, such as their social functions and their relations with language and with dance, let us remind the reader, when approaching traditional African cultures, to be wary of relying too much on the rationality inherent in Western thought, with its tendency to distinguish and to categorise.

I have shown elsewhere that in African civilisations the world is almost invariably apprehended in the multiplicity of its aspects as a dynamic ensemble, as a coherent whole displaying a diversity whose elements are not only not mutually exclusive but rather tend to complement each other. All of these elements are linked by a multiplicity of bundles of relations internal to a universe which implies no separation of the metaphysical from the physical (Arom 1974: 3–6).

Consequently, the notion of art, and that of musical art in particular, in sub-Saharan Africa depends upon quite other mental categories than it does in the West. As Senghor observes:

Negro-African civilization stems from a *unitary* vision of the world. None of the domains into which the 'human sciences' of the West artificially divide it enjoys an autonomous existence. The same spirit prompts and links Negro-African philosophy, religion, society and art. And their philosophy, which is *ontology*, expresses their psycho-physiology.

Art itself is simply one of many artisanal techniques, the one that is most effective for identifying with one's ancestor or for integrating with the vital force of God. For the latter is the source of *life* itself, which in Black Africa is the supreme good. Which is why the word *art* does not exist in the Negro-African languages – I do not mean the notion of art nor the word beauty.

Because it is an *integral technique*, art is not divided against itself. More precisely, the arts in Black Africa are linked to each other, poetry to music, music to dance, dance to sculpture, and sculpture to painting.   (Senghor 1958, rev. edn 1964: 238)

This is a clear statement of the premises upon which any consideration of African music must be based. Indeed, these relations between the multiple aspects of the world, and this search for union or unity is displayed in every activity in which a material aim may only be reached by appealing to the spiritual dimension, or through the intervention of supernatural forces. And

music is the very means man has to make contact with these forces, and to maintain that contact, to have some purchase on them and to render them favourable to him. Which is why it enjoys so important, indeed so essential a place wherever the intervention of these forces is sought – whether it be a question of driving harmful spirits out of the village or of curing someone struck down by an illness whose origin is considered to be extra-human. For there are as many musics and instruments as there are divinities [. . .] So varied are the instruments and so numerous the possible combinations that each music may be said to correspond to a precise function, a function to which the 'liturgical' ensemble in which it is inserted corresponds.   (Arom 1974: 16–17)

2.2   GENERAL CHARACTERISTICS

The frontiers of the Central African Republic do not, any more than the majority of contemporary African states, define an actual 'musical area'. Central Africa is made up of a mosaic of different ethnic groups, coming from various regions, after long migrations. Some of these migrants did not advance as far as did the Central Africans of today, the lands in which they settled today belong to the countries that border on the Central African Republic. That is why the neighbouring countries contain members of the same ethnic families as live in Central Africa, namely, the Banda and the Manja in Zaïre, the Ngbaka in the Congo, the Gbaya and the Kaka in Cameroon, the Azande in Sudan.

For that reason the features listed here as characteristic of the traditional musics now in use in Central Africa should not be taken to be exclusive to this one country, nor to the peoples who, by and large, live within it. On the contrary, a number of these characteristics (especially social function or rhythmic organisation), rest on general principles which hold good for a far wider area than the one under consideration here, some of them even applying to virtually the whole of sub-Saharan Africa.

2.3   THE SOCIAL FUNCTIONS OF MUSIC

As with most African societies, the traditional musics of Central Africa satisfy social functions above all. They are woven into the cycle of individual, familial and collective existence to such an extent that they are an inseparable and indispensable part of the social and religious life of the community.

As a means of communication and an indispensable intermediary between men and the supernatural forces surrounding them, music serves to make contact with the shades of the ancestors, the spirits and the djinns. That is why Central Africans do not consider music to be an aesthetic phenomenon, even though they are quite capable of expressing their tastes and making very precise value judgements about both the music itself and the quality of the performance. But aesthetics remains a secondary question, and is not an end in itself. The European notion of 'Art for Art's sake' has no meaning in the African tradition. Indeed, music only exists here in order to serve something other than itself, and for clearly defined purposes. That is why it is invariably a part of a more inclusive activity, a whole of which it is merely a part, be it the celebration of a cult, a collective work session, a dance for pleasure on the night of the full moon or, simpler still, a mother singing to soothe her child.

All events of any significance, and even many everyday occasions, have some ceremony or display attached to them in which music, being an organic part, has a leading role to play. Conditions vary somewhat, depending upon whether Muslim or Animist peoples are involved, but in every community music plays a crucial role. In every case it is strictly and minutely organised, as much from the structural as the social point of view; only the modes of organisation differ from one society to the next.

Inasmuch as these musics are not abstracted from their cultural context, they may be said to be functional. Consequently, as Alan Merriam notes with respect to the Basongye of Zaïre, the members of an African society know their musical corpus in its entirety: 'Individual songs are recognized instantly in terms of their function. What this means is that music as such does not exist apart from its context or, to the contrary, the context may well determine the conceptualization of the music. This is functionality in its deepest sense' (Merriam 1962: 123). Those functions which demand some musical activity sometimes involve the whole community, sometimes just a small group or merely an isolated individual.

When one is aware of how ill-defined are the boundaries between natural and supernatural, 'profane' and 'sacred', in Africa, and of the manner in which these domains, rather than being mutually opposed, tend for the most part to complement each other, one can grasp how hard it is to produce a classification of musics, according to their functions, in watertight compartments. Such a classification would correspond to no reality. At a very general level, however, it is worth advancing a distinction between two types of music or, more exactly, between two ways of utilising music within a traditional Central African society. On the one hand, then, there are ritual, ceremonial, i.e socially *institutionalised* musics and, on the other hand, there are all those forms of music, whether collective or individual, which are not ritual or ceremonial. By institutionalised musics I mean all those which go to make up an 'institutional' activity and which are a necessary part of it, such that their absence would make it impossible to carry out this activity, or at any rate would cause it to lose its efficacy. I refer here to the various socio-religious and ritual occasions, whether seasonal or connected with specific events.

In Central Africa, such events include birth, that of twins in particular, puberty rites, certain economic activities, such as the inauguration of a big hunt, land clearance, sowing or harvest, or paddling; the installation of a traditional chief or the consecration of a diviner and healer; various rites which are paid to the spirits of ancestors; the curing of certain illnesses; the ceremonies of initiation societies; and, finally, the celebration of funerary rites. All these activities are necessary, indeed indispensable, if a balance with the supernatural powers is to be maintained. That is why the musics associated with them have to be played in a strictly defined manner: there is a strict observance of obligations (regarding the time and the place, etc.), of prohibitions (alimentary, hygienic, sexual), and of the appropriate repertory (specific songs, particular instruments, etc.). As with the performance of music, so too the making of instruments entails numerous ritual constraints.

These institutional musics habitually require the participation of a collectivity, which may range in size from a family, in the most restricted sense, to the entire village. They follow more or less strict prescriptions as regards the role of the participants, the specific responsibilities of some of them, the framework within which they are performed, and the appropriate manner for conducting this performance (specific instruments, specific groupings of instruments, etc.). Finally, so long as a performance of this sort lasts, music will tend to have a dominant part to play.

When the musics are not institutionalised, however, they tend to be more accessible, and more a part of daily routine. The activity which gives rise to them is indeterminate. This is the case with those dances that are for entertainment pure and simple, with some forms of collective work that are stimulated by music, with the mother rocking her child, with the traveller walking to the rhythm of a little *sanza*, or again with the musician–storyteller who narrates myths, legends and chronicles in the evenings. One can define this form of musical practice in terms of its spontaneity and its very great freedom of expression: whether collective or individual, and for all its didactic qualities, it is basically recreational in nature.

When it is spontaneous and collective, this music is mainly employed in dance evenings which bring together all the villagers, events in which everyone has some part to play, be it dancing, playing an instrument, singing, or simply beating time by clapping hands.

When it is spontaneous but individual, music assumes a more intimate character. It gives priority to personal expression, whether in the text or in the music. Above all, it is meant for the pleasure of the performer, and that of any audience.

This form of musical practice leaves much scope for improvisation, particularly where the words are concerned. Taking a popular song as his point of departure, a musician will rapidly jettison all but the melody, which he will thenceforth use as a 'spring-board' from which, by association of ideas, he invents, off the cuff, new words which will tend to reflect his personal preoccupations, his grief and his solitude. Music serves here as an 'escape valve', and 'canalises' grief. It will suffice to mention here two instances of music having this function, both of which are to be found among the Gbaya-Kara, in the Bouar region, in the East of Central Africa. They concern those spontaneous musical displays that occur when there is a death, or when a baby is crying.

When an individual dies, the women members of the entourage begin to weep and lament, but they quickly take up the singing of lamentations which are litanies of a call–response sort. The soloist is the dead person's closest surviving woman relative. In this way her inchoate crying and wailing is 'socialised', taken in charge and given shape by the community. Thus it becomes music.

A similar phenomenon of emergent music takes place when a mother seeks to pacify a crying baby, as Paulette Roulon has recorded (1976: 380). During those brief intervals in which the baby catches its breath, the mother punctuates its crying with a meaningless syllable, an 'oè'. Little by little, a dialogue is set up between cries and responses, the latter being regular and tending towards isochrony. Gradually the child adapts its crying to the pulsation provided by the mother, and this has the effect of pacifying it. This also represents a sort of unconscious musical socialisation, the first stage in the future musician's apprenticeship thus beginning at the earliest possible age.

These two examples clearly show how important music is in moderating excessive individual emotion, which it achieves by taking the person in hand socially, in the second case at the most intimate level, that of the mother–child relation, and in the first case on the largest scale, with the participation of the entire community.

Whilst on the subject of spontaneous individual musics, it is worth mentioning the *ritornelli* that the solitary traveller will perform on a little instrument, a harp or a *sansa*, to pace his journey ('the *sansa* is my bike', people will often say), as also children's singing games and riddles, which are often didactic in character.

There are, finally, mythological or historical narratives (chronicles, legends), which are partly or wholly sung, and which may be heard of an evening in the village, in the course of an improvised entertainment, in front of the hut of a teller or of one of his intimates.

The simple fact of a music being institutionalised or otherwise has no effect on the number of participants needed for its performance. In both of these categories, there are some musics that imply the participation of almost the entire village (in the first category, funerals; in the second category, dances for entertainment). Others entail a less extensive collectivity (in the first category, familial rites; in the second category, paddling); still others simply involve an individual (rites of the ancestral shades on the one hand, lullabies on the other).

There are some musics, however, which even elude this category distinction. For they may become institutionalised at one moment, only to become indeterminate later. This is the case, in particular, with certain repertories bound up with rites of passage which, could perhaps be said to have fallen later into the 'public domain', and which are played nowadays at national festivals.

2.4   MUSIC, SPEECH, DANCE

Music, speech and dance are, for the most part, closely associated. I shall try here to show the points at which they are articulated, one with the other.

It is hardly necessary to say that 'pure' music as such scarcely exists. Indeed, to my knowledge, no Central African vernacular language has a generic term to designate it, nor does it have one for the concepts of *melody* or *rhythm*. Melody is only conceived as clothed in the words that it conveys; it then becomes 'song'. As for rhythm, it is simply thought of as the *stimulus* for the bodily movement to which it gives rise, and, for the most part, is then given the same name as the choreography that it sustains. As numerous researchers (in particular, Hornbostel 1928; Merriam 1959; Lomax 1959) have observed, musical practice in sub-Saharan Africa is conceived as a motor activity, almost inseparable from dance. It is in fact striking to observe just how often, for an African from a traditional milieu, simply to hear music gives rise almost immediately to a movement of the body. It is in the dance, the 'plastic music' of which Senghor speaks (1958, rev. edn 1964: 240), that music, speech and movement find their fullest expression.

This fusion of elements deriving from different orders does not therefore mean that, in Central African societies, there is no clear distinction to be drawn between the 'musical' and the 'non-musical', between that which derives from music, that which *is* music, and that which is not. Such a definition does indeed exist but it is *implicit*. As with many other concepts pertaining to African culture in general and music in particular, it is not expressed or verbalised.

The basic and fundamental characteristic of this country's musics concerns their mode of temporal organisation. I shall therefore propose the following definition, which I have arrived at after a series of enquiries, lasting several years, among a range of different tribal groups.

In this context music is *a succession of sounds capable of giving rise to a segmentation of time during which it flows in isochronous units*. In other words, there can only be music inasmuch as it is *measured*, and 'danceable'. Thus, rhythmic speech, such as is often used in magic formulae, is considered to be music. On the other hand, *unmeasured* melopeias, as for instance certain funeral lamentations which, although based on the degrees of the scale in use in the community in question, are not dependent upon a *tactus*, and are therefore not considered as musical by those who perform them. Whatever is a part of the musical domain necessarily entails a strict division, whether physical or virtual, of time, into regular pulsation.

2.5   LANGUAGE AND MUSIC

Music and language are very closely interconnected, the phonemic structure of the language having a powerful constraining effect on the melodic structure of the songs. Senghor has this to say of Central Africa:

The languages are themselves pregnant with music. For these are tone languages, in which each syllable has its own pitch, intensity and duration, and in which each word may be given a musical notation. Word and music are intimately linked and will not tolerate dissociation or separate expression [. . .] Music cannot be dissociated from speech. It is no more than a complementary aspect of it, is indeed consubstantial with it. In Black Africa, it is music which *accomplishes* speech and transforms it into Word, that higher utterance of man which turns him into a demiurge.   (Senghor 1958, rev. edn 1964: 238)

Indeed, almost all the Central African vernacular languages are tonal. In a tonal language, each vowel can be inflected; the same syllable, when uttered at different vocal pitches or registers, may carry quite different meanings. The Ngbaka language, for instance, has three *level* tones (low, medium, high), to which are added four *gliding* tones (low–high, high–low, low–high–low, high–low–high) (Thomas 1970: 8). It is easy enough to imagine the number of melodic cells that such combinations could generate. Some languages, such as the Monzombo, resort to four level tones, which gives still more gliding tones, and therefore still more melodic combinations imposed by the language itself.

It follows, if the words of a song are to keep their meaning and remain intelligible, that its melody must necessarily remain subservient to them and reproduce their tonal schema. Every change in the words of a given melody, if their tonal schema ever varies, inevitably entails a modification in the melodic line. There is every reason to suppose that the essentially syllabic treatment of sung texts is attributable to these same linguistic constraints. Indeed, with the exception of the gliding tones, whose linguistic realisation requires two or three different pitches, there is one note for each syllable in the text. Given what is said above, it could not be otherwise, since any addition of purely melodic intervals, i.e., those without linguistic justification, would immediately have the effect of reducing the coefficient of intelligibility of the words that the melody conveys. This explains the absence of melismas in societies whose languages are tonal, at any rate where these songs are meant to transmit a verbal message, which is not always the case.

These tonological constraints of language also seriously affect the multipart organisation of vocal musics, a topic to be touched upon later in the present Book (3.5).

2.6   ORAL LITERATURE AND MUSIC

The strict relation between music and language is also evident in another form of expression, that of oral literature, which is almost invariably marked by it. Central African oral literature may be divided, at least as far as music is concerned, into two distinct categories. The first involves chantefables which are spoken narratives, with occasional sung parts. They are performed by the story-teller, with or without instrumental accompaniment, and with or without responses from a 'choir', i.e., from his audience. The second category comprises myths, stories, legends or epic narratives which are *entirely sung* and always accompanied by a melodic instrument (a harp or a *mvet*, a harp-zither) played by the singer-narrator.

2.7   THE MUSICIAN

The peoples of the Central African Republic do not have castes of musicians, nor are there any professional musicians. Alan Merriam observes in this respect that 'Distinctions between the artist and his audience [. . .] are not so sharply drawn as in our own culture. In some parts of Africa the cultural expectation involves almost everyone as potentially equal in musical ability, although this is not the case everywhere' (Merriam 1962: 129). I would maintain that this is the case in Central Africa also.

Music, as we have seen, responds to a social need. It is a practice in which everyone, although to a different degree, participates, or, at any rate, may participate. Except for those performances which are limited by their nature (the cure of certain illnesses, for instance), or which are restricted to those belonging to a particular sex (various associations), everybody may participate as best he or she may in a song or a dance and, if capable of doing so, may play an instrumental part in the ensemble. One can say of a traditional Central African society that every one of its members is, in a virtual sense at least, a musician.

It follows that there is no question of distinguishing the musician from the non-musician. I shall try, nonetheless, to establish a gradation in the mastery of musical technique, by referring to a simple and commonplace example, that of a dance session held for entertainment. Since this sort of performance is not institutionalised, anyone may participate: either in the music, or in the dancing, or in both at once, by singing the appropriate melodies, by simply marking time by hand-clapping, or again by combining song and clapping. Taking part in the dance-movements often requires the simultaneous employment of a rhythm instrument, for the dancers will frequently tie jingles to their ankles or forearms, so that they sound in time with their steps and movements. In addition, the dancers also take part most of the time in the song; indeed, the leader of the dance is usually also the vocal soloist to whom all the other dancers, along with the audience, supply responses. In many cases, the leader holds a pair of bells or a rattle in his hands and knocks them together or shakes them.

All the activities mentioned so far are shared in by men, women and children alike.

The drums, which are played by men, provide the general rhythmical foundation for this music. Now, almost all the men, and often even the boys, know how to beat the different rhythmical patterns which are appropriate to the various socio-musical occasions.

These activities, and the talents that they require, derive from the general culture that each person, given the framework of his society, necessarily possesses, talents that can be summarised as follows: on the one hand, a deep knowledge of one's musical heritage, on the other hand, the capacity to participate actively in its practice, and so in its conservation.

It is somewhat rarer for people to have mastered the technique of playing the often quite complex melodic instruments such as the xylophone, the *sanza* or the harp, but there are nevertheless a fair number of such practitioners. These are true specialists. So, when a ceremony requires that such an instrument be used, people turn to the person who knows how to play it, without his necessarily being rewarded for his playing. Sometimes the fame of an instrumentalist, a real virtuoso, is such that he is known far beyond his village, and this leads him to play elsewhere. In that case, he is rewarded with presents, usually in kind: dried meat, chicken or goat. However, the musician, even if he is a 'specialist', does not consider himself (and is not considered) to be a member of an élite. The mastery of a musical instrument is seen in much the same light as any other manual specialisation, and the virtuoso does not therefore enjoy any special prestige.

Finally, there are certain social functions which demand real musical competence on the part of those who assume them. Thus, the priest in charge of a particular cult, or a diviner-curer has, by definition, to be a good singer, possessing a powerful voice, and at the same time to be a good dancer.

Whether he is an excellent singer, instrumentalist or even a virtuoso, the Central African musician, in a traditional society, has no particular status as such. Just as music has no isolated existence separate from its social context, so its practice, no matter what degree of skill informs it, does not entail any change in status for the practitioner within his own society.

2.8 MUSICAL APPRENTICESHIP

Instrumental music, the use of the voice and dance, all of which, as we have just seen, involve the whole community, imply an apprenticeship and a training. How then is music learnt in traditional societies in Central Africa? The answer is that one learns it just as one learns how to speak! Indeed, for the Central African child, the acquisition of the musical language peculiar to his or her own cultural community runs parallel to the acquisition of language; one could even argue that, in a certain sense, it precedes it.

Indeed, from the very first days of its life, the child can do no other than participate, albeit involuntarily, in the social life of the group. Wrapped in a carrying cloth, the infant is fixed on to its mother's back, where it remains perched all day long, participating in the various activities in which the mother participates, including of course the different ceremonies and dances in which she takes part. Finding itself thus thrust into the musical activities of its milieu, taking part in the dance, since it is 'being danced' by its mother, long before it can stand on its own feet, the infant absorbs and assimilates in the most organic and natural manner possible the rudiments of the music of its own community. The child may be said, in fact, to store up, in a subconscious fashion, the characteristics of this music. This is the 'passive' stage, the first step in its pragmatic apprenticeship, 'on-the-job'. But this is also the stage which marks out the future musician, even if it is not the most important one.

The second stage begins when the child, able to speak and to walk, i.e., to master the movements of his body, of his legs *and of his hands*, feels the need to act, in imitation of the adults and the older children. To this end he is constantly solicited and stimulated socially.

The apprenticeship to musical practice through imitation is widespread in many oral cultures, across the whole world. Without leaving the African continent, let us consider how it is carried out in a South African people, the Venda, settled in the north of the Transvaal, as described by John Blacking: 'From the earliest age, Venda children have every opportunity to imitate the songs and dances of adults, as most music is performed publicly and children generally follow their mothers everywhere until at least the age of three. Their efforts to imitate adults and older children are admired and encouraged rather than hushed up, and spectators often comment when a small child begins to clap or jump about in response to music' (Blacking 1957, quoted by Merriam 1964: 148). Already we see here clearly the link between music and dance, the acquisition of the second possibly even preceding that of the first. Indeed, Blacking notes later: 'Although the melodies are there to be imitated, small children make little or no attempt to sing, and are at first content to imitate only the motor movement' (ibid.: 148).

From this stage onwards, the child tries, somewhat timidly, to participate in the musical activities of his cultural milieu, reaching as it passes for a few snatches of the melody, and trying out a dance step.

The acquisition of motor movements corresponds, as far as dance is concerned, with the mastery of rhythm. It is therefore at this stage that there are set off the first tentative, and still imitative, steps in the learning of an instrumental technique, that of playing on the drums. When drums that have just been used in some ceremony are laid out in the centre of the village, it is a common enough sight to see four- or five-year-old children doing their utmost to produce a sound or two from them. When there is a musical occasion, it is equally common to see eight- or ten-year-old children seated next to the drummers, observing them very closely as they play. Nor is it uncommon to encounter, amongst these latter, boys of no more than twelve years old, carrying out their allotted task quite successfully. This is also the case with those instruments that require a more sophisticated technique.

One can therefore argue that, generally speaking, apprenticeship in music among the peoples of Central Africa occurs through simple observation and imitation. Which means that those who acquire these techniques are all, to some extent, self-taught.

The only criteria for musical appreciation applicable here derive from, on the one hand, the apprentice musician's sense of self-criticism, and on the other hand, the aesthetic judgements furnished by society. Thus, if someone's singing is out of time or if he does not know how to perform a drum part correctly (which is rare), he will not wait to have this pointed out to him, but will discover it for himself and will thenceforth abstain from such a musical activity. On the other hand, villagers are quick to recognise and to value the most talented musicians. I would sum up the situation by saying that, in social terms, there is no more shame in being a mediocre, even a bad musician, than there is merit in being a virtuoso.

There are a number of communities, however, in which there are kinds of music which are not learnt purely by trial and error but are in fact taught in a specific framework. This is the case with the special repertoires linked to initiation rites, the most common of which are the rites of passage which allow children, when approaching puberty, to be admitted according to sex into the community of adult men or women. In many societies this occasion is marked by an initiatory retreat, in the course of which the neophytes are secluded for several weeks, far from the village, in a rudimentary camp. They are subjected there to various forms of teaching, which include an apprenticeship in specific songs and dances. We only have a more detailed musical study of this form of initiation in the case of two peoples, both of whom are a part of the Banda tribe.

For both the Dakpa and the Linda, one of the main activities in the course of this retreat consists in the acquisition both of an instrumental technique and simultaneously of a particular repertoire, which the neophytes have to be capable of performing in various circumstances, when the retreat has ended. These instruments are horns that only produce a single sound and which are consequently only played in large groups (ten to eighteen instruments). The repertoire of these orchestras consists of some fifteen pieces which with recourse to the usual imitation techniques are here taught by a recognized master.

Those initiations which are more specialised, and in general, more secret, may also involve the learning of equally specific and equally secret musical repertoires.

2.9   CONCLUSION

Whatever music is being performed, whether ritual, ceremonial or simply for entertainment, no Central African society has a relationship between musician and listeners that may be compared with that existing in Europe. The radical division prevailing in the West between active musicians and their passive audience could have no meaning here. Music exists either to carry out a function or simply to entertain. But as soon as it is a question of a collective music, every member of the community will, in one way or another, participate, although not always to the same degree. People do not go to 'listen to music', they *make* music together. Some *play* an instrument, others use their voices or their bodies, but everyone does something, everyone participates.

3 Typology

Although each human group has its own musical idiom, the musics of the peoples living in the Central African Republic have many common characteristics. The general principles upon which these different musics are based show a certain degree of uniformity. I shall summarise these general principles as a way of introducing an analysis of the polyphonic and polyrhythmic musics which are the subject of this study.

But before briefly surveying the general features of traditional Central African music, let me remind the reader that, as in most African societies, this music is *popular, oral, anonymous, undatable, collective,* and *for internal use.*

- *Popular* music as opposed to 'art' music because it does not require knowledge of any formal theory on the part of those who inherit it and perform it. The African musician does not verbalise the abstract principles upon which his music is based.
- *Oral* music, because it has no notation and is transmitted from generation to generation by word of mouth and memorisation only.
- *Anonymous* and *undatable* music: its possessors cannot say either who composed the pieces they have inherited, nor when it was first performed.
- *Collective* music, because the whole community, inasmuch as it is a cultural entity, is responsible for its preservation and subsequent transmission.
- Music *for internal use,* because, produced in the society in question, by and for its own members, it constitutes a means of expression and communication – even of communion – that is peculiar to the society, just as much as its natural language is.

3.2 VOCAL AND INSTRUMENTAL MUSIC

The Central African peoples, like so many others in Black Africa, do not generally distinguish vocal from instrumental music. This fact was first mentioned in 1719 by a German missionary, Peter Kolb, writing about the Hottentots of South Africa (Kolb 1719: 529). Indeed, the two tend in most circumstances to be closely associated. However, vocal music is predominant. It is generally supported by either melodic instruments – xylophones, *senza* or harps – or by rhythm instruments – particularly drums, but also rattles, jingles, bells, etc. – and often by orchestral ensembles that include these two types of instruments. Where there are no percussion instruments, they tend to be replaced by hand-clapping, which in certain cases simply serves to mark the beat, and in others produces more complex rhythmic patterns.

Although it is sometimes performed without instrumental accompaniment, vocal music that is strictly *a cappella* hardly exists as such. As soon as the music assumes a social, and *a fortiori*, a cultural function, even if it is performed by only one individual, voice and instrument complement each other: thus, the storyteller, and the poet-chronicler always accompany their narration with a harp, a *mvet* or some other melodic instrument.

The situation is slightly different with instrumental music. Some rare cases do exist where music that is purely instrumental is performed. For example, among two Banda groups, the Linda and the Dakpa, one finds horn ensembles whose use is linked to the puberty rites of young boys, and that execute extremely complex polyphonic music, as we shall see below. When there is a death among the Gbaya-Kara, between the moment when the man dies and that of his burial, which usually follows several hours afterwards, the deceased's heroic deeds are portrayed in warrior dances accompanied by drum ensembles alone, with no vocal music whatsoever. But in such cases, the pieces included in these repertoires are nearly always 'transpositions' or orchestrations of pieces that were originally vocal. In either case, whether instrumental music serves to support vocal music or is played on its own, one can always reconstitute the song, i.e., the monody from which it originates.

There are also instrumental ensembles that within one and the same group are mutually exclusive by virtue of rules of incompatibility. Thus, among the Banda-Linda, drums never accompany horn ensembles. This incompatibility may be caused by differences in the scalar systems of the instruments: among the Sabanga, the xylophone scale is anhemitonic-pentatonic, whereas that of the harp is equihexatonic. These restrictions of the possibility of fusion maintain the autonomy of the instrumental ensembles and of the repertoires, by preventing a mixing of *genres*. In this way, they help to preserve the musical heritage. More generally, the tendency is rather for voices and instruments to move together rather than to diverge as two separate modes of musical expression. Thus, among the Dakpa, there is a repertoire for an ensemble of whistles (each whistle produces only one sound), in whose performance the musicians, within the same piece of music, alternate whistled and sung segments. But the extreme case of symbiosis between voice and instrument is undoubtedly in the utilisation of the *mò.békè* by the Aka Pygmies. This is a small whistle made from a papaya twig, and again, it only produces one sound. In order to obtain real melodies from this rudimentary instrument, the musician regularly alternates the sound produced by the whistle with other sounds sung in a falsetto voice: so fused are the voice and instrument that the listener finds it extremely hard to distinguish between them.

3.3   FORMAL STRUCTURES

All musical pieces are characterised by cyclic structure that generates numerous improvised variations: *repetition* and *variation* is one of the most fundamental principles of all Central African musics, as indeed of many other musics in Black Africa. This principle excludes the process of development, fundamental to European art music, but totally unknown in African musical thought. As Gilbert Rouget aptly remarked: 'There are indeed musics which find in repetition or in variation – and consequently in non-development – their very accomplishment' (Rouget 1956: 133). It is upon extremely simple elements that a process of maximal elaboration is constructed, by using variations that exploit the basic material to the utmost.

Antiphonal and responsorial structures are the dominant characteristics of traditional Central African music. In certain pieces in which the melodic material is more developed, the two techniques may appear alternately. But, very generally, a soloist is contrasted with a choir made up of the whole of the audience.

Musical repetition, in its simplest form, is responsorial or litanical. The soloist sings a series of phrases that the choir punctuates with a response, which is usually shorter than the solo utterance. This response, or consequent, is most often sung in unison, and could therefore in the last resort be provided by a single performer: sometimes it is sporadically in parallel intervals of fourths and fifths.

The other kind of repetition takes the antiphonal form. Unlike responsorial form, there is regular alternation between the two parts: each phrase, having been announced by the soloist, is immediately repeated note-for-note by the audience. In both forms, the solo and choral parts can overlap.

Litanical songs, based upon generally monosyllabic texts, are constructed of melodic units that are usually short and few in number. A typical song will rarely exceed four or five melodic units, which, to the European mind, might be thought to correspond to lines of poetry. In most cases, the durations of these units are identical: these are the periodic units. Many songs have only two melodic units. The originality of their treatment lies in the freedom of their arrangement; they usually have an *open* form, and can therefore be rearranged at will.

(a)   One or two new phrases inserted in the midst of an otherwise similar phrase pattern: ABABABACCAB. . .
(b)   More than one litany pattern occurring in the same song; i.e., another new phrase may appear after the preceding one has been repeated several times. Such a pattern might be: AAAAAA. . . BBBBB. . . CCCCC. . .
(c)   In much African singing, a clear-cut litany is established and then a refrain, sometimes of one phrase, sometimes of more, may occur [. . .].
(d)   Litany pattern preceded by a short through-composed passage.
(e)   Any litany involving more complexity than the simple repetition of one or two phrases should be coded complex litany.
                                                                              (Lomax 1968: 58)

In contrast to strict repetition, there is variation. Whereas the response is clothed in a form that is nearly always invariable, the antecedent, given by the soloist, would seem to be, for its part, extremely variable. From one utterance to the next, the soloist will change, by improvising, either the notes or the words. In the second case, the textual modification of itself entails a melodic modification, given the constraint that speech tones exercise on melodic lines.

The periodic structure is dependent on an extremely strict division of time into segments of equal duration, each segment possessing its own internal organisation within the framework of the piece to which it belongs. The formal structure is thus isoperiodic. The periodic unit is like the basic material of the musical structure, or a kind of mould. Each periodic unit constitutes a musical unit, that can, in turn, be subdivided into two or more melodic and/or rhythmic units.

When vocal music is accompanied by one or more melodic instruments, their part is accordingly based on a periodic unit, itself a repeated formula, whose duration is directly proportional to that of the sung strophe: if the strophe is relatively short, the formula will be of equal duration; if it is longer, there will be repeated occurrences (usually two to three) of a formula of shorter duration. If percussion instruments are added to such an ensemble, their basic periodic unit is generally even shorter, but always remains directly proportional to the sung strophe and the melodic instruments. For example, in a sung periodic unit of a given duration, the melodic instruments will follow a repetitive formula that is half the length, and the percussion a formula that is a quarter of the length.

As for the melodic structure of vocal music in the Central African Republic, it is determined by the tones of the language used in the words of the song. However, a certain disconnection from the tonal system of the spoken language can be operated in the form of 'transpositions', allowing a considerable increase in the number of intervals employed, and so a noticeable enrichment of the melodic material. Generally the melodic line is descending, with conjunct movement; this movement is 'terraced', that is to say the melody rests on successive levels.

Finally, improvisation, which I have described as the driving force behind melodic and rhythmic variations, plays an important part in every group. But there is no such thing as free improvisation, that is, improvisation that does not refer back to some precise and identifiable piece of music. It is always subordinate to the musical structure in which it appears, in respect of mode, metre and rhythm.

Improvisation of text and melody are also closely linked: in any song with more than one verse, as soon as the words change, the melody too must be modified, to follow the language tones. Furthermore, even if the singer allows himself considerable freedom in the enunciation of the text phrases, he is nevertheless constrained, as Kubik has observed, by strict rules requiring a return to the principal phrase from time to time, and by respect for the meaning of the text. Improvisation is inherently limited by the structure of the piece of music, by the speech tones of the sung text, and the text itself; the improviser must, to some extent, also follow the patterns of variation he has learned and developed more or less richly depending upon his musical personality. As Kubik noted in Central Africa on the subject of Zande harp music: 'Like African music in general, it sounds highly improvised to a stranger's ear. But that is an illusion' (Kubik 1964a: 50).

3.4   RHYTHM AND TEMPO

The time organisation of Central African music is analysed in Book V of the present study. I want, however, at this point to summarise some of the general rhythmic aspects found in the vocal and instrumental music of the peoples of Black Africa, as well as their conception of tempo.

Firstly, in vocal music one must always bear in mind that the Central African languages are tonal rather than stressed, which means that they almost never have tonic accents. This absence of stress brings important consequences for the ordering and perception of rhythmic structures by the speakers of such languages, as I shall try to demonstrate below. Suffice it here to say that sung melodies are not subject to regular accentuation, i.e., they are not composed of necessity of a 'strong beat' complemented by one (or more) 'weak beats'. In fact, accent in these melodies is attributable to the following factors:

(a)   intensity: in any row of notes those with the highest pitch stand out dynamically;

(b)   phonetic factors: certain syllables, being more 'open' than others, have greater sonority;

(c)   emotional, prosodic and semantic factors, stemming from the performer's temperament. A word that is emphasised in this fashion will stand out.

As for instrumental rhythm, we adopt the distinction made by the Ghanaian ethnomusicologist J.H. Kwabena Nketia (1975: 125) between two different types, namely 'syllabic rhythms', and 'abstract rhythm patterns'. The first, generally given to melodic instruments (xylophones or harps), correspond with the syllabic divisions in the words of the songs that they accompany, while the second are confined to unpitched percussive instruments (or purely rhythm instruments), especially drums. The rhythmic structure is essentially dependent upon very short patterns, based on a division of time into cyclical units of equal duration, which are themselves subject to an isochronous pulse. This pulse may be realised or implied; and against it are set rhythmic patterns consisting usually of sounds of unequal duration. By superimposing several of these patterns (played by several drummers, for instance), a subtle and complex polyrhythm is created.

Finally, *tempo*, or what Claudie Marcel-Dubois calls 'organic speed or movement' (1965: 204), is the only constant element in Central African musical discourse; all the others (melody, rhythm and instrumental patterns) may give rise to variations. But there is never, within the one piece of music, the slightest variation in *tempo*; it remains constant right to the end, without *accelerando*, *ritardando*, *rubato* or *fermata*. If, for ritual reasons in particular, there are successive pieces of music with differing tempos (during a ceremony for instance) Central African musicians never create a transition from one piece to the next; they juxtapose them, preserving a clean break between the two. Furthermore, even when a piece is slow, the unit of the *tempo*, the 'beat', whether expressed or implicit, is never slow. The basic pulse underlying every piece of music is somewhere between 80 and 140 units per minute (approximately). Finally, it should be borne in mind that unintentional fluctuations in tempo in a musical performance are extremely slight.

3.5   PLURIVOCALITY

The term 'plurivocality' is the equivalent of the German term *Mehrstimmigkeit*, or the term currently used by Anglo-Saxon musicologists: *multi-part singing*. These very general terms have the advantage of neutrality, in that they refer to a phenomenon without indicating by what technical musical process it is realised.

Since the present study concerns *polyphony*, the word must of necessity be examined and defined; this is done in the first section of Book II. But, in the framework of this brief description of the general features of music in the Central African Republic, it is appropriate to review here the musics which, although not *polyphonic* as the category is established here, can nonetheless be characterised as multi-part or simultaneous musics. Only vocal music is considered here. In actual fact, all music of more than one part with implied instrumental participation always shows polyphonic and/or polyrhythmic characteristics; these will be discussed in the relevant chapters below. Apart from polyphonic performance properly so called, the non-monodic songs found in the Central African Republic employ three different techniques, which may be described as heterophony, overlapping, and homophony. There is often a strong link between heterophony and overlapping, such that one is rarely found without the other.

Heterophony is the least structured of these techniques. It consists of simultaneous intervals, consonant or dissonant, usually isolated, that occur at indeterminate points throughout a melody that is performed collectively and *conceived as monodic*. In the Central African Republic, this kind of song is mostly found among Islamicised peoples, whose vocal music is essentially monodic. In the travel journals that André Gide published in 1928, after returning from a long journey in Africa, he gives fine descriptions of heterophonic songs, such as he had been able to hear among the Sara, a group settled along the frontier between the Central African Republic and Chad. Describing a 'tam-tam' at which he had been present the evening before, Gide relates the following impressions: 'But imagine this tune yelled by a hundred persons *not one of whom sings the exact note*. It is like trying to make out the main line from a host of little strokes. The effect is prodigious, and gives an impression of polyphony and of harmonic richness' (Gide 1928: 32). A few pages later, he writes about the song of the paddlers, also Sara, with whom he had travelled in a canoe: 'The notes are never *exactly* sung'. And he adds, in brackets, '(which means that it is extremely difficult to notate the tune)' (ibid: 40). This observation is repeated several times.

Here they never sing in tune. Moreover, when one of them sings 'doh, re', the other sings 're, doh'. Some of them sing variants. Out of six singers, each one of them sings something a little different, without its being exactly 'in parts'. But the result is a kind of thickness of harmony, which is extremely strange [. . .]. As always in French Equatorial Africa, the chorus did not wait for the soloist's phrase to finish, but struck in on the last, and sometimes even on the penultimate note [. . .]. The refrain is attacked on several notes at once. Some voices rise, and others fall. It is like creepers winding around a central stalk, adapting themselves to its curve, without following it exactly.   (ibid.: 40–1)

Gide found 'this polyphony by broadening and overlaying the note' (ibid.: 41) very confusing.

Another reference to the device of overlapping, so common in this part of Africa, as Gide recognised, can be found in an earlier work of his, in the description of an evening dance of one of the riverine tribes of the Ubangi, near Mobaye.

In front of the rest-house at Moussaren, an amazing tam-tam [. . .]. Fine alternating chants gave the rhythm, accompanied and moderated the enthusiasm and the wildness of the pandemonium. I have never seen anything more disconcerting, more savage. A sort of symphony emerged; a choir of children and soloists; the end of each phrase by the soloist was lost in the response from the choir.   (Gide 1927: 61)

These are indeed features that characterise heterophony; a melody whose outline is refracted by a kind of halo created by voices that are, relatively, slightly unfocussed, minute variants, the coming and going of dissonances, to all of which is added the overlapping between solo and chorus parts, that Gide very aptly labelled 'brocading'. Often, in the middle of this process, one of the singers will sustain the note that he has struck, and thus enrich the sound with an intermittent drone.

The homophonic song, which is a multi-part form using parallel movement, is much more elaborate than this. It is the most common plurivocal form in Central Africa and indeed throughout the whole of Black Africa. The name given to the technique involved varies from author to author and from period to period. Kirby (1930) and Schaeffner (1936) call it *organum*; Jones (1959) and Kubik (1968) talk sometimes of *organum*, sometimes of *harmony*, whereas Brandel (1970) only uses the second term; Nketia (1972) calls it *parallel homophony*, and finally Schneider (1934 and 1968), defines it as *tonally linked parallelism* (*tonalgebundener Parallelismus*). Examination of the kinds of existing songs in parallel intervals in Central Africa shows that the last term is the most suitable. Jones states that 'Generally speaking, all over the continent south of the Sahara, African harmony is in *organum* and is sung either in parallel fourths, parallel fifths, parallel octaves, or parallel thirds' (Jones 1959: 217). He adds that the kind of interval that is chosen varies according to ethnic groups; thus, according to this author, certain peoples sing only in thirds, others only in fourths, fifths and octaves. This led him to draw up a 'harmonic map' of Africa, in which he distinguished two main streams; one is made up of peoples who sing in octaves, parallel fourths and fifths, to whom he gives the name '8 – 5 – 4 tribes'; the other comprises those who sing in thirds (ibid.: 219).

Jones talks about peoples who *sing*: this indicates that the principles of parallelism apply essentially to *vocal* music, which is in general the vehicle of words, i.e. linguistic elements. Now, the extensive use in Africa of 'harmonic' song in parallel movement initially derives from linguistic factors. I mentioned earlier the constraint of tonal languages on the melodic contour of song; we should remember that if the words are to remain intelligible, the melody must follow their tonal scheme. This rule applies whether the song is in one part or in several. It follows that the only way to sing in more than one part without infringing this fundamental rule is to reproduce, as precisely as possible, the melodic contour of the song but with a certain 'uncoupling', produced by a change in register, which must remain constant. But, whatever the interval of the uncoupling, the movement of the various parts will always be in parallel.

It was Percival Kirby who in 1930 was first to discern the relationship among certain African peoples between their language and their choral song, and between the latter and the beginning of early Medieval polyphony: 'Speech-tone of the Bantu has not only influenced his melodies, but has also directed the course of his polyphonic thought in a direction analogous to that taken by the polyphonic thought of the peoples of Europe during the early years of the Christian era' (Kirby 1930: 406). It is obvious that this procedure is closely related to that of *organum* in Medieval Europe; but, whereas for the latter this was a dynamic point of departure for the development of a polyphonic language infinitely richer and freer, it would seem that African parallelism is a point of arrival, the result of a development which, because of the constraint imposed upon it by the tonal schemas of the language, must remain dependent upon the language and can evolve no further. For this reason, it would seem mistaken to compare the 'directions' taken by these two kinds of *organum*. Indeed, Kirby recognises this, when, a few pages later, he writes about Bantu music: 'Independent polyphonic movement of parts would not occur systematically until tone ceased to be the predominant factor in language' (Kirby 1930: 406). This statement, made at a time when we knew far less about African music than we do today, is fully borne out by the vocal polyphonies of the Bushmen, the Hottentots, and especially the Pygmies. More immediately, we can now understand why multi-voiced music among certain ethnic groups must follow parallel movements, while instrumental music is not necessarily subject to this restraint.

According to the typology established by Jones, all the Central African peoples belong to the so-called '8 – 5 – 4 tradition', which comprises ethnic groups that sing in octaves, fifths, and fourths. This is confirmed by my own experience and also by that of Gerhard Kubik. In a recent study, having established that 'harmonies of fourths and fifths (and of isolated thirds among some tribes) are concentrated in a large territory in the Central African Republic and to the North of the Congo', the author then specifies 'In the Central African Republic, I have been able to observe that multi-voiced music of the Sango, Manja, Issongo, Monjombo, Mpyemo and to some extent the Gbaya tribes, produced a pronounced harmony in fourths, very often an organum in fourths' (Kubik 1968: 21). Elsewhere in the same work, he includes in this category the Azande. I would further include the Banda and the Ngbaka, to mention no more. Song in parallel fourths is certainly the most common procedure of this country.

As for 'organa in fourths', it seems to me that Kubik's observations need to be qualified a little. I have observed on many occasions that most often the choral parts in the very common alternation of soloist/choir are not always realised *entirely* in *organa* but partly in fourths and partly in fifths. This confirms Jones' observation, who points out correctly that sometimes even 'they are isolated fifths at strategic points in an otherwise unison song' (Jones 1959: 218).

It may help if at this point I recall this 'isolated third', which was mentioned by Kubik, and which Kirby (1930) had already observed. It is a corollary of the very structure of the scales, as Schneider pointed out: 'The harmonic system which has developed particularly strongly in Africa is closely connected with the development of the tonal system. The new notes which are added by polyphony to the *'canto firmo'* represent functional variants of the melodic notes within the given key' (Schneider 1957: 22). Africans are more concerned when adding another voice to preserve the scale – here pentatonic – than to produce a strict parallelism. Therefore, if they wanted to sing strictly in fourths, they would have to modify the scale organisation, which in this case would mean virtually creating another mode; the result would be a 'polytonality' with the following awkward consequences: (a) the concurrence of two pentatonic modes would entail the introduction of the semitone interval, which is so carefully avoided in all the scales, and therefore a rupture in the scale system; and (b) on account of the lack of tonal 'attraction' in pentatonic systems where there are neither 'strong' or 'weak' degrees, there would result a 'modal' unbalance, resulting from the ambiguity created by the two superimposed pentatonic modes.

3.6   SCALE SYSTEMS

In the African tradition, a musical scale is always perceived as a series of successive sounds arranged in *descending* order. This conception, although implicit, is a constant feature in musical practice. I simply mention here, by way of illustration, the tuning of string instruments, harps or *mvet*, which is always carried out systematically from the highest to the lowest string.

Moreover, in this tradition, the terms 'large' and 'small' are substituted for 'low' and 'high'; the higher a note, the 'smaller' it is considered, and the lower a note, the 'larger' it is considered.

The most widespread musical scale is the anhemitonic-pentatonic scale. It is based on the use, within the octave, of the section 1–5 in the cycle of fifths (Chailley 1955 and 1959), and it is characterised, as its name indicates, by the absence of the semitone interval, an absence that probably indicates a wider threshold of intervallic perception than that of European musics.

This scale can be organised in five different ways by simply inverting the sounds that constitute it; these correspond to five different types defined by the position occupied by the close succession of major seconds, that give rise to the only major third of the scale. Brăiloiu (1953: 333–4), following Riemann, calls these *pycnon*. These five types, in ascending order, are as follows:

    (1) C–D–E–G–A
    (2)   D–E–G–A–C
    (3)   E–G–A–C–D
    (4)   G–A–C–D–E
    (5)   A–C–D–E–G

In addition to these constituent notes, there are occasionally added in vocal music what I shall call, following Brăiloiu (1953) and Chailley (1955 and 1959) *pyen* notes, i.e., passing transitory notes that appear alongside the constituent notes but do not exist in their own right. Their absence in the scale is illustrated by the only instrument with fixed and constant sounds found among numerous groups in Central Africa – the xylophone, whose pitched notes cannot be varied. The bars of the xylophone are always and only tuned to the constituent notes of the pentatonic scale.

However, in certain communities, the pentatonic scale is not the only one in use; it may co-exist with other scale systems which are generally linked to particular repertoires and require instruments tuned accordingly. This situation is not peculiar to the Central African Republic; it has been found elsewhere in Africa, notably by Hugh Tracey, who notes that one cannot find, in any one village, different ensembles of instruments capable of playing together, precisely because each ensemble is tuned to a different system (Tracey 1958: 10).

As for Central Africa, Kubik remarks that the Mpyemo, a people settled in the West, use scales of five degrees for certain kinds of music and scales of seven degrees for other kinds; he insists that there is no interaction between the two scales, which 'exist, like foreign bodies, in the same culture' (Kubik 1968: 10). He also confirms that this is true of numerous regions in Central and East Africa (ibid.).

Kubik also notes that in Central Africa (unfortunately he does not specify which people), there is a scale that he describes as 'equipentatonic': that is, it divides the octave into five equal intervals. This is a scale-type that is very remote from the anhemitonic-pentatonic scale, and that probably exists alongside it. I would in fact call the latter 'classical' in so far as it applies the laws of Pythagorian consonance, in contrast to a scale that rejects the fundamental intervals of the fourth and the fifth (Chailley 1955).

The only scale I have found that presents this characteristic comes from the Nzakara people. It has an equihexatonic system:

Ex. 1

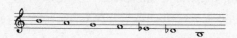

In other words, it is a 'whole-tone scale' which is used in a repertoire of women's songs. Here, too, the system existed alongside the traditional pentatonic scale, which is the one most widely used by this group of people.

Yvette Grimaud, on the other hand, states that among the Kare, who also live in the Central African Republic in the region of Bocaranga, *polysystems* can be found within the same piece of music, although admittedly this is itself polyphonic. She describes a 'solo for *sanza* with jingles and with thirteen metal strips [. . .] where the upper phrase alternates between two systems, the second of which is an anhemitonic-pentatonic distinguished by a *pycnon* whereas the lower phrase oscillates on a *pycnon* from a different scale' (Grimaud 1963: 240). The author provides the following schema:

Ex. 2

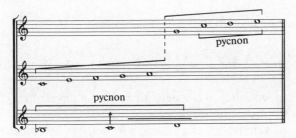

But it is questionable whether this involves a conscious and systematic procedure. My own contact with Central African musics over a period of more than fifteen years, persuades me that this is not the case. Let me simply say that such phenomena seem so rare as to be not a significant part of the scale systems used in that region.

There also exist among the Mpyemo in particular and probably elsewhere, scales that feature what Chailley calls '*mobile* degrees, i.e., during the same piece of music, one is free to choose between several intonations, each of fixed pitch' (Chailley 1964b: 263). But in all cases we must consider the constituent degrees of the scale as being relative, i.e., without reference to any notion of absolute pitch. However this notion is conceived in the West, in Africa it has no existence. But in many cases we may talk of a *constant* pitch, particularly in those repertoires whose performance requires melodic instruments of fixed pitch. Such is the case with xylophones where the pitches given by the bars of the instrument, which are tuned once and for all time, remain, in effect, a constant; in the music in which xylophones are used they enforce both their scale system (which is relative) and a reference to pitch (which is absolute), inasmuch as the realisation of the scale system is, in the last instance, dependent upon the initial tuning and therefore remains constant. This constancy may be maintained for many generations, since the tuning of a new xylophone is always carried out by using an older but identical instrument as a standard.

But this applies to other instruments besides the xylophone. Among some ethnic groups it also holds good for aerophones. Thus, among the Banda-Linda, the xylophone is used as a pitch reference for tuning the horns that perform as an ensemble. The same is true for certain chordophones, as Kubik has observed among the Azande: 'There is no absolute pitch for tuning commonly agreed on by all Azande harpists today. [. . .] When a Kponingbo xylophone was near, the harp was often at the same pitch as the xylophone' (Kubik 1964: 44).

3.7   Musical instruments

The traditional instruments of the Central African Republic display a wide variety of construction methods, materials, uses and types. In this single region there can be found not only representatives of every category known to organology, but also numerous types within each of these categories. I shall not enter into organological and performance details, which are not my concern, and would require a very long discussion, but for the sake of clarity in what follows shall briefly consider the instrument's functions and their uses. I shall follow this with the names of the principal instruments, ranged according to their organological classification.

3.7.1   Functions

The function of musical instruments can be divided into five different categories which are in some cases complementary:

(1)   They serve as a modal and/or rhythmic support for vocal music; this is their most common use.

(2)   They are reserved for the performance of a purely instrumental repertoire; this is the case with the Banda horn ensembles.

(3)   Certain instruments, such as wooden slit drums and whistles, can be used as a means of communication to transmit verbal messages.

(4)   They serve as privileged and often indispensable intermediaries, in order to establish communication between a man or his community and the supernatural powers, and in this role are very often subject to obligations and prohibitions.

(5)   They are symbols of temporal or spiritual authority, and are therefore very rarely or never used, as is notably the case with the Nzakara, where drums represent the ancestors.

3.7.2   Types of use

The instruments in use among the different peoples in the territory are, as I have said, very diverse. Before listing them, it is worth distinguishing between the following two categories: (a) *generic* instruments, those that are common to most ethnic groups in the Central African Republic and are also found in neighbouring territories and beyond, because of the geographical distribution of their users: this is the case notably with different types of xylophones, harps, the *mvet* (harp-*zither*), the *sanza*, as well as a large number of rhythm instruments; (b) *vernacular* instruments: those which are used exclusively by specific peoples and whose use is exclusive to them; these include end-blown and side-blown Banda horns, the *hìndèhú* or *mò.békè* whistles of the Mbenzele and Aka pygmies (already mentioned above) and the *ngòmbí*, the ten-stringed arched harp of the Ngbaka.

Another distinction can also be made between the orchestral ensembles. These can be considered from two points of view, according to whether they are composed only of instruments of the same species (as with ensembles of whistles, horns, families of drums etc.), or are composed of instruments of different organological categories, as is more often the case.

3.7.3   Idiophones

Most types of idiophone are found in this country:

> metal blades used as clappers (Pygmies)
>
> single or double bells, with internal or external clappers, and sometimes with handles
>
> wooden slit drums, used in 'families' of two to four instruments (Banda and Manja)
>
> gourd 'water-drums' (Islamic groups)
>
> a great variety of xylophones with five to ten keys, with gourd resonators, and also some xylophones with mobile keys, which are placed either over a hole dug in the ground or directly across the knees of the player
>
> log drums (Mpyemo and Kaka)
>
> many types of rattles, pellet bells, ankle- and knee-jingles
>
> scrapers (Ubangi river-dwellers);
>
> *sanza*, a set of bamboo or iron tongues fixed on to a base, with or without box resonators, with or without gourd amplifier or additional vibrating elements.

3.7.4   Membranophones

All membranophones are struck directly by the hand or with a stick. They include many kinds of drums, with single or double membranes played either in pairs or in 'families' of up to five instruments of different sizes. The body-shapes and the methods of fixing the skins vary considerably from one people to another: drums are cylindrical with buttoned skins among the Manja, conical with laced skins among the Ngbaka, waisted with pegged skins among the Mbenzele, and hourglass tension-drums among some of the northern Islamic groups.

3.7.5   Chordophones

The chordophones, which are all plucked, include:

> different kinds of musical bows, called 'mouth' bows when the mouth cavity of the player acts as a resonator (forest peoples) or 'ground' bows when a hole dug in the ground has this function (savannah peoples)
>
> the *mvet*, an eight-string harp-zither with gourd resonator, peculiar to the Gbaya, settled in the West of the country
>
> finally, and especially, a great variety of harps, which are, according to Kubik, the 'national instrument' of the country:

In no other African country is it so widespread or so popular. Here the biggest harps in Africa are played: I am referring to the carved ten-stringed harp of the Ngbaka, a tribe living to the south-west of the capital, Bangui.
(Kubik 1967: 44)

3.7.6   Aerophones

Aerophones of the flute type comprise a great variety of whistles of bamboo, wood or horn, with one to three finger holes; end-blown, notched flutes with four finger holes (in certain Islamic groups); globular flutes, of the ocarina type (Ali). The only double-reed instrument is the *algaîtha*, an oboe peculiar to the Hausa (an Islamic group). On the other hand, there is a wide variety of horns, differing as much in their materials, construction and size as in their usage and methods of playing: end-blown trumpets cut from tree trunks (Banda-Dakpa); transverse or 'oblique' horns, made of long, bell-ended roots (Banda-Linda); ivory or horn trumpets with or without a gourd bell. To the same category belongs the long telescoped metal trumpet, known as *kakaki*, used by some Islamic groups, particularly the Hausa, in Central Africa and elsewhere.

3.8   VOCAL AND INSTRUMENTAL TIMBRES

The basic production of Central African vocal songs is like the natural production of sound: a full open voice without vibrato, with no attempt at refinement. The songs being syllabic, the singing voice has only to produce one note to each syllable, or sometimes, due to the nature of the language, two or three but never more. Song therefore is not melismatic, and the Central Africans do not cultivate the art of vocalisation.

However, in an attempt to differentiate vocal timbres, this 'natural' production is used in as many ways as possible. Thus, the men often have recourse to a 'falsetto'. Not infrequently, one hears a song sung entirely in a falsetto voice, or, alternating one verse in a chest voice with another in a falsetto voice. One should also mention the ululations of the women, particularly in moments of joy.

Besides these devices of production, the Central Africans, like people in many other countries, add special effects to their voices. So, for example, they produce a 'tremolo' by hitting the throat with the hand. Or on specific ritual occasions it happens that the singers disguise their voices: by pinching the nose, or hitting the throat, they evoke 'their ancestors' voices'.

In the instrumental as in the vocal fields, the conception of timbre is completely different from that found in European music. In the Central African Republic, as elsewhere in Africa, people like to modify and alter the pure sound of the instrument in order to obtain more complex timbres, more blurred sounds. This is done by adding extra parts to the instrument itself, which are intended to modify the natural timbre. For example, ears of grain are added to the resonating boxes. Or the *sanza* is held inside a calabash that amplifies it and adds what are called 'parasitical' sounds. These are produced by fixing rustling pieces on to the calabash, such as pearl necklaces or coins suspended on cords. On the surface of the resonators of the xylophone bars, one often finds mirlitons made from the membranes of a bat stuck on with resin. Small iron rings are attached to the actual strips of the *sanza*, and vibrating simultaneously with the strips, they produce a characteristic crackling noise. Moreover, in certain trumpet ensembles, the musicians use a sort of flutter tongue effect: a rapid fluttering of the tongue produces a spasmodic exhalation of air that changes the instrument's natural timbre.

3.9   REPERTOIRES

It is not possible to define precisely the number of pieces that make up the musical heritage of a Central African ethnic group, but from my own experience, I would suggest that it is more accurate to speak in terms of hundreds rather than tens. For example, in a single Ngbaka village, for the repertoire of the *chantefable* alone, I collected more than fifty different melodies.

Among these traditional songs, some are suited to, if not reserved for, one or another of the numerous institutionalised, seasonal, social and/or religious occasions; others, undefined, are free from any constraint regarding their performance. The entire musical corpus of a society can thus be classified into a number of categories, that may correspond at least in principle to certain sociocultural functions. This classification is not the product of the researcher: it reflects the implicit taxonomy of the users, and in itself reveals the deep coherence of both social and sociomusical structures.

And so there is a particular repertoire that corresponds to each event that requires musical participation. By repertoire is meant here a collection of musical pieces, vocal and/or instrumental, whose performance requires a particular instrumental grouping, specific that is, to this or that event. In fact, the instrumental setting of the ensemble is usually far more significant here than the vocal setting.

In general, when referring to a repertoire, one uses a generic term that covers the occasion and the performance. The same word can therefore refer to a number of different concepts that are logically associated, such as the name of a ritual, a ceremony, the name of the dance used in it, and also the combination of rhythmic patterns that the percussion instruments must perform in accompanying it. Thus, among the Aka Pygmies, *bòndó* is at the same time the name of the magic ceremony that precedes the departure of the great hunt, the name of the dance performed by the seer during this ceremony, and the name of the polyrhythmic pattern which underlies the dance. Among the Sabanga, who live in Banda country, the word *ngbàkè* refers simultaneously to a choreographic repertoire, a particular dance style and a corpus of songs, but also to the ensemble of singers-dancers and instrumentalists who take part in its performance. Examples of this kind are legion.

Here too it is evident that the idea of function predominates. At times, a single criterion will suffice to define an event that is taking place. For example, an African approaching a village where the sound of drumming can be heard, will state without hesitation 'there is a death over there' simply because he has identified the particular drum rhythm played upon such occasions. Or again, if he sees a group of men travelling and carrying various instruments, the very combination of the instruments will allow him to recognise the ceremony in which they are going to take part, or from which they are returning home.

One should be very wary in the whole matter of classification of the different aspects of African culture. In Africa, mental categories are never as radical as they are in Western culture. One category is not necessarily opposed to another, does not exclude it on the binary principle; on the contrary, two categories may converge to the point where they overlap to some extent, cross each other, reinforce each other, rather than exclude each other. This principle, valid in many areas, is valid in our present concern as I shall demonstrate more fully below.

Book II

African polyphonic music

Introduction

This second Book is divided into two parts. In the first I attempt a classification of African polyphony, and in the second I consider the present state of the subject, in the light of previous studies. My approach to Central African polyphony is based upon fieldwork, and upon initially empirical and always pragmatic observations of the various musical procedures current in a specific geographical area.

It might have seemed more logical to begin with a summary of previous discussions before attempting a classification of these musical procedures. The reason which led me to adopt a different approach is the following one: a summary of the problem could not be attempted until one had defined more exactly what this 'problem' was, or, in other words, what the term *polyphony* could be taken to mean here.

The first part of this book is devoted to a classification of modalities of organisation, because it was this that enabled me to distinguish, out of all the types of multi-part musics observed, those which ought to be considered *polyphonic*. The second part, on the other hand, is a survey of historical records and of all the specialised modern treatments of African polyphony – such as will be defined below – to which I had access. So my approach, while basically synchronic, does nevertheless enable the diachronic aspect to be considered. This other, historical, point of view does indeed lead to an important observation: namely that a number of the musical procedures that are to be found today in an apparently restricted cultural area are not only still quite widespread in Africa today, but were equally widespread as far back as we have reliable testimonies, that is, up to nearly five hundred years ago.

These accounts describe technics of instrumental music that I have myself seen performed time and time again. The specifically dated observations of historians, chroniclers, travellers, missionaries or colonial administrators give us detailed descriptions of apparently identical types of music. This double point of view can therefore provide this part of my study, apart from its strictly synchronic approach (the here and now) with a much broader perspective, both in territory and in period.

1   A classification of African polyphonies

1.1   INTRODUCTION

For many European musicologists, the word 'polyphony' describes a technique of the art of composition that belongs to their tradition alone. In the Western world, polyphony dates from the end of the first thousand years AD. It blossomed in the school of Notre-Dame of Paris around 1200, particularly in the *organa* of Perotin. It has since been established, in various forms, as one of the fundamental techniques of composition in European Art music, of which it was at one time the principal characteristic.

If the idea of polyphony is accepted in such a narrow sense, it cannot be applied to the music of any other civilisation, whether this be the orchestral ensembles of Bali or the choral and instrumental ensembles of Black Africa. Let us quote the radical crew expressed by Pierre Boulez in the *Encyclopédie de la Musique* published by Fasquelle:

> The evolution of music in a polyphonic direction is a cultural phenomenon that belongs exclusively to the civilisation of Western Europe. In the various musical civilisations that preceded it, even those that rested on theoretically solid foundations, true polyphony, the principle of *independent part movement*, which characterises Western counterpoint, is not observable therein whatever certain musicologists say. In so-called exotic musics, one frequently finds [. . .] all kinds of superimposition but these are caused by simultaneous relationships in time, and not *independent* movement of parts.   (*Enc. Fasquelle* 1958: I, 584, 'Contrepoint')

This typically ethnocentric opinion differs fundamentally from that of Jacques Chailley who, in the Larousse *Dictionnaire de la Musique*, recalls that 'until very recently, polyphony was regarded as an invention of the learned Western world, where it was first mentioned in a treatise attributed to Hucbald in the ninth century.' The author continues: 'Today, thanks to the progress made by ethnomusicology, we know that polyphony is found throughout primitive music in a form that is very different from our classical and harmonic conception [. . .] a fact that leads us completely to reconsider the whole question' (*Dict. Larousse* 1957: II, 208, 'Polyphonie'). Those ethnomusicologists who accept the very general etymological meaning of the term often tend to call all multi-part music, whether vocal or instrumental, 'polyphonic' even if there is no obvious organisation. In itself, the concept of polyphony thus embraces procedures as diverse as heterophony, *organum*, homophony, drone-based music, parallelism or overlapping. The shared characteristics of all these procedures is that they all relate to multi-part phenomena. But, *all multi-part music is not necessarily polyphonic*. Therefore, in order to avoid confusion of terms, and until the word 'polyphony' has been precisely defined, I shall use the more neutral term *multi-part* music.

I shall attempt firstly to outline the principal terms generally used to describe the various kinds of multi-part music current in Africa, by examining their distinctive characteristics. This analysis should enable us to specify what, in the framework of the present study, is to be understood by that particular form of multi-part music that we call *polyphony*.

1.2   MULTI-PART, NON-POLYPHONIC PROCEDURES

In the following pages, I investigate several definitions, taken from different authors, of the principal kinds of multi-part musics that I do not consider to be truly polyphonic. I begin with the simpler forms and proceed to the more complex.

1.2.1   Heterophony

At the end of an article entitled 'Über Heterophonie', Guido Adler defines heterophony as 'a rudimentary and unorganised plurivocality'. He then suggests that it should be classed 'alongside the categories of homophony and polyphony as a third stylistic category' (Adler 1908: 24). In *The Wellsprings of Music* Curt Sachs, on the other hand, prefers to include under heterophony, 'every type of part-performance left to tradition and improvisation – *contrapunto alla mente* as against *res facta*' (Sachs 1962: 191). In his *Musiklexikon*, Horst Seeger, having looked at Sach's definition, writes: 'Carl Stumpf introduced the concept of heterophony into modern ethnomusicology as a description of multi-part musics that are oriental and non-European, in which a melody appears in several parts simultaneously, but is as freely handled as the voice or the instrument or the fantasy of the player permit' (Seeger 1966: 1, 389). A more restrictive and so more precise definition is proposed by Willy Apel in the *Harvard Dictionary of Music*: 'A term used by Plato and adopted by modern musicologists (first by C. Stumpf) to describe an improvisational type of polyphony, namely the simultaneous use of slightly or elaborately modified versions of the same melody by two (or more) performers, [. . .] adding a few extra tones or ornaments to the singer's melody' (Apel 1970: 383). For William P. Malm, in his article 'On the meaning of the term "disphony"', heterophony is 'multi-part music in which each part is rhythmically different (like counterpoint), but the difference is caused by simultaneous variations on the same melody by each of the multi-parts' (Malm 1972: 248).

In 'Les langages musicaux de l'Afrique Subsaharienne', J.H. Kwabena Nketia observes that 'This type of organisation is fundamentally linear rather than multilinear: occasional heterophony is to be considered as purely ornamental' (Nketia 1972: 29). In *Origine des instruments de musique*, André Schaeffner, in his description of heterophony, takes up and comments on André Gide's description (already quoted in Book I):

Let me quote three texts from the travel-notes which André Gide published under the title *Retour du Tchad*: 'But imagine this tune yelled by a hundred persons *not one of whom sings the exact note*. It is like trying to make out the main line from a host of little strokes. The effect is prodigious, and gives an impression of polyphony and of harmonic richness. . .

Here they never sing in tune. Moreover, when one of them sings "doh, re", the other sings "re, doh". Some of them sing variants. Out of six singers, each one of them sings something a little different, without its being exactly 'in parts'. But the result is a kind of thickness of harmony, which is extremely strange. . . As always in French Equatorial Africa, the chorus did not wait for the soloist's phrase to finish, but struck in on the last, and sometimes even on the penultimate note . . . The refrain is attacked on several notes at once. Some voices rise, and others fall. It is like creepers winding around a central stalk, adapting themselves to its curve, without following it exactly.'

Gide gives a very clear presentation of the problem. We are not dealing here with polyphony in the classical sense of the term; nevertheless, we encounter a dense harmonic texture that has a kind of halo of dissonance, which slightly blurs the outline of the intended monody. This texture may be produced either by parallel movement in small dissonant intervals, or by contrary and conjunct movements, with a hypothetical trace of the monody in all parts.

(Schaeffner 1936: 327)

These various definitions leave us in no doubt that heterophony, as understood by musicologists, cannot be considered to be the same as polyphony. This is also Marius Schneider's opinion. In an article discussing consonance in primitive polyphony, he writes, 'As long as one of the two voices is merely a schematic duplication of the other, no real polyphony can develop' (Schneider 1963: 150). On this very point, François Michel, in his article 'Heterophony' in the *Encyclopédie de la Musique*, writes:

Heterophony. . . is not a specifically Greek phenomenon, but is a feature of all the traditional musics in the world. Many contemporary ethnomusicologists, properly concerned that due respect be given to the object of their studies, feel that it should be called polyphony; for others, myself included, there is no reason for this to be so. Even if the physical phenomenon of heterophony can be reduced to polyphony by the etymologists, the meaning of the music itself prevents us from accepting *musically* this theory that reduces polyphony to heterophony.

(*Enc. Fasquelle* 1959: II, 466)

I.2.2   Overlapping

In the volumes *Science de la Musique* from the larger *Dictionnaire de la Musique* published by Bordas, overlapping is defined as follows: 'a process employed instinctively by primitive peoples [sic] in the performance of certain monodic songs which require several persons or groups to take part; it occurs when a second soloist (or group) enters before the first has wholly completed its intervention. For a short lapse of time, monody is turned into a rudimentary polyphony by the overlaying of one phrase ending over the beginning of another' (*Sc. de la Mus.* 1976: II, 1046). This description of the process is sufficiently explicit to make any other unnecessary.

I.2.3   Drone-based music

A general definition of the term 'drone' is given by the *Encyclopédie de la Musique*: 'In the popular music of the most diverse ethnic groups, we call a continuous bass on one single note a drone; it is played on one string or pipe of an instrument' (*Enc. Fasquelle* 1958: I, 435, 'Bourdon'). In *Über Mehrstimmigkeit in der aussereuropäischen Musik*, Hornbostel (1909: 300) states that 'this sustained and uninterrupted single sound' serves as a base for the principal melody. Although this process is more frequently associated with instrumental music, it is also found in vocal music. The *Riemann Musiklexikon*, recalling that 'The practice of the drone is very old, and still very widespread in the popular music of Europe and countries outside Europe', goes on to specify that 'The drone is generally applied to the lower register of an instrument or a voice; most often in the form of held invariant notes' (Riemann 1967: III, 118, 'Bordun').

I.2.4   Parallelism

In *Theory and method in ethnomusicology*, Bruno Nettl describes parallelism as the reproduction by different parts, at the same time, of the same musical material at different pitches (Nettl 1964: 152). In general terms, parallelism is considered to be a simultaneous performance of two or more different parts that are separated by constant intervals other than the octave. This technique is widely used in Africa, where the most frequent intervals are the fifth, the fourth, and more rarely the third. From the rhythmical point of view, parallelism in vocal music implies an identical division of syllables in all the parts; in other words, homosyllabism.

1.2.5   Homophony

Like parallelism, homophony creates a similar rhythmic articulation in all the parts, but their movement is not necessarily parallel. The *Riemann Musiklexikon* describes homophony as 'a progression through a series of chords in which all the voices move in a rhythmically identical way or nearly so' (Riemann 1967: III, 378). The *Harvard Dictionary of Music* clearly distinguishes between polyphony and homophony, with the latter being defined as 'music in which one voice leads melodically, being supported by an accompaniment in chordal or a slightly more elaborate style. Homophony is the opposite of polyphony, music in which all parts contribute more or less equally to the musical fabric [. . .] A more suitable term for this style is homorhythmic' (Apel 1970: 390). The idea of homorhythm is also preferred by Malm, who, in an article on the term disphony, writes: 'The clearest distinctions between the fundamental forms of polyphony should begin with the nature of their rhythm. On this basis one can say that if the different parts of the multi-part event have different tones but use basically the same rhythm the style can be called homophonic' (Malm 1972: 248).

1.2.6   Conclusion

The various processes of multi-part music described above apply, as I have said, to a number of musics performed in the Central African Republic. Moreover, some of them have spread across the rest of the continent to the south of the Sahara. But in Central Africa alone, the techniques of heterophony, overlapping and parallelism are so widespread that it would be impossible to describe them exhaustively. Moreover, an inventory of these techniques would only result in a catalogue of variants of the same phenomenon, which because they are so widespread have been sufficiently described in numerous other publications.

The Central African Republic does, on the other hand, contain multi-part musics based on far more elaborate procedures, which are among the most complex in all of Black Africa. It is these musics that I take to be *polyphonic*. So, before going further, it is necessary to consider their specific characteristics, in order to elicit the overall distinctive features that enable us to describe them as polyphonic.

1.3   POLYPHONY AND POLYRHYTHM

1.3.1   General definitions

At this point of our enquiry, by a process of elimination, it becomes possible to outline a definition of Central African polyphony that may then be used throughout the present study. For it cannot be reduced to any of the techniques analysed above, or even a

combination of all of them. Polyphony, rather, unlike them, presents itself as a procedure which is *multi-part, simultaneous, hetero-rhythmic and non-parallel.*

> – multi-part, because it is made up of several (at least two) melodic or rhythmic
> lines that are different and superimposed;
> – simultaneous, because it is not confined to sporadic encounters, as is the case
> with heterophony and overlapping;
> – heterorhythmic, because the rhythmic articulation is different for each
> separate part in contrast to the homorhythm implied in homophony;
> – non-parallel, finally, because of the independent development of each part
> vis-à-vis the others, where both contrary or divergent movements occur, as
> opposed to parallel movements.

Polyphony is therefore defined as *any multi-part vocal or instrumental music whose
heterorhythmic parts are, within the culture of its traditional performers, considered as
the constituent elements of a single musical entity.* This definition is, by intention,
limited in its application to vocal musics and music for instruments of fixed pitch.
In the case of percussion instruments, more frequently of indeterminate pitch, the term
polyrhythm, analogous to polyphony, is used. By this term should be understood
*any multi-part arrangement based on the superimposition of different rhythmic figures
whose interlacing results in a rhythmic polyphony.*

I shall now examine a number of authorities in order to identify, from within Western
art music, approaches to the notions of polyphony and polyrhythm, which will show
that they are not in conflict with what I understand by these terms as applied to African
musicology. It will then follow that ethnomusicology is no longer marginal to classical
musicology in terms of the basic techniques proper to any musical structuration.

Finally, we shall see that in the Central African Republic, regardless of the kind of
polyphony or polyrhythm that is practised, it always involves the principle of *ostinato
with variations.*

1.3.2 Polyphony

At this point, one should decide to what extent my definition of polyphony, based
on actual musics found in Africa, is compatible with those generally given.

The *Encyclopédie de la Musique* gives the following definition of polyphony:
'We name thus the superimposition of two or more vocal or instrumental parts whose
development is both horizontal (contrapuntal) and vertical (harmonic)' (*Enc. Fasquelle*
1961: III, 463). Riemann, however, defines polyphony as: 'An ensemble in which the
different voices have independent melodic roles (the opposite: homophony)' (Riemann
1931: 1031). This idea is further elaborated in a more recent edition of the *Riemann
Musiklexikon* where polyphony is defined as 'the kind of pluri-'vocality' (*Mehr-
'Stimmigkeit'*) in the literal sense, in which the voices, (whether called the *cantus*, the
melodies or the lines) display a melodic and rhythmic independence' (Riemann 1967:
III, 740). For the *Harvard Dictionary of Music*, polyphony is a 'music that combines
several simultaneous voice-parts of individual design, in contrast to monophonic music
which consists of a single melody, or homophonic music, which combines several voice-
parts of similar, rhythmically identical design' (Apel 1790: 687). Finally, in Seeger's
Musiklexikon, we have the following description 'A mode of composition in several

parts in which each separate part has independent melodic and rhythmic figures. These parts, which follow the rules of part-movement and harmony, are treated independently while at the same time combined with one another. Polyphony is based on counterpoint' (Seeger 1966: II, 298).

The same author defines counterpoint as 'a technique of part-movement (*Satztechnik*) which causes several independent melodic lines to sound together and unites them into a more elevated whole' (ibid.: I, 505). The ethnomusicologist Malm, in the article cited above, mentions the necessary conditions of counterpoint: 'If the different parts have different tones but are relatively independent rhythmically, the style is usually called counterpoint or some variation of that term in the language of a given writer. Definitions usually go on to say that, if melodic units of the various parts are similar, words like imitational counterpoint or canon may be used depending on the given musical situation' (Malm 1972: 248).

Finally, let us quote Erich von Hornbostel to conclude this rapid survey. In 1928, in a work entitled 'African Negro Music', this pioneer of ethnomusicology stated that African polyphony was based on a principle of superimposition where 'only the three most consonant combinations of sound, octave, fifth, and fourth are used'. Comparing it to *organum* and other musical forms used in the West during the Middle Ages, the author goes on to make the point that 'This kind of polyphony. . . is based on pure melody, and has nothing to do with harmony as we understand it' (Hornbostel 1928: 41).

1.3.3   Polyrhythm

Riemann defines polyrhythm as 'multiple rhythms, the superimposition of different rhythms in different voice parts' (Riemann 1931: 1031). In *Science de la Musique*, however, it is defined in slightly more detail as 'the superimposition of different rhythms in such a way that there are mutual shiftings of the rhythmic accents, (1976: II, 820). Finally, the *Harvard Dictionary of Music* gives us an even more detailed description: 'The simultaneous use of strikingly contrasted rhythm in different parts of the musical fabric. In a sense, all truly contrapuntal or polyphonic music is polyrhythmic, since rhythmic variety in simultaneous parts more than anything else gives the voice-parts the individuality that is essential to polyphonic style. Generally, however, the term is restricted to cases in which rhythmic variety is introduced as a special effect that is often called "cross rhythm"' (Apel 1970: 687).

It remains to examine one by one the different kinds of polyphonies and polyrhythms found in the Central African Republic. We can then establish points of similarity with those defined by the dictionaries and encyclopedias of Western classical music.

1.4   POLYPHONIC AND POLYRHYTHMIC PROCEDURES IN THE CENTRAL AFRICAN REPUBLIC

1.4.1   Ostinato

If one had to describe in a formula all the polyphonic and polyrhythmic procedures used in the Central African Republic, one might define them as *ostinatos with varia-*

tions. Indeed, with very rare exceptions, all polyphonic musics whether vocal or instrumental are based on this very principle. Certainly the extent and kind of the ostinato differs, as do the means by which the variations which take place in it are implemented. Ostinatos and variations will vary, depending on whether the music is purely vocal or strictly percussive. Nonetheless, whatever the dimensions or the types of music the fundamental organisational principle still remains this one.

Ostinato here means *the regular and uninterrupted repetition of a rhythmic or melodic-rhythmic figure, with an unvarying periodicity underlying it.* This definition, though intended as a description of traditional Central African music, does not conflict with Western musicological definitions of the term. Thus Riemann defines ostinato as 'a technical term that describes the continual return of a theme surrounded by ever-changing counterpoint [. . .] The great masters of the age of polyphony loved to write a whole mass or long motets on a single phrase constantly repeated by the tenor. But the repetitions are not always identical, and the little theme would appear in all sorts of modified forms' (Riemann 1931: 953). Many Central-African musics correspond exactly to this definition. They are indeed musical pieces based on a short phrase, which reappears 'in all sorts of modified forms'. Riemann concludes his article 'It is a very effective compositional procedure, which has always been more or less commonly practised, and traces of it can be found in all forms and at all times' (ibid.: 953).

For the meaning of ostinato as performed in Africa, let us take Rose Brandel's description from the article 'Africa' in the *Harvard Dictionary of Music*: 'The African ostinato, usually quite small in length and pitch range, may be continuous or intermittent, vocal or instrumental, and may appear above or below the main line. Frequently there is a multi-ostinato, two or more ostinatos moving contrapuntally, with or without a longer melodic line' (Brandel 1970: 20). In an earlier article called 'Polyphony in African Music' Rose Brandel was already drawing attention to the contrapuntal character of the device: 'The combination of two or more ostinatos, a direct correlate of the African inclination for 'orchestral' music, distinctly belongs to the contrapuntal, or horizontal, type of polyphony. That is, each ostinato moves in independent melodic and rhythmic patterns' (Brandel 1965: 31). In *Music in Primitive Culture*, Bruno Nettl judges that 'The ostinato patterns are always very short in primitive music, shorter than, for example, the sixteenth-century basses in western cultivated music' (Nettl 1956: 87). We shall see in what follows that this is not always the case in Central Africa.

1.4.2   Imitation

A technique of musical development which is much used in European music, imitation is also found in a number of African musics. Some definitions used in dictionaries and encyclopaedias clearly outline the technique.

In his *Dictionnaire de Musique*, Riemann insists on its formal aspect: 'Imitation is one of the fundamental laws which govern form in the art of music' (Riemann 1931: 609). He states that canon constitutes 'the strictest form of musical imitation' (ibid.: 208). In the Larousse *Dictionnaire de la Musique*, it is defined as: 'the reproduction by one voice, of a part, a phrase or a fragment of music, stated by another voice. The voice which states is called antecedent, the voice which replies is called consequent. Canon

[. . .] is no more than a strict and rigorous form of imitation'. In *Science de la Musique*, the definition is extended to include non-European musics. Imitation is described as:

the repetition of a melodic fragment or entire melody, stated by one voice (the antecedent) and taken up by another (the consequent). The imitation may be strict or free. In the first case, the intervals and rhythms of the antecedent are exactly imitated; in the second case, there may be a certain amount of melodic or rhythmic alteration, which nevertheless allows the listener to recognise the imitation. . . The origin of imitation can be found in the relatively simple polyphonic musics of several primitive peoples, that seem to be derived from alternated songs and heterophony.
(*Sc. de la Mus.* 1976: II, 481-2)

The *Harvard Dictionary of Music* completes the definition of the technique with a historical account of its appearance in European music. Imitation is 'the restatement in close succession of a melody (theme, motif) in different parts of a contrapuntal texture. . . Imitation is predicated on the presence of two (or more) equivalent voice-parts, and it is interesting to note that its history begins with the earliest type of composition meeting this requirement, the *organa tripla* and *quadrupla*, of the school of Notre Dame, c. 1200' (Apel 1970: 402).

Summarising this information, *Science de la Musique* places the emphasis on the relatively late diffusion of the technique: 'In the course of the history of western music, imitation appears for the first time in the 13th century. . . It was not however until the 15th century that it became generally used as a principle of composition' (*Sc. de la Mus.* 1976: II. 482).

1.4.3   Melodic counterpoint

Melodic counterpoint – as distinct from rhythmic counterpoint – occurs in the Central African Republic in vocal music and in music performed by pitched instruments. For the latter, there are two kinds of performance. The first requires an ensemble of mixed instruments; the second requires instruments which are in themselves polyphonic, where the two hands of the musician combine to play distinct rhythmic and melodic parts, providing a counterpoint that is both melodic and rhythmic. This is especially the case with the harp.

As for other inherently polyphonic instruments, the rhythm may be the same in both parts, although the melodic parts are not in parallel movement. Such is the case with the xylophone. Here one finds technique very close to homophony, but the difference is that there is no predominant melodic line, or, more precisely, no hierarchy among the parts. The same principle applies to music played on two xylophones, i.e., in four parts. Although it is not a general rule, all the parts frequently observe the same rhythmic values. It these instruments are included here it is because, in practice, they are always in a relationship of rhythmic counterpoint with percussion instruments, and of melodic counterpoint with one or several vocal parts.

It should be remembered that instrumental music does not generally appear in an autonomous or isolated context. It is nearly always combined with vocal music. The function of the instruments is to sustain the song by providing a framework that is periodic, rhythmic and modal. Sometimes, however, the song is not polyphonic, but a simple monody or a combination of the multi-part techniques defined above as non-polyphonic, namely heterophony, overlapping, drone-based music and parallelism. In these cases, polyphonic elements occur in the instrumental parts only.

As for vocal polyphonies, these are found principally among the different Pygmy groups in the Central African Republic, namely the Aka, the Mbenzele, and others. In the musics of these groups, the songs, because of their periodicity, their internal structure and underlying ostinato are astonishingly close to the principle of the passacaglia.

In the Larousse *Dictionnaire de la Musique*, Armand Machabey has written a short history of this form. The 'melody of a few bars', which was called passacaglia at the end of the sixteenth century became, at the beginning of the seventeenth century a: 'theme and variations, with a bass that was repeated without change or with only slight modifications, until it became like an ostinato bass. Moreover, the short, simple theme. . . moved to the bass part and in turn supported sets of variations'. However, the author says 'the theme of the ostinato bass can from time to time be passed to intermediate or higher voices' (*Dict. Larousse* 1957: II, 166, Machabey, 'Passacaille').

A short ostinato theme, simple but varied – this could well be a description of Pygmy vocal counterpoint. And, as with the passacaglia, the theme is not necessarily confined to the lower part. But, in this case, there is a difference; the theme is often *implicit*, and so there may be a passacaglia without an ostinato bass, even without an explicit theme.

For the term *Basse obstinée ou contrainte*, the *Dictionnaire de la Musique* gives the following definition: 'continuous repetition in the bass part of a short melodic motif. . . This theme accompanies all kinds of variations, whether improvised or notated' (*Dict. Larousse* 1957: I, 82). This definition, if we leave out the reference to notation, applies in all respects to the procedure used by the Pygmies. As in Medieval polyphony, the Pygmies of the Central African Republic – who are in fact the only people there who perform vocal counterpoint – employ contrary and divergent movements and imitation in the voice parts.

1.4.4   Rhythmic counterpoint

Rhythmic counterpoint (or polyrhythm) is to unpitched instruments as melodic counterpoint (or polyphony) is to voices and pitched instruments. In Black Africa, this kind of counterpoint is essentially made up of so-called 'cross-rhythms', i.e., of different rhythmic patterns interweaving with each other. The principle of *cross-rhythm* (a term apparently introduced by Percival Kirby (1934: 54)), involves the combination of two or more rhythmic figures in such a way that they cross rather than coincide with one another. There are nonetheless moments when the different figures correspond, but the overall ostinato pattern that is created emphasises their points of divergence or their oppositions rather than their points of connection.

This phenomenon is produced whenever several percussion instruments play together, no matter how many. In the Central African Republic at least, and within traditional practice, it is rare to find a strictly percussive instrument played on its own, outside a vocal or instrumental context. The rhythmic ostinato patterns are peculiar to the groups to which they belong. These vary not only from one ethnic group to another, but, within one and the same group, from one kind of music to another. In fact, the rhythmic combinatory, which is the result of crossing several individual rhythmic figures, is the defining feature of a musical category, recognisable as such to the members of the social group. Because of their polyrhythmic treatment, these patterns often appear to be very complex, but as Gilbert Rouget rightly says in the *Encyclopédie de la Musique*: 'When reduced to a single instrument, the rhythmic pattern is always simple. But the combination of these patterns in an interwoven texture, whose principles remain to be discovered, produces a complicated rhythm that is apparently incomprehensible.' (*Enc. Fasquelle* 1961: III, 940, 'Musique en Afrique noire') The same observation is made by Curt Sachs in *The Wellsprings of Music*: 'Individually, African rhythms are very simple and become confusingly involved only in their concurrence' (Sachs 1962: 162).

1.4.5   The hocket technique

Riemann defines hocket in his *Dictionnaire de la Musique* as 'a compositional device in twelfth- and thirteenth-century polyphony. In this technique, each voice in turn stops and starts in rapid alternation' (Riemann 1931: 596). The term is more closely described in the Larousse *Dictionnaire de la Musique*: 'A technique of musical composition [. . .] that requires at least two voices. The first voice sings one or two notes then pauses, while the second voice responds with one or two notes and pauses; the first voice sings again, and so on' (*Dict. Larousse* 1957: I, 454).

Although in Western art music of the Middle Ages, hocket seems to have been mainly a vocal technique, it is found in Africa, and particularly in the Central African Republic, essentially in instrumental music, where it is applied with extreme rigour. The device is in fact used there in music for groups of wind instruments where each instrument can produce only one sound, which is tuned to a specific pitch. The combination of the different instrumental parts necessarily produces a rhythmic counterpoint that is here the result of the purest hocketing. From their interweaving there results a polyrhythm with sounds of fixed pitch; i.e., a polyrhythm that is spread over the degrees of a perfectly defined scale.

Thus, by assembling isolated sounds, but in such a way that they are interwoven at extremely precise points, Central African musicians produce very highly structured polyphonies.

In an important study entitled 'The hocket technique in African music', Nketia describes the formal characteristics of this procedure: 'In any music in which the principle here discussed is applied in whole or in part, the resultant – a complex of pitch- or tone-contrasts in a defined sequence, operating within the framework of an equally defined pattern of rhythm – is of particular importance. Each player must have a general awareness of the resultant, as well as the knack of coming in at the right moment'. For this reason, continues the author, 'Analysis of music employing the hocket technique – whether in its simple or more elaborate forms – must emphasise the resultant (or groups of resultants) by showing the interdependence of the separate instruments or the links, both horizontal and vertical, which bind them into an integrated whole' (Nketia 1962: 50–1). This is an important statement because it gives the lie to those theoreticians who have declared that independent part movement does not exist in polyphonic music outside Europe.

Following his description, Nketia points out an aspect which is as much contrapuntal as polyrhythmic in African hocket: 'While the hocket technique in African music may have originally been used for overcoming the natural limitation of particular instruments, it appears to have established itself as a contrapuntal technique which may be applied in more elaborate forms in instrumental ensembles of a fairly homogeneous character. It is the basis of much of what has been described as 'cross rhythm' or 'crossing the beat' in African music' (ibid.: 51).

1.4.6   Conclusion

The five main techniques that are described above have been separated merely for the sake of clarity. Moreover, it can be seen that they are not in conflict with the terminology used in Western musicology to describe similar phenomena. However, these procedures are rarely found in isolation. In fact, an analysis of African musics reveals that, in most cases, they are combined with one another in various ways. This is pointed out by Rose Brandel in the article 'Africa' in the *Harvard Dictionary of Music*: 'The principal African polyphonic types. . . may often intermingle within one piece and may appear in any vocal and instrumental combination' (Brandel 1970: 19).

Throughout this attempt at classifying the different techniques found in African polyphony, I have been fully aware of the reductive and abstract aspects of some of my descriptions. This seemed necessary in order to arrive at a systematic approach to the music concerned. But if we had forgotten, Jaap Kunst, in the conclusion to *Métrique, rythmique, musique à plusieurs parties* would have reminded us of the difficulty: 'How is one to define the difference between homophony and polyphony? Who knows where heterorhythm ends and polyrhythm begins? where exactly is the boundary between heterophony and polyphony? [. . .] The living practice is infinitely superior, in its flexibility and variety of forms, to schematic theories' (Kunst 1950: 37). This distinction and this proviso are the very things that I have tried to define, precisely so that we should arrive at a better understanding of the 'living practice'. Paradoxically enough, in order to grasp and describe Central African polyphonies in their concrete reality, a preliminary abstract classification did in fact seem to be necessary. However, I will now set aside typologies based on abstract criteria, so as to apprehend the main principles that, in practice, govern the performance.

Having thus defined our subject, we can now consider its present state, based on eyewitness accounts and previous studies dealing with polyphonic and polyrhythmic musics performed in the past and today in sub-Saharan Africa.

2 Previous studies: the present state of the subject

Of the principles that may be said to underlie Central African polyphony, some are current in a much wider geographical area, extending from Ethiopia to South Africa.

That is why I have chosen in this summary of previous studies, rather than restricting it to Central African polyphony (which has hitherto been little studied), to devote it to all of sub-Saharan Africa, so as to compare some of the techniques observed or studied elsewhere, both in earlier times and today, with analogous procedures now flourishing in Central Africa. As the reader will see, the documentation concerning this country is very sparse; indeed, out of the hundred or so accounts that I have succeeded in locating, only seven touch upon Central African polyphony. Let me emphasise, nevertheless, that this summary is not exhaustive but is a presentation of the most significant texts that throw light on the subject.

The information available is scattered across some six hundred years. The very first mention of an African musical instrument dates from the fourteenth century, whereas the first description of a performance that would seem to have been polyphonic in character dates from 1497. These descriptions derive from a wide range of sources. They include travellers' tales, as well as the accounts of missionaries, geographers, explorers, ethnographers *avant la lettre*, members of the colonial administration, stationed in various countries. These witnesses, whether they had any musical knowledge or not, always had an opinion about the music that they happened to hear, and they always gave their aesthetic judgement about it.

What all these witnesses have in common is their attempt to give an account, with varying degrees of astuteness or competence, of performances they had attended, and things they had seen and heard. However one judges these works, they are all nonetheless based upon direct observation. Unfortunately the same cannot be said, as we shall see, for that of every specialist.

To this first category of 'impressionistic' accounts there later came to be added the more ample works of specialists, musicians, musicologists, and ethnomusicologists, who have more or less successfully focussed their attention upon African polyphony, from close at hand or at a distance. The various formal studies now available to us naturally belong to this category.

The presentation of these two categories is chronological, so that the reader meets the travellers' narrative first, with the work of specialists subsequently taking the place of that of mere observers.

2.2   TRAVELLERS' TALES AND DIVERSE DESCRIPTIONS

The testimonies grouped here present certain common features. First, when the narrator is describing musical instruments, and even when he presents each of them separately, one can deduce – either by referring to other moments in the same narrative, or by comparing it with other testimonies, or finally by observing present-day practice – that these instruments are played in groups. So it is, for instance, with ivory horns, which, by analogy with the European instruments with which they were familiar, observers often also called 'trumpets'. Whether they are presented separately or in groups, the instruments mentioned are often described in terms of their manner of performance, sometimes even of the technique involved in playing them. Finally, information concerning the manufacture of instruments is in fact extremely valuable, since it shows that instrumental manufacture has altered very little over time.

Apart from this, these testimonies do not claim any 'scientific objectivity' for their account, for the observers often sprinkle them with personal remarks about the manner in which they perceived and responded to the musics they heard. But this subjective bias did not lead me to jettison these aesthetic judgements. For, apart from giving the accounts a certain picturesqueness, they also reflect a number of attitudes typical of the European response to African music. Indeed, some are very adversely disposed towards this music, or even reject it totally; while others are quite open-minded about it, and listen with sympathetic curiosity, and sometimes even with genuine interest.

I have thought it important not to modify the tone of these testimonies. The judgements which they contain are, as the saying goes, the sole responsibility of their authors. I hope the reader will enjoy their often artless flavour.

2.2.1   Before the seventeenth century

The very first reference that we have to African instruments is relevant here, inasmuch as it concerns horns, which are widely used in polyphony.

In a study by André Schaeffner, entitled 'La découverte de la musique noire', we read this: 'As regards Africa, a medieval Arab chronicler, Ibn Battuta, saw the Blacks of Sudan playing several instruments. The narrative of his voyage dates from the fourteenth century' (Schaeffner 1950: 208). A few pages further on, he writes: 'Already in the fourteenth century, Ibn Battuta mentions ivory horns; these have now almost entirely disappeared from the Sudan, but must once have been played throughout almost all of Black Africa'. And, going much further back in time, the author adds: 'In certain tomb paintings in Egypt, dating from the middle of the second millenium BC, the only men with negroid features are musicians or are carrying elephant tusks. Blacks must therefore always have been known for their commitment to music or to the ivory trade' (ibid.: 212). The very oldest narrative of a European traveller's voyage in sub-Saharan Africa, the travel journal of Vasco da Gama (1497–1498), contains the first known testimony regarding musical performances of a polyphonic character:

On Saturday [2 December 1497] there arrived around two hundred negroes, large and small, bringing a dozen horned beasts, both bulls and cows, as well as four or five sheep. And they began to play upon four or five flutes, some of which were high and some low, so well in fact that they played harmoniously indeed, quite surprising for negroes, from whom one expects little in the way of music, and they danced in the negro fashion [. . .]

On Sunday, the same number came again, accompanied by their women and by small boys, and the women stood on the top of a rise beside the sea; they led a large number of bulls and cows there, and, halting at two points, alongside the shore, they began to play upon their instruments and to dance as they had done on Saturday.   (Morelet 1864: 9)

This took place in Mossel Bay, a port to the East of the Cape of Good Hope, and the men whom Vasco da Gama took for 'negroes' were really Hottentots (cf. Schaeffner 1950: 208). Thus, when Kirby notes that 'the Hottentot group had reed-flutes as far back as 1497' (1934: 169), he is referring, in all likelihood, to Vasco da Gama's journal. He thus identifies the 'flutes' mentioned by the Portuguese navigator to the whistles or reed-flutes that certain peoples in South Africa use to this very day.

Another episode in this same journal contains valuable information about musical practice. The expedition had just anchored 'opposite a place called Mélinde', which is today called Malindi, and is to the North of Mombassa, in Kenya. The event recorded by the navigator occurred on Easter Sunday, 15 April 1498. The Europeans were received by the king:

The king was dressed as follows: first, a robe of damask, lined with green satin, and, on his head, a very rich turban; then, two bronze thrones, with their cushions and a canopy of crimson satin, that was round in form, and was fixed to a pole. His page was an old man who wore a cutlass with a silver scabbard; add to this several anafils, and two ivory trumpets, the height of a man, of wonderful workmanship, which one played by blowing into a hole that was drilled into the middle of them; the sound of these trumpets was attuned to that of the anafils.   (ibid.: 36)

This account requires several comments. First the 'ivory trumpets' are undoubtedly transverse horns with a lateral embouchure, for they are clearly described as such. But what are 'anafils'? According to Morelet, who translated Vasco da Gama's journal into French, the instrument is a 'kind of bugle' (ibid.: 19); for Curt Sachs (1964: 12), *anafils* are old Spanish trumpets, the term *anafil* deriving from the Arab *nafîr*. They could in that case be straight end-blown horns as distinct from the 'ivory trumpets', which would be side-blown horns. Be this as it may, Vasco da Gama heard a form of music in which the two types of instruments played at once, and since he was careful to note that 'the sound of these trumpets was attuned to that of the anafils', it would seem reasonable to suppose that these different instruments performed different parts together.

Finally, and this last remark also applies to the following testimonies, these observations 'from the field' are sufficiently exact and convergent that we have no reason to doubt the good faith or objectivity of those who recorded them (in this case, the sailor whose task it was to keep the *roteiro*, the ship's journal of Vasco da Gama's expedition), even though their musical or organological knowledge may have been thoroughly rudimentary.

2.2.2   In the seventeenth century

Almost two centuries pass before an actual sequence of accounts by travellers in Africa is to be found, accounts which thenceforth continue, more or less uninterruptedly, until the second world war.

In 1661, Peter van Meerhoff, a Dutch traveller in South Africa, in the region of Namaqualand, gives an account of his journey. In *The Reed-Flutes Ensembles of South*

Africa, Kirby cites a description that van Meerhoff gives of a huge ensemble of reed-flutes that he heard among the Nama Hottentots:

Towards evening the King (Akambie, king of the Little Namaqua) caused a triumph to be blown, where I stood, in this way, namely, there stood there fully one to two hundred strong men, in a circle, each having a hollow reed in his hand, some long, others short, some thick, others thin, and a man stood in the middle with a long stick, who sang, and the others blew into the reeds and danced around, making very beautiful movements with their feet. The women danced round the ring, and a sound was produced as if one had heard trumpets blown [. . .] This performance continued about two hours with all sorts of dances. Then it ended. The king went with me to our camp, where he smoked a pipe of tobacco or two.
(Kirby 1933: 316)

We probably have to do here with a hocket polyphony, as subsequent descriptions of identical groups will gradually make clear, and as the researches, and above all the transcriptions, of the South African ethnomusicologist Kirby confirm in our own time.

A little later, in 1680, two priests, the reverend fathers Michel-Angelo Guattini and Denis de Carli, published their *Relation curieuse et nouvelle d'un voyage de Congo: fait és années 1666 & 1667*. There one may read that 'One day as we were approaching by river. . . we came across a large number of huts, and heard a great noise of people playing on Drums, Trumpets, Fifes, Cornets, and other instruments' (Guattini and Carli 1680: 86–7). The voyagers learnt that it was a lord and his escort that they saw, following whom 'were several Moors with trumpets and fifes' (ibid.: 88).

This account hardly contains any information as to the kind of music produced by this ensemble. Nevertheless, the range of different wind instruments playing together, and in combination with drums, certainly implies a practice that was both polyphonic and polyrhythmic.

A little after this, during the year 1682, the reverend father Jerom Merolla da Sorrento, a Capuchin and Italian apostolic missionary, made a voyage to Africa, and to the Congo and to South Africa in particular. His account, given in Frank Harrison's *Time, Place and Music*, devotes a whole chapter to music. The missionary begins by describing the course of a procession during a day of ceremonial at a traditional chief's court. He mentions 'ivory trumpets' as long as a man's arm, and gives us some idea as to how these instruments were played:

The lower Mouth [the bell] is sufficient to receive one Hand, which by contracting and dilating of the Fingers forms the Sound there being no other holes in the Body [of the instrument] as in our Flutes or Hautboys.
(Harrison 1975: 95)

The witness must be charged here with a slight error in observation, for the presence and movement of the hand within the bell are actually not meant to 'form the sound', which is produced, through the 'upper' mouthpiece, by the musician's lips. The movement of the hand may, however, modify the timbre and thus give rise to certain sound effects.

In spite of this error, or rather because of it, Merolla da Sorrento's description is still valuable, primarily because it allows us to identify the instruments that he calls 'trumpets'. The holding of the hand inside the bell would imply that these are in fact horns, and very probably side-blown horns. This is a very common instrument in Africa, even today, and its playing position is sometimes not dissimilar to that of European hunting and French horns, especially as regards the insertion of the hand into the bell. Moreover, in contrasting these horns with 'our flutes and hautboys', inasmuch as they lack stops, the Capuchin clearly demonstrates, once we have corrected his error, that the instruments may each only produce one sound.

Now, a few lines further on, the author specifies that a 'concert of these' requires from four to six players (ibid.: 95). We can therefore assert, that their simultaneous playing must have produced a hocket polyphony. The text goes on to describe a portable sixteen-key xylophone, a *marimba*, held by a shoulder-strap that was passed behind the nape of the neck. Various percussion instruments which are played in combination with the *marimba*, and which are mostly idiophones, are then mentioned. This writer concludes his account with the following judgement: 'This Harmony is graceful at a distance, but harsh and ungraceful near at hand, the beating of so many Sticks causing a great Confusion' (ibid.: 96).

During this same period, we hear tell of reed whistle ensembles among the Nama Hottentots of South Africa. Indeed, the Dutch governor of the Cape of Good Hope, Simon Van der Stel, made an expedition to Namaqualand in 1685 and 1686. The journal of this expedition was translated into English, and published by H.G. Waterhouse in 1931 as *Simon van der Stel's Journal of his Expedition to Namaqualand*. Kirby reproduces the relevant episode, which took place on Sunday 14 October 1685, Van der Stel's birthday:

As it was the Honourable Commander's birthday, we fired three rounds in his honour, each round followed by one gun. When the Amaquas learned this, they gave the Honourable Commander a musical entertainment. Their instruments were long, hollow reeds, to each of which they can give a different note, and the sound is best compared with that of an organ. They stood in a ring, about twenty altogether, and in their midst was one who carried a long thin stick in his hand. He led the singing and beat the time, which they all correctly observed. They danced in a ring with one hand to their ear, and the other firmly holding the reed to their lips. Outside the ring of musicians were men and women who danced to the music and reinforced it with handclapping. All this passed off very decently, considering that they are savages.   (Kirby 1933: 317)

This description calls for no further comment, since it repeats, in slightly more detailed form, that given by Peter Van Meerhoff some twenty-four years earlier.

Olfert Dapper's *Description de l'Afrique* was published in almost exactly the same period, in 1686. In this panoramic survey, the author tells of coming to 'a vast country, known as Lower Ethiopia, by contrast with Abyssinia, which people call Upper Ethiopia. . . It begins somewhere to the North of the river Zaïre. . . and eventually finishes at the Cape of Good Hope' (Dapper 1686: 320). Upon arriving at Lovango, the traveller was present at 'a Festival at which the King appeared'. From the description that he gives, the following passage is most relevant to us here: 'To the pomp and magnificence of this display was added the sweet sound of instruments; . . . some were ivory horns whose apertures were an inch and a half or two inches across, and when seven or eight of these horns were blown quite loudly they produced a by no means disagreeable harmony' (ibid.: 331).

It is worth emphasising the connection between the presence of these instruments, fashioned out of elephants' tusks, and those who furnished the raw material for them, who were very probably Pygmies. Indeed, on the following page, we read: 'In the same place we saw Dwarves, with standing there their backs turned to us. They had extraordinarily large heads and they wore a skin drawn tight with a string, which served as a cap. The Negroes assured us that there was a heavily forested Province, where only these Dwarves lived, and that it was they who killed the most elephants. They call these little men *Bakke-Bakke* and *Mimos*' (ibid.: 332). Knowing as we do that the Pygmies are a people of small stature, who live in the great forests, and who are known to be excellent elephant hunters, we cannot have any doubt as to the identity of the 'Dwarves' who furnish the raw material for the manufacture of these 'ivory horns'.

2.2.3   In the eighteenth century

There appeared in Utrecht, in 1705, a book called *Voyage de Guinée, contenant une Description nouvelle et très exacte de cette côte* [. . .] A reading of this text suggests that its author, William Bosman, may rightfully be called one of the precursors of musical sociology.

In his narrative Bosman presents an account of the role of certain instruments, not simply in their strictly musical context, but also, and above all, as signs of prestige. He wrote of the richer Guineans as follows:

Whoever among them wishes to win prestige buys seven of the largest elephant teeth, and makes horns out of them, having his servants learn to play all sorts of songs in the manner of the country, and when they know how to play well, he informs all his kin and friends, that he intends to display all his horns in public. There is then no dearth of people in his house, and they amuse themselves for several days with him; he then brings out his wives and slaves, gorgeously apparelled, and in order to seem still richer, he borrows much gold and coral, and even makes several presents to his friends, so that this day will have cost him a great deal. After this feast, he may, whenever he wishes, have these horns played for his amusement; no one else may do this, unless they have been set up in the manner just described: but if there is someone who desires to amuse themselves, and if they want to have some horns to play, they have to ask if they may borrow them.

(Bosman 1705: 140-1)

A little further on, the traveller gives a number of details both about the different Guinean instruments and the various possible combinations of them, which suggests that there was indeed a polyphonic music. Bosman's personal judgements regarding this music seem to bear this out:

As regards their musical instruments, they have several different kinds, all of which however make a very disagreeable noise; the main ones are horns (of which I have just spoken) which are made out of elephants' tusks and weigh up to thirty pounds a piece, and sometimes more. They engrave on these horns the image of a man or of an animal, but so crudely, that it is hard to make out if it is a representation of a man or an animal that is intended. Around the larger end there are strings blackened with sheep's or chicken's blood, and at the other end a chiselled hole, through which they blow, and produce a fairly pleasing music: they observe, however, the tones and a measure, and change them when they wish; they sometimes play tunes on these horns which, although not very pleasing, are not however painful to hear, such that there is no need to stop up one's ears.

They also have drums, of which there are at least ten different kinds. . . They hit these drums with two hammer-shaped sticks, or else with one straight stick and one's hand; but no matter how they hit them, the noise produced is a highly disagreeable one; and what is most upsetting is that they hit the drum and sound the horn at the same time, and so that the concert may be yet more dreadful, there is a small boy who unceasingly hits the inside of a hollow iron with a piece of wood, which is even more unbearable than the sound of the horns or the drums.

(ibid.: 143-4)

This impressive range of different drums certainly permits the interpretation that, even if these Guineans do not play them *all* at the same time, they elicit different rhythms, at any rate from the different 'families' of instruments. Be this as it may, this valuable text clearly indicates that a polyphonic music is involved, for it states that the 'horns' play at the same time as the drums. Finally, polyrhythm is indicated by the presence, alongside the drums, of a young boy beating 'unceasingly the inside of a hollow iron with a piece of wood', which, I point out in passing, is in fact a metal bell with an external clapper, an idiophone that is very common, even today, throughout West Africa.

The following testimonies are all attributed to Father Jean-Baptiste Labat. From 1728 to 1732 he brought out no less than three works on Africa, amounting to eleven volumes altogether, in which he quotes at length from documents by his contemporaries, notably the Chevalier des Marchais and the Reverend Father Giovanni Antonio Cavazzi da Montecuccolo, to whom I refer below. In the second volume of his *Nouvelle relation de l'Afrique occidentale. . .*, Father Labat describes the construction and use of ivory trumpets in Gambia:

The Negroes of the Kingdom of Galam and of the River of Gambia, and in general in every place where elephants are common, have trumpets made of the tusks of these animals. It should not be supposed that they use the largest of these for this purpose. They would neither have breath enough to fill them nor arms long enough to carry them, since some of them sometimes weigh more than two hundred pounds. They select only the small ones, they then pierce them or scrape them inside and out, until they have reduced them to the desired thickness. They have them in various sizes and weights, in order to produce different sounds: but with all these precautions they only make a confused noise and a din which is more like a charivaria than anything else.

(Labat 1728: II, 331–2)

The main value of this description lies in the observation that the trumpets were cut from tusks of differing sizes, 'in order to produce different sounds', which clearly indicates a *conscious* intention to tune them to different pitches, as the following account confirms.

Indeed, in another work, Father Labat recounts a *Voyage du Chevalier des Marchais en Guinée, isles voisines, et en Cayenne, Fait en 1725, 1726 & 1727* [. . .]; there too we hear tell of ivory 'trumpets', this time assembled in large numbers, upon the occasion of a 'Feast given by the son-in-law of the King of Fetu':

The Governor was about to be seated, when we heard a loud cry followed almost immediately by the sound of Drums and Ivory Trumpets which preceded the Prince and his company. These Trumpets are elephants' tusks of varying sizes, which are laboriously hollowed out, and which are left as thick as is necessary *for the range of different tones that one wishes to produce* [my italics]. If anyone is curious to see these Trumpets, I am able to satisfy their curiosity.

This Prince was preceded by a Drum and by twenty Trumpets.   (Labat 1730: I, 348–9)

In the subsequent volume of this same work, Labat reviews 'the procession held in honour of the Snake, after the King's coronation', a procession that he describes very precisely (albeit through the eyes of one of Louis XV's citizens):

Trumpets. At a reasonable distance there marches the Trumpet major, followed by twenty Trumpets, playing as best they can.

Drums. After the Trumpets there are twenty drums preceded by the Drum major, and who beat as hard as they can; you have to be familiar with this noise not to be stunned by it.

Flutes. The Flutes, which follow the drums, also number twenty, and are preceded by their leader. All of these instruments belong to the music of the King's chamber, and are sometimes heard in succession, sometimes all at once.

(ibid.: II, 194)

These sixty musicians, guided by their three leaders, sometimes play 'in succession', i.e., most probably according to the different musical families to which they belong, and 'sometimes all at once', which of course suggests a massive polyphony.

A little further on in the same book, there are some plates, amongst which are illustrations of various musical objects and instruments, including an end-blown horn, called *Ivory trumpet* (ibid.: 243).

It would therefore seem reasonable to suppose that the 'trumpets' mentioned above were really end-blown horns.

Father Labat, also in this same volume, reiterates a very scornful judgement of polyrhythm: 'The Drums which they [the Africans] use in their armies are the same that they employ in their music; if one can properly give the name of music or of 'symphony' to the charivaria that they produce with their instruments' (ibid.: 245–6). The author then reverts to the question of the construction and playing of the 'ivory trumpets', very probably drawing on the documentation already presented in his previous work, but without seeming any more sympathetic towards them.

The trumpets which are used in war and in concerts are elephants' tusks; they are of various lengths and various diameters; they are more like cornets. The ox-horns which our cowherds and pigkeepers use make a sound which is almost as pleasant as these sorts of trumpets.

There is however a lot of work in these sorts of instruments, since the thickness of the tusk has to be reduced by filing in order to reduce it to what one wants to leave, which is a long labour, and those who play them have to have strong lungs. The different lengths and thicknesses of these trumpets produce different sounds, which seem to me more proper to produce a charivari than a moderately tolerable harmony. So you have to be used to these kinds of noise not to be stunned by them.

(ibid.: 247–8)

Under the voluminous title of *Relation historique de l'Ethiopie occidentale, contenant la description des royaumes de Congo, Angolle et Matamba. . ., traduite de l'italien. . . et augmentée de plusieurs relations portugaises des meilleurs auteurs. . .*, Labat translates, and very probably somewhat adapts, accounts of travels in Africa by the Reverend Father Cavazzi da Montecuccolo, and by various others also.

A whole chapter of this work is devoted to 'the music of the Negroes'. We encounter horns again, but this time cut from antelopes' horns. 'They have another wind instrument which makes a sharp and piercing sound. It is made from gazelle's horns. It is used to summon the troops. This instrument is part of their *simphonie* but to tell the truth the effect is more likely to spoil it, to 'deconcert' it, than to improve their so-called harmony' (Labat 1732: II, 49).

In 1741 there appeared in Amsterdam, in French, a *Description du Cap de Bonne-Espérance: Où l'on trouve tout ce qui concerne l'histoire naturelle du pays; La religion, les moeurs & les usages des Hottentots; et l'établissement des Hollandais. Tirée des Mémoires de Mr. Pierre Kolbe, Maître ès Arts. . .* I should point out that this German missionary – under the true name of Peter Kolb – had published the original version of his memoirs in 1719, in Nuremberg.

This account is of interest in several respects, and primarily because Kolb, whose responsibility it was to make astronomical and physical observations in Africa, would seem to have had a mind that was both enquiring and rigorous, so that he would often appeal to the testimonies of previous authors, and never neglected to compare the opinions presented in their writings with his own. A chapter of his work bears the title 'On the Music and Dance of the Hottentots'. Moreover, Kolb sets out the requisite elements of a truly ethnological description: 'The Hottentots accompany almost all their festivals, and all of their public rejoicings, with music and dances. Since, then, these practices form a part of Religion, it is relevant, before proceeding any further, to give some idea of what their Religion is' (Kolb 1741: 1, 207).

Although they do not directly relate to polyphony, the lines following this introduction are particularly noteworthy. In fact they represent a genuinely quite remarkable testimony, if not a unique one for the period, of the intellectual attitude of a European observer who, at the beginning of the eighteenth century, was capable of setting his own cultural heritage to one side in attending to that of the Africans. A precursor of what today is called 'ethnoscience', Kolb is, to my knowledge, the first to develop *the idea that the Africans have of their own music*, and to take it into account: 'The Hottentots' Music has little charm for the European ear: it has a very small number of different tones, and they have no more than two or three types of instrument. They have, however, so great an idea of music, that we cannot deny this matter a place in their history. Moreover, impoverished as it is, this music suggests that the Hottentots possess a genius and a sensibility that would usefully serve to destroy our prejudices as to their stupidity' (ibid.: 207–8).

This preliminary statement is followed by a description of an instrument called *gom-gom*, which turns out to be a musical bow with a mouth resonator.

Kolb then mentions several of these instruments playing together, though it is not possible for the reader to decide whether this combination resulted in a polyphony in the sense defined above:

When there was a concert of three or four *Gom-Goms* played by accomplished persons, I can assure the reader that I found in it something pleasing, particularly when the tones were low; I found in it a sweetness capable of charming the most delicate of ears. Indeed once, hearing this instrument playing in the dead of night, I was so struck by the delicacy of the tones, that I could not help but give it my complete attention. I thought at first that the musicians must be highly skilled Europeans, who had acquired a very perfect knowledge of this instrument; but you can imagine my astonishment, upon arriving at the place where the concert was, to discover that it was two Hottentots serenading their sweethearts!

And Kolb, anticipating the sceptical reactions of his contemporaries, continues: 'The reader may form what idea he pleases of my taste in music; but I cannot do otherwise than insist that the *Gom-Gom*, however simple and ridiculous it may seem, can become as fine an instrument and produce as charming sounds as any of our own, so long as it is played by a skilled performer' (ibid.: 209–10). Summing up his personal observations, Kolb writes: 'This is all I have to say regarding Hottentot music. In all the Nations that I have visited (and there are few indeed where I have not been) I have never seen another kind of instrument apart from the two *Gom-Goms*, and the Drum or Pot [friction drum]; if you except the flageolet of which I have already spoken' (ibid.: 211).

Kolb like a true man of science, completes his description by citing a slightly earlier testimony, which he then proceeds to refute:

Father *Tachard* has been more fortunate than I, for he mentions several other musical instruments in use among the Hottentots. One of them, according to him, strongly resembles a flute, and the other a cornett. As for myself, notwithstanding the care I took and the researches I made, I never saw anything of the sort. This Author is in fact the only person ever to have mentioned these instruments. I find elsewhere in his narrative several facts that I cannot accept: the reader will judge if my scruples are well-founded. I will begin by presenting his account and I will then add my comments to it.   (ibid.: 211–12)

Kolb goes on to cite some observations made by Father Tachard some forty years before him, specifically in 1682, among the Namaqua Hottentot. He refers to a group of musicians comprising

Fifty young men, with as many young women and girls. The men each carry a flute made out of a certain reed very finely worked, which gave a quite pleasant sound.

The Captain having signalled to them, they began to play their instruments together, mingled with the womens' and girls' voices, and with the noise that they made in clapping their hands.
                                                           (ibid.: 212–13)

This is undoubtedly a large ensemble of reed whistles, identical to that described by Van Meerhoff in 1661.

Kolb also quotes a passage from Father Tachard's work in which he reproduces another account, and this a remarkably accurate one, from Van der Stel:

In the voyage that Mr. *Van der Stel*, the Commander of the Cape, made, which lasted five months, he encountered at twenty-seven degrees of latitude, and at ten or twelve leagues from the ocean coast, a Nation that was very populous and indeed far more docile than any that he had yet found. As Mr. *Van der Stel* had brought two trumpets, several oboes and five or six violins with him, as soon as they had heard the sound of these instruments, they gathered round in large numbers and played their music, by a band composed of nearly thirty persons, who almost all had different instruments. The person in the middle had a kind of cornett which was very long and was made out of a dried and cured ax intestine; the others had flageolets and flutes made out of canes of differing lengths and sizes. They pierce these instruments much as we do, but with this difference, that there is only one hole, extending from one end to the other, and which is much wider than that of those flageolets and flutes in common use in France. In order to tune them, they make use of a hoop which has a small aperture in the middle, and which, depending on the tone they wish to achieve, they move up and down the pipe by means of a stick. They hold the instrument in one hand, and with the other they press their lips against the instrument, so that all their breath may enter the pipe.

This music is simple, but harmonious. When the leader of this ensemble has aligned the tone of all the other musicians' instruments with that of the cornett beside him, he gives them the tune that is to be played and beats the time with a large stick which can be seen by all.

The music is always accompanied by dances, which consist of leaps and of certain movements of the feet, but without the dancers moving from the place in which they are. The women and the girls make a large circle around the dancers, and simply clap their hands, and sometimes [stamp] their feet, in time to the music. The instrumentalists are the only ones to change place whilst dancing, although the Master of the music stands upright and does not move, so as to supervise the harmonies and the rhythm.   (ibid.: 213–15)

Kolb comments upon this quotation as follows: 'The more closely I examine this narrative the less reason I can find for objecting to my own account, for it contains so many absurdities that it is impossible to lend it any credence' (ibid.: 215). We are obliged, however, to lend it credence, for however sympathetic we may find Kolb's personality; it is nevertheless the case that Van der Stel's observations, as recounted by Father Tachard, are well founded. They are in fact corroborated by a host of modern specialists, both in the descriptions given of the musical organisation of this sort of ensemble, as in that of the system of tuning the instruments involved.

2.2.4   In the nineteenth century

In 1800, Mungo Park published his *Voyage dans l'intérieur de l'Afrique, fait en 1795, 1796 et 1797* [. . .]. So captivated was he by the Mandingos' taste for song and poetry that he could not resist drawing up a 'list of their musical instruments', which indicates the polyphonic and polyrhythmic nature of some of them. We thus find: 'the *simbing*, a small harp with seven strings; the *balafou* [*balafon*], an instrument made of twenty pieces of hard wood, beneath which are gourds cut into the shape of shells, which serve to amplify the sound; . . . Apart from this, they use small flutes, elephants' tusks and bells' (Park 1800: II, 31–32).

Published some two years later, Sylvain Meinrad Xavier de Golberry's *Fragmens d'un voyage en Afrique*. . . is in fact an account of a voyage that predates that of Mungo Park by ten years (1785 to 1787). Describing the 'Customs of the Mandingos', Golberry writes:

In each village of Bambouk there is a meeting-place called Bentaba; it is a great market-hall formed by posts placed ten to twelve feet apart, about fifteen feet high and supporting a thatched roof. . . After sunset, the women and girls in turn go to the Bentaba, and the girls give themselves up madly to the pleasure of the dance. . .; it takes place to the bewildering noise of men, women, drums, instruments, hand-clapping, which beat the time.   (Golberry 1802: I, 385–7)

It is hardly necessary to remark that this account implies a polyphonic or polyrhythmic performance.

Later in the work, Golberry mentions the instruments and music of Sierra Leone, which he describes in these terms:

They have in Sierra Leone a flute with four holes, made of a very hard reed, and from which they extract even harder sounds. The Foulha-Sousos of Scherbroo have a trumpet made from a large elephant tusk; this instrument produces a very bright and piercing sound; this trumpet, perfected, could produce a pleasant effect.

Another instrument which they call balafon is built like a spinet. The body of the instrument is two foot thick, four foot long, and eighteen inches wide.

The table is so placed that it leaves a space of six inches between it and the lid of the instrument. This space is occupied by pieces of a very hard wood, polished and calibrated in such a way that each one gives out one of the tones or semitones of the scale. These pieces of wood are held together with little strings of fish-gut, and attached at both ends of the instrument; the musician hits these wooden keys with sticks also made of hard wood, with knobs shaped like drumsticks and covered with skins.

Under the pieces of wood which make up the scale are placed the halves of little gourds which increase the sounds.   (ibid.: II, 417–18)

Would that Sylvain Meinrad de Golberry had stopped there – at the pure organological description. Alas, he went on, showing how far his prejudices blinded his power of judgement:

This instrument is too complicated to have been invented by the Negros, ignorant of the principles of music, and only able to produce on the balafon a confused and detestable noise.

All the blacks of West Africa have instruments; but they are the most barbarous musicians in the world. (Golberry 1802: II, 417–18)

In 1813 the *London Missionary Society* published a report by one of its members, which was entitled 'Observations made in the country of the Great Namaqua', quoted by Kirby. Its author, Albrecht, describes dances performed to the accompaniment of reed whistles, such as he had observed among the Nama of South Africa, one year before, in 1812: 'The music is made by whistles, being cut out of a certain reed and turned in such a manner as to produce a musical sound. If even twenty whistles should be heard at once, they make them all agree. Every dancer whistles on his whistle during his performance' (Kirby 1933: 325). This testimony helps to confirm, across a hundred-and-fifty-year gap, those of Van Meerhoff and Van der Stel. Albrecht's references to twenty or so instruments each producing one note, and to the harmony which their playing produces, seems to indicate that a hocket technique is involved.

Thomas Edward Bowdich, in his *Mission from Cape Coast to Ashantee* (1819), makes a passing reference to the instrumental music of the Ashanti, the polyphonic nature of which did not escape him: 'Few of their instruments possess much power, but the combination of several frequently produces a surprising effect' (Bowdich 1819: 361).

It is Kirby, yet again, who quotes a book by Campbell, *Travels in South Africa*, which was published in 1822. Campbell describes dances performed to the accompaniment of reed whistles that he was able to observe, some two years previously, among the Bechuana of the Lattakoo region. 'About fifteen men were dancing in a circle, each holding and blowing a reed. They leaped like a frog, round and round the circle, keeping time. The King directed the dance, leaping and playing upon a reed exactly like the others, from whom he could only be distinguished by a long rod, which he carried, reaching considerably higher than his head' (Kirby 1933: 330). This description does not specify the resultant sound that these fifteen reed whistles produced, but nevertheless we have so many other testimonies regarding this kind of ensemble, that we have good reason to suppose that the music heard by Campbell was indeed a hocket polyphony.

In the second volume of his *Travels in the Interior of South Africa. . .*, published in 1824, William J. Burchell makes a number of remarks about the Bachapïn, in the town of Litakun, in Bechuanaland, whom he had known some twelve years before. Having attended a concert given by a reed whistle ensemble, Burchell proceeds to describe it in such detail that it is possible for us to deduce the musical system involved:

These *pipes*, which they call *līcháka*, are simply reeds of various sizes and lengths, tuned to concord generally by means of a small moveable plug in the lower end, and having their upper end, or mouth, cut transversely. This mouth is placed against the under lip, and the sound is produced by blowing into them, in the manner of a Pan's-reed. In order to keep the pipe steady, the forefinger rested above the upper lip, and the thumb against the cheek, while the other three fingers held the reed to its place. Each performer had but one pipe, and consequently was master of only one note of the scale; although at the same time, there were among them, several pipes in unison; and it seemed, that those notes of the gamut which were most likely to have produced discords, were rejected from this band. Between the highest and the lowest pipe there might, I imagined, be comprised an interval of twelve notes.

I saw no other instrument but the lĭchákă; nor were these used by any but the dancers themselves, each of whom was furnished with one; and which he sounded frequently though irregularly. In this *music* I could discover no particular air; neither was it possible for me to write it down; as many notes were heard at the same time, joining in, perhaps merely accidentally, or without any preconcerted order. It must not, from these remarks, be concluded that this people are insensible to harmony and melody: a sufficient proof to the contrary will be found in another place. By the dancers keeping time in their movements, a certain cadence was now and then perceptible in their music; but, excepting this, no regularity could be distinguished in their performance; although I doubt not that their ear guided them in some manner, as the general effect of this music was pleasing and harmonious.   (Burchell 1822–4, rev. edn 1953: II, 473)

This description is so finely drawn that one might think it that of a specialist. Burchell was in fact no stranger to music: his mastery of solfeggio enabled him to note down a melody on the spot, although this knowledge, as he himself confessed, was of no use to him here. Nevertheless, his deep intuition led him to posit, beyond the apparent absence of a 'preconcerted order', the existence of a compositional system.

Captain James Alexander's narrative, *An Expedition into the Interior of Africa*, published in 1838 and also quoted by Kirby, also concerns whistle ensembles. I shall refer here only to a large dance with reed whistles that Captain Alexander observed among the Namaqua, during his voyage of 1836 and 1837. Now, Alexander is the first to make the comparison, undoubtedly more by intuition than by reason, between South African whistle ensembles, for which we have references going back as far as 1497, and the Russian horn ensembles that his other navigations had enabled him to hear. This unexpected comparison is of such interest that I shall pause for a moment to consider these Russian ensembles, whose moment of glory came in nineteenth-century Europe.

In an interesting study, entitled 'Russian Horn Bands', Robert Ricks (1969: 364–72) describes how such ensembles came to be formed in the Russian court, a little after 1750. Amongst the court's various orchestras, there was one consisting of French horns and an ensemble of hunting horns, the latter being played by serfs. The French horn orchestra being sometimes unavailable to him, Prince Narichkin, master of the hunt to the Empress Elizabeth, asked the 'musician of the chamber', G.A. Maresch, to teach his serfs to play French horns, and to do it within the year. In order to arrive at a satisfactory result in so short a time, Maresch decided simply to side-step the difficulty. An extremely imaginative teacher, he abandoned the Utopian idea of turning simple serfs into accomplished horn players in the space of a few months, and hit on the remarkably original notion of teaching them to play three-part melodies according to the following principle: each musician would be responsible for one sound only, the second harmonic on his instrument (the easiest one to produce on a horn), and would therefore only have to come in when this sound was required.

This method, as ingenious as it was uneconomical, required as many horns of different lengths as there were different notes to be produced in the work in question; a score accompanying Ricks' article displays a range of four octaves and a fourth, which, in a simple diatonic system, would require thirty-two instruments! Maresch taught his musicians to follow a simplified musical notation that only gave the duration of the notes to be played. He himself conducted the horn players with a small stick, with which he beat not the metre but 'each crotchet', in other words, each beat.

In 1757 Prince Narichkin was able to present a concert given by this orchestra to the Empress; it must clearly have been a great success, for such ensembles multiplied and quickly became known throughout Russia. This highly original manner of playing became quite sophisticated, and famous musicians were astonished by several horn ensembles that played thus. In St Petersburg itself, the composer Louis Spohr heard in 1803 a performance of an overture by Gluck, and expressed his admiration for the precision and the rapidity of the playing. So famous were these ensembles that they came to be heard abroad. In Paris, the famous musicologist Fétis attended one of their concerts in 1833, and devoted an article to the event, which was published that same year in the *Revue Musicale*, under the title 'Concert of Russian Horns'.

Captain Alexander, who had been led to compare the Russian ensembles with a South African reed whistle ensemble, made his voyage to Africa in this very same period. He describes the latter as follows:

A dozen men assembled, and with reeds, which, closed at one end, were from one foot long to seven, like the horns of different sizes of the Russian horn bands, the music of which I used to hear float like that of a grand piano, over the waters of the Neva. Women and girls also came, and throwing off their karosses, stood by. One man then blew on his reed, holding it in the left hand, and with the fingers opening and shutting to undulate the sound, while in his right hand, pressed close to his ear, he held a slight stick to clear the reed. The leader blew strongly, his head stooping forwards, and his feet stamping the ground to beat time; the others blew also to accompany their leader; wild music arose, while the musicians circled round, looking inward, stooping and beating time.

(Kirby 1933: 330)

George Schweinfurth's important works, *Au coeur de l'Afrique, 1868–1871*, was published in Paris in 1875. It contains a very exact, although sometimes somewhat misleading description of the musical practices of the Bongo, a people whom Schweinfurth encountered in the South-West of the former Anglo-Egyptian Sudan. He begins by noting that 'all the Bongos have a great passion for music', and he goes on to specify that 'Everyone, from childhood on, is a musician. The most rudimentary materials will suffice: a mere straw, for instance, will serve to make a pipe' (Schweinfurth 1875: II, 274). He then proceeds to describe their orchestral ensembles, and in the description there are comments that differ strikingly in tone from what goes before:

But for their festivals the Bongos have resources of a quite different order, and form orchestras whose effects may properly be compared with the music of demented cats. The endless blows upon enormous drums, the bellowing of giant horns, whose construction requires the felling of huge trees, form a bass against which one may from time to time make out a shrill blast of small whistling horns, and together these instruments produce an infernal booming that the echo of the desert repeats over a distance of several miles. Hundreds of women and children, armed with gourds filled with pebbles that they shake frenziedly, add their rasping noise to the tumult; or they sometimes replace these bells with sticks of dry brushwood, which they rub against each other.

The large tubes of wood which the Bongos use as horns are called *manyinguys*. They are four to five feet long; the top is closed and decorated with carvings which almost always represent a human head, frequently surmounted by a pair of horns. The lower end is open; and near to the carved figure, in the final quarter of the horn, is the orifice into which the performer blows with all the force that his lungs can muster.

There is another kind of *manyinguy*, which is in the form of a huge bottle. In order to play it, the musician holds it between his knees, like a violoncello; but sometimes the instrument is so large and so heavy that it is placed on the ground, and the performer has to bend over in order to reach the mouthpiece.   (ibid.: 274-5)

Before continuing with the author's account, I point out that he refers to wooden, rather than ivory horns. Does this mean that elephants were less plentiful close to the sources of the Nile, during this period? Be this as it may, this orchestra of horns is identical, down to the last detail, with those to be found today, a thousand kilometres to the West, among the Banda-Linda of Central Africa.

In the course of itemising the various musical instruments and instrumental techniques, Schweinfurth notes:

The Bongo, like all the peoples in this area, make numerous instruments out of the horns of different kinds of antelope. These cornets, which they call *mangâls*, have three holes, like little flutes, and produce a sound much like that of the fife. They also have a wind instrument, which is long and thin, is made of wood and is called *mbourah*. This instrument, which widens towards the mouthpiece so as to form a sound-box, strongly resembles the ivory cornet to be found amongst various Negro peoples.   (ibid.: 278)

Having completed his organological inventory for the Bongo, this explorer presents his somewhat colourful impressions of their 'symphonic song'. Once again, the objectivity of the description of the instruments yields to subjectivity, due in this case to ignorance:

It would be difficult to describe the Bongos' symphonic song with any exactitude. Suffice it to say that it consists of a kind of cackling, a sort of recitative which is sometimes reminiscent of the yapping of a dog, and sometimes of the clucking of a hen, and which is interrupted from time to time by a stream of words muttered at top speed. The beginning is always lively; and then everyone, regardless of age or sex begins to yelp or to bellow as loudly as they can. Gradually the voices, which have been crescendo, subside; the rhythm slows down, and the choir falls away in an extended groaning. It comes to resemble the funereal chants that the cults of the North have said over their tombs, mournful reflections of a leaden sky; when all of a sudden the voices break out again in an indescribable furia, and the contrast is as startling as when the sun, tearing apart the upper clouds, suddenly shines through the rain.

I have often attended these concerts; and upon each occasion the Bongos' music has seemed to me to derive from the instinct of imitation which, in a more or less developed form, is present in all men. Their orgies of sound have always seemed to me to be meant simply to recall the fury of the elements. In order to represent the rage of a tropical storm, no ordinary instrument would have sufficed: they have massed their drums and strike them violently with blows from their clubs. In order to compete with the peals of thunder, the howling of the storm, the streaming of the rain, they form a choir in which hundreds of the most powerful throats combine in song. In order to represent the screams of animals terrified by the storm, they have recourse to their enormous horns; and they take up their flutes and fifes in order to imitate the songs of birds. Perhaps the most characteristic feature of this imitative harmony is the deep rolling of the *manyinguy*, which represents the growling of the thunder. The downpour lashing the foliage, and hurling its huge drops against the branches, is represented by the rattling of pebbles shaken about in the gourds, and by the dry noise of the pieces of brushwood that women and children beat against each other.
                                                                                                                      (ibid.: 278-9)

These final remarks must surely refer as much to gourd rattles as to clicking sticks. They probably indicate the superimposition of different rhythmical patterns, perhaps a rhythmical counterpoint through crossing-over of parts.

2.2.5   In the twentieth century

Henry Junod's account of the Thonga, made at the beginning of this century and reported in his *Life of a South African Tribe* (1906) brings us back to horn orchestras, this time in Southern Africa. Kirby, in his valuable study *The Musical Instruments of the Native Races of South Africa*, quotes this description, which he considers to be excellent. Junod mentions the *bunanga*, which 'consists of an ensemble of ten horns and two drums, the horns having been made by specialists. . . These are carefully tuned to different notes' (Kirby 1934: 85). And he was also the first to observe that 'sometimes three or four orchestras perform at the same time' (ibid.). More than half a century later, in 1974, I was fortunate enough to observe a comparable phenomenon, in the Place de la Préfecture in Bambari (Central African Republic), when three horn orchestras, each consisting of over fifteen instruments, played both together and in alternation. Moreover, the arrangement of the musicians within the orchestra, which Junod describes in detail, was identical in both cases.

Kirby thought the Thonga horn orchestras had derived from the *tshikona*, which is the national dance of the Venda of South Africa, and is accompanied by reed whistles. 'The Thonga have no such reed-flute ensembles, but, in view of the fact that horn-bands, like that described by Junod, have been heard in Barenda Land, I would suggest that the horn ensembles have been modelled upon the ancient reed-flute dance' (Kirby 1934: 85). This hypothesis of course implies that the musical systems employed in the two ensembles are identical, and from an organological point of view, this seems quite plausible, since the horns, like the whistles, only produce a single note each. Thus, once one had pitched the tuning of one on that of the other, horn and whistle orchestras could easily perform an identical repertoire. Let me emphasise that this practice is still current today in Central Africa, among the Banda-Linda in particular, where horn and whistle orchestras co-exist. They both rely upon the same repertoire, the only difference being that, in this case, the horn ensembles came first.

Charles Joyeux's two publications, which appeared in 1910 and 1924 respectively, are also about horns. The first, which is entitled 'Notes sur quelques manifestations musicales observées en Haute-Guinée', and signed 'Doctor Joyeux, doctor in charge of medical aid at Kankan', follows Junod's account by only a few years. Joyeux describes the instruments that he saw among the Malinké.

The horns came from a certain canton in the East, a few days' journey from Kankan. There the musicians are trained and the instruments are made. These horns are made of wood (in certain districts in the South, they are of ivory), hollowed out as flutes are by a red-hot iron rod; they are horn-shaped with a lateral mouthpiece. Sometimes at the end of the horn there is a hole which the player can stop with a finger in order to produce two different sounds: this is the high-pitched sharp horn. The others only produce one note; by blowing very hard they can be made to produce a harmonic which is usually false. The musicians are seven in number. The first plays two notes, the others one, and some notes are played by two instruments at once. The basses are rather like our tuba; the higher ones are like the cornet or piston.   (Joyeux 1910: 49)

He then goes on to describe their forms of collective playing, occasionally interjecting comparisons, which are to say the least unusual, and pejorative judgements about their music:

In order to perform a piece, the leader will play a note on his horn, according to a particular cadence, and the others will thereupon recognise the air that is to be played: each person then plays, in turn, their instrument's note, in the required order, rather like the clowns in our circuses. The leader of the orchestra asserts that the performance of his repertoire is always very carefully done, and he claims to be able to perceive the slightest mistake; indeed, I have seen him exchange angry glances with one of his musicians, as if he had forgotten to count the bars, which would imply that their music obeys some order. But it hardly seems so to a European ear, and you have to have a certain courage to stay and listen to the horrible cacophony produced by this grotesque brass band. There are sounds, usually out of tune, with alternating *forte* and *piano* depending upon whether the note is produced by one or two trumpets, and it is impossible to make out any melodic idea whatsoever.   (ibid.: 50–1)

The detailed descriptions that such commentaries sometimes contain give us all the more reason to regret their tone. Were it not for his endless references to his 'European ear', Joyeux would undoubtedly have recorded other more valuable information. But the facts given above, such as they are, do clearly tally with the present state of knowledge about horn ensembles in other areas of Africa.

Orchestras do exist in which two instruments produce a sound of the same pitch. I have found amongst certain Central African peoples, the Banda-Dakpa in particular, that when two musicians in a horn orchestra play the same note, one uses a normal blowing technique whilst the other plays it in *flutter tonguing*. This explains why there are two instruments for the one note, but Joyeux did not press his 'courage' so far as to observe this phenomenon. As for it being impossible 'to make out any melodic idea whatsoever', it is very probably because the music was a hocket polyphony, which has to be grasped according to a *diagonal* and not a *horizontal* principle, as I shall show below.

Widening his field of observation, Joyeux then proceeds, in the same article, to describe the Malinke musical system:

The scale, at least in the European sense of the word, does not exist. There is no musical unity; the range of instruments is not sufficiently standardised for them to be given a common tuning. All those of the same category produce the same notes and play together; an orchestra is composed entirely of balafons, or of flutes. . ., but the duo, the trio, and the symphony are unknown. The repertoire is different for each, excepting a few very well-known tunes which have fallen, so to speak, into the public domain, and that everyone adopts, in a more or less mangled form.

When a feast brings several orchestras together, it never occurs to them to join together to play the same piece; they each play on their own, to the laughs and cries of the amused crowd, and, shutting one's eyes, one sometimes has the sense of being transported to a travelling fair in one of the Parisian suburbs.   (ibid.: 52)

In leaving Joyeux to his somewhat fanciful comparisons, we should note that his observations are nevertheless of real value. First, when he speaks of an orchestra made up either of flutes or of *balafons* (which are xylophones), this must of course mean that, in such an ensemble, several flutes or several xylophones play together. Now, from what we know of African practice in general, and as I shall seek to show below when two or more xylophones play at once, they are almost invariably following different parts, in polyphony. But it is true that, among the Malinke, the 'symphony' is unknown.

As for the well-known airs that have fallen into the public domain, which everyone takes up 'in a more or less mangled form', they are very probably musics that once had a function and have now lost it, and are now therefore 'banalised' (cf. Book I, 1.3), and very probably performed in heterophony.

The very fact that these musics are, above all, functional, explains why, when 'several orchestras are together, it never occurs to them to join together to play the same piece'. This is quite simply because they are not supposed to do that. Indeed, the traditional socio-musical taxonomy requires that, for each organological category (whistle *or* flute *or* horn ensemble, etc.), there should correspond a kind of functional music, a specific repertoire, tied, in many cases, to a particular scalar system. That is why two different ensembles do not play together, their repertoires being dissimilar and their systems of tuning often being, in addition, incompatible.

Taken singly, however, Joyeux's remarks are accurate. It is true, for instance, that 'the scale, at least in the European sense of the word, does not exist', for the simple reason that there are several of them. It is also true that 'the range of instruments is not sufficiently standardised for them to be given a common tuning', for the simple reason that, from the point of view of tradition, some instruments are not supposed to be played together. And if 'all those of the same category produce the same notes and play together', the social or religious function associated with each of these instruments requires that it should be so. This is also the reason why 'an orchestra is composed entirely of balafons, or of flutes', and also the reason why 'the repertoire is different for each'.

Unfortunately Joyeux confined himself to simple facts, without trying to establish any relationship between them, still less placing them in their ethnological context. One can see how direct but partial observation, linked to hasty deductions, leads to an erroneous interpretation.

In his 'Etude sur quelques manifestations musicales observées en Haute-Guinée Française', published in 1924, this same Doctor Joyeux again discusses the Malinke horn ensembles, concentrating this time upon the modalities of instrumental performance:

The instrument is called *budu* in Malinke. It has a lateral mouthpiece and generally only produces one note. The native orchestra consists of several musicians: the one I saw contained seven people. . . The bass horn is played by the leader of the orchestra, who is incontestably the worst performer in the whole company. [. . .]

Here is how the performance is conducted. The instrument played by the leader plays several notes; the musicians recognise the piece and the highest pitched horn launches into it; then the others begin, each playing its note. They thus play pieces in which each note is played by a different musician. But the *mi* is given by two horns (third and fourth), which always play together; the same goes for the *fa* (fifth and sixth). These notes therefore dominate the melody, in the midst of a general hubbub which is pierced by the notes of the high pitched horn.

They play standing upright, in a line, or else turning in a circle. In the former case, the drums are placed on the far right, then comes the leader playing the bass horn, next, the high horn, the instrumentalist giving the *doh* sharp, those who give the *fa*, and, finally, the remainder, who stand on the left. They do of course always require a complete contingent in order to play; they therefore have pupils in their villages who are ready to replace them if need be. The pieces played are necessarily slowish, and the natives seem to recognise them. In any case, these musicians' wives, who sing while their husbands are playing, can make out the different pieces, as I confirmed by questioning each of them in turn. Nevertheless, it is impossible to grasp the relationship between what they sing and what the horns play; this grotesque band creates the most terrifying cacophony imaginable. However, the leader claims to be able to recognise the least lapse in a performance.   (Joyeux 1924: 178)

These observations call for a certain amount of comment. First, as regards the order in which the horns enter, with the highest beginning and the others following. This description accords with what we know of the practice of the Banda-Linda of Central Africa, as I show below. The fact that each note is produced by a different musician confirms that each horn only sounds a single note. We therefore have to do with a hocket technique, such as we find in whistle orchestras in South Africa, and in the horn orchestras that occur in Central Africa, as well as in other countries. Finally, the notes *mi* and *fa*, each produced by two horn at the same time, would again seem to correspond to two ways of producing the same sound, the one a simple exhalation and the other a flutter tonguing.

The description of the playing of the orchestral ensemble is actually very interesting. For the musicians who play in whistle orchestras in, for instance, the village of Wadimi, near Ippy, in Banda-Linda country (Central Africa Republic), are disposed in exactly the same arrangement. Yet the two instances are separated by some fifty years, and by four thousand or so kilometres.

There is nothing surprising about these musicians needing a full complement in order to play, for in this type of hocket polyphony, the absence of any musician implies by definition the disappearance of one of the degrees that constitute the musical scale.

But Joyeux's remarks about tempo are more surprising. In other parts of Africa, the hocket principle in no way entails a particularly slow pace; on the contrary, what is striking is the quality and rapidity of the musicians' reflexes, inasmuch as they come in decisively, at the appropriate moment, and with their own particular note, in musics whose tempo is usually very fast.

Let us conclude these quotations with the following lapidary statement of Joyeux: 'The horn repertory is of no intrinsic interest to the ethnographer: airs in honour of chiefs, for marriages, for circumcisions, are about all they have to offer, and it is impossible at present to elicit anything else from them' (ibid.: 178).

In Torday's *On the Trail of the Bushongo* (1925), which is quoted by Kirby, we are given a much more precise and exacting account. Torday describes ensembles practising hocket polyphony, such as he observed among the Luba, in the Congo:

Luba songs are very pleasant to our ears, and the execution of their orchestras is splendid; no chief would be without one. The 'leader' plays the marimba, a xylophone consisting of a board of keys made of hard wood and tuned to the pentatonic scale; under each key a calabash is attached which acts as a resonator. The 'leader' plays the melody with some ornamentations common to instruments played with hammers. Next in importance to him are the flautists; there must be at least five, but generally there are many more. Each note of the scale is represented by one or more flutes, and each flute can play but one note; the success of the performance depends on each musician playing his instrument at the right moment. We have here an organ every pipe of which is sounded by a different organist. The ensemble is generally perfect. The rhythm is accentuated by drums, gongs and rattles.   (Kirby 1934: 169–70)

Although brief, this description is at least as valuable as that of Joyeux, not least because the observations contained in it are so much more objective.

André Gide's account, as can be imagined, creates a quite different atmosphere.

His *Voyage au Congo. Carnets de Route*, published in 1927, contains the very first observations of polyphonic music in the Central African Republic itself, formerly called Ubangi-Chari. Gide attended a musical performance in the village of Bakissa-Bugandi, in the region of Carnot:

This evening a tamtam is being organised in the village not far from where I am. . . There was a meagre fire of brushwood the middle of a big circle; a round dance to the beat of two drums and three resonant calabashes, filled with hard seeds and mounted on a short handle, so that they can be shaken rhythmically. The rhythms are subtle, irregular: there are groups of ten beats (five and five), succeeded in the same space of time by a group of four beats – with the accompaniment of a double bell or a metal castanet. The instrumental players are in the middle.   (Gide 1927: 142)

It is well known that Gide had a very solid musical background, but his testimony is nonetheless very remarkable. It is a real achievement to have noted, and to have described in some detail, the groups of rhythmical units, which clearly indicate that a precisely described polyrhythm is involved. The scene probably took place among the Gbaya tribe; but quite similar rhythmical phenomena may be found amongst other Central African peoples, the Banda-Linda in particular. In the chapter devoted to polyrhythm, I describe an ensemble consisting of three drums and some ankle-bells, which follows much the same system as that described by Gide.

Gide also describes a Banda-Dakpa horn orchestra, whose playing accompanied the rites of passage of young boys:

This morning, as soon as we were up, a dance, given by the Dakpas. Twenty-eight little boy dancers from eight to thirteen years old, painted white from head to foot; on their heads a kind of helmet stuck all over with forty or so red and black spikes; on their foreheads a fringe of little metal rings. Each held in his hand a whip made of rushes and plaited string. Some had black and red checks painted around their eyes. A short skirt of raffia completed this fantastic get-up. They danced gravely, in Indian file, to the sound of twenty-three earthen or wooden horns of unequal lengths (thirty centimetres to one metre fifty) which can each make only a single note. Another band of twelve older Dakpas (these were all black) performed their movements in the opposite direction to the first.

A dozen or so women soon joined in the dance. Every dancer moved forward with little jerky steps which made the bangles around his ankles tinkle. The horn-players formed a circle, in the middle of them an old woman beat time with a feather brush made of black horse-hair. At her feet a great black demon writhed in the dust in feigned convulsions, but without ceasing to blow his horn. The din was deafening, for, overpowering the bellowing of the horns, everybody except-ing only the little white dancers, sang or shouted at the top of their voices, unwearyingly, a strange tune (which, by the way, I noted down).   (ibid.: 68–9)

I ought to mention that the Dakpa, to make their horns, use the naturally hollow roots of a particular kind of tree, but even the longest of these roots is not long enough to make the lower pitched instruments. The clay horns mentioned by Gide are therefore very probably the lowest pitched of the instruments that the Dakpa use, which are always constructed out of this material. At Bakala I myself witnessed the manufacture of horns such as these, out of clay, and I also saw the 'feigned convulsions' of the musicians' leader, which are indeed a traditional function of his.

In *La croisière noire. Expédition Citroën Centre-Afrique*, which also appeared in the same year, 1927, Georges-Marie Haardt and Louis Audouin-Dubreuil recount their travels. In the same country, in the same town, amongst the very same people, and in identical circumstances, these travellers met an orchestra altogether comparable to the one described by Gide. Here is how, in their turn, they described it:

A little further on, at Bambari, we were to have the unhoped for opportunity to be present at these initiation dances. The cinema has resources which the book does not have, in order to create the impression of such an extraordinary sight; and the film in which Léon Poirier has preserved the vision of this infernal ballet cannot be replaced by any description. Words are not the equal of images when it is a matter of evoking unknown shapes, new rhythms.

Neophytes painted white, preliminary flagellation, performance of the rite by the witch-doctor in the bush, wild dances in headdresses with phallic points and the adult man's body-cloth – you have to see it to feel the frenzy of this sensual whirlwind which mounts to rapture and orgy, during the warm night, to the sound of horns hollowed out from branches, veritable forest organs, with their heroically dissonant clamour.

There are sounds of the flute, blasts on the trumpet, soft phrases on the oboe, rumblings as of a bassoon coming from treetrunks which need two people to blow them until they fall down drunk with exhaustion and *dolo* [millet beer]. All this fairground racket is not a cacophony; a savage harmony, sometimes disagreeable like the sound of wild animals, a true concert of rutting beasts.   (Haardt and Audouin-Dubreuil 1927: 117–18)

Without knowing it, these authors were engaging in a veritable oratorical joust with André Gide. . . The two accounts do, at any rate, have in common a wish to avoid ethnocentrism. Even if the second text advances some slightly naive analogies with certain Western instruments, its authors lack neither curiosity nor interest respecting the musical facts that they happened to have witnessed. I simply point out that if some of the horns seemed to them to be actual 'tree trunks which need two people to blow them', the musicians must have set these instruments vibrating by blowing alternately, not together.

Henri-Philippe Junod, son of the Henri A. Junod, mentioned above, wrote an article entitled 'The Mbila, or Native Piano of the Chopi Tribe', which was published in 1929. Both were Swiss missionaries, and the son, like the father, took a strong interest in the customs and music of the people of South Africa, where they exercised their ministries.

The article describes the Chopi xylophone ensembles, and the author tackles the subject in the spirit of a true researcher, even going so far as to sketch out some rhythmical analyses. Henri-Philippe Junod describes an impressive array of xylophones (which he calls 'pianos'), in which the instruments are categorized according to their respective registers: 'The band itself consisted of 17 pianos of the usual types: 14 *tfilandzana* of the ordinary sizes, placed in two rows. . . Behind the rows were two bigger *timbila* or *mabinde* – and behind these one *tfikhulu*, the big bass with its large keys' (Henri-Philippe Junod 1929: 284).

Further information about this type of ensemble was given by Henri-Philippe Junod to his father, who published it in a note to the French edition of his book *Moeurs et coutumes des Bantous* (1936). This sheds light on the very rigorous character of the internal organisation of these ensembles:

All the xylophones that my informant saw in Chopi country began with a *re* or a *mi* flat. These were *tfilandzana* or ordinary xylophones, which play the melody and which one might term *soprano* xylophones. The Chopi orchestras use three other kinds of xylophone, the *didole*, or *alto* xylophone, which usually has ten keys and whose lower key is a fourth below the lower key of the ordinary xylophone. This instrument plays the melody in an accompaniment four tones lower than the soprano. Then comes the *dibinda*, or *bass*, which reproduces the *tfilandzana's* part exactly, but on the lower octave. Lastly, there is the *tfikhulu*, or *contra-bass*, which has four or five enormous keys. This is clearly a genuine four-part orchestra, an authentic product of the musical genius of this particularly gifted tribe.   (Henri A. Junod 1936: II, 236)

Of all the writers that I have quoted so far, Henri-Philippe Junod, along with Peter Kolb some two hundred years earlier, most deserves notice. Indeed, Junod seems to have been the first, speaking of the music of an African people, to use the term *polyphony*, until then jealously reserved for Western music. But his real achievement is to have postulated a rule-governed musical system. He begins by arraigning Western ethnocentrism in terms which, unfortunately, have lost none of their relevance over the years:

It is a very great pity that we missionaries and white people in general have seen nothing better than to impose upon natives our occidental principles without trying to understand and develop the native ones. Many thought, at the beginning, that native songs were purely and simply mistaking the right laws of harmony, whereas it is now perfectly clear that native music is governed by law, and by a peculiar and most interesting system of polyphony. We have often thought that primitive people were actually primitive in all the manifestations of their genius. This is probably erroneous. Every student of Bantu, acquainted with the strict laws of primitive society and family relationship, as well as with the most delicate laws of primitive languages, knows that primitive polyphony, far though it may be from our Western harmony, is nothing like cacophony. The gramophone records already collected furnish proof of this statement. But of course with more material and a thorough study of the question it will be possible to realise more fully the interest and value of native music.   (Henri-Philippe Junod 1929: 282)

Two years later, there are two more testimonies regarding Central African polyphony, a type of music that would seem to have been overlooked by travellers until 1927.

The first comes from Father Daigre who, in a study entitled 'Les Bandas de l'Oubangui-Chari' (1931), devotes much of his attention to musical performances. In his inventory of this people's musical instruments, there is a brief description of the horns and of their use: 'The *mbéa* are wooden horns, from 0 *m* 20 to 1 *m* 70 in length, with which they produce sounds of every variety. The players form into series of from fifteen to twenty instruments, which constitute a veritable orchestra. They are used for circumcision ceremonies, in particular' (Daigre 1931: 655). Daigre does not specify to which Banda sub-group this instrument belongs; but the term '*mbéa*', which means horn only in the Banda-Dakpa language, enables us to repair this omission.

On a later page, Father Daigre emphasises the importance of musical performance during the adolescents' rites of passage:

The ceremonies of circumcision are invested with more solemnity than those of excision. They differ primarily in that the boys have to live far away from the settlement, in a deserted spot called *aba* to which their fathers carry their food every day.

They stay there until the wound is completely healed, under the watch of elders, and sheltered from the eyes of women and the uncircumcised, whose sight alone would cause their death. After several days, they cover their whole body with white clay, put rings of liana around their necks, wrists and ankles, put on tricorn headdresses of palm-leaves, and in this strange gear, two sticks in their hands, they execute the sacred consecrated dances under the constant threat of the long whips of their guardians who subject them to an ordeal which is stoically borne.

All the day and for much of the night the joyful refrains ring out, accompanied by the tam-tam or the *mbéa* orchestra. . .

Leaving the *aba* the newly circumcised make a solemn entry into the village where they perform their dances. It is a memorable day in the life of a Banda. (ibid.: 667–8)

Félix Eboué, who was an administrator in Central Africa, and who was very attentive to the music there, provides us with our second testimony. In his *Les peuples de l'Oubangui-Chari. Essai d'ethnographie, de linguistique et d'économie sociale* (1933), Eboué emphasises the part played by the horn orchestras in Banda rites of passage:

We know that the *ganza* are those who have been circumcised. After the cicatrisation of the wound, they devote whole weeks to rejoicing. . . They dance on their own, and the music that they play, on wooden horns, is not meant to make the others present dance. . .

This *ganza* music is particularly surprising, in that it is agreeable to hear, and is produced by a veritable symphony orchestra. The instruments are wooden horns, with a hole pierced at one end, and with the other end forming the bell; the performer holds his instrument in his right hand, his left hand is placed in front of the bell and serves, depending upon the variations in its position, to modify the volume of the instrument. The artist thus obtains a wide range of nuances and expressive qualities from his instrument.

An orchestra usually comprises ten or so musicians, who are supervised by the leader of the orchestra. The *ganza* play, and at the same time dance on the spot, or else while moving, or else turning around, depending upon the scene which they wish to mime. No drums accompany them, and the tune played may be *translated* by any local member of the audience who has a little experience. It is *translation* and not interpretation, a translation that local people can produce *simply by listening to the music*, and without watching the scene as it is represented.

The *ganza* musicians play in time and pay careful attention to the orchestra leader conducting them. (Eboué 1933: 78)

Like Father Daigre, Eboué does not give the name of the Banda sub-group he is discussing. But the passage contains two clues which enable us to identify it. The writer informs us, on the one hand, that the *ganza* music 'is not meant to make the others present dance' and also that 'no drums accompany them'. Of the numerous Banda sub-groups, only two employ horn orchestras in comparable circumstances, namely, the Dakpa and the Linda. Now, among the Dakpa, the playing of the horns is accompanied by a wooden slit-drum, which is meant to cause people to dance. It can therefore only be the Linda who are described here.

Moreover, when Eboué states that 'the tune played may be *translated*', it would undoubtedly have been more appropriate for him to have written 'may be *recognised*'. For what is really involved here is an *identification* of the melody by the audience, and not a translation in the strict sense of the term. This is probably what the author meant in writing of 'a translation that local people can produce *simply by listening to the music*, and without watching the scene as it is represented', and indeed by placing particular emphasis on the italicised part of the statement. The pieces that these orchestras play correspond to *monodic* popular songs which have been treated in a particular manner, really adapted and given an instrumentation, so as to be played by horn ensembles. It is the tunes of these popular songs that the listeners are so quick to recognise. I shall try to account for this process of transformation when I return to Banda-Linda hocket polyphony.

Eboué's reference to the presence of an orchestra leader calls for a comment of a more general sort. I have often wondered when attending musical performances given by horn ensembles in Banda country, whether the presence of a band leader was not a very recent thing, attributable perhaps to a film show or to a military parade which the musicians might have watched. Now, Eboué's observation confirms that this function goes back at least fifty years, to a period when cinema, and indeed military bands, were as yet unknown in the heart of the Central African savannah. One can therefore assume that this technique, and the point is an important one, goes back much further than that, Joyeux's account (1910), along with that of Van der Stel (prior to 1682), lends further support to this conclusion.

The final traveller's narrative that I present here dates from 1936. I refer once again to *Moeurs et coutumes des Bantous* by Henri A. Junod (the father of Henri-Philippe). The author gives two descriptions of a horn ensemble among the Tonga (or Thonga) of South Africa. He maintains that, in some of the Tonga clans, this type of ensemble is used for an 'official fanfare', which is known as the 'bunanga'. Henri A. Junod's description once again implies a hocket polyphony.

These instruments are made by specialists. . . and form a kind of orchestra (*simo*) composed of ten instruments. To play them well one must have acquired real virtuosity. The players stand up around two drum-players. The big drum gives the rhythm: when it slowly beats 'ton-ton-ton' the ten musicians have to dance in a circle, moving one behind the other, both playing and making certain faces and certain gestures. When the big drum beats slower and softer, they have to form a line and walk slowly. The drum accelerates the rhythm; then they come back to the centre and make a ring again, dancing faster and faster. The players follow each other in a given order; at the head walks the man holding the biggest horn with the deepest sound, at the tail-end walks the man with the smallest horn with the highest sound.   (Henri A. Junod 1936: I, 401)

This narrative, like so many of the others given above, contains more ethnographic than musicological observations, but it marks the decline of 'the age of the traveller' and the birth, however gradual, of truly specialised research. Indeed, whilst Henri A. Junod's account dates from 1936, it was since 1930 that the results of the first ethnomusicological field studies were published. These studies were written by Percival R. Kirby, who had worked in the same part of Southern Africa as Junod.

Horn ensembles have taken up a large part of the accounts quoted above. It will therefore come as no surprise that the last description given here is devoted to them, but this time, and as a kind of *coda*, from a folkloric rather than polyphonic point of view:

The players of the *bunanga* receive a methodical instruction before playing in front of the chief. When they have prepared the pieces for their programme, they all proceed to the capital in order to take part in a musical competition, with each under-chief conducting his own group. The councillors act as judges. Each *simo* plays in turn. The judges discuss their respective merits, and when they have arrived at a decision, they call upon a young man to announce the result of the competition. This proclamation is known as *kεu tjema chivangeu*, 'cutting the contest', and is conducted in a very curious manner. The herald carries an axe in his hand, and pronounces the verdict at the top of his voice: 'Such-and-such played badly; such-and-such, better; we pronounce the son of such-and-such the winner of the competition'. ('*Nkino hi nkhensa wa ka man*'.) He then strikes a tree trunk with his axe, as if to confirm his decision, and flees; he does so in order to avoid the protests and insults of those who did not carry off the victory.
                                                                      (Henri A. Junod 1936: II, 232)

I conclude this historical survey by emphasising a point that has emerged from the collocation of the various accounts reported here. I begin by calling upon Kirby's description of his visit to Bechuanaland in 1931. He heard a reed whistle ensemble at Kanye, and gives a very detailed account of the tuning system employed. Now, the striking thing to note is that this system corresponds exactly, both with Burchell's eye-witness account of 1812, and with what Van der Stel said before 1682.

This system of tuning, if we accept the description given by a researcher who studied it in South Africa in 1931, in no way differs from that in use in the same part of Africa amongst the same instrumental ensembles some two hundred and fifty years before. And this does not merely apply to the tuning, but to the musical system too, since Kirby notes 'I found it impossible to note down the music completely on the spot at first hearing, and sympathised with Burchell, who had found the same difficulty under very similar circumstances' (1934: 149).

The remarkable consistency of these accounts on the same subject gives us a historical perspective that enables us to assess the endurance of a musical system across time.

We do, admittedly, have far fewer mutually supporting accounts of this type of music than we do for other African polyphonies. I would, nevertheless, by extrapolation risk the hypothesis that some polyphonic procedures known today in a particular place – if you take into account their oral transmission, their relation to specified social functions, and their persistence amongst peoples whose way of life has not undergone any profound modifications – cannot be so different from what they were some hundreds of years, and even – who can say? – longer ago.

2.3 SPECIALIST STUDIES

The works published by musicologists and ethnomusicologists on African polyphony and polyrhythm in the last fifty years constitute a fairly motley collection. They rest on very different bases – as to the theoretical presuppositions and objectives of the writers – and also function at different levels, since they include both very precise descriptions and significant attempts at synthesis. Moreover, they employ very diverse analytic methods. So before undertaking a critical examination, it seems appropriate to give a brief account of the order in which they are presented. It was possible to classify these studies according to the main topics of which they treat, namely counterpoint, hocket, pure polyrhythm and so on. One might also have presented, chronologically, the works of each of the most eminent researchers, and one might then have proceeded to survey all the other publications that had, to a greater or lesser degree, shed some light on African polyphony. One might also have distinguished between ethnomusicologists with the benefit of direct contact in the field with the music, studied in its cultural setting, and musicologists whose research depended entirely on 'second-hand' materials – recordings made by others – whether archive documents or commercial records.

But it seemed nevertheless that the least arbitrary approach was to observe, as above, a rigorously chronological order. Indeed, this seemed to be the most appropriate way of noting what one researcher might owe to another (errors included) in the advance of our knowledge, and, consequently, of throwing some light on the present state of our understanding of the subject.

2.3.1   From 1922 to 1940

The first study, so far as I know, in which any musicologist treats of African polyphony dates from 1922. In an article devoted to 'La musique chez les Nègres d'Afrique', published in the first part of Lavignac's *Encyclopédie de la Musique et Dictionnaire du Conservatoire*, Julien Tiersot, relying on various earlier accounts, describes the *rhythmic polyphony* which characterises this music: 'The vocal chants are often supported (in dances, in particular) by an accompaniment by rhythmical instruments, and these instrumental rhythms are superimposed in such a way as to form amongst themselves, and with the voice itself, aggregations which constitute a very complex rhythmical polyphony' (Tiersot 1922: v, 3224). Tiersot goes on to acknowledge the interest of instrumental and vocal polyphonies, without going so far as to recognise the men who produce them:

It happens in certain cases that instruments of fixed pitch combine in superpositions of intervals which create true chords and constitute a real harmony.

Finally, we have noted cases – perhaps exceptional but certainly very significant – of perfectly characterized vocal harmonies, which constitute a proof that the notion of chords formed by the movement of several simultaneous vocal parts is not unknown to peoples recognised as being at the bottom of the scale of civilisation.   (ibid.)

Two years later, in 1924, Dr Charles Joyeux published his 'Etude sur quelques manifestations musicales observées en Haute-Guinée Française', discussed above (cf. *supra*, 2.2.5). This publication included in the text some 'Notes relatives à la transcription des phonogrammes', phonograms that Joyeux had brought back to France after his stay in Africa. A musicologist, Marguerite Béclard-d'Harcourt, was responsible for the 'Notes' and musical transcriptions. One of the cylinders recorded by Joyeux reproduced a polyphonic piece for six xylophones, but the piece was so complex that the musicologist had to abandon her attempt to transcribe it. 'Played on the phonograph, this cylinder is remarkable and I regret being unable to transcribe it. The extreme speed of the balas [xylophones] and the confusion which arises from their playing together makes notation practically impossible' (Béclard-d'Harcourt in Joyeux 1924: 187). The author of these 'Notes' does nevertheless give a very precise account of the principles governing the organisation of this piece:

Alongside these *balas*, but completely independent rhythmically and melodically (although tuned to the same intervals), there was the virtuoso's *bala*. He suddenly launched into very rapid diatonic outlines of scales and repeated notes, produced by striking the same key with two hammers in turn, his part being superimposed upon that of the others. He sometimes seems to be in the grip of a genuine frenzy, passing from sharps to flats and back with a disconcerting speed, and with a distinctive fantasy. There results from this ensemble: an obstinate rhythmical accompaniment on three or four notes by the *balas* that form the orchestra, and, on the part of the virtuoso, a hurried melody, a flood of notes that floated on the surface of this accompaniment without mingling with it. This was a very curious ensemble which, unfortunately, it was almost impossible to notate. The rhythmical shiftings observable in it were simply produced by the shifting of accents, but the quantities remained the same.   (ibid.: 188)

By virtue of this brief description, Marguerite Béclard-d'Harcourt seems to be, unknowingly, the forerunner of the study of African rhythm; she makes a number of crucial observations of fundamental importance, whose implications went unnoticed by most ethnomusicologists at least until the 1960s. Indeed, in speaking of the 'obstinate rhythmical accompaniment on three or four notes by the *balas*', she seems to have been the first person to have observed the *ostinato* principle so common in sub-Saharan Africa. She is also the first, and this is the crucial point, to have noticed that the rhythmical shiftings are simply due to the shifting of accents, and also to have brought out the correlation between these shiftings and the constant nature of the quantities within which they are effected. Now, this constancy in the quantities is itself a constant of the metrical structure of most African traditional musics, and, as a corollary, of that of the polyphonies.

In an article published in 1928, entitled 'African Negro Music', Erich von Hornbostel insists upon the need to distinguish between harmonic polyphonies and melodic polyphonies. He notes that African polyphony develops, from the basis of pure melodies, into forms that were undoubtedly current in Europe during the early part of the Middle Ages (Hornbostel 1928: 62). This analogy with Medieval polyphony, which Hornbostel was apparently the first to propose, was taken up later by numerous other researchers. Percival R. Kirby proposes the same idea in 1930, in his article entitled 'A Study of Negro Harmony'. Having noted the influence of African tone languages upon the music in general, and upon the parallel arrangement of the voices in particular, Kirby observes: 'Speech-tone of the Bantu has not only influenced his melodies, but had also directed the course of his polyphonic thought in a direction analogous to that taken by the polyphonic thought of the peoples of Europe during the early centuries of the Christian era' (Kirby 1930: 406). This crucial observation leads Kirby to conclude that: 'Independent polyphonic movement of parts would not occur systematically until tone ceased to be the predominant factor in language' (ibid.).

Three years later, in 1933, the same scholar published an important study, entitled *The Reed-Flute Ensembles of South Africa: A Study in South African Native Music*. It contains the description, in chronological order, of a great number of reed-flute ensembles as seen by travellers from Vasco da Gama in 1497 to Kirby himself in 1930. In the historical section of the present survey (cf. *supra*, 2.2), I have reproduced those accounts given in Kirby's book which were relevant to the present discussion. At this point, we meet, for the first time, the work of the Reverend Arthur Morris Jones, a missionary and ethnomusicologist. He lived for a long time in Zimbabwe (then Rhodesia), and published numerous works devoted to African polyrhythm.

In 1934, A. M. Jones published a study entitled 'African Drumming: A Study of the Combination of Rhythms in African Music', in which he criticised the article by Hornbostel cited above, giving a polemical discussion of Hornbostel's transcription of a polyphonic piece played by the Pangwe of Gabon. He throws light, not without a certain lyrical note, on certain aspects of African rhythm: 'Anyone who cares to take a course of African drumming will speedily be convinced that what he has to play on his own drum is a *perfectly simple* rhythm. The other players are also playing *simple rhythms*: it is the combination of these simple rhythms which makes the glorious African rhythmic harmony, which to the listener often sounds beyond analysis' (Jones 1934: 2). Turning directly to the transcription proposed by Hornbostel, Jones happens to make use of the notion of polyrhythm, which he attempts to define:

The present writer regards the piece as 'poly-rhythmic', i.e. made up of voices each carrying their own inherent rhythm, and having different starting-points. . . There can be no doubt that if we are to solve the problems of African rhythm, we must regard it as 'poly-rhythmic', i.e. a combination of rhythms having their own starting-points and their own individuality.

(ibid.: 8)

In this same year we find Kirby using the terms *cross-rhythm* and *rhythmical counter-point* in writing about xylophone music, and also *polyrhythm*, in relation to the hocket music of the Venda reed whistle ensembles. These observations occur in his very important work *The Musical Instruments of the Native Races of South Africa* (1934). Like Jones, Kirby observes that the different rhythmical parts are simple enough when considered in isolation, the complexity of the ensemble deriving from the manner in which they interweave; he makes this observation in the light of his own experience of playing several African instruments.

The second tune was a much more complex affair, and it took some time for me to realise how it was constructed; for, when heard, it presents to the ear a bewildering cross-rhythm. Yet, dissected out, as it must be when one is being taught to play it, it becomes quite clear, although far from easy for a European player to execute. It is based. . . upon the direct and deliberate opposition of two distinct rhythmic schemes, and provides an excellent example of a very attractive form of rhythmic counterpoint.   (Kirby 1933: 54)

Kirby later arrives at the notion of polyrhythm in reed whistle orchestras, whose music seems to him to be like 'a twentieth-century survival of the practice familiar to European musicians as the *organum* of the Middle Ages' (ibid.: 159). It is worth noting that this writer seems to have been the first to have produced a genuinely ethnomusicological description, giving an account both of the circumstances in which the performance was held and of its actual technical execution; of the local names of the instruments and of their grouping in 'families'; of their system of tuning and of the scales employed; and not forgetting the principles embodied in the music (ibid.: 135–70). We should also note that Kirby was the first to succeed in presenting a true score of a complex polyphony, one used in a piece for nineteen whistles and three percussion instruments (ibid.: 160).

It was in 1934 also that the first volume of Marius Schneider's famous work, *Geschichte der Mehrstimmigkeit*, devoted exclusively to vocal polyphony, was published. The author, it must be said, is not fundamentally concerned with questions of ethnomusicology. His main aim is to trace the sources of Western polyphony. Inasmuch as he was a disciple of the German diffusionist school, whose central notion was that of *Kulturkreise* ('circles of culture'), Schneider held the theory that most of the cultural features peculiar to a society have been, at a given historical moment, borrowed, directly or indirectly, from other societies, and subsequently adopted. This diffusionist theory also has it that these elements derive from a limited number of 'centres of diffusion' or 'cultural foci', considering how rare true inventions are.

So for lack of documents throwing any light on the prehistory of the medieval *organum*, Schneider devoted himself to an investigation of the polyphonic procedures in use among those populations held to be representative of the various original *Kulturkreise*. These latter are the 'natural peoples', hence the title of this first volume, *Die Naturvölker*.

But what is a 'musical cultural focus'? I turn to Bruno Nettl to answer this question. In *Music in Primitive Culture*, he discusses Schneider's work as follows:

In this survey, the majority of the primitive styles using polyphony have been classified under four 'areas' that correspond to the *Kulturkreis* concept – they are noncontiguous and supposedly delimit historical periods as well as geographic cultural boundaries. The areas were determined on the basis of two main criteria: the similarity or diversity between the tonal organisation of the individual parts; and the equality or inequality of the importance of the individual parts. . .

Schneider believes that each area is at a stage of musical development through which all areas pass at some time, the view taken by the *Kulturkreis* school.   (Nettl 1965: 79–80)

To realise his project, Marius Schneider used the archive recordings preserved in the *Berliner Phonogrammarchiv*; his study is based on the analysis of these recordings, from which he selects 289 transcribed examples, drawn from the peoples of every continent. So far as Africa is concerned, Schneider thinks the most striking feature of this continent's polyphony is homophony. He also makes an entirely justified distinction between the music which he calls 'Negro' and that of 'persons of small stature' (*kleinwächsige Leute*), in which category he includes Pygmies, Bushmen and Hottentots.

There are several reasons why this work made such a stir. Its publication, at a time when little was known of 'exotic' musics, did much to make them better known, particularly through the transcriptions and analyses that feature in it. Moreover, the method employed – a kind of musical archaeology of the present – constitutes one of the first applications of diffusionist theory, if not the very first, to musicological research. In any case, it would not do to underestimate the attraction of any new universalist theory. But while one has every sympathy with the methodological presuppositions that lead Schneider to enquire into civilisations with an oral tradition, one must express reservations about the application of this method.

My first reservation concerns the actual material upon which Schneider had to work. These are undoubtedly heterogeneous documents, recorded for the most part by *travellers*; but it is not clear that the few samples they were able to collect among any particular people would faithfully reflect the various polyphonic procedures practised there. Four or five specimens from the repertoire of a particular people certainly do not allow us to draw conclusions about the polyphonic principles used by it, especially since the examples transcribed tend, moreover, to be in a fragmentary form. It must also be said that some three hundred fairly brief examples hardly suffice to support a supposedly universal theory.

Finally, some of the theoretical points that Schneider makes are clearly wrong. I shall only cite one example, concerning African hocket polyphony, in which Schneider discerns a European influence. Indeed, he holds that African hocket is *harmonic*, in the Western sense of the word, but since, quite rightly, he does not consider African music to derive from that harmony, he is led, as a good diffusionist, to see in it a borrowing from the 'cultural focus' of Western art music.

However harsh this criticism of diffusionist theory may seem, it is shared by most contemporary ethnologists and ethnomusicologists. Hence Bruno Nettl, summarising Schneider's work in *Theory and Method in Ethnomusicology*, notes that this author's perspective is hard to accept (Nettl 1964: 39).

In an article published in 1936, entitled 'The Musical Practices of the Auni and Khomani Bushmen', Percival R. Kirby gives a succinct account of the vocal polyphony of these peoples. Among the features mentioned are counterpoint, yodelling and the absence of words, all of which recur among the Pygmies.

A. M. Jones, published 'The Study of African Rhythms' in 1937. This article has the merit of including a complete transcription of a song for two voices, accompanied by four drum parts and hand-clapping. Its author again refers to cross-rhythms, and again emphasises that, in a polyrhythmic music, the main beats of each of the drums occur at different times (Jones 1937: 299). I cannot follow Jones on this point, which will be discussed in detail in Book V, devoted to the organisation of time in African music.

2.3.2   From 1940 to 1960

In an article published in 1949, entitled 'Canon in West African Xylophone Melodies', George Herzog tells of his surprise at having found, in 1930 and to the East of Liberia, melodies in canon form, played on a xylophone. The author observed two musicians, seated face to face, who played on the same instrument, a xylophone with six keys placed on trunks of a banana tree. Having listed the various polyphonic procedures (rhythmical ostinato, canon, hocket) which may be used in the playing of this instrument, he mentions that 'There are a few examples in which ostinato, canon and hocket are combined in various ways, and a few in which *the two players play two independent pieces at the same time* (my italics)' (Herzog 1949: 197). One may nevertheless wonder how Herzog arrived at this conclusion. One of two alternatives must be correct. Either what he thought to be 'two independent pieces' actually consisted of two independent *parts*, and so formed a coherent whole when played simultaneously, so that one has to do with a piece of music whose polyrhythmic organisation has simply eluded the observer. Alternatively the two musicians, in a gamelike manner, may have superimposed two totally unconnected pieces, in which case their combination, being fortuitous and unmusical, is of no concern to ethnomusicology.

In 1950, Herbert Pepper published a study entitled 'Musique Centre Africaine'. This contains a fragmentary transcription of a piece for five xylophones collected in Gabon, though Pepper unfortunately does not specify its ethnic origin. It also includes a transcription of passages from a Bembe (Middle Congo) 'fetishist ceremony', known as *Mumpa*. This was a five part polyphony, involving a solo vocalist, a choir singing in unison, a drum, a rattle, and a pair of wooden bells – so, two melodic and three rhythmic parts. In the same work Pepper describes horn and whistle orchestras, and makes a specific reference to the Banda of Central Africa:

They all follow the same technique. Consisting of about a dozen performers, the listener is left with the impression of a single breath, for each performer, owing to the poverty of his instrument, is only able to produce one or two sounds, and therefore has to allow his neighbour to continue the musical phrase, which, when literally translated, again reveals its secret.

(Pepper 1950: 565)

The reader will note the recurrence here of the word, and also the concept of the 'translation' of music, which Félix Eboué applied to Banda horn ensembles (cf. *supra* 2.2.5). The coincidence is easily explained when it is known that Pepper carried out some of his researches in Bambari, the 'capital' of Banda country, during the period when Eboué was posted there. We cannot tell which of the two first used the idea of 'translation', an idea, which, as I have pointed out, simply means the *identification* by the audience of the pieces played by the orchestra.

An article by Friedrich Hornburg, 'Phonographierte Afrikanische Mehrstimmigkeit', published in the same year, also contains transcription. These are of polyphonic music taken from archive documents of performances of the Tiv (Nigeria), recorded before the Second World War. Hornburg also presents detailed analyses, interval tables, statistics, etc. Of the nine pieces that he publishes, four are polyphonic. But unfortunately Hornburg seems not to have understood the principles upon which their rhythmical organisation is based, for he has no hesitation in writing: 'So divergent are the vocal and instrumental parts that they cannot be subsumed under any common denominator' (Hornburg 1950: 176).

This seems to be a hasty conclusion, given the brevity of the examples transcribed and the small number of pieces noted. One cannot advance definitive and wide-ranging assertions on the basis of four polyphonic pieces, selected at random from the musical heritage of a people who obviously have many more pieces of music. I find it hard to accept the notion that, in sub-Saharan Africa at any rate, there could exist polyphonies without a 'common denominator' between vocal and instrumental parts.

Marius Schneider's article, 'Ist die vokale Mehrstimmigkeit eine Schöpfung der Altrassen?' (1951), is a summary of the diffusionist ideas that he had outlined some seventeen years before, in the first volume of his *Geschichte der Mehrstimmigkeit*.

In 1951 André Schaeffner published a work entitled *Les Kissi, une société noire et ses instruments de musique* in which the Malinke horn orchestras in the Kankan region of Guinea are discussed. This ethnomusicologist's observations about tuning methods and performance are so detailed and plentiful that they bear out those of Dr Joyeux in every respect (cf. *supra* 2.2.5), so that we can safely assert that the same type of polyphony was employed in the same place for several decades.

In 1952, Rose Brandel published an article entitled 'Music of the Giants and the Pygmies of the Belgian Congo'. She began by describing the rhythmical system of the Watusi royal drums. She went on to mention Bahutu vocal polyphony, which included pieces with three melodically independent voice parts, in genuine counterpoint. The third people discussed, the Batwa Pygmies, are also said to have three-part vocal counterpoint. This study, which includes several brief transcriptions, is based on gramophone records.

A year later, in London, an important ethnographic study, entitled *Tribal Crafts of Uganda*, was published. The second half of this work, *The Sound Instruments*, was written by Klaus P. Wachsmann, and was devoted to Ugandan musical instruments. Surprisingly enough, this writer says nothing about the instrumental techniques employed in the only two polyphonic ensembles mentioned: an ensemble consisting of sixteen reed whistles covering a range of over three octaves (Wachsmann 1953: 343), and an orchestra of eight side-blown horns with calabash bells (ibid.: 358). This book abounds with descriptions of instruments, but unfortunately one can learn almost nothing about the music that they play.

Another study by A. M. Jones, 'African Rhythm', was published in 1954. He once again presents his interpretation of those cross-rhythms whose 'main beats' are supposed not to coincide. In fact he gives many examples of extremely interesting rhythmical combinations, but employs an excessively complicated system of notation, to which I refer below.

The musicologist Paul Collaer published some 'Notes sur la musique d'Afrique Centrale' (1954) which, in spite of their brevity, provide an excellent survey of the music of this region. Having stressed that the practice of polyphony is more widespread in traditional Africa than in European folk music, the author goes on to say that 'Classical musicologists have made out that polyphony is European in origin. But in fact there are three main centres of polyphony: Mediterranean Europe, Black Africa, and Polynesia' (Collaer 1954: 268). Collaer focusses his attention upon the form of polyphony to be found in Zaïre, and tells us that it contains 'a music remarkable for its melodic invention, and involving every form known to European polyphony from the thirteenth and fourteenth centuries onwards: gymel, organum, conductus, faux-bourdon, and not excluding the technique employing alternating and complementary voices known as "hoketus"' (ibid.: 269). Collaer is convinced that black African music, like European music, developed out of the most primitive forms:

The Blacks organised sound in the same manner as the Europeans, and independently of them. They discovered the diatonic scale, often with the same intervals as the Europeans had adopted, and black polyphony went through the same stages as the European. But the Blacks stopped short at the forms used by the Europeans in the twelfth century. . . One wonders why the Blacks should have stopped when the Europeans have continued. It is, to my mind, because a musical writing was invented, along with a notation agreeing with the chosen system, that Europeans were able to find more complex polyphonic combinations, and to experiment in a domain in which music burdens itself with an increasing number of factors of a purely intellectual order, to the detriment of its rhythmical and melodic richness.

This analysis concludes with some most pertinent considerations:

From this moment on, European classical music has become more and more intellectual, gradually restricting the circle of men that it represents and addresses, until finally it becomes the music of man in isolation.

The Blacks have taken that form of polyphony that is orally preserved and transmitted as far as it will go. Their art is still a collective creation, and their music still represents the ethnic group from which it stems, and it is still a direct expression of a people's vital energy.

(ibid.: 269)

Two articles by Jean-Noël Maquet, 'la musique chez les Bapende' (1954) and 'La musique chez les Pende et Tshokwe' (1956) are worth mentioning, if only to ensure the completeness of this survey. They contain several brief transcriptions of two- and three-part songs collected in Zaïre.

In 1957, Yvette Grimaud and Gilbert Rouget published a joint ethnomusicological study, entitled *Note sur la musique des Bochiman comparée à celle des Pygmées Babinga, d'après les enregistrements de la Mission Marshall au Kalahari (1954) et de la Mission Ogooué-Congo (1946)*. Gilbert Rouget compared and contrasted Pygmy and Bushman music. He noted that they shared the use of yodelling, vocal polyphony and 'the systematic use of a vocalised song in which there is never, or hardly ever, recourse to words as support for the sung melody' (Grimaud et Rouget 1957: 2). In trying to make sense of the 'troubling kinship' between Pygmy and Bushman music and dance, Rouget asked this question: 'Must we conclude that Pygmies and Bushmen derive from a common stock, and that dance and music is all that now remains of a common cultural heritage?' (ibid.: 3)

This same booklet contains an analysis by Yvette Grimaud of the musics of the two peoples. Highlighting the features that they have in common, she notes:

One of the most important of these is undoubtedly the form of development that could perhaps be called concentric, and which would seem to be peculiar to these musics. It operates within a sort of melodicorhythmic *loop*. Each of these loops is continuous and is integrated within a larger cycle whose movement is powered by a number of infinitely renewed and mobile detail.

(ibid.: 5)

Amongst the other features that these two musics have in common, Yvette Grimaud draws attention to:

- the relatively extended voice range;
- the frequency with which a melody is developed by disjunct intervals. . .;
- devices such as imitation, augmentation, contraction and extension of intervals, echo effects and ornated counterpoint;
- the superposition on an *ostinato* rhythm of diverse rhythmic structures.

(ibid.: 5–6)

This study includes fragmentary transcriptions of polyphonic pieces, some of which have as many as seven vocal parts and two percussive parts.

In *African Music in Northern Rhodesia and Some Other Places*, a small book that came out in 1958, A. M. Jones discussed in some detail the notion of 'main beats'. He observes that, when we listen to an African percussion ensemble, 'we hear not one rhythmic pattern but many distinct rhythms intertwined, each with its own main beat which does not coincide with the main beats of other instruments' (Jones 1958a: 8). In 1959, the same author published *Studies in African Music*, a synthesis of all his previous works. This huge endeavour must be considered, as the ethnomusicologist Miecyslaw Kolinski observes, as one of the 'most important contributions to our knowledge of African music south of the Sahara' (Kolinski 1973: 496). I would go so far as to say that it is still the most important work on the subject. It consists of two linked volumes, the first of which contains a series of essays concerned with various subjects, but with an emphasis on the homogeneity of African music; its central part is devoted to the analysis of the various musics whose transcription is presented in the second volume. The latter, which is some two hundred pages long, actually contains nothing but scores, which, for the first time, are complete. They reproduce mainly dance musics whose structure is polyrhythmic, and is often extremely complex. Most of the pieces transcribed contain, apart from the melody, which is generally monodic and responsorial, six or seven rhythmic parts: three drum parts, one of which is the master-drummer's, and one or two bell parts, in addition to which there are various hand-clapping parts. All these musics come from the Ewe people, who live in Ghana, excepting the *Icila* dance, which was recorded among the Lala in Zimbabwe.

The transcription of such complex polyrhythms was only possible because of the employment, by Jones, of a specially designed electro-mechanical apparatus. I shall describe this in Book III, in the chapter devoted to the problem of transcribing polyphonic music. From the very first pages of his book, Jones warns us against ethnocentrism: 'As we begin our study, we invite the reader to lay aside his own musical concepts and to approach this novel territory with an open mind. If, by the end, he has begun to look at African music from the African's own point of view, that will be our reward and his enrichment' (Jones 1959: I, 15).

In spite of this laudable attitude, Jones himself did not succeed in totally divesting himself of the ethnocentrism that he so properly condemns. Thus, in his review of *Studies in African Music*, Kolinski notes: 'Jones's treatment of African metro-rhythmic structures results from a radical application of a widely accepted Western misconception on the nature of metre, leading to a basic misrepresentation of one of the most characteristic traits of African music' (Kolinski 1960: 107). This criticism was refined in an article that appeared in 1973, entitled 'A Cross-Cultural Approach to Metro-Rhythmic Patterns'. Kolinski holds that Jones arrives at a remarkably distorted interpretation of African metro-rhythmic structures, mainly because he analyses them in terms of 'the mistaken notion of accent' in Western music (Kolinski 1973: 496). The mistaken notion to which Kolinski refers concerns the organisation of time into bars. It is attributable to the effects of notating music graphically, in those societies that have written musics (cf. Book V). As is well known, Western notation arranges musical time in 'measures', which are divided by barlines; the note immediately following the barline constitutes what is called a 'strong beat' and implies a certain accentuation. Time and time again Jones insists, both here and in his previous works, that there is no regular reiteration of accent in African music. He holds that African melodies are 'additive', whilst their time-background is 'divisive': 'The African is not concerning himself with preserving a regularly recurring divise rhythm to which the inherent stresses of the melody shall agree. True, where there is a regular clap, there is divise rhythm: but the African whilst strictly regarding it as a metrical background, is not in the least using it to indicate any accentual stress in the melody' (Jones 1959: I, 20).

This metrical background, to which Jones so often refers, is the equivalent of a metronomic unit which has two functions: it serves as a standard for the organisation of the various durations of each part, and as a common denominator in the ensemble of all the parts in a polyphony. In African music, it manifests itself as what Jones calls a 'clap', i.e., a beat (either implicit or realised in the form of hand-claps) corresponding to a regular succession of isochronous units and – the crucial point – implying no notion of accentuation. Jones is emphatic about this last point: 'The clapping has no accented beats' (ibid.: 167).

Even in the first pages of his study Jones had placed great emphasis on the purely metronomic, i.e., neutral, character of this metrical background: 'The claps carry no accent whatever in the African mind. They serve as a yard-stick, a kind of metronome which exists behind the music. Once the clap has started you can never, on any pretext whatever, stretch or diminish the clap-values. They remain constant and *they do not impart any rhythm to the melody itself*' (ibid.: 21). Now, once Jones introduces into his analysis the opposed notions of 'additive' and 'divisive' rhythms, the claps seem to lose their neutral quality. Thus, with respect to a song accompanying a children's game: 'The melody being additive, and the claps being divisive, when put together they result in a combination of rhythms whose inherent stresses are *crossed*' (ibid.: 21-2). From being metronomic, these claps have, owing to the 'inherent stresses' with which they have been provided, become rhythmic. This confusion causes Jones to adopt a system of bimetrical notation for the transcription of songs: 'There is going to be one kind of bars for the claps and a varying bar-system for the melody so as to indicate where the melodic stresses lie. This we think is inevitable in dealing with additive music' (ibid.: 21). But if the claps are given no accentuation, into what 'kind of bar' should one insert them? In other words, what is to determine the number of claps per bar?

As we have seen, the status of this beat, which is so clearly defined in other contexts, turns out to be very ambiguous once the melody for which it is supposed to serve as metrical background is an 'additive' one. However, Jones insists that it really is the song which depends on the claps and not the other way around, whether the beat is realised or not. The proof is that 'the singer, if no one claps, will be making the claps mentally' (ibid.: 20). These claps become even more ambiguous as the work progresses, inasmuch as they no longer seem to be *isochronous* metrical reference points, but constitutive elements in rhythmical figures, i.e., based upon non-identical durations, or *heterochronous* (ibid.: 26, 33, 142, 211 and elsewhere). Jones even goes so far as to superimpose various schemas of claps in rhythmical counterpoint.

As to the beat's function as regulator between melody and percussive parts, Jones asserts that 'the hand clap is the rhythmic link between the song and the other instruments' (ibid.: 69). Would it not therefore be more appropriate to employ just one metric system, including both claps and melody, so demonstrating the remarkable rhythmical independence of these 'additive' melodies with respect to the relentless beat which forms their backbone? For, in order to transcribe these melodies, Jones precedes each stressed note with a barline. This approach of course gives rise to a sequence of bars with an endlessly varied number of time signatures. Thus, the melody of the *Nyayito* dance (ibid.: II, 11–40) is divided into bars of 3/8, 2/4, 6/8, 1/4, 3/4, 7/8, and even 1/8, which are constantly switching.

Because he considers each instrument to have a specific 'main beat', Jones, when he transcribes the instrumental parts, ascribes a different time signature to each of them. The seven rhythmical parts of the *Nyayito* dance are represented as follows: we read 12/8 for the double bell (with 6/8 added in square brackets); the first drum follows this 12/8 time, whilst the claps are defined as 6/4; then comes the master-drummer's part, which is defined in terms of a constantly alternating 5/8, 3/8, 2/4, 5/4, 6/8, 3/4, and 1/4; of the three remaining drum parts, two are given as 6/8, followed shortly after by a 3/8, and then again by a 6/8, followed this time by a 4/8; the last drum, however, stays in 3/8. Now, if the hand clap constitutes, as the author says, 'the rhythmic link between the song and the other instruments', how is one to justify such a complex notation, when the reality is, as Jones himself admits, far more simple: 'It is not a platitude to insist that normally in African music all rhythms are compounded of notes whose value is a simple multiple of the basic unit of time, and that the whole complex structure rests on this simple mathematical basis' (ibid.: I, 24).

A consequence of the system of notation adopted here is that the barlines indicated in the various instrumental parts only rarely coincide with each other. Score reading therefore becomes very arduous, and the polyrhythmic organisation of the ensemble may be discerned only with great difficulty. I feel bound to accept the criticisms of Jones's work made by Kolinski. It is indeed because Jones has a mistaken conception of African metro-rhythmic structures that he describes *polyrhythmic* performances (cross-rhythms) in terms of *polymetric* devices (superimposition of bars of different value). In Book V I shall attempt to show just how different these two notions are.

Apart from these critical remarks, which one could not in honesty leave unsaid, *Studies in African Music* remains to this day the major contribution to the technical study that is, the musicological study of African rhythm and polyrhythm.

Also in 1959, Gilbert Rouget issued a record *Musique pygmée de la Haute-Sangha*, taken from recordings made in 1946 at the Ogooué-Congo Mission in the Ouesso region of what is now the Peoples' Republic of Congo. The notes accompanying this record contain much information regarding the practice of music among the Bangombé and Mbenzele Pygmies. In his comments, Rouget rightly insists on the polyphonic character of their song: 'When two or three Pygmies are gathered together, they always sing polyphonically; I have never heard Pygmy choral singing in unison' (Rouget 1959: 1). As for ways of performing the music, he says later: 'As is the rule with these Pygmies, the women form a separate group, sing with drum accompaniment, but do not dance. The men sing and dance, but their part in the choir is distinctly less important than that of the women' (ibid.: 2).

2.3.3   From 1960 to 1970

In her 'Note sur la musique vocale des Buchiman !Kung et des Pygmées Babinga', published in 1960, Yvette Grimaud elaborates upon the theme of her 1957 'Note', which she had published in collaboration with Gilbert Rouget. It contains transcriptions and analyses of three polyphonic pieces, namely, a Bushman song (three women's voices and hand claps), a Bushman women's choir (four voices and hand claps), and a mixed choir of Babinga Pygmies (three voices, three drums playing in unison, hand claps, and the chinking of metal blades). These transcriptions were made from gramophone records, and one can well imagine the arduous nature of such work, given the tangled polyphony peculiar to this kind of music. The author therefore deserves all the more credit for what she has achieved.

Having recalled the 'concentric' development of these songs, Yvette Grimaud proceeds to describe their rhythmical organisation:

There is another element which plays an important role in these structures, namely, the superimposition of different beats. Bushmen and Pygmies are quite happy to have rhythmical arrangements based upon long values coexisting, within the same polyphony, with others based upon short values, and this is done with such freedom that each of the lines of the vocal polyphony seems to belong to an independent rhythmical complex.   (Grimaud 1960: 110)

But Grimaud quite properly notes that, in spite of this apparent independence, the various structures are nevertheless built up in tiers 'upon an *ostinato* – a rhythmical foundation which serves, so to speak, as common denominator (ibid.: 112)'. Proceeding with her analysis of the Pygmy choir, Grimaud observes: 'As is the case with the Bushmen, one can discern a range of superimpositions of melodic and rhythmic elements in the course of the development of the piece, the arrangement of these elements being slightly modified with each repeat of the period' (ibid.: 121). Thus we are told that it is 'the rhythmical and melodic variants [of certain periods which] alter with each repeat. Sometimes they occur right at the beginning of these repeats and *modify the length of the periods* (my italics). There is consequently a dislocation in the coincidence of the superimposed parts' (ibid.: 122). I cannot accept this statement as it stands. For if all the constitutive, i.e., melodic and rhythmic, elements participate in a constant modification of the length of the periods, it is no longer clear what the term period can mean. Now, we know that among the Pygmies of Central Africa, polyphonic song is *always* based upon a very strict periodicity though this, given the complexity of the contrapuntal and polyrhythmic texture, as well as the overlapping of the repeats, is admittedly not always easy to discern.

The following year, in 1961, Rose Brandel published *The Music of Central Africa: An Ethnomusicological Study*. This work is entirely based on the transcription and analysis of gramophone records, and covers a part of former French Equatorial Africa, along with Zaïre, Rwanda-Burundi, Uganda and Tanganyika. Despite the title, this book contains no reference to music from what was then the Central African Republic. This lacuna is probably attributable to the lack of records of the traditional music from this country at this time. The book is divided into two parts, with a few plates in between. It contains a hundred pages of text, and fifty-two transcriptions, which take up almost a hundred and fifty pages. A number of these examples involve polyphony, from various different peoples. Particular mention should be made of a Bapere ensemble consisting of five horns and two drums, and a Mambuti Pygmy ensemble consisting of six whistles and a drum, both of these ensembles coming from Zaïre, and a Kukuya horn ensemble with solo vocalist and drum, from the Ouesso region (today the Congo People's Republic). All of these pieces were transcribed by ear, from records. A large number of these transcriptions reveal that Rose Brandel took into account the principle of periodicity, which is so basic to the music of this region. But some of the other transcriptions, astonishingly, bear no trace of it.

Rose Brandel, like Jones, often alters the time signature of the different bars, which gives rise to an unnecessarily complicated notation. It seems that it is because she wants to respect the music's inherent stresses, which are often irregular, that she adopts this notation, but it soon becomes apparent that these stresses do not appear in the score on those notes which follow the bar lines. It is also unfortunate that Rose Brandel chose to present a large number of fragmentary examples, instead of publishing a complete transcription of some polyphonic pieces. She also advances several ideas respecting the nature of African rhythm to which she returns again and again. She begins by discussing 'hemiola style', which she defines as follows:

The present writer has employed the phrase, 'African hemiola style', in describing the rhythms of this area, and it would seem that the phrase is a useful one.

As used in European musical tradition from the Renaissance onward, the term 'hemiola' refers, of course, to the rearrangement or regrouping of note-values in two measures of triple time, more specifically, the interplay of two groups of three notes with three groups of two notes. This is accomplished without any durational change in the basic pulse unit, so that two groups of 3/4 for example, may become three groups of 2/4 without any metronome change in the quarter note. The important overall effect here is the quantitative alternation of two 'conductor's' durations, one of which is longer or shorter than the other. This exchange of 'long' and 'short' is always in the ratio 2:3, or 3:2, i.e., the longer duration is always one and one-half times the length of the shorter duration.   (Brandel 1961: 15)

As the reader will have gathered, Rose Brandel is here adopting Jones's polymetric conception. In Book V, which is devoted to the organisation of time in African music, this conception will be critically discussed. The opposition that Brandel sets up between 'syncopated' and 'hemiolic' notation commits her, if she is to avoid ties running across the barlines, to a *heterometric* system of scoring, which in some respects mis-represents the metro-rhythmic reality of the music that she is transcribing. She thus transcribes the five bars that go to make up a Mangbetu choral song, on account of their 'hemiolic content', as 3/8, 5/16, 6/16, 7/16, and 3/8; and preceding these, she puts a *double* metronomic indication, namely, ♪ = 224 ♪. = 150. But she also transcribes the same example using a 'notation implying a syncopation', which is obviously simpler, entailing the metronomic setting: ♩ = 112. Now, the melody's inherent stresses do not fall systematically upon the 'strong beats' in 'hemiolic' any more than in 'syncopated' notation. It is therefore hard to see what is the advantage of the system of hemiolic notation.

Approaching the problem of periodicity in the musics of this region, Rose Brandel very properly notes that: 'Central African hemiolic patterns. . . are, when repeated (whether the melody is the same or not), slightly varied in their inner groupings, while kept intact in their overall length' (ibid.: 76). Nevertheless, I find it hard to agree with her evolutionist conceptions regarding these musics, whether they touch upon their melodic, 'harmonic' or rhythmic structure. A detailed discussion of this latter point, and of the notion of 'syncope' in particular, will be presented in Book V.

It is worth noting that Jones himself made certain criticisms of transcriptions made in an earlier study by Rose Brandel (1952), which she reproduces unchanged in the book now under discussion: 'She shows that she is aware of the 'polyrhythm of the drum music' though she does not seem to realise the fundamental principles involved' (Jones 1959: 4).

Zygmunt Estreicher's remarkable study, 'Le rythme des Peuls Bororo', published in 1964, is the exception which proves the rule. It should give pause to the temptation to condemn *a priori* those researchers who work on documents collected by others. It was by working with such recordings that Estreicher succeeded in identifying the structure of the main metrico-rhythmic system of Bororo Fuebe music, as featured in a boys' dance accompanied by hand claps. This study represents a valuable contribution to our knowledge of African rhythm. Estreicher was moreover the first scholar, when speaking of different interpretations of the same rhythmic pattern, to use the concept of the *model*, this latter being either realised or simply implicit.

Whether they depart from it or move towards it, the musical motifs always represent an inter-pretation of the basic pattern. . . Moreover the interpretation of the implicit model often takes quite perceptible form. So the basic pattern does not seem to impose any schema of accentuation; the Bororo take advantage of this to introduce accents, placing them at quite freely chosen places. . .

The Bororo are also free – and this is the essential point – to suppress certain notes in the basic pattern. In this way, they transform the rhythm of the handclaps considerably.

(Estreicher 1964: 188)

He emphasises the polyrhythmic nature of this pattern, which is produced by the crossing of distinct parts, a fact which he takes to be crucial: 'The *basic pattern* results from the coming together of two *complementary patterns* performed by two separate ensembles.' And he notes that 'both of them employ the same metrical values' (ibid.: 188). As for the schema of the basic pattern, 'it may be likened to a canvas meant to be covered with a musical embroidery whose motifs it will support and direct' (ibid.). Estreicher gives a very clear explanation of the function of this pattern:

The basic pattern, this internal 'motor' regulating Bororo rhythm, cannot therefore properly be compared with a motif in the European sense of the term, for it seems to serve simply to mark the moments as they pass, indeed to measure duration as a metronome does, but not to express a musical thought. It comes closer to the European bar, inasmuch as it determines and hierarchises duration. Nevertheless, the hierarchy that it establishes between beats is subtler than a quantitative division between strong and weak beats; these do not feature, moreover, in the actual Bororo schema, but in its free applications. It is then that even or odd, regular or asymmetrical structures may emerge, which, in European music, would seem to be a primary datum but which, in Bororo music, already have an expressive value inasmuch as they are the free expression of an implicit basic system.   (ibid.: 192–3)

There is indeed an implicit reference since, as Estreicher emphasises, 'the basic metrical pattern would seem to be ever present in the minds of the Bororo when they are making music'. And he goes on to make the point that 'in the thousands of patterns transcribed, I found no irregularity' (ibid.: 193). That these patterns, though implicit, are permanent, is borne out by numerous other factors: 'Thus, to give an example, when you have a song that for long periods is not accompanied by hand claps, some isolated claps can nonetheless still be heard. These always coincide with the implicit pattern' (ibid.: 193).

This study closes with fifteen transcriptions, each comprising three rhythmic parts. They are often no more than fragments, but these extracts provide a very clear illustration of the procedures that Estreicher has identified. And the 'interpretational schemae' included in the body of the article (ibid.: 189–91) are sufficiently telling to make it clear that this researcher has attained a remarkably acute understanding of the principles underlying the main metrico-rhythmic system of the Bororo Fulbe.

In the same year, Gerhard Kubik published 'Harp Music of the Azande and Related People in the Central African Republic', which is the first publication devoted to Central African polyphony. This work contains fragmentary transcriptions of fifteen pieces for voice and harp (Kubik 1964a: 59–76). Kubik was able to make these transcriptions in the course of a long stay in the field, during which he devoted himself to learning, in contact with local musicians, how to play the harp.

Although it is mainly concerned with the analysis of music for the harp, this article is also meant to be didactic, for Kubik describes the instrumental technique involved in playing the pieces transcribed, even going so far as to specify the fingerings to be used.

There is one innovation that Kubik introduces, as regards transcription: instead of indicating the metre in the traditional manner (4/4, 6/8 etc.), as so many ethnomusicologists once did, and indeed still do, Kubik mentions in the 'time signature' the total number of minimal values that the melodico-rhythmic pattern includes (for example, 24 quavers) and inserts vertical barlines only in order to separate each reiteration of the pattern. Inasmuch as it disregards the notion of 'measure', this approach eliminates any implication of a regular accentuation by 'strong' beats.

One must admire the patience and determination of a researcher who entered into a long apprenticeship in Azande harp playing, but one may have some reservations about his ideas on an aspect of African music which seems to me to be fundamental, namely, metrical organisation. Indeed, I do not see how one can follow Kubik in what he chooses to term 'an *ambivalent conception of metre* or, more simply, an ambivalent beat' (ibid.: 49–50).

In this respect, Kubik's article raises an important question. In one of the pieces analysed, the parts played by the two hands of the harpist being in a relation of two to three (in accord with the 'hemiolic principle' advanced by Rose Brandel), Kubik asks:

How does the harpist *think* about the above bimetric pattern? Where does he feel his beat? (if he feels one at all). Does he feel it in accordance with the right or the left hand's part?

This is, indeed, a difficult question to answer scientifically. Although personally it is entirely clear to me where the beat is. How can I prove it to the sceptical reader?. . . Theoretically there are three metrical conceptions possible for the harp pattern. . . How can we look into the harpist's mind?

(ibid.: 49)

The reader in turn may wonder why, if Kubik feels so clearly where the beat is, the same cannot be said for the African harpist, whose music, after all, this is. As for reading the musician's thoughts, there is no need. I shall demonstrate in Book III how one can identify the beat of a piece of African music, so long as it has a metre.

Kubik's article also has the virtue of bringing out another aspect of the organisation of African polyphonic material, namely, its internal economy. He points out that the same melodic material is used in both sung phrases and in the melodico-rhythmic pattern that the harp plays beneath them. 'In Azande harp music the voice part can 'pull out' any notes of the total pattern of the right and left hand parts and duplicate these either in unison or at an octave. . . One can hear the voice part looming out of the notes of the instrumental part' (ibid.: 51).

For the sake of completeness, I ought also to mention Robert Günther's work, *Musik in Rwanda: Ein Beitrag zur Musikethnologie Zentral-Afrikas*, also published in 1964. This book is based upon archive recordings, and considers the music of four different peoples, the Twa, the Hutu, the Fulero and the Tutsi. It includes the transcription and analysis of thirty or so pieces, of which only one – for voice and *sanza* – is truly polyphonic in character.

Yvette Grimaud published another article, also in 1964, entitled 'Etude analytique de la danse "Choma" des Bochiman !Kung'. It contains a reformulation of ideas expounded in previous publications, notably concerning 'the superposition of different rhythmic structures on a basic *ostinato* which sometimes undergoes slight modifications (Grimaud 1964: 175) as well as the process of 'loop' or 'concentric' development' (ibid.: 175–6). This article includes a transcription of the first thirty-two 'groups' of the piece analysed, a term that the author prefers to that of 'bars'; the piece consists of six vocal parts accompanied by stamping of the feet.

In an article entitled 'The Polyrhythmic Foundation of Tswana Pipe Melody' (1965), Christopher Ballantine presented an account of a South African reed whistle ensemble – the *ditlaka* studied by Kirby in 1933 – that produce a hocket polyphony which is relatively simple in structure. Ballantine defines his quite personal position as follows:

My theory is that these tunes are produced by the *application of polyrhythmic techniques* to the pipe ensemble. Stated differently, this means that the Tswana, in the creation of at least some of their pipe pieces, do not proceed from melodic considerations – do not first think of a melody and then play it, with the addition of a few 'harmonies' on their pipes – but begin with one, or in some cases, two rhythmic schemes, which are then played by the pipes in a polyrhythmic way.   (Ballantine 1965: 55)

It was Kirby's opinion that this form of hocket is derived from *melodies* and my own experience of an altogether analogous musical practice, though in another region of Africa, seems to confirm this. Therefore, Ballantine's argument does not seem very convincing, and even less so given his somewhat obscure presentation of the steps by which he arrived at this 'theory'. His conclusion, moreover, is much more qualified:

I cannot assume that *all* Tswana pipe melodies are made according to my polyrhythmic theory. . . It is indeed possible that some Tswana pipe melodies may be founded on song, as Kirby argued, but the proportion of vocally inspired pipe melodies to those based on polyrhythm can be established only by further investigation.   (ibid.: 80)

This article contains the transcription of seven pieces, each of which is two or three bars long.

A subsequent article by Gerhard Kubik, 'Transcription of Mangwilo Xylophone Music from Film Strips' (1965), has several points of interest. First of all, it contains an account of a new method of transcribing instrumental music, based upon the use of silent films. I discuss this below, in Book III. Moreover, Kubik here outlines the principles of what he calls 'interlocking style'. *Mangwilo* music, which is found among the Alomwe and Ashirima peoples in the North of Mozambique, seems to him an excellent illustration of this style. There are two musicians seated opposite each other, at different points along the one xylophone, and each of them has to interpose his own part in the silences left by the other, usually at equally spaced intervals.

Here too Kubik invokes the highly contentious notion of 'metrical ambivalence':

The players sitting opposite each other do not feel one metre held in common, but each of them feels that his own beat or pulse is the basis. These two 'individual pulses' interlock. To get the music started, the second musician has to 'fall in between' the pulse of the first one and at the same moment start thinking of his own pulse as the basic one. In 'interlocking style' music, each of the two players interprets the pattern of the opposite one as 'off beat' and his own as 'on the beat'.   (Kubik 1965: 39)

Kubik has some difficulty, however, in justifying his argument. Indeed, having established that all the notes belonging to the part called *wakulela* fall exactly half way between those played by the *opachera* part, which are thereby subdivided, Kubik asks 'Which, then, is the *wakulela*'s pulse?' (ibid.: 40) However, a few lines further on, when he explains the principles of the system of notation he has used, he says: 'We have marked all the notes on which the beat is *felt*' (my italics) (ibid.). A confusion of this order seems to derive from a methodological error. Indeed, what Kubik has done is to present a description in which actual observations are mingled with extremely hypothetical interpretations of phenomenae relating to musical *perception*. We still lack the appropriate instruments for such an investigation, either in ethnomusicology or in classical musicology. The article concludes with transcriptions of the seven short pieces that had been analysed.

Mention also should be made of an article published that same year (1965) by Rose Brandel entitled 'Polyphony in African Music', in which she summarises the arguments first presented in *The Music of Central Africa* (1961).

In 1966, A. M. Dauer published a study entitled 'Afrikanische Musik und völker-kundlicher Tonfilm – Ein Beitrag zur Methodik der Transkription'. Like Jones and Kubik, Dauer outlines a new method for transcribing instrumental music, this time based upon the decoding of the synchronised soundtrack of films; the advantages and drawbacks of this method will be examined in Book III. Dauer applies this new method to the *djele* dance music, which is found among the Djaya, a people based in South Hwaddaï, in Sudan. Apart from the fact that it gives a complete transcription of the *djele* music (which comprises two sung and three percussive parts), the real virtue of this study lies in its competent structural analysis of the piece in question. Dauer uses the system recommended by Kubik (1961) for his transcriptions, employing an *overall metre* for the melodico-rhythmic patterns, and so avoiding the inadequacy of a Western bar system.

In 1967, Nicholas M. England published a very interesting article, 'Bushman Counterpoint', whose title itself is of interest here. He gives an account of the musical techniques employed by the Bushmen in the course of their vocal polyphony:

As they severally alternate the musical materials in what might be called an extended *Stimmtausch* technique, the singers bring into being a contrapuntal complex that constantly changes throughout the performance as the musical period. . . is repeated again and again until the performance is terminated.
   This interchanging of melodic phrases is a common method of music making in Bushmanland.
(England 1967: 60)

The fact that elaborated *Stimmtausch* technique features in traditional African polyphony is of such interest that it is worth pausing to consider the question in greater detail.

In the *Riemann Musiklexikon*, *Stimmtausch* is defined as the 'cross-exchange of melodic fragments between two or more voices in the same register' (Riemann 1967: III, 907). It was a known technique since the Middle Ages, but it seems to have been little used before the sixteenth century. Edmond de Coussemaker, in his *Histoire de l'harmonie au moyen-âge*, recounts that Jean de Garlande, the great theoretician of music in the thirteenth century, called it 'repetitio diversae vocis est idem sonus repetitus in tempore diverso a diversis vocibus', which literally translated means the 'repetition of a different voice which is the same sound repeated at a different time by different voices' (Coussemaker 1852: 53).

Coussemaker regards the development of this technique as 'one of the strangest things in the history of Medieval music', and goes on to explain in more detail what he means: 'By 'repetition of a different voice', Jean de Garlande means what we would call double counterpoint. The example that he gives [and Coussemaker conscientiously reproduces it in both the original and modern notation] can leave us in no doubt about this' (ibid.: 53). Coussemaker then proceeds to emphasise the importance of double counterpoint in the history of harmony, and its avatars:

Whether one considers this ornamented descant, which Jean de Garlande terms 'repetition of a different voice', to be 'double counterpoint', 'canon' or 'imitation', it is clearly one of the most important facts in the history of harmony. It has remained unknown to every historian of music. We still know of no relic of this genre of composition for any period prior to the end of the fourteenth century. There is nothing comparable either in the compositions of twelfth, thirteenth, and fourteenth century musicians that have so far been discovered [the date is 1852], nor in any of the known documents. The first traces of imitation and canon are found in the compositions of Dufay and Eloy, two of the most celebrated musicians of the end of the XIVth centuries and the beginning of the XVth.

Coussemaker goes on 'As for double counterpoint, we need to look as far as the middle of the 16th century before we find its use and its theory' (ibid.: 54).

It becomes clear in what respect the observations of the practice of this same procedure by the Bushmen add a new dimension to our understanding of African polyphonic techniques. Indeed, when musicologists and ethnomusicologists appropriately compare certain principles of African polyphony to those of European polyphony, it is usually *organum* that they have in mind; that is, a product of the *Ars Antiqua*; they never approach the *Ars Nova*. Now England's observations establish a parallel between an African oral technique and an organisational principle of European 'art' written polyphony which was practised not only later than the *Ars Antiqua* but also later than the *Ars Nova*, since *Stimmtausch* only appears, both in use and in theory, in the sixteenth century.

England's study also contains a number of important details about the modes of elaboration in Bushman vocal polyphonies. For instance on the topic of the arrangement of the melodic parts, he writes that 'there is absolutely no constraint on any participant to perform any one specific musical line at any one specific moment, and that applies in all repertoires' (England 1967: 61). The polyphonies in use among the Pygmies of Central Africa have voice parts which are equally unconstrained.

This is only one of the analogies between Bushman and Pygmy polyphonic structure. Others have been brought to light in the writing of Yvette Grimaud and Gilbert Rouget (1957 and 1960; cf. *supra* 2.3.2 and 2.3.3).

England presents some equally valuable information regarding the manner in which Bushman polyphonic songs are created. It turns out that, for these people, the medicine man is the composer. The melody of a song comes to him, either at the crisis point of a trance, or in a dream: it is then incumbent upon the medicine man to transmit this melody to the women of the community. At this stage, the song is still extremely simple, i.e., made up exclusively of long values:

Thereafter, the women will rehearse the song, elaborating the basic melody according to their usual polyphonic habits: they will insert tones, shorten and prolong rhythm values, etc., until they arrive at a melody (or melodies) that please them and the Medicine Man composer [. . .] Thereafter, in full performance of the song, the women might add extensions in order to weld the many, many repetitions of the musical period into a tighter whole, or they might make deletions that will change the emphasis or direction of the melodic lines.   (ibid.: 61)

As to the Aka Pygmies, beyond the proliferation of parts which is so typical of their music, and beneath the contrapuntal elaboration of the song, one can always find a very simple melodic line, constituted – as is the case with the Bushmen – of long values only.

England's article also contains seven fragmentary transcriptions of vocal polyphonies, employing up to seven different voices.

In 1967, David Rycroft also published an article concerned with vocal polyphony, entitled 'Nguni Vocal Polyphony'. He discusses the main Nguni peoples of South-East Africa, the Zulu, the Xhosa and the Swazi, whose cultures are linked. Rycroft emphasises the temporal relations between the various parts of the vocal polyphonies, and the manner in which the voices are organised as a function of the text. The article is accompanied by several brief transcriptions, whose presentation, in the form of circles, is intended to allow one to visualise more easily the cyclical nature of the music described.

In *Mehrstimmigkeit und Tonsysteme in Zentral- und Ostafrika*, published in 1968, Gerhard Kubik focusses upon homophonic multi-part music. But polyphony in the strict sense is only touched upon in passing.

2.3.4   From 1970 until the present time

The second edition of the *Harvard Dictionary of Music* was published in 1970, with Rose Brandel contributing the article concerned with Africa. It contains the same topics that the author had developed in her previous publications; complexity of rhythmic structures, 'African hemiola style', polymetre, hocket, ostinato and multi-ostinato.

Pierre Augier's 'La polyrythmie dans les musiques du Sahara', published in 1971, may seem out of place in the present survey. For most authors, when referring to African rhythmic structure, restrict their field of study to the sub-Saharan area. Whereas Augier's study demonstrates that the 'typical rhythmic pattern' (which Jones calls *standard-pattern*), which serves as the basis of innumerable polyrhythmic developments in both West and Central Africa, also applies in North Africa, and in Algeria in particular.

'Three Principles of Timing in Anlo Dance Drumming', an article published by Hewitt Pantaleoni in 1972, is concerned with the principles of rhythmic organisation in the music of the Anlo, who live in Ghana. Discussing the polyrhythm produced by an ensemble consisting of three drums and a bell, Pantaleoni explains the nature of the unifying principle common to these four instruments and also to the dancers. This article also contains a lively discussion of several other theories of African rhythm, in particular those of Hornbostel, Jones, Waterman, Koetting and Nketia. It features four extracts from rhythmic transcriptions, presented in graph form.

In an article entitled 'Les langages musicaux de l'Afrique Subsaharienne. Etude comparative', published in 1972, J. H. Kwabena Nketia begins by describing the various types of plurivocality (heterophony, parallelism, homophony), and then proceeds to those 'polyphonies which are more contrapuntal in nature', whether in vocal or in instrumental music.

In vocal music the parts are organised in such a way that each begins at a different moment but overlaps the other phrases in certain positions when they complete the melodic cycle. This style, which can be very complex, characterises the vocal polyphony of the Zulu, the Xhosa and the Swazi of South Africa.

Concerning polyrhythms, Nketia writes:

It is clear that the organisation in different parts is not restricted to polyphony. It may also be expressed in polyrhythmic forms according to a number of procedures parallel to the above, with, however, the peculiarity that the desired contrasts are not only of a tonal order but are also in opposition rhythmic structures.

He specifies: 'It is clear that there is absolutely no question here of rhythmic parallels.'

The most recent publication noted here dates from 1973. In 'Two Lullabies from the Babinga Mbenzele Pygmies – Transcriptions, Analysis and Commentary', Lamar Gene Strasbaugh considers two pieces that I know very well, since they derive from a set of gramophone records taken from my own recordings.

It is understandable that I embark upon a more detailed discussion than with other authors mentioned above. I have two reasons in particular for discussing this relatively short article at some length. First, since this music was collected by myself in the field, I am in a better position to present a fairly severe criticism of Strasbaugh's opinions than with the more significant of the publications discussed above. And, in widening the terms of the debate, my observations imply a more general critique of the majority of the studies based on second-hand documents.

Among the lullabies considered by Strasbaugh, only the second is polyphonic; it is a two-part counterpoint performed by two women. I propose to discuss the first lullaby as well, because the underlying musical system is identical to that of the polyphonic piece. Strasbaugh begins by setting out his objectives: 'In the accompanying analysis, my interest is directed towards a structural examination of the transcriptions (Strasbaugh 1973: 79).

Outlining the principles that he has followed in producing a notation of the rhythm of the two lullabies, he writes: 'In the first, I chose to present the rhythm as a loose series of individual values and not to attempt a finer rhythmical organization' (ibid.: 88). Now, from the structural point of view adopted by Strasbaugh himself, this approach is inadmissible since, by definition (cf. Book I 2.4), the Mbenzele Pygmies do not perceive their music, any more than other peoples in this region do, as 'a loose series of individual values', but on the contrary as a set of proportional values arranged within a strictly periodic framework.

In his examination of scales, Strasbaugh is a little more hesitant:

With the discussion of the tonal system employed, I have arrived at the point which unveils perhaps the greatest portion of subjectivity in the entire transcription. . .

In view of the fact that on untold occasions, tones which deviate by a semitone or more from one another are embedded in similar formal components – motifs or entire phrases – I have come to regard these unlike tones as functionally identical. . .

All Pygmy scales are, of course, untempered, and their notation is approximate. After spending countless hours with the music transcribed here, I hope to be able to approach a correct description of the scales intended by the Pygmies.   (ibid.: 91–2)

In spite of these laudable intentions, Strasbaugh is nevertheless led to assert, a few lines further on: 'My subjectivity enables me to transpose certain passages which simply do not fit into the overall scheme at the tonal level at which they are transcribed' (ibid.: 92).

Unfortunately, Strasbaugh gives no clue as to the method that enabled him to arrive at this 'overall scheme'. So it is that he produces the following scale, which gives *six intervals of a semi-tone* (ibid.) for nine sounds:

Now, my own experience among the Mbenzele themselves, as among other Pygmy groups, has left me in no doubt as to their general use of a single type of scale, namely, the *anhemitonic-pentatonic*.

Could the scale presented above be an exception to this rule? To answer this question, I went back to the records and listened to them once again. I then checked my response by employing a method recommended by Jacques Chailley: having copied the two pieces on to tape, I listened to them at double speed, when the intervals of the scale stand out much more clearly. This procedure left me in absolutely no doubt as to its being an anhemitonic-pentatonic scale. Reduced to their constitutive values, the notes produced by the Pygmy women may thus be set out in terms of the following scale:

In order to deny that this scale is anhemitonic in character, Strasbaugh referred to a passage in his transcription, where he picks out a sequence of three consecutive leaps up a perfect fifth – each beginning a whole step lower than the previous one (ibid.).

Now, what Strasbaugh treats as a D sharp is, *from the structural point of view*, the note E, so long as one takes into account the margin of tolerance that every musical system allows in its realisation. Thus, in an anhemitonic-pentatonic system, D sharp and E are, in Strasbaugh's own terms, 'functionally identical'. We can then read it as follows:

Moreover, once we have corrected this error, the fragment in question gives us the very five intervals that constitute the anhemitonic-pentatonic scale.

Also, it is quite surprising, in so restricted a work, to encounter such peremptory assertions as this: 'There are countless additional musical aberrations which could be listed here' (ibid.: 94).

I have passed several weeks not merely among the Mbenzele but actually in the camp in which these lullabies were recorded, and I never came across a single musical aberration. On the contrary, within the extreme rigour of their metrical, rhythmic, contrapuntal, and of course scalar organisation, I have always been struck by the great liberty enjoyed by these musics. But let me leave it to Jones, in his *Studies in African Music*, to pass comment on this sort of ethnomusicology:

Experientia docet, and no amount of theorising can take the place of musical contact with living Africans. African music has been little served by writers who, following the lead of the Hornbostel school, tend to rely on their powers of abstract analysis largely from gramophone records, and whose articles though couched in learned language are based on no real first-hand knowledge. What *is* scholarship in this field? Is it the ability to write in the idiom of professionalism? Or is it the possession of first-hand knowledge? Why should it not be possible to say in plain language just what the African does, *provided we know what it is*? (my italics)

(Jones 1959: 1, 5–6)

This assertion is echoed, in a gentler tone, in Merriam's *Anthropology of Music*:

There have in the past been extended studies in ethnomusicology based upon a small sample of commercially issued materials; while the proof of the accuracy of such studies remains to be ascertained, it seems extremely doubtful that we can give them much credibility. Armchair ethnomusicology is, I hope, a thing of the past.   (Merriam 1964: 39)

Book III

Technical tools: methods of recording polyphonic music for transcription

1   The need for transcription

Western culture has been shaped for the past several thousand years by its use of
writing as a vehicle for thought, making a written support indispensable for any
academic study. Music is no exception to this rule, and would seem extremely difficult to
analyse in depth unless first reduced to the form of a written score, i.e., a transcription
in the case of music from an oral tradition. The essential transience of music requires
that its movement through time be fixed in writing as a substantive 'reference text'
for the living reality. This is what the ethnomusicologist's attempts at transcription
aim to provide, whatever the geographical or ethnic source of his material. If this is true
of monodic music, it is even more so in the case of polyphony, where the simultaneity of
events results in a much more complex musical lattice. Transcription is thus all the
more necessary, though commensurately harder to achieve.

In his *Theory and Method in Ethnomusicology* (1964), Bruno Nettl highlights
both the need for transcription and all the intrinsic difficulties attending it. He distinguishes two main approaches to the description of music: the first consists of analysing
and describing what one hears, while the second involves *writing down* what one hears
and then describing the audible phenomena, relying on the observations contained in
the transcription. In Nettl's words (1964: 98),

If human ears were able to perceive all of the acoustic contents of a musical utterance, and
if the mind could retain all of what had been perceived, then analysis of what is heard would
be preferable. Reduction of music to notation on paper is at best imperfect, for either a type
of notation must select from the acoustic phenomena those which the notator considers most
essential, or it will be so complex that it itself will be too difficult to perceive. But since human
memory is hardly able to retain, with equal detail, what was heard ten seconds ago along
with what is being heard in the present, notation of some sort has become essential for research
in music.

Mantle Hood agrees: 'Any serious determination of the musically significant ultimately
must depend on notation and transcription' (1963: 190). In an article on the transcription of African music, A. M. Jones too, affirms that: 'This business of transcription
is the key to the whole understanding of the African musical systems' (1958b: 11).
In his conclusion, he stresses this point when he says:

We have, however, emphasized the importance of transcription because of the great need of
trustworthy transcriptions if the principles of African music are to be fully understood and
if progress is to be made in the ethnographic and comparative studies of the distribution of
African musical techniques. Unless a music score can claim a high degree of accuracy it is
valueless for the study of African music [. . .].

What we need above all things at the present time in the field of African music is accuracy –
accuracy of transcription leading to accurate and definite statement of facts.   (ibid.: 14)

Jones returns to this subject in his *Studies in African Music* (1959: 1, 7) where, right from the introduction, he emphasises the need, not just for transcription, but also for writing out complete scores. He rejects illustrative examples or fragments as inadequate representations of real African music:

What we need are reliable scores of African music so that all musicians may see what it is like. This is precisely what has not been available. One can find in the literature of African music short isolated extracts illustrating this or that feature and perhaps a few songs [. . .]. To commend African music to the musicians of the world we need some full scores so that people may study whole complete pieces of African music.

Full transcriptions are required 'to answer the simple but fundamental question, "When the African makes music, what exactly does he do?"'

2   The difficulties of transcription

In our discussion of earlier works on the subject, we noted that little attention has been devoted to African polyphony. Unlike many other aspects of music transmitted by oral tradition, reference transcriptions of African polyphony are rarely available, and when provided are only fragmentary at best. This seems to be mainly attributable to the difficulty of transcribing this kind of music. Several experts, among them Bruno Nettl (1964: 84), have pointed out the problems involved:

Special problems in eliciting appear when the musical structure is complex, especially if a performance is by several singers, instruments, etc.

It is almost impossible to transcribe a record on which several xylophones of equal size are playing together if one does not know the number of xylophones. Even when the number and size of the instruments is known, it is extremely difficult to notate what each individual one is playing. It may be possible to reproduce the overall acoustic impression, but this may be misleading.

Gerhard Kubik (1961: 200) is equally sceptical about transcribing African instrumental music: 'Transcription of African instrumental music from tape recordings poses enormous problems. In most cases, it will lead to incorrect results.' In a subsequent publication on xylophone music (1964a), Kubik reaffirms that transcription from tape recordings is impossible. He suggests instead that an attempt be made to learn to play an African instrument before transcription is undertaken. We will return below to the effectiveness of this approach.

Dauer (1969: 229) cites the same difficulties in justifying his own method of transcription involving the use of films: 'While the transcription of simple musical forms by ear or from tape may be quite possible, it is not practicable in the case of complicated music without simultaneous control by the eye. Too many sound events may occur at the same time or follow immediately upon one another for aural differentiation alone to be sufficient.' The main problem is how to separate the parts in the polyphonic whole from one another. It might appear that it would suffice to record and transcribe them individually. But this would still teach us nothing about the essential question of how the parts are organised with respect to one another, and how they fit together. This is what Jones points out (1959: 1, 13) with respect to African percussion music: 'It is one thing to know what is the rhythm-pattern of each instrument; it is quite another to determine their exact metrical relationship.'

3   Earlier methods

Four techniques have been proposed to solve the problems of transcribing complex polyphonic phenomena. All of them require, for one reason or another, that the investigator spend time in the field. The first is propounded by the American school following Mantle Hood, and is called *performing*. It involves learning how to play traditional music and using the knowledge acquired in this way to transcribe it. The second requires the kind of special technical equipment developed by A. M. Jones for his own use. The third involves the use of films, which may be either silent or synchronised with a sound track. These are subjected to frame-by-frame analysis. The fourth and last consists of a special use of conventional stereophonic sound recording equipment to obtain a measure of separation of the parts in the polyphonic whole.

We will now discuss each of these techniques in turn and point out what we take to be their individual advantages and drawbacks.

3.1   PERFORMING

As we have said, this technique involves learning to play an instrument used to perform the music under study, and using the acquired knowledge as a basis for analysis. In the preceding Book, we noted that Gerhard Kubik (1964a) recommends this method. He advises the investigator to get advanced knowledge of how to play an instrument from the traditional musicians in their own cultural setting. Kubik himself followed this procedure in studying the xylophone in Uganda and the harp in the Central African Republic. Mantle Hood, who first propounded this method, has, of course, also used it. In *The Ethnomusicologist* (1971: 235-7), he describes how he went about learning drum formulae from an Ewe master drummer in Ghana, to gain an understanding of the nature of African polyrhythm. There are several clear advantages for the investigator in this approach, the primary one being the chance to familiarise himself *from within* with music which will initially be foreign to him. He learns to memorise and perform an orally transmitted form of music, just as a native would. He tries, as it were, to make this music a part of himself. There are nevertheless various disadvantages to this method, not all of which are immediately apparent. Some are practical, and others theoretical.

Practically speaking, the investigator is subject to several inevitable constraints, the first of which is limited time, with regard to both the overall duration of his apprenticeship, and the length of the individual trips into which his field work will, in all likelihood, have to be divided. But however much time and effort he may be willing to put in, there is still nothing to prove that his apprenticeship will not be slowed by his own limited talents as a performer, which he may only recognise after his apprenticeship has already begun. It is, in fact, quite unlikely that he will manage to perform the music of another culture with the same ease as a native musician, just as a linguist studying an 'exotic' language will not learn to speak it as well as someone who has it as his mother tongue.

It is important to remember that the investigator is a product of his own cultural background, which will impose certain limits on his performing ability. Even the musicologist who is an experienced performer on an instrument from his own culture will find it hard to pick up the entirely new and different principles prevailing among the people whose music he wants to study, imbued as he is with the principles of his own music. This is particularly true of polyrhythm and rhythm based more on the organisation of durations than on accentuation (see Book V).

Furthermore, even if we admit that the investigator can learn all the parts in a polyphonic or polyrhythmic piece, to the extent of mastering and being able to perform each of them individually, he will still not be certain of understanding precisely how these parts fit together and how they are to be interwoven. This could be a serious obstacle to his overall apprehension of the piece as a single composite entity.

And finally, even if an ethnomusicologist were to devote all the necessary time, effort, and talent to his task, independently of any negative effects of cultural conditioning, and thereby manage to obtain a full understanding of a small number of polyphonic pieces, would this represent knowledge of all the music of a given people, or of the entire polyphonic corpus of that society?

It is clear from the above that, since we can only learn a limited number of pieces by this method, it would never enable us to obtain more than a fragmentary knowledge of the polyphonic repertory of a given society. Furthermore, the inherent restrictions arising from the investigator's own cultural origin mean that his status as a researcher will be undermined when he takes up the role of apprentice. He may well be unable to obtain a proper understanding of the music he has in view, when he abandons his position as an external observer and tries to slip inside the system he intends to describe. His situation will definitely be uncomfortable, but worse still is the danger of losing his bearings. In taking up the practice of the music of another civilisation with which he is initially only imperfectly acquainted, and which he can only find irremediably foreign, he is starting out with a heavy handicap with respect to any native beginner. Not only does he not yet know how to manipulate the instrument he wants to learn to play, he does not even have (and will, in fact, never obtain) the cultural foundations acquired by native musicians during early childhood. In what way, then, will he 'lose his bearings'? In that, before he manages to get at the music from the inside (if indeed he ever can), the technical problems resulting from his apprenticeship will make it impossible for him to continue seeing it from the outside. When he becomes directly involved, he will no longer be able to distance himself and retain his admittedly often intuitive overall grasp, which nevertheless proves indispensable in research, and should not, in our opinion, be exposed to muddling.

The apprentice musician will moreover be unavoidably tempted to dispose of any technical difficulties he may encounter by means of the physical and/or mental resources proper to his own ways of thought, cultural references, and personal musical experience. There is thus nothing to guarantee that what he comes out with will be *pertinent* within the musical system under study. He could, for example, easily be largely unconsciously projecting Western criteria on music which makes no use of them and will therefore not regard them as pertinent. This is clear from some of the research based on this method. We have already mentioned Kubik's (1964a: 49) idea of 'bimetry', which showed him to be incapable of assuming or admitting that superposed figures could move in counterpoint (i.e., polyrhythmically) without actually making use of different metres.

Finally, just as no one expects an ethnolinguist to have a native's ability to speak the language he is studying, or a musicologist specialising in a given field of art music to be a concert performer, so an ethnomusicologist should not be obliged to perform the music he studies. His job is to provide the clearest description he can on the basis of a proper understanding of its structure, as obtained through well-founded analysis. The surest way to this end would seem to be the method of observation and experimentation which, by definition, requires an outside observer, and combats subjectivity by requiring the investigator to maintain a *neutral* attitude towards the object of his study. This is not to say that he should avoid taking an active role, asking questions, checking results, even provoking the performers, and nothing prevents him from participating in native musical activities. But he must in no case forget that his sole purpose is to *understand*, which here means trying to grasp the principles governing the music he is studying, independently of any technical problems involved in performing it.

3.2   SPECIAL APPARATUS

The idea of constructing special apparatus suitable for transcribing polyrhythmic phenomena was put forth by A. M. Jones, who developed several devices during his twenty-one years in Rhodesia.

In an article published in 1937, he states that, after learning the individual patterns for each drum accompanying two Bemba dances (thus applying a precursor of the performing technique), he was still unable to transcribe a single case of simultaneous song, hand-claps, and drum percussions. Seeing that, despite seven years of effort, he had not yet grasped the relationship among these three components, he came to the ultimate conclusion that 'the subjective method here shows its inherent incapacity' (1937: 299). He considered the transcriptions available in the 1930s unreliable, and judged them harshly: 'It is, one hopes, not uncharitable to say that there is hardly an example of African rhythm in existence on which one would feel safe enough to build a theory' (1937: 299).

Finding himself unable to obtain a coherent transcription, Jones tried to solve his problem by inventing equipment which could produce rigorous results, i.e., make an accurate recording showing the rhythmic correlations among the percussion instruments. He could then use the signs automatically registered on a roll of paper by the apparatus as a basis for a transcription in conventional musical notation. With his machine, Jones managed to transcribe the rhythm of each individual drum, the exact relationship of these rhythms to one another, the precise rhythm of the hand-claps, and the latter's relationship to the rhythms of the drums.

Jones precedes the description of his equipment with a section entitled 'A scientific approach to the problem of recording', where he asserts that research should be *objective* and impervious to the investigator's personality. It should be conducted with the help of physical experimentation, such that the same experiment carried out by different people will yield identical results on each occasion. These results should be *measurable*, in numerical terms, if possible. The scientific investigation of African music should be based on this kind of approach:

> In so far as music is constructed on regular rhythms, it is based on something which can be counted, and indeed counted with the utmost arithmetical precision. [. . .]
>
> Approaching African music in this scientific frame of mind we find that we are, of all investigators, most fortunate. For one of the chief characteristics of African music is its rhythms, which are not only invariably present, but also invariably regular in structure.   (Jones 1937: 302)

There can be no doubt that Jones carried out admirable pioneering research under material conditions far more difficult than the ones we are now accustomed to. We need only recall that he took the power for his first machine from his automobile engine's alternator, to see how 'archaic' his system was.

As technology improved, Jones was able to develop more elaborate equipment which he put into use some twenty years later. Here is his own description of his electric tracer and how to use it:

> The prime task is to ascertain the exact rhythm of each instrument. For this purpose our drum recorder was adapted for laboratory conditions. It was provided with two small wooden boards on which were fastened some metal plates. One board was for the bell-pattern, and one for the drum or clap or other instrument. The two operators had in each of their hands a brass pencil. By touching the metal plates with the pencils an electrical contact was obtained. This in turn operated the drum recorder so as to make a mark on a moving strip of paper [. . .]. The rhythm of each instrument was taken in turn. It was played simultaneously with the bell-pattern into the drum recorder and so, after some twenty seconds, we had on the paper strip an unimpeachable record of what had been played. This we then converted to the conventional notation of music. It was in this way that we reduced the intangible, evanescent, counterplay of rhythms in an African dance to an objective, stable, and visible form.   (Jones 1959: I, 13–14)

It should be noted that the 'bell pattern' Jones mentions is one of the most widespread formulae in all of sub-Saharan Africa, the one he says serves as the *standard pattern* in Ghana. It constitutes the reference for all the often extremely elaborate formulae improvised by the master drummer which Jones was trying to transcribe. As Jones himself says, it worked like 'counter-rhythm'. With his apparatus, he was able to write the first full scores for any complex African polyrhythmic music. These scores, which comprise the entire second volume of his work, furnish the basis for his study. Unfortunately, however, his device, though useful, does not solve all the problems of transcription. Specifically, it cannot deal with melody. This is clear from Jones's work, where all the transcriptions are either of monodic songs taken down by ear, or of polyrhythmics. His device is thus all the more incapable of dealing with vocal polyphony. Its possibilities, while considerable, extend only to the analysis of rhythmic structures.

There is another important point to be made about Jones's methodology. We have seen that Jones rightly espoused the ideal of scientific objectivity. Yet his transcriptions were not obtained in the field in Africa, but in a London laboratory to where Desmond Tay, his Ghanaian master drummer, performed in succession the component parts of each polyrhythmic piece. There is no particular fault to be found with this, but more unusual is the fact that, though Jones states that at least two performers are required, he fails to give the name of the second musician, who has the fundamental job of playing the 'standard pattern' providing the framework for the master drummer's performance. To find the reason for this omission, we must turn to the very last page in the book. There we find a photograph of a recording session showing Desmond Tay, the drummer, and. . . A. M. Jones himself, both sitting pencil in hand on either side of the device!

We can guess how hard it must have been for Jones to get another African musician to London. Seeing, however, that the 'standard pattern' is more than a mere metronomic punctuation of time (it is in fact the asymmetric rhythmic formula: ♩ ♩ ♩. ♩ ♩.), and given how hard it is to sustain even the tempo of such complex music on account of its rapidity, we are entitled to worry about how objective these transcriptions can be, regardless of the author's stated commitment. Such worries could have been avoided if Desmond Tay had been able to perform with another drummer from his own ethnic group as a partner.

We have already suggested that the investigator using this method ends up withdrawing his experimentation from the social context in which the music he studies is normally produced. The master drummer was thus not only removed from his own cultural setting and conveyed to a laboratory in a foreign country; he was even deprived of the physical and motor conditions of traditional musical performance. The musician is thus called upon to exchange his vital contact with the skin and resonator of his drum for a table of metal plates and a pencil to hit them with.

When Jones's device was ready for use, W. Tegenthoff wrote a description of it, stressing its scientific importance, in *Aequatoria*. Jones quotes some of his remarks:

The acoustic data are transformed into a visual image by means of electromechanical devices which simultaneously plot each of the instruments. This makes it possible to give even the most complicated polyrhythmics a graphic form in a scientifically accurate way.

No one can doubt that Jones has found a way of solving the main problem in African music. But how many others will be able to use it?   (1959: 1, 8)

Jones has a ready answer: 'The reply to this last sentence is that no one *will* be able to penetrate and to transcribe African music unless and until he has some such apparatus at his disposal' (ibid.).

This peremptory affirmation is inclined to discourage new initiatives and preclude advances in methodology. We will see below that it is now possible to provide transcriptions not only of polyrhythm, but even of instrumental and vocal polyphony, with no other special equipment than a pair of ordinary portable tape recorders.

3.3   CINEMATOGRAPHIC TECHNIQUES

Two different methods have been proposed for applying cinematographic techniques to the transcription of African instrumental polyphony. One uses silent film, and the other requires a synchronised sound track. To our knowledge, the only users of these techniques have been their respective inventors, G. Kubik and A. M. Dauer.

Gerhard Kubik was the first investigator to perceive that the ability to decompose and reconstitute continuous motion provided by his 8mm film camera could be put to a special use in the study of very rapid gestural activity such as xylophone performances, which air almost impossible to transcribe by ear alone. He describes his method in an article entitled 'Transcription of Mangwilo xylophone music from film strips' (Kubik 1965).

He worked with two xylophone players positioned on opposite sides of their instrument. First of all, he identified the note produced by each of the bars and numbered it on a diagram. A complete recording of the piece he wanted to transcribe was then made to serve as a reference and to provide a basis for deciding whether the filmed portion was sufficiently representative of the entire piece to be transcribed.

A transcription can be obtained by first preparing a graph for each musician with the abscissa graduated into units of time equal to the distance between two consecutive frames, and the ordinate showing the notes of the xylophone bars. The investigator can then go through his film frame by frame and plot almost exactly when the sticks strike the bars. This will allow him to see which player strikes which bar with which hand at precisely what instant.

The material labour involved in this method is, however, enormous, to the extent that Kubik himself (1965: 43) was led to admit that: 'Had we been able to film the complete items and transcribe everything in extenso our gain would have been little compared with the enormous effort of writing it down'.

Dauer later used more elaborate motion picture equipment to analyse polyrhythm. He linked two 16mm cameras to a tape recorder to obtain a synchronous sound track. Incidentally, he took a whole team of technicians along to work with Djaya musicians in the Waddai region of Chad, a luxury few ethnomusicologists will be able to grant themselves.

Dauer's method was a considerable improvement on Kubik's. It provided the investigator with correlated sets of auditive and visual data, thereby facilitating the identification of the part played by each instrument and the process of analysis (Dauer 1966).

Kubik and Dauer thus seem to be the only investigators to have used cinematographic methods to study polyphony, the field which concerns us here. Yet their only publications have been transcriptions of a few short polyphonic fragments by Kubik (1965), and a single piece by Dauer (1966). This suggests how real were the difficulties they report having encountered in trying to apply their methods. Nevertheless, with a team of technicians and suitable high-quality film and recording equipment, the investigator can obtain extremely useful material in this way.

Unfortunately, this method, like Jones's, is not applicable to all types of polyphony. It works with percussion instruments and polyphonic instruments with fixed pitches, such as the xylophone and the *sanza*, but is infinitely harder to apply to string instruments and, in general, all instruments producing sounds which are not directly dependent on the position of the hand or finger. This holds as well for wind instruments with holes which are not all on the same plane. Finally, it is useless for determining the points of onset and extinction of notes in vocal polyphony, and consequently, cannot isolate the contents of each part. The investigator here finds himself back in the situation of having no more than a recording, and obtains no advantage whatsoever from the cinematographic factor.

There is thus a very long process leading from data-gathering to obtaining the final score. Notwithstanding the costly and complicated technical equipment required, and the uncertainties of accidental failures such as improper film exposure, this method is still inappropriate for dealing with certain polyphonic phenomena. These limitations suggest why no further steps in this direction have been taken.

3.4   SOUND RECORDING ON SEPARATE CHANNELS

When the mass production of stereophonic recording equipment began during the 1960s, many investigators recognised that it would be of more use to them than special apparatus or techniques unrelated to sound recording they might develop. As the new equipment came into everyday use, specificity was sought in its applications alone.

In a 1963 article on the problems of field work, Mantle Hood points out that, despite rapid advances in the field of sound recording technology, some needs of research had still to be met. He recalls (1963: 190) that the ethnomusicologist Nicholas England had stressed [. . .] the urgent need for a four or six-channel tape recorder in making tapes for analytical purposes among the Bushmen. He then describes how he used a small mixing desk and five microphones to record African groups in Ghana, but notes that the result was still monophonic, though with improved definition. He accurately observes that if each mike were capable of recording on a separate channel this would greatly facilitate analytical studies.

Dauer (1966: 448) also considered the advisability of exploiting the use of separate channels and making multi-track recordings of musical events with several 'layers', so that polyphonic vocal parts could be separated or synthesised as desired.

Ladislav Leng expressed the same idea three years later in an article on the technical problems involved in recording several-part folk music. He, however, was reflecting on methods of analysis and transcription for application to European folk music, and cited the inadequacy of monophonic recordings for the study of the two- and three-part polyphony of Slovak string instruments. He suggested recording stereophonically, using two or more channels and microphones, so that the instrument parts could be separated: 'The essential feature of new recording methods for several-part folk music is multi-channel analytic recording' (1969: 174).

Unfortunately, none of these ideas was ever applied. The reason for this is simple: even now, there are still no miniaturised, *autonomous* (i.e., portable for field use) versions of the kind of multi-track magnetic recording devices that are in ordinary use in professional studios. If such equipment had been available in the 1960s, our knowledge of African polyphonic music might well have made huge strides forward at the time.

The methods of analysis and transcription briefly examined above all have limitations of some kind. Moreover, none of them can be used for polyphony involving the human voice or certain string and wind instruments. To achieve our aim of providing an analysis of Central African polyphony, we therefore had to find some method which would both apply to all types of vocal and instrumental polyphony found in the region, and properly reflect the musical reality. It seemed obvious that such a method should be based on sound recording techniques which could be applied *in the field*. Currently available autonomous equipment does not, however, allow simultaneous separate recording on more than two channels, however many microphones are used. In one way or another, we always come back to the problem of having to separate out the parts of a whole.

It then occurred to us that, instead of recording with several microphones on a single occasion, we might try *recording with a single microphone on several occasions*. This would involve applying the so-called "playback" technique, i.e., the diachronic reconstitution of a set of musical events which take place synchronically in real situations.

4   Towards a new method

We are now about to describe a new method which has enabled us to obtain the results presented in this work. It came, not as a brainstorm, but as a result of the kind of long and sometimes tortuous processes, as is often the case. The reader may find it helpful if we outline the main stages in the process which led to its development; we therefore hope he or she will excuse the personal nature of some aspects of the following presentation.

In 1967, we were working on the monodic song-tales of the Ngbaka people in the Central African Republic. These pieces have no regular accentuation and are performed *a cappella*, i.e., they contain no *materialised* metric or rhythmic point of reference. We were faced with the problem of finding out how to determine the periodicity of these songs, which meant discovering the key to their temporal organisation. It occurred to us that an answer to this question might be found if we first recorded the song and then asked the singer to record the same piece again, this time clapping his hands. We naturally avoided telling him exactly how this should be done. The Ngbaka performer would then straightforwardly provide us with the basic pulsation for the piece involved. We hoped to obtain a new recording in this way, containing enough metric reference points to enable us to transcribe the durations within the song. The singer's handclaps must be intimately connected with the music, and could therefore leave no doubt as to their accuracy, and consequently, their validity as reference points.

Unfortunately (actually quite fortunately for us), things were not so simple. For when the musician re-recorded his song, his version was not identical to the earlier one. Instead, he introduced variations involving changes in the way some of the melodic segments were combined. Although the differences were slight, the second version would not necessarily suffice for accurate location of the pulsations in the earlier version with no accompanying handclaps. Our problem was to get a recording where the hand-claps could be made to coincide with the original version without ruining it. We therefore decided to have the musician listen to the recording of the song he had just sung and clap his hands in time (this he could do without difficulty), while we recorded this superposition on another tape. This yielded two documents, the original recording of the song for analysis, and a reproduction of poor technical quality which nevertheless clearly showed how the singer's hand-claps should be superposed. This gave us exactly what we wanted: both a culturally authentic document, and a separate working document which contained an exact replica of the former.

When subsequently faced with the subtle problem of transcribing polyphonic music, we tried to adapt our earlier procedure to the investigation of simultaneous musical phenomena of much greater complexity. We did this by first recording one of the polyphonic parts, and then proceeding with another part as we had previously done with the hand-claps, so as to obtain one recording of the individual part and another of two superposed parts. The problem was then to extract the second part from the second recording so as to get two separate parts. Since, however, we only had two monophonic recorders to work with, we carried on to get at least a set of useful results. We then found a way of isolating the second part, which could also be generalised and used to separate out any part in even the most complex polyphony (Arom 1973).

By way of example, suppose we want to obtain separate recordings of all the parts played by a group of n drums, which we will designate as drum 1, drum 2,. . .drum n.

We use one recorder (A) to make a series of recordings of each individual drum part. The output jack of recorder A is then connected to the input jack of a second recorder (B), to which a microphone is also fitted. Drum 2 listens through headphones to the part played by drum 1, as played back by recorder A, and simultaneously plays his own part. This is picked up by the microphone of recorder B and is thereby 'mixed' with the part played by drum 1, which is being re-recorded on B through the input jack. This gives us one recording each of drums 1 and 2, and a mixed recording of both. However, when drum 2 can hear drum 1, he will not perform his own part exactly as he did when playing alone.

If we now try to repeat this operation working with drums 2 and 3, we are likely to find that drum 3 also varies his part somewhat, and that the same thing happens with every pairwise step down the line.

This procedure thus leads inevitably to serious problems in both transcribing the individual parts and obtaining the complete score (e.g., for drum 2, should we use the version recorded separately on A or the one mixed with the part for drum 1 on B?). These problems could be solved by using a third recorder (C), unconnected with A or B, to obtain another separate recording of the part played by drum 2 while listening through the headphones to drum 1. At the next stage, this separate recording of drum 2 was played for drum 3 on A. At the same time, the parts played by drums 2 and 3 were mixed on B, and drum 3's part was recorded separately on C.

After n operations of this kind, we had thus obtained:

- a separate recording of each of the n drum parts (note that, with the excep-

tion of the part played by drum 1, each has been recorded *as performed when mixed with the immediately preceding part*).
- n − 1 mixed recordings.

Each drum part included in a mixed version is thus the same as the one recorded separately. The requirements for coherent transcription are thereby satisfied.

In this way, we were able to conjoin a field method and a laboratory technique in a single process, so that we could actually do laboratory work *in the field*. We would thereby hope to escape, at least in this area, from the awkward situation pointed out by Alan Merriam (1964: 38):

Despite the fact that ethnomusicology is both a field and a laboratory discipline, and that its most fruitful results must inevitably derive from the fusion of both kinds of analysis, there has been both an artificial divorcing of the two and an emphasis on the laboratory phase of study.

In trying to restore field work to its rightful position, we encountered some of the difficulties inherent to experimentation in the social sciences, but we also recovered the invaluable advantage of being able to subject our results to immediate checking, as we will see below.

5   Theoretical assumptions

At this point, we must set out the theoretical foundations of our method. We will first have to state a postulate. Any polyphonic piece of music can be looked at as a complex sound structure characterised by the superposition of a given number of coherently related monodies. This leads us to the following assumption: insofar as a polyphonic piece is based on a coherent structuring of all its parts, each of these parts must be coherent in itself. If this is true, each part should be playable separately, i.e., have its own individual existence in sound, just as it exists in the mind of the person who performs it. By this hypothesis, if we can isolate each part and determine the points at which it fits together with the others (or at least one other), we may assume that we have all the elements we need to reconstitute the polyphonic structure. For insofar as the relationships between parts, or between any part and the whole, are coherent, the number of linkage points must be relatively small. The whole can thus be reconstructed, even without the complete set. These interrelations are furthermore based on the principle that all the musicians performing a polyphonic piece will start to play or sing their parts, not simultaneously, but consecutively. This principle holds not only for traditional African music, but also for almost all known forms of orally transmitted polyphony. The only reference used by the individual musician will thus be the part of the musician (or one of the musicians) who has already come in.

The order of entry varies from one repertory to another. It may be fixed by tradition or remain undetermined. This should be ascertained during a preliminary investigation. If the former, it will be sufficient to make partial recordings in the proper order of entry. The second musician comes in after the first, whose part will necessarily be his reference. The sole reference of the third musician, who comes in after the first two, can then be the part of the second, and so forth. If the order of entry is not determined by tradition, the problem is even simpler. The musicologist need only ask which musician wants to start, and in what order the others will follow.

In practice, however, these theoretical principles are applied differently, according to whether the music is strictly percussive with no assigned pitch, is played by wind instruments using the hocket technique, or by instruments which are themselves polyphonic, or is vocal polyphony. We will return later to this point.

Experimental working conditions must, however, also be recognised as involving certain difficulties. First of all, when traditional musicians are removed from their normal performing situation, they tend to restrain their creative impulse and thus show less of their sense of improvisation, which is one of the essential factors in orally transmitted music. On the other hand, paradoxical as it may seem, the experimental situation has the advantage of this very drawback. With less stimulation than in the traditional performing situation, the musicians will improvise less, and stick more closely to a 'basic pattern' with fewer variations, which will therefore be structurally more fundamental. The structural models used by the musicians as references will thus stand out more quickly and clearly. This point is of particular importance to the investigator dealing with music which is not subjected by the musicians themselves to theoretical analysis or verbal formulation, for his job is precisely to discover the basic structures whose *realisations* are the actual improvisations he hears performed. By being somewhat inhibitory, the experimental conditions actually turn out to be quite useful in helping to reveal the invariant foundations underlying spontaneous musical expression, i.e., in giving access to the models to which the musicians refer.

With the help of this experimental situation, a new dialogue is also set up between the investigator, who can escape from his position as an outside observer of the material he is studying, and the musicians, who are no longer relegated to the role of mere informants with no part in the research activity. Rather, they now accede to the position of scientific collaborators in conducting experimentation intended to obtain a diachronic reconstitution of an intrinsically synchronic musical event, where they also furnish an order of entry known to them alone (or at least only partially available to the musicologist).

Needless to say, the investigator must be extremely careful in applying an experimental method to the study of the musical heritage in an oral culture, and unfailingly respect all aspects of the tradition. Supposing the required experimental conditions obtain, the investigator then need only take proper precautions to make sure not to skip any phases of the method. This is a mere technical problem, to which we now turn.

6 Technical equipment: description and use

This work could never have been written if we had not developed a suitable method of transcribing Central African polyphony (Arom 1976). All our analyses depend on it. Now that we have made its practical and theoretical principles clear in the preceding two chapters, we are ready to provide a narrower technical description of how it is to be applied.

6.1 EQUIPMENT

The equipment required is entirely conventional and easily found in specialised shops. It is lightweight, autonomous (i.e., has a built-in power supply), strong, and easy for the user to operate alone. The following components are required:

- two portable stereophonic tape recorders, one for playback and the other for recording. The latter must have an input jack and a microphone jack which can be used simultaneously and applied to either of the two tracks
- a cable connecting the output jack of the first recorder to the input jack of the second
- a microphone equipped with connecting cable
- several sets of headphones
- a terminal box and cables so that the headphones can be connected to the proper jack of one of the recorders.

Fig. 1 shows how this equipment should be laid out for use.

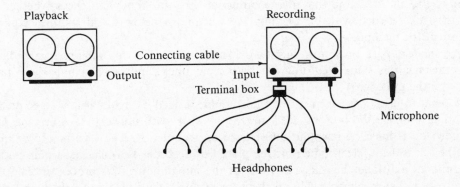

Fig. 1

6.2   THE RECORDING PROCESS

It should be clear by now that the analysis of any polyphony involving more than two musicians becomes very difficult. Two can be properly recorded at the same time, one on each track, by a stereophonic recorder, as Leng suggested in 1969; but there is no room for more.

Let us consider the general case of any polyphonic piece involving n musicians. We will describe the first steps in the process, up to and including the point where the third musician comes in. The process must, of course, by repeated as many times as are required, until all n performers have taken part.

The first step is to make a conventional recording of the entire piece according to standard ethnomusicological procedure. This recording may be either mono- or stereophonic; this has no bearing on subsequent steps. We now have a reference document to be submitted to analysis; we will call it the *tutti recording*.

The equipment should now be arranged as follows for the second step in the recording process: the tape containing the *tutti recording* must be rewound to the beginning and placed on recorder A for playback. Recorder A must be connected by cable to the input jack of recorder B so as to feed its bottom track. The microphone should then be connected to the proper jack on B so as to feed the top track. A clean tape must be fitted on B.

Sets of headphones must be given to the first musician to perform (musician 1), to the investigator so that he can keep tabs on the musical and technical aspects of the process, and to other musicians: the most experienced ones, the other performers, those who are best acquainted with the piece, and the oldest members of the group, all of whom will thus be able to check what is happening. We are now ready to make the first recording by playback.

Musician 1 hears recorder A playing the tutti recording through his headphones, and plays his own part again in time with it. Since he is guided entirely by the recording he has just made, his timing will be absolutely identical. This performance is recorded through the microphone on the top track of recorder B, while the tutti recording is copied from A onto the bottom track.

The other headsets enable the investigator, and particularly, the other musicians, to listen to the musician and the tutti recording at the same time, and check whether or not they are satisfied with his playing. We will return below to this built-in control feature of the method.

The musicologist thus now has two documents: one is his reference recording; the other has this same recording on the bottom track, and the first musician's part alone on the top one.

No change in the arrangement of the equipment need be made at any stage of the recording process. We now proceed directly to work with musician 2. The tape just recorded on B must be rewound and placed on recorder A. The tutti recording may now be set aside. A clean tape must be placed on recorder B. Musician 2 puts on his headphones and takes his place in front of the microphone. The process is then the same, except that musician 2 will only hear the recording by musician 1 (which we know he uses as his reference) through his headset. Recorder B will thus record the second musician's part on its top track, and a perfectly synchronised recording of the first musician's part will be copied from recorder A directly onto the bottom track.

This new recording will give us the completely synchronous, but separately recorded, individual parts of musicians 1 and 2. The musicologist can thus hear a playback of either musician 1 alone (on the bottom or righthand track), or musician 2 alone (on the top or lefthand track), or both of them together in the "stereo" position.

A decision now has to be made before recording musician 3: he can choose to play to either musician 1 or musician 2, according to which track is selected on recorder A, or to both (if A plays back both tracks simultaneously), or even to the tutti recording, which can be put back on A. Whatever the case, a new recording will be obtained with musician 3 alone on the top track and his preferred reference music on the bottom one.

A piece with n parts will thus require $n+1$ recordings: first the tutti recording, and then n recordings of each of the performers (see Fig. 2).

We have, however, already remarked that this general procedure can be applied in different ways according to the type of music involved. It can be used exactly as described above for simple polyrhythmics such as drums coming in consecutively in a given order, for polyphony created by several instruments, each of which plays a single note (the hocket technique), or even for purely vocal polyphony.

This is, however, no longer true of intrinsically polyphonic instruments with fixed pitches such as xylophones, *sanzas*, and harps. Analysis is complicated in these cases by the fact that a single musician performs two parts simultaneously, one with each hand. To deal with this situation, we have extended the method described above, and developed a more general procedure, valid for all heterogeneous instrumental and vocal ensembles of music-producing sources of any number or kind. The procedure presented thus far is consequently a specific case of this general method.

6.3   RECORDING POLYPHONIC INSTRUMENTS

Intrinsically polyphonic instruments will often produce an extremely complex contrapuntal lattice of two closely interwoven parts, each played by one of the musician's hands. It is then practically impossible accurately to disentangle these parts, and determine how they are related melodically and rhythmically. The basic idea is to treat each of the musician's hands as we did each individual player before. The procedure therefore consists of obtaining a tutti recording, and then recording each hand separately on a different track on recorder B. It is true that musicians are not accustomed to play only the part for one hand, because the characteristic patterns their instruments produce result precisely from a combination of the two. There is thus usually a minor technical obstacle. Experience has shown, however, that in most cases, an African musician will need only a few minutes to get over this difficulty, and play each part separately without inhibition. It may be added that such practiced and skillful musicians will often see this new difficulty as challenging, be stimulated by it, and take pleasure in overcoming it.

The procedure may thus be summed up as follows:

- the *tutti recording*: the piece is performed with both hands
- the first hand recorded alone: the musician hears the *tutti recording* through his headset
- the second hand recorded alone: the musician hears only the recording of his first hand.

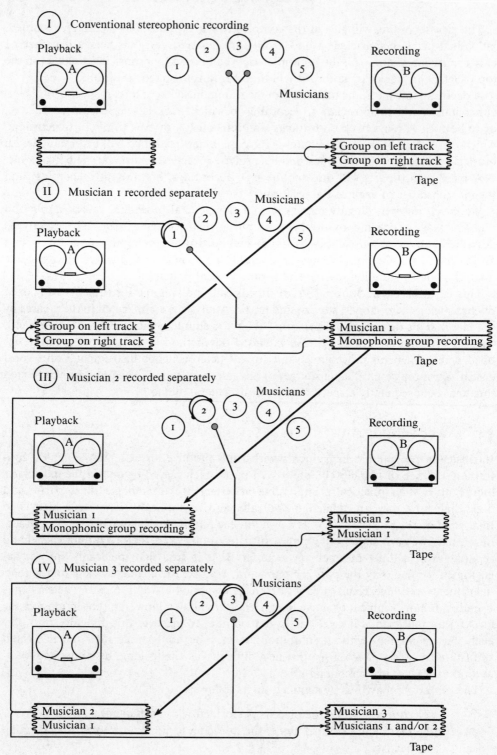

Fig. 2

When the latter two recordings are played back together with the recorder set for 'stereo', the piece as played simultaneously by both hands can be reconstituted, and should be comparable to the reference recording.

6.4   RECORDING HETEROGENEOUS ENSEMBLES

There are no special problems in applying the procedure to groups comprised of different kinds of instruments (melodic instruments and percussion instruments without a given pitch). If, however, there are intrinsically polyphonic instruments in the ensemble, we will have to go back to the preceding procedure.

The final case to be considered is that of a heterogeneous ensemble including voices and *melodic* instruments. There would be a problem here if the voices began to sing before the instruments came in, for they would then have no prior pitch reference. But the music itself is so coherent that this is *always* avoided: when a piece calls for a combination of fixed-pitch instruments and voices, the former will invariably start. The investigator need only follow the normal order of entry. When vocal polyphony is directly superposed on various percussion instruments without specified pitch (the usual case in Central African Pygmy music), the percussion instruments can be recorded first, assuming the musicians agree, and then the singers in their traditional order of entry.

6.5   ASCERTAINING THE TEMPORAL REFERENCE

Collection of material in this way gives the musicologist access to each part separately, to each one superposed on one or more other parts, and in some cases, to a synthesis of the entire set of parts. But this is still not enough to provide a score, which cannot be written until the musicians' basic reference pulsation (or beat) has been determined, i.e., the *metre*, in the *metronomic* sense of the word. The *metre*, however, is usually only immanent and underlies the music we hear; a way must therefore be found to materialise it. Not only does it provide the investigator with the isochronous reference points he needs to transcribe this music; it also allows him to determine the intrinsic tempo of the piece.

We have found the simplest and most accurate way of doing this is to ask one of the performers to listen to a playback of all the recordings of the individual parts, and to superpose hand-claps on them. Hand-claps can, of course, be replaced by any other kind of percussion, such as beating a pencil or wooden stick on a table, provided the sounds produced are sharp enough. (The danger is that intrusive resonance or reverberations may mask the purely musical material being measured.) The sole purpose of this operation is to obtain *audible markers* of the time intervals. The hand-claps, or whatever other materialisation of the beat may be chosen, will be recorded each time on the top track of recorder B. The lower track will copy from A the musical part to which the beat applies, so that the two will be synchronous. This procedure is diagrammed below:

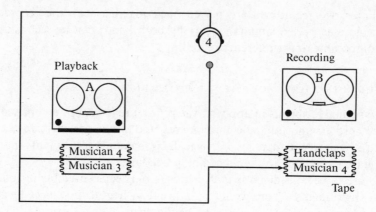

Fig. 3

When this procedure has been followed for each of the recorded parts, we will then have a new set of recordings where each one is correlated with the *beat they all have in common.*

It must be stressed that the traditional musicians themselves must materialise the beat if we are to be sure of having the metre as they conceive of it. The musicologist should therefore keep apart from this operation. He should explain as clearly as possible what he wants done, but not try to show them how to do it. To do this, he may give an example of isochronous beats with no accompanying music, or if this does not work, show them what beats are and how they work for music from a different community, such as a folk song from the investigator's own musical tradition.

In our own experience, we have had no trouble getting the metre, by simply explaining what we want to achieve and how much we need it to understand the music, and then giving a quick demonstration, if required. When there are many documents to be 'measured' in this way, it is wise to have the musicians take turns so that they can retain the necessary power of concentration. Performing an operation of this kind out of context and in experimental conditions requires very close attention on the part of the 'punctuator' listening to the music through his headphones. A musician accustomed to giving free rein to his creative imagination will furthermore find that merely applying equi-distant percussions is a boring or even frustrating operation.

This procedure must be controlled throughout by other musicians, including those who made the recordings that are being submitted to 'postsynchronisation'. They, too, should be provided with headphones and check whether or not the beat is right. Through his constant visual contact with the musicians around him, the investigator can immediately detect the slightest error from any changes in their facial expressions. Once these operations are completed, the musicologist will have all the material he needs to proceed to analyse any piece of polyphonic music:

- the conventional recording
- separate recordings of each part
- recordings providing the superposition of the basic beat on each of the latter
- recordings of the combinations of the parts.

The music can now be transcribed and written in the form of a score.

7 From recording to transcription

The method we have described is based on collecting culturally relevant documents. The musicians play their traditional instruments, the proper order of entry for each piece is respected, and temporal reference points are materialised according to internal criteria, such as superposition of the beat by the musicians themselves (an entirely immanent criterion from the cultural standpoint), rather than external ones, such as the use of a metronome or other chronometric systems involving the use of mechanical apparatus. With only material of this kind available, the transcription will have to depend on the musicologist's ear alone, rather than on instruments for measuring pitch and duration on a scale of discrete frequencies.

The method of transcription itself is based on the same theoretical assumptions as the recording method, but works in the opposite direction. It aims to reconstitute the entire piece in writing as a synthesis of the separate parts collected in the field by the recording method, which allowed us to 'take the music apart' into a temporal sequence of elements.

The first step in transcription is to organise the durational reference points. Extremely useful for this purpose is lined music paper which is also graduated with fine vertical lines. These can be used to show the arithmetic ratio of the durations: a given number of lines will mark the duration between two isochronous pulsations, which can be represented, for example, as a crotchet or a dotted crotchet, depending on whether the basic value contains a binary or a ternary division. We then prepare a strip of such paper long enough to hold a representative fragment of the piece, and with as many staffs as there are parts.

The first part may then be transcribed from the recording with the superposed beat. Vertical marks must be made to show exactly where the beats fall (i.e., the fundamental pulsation). The remaining parts are then consecutively transcribed on the staffs below in the same way. This means they are transcribed in time with the superposed pulsation, but have not yet been synchronised among themselves. This is merely a part-by-part transcription provided with a *homogeneous metric representation*.

Once the individual transcriptions are completed, the paper can be cut horizontally into smaller strips, each containing a single part. We now turn to the recordings where the parts are superposed in pairs, starting, of course, with the superposition of parts 1 and 2. We then slide the strip for part 2 along beneath part 1 to the point at which the two coincide, exactly as they do on the recording. This brings the two parts into the proper relationship, and their individual metric pulsations should now also coincide. If the two transcriptions are correct and they have been made to coincide properly, they will, being concomitant, then match perfectly throughout the entire piece. The two strips can now be attached with adhesive tape, and the operation can be repeated for each of the remaining parts.

At the completion of this task, we obtain a score showing the totality of our individual recordings. If our basic assumption is correct, and we have made no mistake at any point in the procedure, the contents of this score represent *one of the piece's possible realisations*.

8   Checking the results

Conducting research in this way under experimental conditions calls for extreme caution. That is why checks and controls must be included in our procedure and applied throughout the experimental process. Brief reference has already been made to one kind of check, namely, the fact that headsets are provided to enable various people to monitor the recording operation: the musicians, the head musician (where the function of leader exists), the masters, and the elders, all of whom have an intimate knowledge of the music from having been involved in it. They listen through their headphones to all the individual performers being recorded. The investigator must maintain constant visual contact with them so that, if they object to any musical event, he will see their opinion reflected with such speed and clarity on their faces that he will immediately know there has been a mistake. If the investigator himself thinks he has heard something wrong during the performance, he can direct a questioning glance at them, and they will either confirm his impression or let him know that everything is as it should be. Clearly, this constant questioning of the accuracy of the output in no way relies on the investigator's theoretical assumptions, but is based entirely on the proper of improper performance of musical material within a given group, i.e., on culturally relevant criteria.

There is a second sort of checking procedure built into the method. If a musician makes a mistake which gets by even the kind of monitoring described above, yet is serious enough to affect the coherent musical organisation of the piece, the next musician to record, who uses the erroneous part as a reference, will obviously be bothered by it in his own performance. This is an additional guarantee, although long experience has shown that it is very rarely required.

These two forms of checks naturally apply to the recording of both the individual parts and the beat, the latter being no less important for collecting accurate and coherent musical data.

One final kind of checking can also be done when dealing with polyphonic ensembles involving a fairly small number of parts. If the parts can be cumulatively superposed, i.e., if each musician can be provided with the full set of parts prior to his own as a reference, the entire piece can be reconstituted by this synthesis.

With both recorders set for playback, the musicians (and other members of the community) can listen to the reference version (the initial complete recording we call the *tutti recording*) and to the version subsequently obtained by conjoining the individual parts. The listeners can hear the two versions consecutively *without being told which is which*; the musicologist then asks them whether they approve of both, whether only one is right (and in this case, which one), or whether neither of them is. If both versions are accepted as correct (disregarding remarks that are bound to be made on the poorer technical quality of the *synthetic* version), this may be taken as an additional check on the validity of the experimental version.

The investigator may also make a general check of the coherence of his data and theoretical assumptions, and even the accuracy of his transcription. To do this, however, he will need to have enough time to transcribe the piece he is studying in the field when he has completed his analytical recording. When the transcription is finished, he can have the musicians listen to one of the parts (or some combination of them) while he sings another one from his score. If this check is to be valid, he must be careful to superpose his own part on some part other than the one which was used as a reference, at the time of recording, for the part he is singing.

9   Potentialities

The method described can be used to decompose polyphony into a coherent set of elementary monodies. It is therefore the first method to be devised which is capable of providing students of musicology, acoustics, and organology with a recording of the individual parts in any piece. It thereby makes it possible to conduct laboratory studies which were previously restricted to monodic music: pitch analysis, decomposition of the frequency spectrum by real-time analysis, sonographic studies of harmonics and overtones, and melographic recordings of melodic curves. It also constitutes a new tool for ethnomusicological research into the musical psychology of peoples with orally transmitted polyphonic traditions, particularly, into how far the musicians consciously develop their polyphony and what individual limits are placed on their musical 'productivity'. A few of these possibilities will now be illustrated by specific examples.

We wanted to find out to what extent each of the singers in a group of Pygmies was conscious of the polyphonic structure of a specific piece, i.e., of its metric, rhythmic, modal, and vertical, i.e., 'harmonic', organisation. After recording the first singer in the traditional order of entry, we asked each of the remaining performers to develop a counterpoint to the melody of this initial 'cantus firmus'. This was done by about ten people. We found that, despite (or perhaps because of) the experimental conditions, all were perfectly clear about how the metre, rhythm, mode, and vertical organisation of their parts should be directly related to the 'cantus firmus'.

Conversely, it is impossible, by merely listening, to determine how Pygmy vocal polyphony is organised, despite the obviously coherent relationships among the undeterminable number of voices. When someone starts up a song, his melodic line takes only a few seconds to be absorbed and disappear within the vocal mass, and may well never be taken up again by anyone else. All indications are that the singers are capable of developing polyphony in accordance with a melody without having to hear it, just as instrumentalists can establish a polyrhythmic structure with respect to an implicit or underlying beat.

What we have to discover is the melody used as the reference for the polyphonic construction. Here again, our method can provide an answer. We simply ask a singer to listen to the *tutti recording* of the vocal polyphony through his headset, and to superpose the 'real melody' of the piece. We will thereby obtain a recording of the implicit model, the 'cantus firmus'.

A given individual's 'contrapuntal stock' for each piece can also be determined. We thus asked a Pygmy musician to sing in counterpoint over a recording of himself singing a certain melody, and to do so as many times as he could think of different parts. He provided four, and then made the particularly revealing comment, 'I could sing more, but I would just be repeating things I have already done'. He had, however, simply omitted the 'cantus firmus' for the piece, probably thinking we were more interested in his own virtuosity than in the structure of the music.

The preceding three examples suggest a few of the possibilities opened up by this method in the investigation of problems of polyphonic awareness and perception in musical psychology. Within the more limited framework of the present study, however, the method will also enable us to determine the set of improvisations which are permissible within the structure of a given piece. The 'stock' of variations available not only to the individual musician, but to the entire community, can also be determined for any piece in the corpus.

The investigator will, in fact, encounter a sort of stereotype after listening to a number of recordings of individual parts in a given piece. Once the listener familiar with music of this kind has seen how each musician gets through his initial statements, he will be able to predict the musical events which are likely to occur further on. There is a saturation point beyond which new variations will become very rare. The method also reveals a process of centonisation within each melodic line. There will be a set of elements for assembly, which can appear in any part, though only at specific places within the periodic musical structure.

The reader will recall that we pointed out a paradox when we described our method above. This was that experimental conditions tend to inhibit some musicians; but if this is a disadvantage to the extent that improvisation plays an important part in this kind of music, it also allows much quicker and clearer access to its structure. There is, however, a related paradox, in that the opposite effect can also happen. A musician normally plays or sings in a group of twenty or thirty people within which he fulfills his musical function as best he can; he does not, however, think of himself as an 'artist' in the sense of someone who makes an original personal contribution. When he suddenly finds himself in the situation of having to play or sing alone, with the elders, the other musicians, the musicologist, and other curious villagers looking on, he may be stimulated much more than he would be as just another member of the group. Without actually modifying the musical nature of his part, he may then give free rein to his own personality and his talent as an improviser. He is quick to observe how those around him react, particularly the musicologist, whose expression will respond to any variation. This will stimulate rather than inhibit him, and make him, in theatrical language, 'ham it up' and produce improvisations which would rarely be heard in a traditional performance.

We are thus presented with the notable paradox of a method which is both capable of detecting the implicit structure of a traditional work of polyphonic music, and producing the opposite effect of stimulating the production of variations, thereby enabling the investigator to achieve a better understanding of how the music works by comparing these two sides of the same situation.

10   Anthropological validity

The method of polyphonic analysis described above is experimental. The question must now be raised whether the use of this kind of experimentation in ethnomusicology is acceptable. Before proceeding, we may remark that the procedure receives initial support from the fact that a number of experiments involving the same object have yielded, perhaps not identical, but at least extremely similar and equally revealing results. Paradoxically, the theoretical assumptions of the method are confirmed in its application. We may summarise these assumptions as follows: each part in polyphonic music is itself a coherent entity; these parts also fit together in a coherent way; and the way they fit together two by two remains unchanged, however many times we record them. We furthermore assume that the combination of all the parts is equivalent to the set of the individual parts and to the set of all possible combinations of these parts. In applying the method, we can confirm each and every one of these hypotheses.

The procedure consists essentially of obtaining a diachronic reproduction of a synchronic event. The fundamental principle of the successive entry of voices or instruments, which characterises the polyphony and polyrhythmics of this part of Africa, is nevertheless respected, even while the music is being 'disassembled'. In some cases, entries take place in indeterminate order; in others, they are strictly ordered in connection with the structure of the piece, and can be indicated by the musicians. The musicologist has no part in this breakdown, and is a mere spectator to the musical performance. The method follows this order step by step. The procedure has the further advantage of being applicable in the field, i.e., in the musicians' own cultural setting. The members of the community who take no part in the performance itself can thereby also offer their opinion and provide immediate confirmation as the experiment proceeds.

If the experimentation were based on principles incompatible with the structure of the music under study, the musicians would, in all probability, refuse to go along with it, or would at least let their doubts be known. The fact is, however, that they not only allow the experiments to go ahead, but also take an active part in them, with obvious enjoyment. There have even been several occasions when people from neighbouring villages, or musicians who are only passing through, ask to take part in such experiments and suggest the musicologist come and work with their own music using the same recording method. The confirmation the method thus obtains is far from negligible.

All ways of checking the results are based on the internal coherence of both the method and the music itself. We may recall that checking is carried out at two different times during the experimentation, first during the recording session, and again when the synthetic production is complete.

The coherence of the method is guaranteed by its permanent checking mechanism: if a musician makes a mistake, the next one to enter will be obstructed and will be unable to perform his part properly; and this in turn proves that the polyphony itself is coherent. At the same time, the psychological behaviour of all the participants in the recording process, whatever their role, constitutes a further guarantee that each phase of the procedure is reliable: the facial expressions, comments, and reactions of the other members of the community (elders, master musicians, assistants) are indicative of the accuracy and quality of the recorded performance.

When the recording is completed, the investigator can submit the result to the judgement of the musicians and the other inhabitants of the village, or even to people from neighbouring villages who are unaware that they are listening to a synthetic production. My own experience has been that this production is accepted by everyone, not only right after the recording is completed, but weeks and even years later (in one case, I rechecked after four years).

In conclusion, it should be stressed that the conditions under which this experimentation is done bring about a major change in the investigator's relationship with the local musicians, insofar as the latter are actually converted into his scientific collaborators. As specialists in the music under study, they are the ones who direct and supervise the application of the analytical method, and thereby provide a guarantee of accuracy at every step of the procedure.

1 Gàzà kõfẽ, dance for the passage rites of the young Banda-Dakpa boys

2 *Playing the* sanza

3 Kálángbá, *Banda-Dakpa xylophone*

4 Ngòmbí, *Ngbaka bowed harp*

5 Kpòlò, *Ngbaka double bell*

6 *Re-recording session of Ngbaka harp songs*

7 Āngɔ̄, *Banda-Linda horn orchestra*

8 Banda-Linda horn orchestra, detail

9 Re-recording of the Banda-Linda horns, two by two

10 Re-recording of the Banda-Linda horns under the supervision of the 'master of the horns'

11 *Re-recording the* mānzā *xylophone part (right hand) from the* ngbàkè *repertoire of the Sabanga*

12 Re-recording the ngàsà *drum part from the* ngbàkè *repertoire of the Sabanga*

13 *Re-recording of the ankle jingles part of the dance associated with the* àgā tɔ́rúmɔ̄ *ritual of the Banda-Linda*

14 *Aka Pygmies singing in choir*

15 *Aka choir with percussion (drums and iron blades)*

16 Aka men striking the mò.kóngò

17 *Aka man striking together two iron blades,* dì.kétɔ̀

18 *Aka man re-recording a vocal part*

19 *Materialisation of the pulsation by two Aka men*

20 *Aka Pygmies controlling the accuracy of a re-recorded piece*

Book IV

Theoretical tools

1 The notion of relevance

1.1 WHAT IS RELEVANCE?

Having developed a method and shown it to be well-founded, we now have the technique we need to transcribe and analyse polyphony. We can record unwritten polyphonic music part by part, and our recordings enable us to see how the parts combine and interlock. They thus provide the raw material for further research; however, analysis as such cannot begin without a *transcription*.

We now come to a fundamental methodological question. Do we want a rational and meaningful transcription based on the way the people who use the music perceive and understand it, i.e., do we really want to follow through with our stated purpose of setting aside whatever Western notions we might be tempted to project onto African music? If so, before we actually start to transcribe, we must develop another device to enable us to determine what we can and ought to extract from our recorded material. Referring only to criteria present in the musical tradition under study, the investigator should be able to decide which data in the raw material are meaningful, and which are not. We therefore require a device like a sequence of filters, which can separate out whatever is meaningful. This device must operate on the basis of the notion of relevance.

The musicologist has, in fact, a choice of two alternatives. He may remain as close to the recorded material as he can and try to note every detail with maximal accuracy. This approach, while apparently convincing from the acoustic standpoint, nevertheless suffers from the fact that there is no limit of ultimate accuracy, as transcriptions like Bartók's have shown. The other possibility would be to try to determine beforehand what the members of the community consider to be meaningful in their own music. In this case, the analysis will no longer integrate every acoustic feature, but will refer only to the ones the users themselves find meaningful. This approach will obviously have to be based on prior knowledge obtained by work in the field. The resulting transcription will provide a visual representation of the features which are relevant within a given musical system, and should allow us subsequently to identify structural features, syntactic rules, and the principles governing function and combination.

For an element to be relevant, it must be an essential and inalienable part of a musical structure. Our problem is, first of all, to determine what makes a given element in a musical structure relevant, and then to identify the structural levels at which different sets of elements are assigned this relevance.

Our aim is to get a transcription containing only relevant elements. It is senseless to try to discuss a transcription independently of the problem of relevance, as there is a close dialectical relationship between the two. While the concept of relevance must be discussed first so that it can act as a guide to transcription, it will be impossible entirely to avoid anticipating somewhat on the subsequent discussion of the problems of transcription itself.

The question is, what degree of significance should be assigned to each item of information the ethnomusicologist collects? According to Chailley, there should be 'a *basic distinction between the formal appearance of music and its substantive reality*' (1964a: 47). He regrets that investigators are not always 'capable of perceiving the meaningful reality underlying the many extrinsic forms of ornamentation, one-off variation, and uncircumscribed freedom, but neglect it in a premature search for the unusual in a world where the banal has yet to be recognised and understood.' He then issues a warning:

Of all forms of music, folk music is the one that most hides a subjective content which the performer communicates to a listener from the same culture, through a disguise of external artifices which the latter cannot, properly speaking, even hear. The tape recorder, however, cannot make this distinction. It hears and repeats everything. We in turn train our ears to work like tape recorders, and our hand to write like an oscillograph. This sometimes leads to dangerous illusions. One of the worst of these is perhaps *to take the 'snapshots' our recordings provide for eternal portraits.*

Referring specifically to our own subject, he adds:

Polyphony is like ornamentation and rhythm: there are times when *what the ear hears materially is only a deformation of the musical reality.* The latter is all that counts for the performer, and is all the hearer who understands the rules and conventions actually hears.

The problem of relevance is perfectly summed up in the preceding remarks, to which we fully subscribe. They cover the principles of both transcription and the underlying analysis. As Chailley rightly concludes, 'If we listen to a recording of this kind of polyphony, and analyse or draw upon it as if it were a Bartók string quartet, we will be denying its very *raison d'être.*'

Several musicologists have already devoted attention to the question of relevance. Hood (1963: 188–9), for example, says, 'I want to repeat the overriding question "What is *musically* significant?" Not "What is *symbolically* significant?"' To clarify the distinction between the two types of problem, he adds, 'The latter question is more the concern of the anthropologists.' He concludes by asking, 'What in terms of the musical tradition itself has significance?'

The importance of this question is clear in the light of List's (1963: 195) remarks: 'Theoretic concepts concerning music are not present in all cultures. Where such concepts do not exist it is difficult to determine from the culture itself what elements in style are most significant musically.'

What then is relevance, or as Merriam (1964: 49–50) puts it, what is 'truth' in anthropology?

Within any given culture there is what often seems to be almost infinite variation in the details of any given behavior or belief, and this applies as well to music as to any other aspect of culture. Given the fact that the investigator cannot possibly consider every minute variation because of the simple limits of time, how can he ever know what is the 'proper' or 'correct' version of a song? The answer lies in the distinction to be made between an absolute correctness and an understanding that such an absolute probably does not exist. What is important is not the search for a single truth, but rather 'the limits within which a culture recognizes and sanctions variations in a given mode of behavior' (Herskovits 1948: 570). That is, the ethnographic or ethnomusicological "truth" is not a single fixed entity, but rather a range of entities within a particular distribution of variation, and it is the limits of the variation, rather than a supposed absolute, which lead to an understanding of the phenomenon.

Merriam narrows the problem down when he says: 'We want to know what a musician sets out to do each time he plays a certain piece of music, not *exactly* what he did on one particular occasion.'

The trouble is that the theory is *implicit*. The outsider trying to understand the music of a given culture or people is ignorant of its underlying rules. As Molino says, 'What the observer comes face-to-face with is the heterogeneity of the musical data' (1975: 53).

Constantin Brăiloiu has also made several references to the absence of explicit theory in folk music, particularly in his 1958 and 1959 articles. In the latter, he writes: 'Unlike the "composer" who knows the significance of every note he writes, the unclutivated musician is unaware of any "method". . . and can give no explanation of any technical procedure or theoretical concept. He remains fully within the bounds of empiricism' (Brăiloiu 1959: 89). In a subsequent passage, Brăiloiu (1959: 91) nevertheless remarks that all the members of societies with orally transmitted traditions possess the mechanisms which underlie their musical systems and know how to put them into operation.

There is an interesting comparison to be made here between traditional African music as we see it today, and the situation in the Western world in the thirteenth century, as reflected in Aubry's (1909) study of troubadour songs. The former is *oral* music which the investigator must first collect if he wants to find out how it is constructed; the latter is *written* music, but the notation is incomplete: 'The ancient manuscripts containing motets and troubadour songs show no indications of rhythm' (Aubry 1909: 190). Aside from this obvious difference, there are, however, close resemblances, first of all in the general situations: in both cases, there is a code, but an implicit one. Aubry makes this clear for the troubadour songs: 'I have come to the conclusion that rhythm is intrinsic and latent in the documents of that period; that it existed but in no way appears in the notation' (ibid.: 190-1).

But this is not the only similarity. The activities of a musicologist working on medieval music, such as Aubry, and an ethnomusicologist facing the complexity of African polyphony as it is today, follow the same general plan: working under identical limitations, they try to uncover implicit laws which the performers themselves cannot state theoretically, although they make systematic use of them in practice. 'In the thirteenth century, observance of these laws must have been so natural that theoreticians neither stated them nor remarked upon them: we can only assume that dilettantes, composers, and singers all made instinctive use of them' (ibid.: 199).

The documentary sources available to Aubry lacked any indication of rhythm, but he was able to reconstruct this implicit feature by extrapolation:

Some manuscripts contain monodic songs and motets for several voices. Both kinds of pieces are written by the same hand, using the same notational system. But rhythm is unwritten.

The same motets are, however, found in other unquestionably measured manuscripts. They must then be measured in the same way in the anthologies where the notation gives no indication of metre, and the troubadour songs in the same manuscripts as the motets must also be measured, since the notation is identical.   (ibid.: 191-2)

His concluding remark on how he worked out the implicit rhythmic laws in troubadour songs is: 'I have been able to discover the main laws by an experimental method through textual study, i.e., *a posteriori*' (ibid.).

The existence of theory in civilisations with an orally transmitted tradition, though entirely implicit, can nevertheless be demonstrated from the fact that *the users never miss a mistake*. They will immediately remark on and correct even the most minor error. If there can be a mistake, it must be with reference to some sort of theoretical framework. As Jakobson says,

A Serbian peasant reciter of epic poetry memorizes, performs, and, to a high extent, improvises thousands, sometimes tens of thousands of lines, and their meter is alive in his mind. Unable to abstract its rules, he nonetheless notices and repudiates the slightest infringement of these rules. . . Meter – or in more explicit terms, *verse design* – underlies the structure of any single line – or, in logical terminology, any single *verse instance*. Design and instance are correlative concepts. The verse design determines the invariant features of the verse instances and sets up the limits of variations.
(1960: 364)

List (1963: 196) has suggested that the investigator's task would be much simpler if he could get his informants to show him how their culture distinguishes between those elements which are significant from a musical point of view, and those which are not: 'Music is a product of culture, not of nature. Our perceptions are limited. We cannot overstep the thresholds of audibility or feeling nor can we react to frequencies outside a certain gamut. Past this what is music is determined by the culture, not by the harmonic series.'

Blacking (1964, quoted in Ballantine 1965: 54) also remarked that even the 'simplest' music is a cultural product. Among the Venda people of South Africa, for example,

Venda music is not 'natural' but highly artificial, and it has to be learnt by aural experience and physical participation. When a Venda sings, he is expressing cultural particulars, rather than psychophysical universals. Although the Venda cannot explain the theoretical framework upon which they build their performances, they know very well, by training and not by instinct, what is right and what is wrong, and what is acceptable or unacceptable according to the canons of Venda music.

Estreicher (1957: 83) writes with respect to the formal organisation of music in an oral tradition that 'It may be assumed that every musical structure is in some way simple, particularly in the case of collective music, which is transmitted orally from one generation to the next.'

If a human group really has a common shared musical system based on canons, these must in fact be simple at some level of abstraction, no matter how complex the musical performances themselves may appear to be. We may notice how this idea ties up with Jacques Chailley's remarks quoted above.

The foundations of such music, while usually simple, are nevertheless quite difficult to discover. This is mainly a result of the extent of variability permitted by the lack of a written reference. Two successive performances of the same piece are almost never identical. There are, however, always systematic data somewhere, in some form or other. This is what Brăiloiu meant when he wrote: 'Whether it be scales, rhythms, or structures, these building blocks always turn out, when subjected to close examination, to be governed by an intelligible principle giving rise to a given set of procedures, which we could also call a *system*' (1959: 90–1). In an earlier publication, he develops the idea that an abundance of variations in any system always disguises a simple basic structure:

In the absence of any irrefutable counterevidence, we must accept that we can only collect variants, and that an ideal archetype is latent in the minds of the singers, who provide us with ephemeral incarnations of it.

We have to discover the essential properties of this archetype, which would not be what it is if the musicians could disguise all of its elements simultaneously. We must therefore assume that its basic structure cannot be altered by improvisation, which can only proceed freely insofar as it does not affect any of the features which make the abstract model recognisable.

Comparison of variations will automatically bring out which parts of the melody are inalterable and which are ductile. Likewise, the comparison of different performances of a given song will reveal the extent to which the individual can intrude from one theme to another, one human category to another, one environment to another, one period to another, one state of mind or set of circumstances to another, and of course, one musical genre to another – the latter being the primary artistic and psychological question.   (Brăiloiu 1949: 319–20)

In this passage, Brăiloiu makes an important point: the investigator's task is to discover essential properties, i.e., a *model*. The use of the term 'archetype' successfully brings out the idea that, in the course of a given performance, variations cannot be applied simultaneously to *all* its elements. There are thus limits to improvisation. If infinite improvisation were possible on a given model, the piece it represents would become irrecognisable. The model is precisely what preserves the identity of a piece of music.

If folk music is to stick in the memory, it must make use of inflexible patterns; but to remain a 'popular' art form, it must allow these necessarily summary patterns to be infinitely adaptable by individual temperaments: that means variation, which writing does away with. Variation also shows us how folk music gets far-reaching results from relatively limited means. Intensive or even. . . systematic (in the strict sense) utilisation of these means stands in the stead of richness.
                    (Brăiloiu 1949: 330)

The goal of analysing music from an oral tradition must be to describe not so much the abundance of variation as the basic elements which allow it to subsist from generation to generation.

With few exceptions, all folk music is organised so as to develop variations from an *implicit* model. Jones (1959: 1, 127), for example, writes of his transcriptions of patterns of African drum rhythms that:

All the music on the scores is what one master drummer played on one particular occasion when we recorded him. Other master drummers might play these patterns in a slightly different way, though *essentially* it would all be the same. [. . .]

No two African performances are identical. What we have done is to take, as it were, a series of snapshots of African dance-music.

We have then nothing to work on but 'snapshots' of African music, or for that matter, practically any other music from oral traditions. One of our primary aims is to find out what such snapshots all have in common.

Brăiloiu has made remarks which fit in well with the 'snapshot' metaphor. Speaking of the features of a body of oral tradition, he says:

Without the help of the writing, there is no other way to preserve a creation than by obtaining the universal consent of its guardians, which itself can only result from the uniformity of their tastes. A body of oral tradition depends on someone's will to retain it in his memory and reproduce it in concrete form; tradition and the individual human being have a single life. Not being fixed once and for all in written form, the tradition is not complete, but in the making, and is being perpetually remade. This means that every individual realisation of a melodic pattern is equally genuine and has the same weight on the scales of judgment. It also means that 'instinctive variation' is not just an urge to vary but the necessary consequence of the lack of an unchallengeable model.   (Brăiloiu 1958: 88)

This is why no piece is ever performed twice in completely identical fashion. Brăiloiu clarifies this point with a simile comparing music based on the principle of variation on a stable underlying model, with a traditional house.

A house just built on a traditional plan is new only in its material reality. Little matter when it was finished, it is already centuries old in its spiritual reality. It is a variation on an architectural type, just as a song is a variation on a melodic type. The less the builder's or singer's environment has been subject to foreign influences, the less it has absorbed infiltrations, the better those types will be able to brave the passage of time.   (ibid.: 89)

This implicit, underlying system which is capable of braving time and history shows up in each of the music's constituent elements, at each and every level. This is already clear at the simplest and lowest level of musical structure: that of the set of sounds used in the music, i.e., its scale, or scalar system.

A scale is a sequence of pitches and intervals. While these can be measured *physically* by electroacoustic means, the organisation of pitch contrast into a system and the relationships among the degrees are a *cultural*, not a physical phenomenon. Kirby was already aware of this in 1934. When he described how flute orchestras use the hocket technique, he noted that, while such music is governed by the same principles among the different peoples of South Africa, 'the tuning of the reed-flutes, however, would appear to indicate distinct differences between the various peoples who play them' (1934: 169).

Brăiloiu has also discussed this dichotomy of the physical and the cultural and criticised those who, invoking 'scientific principles', deal only with the physical side of musical scales and treat them as mere acoustic phenomena. He comments ironically that, when the phonograph was invented,

people thought themselves on the threshold of a truly scientific age. With a bit of complementary equipment, uncertainty could be banished forever. The reign of the irrefutable was about to begin. Even in its original rudimentary form, the new equipment drew such a clearly indelible demarcation line between past and present that machine worship quickly invaded many minds and still exercises control over some. In 1912, there was already an authority on the subject to assure people that the absolute pitch of sounds could now be measured with 'physikalisch' accuracy. How? By tuning them (if they will let themselves be tuned) with a graduated tuning fork and then calculating its vibrations. But the ultimate judge of tuning is the ear, and the ear is not a physical measuring instrument.   (1958: 24)

More recently, Wiora has reaffirmed the primarily cultural nature of musical scales;

A scale is a preconceived model which voice, hand, and ear obey when they play the game we call 'music'. . .

Intervals and scales are the result of an intention. A scale is an *Intentionat*. It is a system which serves as a norm within the limits of a style. It is a *regula*, to use the medieval expression. . .

Ellis's sets of figures in 'cents' and E. von Hornbostel's structural formulae are only scales insofar as they represent models in the minds of singers and musicians. Robert Lachmann has already. . .pointed out that a scale is not a material object but a model or project to be materialised. It acts as a norm among primitive peoples as well, only it is not codified.   (1963a: 38–9)

Estreicher, too, was aware of the idea of a *preconceived model* when, in a study of the notation of oral music, he wrote

The musician-performer attempts to materialise a specific musical structure. His deviant intonations, the occasional interruptions in his production, etc., do not count for him. . . With respect to the formal aim (*res facienda*), the actual execution (*res facta*) is always imperfect. (1957: 91)

If transcription cannot attain the *res facienda*, should it then be no more than an exact written reproduction? Estreicher rejects this idea: 'A musical transcription which makes allowance for the performer's inaccuracies. . . takes over all his imperfections and becomes inaccurate itself (ibid.).'

In a similar vein, Ballantine (1965: 52–3) explains why he thought it unnecessary to make stroboscopic measurements of the pitch of each individual instrument in the Tswana flute orchestra he studied:

While each pipe can technically produce only one note, in practice it is possible, depending on the way a player blows, to alter its pitch by as much as a semitone; and Blacking has pointed out the invalidity of making pitch measurements upon people to whom the concept of an isolated tone is foreign. . . . For the Tswana, intonation can only be judged during performance, and discrepancies here are relatively slight.

The latter remark is particularly important. Since there is always a gap between intention and realisation, and moreover, the pitches of the flutes can only be determined in the course of a group performance, it is obvious that the way the sounds contrast with one another is the only basis for defining the scale as a system. If there are not at least two sounds being played, there is no way of properly locating them. When the musicians start to perform, however, a sort of 'homing in' takes place. The pitches find the right places, and the scale is constituted. The same phenomenon can be observed in the Central African Republic in horn or flute orchestras of an identical type. Each instrument alone can vary by more than a semitone from the note it plays when all the instruments perform together. Only a few seconds into a group performance, however, the degrees can be clearly perceived to stabilise, the sounds at octave intervals converge, and the anhemitonic pentatonic system characteristic of this region takes shape.

The basic difficulty is still how to determine the *margin of tolerance* within which the hearer can still mentally correct the fluctuations in the performance and pick out the scale being used. This problem is not, by the way, limited to music from outside Europe. The same phenomena can be observed in Western music, both popular and cultured. While margins of tolerance may vary from one civilisation to another, from one genre to another, or from one kind of scale to another, they are nevertheless universally present.

In the course of a discussion which took place at the conference on 'Resonance in musical scales' held in Paris in 1960, Chailley stressed the importance of the phenomenon of tolerance by citing a particularly telling example:

On one of Georges Brassens's recordings, *L'enterrement*, the sol in a mi-do-mi-sol-mi-do arpeggio is consistently too high. Since this occurs in each verse, it is not simply a case of being off tune, but rather a psychological or physiological phenomenon which involves a gap between what the singer 'thinks' and what he 'produces'; for it is clear from the accompanying guitar that he is 'thinking' an exact fifth. Actually, however, this fifth is always nearly a semitone higher.

(1963: 182)

The entire problem of the relevance of a scalar system is clearly captured in this striking example. First of all, we know what system or *code* the singer is using (our ordinary major scale), and this enables us to judge what the margin of tolerance can between what he is 'thinking' and what he actually performs. Next (and this is extremely important), the two 'instruments', the singer's voice and the guitar, are in conjunction. Now in this case, *the same person* happens to be singing the vocal part and playing the accompanying instrument. If we do not want to accept that the gap between the voice and the guitar is a form of tolerance, we will be forced to say that the same performer is simultaneously making use of two different scalar systems.

Chailley rounds off his proof as follows: 'This illustrates the difficulties musicologists face when they listen to the material content of a tape on their recorder, but are not party to the composer's own mental background. Overzealousness may lead them to make some very foolish statements.' If anyone thinks this example is meaningless because it involves popular music, we may note that it is quite easy to make similar observations concerning any performance of cultured music. Lajtha cites a telling example:

Anyone who wants the principle of physically precise intonation to be strictly applied, would have trouble finding a classical musical composition, even performed by a major artist, which is never off tune. This is particularly true of stringed instruments and vocal parts, where the individual musicians can determine the pitch and quality of their intonation. I would even say that concert violinists and great opera singers who play and sing off tune do so intentionally when they go slightly higher or lower on a note or succession of notes to accent the expression of a musical phrase, while of course respecting the specified harmonic line.   (1956: 146)

There is no difference whatsoever on this point between ethnic music, Western folk music, and the cultured music of our concert halls. As Estreicher (1957: 91) says, 'With regard to the absolute pitch of sounds, there are certain limits of tolerance within which all sounds are 'the same' for the musician, even though they may be different for the well-equipped acoustician.' He suggests that 'it is up to the investigator to decide how far he should take his precision in each case', and concludes that 'it is clear that taking precision too far would be nonsense from the musical standpoint'. In this he agrees with Chailley (1959: 139), who defines tolerance as 'the subjective assimilation of approximate sounds to strictly precise ones.' As Chailley rightly stresses, this assimilation 'varies according to the society and the individual'. A musical scale is thus definitely a cultural product, as Lévi-Strauss shows:

Hierarchical relationships among sounds are brought out as soon as a specific kind of scale divides up the sound continuum. These relationships are not imposed by nature, for the physical properties of any musical scale are far more numerous and complex than the ones a given system will choose as its own distinctive features. It is, of course, true that any modal or tonal system (even polytonal or atonal ones) will, like a phonological system, be based on a given number of physical and physiological properties; it will select a few of these from among the probably unlimited number of available ones, and make use of the contrasts and combinations to which they lend themselves in order to make up a code which can be used to distinguish meanings.

(1964: 29–30)

If we move from the question of scales to the field of rhythm, we again encounter the contrast between intention and realisation and its corollary, the notion of tolerance. Chailley (1964a: 49) reminds us that, here again, the musical reality is generally much simpler than it appears.

This may be precisely what our sophisticated mentalities dislike about it, just as we dislike a simple 4/4 notation using crotchets and quavers of a song with a simple melody thought of in 4/4 time with crotchets and quavers, but performed with considerable freedom of rhythm and ornamentation, which we feel we have the power to capture in an incomprehensibly complex notation.

In fact, our complex notation. . . will sometimes be even more of a betrayal than the simple one. Simplicity is a virtue often derided, but one which both musicology and music are greatly in need of today.

The concordant remarks of the various authors we have quoted show how important it is to distinguish what belongs inherently to the structure of a given musical language from the features pertaining only to the material realisation of this structure. Minor gaps between intention and realisation are to be observed in the domain of rhythmic organisation, just as in the matter of scales. That is why the investigator must here again refer to a *cultural consensus* in order to determine what the significant elements are in a rhythmic system which is foreign to him. Jones laid particular emphasis on this point. In one passage (1959: I, 20), he mentions that the underlying beat in African songs can either be materialised or remain *implicit*. In the latter case (the usual one), the singers have it in their minds. The investigator must therefore obtain a materialisation of it, so that its structural role in the piece can be determined. Now Jones observed that if he recorded a piece from a given group several times, at intervals of an hour, a week, a month, or a year, whenever he asked a member of the same culture to clap his hands to show him the beat, it always fell on the same syllables and at the same points in the period. This means that, whatever divergencies may occur in performance, there is an implicit temporal reference for each song which is strict and permanent, and therefore *cultural*.

Chailley (1964a: 48) warns us, however, that, whether we are dealing with melodic or rhythmic structures, there will be 'a formidably complex problem of noting such phenomena'. He accurately remarks that the problem of transcribing oral folk music is not unlike that of noting ornamentation in vocal and harpsichord music during the classical period. The musicians of the seventeenth and eighteenth centuries found a logical way of solving this problem:

This consisted simply. . . of noting the actual musical content, divested of artifices, in the principale so as to be easily perceptible to both reader and analyst. Then there would also be either a detailed description of one or two developed examples as specimens, such as the ones Monteverdi provided for *Orfeo*; or treatises or tables of ornamentation, with explanations as to how they should be used and read, allowing variation from one performance to another.

The modern performer of this music must therefore be aware of the way the culture of the time allowed notation to differ from practice, and apply the rules enabling him to switch back and forth. This led Chailley to castigate the 'frozen and amorphous performances' resulting from modern editions of works of the Baroque period, and their 'false accuracy', whose only effect was to bring about 'a sterilisation as in a laboratory beaker, which destroys the germs of living music'. He warns that

in all our investigations, we cannot be too wary of subtle traps created by the temptation to base our analyses on contexts which are entirely foreign to the nature of the object under study, so that what we actually depict are imaginary beings absolutely unrelated to the ones we hoped to describe.

Difficulties of this kind are not restricted to music. They appear much more generally in the study of any semiological system of which the investigator has no prior knowledge. This is, for example, the case of unwritten languages. This similarity is not accidental. Music and language, indeed, have a number of common points. Both may be considered as 'organised sound, or more specifically, as culturally moderated systems of recurrent and structured arbitrary sounds' (Springer 1971: 31). This definition gives a clear statement of the problem. Springer too believed that an essential distinction must be made between the system and its execution, i.e., its actualisation or realisation. The code/message and system/text dichotomies which have been borrowed by linguistics from information theory, are present here as well.

Springer remarks that this distinction is directly applicable to music, and correctly adds:

The problems of sameness, which are complex in music, would be even more difficult to solve without it. We would be deprived of the entire social framework of norms, tolerances, and deviations, and the rôle of the individual as both conditioned by, and creator of norms would be obscured.

The creation of both language and music requires that a very limited choice be made from among the amorphous mass of potential raw material, a choice which is reinforced by each linguistic and musical community. It will never make full use of man's biological possibilities in the matters of articulated sound perception and production. With training, natural skill, and concentration, the human ear can distinguish, and the vocal organs can produce, a much larger number of sounds than any code requires. Nevertheless, the human being is normally conditioned to record and retain only those sounds belonging to his own code.   (1971: 32-3)

At this point, we should perhaps recall how a code is to be defined. We borrow Eco's (1972: 13) definition: 'We define a code as any system of symbols which is intended by prior accord, to represent and transmit information from a source to a destination.' Eco adds the following comment: 'One of the hypotheses of semiotics is that underlying each of these communication processes are rules or codes which rest on some cultural convention.' A code may thus be considered to be a system of cultural references. This means that the musical code of a given population can be seen, in Molino's (1975: 55) words, as the 'conventional matrix' out of which that population constructs the entire body of its musical creation and practice. We therefore define as relevant *everything in this system of references which is meaningful to its users*.

We must now determine how relevance can be defined within a strictly musical system.

Our first task is to distinguish how much of a given sound event is strictly physical and acoustic, and how much is culturally shaped. We should observe that this distinction between the physical and the cultural can be made in any human society whatsoever. If we restrict ourselves for the time being to the field of cultured Western music, we find that the distinction applies quite differently to the works of different composers. Mâche writing on differentiating acoustic events from cultural relevance, remarks in this particular connection that

musical objects cannot be defined *a priori*, but only in context with respect to the entire aesthetic project containing them. The important thing is not to get an exhaustive picture of the multi-dimensional values to be found in them, but to see how they work. . . A *forte* bass drum roll is always a *forte* bass drum roll for the acoustical engineer. But it works differently for the musician, and has a different relevance when it appears, for example, at the end of a Verdi opera melody, from when it appears in the middle of a work by Varese. The primary effect of the roll in Verdi will be dramatic, but in Varese, it may be there simply to contrast with a flute note. The important thing is the function. We could conceive of a kettledrum roll and a double bass tremolo as being the same musical object, despite the fact that their acoustic parameters are quite different. A musical object is not like a preexistent three-dimensional part of some construction set (i.e., the work as a whole). Rather it can only be defined at the same time as the work itself, which conditions it more than it is conditioned by it.   (1971: 76)

As early as 1932, Jakobson called attention to the distinction between the strictly acoustic side of a piece of music, and its underlying systematic structure:

In music, a note functions as one in a system of notes. It may have many realisations (the acoustician can determine exactly how many), but from the musical standpoint, the deciding factor is that the piece has to be recognised as identical.

The relationship between a musical value and its realisations is thus exactly the same as the one that holds between a phoneme in a linguistic system and the articulated sounds which represent that phoneme in speech.   (1932, 1971: 552)

Since each human society develops its own musical code, we can only approve of Molino's (1975: 53) lapidary definition: 'Whenever sound is shaped and recognised by a culture, it is musical'. If several different realisations of a single piece are recognised as identical, or more precisely, as *equivalent* within a given culture, then that culture bestows the same value on them.

Saussure defined the nature of the link between the notions of *value* and *identity* in semiology as follows:

In semiological systems such as language, where the elements hold one another in reciprocal balance according to specific rules, the notions of identity and value merge.

That, after all, is why the notion of value includes those of unit, concrete entity, and reality.   (1916, 1971: 154)

We will examine below some cases of diverse realisations of musical elements such as rhythmic or melodic formulae, and see how the members of a cultural community can treat apparently 'different' pieces as identical, i.e., as having the same value in the system they take as their reference. Here we come to a particularly delicate aspect of the analysis of music from oral traditions, particularly in view of the fact that, unlike language, music is a purely formal system and is not bound to any external meaning.

The operation by which participants in a culture come to consider different musical realisations as identical is not confined to civilisations with oral traditions. It appears in Western music as well, as the history of the period of the first written examples of this music confirms. Chailley demonstrates this when he writes, 'Almost all medieval manuscripts of monodies are 'musical dictations' taken down from performance. That is why, aside from copies of archetypes, two versions of any single text are so rarely identical from one manuscript to another' (1967: 109). Examples abound in cultured European music. The most striking one is undoubtedly the realisation of the figured bass parts in the seventeenth and eighteenth centuries. The term 'realisation' already implies that there are different ways of materialising or actualising the musical text: any realisation of a figured bass part is nothing but one of many possible versions of a given model.

This is the same kind of phenomenon that Aubry observed in the field of monodic troubadour songs. But while the versions of these songs all derived from an *oral* creation, the figured bass part provides a definitive and irrevocable *written* model which can give rise to as many versions as there are realisations. The difference between this situation and the one faced by the ethnomusicologist lies in the fact that the model according to which the realisations are obtained is given in one case, but remains implicit in the other. In both, however, the operation of identification discussed above takes place in the same way. All the realisations of a figured bass part thus have the same value in the system of reference provided by cultured Western music in the seventeenth and eighteenth centuries. They are recognised as identical despite their individual features.

The same is true of any work of music in general, whatever period it may be taken from. Consider, for example, the various recordings of Berlioz's *Symphonie fantastique*: whatever their differences, each recording is derived from a single entity, which is the symphony itself. Berlioz's score is the *res facienda*, while each interpretation of it is a *res facta*, which we call a 'version'. Although every performance is a version, the work itself remains unchanged by the multiplicity of interpretations imposed on it. The proof of this is in the fact that the music lover can immediately identify each version as being the *Symphonie fantastique* and nothing else, however large a margin of difference may exist between any two of them.

Mutatis mutandis, the problem is essentially the same in the field of African music. Each time a rhythmic pattern is performed by a different master drummer, it seems to be different. But each of these realisations is just another version of the same model, the same entity: *the pattern itself* insofar as it can be distinguished from all the other musical patterns in the same musical language. From the viewpoint of cultural relevance, there is no more reason to distinguish between any of the possible versions of an African rhythmic pattern, than between any two interpretations of the *Symphonie fantastique*. What we refer to as the model is not the written text, but Berlioz's work as an auditive entity, i.e., the set of features common to each of its realisations, which allow us to identify it. It is important not to confuse the material score and the abstract model, although this confusion is widely sustained by our writing-based civilisation. If Berlioz wrote a score, it was because he had no other way of transmitting the 'pattern' of his symphony to the performers.

Ethnomusicology faces a similar problem, but proceeds in the opposite way. In our civilisation, the mental vision of music must go through a written stage in order to be expressed orally, but the analysis of music from oral traditions must be based on live performances. The only reason for writing them down is to help us understand their internal logic.

Cultured Western music thus proceeds from the code to the message, while the ethnomusicologist's research takes him from the message (or more precisely, *the messages*) to the code, as we have shown elsewhere (Arom 1969: 173–4).

Let us now return to the field of African music. Kubik (1964a: 58) has expressed ideas similar to those already mentioned. In discussing his scores of Zande harp music, he remarks that, while two performances of a given piece are never identical, the melodic 'material' remains the same. In Africa, this relationship of a model to its realisations also prevails in the constitution of musical instruments. Nowadays, a missing drum for any ceremony will often be replaced by some everyday object with suitable percussive characteristics. In our own experience, we have seen traditional drummers accompany ritual music on an object as untraditional as a lorry silencer. This may seem absurd, given how foreign such an object is to the tradition in terms of its shape, material, function, and sonority. But it must be understood that the culturally meaningful, i.e., *relevant* point here is not the object itself, but the use to which it is put. The rhythmic formula played on this utensil must be the proper one for the ritual. Neither the morphology nor the tone of the instrument are relevant; only the musical message it transmits. Culturally speaking, the acoustic results are assigned the same value and treated as equivalent. Bright (1971: 73) presents the problem of the *cultural judgment of equivalence*, which we believe to be essential, in these terms:

In a given musical culture, what is the possible range of variation for a musical work within which such variation will be accepted by the members of that culture?

He replies,

If we find that, in a specific context, two different events (whether they be single notes or longer sequences) are accepted as equivalent or equally correct, then we should consider them to be variants of a single musical 'phoneme' (or 'morpheme' or whatever) and there upon determine the inventory of basic units of the same type.

If we make a list of the acoustic events which, though different, are accepted as equivalent in a specific context, we can then start to distinguish *units*. When we can define such units, we have clearly taken a major step forward in our study of the musical system.

How then do we go about drawing up the inventory of these basic units? We should first recall that music, like language, is a semiological system. Units in either one can only be defined by their mutual relationships: 'In any semiological system, a sign consists of no more than what makes it different. Difference is what determines not only kind, but value and unithood as well' (Saussure 1916, 1971: 168).

We have seen that musical events are identified by the participants in a given culture, not by virtue of their physical or acoustic reality, but rather by the role they play in the operation of the system. This is precisely what gives them their relevance.

Musical units are formally discrete, i.e., *differential*. That is why a musical scale contains a *finite* number of sounds, just as a language uses only a finite number of phonemes. As we will see below, the same is true of rhythmic structures.

We have not been developing the analogy between music and language simply as an *a priori* exercise in applying the principles of linguistic analysis to another discipline. Rather, as Molino says,

these are not simply analogies but homologies, in the strict sense of the word, between language and music. Not that music is a language, or language a kind of music; such a view would lead us into all the impasses of musical analysis which blindly copies linguistic models. But language and music *are* examples of a symbolic form, and as such, have a certain number of common properties. Musical analysis and linguistic analysis are both semiologies. This explains the many similarities. . . between the two domains, based not on some privileged status of one or the other, but rather on the existence of a common set of problems and the fruitfulness of systematic comparison.

(1975: 53)

Linguistics has a tried and tested methodology. Some of its procedures apply particularly well to our subject, namely, those which allow the delimitation of discrete units. We should nevertheless recall that, as Eco (1972: 16) says, 'music raises the problem of a semiological system with no semantic depth'. It is thus clear that, as soon as language's characteristic semantic element comes into play, even distant analogies with music must be abandoned. That is why, according to Ruwet, 'since the meaning of a musical work is immanent, it can only appear in the description of the work. . . The only way to approach the study of its meaning is through the formal study of musical 'syntax' and a description of the music's material aspect at all the required levels' (1972: 12).

For Jakobson,

instead of aiming at some extrinsic object, music appears to be *un langage qui se signifie soi-même*. Diversely built and ranked parallelisms of structure enable the interpreter of any immediately perceived musical *signans* to infer and anticipate a further corresponding constituent (e.g., series) and the coherent ensemble of these constituents. Precisely this interconnection of parts as well as their integration into a compositional whole acts as the proper musical *signatum*. . . The code of recognised equivalences between parts and their correlation with the whole is to a great degree a learned, imputed set of parallelisms which are accepted as such in the framework of a given epoch, culture, or musical school.

(1971: 704)

The ethnomusicologist's main task is thus to discover Jakobson's 'code of recognised equivalences'; in other words, the set of parallelisms which make it possible to define the units of the 'compositional whole'.

The code of equivalences is a cultural phenomenon and can only be determined internally, from the standpoint of the culture in which it has developed. The investigator's first task is thus to find out what parameters the natives make use of to decide what belongs to the code and what is outside it. This is an indispensable stage, for, as Jean-Claude Gardin says, 'If we have no indications concerning the corpus of texts within which the individuality of the one (or ones) we have in view is to be established, there is no way of knowing whether or not we are stating that individuality in a relevant way' (1974: 23).

All of the above leads us to the conclusion that the description of a musical system should aim at defining units, or individual elements, which are meaningful for the system's practitioners. But an investigator to whom that system is foreign can only determine its units by starting with a heterogeneous, empirically constituted set of pieces. The raw data he collects in the early stages can only be submitted to forms of measurement which are 'objective', i.e., independent of internal criteria. To return to the example of linguistics, we may remark that the first stage in the description of a language with only an oral tradition is to attempt to determine its phonemic system. At the beginning of his study, the linguist has only external, physical, acoustic, objectively measurable, i.e., *phonetic* criteria available to him. When he has worked out what distinguishes one phoneme from another *in that language*, he will have its *phonological* or *phonemic* system, i.e., the set of its *smallest discrete units*. He will then have a list of the ultimate units in the language he is studying, and an understanding of how the sounds it uses are functionally organised; and furthermore, he will have obtained this list by means of criteria which are inherent to the language, and therefore *relevant* within it.

1.3   EQUIVALENCE CLASSES

The American linguist Kenneth L. Pike was the first to suggest applying a distinction similar to the phonetic/phonemic one to cultural domains other than language itself (see particularly Pike 1954). This generalisation was intended to allow the systematic organisation of any structured form of human activity to be determined by a study of its contrasting constituent elements. Pike's suggestion has proved to be well founded. Whatever his subject of research may be, the investigator dealing with cultural facts which are foreign to him will always find himself in a situation similar to that of the linguist, as we have described it. His approach will also be the same, for in order to discover the system, he will be obliged to go through a stage of *provisional* conceptualisation analogous to phonetic study. Only the object to which the approach applies has changed.

That is why Pike suggests a more general terminology to illustrate the analogy of approach and underscore the identity of method. To designate these two stages of research, he removed the 'phon-' portion of each term (which connects them directly with linguistics) and retained only the suffixes '-etic' and '-emic'. These terms, freed of strictly linguistic connotations, could then aptly be applied to other domains, among them our own.

Roulet discusses Pike's ideas in a theoretical context and gives a clear statement of the dialectical relationship between the etic and emic stages of research:

Pike clearly shows that the ideal of a neutral and objective description is utopical, for every investigator is conditioned by his prior training and cannot help applying a predetermined pattern of thought to his subject, no matter how he may try to avoid doing so. Since there can be no naive viewpoint, it is better to make explicit allowance for this fact in the method of analysis (in the form of the etic stage of description), and then aim later at achieving an internal view of the subject, i.e., an emic viewpoint. (1974: 42)

We should note that Pike ascribes two meanings to the term 'etic'. In the first sense, etic units are the result of the preliminary description, as we have already described it. In the second, 'an etic unit is a free or complementary variant of an emic unit' (ibid.: 44).

The first point to remark is that this definition introduces an element of hierarchical organisation into the levels of description. Let us repeat that our research aims to achieve an emic description of the system under study. Pike defines the basic features of such a description as follows:

Emic descriptions provide an internal view, with criteria chosen from within the system. They represent to us the view of one familiar with the system and who knows how to function within it himself. . .

The discovery or setting up to the emic system requires the inclusion of criteria relevant to the internal functioning of the system itself. . .

Emic criteria are relative to the internal characteristics of the system, and can be usefully described or measured relative to each other.   (Pike 1954: 38)

From our own point of view, there are two particularly important distinctions to be made. The first is: 'Non-integration versus integration: The etic view does not require that every unit be viewed as part of a larger setting' (ibid.).

Etic elements are part of an unlimited set of narrow descriptive features. Emic features, on the other hand, allow the establishment of equivalence classes containing the features observed on the etic level. These classes are defined according to the principle of cultural relevance. Consequently, 'The emic view insists that every unit be seen as somehow distributed and functioning within a larger structural unit or setting, in a hierarchy of units and hierarchy of settings as units' (ibid.).

The etic/emic contrast thus represents not only a distinction between the external and internal points of view, but also, once the internal organisation has been determined, a difference in degree of generality. The essential point to remember is that the contrast between etic and emic factors in a system can be established on more than one level. An emic element on any given level will become a free variant on the next higher one.

Pike's second distinction is just as important as the first. It concerns the problem of making decisions of *identity* and *difference*, and establishes a contrast between the notions of measurement and system: 'Two units are different etically when instrumental measurements can show them to be so. Units are different emically only when they elicit different responses from acting within the system' (ibid.).

Pike goes on to say that, while etic data give the investigator access to the system and are therefore the starting point of his analysis, the final description or statement of results should be in terms of emic units (ibid.).

The idea that there is a hierarchy of levels of description is essential to our study. We can restate it as follows:

 – by definition, each emic unit on a given level n is also a free (etic) variant of an emic unit at level $n+1$;
 – these levels extend upwards from the organisation of the smallest units in the music of a given population, to a characterisation of its style.

The investigator should thus provide descriptions of each level in the system under study by proceeding from bottom to top.

The analytical method based on the etic/emic distinction ultimately rests on the possibility of defining classes *with respect to a given equivalence relation*. This operation requires that the investigator choose a specific standpoint, or define a criterion that will allow him to recognise in his corpus the auditive data which the users judge to have the same value (or be equivalent), and then place them in the same class. Initially, he should repeat this operation with each of the criteria available to him. Only later will he be able to support and confirm his results on the basis of the convergence of several criteria. He should, for example, first try to find out what scale is being used. This requires classifying the various pitches so that the distinctive sounds can be determined, since these contrasts are precisely the basis of the scale. As Molino says, the makeup of the scale emerges 'when we find, on the one hand, that an entire class of sounds constitutes an equivalence class (whatever their concrete, 'etic' differences, they are 'the same'), and on the other, that this class contrasts with other classes of sounds' (1975: 41).

Needless to say, the distinction between etic and emic elements will be meaningless unless we can say at what level it is to apply. For example, the degrees of a scale should be considered emic with respect to the pitch continuum, which is etic. But the degrees used in a melodic motif (located on the next higher level) are etic variants with respect to the melody itself. These melodic motifs, which are frequently interchangeable in Africa, themselves form equivalence classes with respect to the emic entity of the song they come from. On a higher level still, the song is included in a set of songs associated with a social and/or religious function, which constitutes a repertoire in native taxonomy. This will be the case, for example, with a set of songs that can be performed prior to the departure of a collective hunt. This set is a class, with respect to which any song in it is a free or complementary variant. A class of this kind contrasts with other classes on the same level in the musical heritage of these people, i.e., with other repertoires used for different ritual functions. If we go another step higher, we reach an abstract entity consisting of the set of repertoires, i.e., the entire musical heritage of the people in question. The repertoires linked to different social and religious functions are in turn equivalence classes with respect to this entity. We could go higher yet by generalising over an entire geocultural area. The musical traditions of different populations then become contrasting classes with respect to this next higher level in the hierarchy.

Proceeding step by step, we can thus arrive at a stylistic characterisation of the music of a given population, i.e., determine the set of intrinsic features which distinguish it from the music of any other population. The characterisation of a musical language, like that of a spoken language, can only be based on the principles of differentiation and contrast.

1.4   ASPECTS AND LEVELS OF RELEVANCE

We have seen that, to set up an equivalence class, the investigator must select a point of view, i.e., define a criterion. We have also shown that this basic operation makes it possible to reveal different levels in the organisation of the musical material. Each of these levels of relevance may intersect with factors which are also relevant on the basis of another criterion. This will depend on the investigator's angle of approach, and on the breadth and depth of his field of observation. His full set of data will enable him to focus on a set of relevant distinctive features which will ultimately confirm each other by virtue of their *convergence*.

We could, for example, take different angles of approach to the social and religious functions with respect to which a set of pieces of music constitutes an equivalence class. In terms of organology, we will find that each function requires a specific set of instruments. This is a relevant feature with respect to organology. If we turn to the question of musical organisation, we may find that a single rhythmic formula underlies all the songs assigned a given function. It will enable anyone at a distance to know, as soon as he hears it, what ceremony is going on in the village. It is therefore another relevant feature of the social and/or religious function in question. This function may also be approached from the standpoint of the texts. It is obvious that each function requires a set of songs with words shared with no others. This kind of cluster of convergent features (instruments, rhythmic formula, words to songs) enables us to define musical individuality and distinguish units on a given level.

There is an abundance of examples to illustrate this view. In the sphere of organology, there is Schmidt-Wrengler's observation on Chokwe music from Zaïre that 'the rhythmic and dynamic base is provided by a group of drums whose composition varies with the type of dance' (1975: 49). But the same musical reality can be observed from the standpoint of rhythmic patterns; thus, Schmidt-Wrengler remarks that 'a given type of dance has no more than one fixed rhythmic pattern, though it may vary in some details; it is, however, accompanied by countless different songs' (ibid.: 48). Given that each type of dance corresponds to a specific social function, we can say that each class of Chokwe songs connected with one of these functions has its own rhythmic pattern.

Merriam also remarks that, for the Basongye people of Zaïre, 'Individual songs are recognized instantly in terms of their function. What this means is that music as such does not exist apart from its context or, to the contrary, the context may well determine the conceptualization of the music. This is functionality in its deepest sense' (1962: 123).

Merriam wonders whether other African peoples conceptualise their music in the same way. We can assure that, as far as the music of the Central African Republic is concerned, the answer to his question is definitely, 'yes'.

1.5   RELEVANCE FOR THE PURPOSES OF TRANSCRIPTION

We have seen that the identification of relevant features is an indispensable stage of ethnomusicological research. But the principle of relevance has a wider use. It should not be limited to the observation of music and recording of data. It should also apply in the matter of transcription. Several scholars have already noted this. Thus, according to Nettl, 'Transcribing involves consideration of what is significant and what is incidental in a music (1964: 101). He also believes that 'It should be possible to move from transcription of all musical phenomena perceived by the transcriber to another transcription which gives only the essentials' (1964: 104).

In a subsequent publication, Nettl indicates what makes transcription and analysis inseparable: 'Transcription and analysis should go together, since the identification of relevant features is already a decisive stage in the definition and description of a musical style' (1971: 63).

The main obstacle to the analysis of African music is its rhythmic complexity. It is therefore not surprising that numerous scholars have wrestled with the problem of how such rhythms should be noted. For example, the Ghanaian ethnomusicologist Nketia writes: 'The African approach to rhythm raises important problems of notation, in particular the use and interpretation of bar lines, time signatures and ties, and the definition of such concepts as accents, time, meter and so forth' (1963: 3). He mentions that different opinions have been expressed on this subject, and adds that, in the analysis, 'Much has depended on the transcriber's understanding of African rhythm and his ability to feel or perceive this rhythm in movement' (ibid.).

Jones (1937: 297) was the first to make the important observation that the rhythmic transcription of an African song will only be accurate if it matches the handclaps which materialise the underlying beat. Much later (1959: 1, 38), he states that it is practically impossible to transcribe irregular durations accurately without a temporal reference: 'There *must* be a *regular* counter-rhythm against which to measure them.' He then adds: 'This counter-rhythm must be supplied by the African.'

It should thus be clear that, if the investigator is not careful to compare rhythmic events with their temporal reference, or 'counter-rhythm', he will almost invariable come out with a transcription which is not relevant. This is the case with the transcriptions by Rose Brandel, Yvette Grimaud, L.S. Strasbaugh, and others.

There are, however, other investigators who have recognised this side of the problem, as a glance at their transcriptions will suffice to prove. Zygmunt Estreicher, like Dauer, is one of these, though his considerations extend beyond the dimension of transcription alone. He raises (1957: 91–2) the much broader question of whether the Western system of notation is suited to traditional music:

The inadequacies of musical notation are often cited in conjunction with proposals to make it more accurate. Let us merely make mention of the counterstatement that musical notation is often too accurate to express an imprecise auditive impression. . . In the score, however, a note must be located in a precise position and express a precise duration. We then find ourselves in the same situation as a draughtsman who is called upon to make an exact drawing of an object which he only knows from a blurred photograph.

As technology has progressed in the field of physical measuring instruments, some musicologists have justifiably hoped to solve this problem by using such devices. Lajtha was among those advocating this approach:

We should have pitch-measuring machines built especially for folk music so that we can deter-mine tone by a physical procedure. The recording of a folk tune would thus yield a graphic image something like a seismogram, and provide precise indications regarding the pitch and duration of tone, and thereby, rhythm.   (1956: 147)

Lajtha was, however, aware that a device of this kind entailed the risk of introducing irrelevant information into the transcription, and therefore went on to say:

But as long as folk songs are noted normally, every effort must be made to avoid overloading the already extremely complicated image of contemporary, scientifically exact notations with superfluous signs.

He then illustrates his remark with a reference to the techniques developed by his famous fellow countryman, Béla Bartók, whose extremely scrupulous notation of folk songs recorded even the slightest fluctuations in pitch.

Béla Bartók frequently used the sign 'b/2' to indicate that a tone in a melody with tonic G was between B and B flat. This would lead us to believe that our peasant lad or girl was capable of exactly dividing the interval between B and B flat. But when the notation was rechecked, it turned out that the pitch of the b/2 tone was never the same in any of the airs. Some of them were closer to B and others to B flat.

This means that the use of an additional sign here has not resulted in a more precise knowledge of the system. In other words, with all due respect for the accuracy of Bartók's work, this sign is not relevant.

The well-founded criticism of excessive accuracy in notation naturally leads to doubts about the systematic use of electroacoustic machines. No matter how precise their readings may be, they cannot, or at least not yet, be treated as relevant. Brăiloiu (1949: 316–7) writes of this shortcoming: 'The thoroughness required in the examination of acoustic data cannot come from machines alone. Records, films, oscillographs, potentiometers, or whatever, all require the assistance of intelligence' (1949: 316–17). By *intelligence* Brăiloiu means the faculty of judgement. Having said this, he wonders, 'Will the accuracy a graph of this kind is likely to have make up for the major drawback of driving all those who have good reason to treat this device as no more than an auxiliary (perhaps a valuable and even an indispensable one, but still an auxiliary) away from a science whose object remains, in spite of all, an art?'

The mere fact of raising this question shows how sceptical Brăiloiu was of the validity of transcription methods which make exclusive use of physical measuring instruments. He feels there is no reason to note slight fluctuations in pitch unless they, like the other parameters of musical reality, can be shown to occur systematically:

The mathematical measurement of pitch is only worthwhile when deviations are themselves part of a system; in such case, there is nothing to prevent thorough checking by the use of graphs or any other means. But if they are haphazard and unstable, it will be wise to recall that cultured performers, both singers and instrumentalists, make frequent use of floating intonation for expressive purposes.

This is particularly the case in cultured Western vocal music, where expressive intonation is not codified as it is in some Asian traditions. Its nature and frequency are closely dependent on how the work is composed and on the style of the period; but regardless of the style, it always depends solely on individual choice and the personal preferences of the performer. It would, for example, be quite instructive in this regard to see what conclusions concerning scales could be drawn from a graphic representation of a Schubert *Lied* sung by any of the great contemporary singers.

Extreme caution must therefore be exercised in this matter. Hood (1963: 191) stresses this. While admitting that physical laboratory measurements are often indispensable for improved understanding of some musical phenomena, he sustains that what is musically meaningful is ultimately dependent on strictly musical considerations.

List also supports this idea when he says. 'The hand notation is a product of the human mind which attempts to synthetize the data heard and to offer an intelligible description of the whole in symbolic guise' (1974: 371). That is why he believes it should take precedence over electronic equipment, which is incapable of making judgements.

Nettl made this same point ten years earlier, noting that electronic instruments are not selective: 'They record everything regardless of its importance, and selection of the essentials must be made later by the scholar' (1964: 102).

Over the last few years, attempts have been made at transcription using the latest of physical instruments, the computer. Even with such highly sophisticated equipment, the automatic transcriptions obtained are subject to question.

A computer must obviously be properly programmed to process the data and recognise characteristic features. But does not writing a programme involve prejudging what is characteristic on the basis of the relevant features thrown up by prior analysis? We thus support List's conclusions to a study comparing transcriptions made by ear with others made by a machine. His experiment taught him that, with respect to the musical parameters of pitch and duration which he considered. 'The capability of the unaided human ear should not be underestimated. The evidence indicates that transcriptions made by ear in notated form are sufficiently accurate, sufficiently reliable to provide a valid basis for analysis and comparative studies' (1974: 376).

We should also note that this debate refers only to the transcription of monody. Despite some attempts (at the University of Uppsala in Sweden, for example), no device has, to our knowledge, yet been able to furnish even partially satisfactory results for polyphonic music. In this domain, the ear remains our only recourse for the time being.

In view of the obvious limitations to graphic representations, we should make it clear that, when we transcribe a musical event, we are not 'photographing' it. What we are doing is revealing its relevant features, and exposing the characteristic elements which allow it to be identified. In this view, a transcription is to a recording as a drawing is to a photograph: it is a representation containing nothing but the essential. Experience shows that it is much easier to get a clear idea of the shape and outline of an object from a drawing than from a photograph. That is probably why, even nowadays, most technical works are still illustrated by drawings rather than photographs. A drawing retains the set of the object's relevant features and only these.

2   Description and analysis

2.1   INTRODUCTION

In the preceding chapters, we have insisted on the fact that the music we are considering here is always based on a system or *code*. We should, of course, recall that 'a code has two essential parts: a set of elements and a set of rules defining how these elements must operate and combine' (Ruwet 1966, 1972: 102). It is therefore obvious that a code implies a theory, and we have already indicated several times that the theory is *implicit* rather than explicit in traditional African music. All the investigator will encounter there at first are sets of elements, messages.

His description can thus only start from sets of messages, each characterised by a cluster of relevant features which distinguish it from the others in the same cultural setting. Let us also recall that, in Central Africa, these sets are generally musical categories or special repertories defined by a social function, a particular vernacular name, a certain vocal and/or instrumental ensemble, and very often, a characteristic rhythmic formula.

The first step of a description is to pick out what distinguishes each set of messages from all the others, to determine what characterises it, and discover its relevant features. The way the elements comprising each of the pieces in the set are organised must also be determined: in their syntactic aspect, the individual parts in polyphony, and in the aspect of musical simultaneity, the poly-phonic and poly-rhythmic combinations. At the next lower level, the description should provide a characterisation of each operational unit in each part in a given piece, i.e., it should define the smallest formally relevant elements, or 'morphemes'. This stage of the description proceeds from the whole to its parts and is strictly analytic. The investigator must try to establish the *model* underlying each part in each piece in his set. This will enable him to work out the overall model of simultaneity which reflects the coherence of the entire polyphonic piece in terms of a set of coherent parts.

The second step of the description consists of reconstructing a simulation of each piece in the set, by engendering an *artifact* from the models obtained. If these imitations have exactly the same features as the ones defined during the first stage of the description, and if the users are willing to allow them to be included in the set of messages which provided the starting point for the operation of modelisation, the description may reasonably be accounted correct.

This method, which is taxonomic in its first stage and generative in its second, is designed to guarantee that what is essential in a piece, i.e., its structure, will be revealed.

A few clarifying remarks are required on the purely formal approach developed in this method of analysis.

Molino writes of the set of symbolic processes requiring a network of interaction among individuals that 'language, music, or religion, all require a threefold analysis of their existence, without which no exact knowledge is possible' (1975: 47). Any object of the social sciences 'is inseparable from the processes of both production and reception, which are as essential to its definition as the properties which define it as an abstract object, unlike the situation in the physical sciences'. The central element in this triple analysis is obviously the nature of the object itself; this is flanked by production and reception. The object is organised matter. There is a dimension of symbolic analysis for each of its three modes of existence: poietic analysis, aesthesic analysis, and 'neutral' analysis'.

The approach we have described above falls mainly into the last of these three dimensions. We have intentionally concentrated on the material or 'neutral' analysis of Central African polyphony. While Molino's division can be profitably applied to cultured Western music, it will not always work well in the case of music from an oral tradition. No overall analysis of the processes of production is indeed possible in a traditional African society, where music is a collective and anonymous phenomenon. And we have no historical information whatsoever on how this music was contrived and developed.

Though we must abstain from such an analysis, our approach will necessarily involve the processes of production to some extent. In music of this kind, where variation is so prevalent, it is hard to dissociate performance from production; they imply each other to a considerable degree.

The same is true of aesthesic analysis on the other end of the spectrum. Traditional

Central African music is for the internal use of the community. It may even be restricted to the musicians who perform it. This is the case, for example, with Banda horn music which is performed at the initiation camp and is not intended for an audience.

An aesthesic study of a musical language would furthermore require a study of the users' psycho-physiological modes of reception. It would, for example, be fascinating if we could analyse the physiological effects (trances or crises of possession) on listeners to some forms of African ritual music. Currently, however, the psychology of musical perception does not, to our knowledge, have any means of carrying out such a study, even in the field of Western cultured or folk music. There is still no reliable method of apprehending the diversity of perceptions, images, and thoughts provoked by listening to music. We know, for example, that the same work can have a different 'meaning' for each of a thousand people in a concert hall. There is thus even less chance of proving any well-founded hypothesis concerning musical perception among groups or people whose way of life and symbolic representations are so different from our own.

The musical material itself, its organisation and structures, are thus our only handle on the real world, and provide the only ground solid enough for descriptive investigation to proceed upon. As we have already shown (see section 1.4 above), this should not be taken to mean that the search for relevant features takes no account of extramusical data. We will, however, deliberately avoid placing the aspects of production and reception in the forefront. We will limit ourselves to formal musical analysis, based on the strictest possible principles of segmentation.

2.2 DEFINING THE PROBLEM

The aim of description and analysis is to characterise a musical tradition, a repertory, or a given piece. We use 'characterise' to mean the act of defining the individuality of the object under study, i.e., its identity and distinctive properties with respect to other traditions, other repertories, or other pieces.

We can carry out this characterisation in several ways. No aspect should automatically be excluded from the description. It should, on the contrary, contain whatever apparently relevant properties analysis may bring to light, as all of them will be needed to explain the intrinsic workings of a musical tradition, repertory, or piece.

When we speak of 'intrinsic workings', we mean *the kinds of relations which exist among the various parts of the musical material*. To describe these, we must observe their temporal progression in the case of monodies, and also their combinations, in the case of polyphony. As Gardin (1974: 22) says, we require an explanation which should 'start by *showing how things differ among themselves*'. But, he asks, 'Differ in what respects?'

Let us take the example of literature. A scholar studies a text. He knows something individuates it, but is as yet unable to say precisely what it is. He must, however, characterise his text with respect to others which are outside his study but nevertheless related. If he tries to list every feature of his text,

his list will, properly speaking, be infinite, since the commentator is free to define the universe of texts contrasting with his own in any way he likes, in relation to that which he perceives as its individuality.

We need some idea of the universe in question; otherwise we will already find ourselves unable to judge the 'relevance' of our analysis at this early stage.   (ibid.: 22)

We lack certain references in the field of traditional African music: we have no historical data on how this music came into being, and are almost completely ignorant of how it is perceived by the users and how it fits in with other features of the mental life of groups or individuals. It follows that a method of characterising a musical tradition, repertory, or piece should not require the investigator to have prior knowledge of the empirically constituted 'universe' within which he defines his contrasts.

We must now state how such a characterisation can be obtained. Since we are dealing with *oral musical texts*, our analytical tools should be comparable to the ones the linguist uses to analyse texts.

Gardin (1974: 19) says, 'A method of textual analysis is the expression of a theory.' But a theory is valid only if we can 'make predictions from it, and submit them to empirical tests proving that the theory (or method) gives us a grasp on the objects it deals with'. To have a proper 'grasp' on our own subject, we must remain mainly within the domain of the musical material itself. That is where our analytical method can work with the least 'theoretical insecurity'.

The Western investigator faced with traditional extra-European music is, indeed, in a very peculiar situation, which Molino (1975: 51–2) analyses as follows:

In Europe at the beginning of the twentieth century, music was thought to be both a rational and a natural system. It had a twofold existence, both as music one could hear, and as written music in the form of a score. It consisted of a set of conditions: technical (the instrumentation), social (the concert), and psychological (musical expectations, which P. Schaeffer calls 'listening intentions'). The proper approach to the study of musical data was thus to start from these conditions and to explain any music whatsoever by reducing it to them. That is why, even when musical analysis approached logical coherence, it remained an offshoot of a musical system which it could not conceive of bringing into question.

Given these facts, 'classical' methods of analysis,

which were worked out in parallel with the development of the Western system,. . . effectively explain works based on this system, but founder when dealing with works from outside. This is particularly the case with music from oral traditions. . . which poses a preliminary problem of notation, a problem which has already been solved by definition in the Western system. Furthermore, classical analysis rests on an immediate familiarity with the tonal system, enabling numerous factors to be taken for granted and left in the dark. Since composers and analysts have in common their command of the system, there is no need to make every step explicit; in fact, analysis is a stage or part of a composer's or performer's apprenticeship. The principles of analysis are not much different from the rules for production of a work if indeed they can be distinguished at all. This is clearly no longer the case with music from an oral tradition: the analyst finds the system he wants to describe is foreign, and faces problems similar to those encountered by the field linguist.

The ethnomusicologist has no prior knowledge of the system he intends to study, or of its underlying code. Unlike the musicologist analysing a message in a code he knows, he must work out a method which can take him from a description of the message to the discovery of the code. This is, as Ruwet (1966, 1972: 100) notes, an analytical procedure:

It will, in principle, be required whenever we are dealing with an unknown language, a myth or music of exotic origin, and so forth, and are given only the message. The analyst's task is then to take the corpus (i.e., the set of messages) apart and manipulate it in different ways until he can establish the units, classes of units, and rules of combination which make up the code.

This process must obviously take in the entire set of levels of characterisation or description which comprise the organisation of the musical material. Thus, 'analysis takes the form of division into ever smaller parts defined by their reciprocal relations, until it comes out with the ultimate indivisible elements' (Ruwet 1966, 1972: 103).

We may, however, remark that we are not always required to reach these 'ultimate indivisible elements'. There are times when we are forced to stop at a much earlier stage. When segmentation is carried beyond a certain limit, it may no longer have meaning for the participants in the musical tradition under study, and thus lose its relevance.

Unlike conventional musicological analyses which make use of many factors without always having to make them explicit, ethnomusicological analyses must follow explicit procedures which can be repeated and will allow the elements in the corpus to be reproduced. Only when he has reached this point can the investigator be sure that he has developed a suitable characterisation of his corpus.

2.3 SEGMENTATION PROCEDURES

We have already remarked that, insofar as music has no semantic depth, it is considerably different from language. In Jakobson's words, 'instead of aiming at some extrinsic object, music appears to be *a language which signifies itself* (*un langage qui se signifie soi-même*)' (1971: 704). The "meaning" of music can only be perceived through its form, i.e., some predefined object. This is the essential feature of all musical discourse.

The distinction between form and substance makes it easier to understand the difference between language and music. If, as Saussure (1916, 1971: 169) says, '*language is a form, and not a substance*', music is a both form *and* a substance, precisely because it has no semantic depth. Neither can exist without the other. Its form can only be defined by its substance, and vice versa.

2.3.1 The principle of repetition

We must now define how a form can be 'segmented'. In the case of music, this operation will be based on its substance, whose parts must be examined to find out which ones are alike or identical, and which are entirely different. This procedure again presupposes a prior definition of what should be considered identical from a *cultural* viewpoint.

Two elements in any mode of expression which naturally involves a succession of events can appear to be identical only if they are repeated. The first criterion of identification will thus be the *principle of repetition*. The flow of music is organised in ways similar to language, particularly poetic language, as Jakobson says: 'Only in poetry with its regular reiteration of equivalent units is the time of the speech flow experienced, as it is – to cite another semiotic pattern – with musical time (1960: 358).

As Ruwet has also noted, 'musical syntax is a syntax of equivalences: its units are related by a full range of equivalence relations' (1966, 1972: 134).

For Jakobson, the 'poetic function' takes the form of a projection of associative phenomena selected on the vertical axis of equivalences (the *paradigmatic* axis) onto the horizontal axis of speech (the *syntagmatic* axis):

The selection is produced on the base of equivalence, similarity and dissimilarity, synonymity and antonymity, while the combination, the build up of the sequence, is based on contiguity. *The poetic function projects the principle of equivalence from the axis of selection into the axis of combination.* Equivalence is promoted to the constitutive device of the sequence. In poetry one syllable is equalized with any other syllable of the same sequence; word stress is assumed to equal word stress, as unstress equals unstress; prosodic long is matched with long, and short with short. . . Syllables are converted into units of measure, and so are morae or stresses.

(1960: 358)

The preceding text is now classic and is frequently quoted. It is, however, rather surprising that another equally important text has apparently been ignored by musicologists, although the very title of the work in which it appears might have awakened their curiosity. It is Bachelard's *Dialectique de la durée*.

Bachelard examines the question of the organisation of musical time from the standpoint of the psychology of perception in nontechnical language. In the incisive passage quoted below (Bachelard 1950, 1963: 114–5), he extends his essentially philosophical approach to a discussion of *repetition*. There are several valuable intuitions to be gathered: first of all, he remarks that we can recognise a melody before we know what it is. He also says that only repetition gives a rhythmic figure its meaning; without it, the as yet unformed temporal structure remains in the realm of the *possible*, disconnected and unmotivated, i.e., without *relevance*. He then shows how the *symmetries characteristic of music and poetry are established*:

The continuity of a melody must be *learned*. It cannot be *heard* at first try. Awareness of musical continuity comes through recognition of a theme. Here as elsewhere, recognition precedes cognition. Lionel Landry has rightly remarked, 'A rhythmic figure cannot have its full qualitative value for someone who has only heard it once'. At the first encounter, the first time the sounds unfold, the temporal structure is not properly *formed*. Musical causality is not yet established. Structure and causality are posited in the realm of the possible rather than in the real. The whole is as yet disconnected and unmotivated. The recurrence of the impression is what provides formal causality. For the metaphysician, this formal causality is the counterpart of Landry's *qualitative value*.

This *reformation* is truely form-giving. It can bring poetical and musical symmetries into being from dissymmetric subordinate form. Raoul de la Grasserie shows this when he says, 'Let us suppose two hemistichs have an unequal number of syllables in two successive verses. If the inequality appears in the second verse in the same form, the same rhythmic pattern recurs, and *internal inequality* becomes *external equality*'. In other words, the identity of the complex entity transcends the diversity of individual detail. Continuity is created by grouping. Poetry or, more generally, melody is thus able to *last* because it regularly *starts again*. Melody plays a dialectical game with itself: it gets lost only to find itself again. It knows it will be absorbed into its initial theme. It thus gives us, not a real duration, but the illusion of a duration. In some respects, melody is temporal perfidy. It promises us a future, but then confirms us in a certain state. By bringing us back to its beginning, it gives us the impression that we should have foreseen its course. Properly speaking, however, it has no source or centre of expansion. Its beginning, which we identify through recurrence, is, like its continuity, a value created by composition.

All cultured Western music is based on the reiteration of similar elements. There are countless examples, from medieval isorhythm to the post-Romantic *Leitmotiv*. Let us mention only three of these. First, the theme of a sonata: whether the theme is repeated in identical form or is modified in the course of the movement, the listener can identify it as being *the very same theme* on each occasion; it may have been enlarged, developed, or even metamorphosed, but is nevertheless immediately recognisable. Next, on a wider scale, the *da capo* form, which, as its name indicates, is based on the principle of repetition of larger units. And finally, a specific example, the first movement of Beethoven's Fifth Symphony, which is built upon the almost uninterrupted repetition of a single rhythmic figure, stated by the full orchestra at the very beginning of the work.

If we write musical figures (whether melodic themes or rhythmic cells) and their repetitions on a vertical (or paradigmatic) axis, we will be able to visualise (rather than simply hear) how each one resembles its subsequent restatements.

In the field of ethnomusicology, Gilbert Rouget was the first to provide a theoretical foundation for using the principle of repetition to delimit musical units. In a discussion of the transcription and analysis of ritual songs from Dahomey, he writes:

There are a variety of approaches to a given type of music. I feel that, for each type of analysis envisaged, there should be a specific transcription technique which picks out the desired features and leaves the others aside. Dividing music into a sequence of units designated by framed letters has nothing to do with melodic analysis.

In each of these pieces, some fragments are repeated and others are not. My segmentation is based on the presence or absence of repetition. *When a sequence of sounds is stated twice or more, with or without variations, it may be treated as a unit* [italics added]. Correlatively, any sequence of sounds stated only once, however long it may be and however many apparent junctures (particularly rests) it may contain, must also be treated as a single unit.

(Rouget 1961: 10)

While Rouget was the first to make the criterion of repetition *explicit*, it had already been applied in practice as early as 1931 by Constantin Brăiloiu. Brăiloiu presents a transcription of a Romanian dirge in the form of a paradigmatic table, in the following terms:

It is well known that a folk melody is almost always a short period which the performer repeats as often as necessary to reach the end of his text. But each time, he makes more or less perceptible changes in the rhythm, melodic line, or even the overall structure, which may be called variations. The study of such variations is still in its beginnings, but is perhaps the most difficult, and certainly the most important problem in folk music. We are here approaching the very sources of folk creativity. . .

The melody is composed of three phrases and was sung ten times in all. It is written in full on the first staff. When there was no change in the melodic line, only the text of the repetitions has been transcribed, with each syllable exactly below its corresponding note. Where changes appear, the variations are noted beneath the original melodic formula. Rhythmic variations are indicated in their proper place by signs of duration alone. The way the *Variationstrieb*, or urge to vary, works can be discerned at a glance. The parts of the melody it attacks preferentially (the dark spaces), and those it avoids (the blanks), are immediately visible.   (1931: 22–4)

2.3.2   The principle of commutation

Given the principle of repetition, our next task is to carry out a segmentation and systematically group similar events together. Ruwet (1966, 1972: 112) speaks metaphorically of a 'machine for locating the elementary identities' which goes over the musical text and 'picks out the identical fragments'. These are then placed one above the other in columns on paradigmatic axes. As Lévi-Strauss (1964: 39) perceptively puts it, these columns represent 'large clusters of relationships which we indistinctly perceive to have something in common'.

This is how we start picking out units at the most general level. At this stage, the way in which the sequences are conjoined is of little importance. The essential thing for the time being is to recognise similar elements.

The next step is to examine these 'clusters of relations' individually and determine whether the elements they contain elicit a *cultural judgement of identity*. If the elements in a 'block' of this kind have the same value from the cultural standpoint, i.e., if they are *equivalent*, they may be considered *identical* by virtue of the principle of relevance. If identical, they are interchangeable, in which case we say that the terms of the given paradigm can *commute*. By commutation, we mean both *the operation consisting of the substitution of the terms in a given paradigm one for another, and the principle making this operation possible*.

Ruwet (1966, 1972) bases the segmentation procedure on two criteria which he calls *repetition* and *transformation*. While we have no hesitation in adopting the first of these criteria, we will carefully avoid making use of the second. Even more important than the close association of this term with a particular school of linguistic thought, is the fact that there is no limit to transformation. A motif or theme can be transformed until it is no longer identifiable. But the members of a paradigm have precisely the common property of being *variations* on an (often implicit) underlying model.

In any piece of Central African music, each musician's margin of variation depends directly on what possibilities of commutation the structure of the piece allows, for two elements can only commute if they belong to the same axis of equivalence or paradigm. Such music is thus divided up into classes of interchangeable elements. Each of these is part of a larger entity composed of several juxtaposed classes. The whole constitutes the period, which defines the structure of the piece. It is a temporal sequence of a given number of elements, each of which is taken from one of the classes. Clearly, then, each class is characterised by the position it occupies within this temporal structure. Commutation can take place at each position, with one element replacing another. This is why a piece of traditional music is practically never performed twice in a fully identical way.

This is true of monody and even more so of polyphony. The latter, however, is much harder to analyse because several melodic or rhythmic lines are flowing simultaneously. A variation in any of the parts, however small, will thus produce a change in the acoustic aggregate. It is easy to see that a theoretical construct accounting for all the variations in a single performance would need to manipulate a huge number of facts. From our own standpoint of *cultural relevance*, however, these minor variations are no more meaningful in a polyphonic piece than they are in monody. On the contrary, the more parts there are, the less perceptible these small variations naturally become. At each moment in the production of the period or musical phrase, the Central African musician instinctively chooses the most suitable element from a paradigm or relevant stock. The elements of a given class are not interchangeable with those of any other; there is no permutation, only *commutation*.

Each set of interchangeable elements thus constitutes an equivalence class, a formal class, or in linguistic terms, a 'distributional class'. Precisely because there is a *distribution* within a statement, a period, or a musical phrase, there can be no permutation. Each element comprising the statement, period, or phrase can only appear in one position.

It will be noticed that the members of a paradigm must be both similar and dissimilar. They all have at least one common and one varying feature. The latter is what makes it possible to distinguish among them. The position occupied by this differential feature in the paradigm constitutes a 'substitution point'. From the preceding definition, it is evident that each substitution point corresponds to a distributional class.

These notions were incorporated by Kenneth L. Pike into his theory of *tagmemics*. Though the term is rather abstruse, the content aptly applies to the musical reality we are dealing with. Pike believes that the basic feature of a grammatical constituent is neither its form nor its internal structure, but the *position* it can occupy in a higher-level construction, this position generally being associated with a specific *function*. Consequently, 'a grammatical dichotomy into morphology and syntax is not as crucial or basic to linguistic structure as a division into (a) patterns, (b) points in patterns, and (c) lists of potential replacement elements at those points' (Pike 1949: 124, quoted by Roulet 1974: 54–5). This division corresponds exactly to the nature of Central African music. If we take the structure of each piece as a *construction*, each paradigm in it represents one of the *points in the construction*, and the sets of members of each paradigm are the *lists of elements which can be substituted for each other at those points*.

Pike's threefold division does not make explicit use of the idea of 'equivalence classes'; it is obvious, however, that it takes over the content of this notion. By definition, the elements located at the same substitution point constitute an equivalence class; conversely, all the elements belonging to an equivalence class can be substituted for one another.

Granger (1967: 111) gives the following philosophical definition of the concept of 'equivalence': 'The relation of *equivalence* defines a subclass of undifferentiated objects within a set which satisfy the intuitive notion "qualitatively identical"'. By the principle of relevance, the expression 'qualitatively identical' should here be replaced by '*culturally* identical'. Granger goes on, 'This relation is naturally likely to be determined by purely formal properties.' This is precisely the case with music, whose units, as we have seen, can only be defined on the basis of a formal comparison.

The scope of Pike's theory extends far beyond the domain of linguistics, and his method can be applied in many other fields. Pike himself wanted to expand it into a generalised theory of human behaviour. As Roulet (1974: 24) says, he shows that 'every human activity can be analysed in the same way into a given number of substitution points, each of which is characterised by a given function and occupied by a given class of elements'. The same type of analysis can thus easily be applied to a piece of music, or to a musical repertory; for at the next higher level, each piece appears as a commutable element belonging to the equivalence class consisting of the set of pieces in the repertory.

Pike's notion of 'function' applies, in the field of African music, to a complex of social and musical factors. For example, as we have seen, the songs and dances in use among a given population fall into categories determined by both a specific set of circumstances and a particular rhythmic formula.

Bloomfield (1933: 185, quoted by Roulet 1974: 56), whose linguistic theory prefigured Pike's, describes the formal relation between the notions of *position* and *function* as follows: 'The positions in which a form can appear are its *functions* or, collectively, its *function*. All the forms which can fill a given position thereby constitute a *form-class*.' The boundaries of our approach are now clear: since there is no way of reaching the *signifié* of music, our analyses must be founded primarily on formal criteria.

2.3.3   The definition of units

What then is a unit? Let us say that all the elements in a paradigm, i.e., which can be substituted for one another, constitute a unit. In other words, any formal class, defined at whatever level on the basis of a cultural judgement of equivalence, is a unit.

We must now establish a hierarchical ordering of levels. Let us recall that, according to Pike, a construction, the points in this construction, and the elements which can appear at these points are all units. At the next higher level, each construction becomes in turn a substitution point in a larger unit defined in the same way. This sort of 'bottom up' analysis involving a progressive enlargement of the field of observation can be repeated as often as the datum and the context require. If however we proceed from top to bottom, we first define the units at the highest level (I) and then repeat the segmentation operation to determine the units at level II, and so forth, 'until we reach the units which are identical with the elementary ones' (Ruwet 1966, 1972: 155).

In Central African music, we will treat the last point of substitution recognised as such by the users as an elementary unit. It will thus constitute the *smallest relevant unit*. If we try to segment this unit into subclasses, we will find that commutation will invariably be meaningless, for the equivalence classes which occupy the substitution points are defined precisely on the basis of the principle of cultural relevance. Once the segmentation procedure has reached the smallest relevant units, we must accept that it can take us no further. This is therefore the end of the analysis. We will not pursue it beyond what the traditional observers themselves consider to be relevant. We will, in other words, not go beyond this threshold in delimiting units, and will describe neither sequences of individual notes nor occurrences of intervals. We will restrict ourselves at all times to the *smallest relevant units*.

In the field of vocal music, there is, if need be, an additional justification for this position: namely, the restrictions which tone languages impose on melodic profiles. When a singer varies or improvises the words to a song, the melody *must* adapt itself to the tone patterns of the language. Calculations and statistics on the occurrence or frequency of this or that interval are consequently purposeless, and give unjustified musicological import to a phenomenon whose relevance lies essentially in the field of linguistics.

Blacking showed he was aware of this when he remarked with regard to the words of children's songs that 'The sequence of descending or ascending intervals is considered more important than their exact pitch, because in certain parts of a melody they are expected to reflect changes in speech-tone' (1971: 99).

This does not, however, mean that our analyses will systematically ignore the intervals in the songs we study. It merely implies that the scales they use and the relevance of their constituent degrees must be clearly defined. The important factor here is not the direction of the intervals but their order of magnitude. One population may well prefer to proceed by conjoint intervals in its songs, and another by disjoint intervals; this is a true differential feature which can help to characterise a style of vocal music. But counting intervals and calculating their frequency of recurrence is not relevant to the kind of analysis we are proposing.

A single note is thus even less apt to be treated as a basic unit. Molino rightly considers the individual note to be

an 'amalgamation' of heterogeneous characterisations: it serves to indicate absolute pitch, virtual intervals, virtual degrees and functions, and rhythm-bearing durations, all at the same time.

That is why the individual note can never be taken as a unit in itself: its primary properties (intervals, degrees and functions, rhythms) remain virtual as long as it is not conjoined to at least one other note.   (1975: 55)

But in the music we are discussing, two or even three notes are generally still not enough to constitute a unit. As Reinhard (1968: 44) correctly notes, the musician in an oral tradition does not perceive a melodic or rhythmic motif as a sequence of isolated sounds, but rather as an indissoluble whole.

Aside from the segmentation procedure described above, there is another way in which the analyst can go about delimiting the units in Central African music; that is by examining their period, or more strictly speaking, the musical duration containing this period. Let us recall that such music is always measured (refer particularly to Book I, 3.3 and 3.4), and always takes the form (though at quite different levels) of a varying ostinato. This means that a cycle will have a specific duration within which a given number of beats can always be counted. The way units are delimited can thus be confirmed by the fact that each repetitive element, whether or not it contains variations, fits into the same time span each time it appears. Any musical construction, and any substitution point in it, can thus be equally well defined as a *temporal matrix*, since its content, however it may be internally distributed, always spans an invariant whole number of isochronous units or beats. The same is true of rhythm. The repetition of a basic rhythmic figure can be confirmed by its periodicity, i.e., by the *invariant* number of beats underlying it. Conversely, as long as the period remains incomplete, the figure is unfinished and cannot be said to exist for the users, they are still unable to identify it. This again sets a lower limit beneath which analysis should not be pursued.

Blacking reports this feature too, in his description of a Venda children's song: 'There is not a rest on the fourth beat but a *total* pattern of four beats which can be repeated any number of times, but never less than once if it is to qualify as "song" and not "speech"' (1971: 98). Blacking thereby indicates that no unit is relevant unless it is heard *in full*. Otherwise, it lies beneath the lowest level of meaning. The construction can only be identified, i.e., *re*cognised, when perceived as a whole (this means, in practice, when another repetition of it has begun).

The basic principle we use to delimit units for our analyses is always the cultural judgement of the user populations. This principle is verified anew every time we return to the field. Verification is, of course, obtained for all material as we collect it, but also (and more importantly) for material collected during previous visits. It thus becomes possible to collate earlier documents, whose relevance has already been determined, with new ones.

2.4   PROVING THE VALIDITY OF ANALYSIS

The purpose of our analysis is to characterise a musical object (piece or repertory) by revealing its distinctive features and thereby stating what individuates it. Once the analysis is complete, the results need to be checked. To do so, we must have the *model* of the object under study, i.e., the pattern underlying each of its realisations, the 'skeleton' consisting of all the relevant features of the object, to which its substance can be reduced.

However schematic the model may be, it should clearly reflect the individuality of the object. If it meets this requirement, it is valid. But to show the analyses themselves to be valid, we must be able to produce new objects from the model, i.e., new realisations which will be, culturally speaking, identical to the original object. Such confirmation is provided by the users of the repertory themselves. If the result is positive, this is proof that the analysis has been correctly carried out from beginning to end.

The deductive phase must thus be followed by an inductive one, i.e., after working from object to model, we must now proceed in the opposite direction, and derive the object from the model to show that the latter has been correctly inferred. As Gardin (1974: 106) says, 'the model should be expressed in a language with signs and a grammar that will enable us to reconstitute, or even reproduce, the object it characterises. . ., i.e., to restore it or relocate it among all the other known (ideal) objects in the field of reference'. If we can produce a model satisfying these conditions, we have the elements of the code.

The model thus stands at the turning point between the processes of analysis and verification. It is the goal of all analytical procedures and the starting point for the process of proving the analysis to be valid. The model is ultimately an all-embracing but simplified representation of the object. It characterises it while condensing it into a representation that reveals its individuality, i.e., the set of its relevant features and only these.

The re-production of a synthetic form of granite which is just as genuine (i.e., endowed with the same properties) as the natural kind, is the only irrefutable proof that the mineralogical model was correct. The re-production of a 'fake' poem *which knowledgeable people say is genuine* [italics added] is the only irrefutable proof that the literary model was right.

(Gardin 1974: 27)

Modelisation has an additional advantage in our own field. When each of the pieces in a repertory has been modelised, and when the principles governing the production of realisations of each piece from its model have been determined, the detailed description of each individual piece becomes superfluous. Knowing the functional principles common to all the pieces in the repertory is in itself sufficient to fill the gap between the model and its potential realisations.

In Book VI, we will return to a detailed discussion of how analyses are substantiated by the procedures of modelisation and production, which have only been treated here from the methodological standpoint.

2.5   CONCLUSION

Analysis and checking procedures are ultimately intended to reveal the *structure* of the music under study. But what precisely is structure? Eco (1972: 322), following Aristotle, describes it as 'at the same time a set, the parts of that set, and the relationships among these parts; . . . structure is a system in which everything is connected, the whole as well as the system of connections'. Every piece of truly polyphonic music, from a Bach fugue to pygmy counterpoint, provides the finest possible illustration of this definition.

Granger, however, gives another one which is more appropriate to our own field:

A structure is an *abstract entity* by means of which a concrete cognitive activity defines a form of *objectivity* at a specific stage of practical action. Looked at in this way, structure is not in things; but it is also not in the mind alone as a model for, or reflection of being. It is the result of a subject working up an experience, and itself helps him accurately to pick the thing out of that experience by investing it with the status of an object.   (1965: 255)

As Caillois says, the possibility of picking an object out in this way is due precisely to the fact that

the relations which bind concrete data together are simpler, more easily intelligible, and more stable than the elements themselves, always so mysterious and impenetrable. . . It is thus a matter of recognising a flexible framework which retains its identity beneath whatever contradictory appearances it may take on. It relies on the unchanging laws of *symmetry* and *substitution* [italics added] to hold together the linkage points and reveal their secret complicity.   (1974: 22)

3   The question of transcription

3.1   THE LIMITS OF WRITTEN NOTATION

The need for transcriptions in the analysis of Central African polyphony has already been made abundantly clear. This should not, however, obscure the many limitations inherent in the notation of orally transmitted music. In fact, we here encounter the infinitely wider problem of reducing any oral expression whatsoever to a written form of symbolisation. 'Writing veils language; it disguises rather than clothes it' (Saussure 1916, 1971: 51–2).

Senghor extols the virtues of the oral transmission of culture in Africa: 'Black Africa has had the good fortune to ignore writing, even when it was not unaware of its existence. . . For writing impoverishes *reality*. It crystallises it into fixed categories and freezes it, when reality is properly *alive*, fluid, and shapeless' (1958, 1964: 238–9).

Whether it be language or music, writing is responsible for *immobilising reality in a univocal way*. Chailley (1967: 118) also stresses the limits to notation, and defines the role of the 'written sign' in music as follows:

Until very recently, it was never expected to represent every detail of music. It was only intended to transmit a fleshless but indispensable skeleton of 'note music'. The recipients were then to make use of their own sensitivity and intelligence to bring it alive again according to their own lights. This is why, from generation to generation, music has always remained a living being, despite being on Paper. The 'written' skeleton has been filled out with one kind of flesh after another, as Man passes on to men the only message in music that counts: the one that sets the limit beyond which machines, even the most wonderful of machines, can no longer rule.

Chailley is here referring to Western composers who start with a mental idea of their works and then commit them to a written notation, from which they can come to life again in performance.

As we have seen, the opposite procedure is followed in ethnomusicology: the investigator starts with a living musical reality produced by traditional performers. Through his notation, he tries to reveal the structural principles on which this reality is based. In this field, even Estreicher (1957: 91), himself a stickler for accuracy in musical transcription, recognises limits to written notation: 'It should never be forgotten that a score is nothing but a projected shadow of the music itself, a flat and colourless silhouette of a living being.'

All these observations lead to the same conclusion: in oral expression is life, of which writing is only a pale reflection.

The transition *from writing to oral expression* involved in an act of interpretation is represented as a 'resurrection' in Western musical practice. The performer brings alive music hitherto frozen in notation. In the transition *from oral expression to writing* involved in an act of transcription, however, the ethnomusicologist performs an 'autopsy' (Arom 1969: 174).

As Seeger (1958: 24–5) has remarked, there are two different ways of conceiving the function of written music. The one used by all cultured Western music is *prescriptive*. The other one, which allows us to show how living music works, is *descriptive*.

3.2   TOWARDS A RELEVANT TRANSCRIPTION

The transcription of music from oral traditions, being *descriptive*, is not, of course, intended for subsequent performance. We would be likely to get only some kind of parody. Its only purpose is precisely to provide a description. This has given rise to the question of whether the transcription should contain every possible acoustic detail of the performance, or should be restricted to meaningful elements. In other words, should it be a kind of photograph reflecting the acoustic reality as accurately as possible, or should it be like a sketch containing only the relevant features? We, of course, favour the latter alternative.

Obtaining 'sketches' of this kind requires prior knowledge of the principles underlying the organisation of the music under study. Such knowledge is the result of long experience and constant checking of the investigator's intuitions and hypotheses against the musicians' practice.

All aspects of acoustic reality cannot, of course, be transcribed. There are certain parameters which are essentially impossible to reduce to written form. This is true, for example, of tone colour. A score marked for 'oboe' or 'horn' indicates the notes each instrument is to play, but leaves it to the reader's memory and imagination to restore the missing dimension suggested by the mere names of the instruments, each with its own characteristic timbre. *Western scores restrict themselves to essentials.* Likewise, the scores in this study will only represent the parameters which are necessary and sufficient for the description of Central African polyphony. These are: *pitch*, *duration*, and *period*. With these alone, we consider ourselves able to give a satisfactory picture of the structural principles of this music.

To write *pitch*, we must first determine the scales being used. All the music we will be dealing with here uses *anhemitonic* pentatonic scales in which the smallest interval is a full tone. That is why we will pay no attention to the inevitable tiny deviations of intonation from this norm. Only the notes comprising the scale will be used in the transcription.

This decision is imposed upon us by the principle of relevance. If, for example, in four-part polyphony, we hear a major seventh (which is excluded by definition from an anhemitonic scale) in one part, while the other three sing an octave interval in the same sequence, it is obvious that the latter is the one the singer *intended*, and that its second note has involuntarily come out too low. To respect the scalar system, the note the musician intended to sing should therefore be noted, instead of the one physically emitted.

Three criteria must be considered in the transcription of *durations*:

(1)   the period and its relationship to the beats
(2)   the way the beats are subdivided
(3)   the actual durations.

Let us examine each of these in turn.

We should first recall that Central African music is cyclic or repetitive. Each piece therefore has a period. As we have already seen, this is confirmed by its invariant number of beats: a period can be determined by reference to the musical material it contains, which always spans a given number of beats.

The second criterion refers to whether the beats are divided into binary or ternary values, according to the number of *minimal metric units* they contain.

The third and last involves the notation of durations, for which greater strictness is required. A smaller margin of tolerance must be allowed than in the case of pitch, because we have no norm or *scale* of durations comparable to a pitch scale. In the absence of any standard, the durations should be noted exactly as they appear in the performance. It should be remarked that, while relevance does not appear at this level, it nevertheless determines the relationship between the express durations and the internal organisation of the beats, and the way they are distributed within the period. By noting durations exactly as they are physically realised, we do not reject the idea of a system, since the division of the beats into binary or ternary elements is itself subject to the principle of relevance.

We have made the deliberate choice of using transcriptions made by ear to reduce complex musical phenomena to their cultural reality. It might be asked why we have not used the electroacoustic equipment mentioned in some works on ethnomusicology (in particular, see Nettl 1964: 101-2). The answer is, to avoid collecting data so full of detail as to make it almost impossible to distinguish the essential from the extrinsic. We have already seen that, to interpret the data provided by a machine of this kind, the transcriber will be required to make choices depending not just on his ear but on his judgement as well. But the only basis for judgement is the knowledge the investigator *already has* of the music he wants to transcribe. This brings us back to our starting point, and obviates the need for a machine as intermediary.

We might add that on one occasion we actually attempted to clarify some extremely complex drum patterns by using an electroacoustic device. The results we obtained from the decoded graphs were so irrational, incoherent, and powerless to show the slightest proportional ratio among the durations, that the drummer's formulae resisted any inclusion in periods based on isochronous values. Yet even a novice listening to the recording of the drum accompanied by handclaps showing the beat would quickly conclude to the existence of a temporally structured periodic frame.

Given this outright contradiction between experience and the results furnished by our equipment, we found ourselves forced to retranscribe all the recorded documents, this time by ear. We take this as further proof that such devices, *by their inability to evaluate a margin of tolerance*, are not yet at a stage where they can be useful for the study of traditional music. This observation should surprise no one; the situation is exactly the same in our own cultured music. In performing a symphony, the musicians never play the strictly proportional durations indicated in the score, nor does the conductor act as a metronome. This in no way prevents the listener from perceiving the tempo of the work and the relationships of the durations which divide up the musical substance.

We thus support List's position: 'Since music is man made, what is musically significant must be phenomena which man can hear, not phenomena which he cannot hear' (1963: 196). This is once again justification for the practice of transcribing by ear.

We may end this discussion by noting that the accuracy of laboratory equipment should not be overestimated. List remarks that machines are not always as precise as we might think: 'The ear can make distinctions which cannot be made by the spectograph. The stylus of the melograph does not always react with the speed necessary to exactly mirror the signal received. Electronic devices are in certain directions more limited than the ear' (ibid.: 196).

We have often had occasion to observe the truth of this judgement. Anyone who watches a melograph record a melody can see how often the stylus will hesitate, showing that it follows the music with less accuracy and slower reactions than the human ear.

3.3   Notation

It may reasonably be asked whether it is not improper to notate music so different from our own with the same signs. Experience quickly shows, however, that the parameters we have mentioned as relevant (pitch, duration, period) can easily be expressed by conventional notation.

With respect to pitch, Central African polyphony uses a scale divided into five degrees. Being somewhat simpler than our own, it can be fully captured by this notation. African rhythms, though more complex, are ultimately based on multiples of binary or ternary minimal values. While the distribution of durations in the parts inevitably involves some complications of notation with respect to ordinary usage (particularly the frequent use of ties to express certain values), our conventional signs are still quite capable of accurately representing these durations.

Finally, the Western system has the advantage of being already familiar to the reader and thus requiring no prior training for consultation of our scores. This essentially practical advantage should not be the least of our considerations.

In any case, it is clear that, as Estreicher puts it, 'transcription aims at an unattainable ideal; therefore, no transcription is more than a compromise' (1957: 92). The analyst is thus obliged to 'choose, out of all the possibilities of presenting the same acoustic datum, the one which is conceptually most satisfying', and try 'to provide the fullest and strongest possible support for the reader's intuition and reasoning'.

3.4   DEFINING A *SCORE* OF MUSIC FROM AN ORAL TRADITION

Before we discuss the purpose of scores representing music from an oral tradition, we should briefly recall the general features and function of scores in written traditions.

In the Western world, for example, scores are normative. They are intended to show how music conceived by somebody else should be performed. They must exist prior to performance of a work, and therefore require a suitable system of signs, or code, which is the basis for musical notation. As a coded graphic representation, the score can express all relationships of pitch, duration tempo, and dynamics, and suggest the special colouring of each vocal and instrumental part. It is the means of materialising the message so that the acoustic event of hearing the work can take place.

The ethnomusicologist dealing with music from an oral tradition, however, has nothing but materialised messages (or sets of messages), which he scores in order to reveal their underlying code. A score in this case is a reduction to writing of an acoustic event *which has already occurred*. While the score of a work of cultured music is the link between the abstract thought of the composer and its materialisation, the score of music from an oral tradition is the link between living musical reality and an abstraction of it. In both cases, the score links messages with a code, but in one, its purpose is the reproduction of the message from the code, while in the other, it is the discovery of the code through a study of the message or set of messages; and after the code has been determined, the score remains indispensable for showing the relationships between the code and the multiplicity of messages it is capable of engendering. In cultured Western music, the performance of a work is perceived only in terms of its respect for the score, the definitive textual reference from which no deviation is allowed. In most music from oral traditions, however, there is no definitive text. Two performances of a given piece will differ, often considerably, even though the users treat them as identical. There is a 'text', but not a univocal one.

We may therefore ask what status we should grant to a score of music which, by definition, is not based on an invariant text. A reply to this question requires a discussion of the different types of scores which, we suggest, can be provided for music from oral traditions, and of the uses to which they can be put.

The etic score

This is the most detailed transcription. The transcriber tries to capture everything he hears, i.e., to pick up every perceptible acoustic phenomenon and express it as accurately as he can. In sum, it is a kind of phonetic transcription like the one Bartók used for notating folk songs.

The disadvantage of this method is that it results in heavily overloaded scores requiring numerous diacritics which are hard to read, and worse still, make it impossible to distinguish the elements which are relevant from ones that are not. This defect is particularly serious in the case of polyphonic music. That is why we feel such scores can throw no light on our subject. The time required to draw up such documents furthermore seems out of all proportion with the results that can be obtained from examining them.

This procedure, which has little to contribute to the understanding of the principles at work in the music being transcribed, has therefore been set aside.

The emic score

This is a transcription which makes allowance for the margins of tolerance exercised by the users. The melodic and rhythmic deviations which they consider meaningless are restored to the norm on the basis of a cultural judgement of relevance. This is, in sum, the equivalent of phonemic notation in linguistics.

Several pieces from a single repertory need to be transcribed to obtain a group of messages belonging to one and the same set. Even if the code underlying this set has not yet been fully determined at this point, major steps can be now taken towards discovering it, as compared with the preceding type of transcription.

Writing an emic score is thus an absolutely necessary stage in the process of characterising a musical repertory.

The modelised score

In some cases, further investigation will lead to the moment when the musicians finally materialise their ultimate reference for the construction of messages, i.e., the *model* underlying each of the parts in the polyphonic or polyrhythmic piece under consideration. It then becomes possible to write a score showing this structural reference which is common to *all* its realisations, however many variations they may allow.

Since our main aim is to discover such structural principles, we could make it our only goal to obtain scores of the latter type. The fact that the models they contain may well be the very basis of the transmission of musical knowledge makes them even more essential. It is indeed often the case that children are familiarised with the traditional repertory by the direct acquisition of these highly simplified forms.

We would nevertheless be wrong to content ourselves with writing only modelised scores. As we have seen, one of the main characteristics of oral folk music is its variability. This is particularly true of all Central African music, whether it be monodic or polyphonic, predominantly melodic or predominantly rhythmic.

This intrinsic variability considerably reduces the practical value of the modelised scores alone, since they tell us nothing about the processes by which the models they contain are realised. That is why we feel the best way to show both *how* and *with respect to what* the variations are produced will be to provide a double scoring of each piece whenever possible. On the one hand, there will be a modelised score which will be very short owing to the repetitive nature of the music, and on the other, an emic score showing the different shapes the model can assume when it is realised. This will allow the reader to inspect both the close relationship between model and realisation, and the distance separating them. It is essential to note that, with one exception, all scores of both types in this work have been obtained from recordings made in the field, and that the emic version *as well as* the modelised version have been approved by the users.

In conclusion, we propose the following definitions of the two types of scores we will be using:

- by *emic score*, we understand the reduction to writing of one of the possible realisations of a polyphonic piece of music, in a way that respects the cultural judgement of relevance;
- by *modelised score*, we mean the vertical arrangement of the basic constituent parts in a polyphonic piece; this set, as presented in its barest possible form, constitutes the model for each realisation of the piece, and is identifiable, insofar as it enables the users to distinguish it from any other one.

3.5   DEFINING A *PART* IN ORAL POLYPHONY

We have seen that Central African music is repetitive and periodic. The material contained in each period thus remains *essentially* the same throughout a performance. This allows it to be modelised. We may thus say that a polyphonic or polyrhythmic *part* is any individual realisation (with or without variation) of material contained in the recurrent framework of the period. The ways of linking periods in sequences are in fact only ways of restating the same overall material. We may recall that this material is distributed over a number of substitution points (or paradigms) within the period, so that the elements it contains can commute.

The score showing how the polyphonic parts are conjoined can thus be accompanied by a representation of the principles of internal organisation which characterise each part, in the form of a paradigmatic table. The material *in its modelised form* will generally appear at the top of the table; below will be a vertical column showing a number of possible realisations of each part, all of which are interchangeable, provided their position in the periodic structure remains the same.

This procedure seems simple and expressive enough to show both the resources and the limitations of the principle of variation, and to indicate how commutation and concatenation take place.

It also becomes possible (although this is not our main objective) to engender new versions of polyphonic pieces from the parts transcribed and the models showing how they fit together. It will suffice to arrange the realisations shown in the paradigmatic column for each part in a different order from the one represented in the transcription. There are thus many possible combinations which could give rise to as many emic scores. If any of them were performed, the members of the community which provided the model for it would immediately identify it. We have tried this very experiment many times in order to check the validity of our transcriptions.

This operation is merely an imitation relying on a written score *of what the Central African musicians do themselves when they perform their polyphony* orally.

3.6   CONCLUSION

A double transcription including an emic score and a modelised score is required to explain the structure of an individual piece of music and its materialisation. We have, however, seen that each piece becomes a free variant at the next higher level, i.e., the level of the repertory containing a given set of pieces. That is why the emic scores should be set aside, and reference should be made to the modelised scores alone to obtain a characterisation of this set. A comparison of all the modelised scores will immediately reveal the common features which distinguish them from pieces belonging to other repertories. This will enable us to construct an abstract model characterising this larger set.

Since modelised transcriptions are schematic representations, they constitute a particularly appropriate tool for describing the stylistic features of a repertory or even of the polyphonic music in general of a given population. From this standpoint, a modelised score shows itself to be as far from an emic transcription as the latter is from an etic one. This remark must be qualified in one extremely important way: both kinds of scores we use are relevant, differing only in *level of relevance*, while etic scores by definition never are. By the same principle, the stylistic characterisation of the musical heritage of a given population can in turn be compared with those of other populations. This operation would yield a stylistic description of the music of an entire geocultural area.

Book V

The organisation of time in African music

A brief survey of Western rhythmics

> The beat acts as a signal, not as mere duration. It binds into coincidences, binds rhythms into instants that will stand out.
>
> Bachelard, *La dialectique de la durée*, p. 122

1.1 INTRODUCTION

This Book deals with the temporal structure of African music, particularly African polyphony. All polyphonic music requires a temporal reference unit to provide a common denominator for its parts. We will therefore be discussing *measured* music, i.e., music *comprised of durations with proportional values*.

Let us recall that the distinction between measured and unmeasured music has a long history. It existed in the cultured music of the ancient Greeks, and in medieval musical theory, in the contrast between the *cantus mensuratus* (measured chant) and *cantus planus* (plain chant). Closer to our own times, it can be found in classical opera, where arias or measured pieces alternate with unmeasured *recitativo secco*.

Measured music, sometimes referred to by the Italian expression, *tempo giusto*, is thus defined by contrast with unmeasured music. The latter is not governed by fixed quantities, i.e., the values of durations are not strictly proportional. In unmeasured music, a note is only meaningful in its position with respect to preceding and following notes, i.e., in a melodic pattern. In measured music, however, all durations are strictly proportional.

According to Rousseau's (1768: 283) dictionary, the term *measured* 'corresponds to the Italian *a tempo* or *a batuta*'. Proportional durations must be based on a reference unit. Different epochs and civilisations have had different ideas of such a unit. Ancient Greek music was based on a *chronos prōtos*, the smallest indivisible unit of duration, whose multiples formed the *foot* and the *metre*. In the West, this unit is the beat provided by the conductor, whence the term *batuta* in Rousseau's definition of *measured*.

It is obvious that music composed of several simultaneous vocal or instrumental parts needs a temporal regulator to provide cohesion. All the parts must use the same reference unit. This is the sense of Bachelard's metaphor in the epigraph to this Book, which speaks of the beat 'binding into coincidences'. The purpose of the beat is to mark time or set the tempo. That is why Rousseau juxtaposes the two notions of *time* and *beat*.

The beat is thus a unit of measure. We may, however, hasten to remark that it has nothing to do with 'measure' in the sense in which this term has been used in Western music, since the beginning of the seventeenth century, to refer to the way music is *written* and designate an arrangement of a given number of basic values into groups separated by vertical bars. This latter sense of the notion of measure has sharply constrained all cultured Western music from the Baroque period to the present day. Only in the twentieth century have a few composers like Stravinsky and Bartók tried to break out of this mould. Even today, however, freedom from this constraint has not been fully achieved. Schools of music and conservatories still teach this system, particularly the contrast between 'strong' and 'weak' beats. The definitions of *measure* in musical dictionaries and encyclopedias are also based essentially on this antonymy. Its grip even on contemporary music is such that musicians seem blinded to all other possibilities. The greater complexity of modern music means that, when making use of conventional notation, it becomes even more dependent on this idea of measure.

The goal of being able to perform complex music is no justification for such a constraint, as the history of music will show. At the time of the *ars nova*, when composers like Philippe de Vitry and Guillaume de Machaut had brought polyphony to the pinnacle of refinement, the notion of measure as it is understood today was still unknown. All extant texts concord in showing that there was nothing but a temporal reference unit which synchronised the parts during performance and indicated the tempo as well. This unit, which prefigured Rousseau's *batuta*, was called the *tactus*, or 'touch'.

The arrangement of durations in most African music is still based on the same principle as the medieval *tactus*. No use whatsoever is made of the notion of matrices of regular contrasts of strong and weak beats. African music is thus based, not on measures in the sense of classical musical teaching, but on *pulsations*, i.e., on a sequence of isochronous temporal units which can be materialised as a beat.

The outlook of Western musicians and most musicologists depends so heavily on the notion of measure that, as we ourselves have experienced, they find it extremely hard to get their bearings in the flow of African polyphony and polyrhythmics, even when they can intuit the presence of an order. This disorientation stems from the fact that the Western listener finds it extremely hard to conceive of a musical structure without a regular (or sometimes irregular) underlying alternation of strong and weak beats. Despite this, there was, as we have seen, a time when European music worked more or less in this way. To give a better idea of how African rhythmics are organised, we will therefore briefly sketch the development of temporal organisation in the history of Western polyphony.

We will turn first to Chailley's (1961: 249–55) description of this process. He says that, in the Middle Ages,

plain chant, like secular music, was sung by choirs without a leader.

When polyphony was introduced, however, some kind of regulation had to be provided to hold the parts together. At first, polyphony was performed by soloists who managed to keep their parts in time simply by maintaining close physical contact with their partners. Even today, the folk singers of some populations handle polyphony by the same technique: they bunch together, take a glance at each other at the start, and then proceed by feel.

The way the pygmies of the equatorial rain forest sing their polyphony supports this observation: they too stand tightly together with their shoulders touching.

When physical contact is no longer sufficient,

folk musicians reinvent the ancient method. . . of tapping their feet.

We know that this is how the beat was provided in Antiquity, and in fact, the rhythmic unit of verse in ancient metrics is still called the 'foot'.

In the West, the first mention of a materialised beat dates from around 1275. Chailley cites a report by a priest from the Perigord region named Elie Salomon:

In his musical treatise, he describes four cantors performing four-voice polyphony, probably of organum or conductus type. They are dressed in silk copes and standing close together in the choir before a single lectern. The lead cantor, probably the *tenorista*, is in the middle. He simply bends a finger to mark each division of time.

Chailley stresses

the importance of this ancient conception of the 'beat': there are none of the groups of two, three, or four that appear in our classical 'measures'. Each unit is individually marked by one in a sequence of finger movements, just like a schoolmaster beating time by clapping his hands or striking a desk with a ruler. . . This is the *tactus*, the essential principle of 'measure' in ancient times.

It remained predominant for four centuries. Even the conductor's baton was originally intended merely to mark the *tactus*.

When, in the seventeenth century, opera began to make use of large groups of instrumental performers, choirs, and soloists who had to be controlled on a spacious stage, some way had to be found of transmitting the *tactus* to them. . . The baton is likely to have come into use in both the theatre and the church for the prosaic purpose of making a louder noise on the lectern so that the singers could hear it more clearly at the back of the stage or tribune.

Though use of the *tactus* extended into the eighteenth century, another hierarchical form of measure had already begun to gain ground during the preceding century. It was only able to achieve a dominant position, however, as a result of contemporary developments in the way music was written. 'Grouping beats into measures only became possible when the notion of the 'measure' as a graphic notation in the form of bars invaded musical instruction in the course of the seventeenth century.' Even today, this notion, which arose out of a mere graphic convention, continues to exercise a decisive influence on Western cultured music.

Unlike the Western musician, who refers to a beat materialised by a gesture (formerly associated with a sound), the traditional African musician will not exteriorise his temporal reference. For him, the 'beat', his analogue of the *tactus*, is an integral part of his music and *under*lies it. What kind of temporal organisation prevails in African music? Or as Jones says, 'We want to know not only what the African plays but also how he feels about it, in other words its internal musical organisation as he sees it' (1959: 1, 123).

Waterman (1952) suggests that there is a 'metronomic sense' at the basis of African rhythm. This sense is part of the 'perceptual equipment' which musician and listener share, having acquired it in the process of assimilation to their own culture. Waterman therefore calls it a 'cultural pattern'. Since almost all African music is dance music, he logically concludes that there must be a relationship between dance movements and the accompanying musical pulsation.

Merriam accepts Waterman's suggestion and comments, 'Given the acknowledged rhythmic and metric complexity of African music, the logic of the proposition appears in the fact that there is no reason to suppose that the African listener could not become fully as confused as the Westerner, were there not in operation some orienting principles' (1962: 126). He states, however, that no confirmation of such orienting principles is forthcoming from Africans themselves, and that Waterman's hypothesis cannot therefore be proved.

A proof does, however, exist, and is stated in our methodological presentation (see Book III, 6.6.5, 'Discovery of the temporal reference unit'). When the musicians superpose hand-claps on the recording of a piece they have just performed, they are materialising Waterman's 'metronomic sense'. This is the proof Merriam was looking for. The metronomic beat, materialised by the Africans themselves, is intrinsic to the music and thus a 'cultural pattern'.

We will try to provide an answer to Jones's question as to how the African feels about his own music at the end of this Book. For the time being, it will be helpful to start with a look at the concepts involved in the temporal organisation of Western music. Just as an anthropologist studying another culture may be led to question the 'immutable' nature of some aspects of his own civilisation, so an ethnomusicologist should adopt a new perspective when it can shed fresh and unexpected light on one of the basic elements of his own musical culture. African rhythmics has thus led us, involuntarily at first, but later with a clearer purpose, to subject certain long-established musicological concepts to a critical reappraisal. The first thing we discovered in this process was the extent of terminological confusion.

1.2   TERMINOLOGICAL AMBIGUITY

1.2.1   On certain confusions

Anyone who consults the literature on African music will quickly see that a certain number of terms relative to temporal organisation appear quite frequently, e.g.,

- rhythm or rhythmic
- metric, metre, measure
- stress, weight (*Gewicht*)
- strong or heavy beat, main beat, weak or light beat
- syncopation
- beat, pulse, clap
- isometric, heterometric, polymetric
- isorhythmic, heterorhythmic, polyrhythmic
- additive and divisive rhythms
- pattern.

All these terms are, of course, taken from the vocabulary ordinarily used to describe cultured Western music. This is only normal insofar as ethnomusicology is still in its early stages and has not yet had time to develop its own terminological tools.

One of the essential features of most traditional African music is the absence of *regular* accents. Marguerite Béclard-d'Harcourt (1924) was already aware of this, as were many later investigators such as Jones (1934, 1937, 1954, 1958, 1959), Nketia (1963), Estreicher (1964), Kubik (1964, 1965, 1967, 1969, 1974), Belinga (1965), Dauer (1966), and Pantaleoni (1972). All terms implying a contrast between strong and weak beats should thus be excluded from the vocabulary applied to such music.

This means that terms such as *metric*, *metre*, *measure*, *strong* and *weak beats*, *main beat*, *weight*, *heavy*, *light*, *syncope*, *isometric*, *heterometric*, and *additive* and *divisive rhythms* should be dispensed with as foreign to it. The description of rhythmic phenomena in music with no regular stress should, in our opinion, limit itself to the use of the following terms:

- rhythm or rhythmic
- accent
- 'contra-tempo' (*contre-temps*)
- beat, pulsation, or clap
- isorhythmic, heterorhythmic, polyrhythmic
- pattern.

This reduced set of terms is, not surprisingly, nearly the same as the one required to describe the rhythms which held sway in Western music from the *ars nova* to the Renaissance. It contains the vocabulary which is necessary and sufficient to explain the workings of most rhythmic systems in use in sub-Saharan Africa. All of these terms will be carefully redefined below.

Even ethnomusicologists recognising the absence of regular stress will often make use of inappropriate terms. One of the reasons for this is that there are ambiguities in the terminology, even as it applies to Western music. Most of these terms either designate more than one notion or partially overlapping ones. New, exclusive definitions are clearly required.

We have already quoted Chailley's (1961: 255) view that it only became possible to group beats together in 'measures' when the use of bars invaded the written material of musical instruction in the seventeenth century. Once the notion of measure was established, no composer could escape it. They were forced to fit the metric structure of their works into the available frameworks, and have ever since submitted their choice of a metric pattern to the constraints of measure. The bar thus became a part of the composer's set of material and conceptual tools. Even someone like Beethoven would think musically in terms of bars, and there would be nothing haphazard in his choice of 3/4 rather than 6/8, despite there being no difference in the *quantities* of these measures. This shows that measure is more than mere bondage; it is also a foundation for rhythmic organisation *governing the first and most elementary level of rhythmic arrangement*.

The ethnomusicologist finds himself in a situation similar to the composer's. When translating oral music into written form, he will naturally try to fit what he hears into the metric patterns provided by conventional notation. This, however, will deform traditional music with no regular accents by suggesting, in the writing system, a contrast between strong and weak beats. The use of ambiguous, equally conventional terminology is only a by-product of this original deformation.

Ethnomusicologists who have put the available tools to uses for which they were not intended have been led into incoherences. We find, for example,

- indications of measure (6/8, 4/4, and so forth) heading transcriptions
- the use of bars, suggesting that the first beat in each measure is accented
- the description of overlapping measures as *syncopation*
- and the interpretation of metric structures which can be segmented into equal parts (2/4, 3/4, 6/8, 4/4, and so on) as 'divisive', and of asymmetric structures (resulting from the combination of *unequal* binary *and* ternary parts, e.g., 5/8, 7/8, 11/8, etc.) as 'additive'.

This situation is a result of the conditions under which ethnomusicology has been developing. It has had to make use of concepts which are not only borrowed from a somewhat different discipline (Western musicology), but have also become quite ambiguous through historical change and semantic shifts.

There is, in sum, confusion at two different levels. First of all, investigators have been imposing on African music notions which are were originally applied to only to Western music; secondly, the available terminology is not univocal. The latter problem arises essentially from the different meanings assigned to the term 'metric', and to an overlapping between the notions of metrics and rhythmics. This has resulted, as we have seen, from changes in musical notation, primarily the progressive replacement of the notion of *tactus* by the notion of 'measure'.

Chailley has described the consequences of this transformation as follows:

The old *tactus* based on juxtaposed 'beats' did not entirely disappear, but slowly gave ground to the procedure of grouping beats together which later became our 'measure', named from the fact that it took over the signs of the earlier 'mensuration'. The bar, which was originally nothing but a visual reference mark,. . . came into general use towards 1625. It helped to reestablish or reinforce a new hierarchy of strong and weak beats, which lost little time in fitting music into a corset of symmetry that did away with much of its earlier flexibility. And the practice of counting the new measures took over.

(1967: 106)

The notions of bar and strong beat are, in fact, so compelling that most dictionary definitions of rhythm do not even allow for the possibility of proportionality with no regular accent. 'Rhythm' is always cross-referenced with 'metrics' and vice versa, in accordance with the assumption that one is inconceivable without the other.

To help us redefine these terms in a way that will avoid contradiction, we should perhaps look back at the origin of the confusion. As we do so, we will find that the notions of metrics and rhythm necessarily interlock.

1.2.2   On the different kinds of metre

Differences in the meaning of the term 'metric', and confusions of the kinds of metre with the various definitions of rhythm, have been present in musicological terminology from Antiquity to the present day. That is why so much space must be devoted to these notions in this Book. Additional justification is provided by the fact that nearly all works on the problems of rhythm begin with a warning against such confusions. One of the oldest treatises in the Western tradition, St Augustine's *De musica*, written in the fourth century AD, already contains such a warning. In the dialogue captioned 'From rhythm to metre' (*De musica* III, i, 2), the Master enjoins his disciple to distinguish these two notions: 'these nouns [i.e., *numerus, mensura*] are used in a broad sense in our own language, and we must avoid being ambiguous. . . We must distinguish in words those things which are themselves different in reality.' Or again (*De musica* v, ii, 1), 'One thing is the improper use of a name permitted by some sort of proximity, and another is giving a thing its proper name.'

The term 'metre' as used today has at least three different, if not contradictory, meanings.

(a) *Measure* in the simplest sense means *metrum*, i.e., the specification of time intervals by comparison with a constant value used as a reference unit. These intervals are obtained either by multiplication (as in the ancient Greeks' *chronos prōtos*) or by division (as with the principle of Western music in the Middle Ages).

(b) In *versification*, 'metre' means *a succession of different durations arranged into a figure*. Emmanuel (1926: 106) defines metrics in this sense as follows:

When rhythmics is taken in relation to words alone, it is called *metrics*, and consists of stylising and standardising the natural rhythm of language. It is, so to speak, the science of *metres* or *measures*, whose elements are long (♩) and short (♪) syllables.

This definition is explicitly limited to speech alone, and refers to measuring verse. We can see, however, that it makes use of the notion of rhythm, which brings us to the crux of the problem, namely, that metrics is inseparable from rhythmics.

In another work, Emmanuel (1921: 380) says, 'Metrics, which borders on music on account of its rhythmic aspect, has verbal rhythmics as its sole object.' He thus suggests that the primary sense of 'metrics' applies to verse, not music.

In the dictionary *Science de la Musique* (1976: II, 608), metrics is defined as

the science which studies the rules for measuring verse, i.e., quantity, kinds of feet, and ways of arranging verse in stanzas. The term is applied primarily to ancient Greek and Latin poetry, and to prosody. *By extension* [italics added], the term can also be used in music, e.g., to define the arrangement of units of time in measures.

(c) In *music*, 'metrics' is in fact used to refer to the way beats (in the sense of *tactus*) are ordered within a larger framework of reference, a matrix of temporal organisation, or a *measure*, with precise relative indications not only of the quantities it contains (as 2/4, 4/4) but also of the way these quantities are divided up (as 3/4 or 6/8). The ranking of quantities is a natural consequence of the arrangement into measures. But we must not forget that this ranking is a result of what was originally only a graphic convention.

Most works on musicology and the history of music use the term 'metric' indifferently in any of these meanings. It is rare to find an author who will take the trouble to define beforehand exactly which sense he assigns to it. It seems to be taken for granted in whatever meaning it may have. A closer look will, however, immediately show it to be ambiguous.

Kunst (1950: 8) noticed this long ago:

For centuries, metre in European music has taken the form of what are called measures.
There are thus at least two meanings to the term measure: sometimes it means metre, but usually it designates the part of a composition bounded by two bars.

1.2.3   Rhythm and measure

Let us now turn to the terminology concerning rhythm. There are so many meanings for this term that it would be useless to try to enumerate them all. Unlike 'metric', they have no common denominator. This led Apel to affirm, 'It would be hopeless task to search for a definition of rhythm which would prove acceptable even to a small minority of musicians and writers on music' (1946: 639).

Cooper and Meyer start from the premise that

the development of a fruitful approach to the study of rhythm has been hampered by a failure to distinguish clearly among the several aspects of temporal organization itself. The resulting confusion has created a correlative ambiguity of terminology. Since clear distinctions and unequivocal terminology are necessary if the analysis of the rhythmic structure of music is to move beyond its present moribund state, our first task must be one of definition   (1960: 1)

We will see below that, while their criticism is well founded, their own definitions are not always free of ambiguity.

Kolinski (1973: 494) returned to the subject of this confusion. He claimed to have inventoried some *fifty different meanings of the word 'rhythm'* in the musicological literature (entirely apart from the contradictory interpretations of the term 'metre' and its correlations with 'rhythm'), and wondered why there was still such confusion. Chailley (1951: 95) deplored this as much as Kolinski: 'Musical theories too often confuse two entirely different things: *rhythm* and *measure*.' So did Benary (1973: 8) when, sixteen centuries after St *Augustine*, he wrote: 'There is, however, still no obligatory terminological distinction between metrics and rhythmics.' We must therefore give a little further attention to the term 'metric'.

For Cooper and Meyer, measure is 'an ordering framework of accents and weak beats within which rhythmic grouping takes place. It constitutes the matrix out of which rhythm arises' (1960-96). Having defined measure in this way, they ask whether the notion of rhythm determines the notion of measure, or vice versa. They examine this question from the standpoint of both composer and performer and conclude: 'For both composer and performer – as well as for the listener – meter establishes a structured continuum of accents and weak beats which acts as a basis for rhythmic and melodic expectation; that is, it becomes a norm in the light of which both the regular and irregular are apprehended and felt.'

According to the *Riemann Musiklexikon* (1967: III, 933), the measure combines several note values into a unit which acts as a 'reference pattern' and has parts ranked by accentuation. Under 'Bar' in the same work (ibid.: 934), the note immediately after the bar is said to be the 'fulcrum' of the measure.

Apel describes the measure as 'the pattern of fixed temporal units, called beats, by which the timespan of a piece of music or a section thereof is measured. . . Meter is indicated by time signatures. For instance, 3/4 meter (or 3/4 time) means that the basic values are quarter notes and that every third quarter note receives an accent' (1970: 523).

Herzfeld says 'Measure is a standard reference unit which also implies rules of accentuation and is thereby related to metrics (vd. Accent). The first note after the bar is always accented, and may be followed by one or two unaccented notes' (1974: 541). When we consult "Accent" as suggested, we find,

Certain beats in the measure receive natural accentuation: the first in 3/4 time, the first and third in 4/4 time, the first and fourth in 6/8 time. These accents require no special marking, as they are taken for granted. If, however, the accent deviates from the rule by being shifted onto another beat, this must be marked.

We may conclude this brief survey of definitions of measure by quoting *Science de la Musique* (1976: II, 606): 'In the widest sense, "measure" designates an aspect of rhythm, namely, the arrangement of its constituent durations according to rational proportions.'

1.2.4   Accent, weight, and stress

Comparing these definitions, we find that all of them provide for accentual ranking within the measure; furthermore, they accept that the presence of accents in itself implies the existence of rhythm. From this standpoint, it is clear that all metre *is* rhythm, since most of these writers believe that accentuation is the foundation of rhythm. Benary (1973: 86) thus writes, 'The basic conditioning factor of rhythm is accent.'

This is also Cooper and Meyer's (1960: 8) opinion. Having defined accent as 'a stimulus (in a series of stimuli) which is *marked for consciousness* in some way', they go on to say, 'The difference between accented and unaccented beats lies in the fact that the accented beat is the focal point, the nucleus of the rhythm, around which the unaccented beats are grouped and in relation to which they are heard.' While Benary (1973: 86) takes accent as the basis of rhythmics, 'the basic conditioning factor of metrics is weight. Accent and weight usually coincide. They are ranked together in the measure.' We might then wonder how accent and weight differ, if they are supposed to coincide. Should the first beat in a measure be said to have accent, weight, or both?

To return to Cooper and Meyer, we find that, having defined 'accent', they introduce an ambiguous term, 'stress' (which can mean either 'tension' or 'emphasis'), while warning the reader to avoid a possible confusion: 'Accent must not be confused with stress. The term "stress," as used in this book, means the dynamic intensification of a beat, whether accented or unaccented. Thus a stress, no matter how forceful, placed on a weak beat will not make that beat accented' (1960: 8).

Two questions now arise. First, what is the difference between 'stress' and 'accent' when both fall on the first beat in a measure? Then, if 'stress' on a weak beat does not 'accent' it, though it does involve a 'dynamic intensification', how is it perceptible? The problem becomes even more complicated when Cooper and Meyer turn to the causes of accentuation. After emphasising that definitions should be free of ambiguity, they write,

Though the concept of accent is obviously of central importance in the theory and analysis of rhythm, an ultimate definition in terms of psychological causes does not seem possible with our present knowledge. That is, one cannot at present state unequivocally what makes one tone seem accented and another not. . . In short, since accent appears to be a product of a number of variables whose interaction is not precisely known, it must for our purposes remain a basic, axiomatic concept which is understandable as an experience but undefined in terms of causes.

(1960: 7)

While allowing that there is no way of knowing 'what makes one tone seem accented and another not', they affirm that accent can be defined on the basis of its role in a given musical context, and point out one of its features: 'In order for a tone to appear accented it must be set off from other tones of the series in some way.' This brings us back to the question raised above: since an accent can only be perceived by contrast with 'unaccented', and 'stress' is defined as 'dynamic intensification', what is the difference between them?

1.2.5   Measure and symmetry (*carrure*)

This question is the basis of Kolinski's criticism of Cooper and Meyer: 'Unfortunately, this intricate concept of intertwined stresses and accents does not do justice to essential aspects of metro-rhythmic structure' (1973: 498). Kolinski feels that the fundamental cause of confusion between metrics and rhythmics lies in the role assigned to accents in metrics: 'According to the most widely accepted theory, it is the more or less regular recurrence of accents that creates metre' (ibid.: 495). To show the inaccuracy of Cooper and Meyer's theory, he gives the following counterexample: 'The metric structure of a piece played on an organ or harpsichord can be recognized with the same ease by mere listening as that of a piano piece, without the guide of any accentuation.'

If we try this out in practice, the result is not so clear as Kolinski would have it. Certainly, the metric structure of most works from the Baroque and Classical periods will be immediately perceptible. But we would then like to know *how* we manage to recognise it with no help from accent. What allows us to identify the metric structure of an organ or harpsichord piece is a set of characteristic features in the musical language of the time. By the polarities of the intervals, the interplay of harmonic tension and release, the symmetry of the phrases, and the restatement of melodic and rhythmic features, the *knowledgeable listener* can *infer* the metric structure without the help of accentuation, because this structure always concords with the remaining stylistic features of the work. This is succinctly stated in the article on 'Rhythm' in *Science de la Musique* (1976: II, 905): 'Tonal and rhythmic functions mutually condition and modify each other. Both these means of accenting (which are not the only ones) can help to determine the metric accents which an organising intelligence will perceive.'

The article on 'Measure' (*Science de la Musique*, 1976: II, 607) makes the same point: 'Measure has had a near stranglehold on Western music from the beginning of the Baroque to the end of the Romantic period, in parallel with the supremacy of harmonic tonality (*the two are not unconnected*) [italics added].'

As a counterproof to Kolinski's, we could thus suggest having a *novice* try to identify the metric structure of a work played first on an organ or harpsichord, and then on a piano. He might well be successful in the case of the piano, but probably less so in the case of the other two. It is, however, quite likely that someone familiar with the work's general style would be able to discern the metric structure, even without accents. This would show that the listener's 'organising intelligence' is capable of making up for the absence of accentuation and, therefore, that metric structure is indeed determined by a set of structural features.

One of the features that is most helpful in perceiving metric structure is undoubtedly symmetry. The article on 'Rhythm' in *Science de la Musique* (1976: II, 906) says of *carrure* that 'by clearly indicating the end of a span, it is extremely useful in clarifying the significance of musical movements'. Contrary to the position of other theoreticians, who see it as 'a rational principle imposed from without,. . . it is imposed from within, like a flowering of the sense of cadence. Rationality here governs musical activity.' The author of this article cites several examples, including the particularly enlightening one provided by Bach's *Goldberg Variations*. An analysis of this work shows the importance of symmetry: each variation has thirty-two measures, and is divided into two equal sixteen-measure parts. Each of these parts is broken down into two eight-measure periods, and each period contains two four-measure sections. The segmentation can be continued down to the level of the individual measure, which itself constitutes a basic harmonic unit, insofar as the beginning of each measure is marked by a change of chord.

When the *Goldberg Variations* are played (as intended) on the harpsichord, which cannot produce dynamic accentuation, the correlation of harmonic development, melodic movement, and temporal organisation does indeed enable the listener to perceive the metric structure.

1.2.6   Measure, *tactus*, beat

We have seen that all the authors we have quoted agree that the measure has rhythmic properties, since it is based on the regular repetition of accents. In this part of our discussion, we will, however, temporarily set aside this view of the measure as implying internal ranking. We will limit ourselves to a single aspect, namely, the use of the measure as a graphic framework for reading and writing musical texts. Justification for this approach can be found in the fact that the measure was originally nothing more than a way of assembling of a given number of beats. These beats derived from what was known as the *tactus* in the Middle Ages.

The *Encyclopédie de la Musique* (1961: III, 1316) reminds us that *tactus* in Latin can have the sense of both touching and striking. It refers to the 'bending of a finger' to mark each of what Chailley calls 'individual beats': 'They did not count, let us say, 1, 2, 3, 1, 2, 3,. . . but rather 1, 1, 1, 1,. . . .' (1961: 252). It is found in modern conducting as the *one-beat technique*.

The *Encyclopédie de la Musique* gives a similar description: 'In the sixteenth century, and as late as the eighteenth, the *tactus* was entirely different from what is known today as "measure" (*Takt* in German). It was not a group of several of the units of time marked off by a baton; it was a single one of these units.' The *tactus* was the unit of length used in the proportional music which originated around the twelfth century. Auda describes this music as follows: 'Proportional music is incompatible with the *isochronal structure* of strong and weak beats, and with symmetry [*carrure*]. The rhythmic and melodic accents are freely placed in each part. It is *ordered rhythmic music* where values and lengths of notes are *counted individually* rather than in *sets*' (1965: 1-2). In proportional music, Auda says, 'there is only *one way* of beating the *tactus*, using the two movements, up and down. . . A *beat* is always a *measure* in proportional notation, but not in modern music.'

Sachs (1953) emphasises that the two movements have equal value and do not allow accentuation. To support this, he quotes (1953: 217-8) a treatise by Tomás Sancta Maria called *El arte de tañer*, and published in Valladolid in 1565, which says that the beat 'which strikes up high does not have anything to hit against, as that which strikes below. . . Both of them are struck with equality, that is, the low *golpe* beat is not struck more forcefully than the high, nor vice versa.'

A century later, Fr. Mersenne (1636: II, 324) writes: 'Beating time, which St Augustine and the other ancient Latin writers called *plausus*, is just raising and lowering the hand to show how much time should be given to each note; for example, the semibreve normally lasts the time it takes to raise and lower the hand, or the foot, or anything else.'

Souris (1961: III, 787) gives a definition similar to Mersenne's: 'A unit of duration chosen as a reference to govern the pace of performance.'

It is clear from the above that the *tactus* is similar to what we now call the 'beat', and Souris confirms this:

The beat is a neutral pulsation with no metric accentuation. There may be some internal division within the beat. . . Under the name of *tactus*. . ., this unitary beat sufficed to control the performance of the extremely complex polyphony of the Renaissance. . . As a general rule, the bars of the *tactus* remained independent of metric accentuation and polyrhythmic structures. . . The principle of the measure was grafted onto the *tactus* at the beginning of the seventeenth century, and has given rise to serious confusion.   (1961: III, 787)

Souris also says that the "tempo" is 'organised on the basis of the pulsations in the measure'. These pulsations are the beats, or what used to be the *tactus*. Incidentally, Souris shows considerable insight, when, in the same article, he says, 'We may assume that the tempo of highly structured music can be passed on orally with perfect accuracy in civilisations which do not use writing.' This is what our experience over more than twenty years has shown to be the case in Central African music.

The function of the *tactus* has remained the same in Western musical practice, where 'beating time' still refers to a materialisation of temporal units. Rousseau (1768: 51-3) stated this explicitly: 'BEATING TIME: marking the beats in the measure by movements of the hand or foot to fix their length and make all similar measures perfectly equal in temporal value during performance.'

Keeping time was more than just a visual indicator in the seventeenth century. An auditive signal was also a technical requirement to assure the synchronisation of large vocal and instrumental ensembles. Rousseau, however, was unhappy about this: 'How the ear suffers at the Paris Opera from the constant unpleasant sound made by the baton in *beating time*!. . . This, however, is an unavoidable evil, without which it would be impossible to perceive the beat; nothing in the music itself indicates it. . . Good taste even consists in making it imperceptible.' This is the occasion for Rousseau to let fly one of his characteristic sarcasms: 'The Paris Opera is the only theatre in Europe where time is beaten but not kept; everywhere else it is kept without being beaten.'

This distinction between 'beating' and 'keeping' time is particularly important for our purposes. Rousseau might have been surprised to learn that his remarks apply far beyond the limits of cultured Western music. He continues as follows:

There is, in this matter, a widespread misconception which a little reflection could easily eliminate. People imagine that someone listening to a song instinctively beats the time because he feels it so strongly. But the fact is that it is not clear enough, or he does not feel it strongly enough, so he tries to replace what is lacking to his ear by movements of hand and foot. As soon as the cadence starts, most French people will twist and turn and make a terrible racket to help *time* along or help their ear to perceive it. Take Italians or Germans and you will not hear the least noise nor see the slightest gesture in time with the beat. Could it be that Germans and Italians are less sensitive to *time* than the French? Some among my readers will leap to this conclusion. But will they also say that the most talented musicians are those least able to perceive *time*? They are unquestionably the ones who *beat* it the least. And when, through practice, they become accustomed to feeling it constantly, they do not *beat* it at all. This fact is there for all to see. Some might also say that the same people whom I reproach for *beating time* simply because they cannot feel it strongly enough, no longer *beat* it when it cannot be perceived in the music. And there I reply that this is because they can no longer feel it.

These remarks obviously have a polemical side, but the underlying theory has a much broader scope and, strange as it may seem, applies nicely to African music. Traditional African performers feel no need to materialise in any way the temporal reference unit which governs their music. The fact that they do not beat time does not mean that they are clumsier than people who do, but rather that they have such a perfect command of their rhythm that they no longer need any auditive or visual indication of the beat.

Benary (1973: 21) says, 'Metre is a continuum'. This statement nevertheless contradicts his assertion (1973: 20) that 'light and heavy are the smallest metrical building blocks'. If metrics is indeed based on an alternation of 'heavy' and 'light' beats, the term 'continuum' is inappropriate, as it implies either a homogeneous flow *with no discontinuities* or a series of identical and perfectly equidistant discrete elements. An alternation of two kind of beats cannot be a continuum.

There are, in fact, many writers who use the term 'isochrony' to refer to a regular sequence of beats in a metric framework, but then define the measure as ranking accented and unaccented beats. This is a conflation resulting from the inclusion of a foreign element in the notion of isochrony, namely, the idea of accentuation. 'Isochrony' itself means only equality of duration and has nothing to do with accent ranking. But musicologists often use this term in connection with measure to mean not only that a given quantity never changes, but also that it is structured in a given way. This conflation results in ambiguity; for were we to accept this viewpoint, could we allow that twelve crotchets arranged into four three-beat measures are 'isochronous' with twelve crotchets played at the same tempo, but arranged into three four-beat measures? In the primary sense of the word, we could, but then we would have to refrain from using it in connection with 'measures'. On the other hand, we certainly could not, if we want to include accentuation in the idea of isochrony. This is clear from the fact that, even for a theoretician of medieval music like Auda 'proportional music is incompatible with the *isochronal structure* of strong and weak beats' (1965: 1). Accuracy aside, this statement shows how far terminological confusion has gone: paradoxically, proportional music, which is based on the *tactus*, a reference unit implying *unaccented* equidistant beats, and thus 'incompatible with the isochronal structure of strong and weak beats', is itself the only truly *isochronous* music in the primary sense of the word.

The measure assembles a given number of beats (*in the sense of tactus*). The only mark indicating a sequence of measures is thus accentuation. We must therefore now discuss the prevailing confusion between the ideas of *beat* and *measure*.

Let us start by looking at the first of these notions. Cooper and Meyer use the word 'pulse' to refer to the beat as a temporal unit: 'A pulse is one of a series of regularly recurring, precisely equivalent stimuli. Like the ticks of a metronome or a watch, pulses mark off equal units in the temporal continuum'. They rightly emphasise that pulses must be absolutely equal: 'All pulses in a series are by definition exactly alike' (1960: 3).

If we now compare Cooper and Meyer's remarks with Benary's, how are we to define a temporal continuum: as a sequence of pulses or measures? In the former case, time is organised on the basis of the notion of *tactus*; in the latter, on the notion of *metre*. As Cooper and Meyer themselves remark, 'Although pulse can theoretically exist without either meter or rhythm, the nature of the human mind is such that this is a rare occurrence in music' (ibid.: 3).

While this assertion is valid for Western music, it is hardly applicable to many forms of extra-European music. It is, however, right to say that the pulse is 'an important aspect of musical experience. Not only is pulse necessary for the existence of meter, but it generally. . . underlies and reinforces rhythmic experience' (ibid.: 3–4). Metre, according to Cooper and Meyer, is

the measurement of the number of pulses between more or less regularly recurring accents. Therefore, in order for meter to exist, some of the pulses in a series must be accented – marked for consciousness – relative to others. When pulses are thus counted within a metric context, they are referred to as *beats*. Beats which are accented are called "strong"; those which are unaccented are called 'weak'.   (ibid.: 4)

While this definition is quite accurate, we later (1960: 88) find a curious remark which is made even stranger by its being presented as a warning:

A word of caution seems in order here. Even in the music of the seventeenth through the nineteenth centuries time signatures and bar lines do not always accurately reflect the real metric organization. At times composers have used them somewhat casually – as a convenience – relying upon the performer to interpret and communicate the true metric structure.   (ibid.: 88)

This raises an important question: if the purpose of metre is to arrange beats within a particular framework which the composer has selected from among several possibilities, and if there is no written indication of the metric structure of the work, how can we tell what the 'right' one is? How can the reader recover it? The terminological vagueness is such that not only are different authors in disagreement, but some even manage to contradict themselves within a single work.

1.2.7   What is rhythm?

As we have seen, three levels of temporal organisation can be distinguished: the *beat*, the *metre*, and the *rhythm*. Having dealt with the first two individually and in relation to each other, we must now examine rhythm in the same way, first by reviewing generally accepted definitions, and then by seeing how metre and rhythm are related.

Herzfeld says,

Rhythm must be distinguished from measure [*Takt*] and metre [*Metrum*]. Rhythm is part of the musical *Gestalt*. The model for musical rhythm is the lilt of language with its ups and downs, its contrasts of stress and absence of stress. Music concentrates these differences in the length of sound. . . Rhythm, of course, implies only a relative ordering of time. Absolute values measured in physical time derive first of all from the tempo. Rhythm is also not an independent feature. It cannot be conceived separately, but is rather a temporal ordering to which the notes are submitted. (1974: 445)

Language is thus held to be at the origin of rhythm.

Cooper and Meyer propose the following definition: 'Rhythm may be defined as the way in which one or more unaccented beats are grouped in relation to an accented one' (1960: 6). According to this view, rhythm is based on accentuation alone. Accented beats are furthermore viewed as 'cores' around which rhythm is organised. Closer examination will show that this definition takes over all the elements of the definitions of *metre* already quoted above, including Cooper and Meyer's own. This suggests that all of these authors base rhythm on metre alone, i.e., imply that there can be no measured rhythm without metre and regular accentuation. Cooper and Meyer's definition continues as follows:

The five basic rhythmic groupings may be differentiated by terms traditionally associated with prosody:

a. iamb ‿ —
b. anapest ‿ ‿ —
c. trochee — ‿
d. dactyl — ‿ ‿
e. amphibrach ‿ — ‿ (ibid.)

But Greek versification, which has given us these terms, while it does involve grouping elements into figures, is nevertheless characterised *by not relying in any way on accentuation*. It is surprising that Cooper and Meyer should give figures based on a long/short contrast as examples of 'basic rhythmic groupings', when in the same paragraph they define rhythm as being based on accented and unaccented beats. Regarding the latter contrast, they go on to say, 'Since a rhythmic group can be apprehended only when its elements are distinguished from one another, rhythm, as defined above, always involves an interrelationship between a single, accented (strong) beat and either one or two unaccented (weak) beats' (ibid.) Their work contains several other references to the contribution of accent to rhythmic organisation, e.g. (1960: 125), 'The possible elements in a rhythmic group are upbeat (or anacrusis), accent, and afterbeat.'

The article on 'Rhythm' in *Science de la Musique* (1976: II, 903) says,

Rhythm is the temporal aspect of music, the source of its temporal unity. It is what gives oneness to the flow of music. It provides the underlying coherence holding together the moments into which music can be broken down by analysis, and allows it to exist. . . But rhythm involves the structuring of a sequence of musical acts. It is the temporal form of music, the particular way in which it achieves its existence in time. . .

In the narrow sense, rhythm is the order and proportion of durations in terms of long and short. In the wider sense, it is the flow of music in its entirety. It is not something that propels a previously motionless entity, like a force driving a machine. It is the temporal condition of the existence of the events which take place in the realm of sound. . . We must therefore recognise that there are rhythmic functions, and that musicians do not compose using lengths of time, but values. Cadence, measure, phrases, forms, tempo, all of these features which are part of rhythm in the wider sense, arise out of the network of relationships among values in terms of succession and simultaneity.

Here for the first time we find a reference to measure as a *rhythmic* function. The article continues as follows:

The organisation of rhythm implies diverse forms of periodicity, i.e., the predictable recurrence of an event in essentially identical but existentially different form. This is what 'rhyme' means (a doublet of 'rhythm' dating from the twelfth century). Periodicity, which is initially perceived in the equality of time between beats, suggests that measurable units can be found in rhythm. From the metric standpoint, rhythm, once established, is measured as an object by assigning the number 1 to a pure duration, which can be summed if it is short, or divided if it is long.

While this definition is accurate enough, another statement in the same article restricts its usefulness in at least some respects, and is open to question: 'Rhythm is completely cadential, like our own motor activity.'

The doubtfulness of this affirmation is increased by the author's attempt to support it with an example from dance: 'Whenever man tries to project his sense of existence and his feelings on to bodily space in dance, or on to auditive space in music, he organises his activity by rhythmic cadence.' African reality shows that neither dance nor the supporting music require an alternation of strong and weak beats. If by cadence we mean a 'regular structure of musical time which appears in the rhythm of strong and weak beats, measures, or periods' (*Science de la Musique* II: 133), no use whatsoever is in fact made of this notion.

The author of the article on 'Rhythm' is on sounder footing when he goes on to say, 'The cadential organisation of values and measures is not all there is to musical rhythm. It is merely the foundation on which musical rhythm (motifs, phrases, periods, form) can be freely built.' We see again that, when present, measure, far from being excluded from rhythm, actually provides the foundation for it.

1.2.8   Rhythm and metre

Cooper and Meyer (1960) devote an entire chapter to rhythm and metre. They start by describing how the two are related:

The interaction of rhythm and meter is a complex one. On the one hand, the objective organization of a piece of music – the temporal relationships, melodic and harmonic structure, dynamics, and so forth – creates accents and weak beats (unaccents) and defines their relationships. And these accents and unaccents, when they occur with some regularity, would seem to specify the meter. In this sense the elements which produce rhythm also produce meter. [. . .]
   On the other hand, meter can apparently be independent of rhythm, not only in the sense that it can exist in the absence of any definitive rhythmic organization, but also in the sense that rhythmic organization can conflict with and work against an established meter.   (1960: 88)

This passage raises more than one question. First of all, what are the criteria for the 'objective organisation' of a piece of music? The measures provide a regular organisation which 'creates accents and weak beats. . .and defines their relationships', and 'would seem to specify the meter'. But when the authors conclude that 'in this sense, the elements which produce rhythm also produce meter', they are putting the cart before the horse. If metre can be defined by the relatively regular repetition of accents, the proper conclusion would be that *the elements which produce metre also produce rhythm*. In short, what they call metre is actually already *rhythm*. It is therefore wrong to affirm that metre 'can exist in the absence of any definitive rhythmic organisation'. This contradicts not only musical reality (is, for example, a melody in 4/4 containing only crotchets rhythmless?), but even their prior reasoning. In Cooper and Meyer's, and in many other theoreticians' usage, metre is actually an integral part of rhythm. We will shortly see that *metre* and *rhythm*, while apparently differing in meaning, actually refer to different levels of organisation and complexity of a single phenomenon.

Benary (1973: 16) makes the following distinction between rhythm and metre:

'Heavy' and 'light' in metrical language correspond to 'stressed' and 'unstressed' in rhythmic language. . .
    As a rule, rhythmic accent and metric weight coincide. No distinction can thus be made between accent and weight in the 'stress' applied to the value of a measure. . .
    Rhythm is related to metre as accent is to weight. As we have said, accent and weight coincide as a rule.

If, as Benary says, the two cannot be distinguished, how do they differ? The beats immediately following a bar in a score are easily treated conceptually as 'heavy', but can 'heavy' and 'accented' beats be distinguished by ear? More generally, what criteria can be used to decide whether any beat which is more perceptible than another is heavy or accented?

The article on 'Accent' in *Science de la Musique* (1976: 1, 5) says, 'The initial beat in a measure is accented, i.e. becomes the strong beat, only if it corresponds to a downbeat. This is far from being necessarily the case. *It therefore seems erroneous to try to set up a distinction between a metric and a rhythmic accent* [italics added].' This would seem to be the most sensible reply to the difficulties arising from Benary's position.

As an ethnomusicologist, Reinhard writes, 'Rhythm and metre. . . are not just closely intertwined and even often impossible to disentangle; they are also extremely hard to define' (1968: 40). He suggests that rhythm only frees itself from metre when it extends beyond the framework of the measure. The notions of metre and rhythm are so dependent upon each other that no definition can assign them different domains. Reinhard noted this without explaining it. Benary, too, was unable to resolve the problem. This is clear from the fact that he gives up on defining any difference in the very chapter he heads 'Definition':

Since the forms in which rhythm and metre appear partially overlap, a definition of either without reference to the other is neither possible nor useful [*sic*]. Hence, the following study will not aim at a scientifically suitable definition by definitively contrasting rhythmic and metric factors, but is intended as far as possible to provide the practising musician with a helpful clarification of whatever may seem essential.   (1973: 88)

These passages show how unsuitable conventional terminology is for dealing with these two notions. All the authors quoted insist on distinguishing them, but are unable to develop a clear view of either. Another noteworthy point is the unanimous support for the idea of metre as implying a regular repetition of accents. This leads to some rather hasty conclusions like Benary's: 'It is impossible to make music without weighting. The ear weights, for it could not otherwise perceive musical duration' (1973: 79).

A generalisation of this sort is all the more surprising in that most writers cite cases of music to which it does not apply. These include Medieval and Renaissance polyphony, which they realise are based on the principle of *tactus* alone. How is it possible to say that the ear cannot perceive musical duration without recourse to 'weighting', when it is a well-known fact that the rhythmics of the *ars nova*, despite its complexity, involves no regular accentuation? Even without expecting the theoreticians of rhythm to go so far as to take account of extra-European music, we can only wonder that they can so easily ignore a procedure which was still current in the West only four centuries ago.

1.3   *A LA RECHERCHE DU TEMPS PERDU*

Rhythm in cultured European music could never have been confused with the alternation of strong and weak beats before the second half of the seventeenth century. Prior to that time, rhythm was ordered according to other principles, which can be traced as far back in time as the availability of written documents will allow. It will therefore be helpful to return to the origins of our own music and examine these principles, which have suffered only four centuries of disuse, for they are the basis for a conception of rhythm which some modern theoreticians seem to have entirely forgotten; even more, they still govern most traditional African music.

Our main guide on this quick trip back through time will be Maurice Emmanuel, whose works have still not received all the attention they deserve, fifty years after their publication. He describes (1926: 124) the kind of rhythm in use at the beginning of the sixteenth century as follows:

In the sixteenth century, the bar was not yet in use; partitioning, and even vertical alignment, were not indispensable to either eye or mind in reading a score. It was customary to beat *time*, nothing else. The intrinsic structure of a piece would thus give rise to measures which could be heard *but not seen*. This made it possible to conceive of rhythm as based on beats, but not on beats marshalled into measures.

The French Renaissance was a time of

measured poetry in the ancient manner which the French masters of the sixteenth century wanted to model on Greek and Latin lyric verse. . . By trying to write in *long* and *short* syllables, the humanist poets of the Renaissance showed their ignorance of the fundamental change their language had undergone since ancient times. . . But their rhythmic transcriptions will often turn out to be accurate, because they simply took note of the alternation of long and short syllables in ancient poetry without trying to fit them into isochronous measures.

Emmanuel (1928: II, 433) says, however, that in the second half of the sixteenth century,

when polyphony was going through a period of outstanding development, a renewal of dance also took place in Europe, where elegance and sensuality had become widespread. Both the smaller and the larger courts went wild over it, and got professional musicians of common origin to compose programmes based on folk rhythms and melodies.

The development of dance favoured the introduction of measuring in bars and thereby contributed to halting the impetus of Renaissance rhythmics:

If musicians had taken no more account of measuring in bars than painters did of the cross-ruling of their drawings when they transposed them onto the canvas, there would never have been any confusion between rhythmics and metrics; the bars scattered throughout the score originally had no other import or effect. When, however, the unfortunate spread of measuring into bars, which dance musicians found so helpful, made it the sign of a rhythmic choice for any musician whatsoever, the sixteenth-century advances in rhythm were jeopardised. It was of little help that great musicians, starting with Bach, should have shown their disdain for the use of bars by bending them to their own uses. The die was cast: bars and symmetry gained ground apace. Triumphant, they lent each other help and support, and even managed at times to mislead great masters. For the general public, they became dogma. Between them, they did away with everything the Renaissance had recovered of ancient free rhythmics.   (ibid.: 436)

In less than a century, the bar grew from a mere indicator into a dogmatic theory. Long before Bach, the *tactus*, though still in use alongside the new system, had given up its role in governing rhythmic organisation. This development is all the more remarkable in view of the importance of the *tactus* as the sole unit of measure throughout the Middle Ages.

Though the *tactus* enjoyed a special ascendancy during Medieval times, the basic principle was in use long before. St Augustine, writing on beating time in the fourth century AD (*De musica* II, x: 18), already distinguishes the rising and falling movements which impose isochronous durations on the flow of time: 'The hand in clapping first rises, then falls. One part of the foot thus corresponds to the raising and the other to the falling.'

In the notes to their edition, Finaert and Thonnard (1947: 498) add,

The Master prefers equality coupled with variety to perfect equality, which would be monotonous; however, the length of time must be the same. This is an exceptionless rule required of him by mathematics. . .

Like other Latin grammarians, St Augustine makes no mention of strong and weak beats or of accentual differences in the foot. . . This point is extremely important for a proper understanding of the *De musica* and rhythmics in general in Antiquity. We will see below how St Augustine bases his theory of silences on the rule of rhythmic unity.

Augustine himself (*De musica* IV, xvii: 36), states this theory as follows: 'Some metres are connected in such a way as to reject any insertion of silence. . ., while others require that there be silence between them.' Elsewhere (ibid. III, viii: 17), the Master says to his Disciple, 'Remember then that these spaces of silence must be a fixed part of the metre, so that, when you find something is lacking for a proper foot, you must ask which of the two parts requires an additional measured silence to make up for it.' Again (ibid. IV, xiv: 24), 'However, in those rhythms which are not formed by words, but by some plucked-string or wind instrument, or even by the tongue, it makes no difference after which note or percussion the silence comes, provided that it is allowed by the above-mentioned rules.'

Let us remember that St Augustine was writing at the end of Roman times, which had seen the progressive degeneration of poetic and musical canons. Augustine, far from taking the art of his own time as a model, protests vigorously against this decadence. As Finaert and Thonnard (1947: 498) say, 'the *De musica* is an attempt to restore purity to the rules of ancient "music"'.

What was this ancient music like? Emmanuel tells us that Greek and Roman melodies were almost entirely homophonous, which made it impossible for musicians to mark rhythmic divisions by the richness of combinations in the accompaniment.

This led to stamping the foot on the stage floor to mark the start of the downbeat, and probably its subdivisions as well (perhaps a sound for every beat?). It may even be that the upbeat too was indicated in practice by a sound such as snapping of the fingers. . . The members of the Roman chorus wore sandals reinforced with iron whose rhythmic pulses sometimes made the stage floor give way: the kind of 'strong beat' our own theoreticians would love! Closer consideration shows, however, that those percussions have nothing in common, particularly with regard to position in the measure, with the ones which dominate our own music teaching. Their role is simply to make the divisions of the measure perceptible in both its weak and its intense parts.

In any case, the important thing here is not the precise procedure of beating time, nor how the main gestures could be broken down into secondary ones to mark divisions within the measure by auditive or other means, but the theory itself which reflects the nature of rhythm.

The theoreticians say that, however long a measure may be, it is made perceptible to the performer by two gestures by the orchestra leader (accompanied, if need be, by auditive indications). These two gestures are the upbeat and downbeat, represented by lifting the foot or hand, and then letting it fall again.   (Emmanuel 1921: 484)

According to Wegner (1956: v, 877), the Greeks of the Hellenistic period (starting in the third century BC) had, alongside instruments such as *crotala* and cymbals, another idiophone called a *kroupezion*. It also sounded by striking its parts together, but was operated by the foot: 'Demosthenes (*Meidias* 17) was the first to mention the *kroupezion*, but only speaks of it as a training instrument. Later authors say somewhat more precisely that it was used to mark the beginning of a piece, and particularly for the continuous marking of the measure.'

The *kroupezion*, which is pictured in the imagery of the Hellenistic period, acted principally as a metronome. Only later did it become a full-fledged instrument. Wegner (1956: II, 877) says that it only appeared in Roman orchestras, where it was called a *scabellum*, in imperial times.

Emmanuel (1921: 484) writes that, whether a percussion instrument or a simple movement of the arm is used, 'the start of the downbeat might be called the *ictus* of the metre. This corresponds to the fall of hand or foot. There is usually an accompanying sound, but it is no more necessary than it is to the first beat of our own measures as indicated by the downward motion of a conductor's hand.'

Let us turn to *Science de la Musique* (1976: I, 481) for a definition of *ictus*:

The term *ictus* appears in texts by Horace, Ovid, and Aristides Quintilian concerning metre, which was an integral part of the general theory of Greek and Latin music. The *ictus pollicis* is a percussive gesture by the leader which transmits both an auditive and a visual signal to the chorus. The *ictus* is reinforced in dancing by the use of the foot-operated *scabellum*.

The *ictus* was no more than a marker and was nothing like what is now known as a 'strong beat'. As Emmanuel (1921: 537) says, 'Greek rhythmics only made use of the *strong beat* in a small number of special cases, such as diverse sorts of marching rhythms.'

Greek rhythmics is in fact based entirely on the principle of the *chronos prōtos*, which is quite different from the idea of a strong beat. According to Tiby (1960: I, 384), the *chronos prōtos* 'may not contain more than one syllable, note, or dance step, nor can it be decomposed in any way. . . . A uniform sequence of notes has no rhythm until certain notes are separated by an equal number of units, and are made to stand out, giving rise to equal groups beginning with an ictus.' He says that the term *chronos prōtos* is taken from the works of Aristoxenes of Tarentum, writing in the fourth century BC. Eight centuries before St Augustine, Greek rhythmics were thus already based on the maintenance of strict periodicity. As Tiby (1960: 1, 387) says, 'the Greeks had signs to mark silences, which were, of course, considered to be an integral part of the foot.'

Emmanuel takes us even further back in time on the basis of this idea:

To explain this choice of the *chronos prōtos*, we must recall that ancient Greek, a daughter of an even older Indoeuropean language of which the Vedic poems were also an offshoot, was not accented like Italian or German. Its accents were *pitch accents*. This means that they were marked by a quick rise in the pitch of the voice without harshness, stress, *ictus*, or lengthening of the syllable bearing it. (1926: 104–5)

He quotes Meillet in describing Indoeuropean as

an ancient language 'of which not a scrap remains, nor the slightest memory of the people who once spoke it'; however, nearly all the ancient and modern languages of Europe derive from it, and a comparison of their similarities allows us to arrive at 'a fairly accurate definition of the general features of this parent language'. (ibid.: 110)

Meillet says that

every syllable in Indoeuropean had a fixed long or short quantity (with a few exceptions in final position). The contrasts of quantity were constant and quite clear to the ear. The metrics of Vedic and ancient Greek thus rest solely on the regular repetition or recurrence of short and long syllables in specific positions, together with a few rules regarding the end of a word. In other words, *the rhythm to Indoeuropean was purely quantitative and did not involve stress*. (1903, 1937: 143)

Emmanuel again quotes Meillet as saying,

Speakers of modern languages which use stress, such as German and English (which have very strong stress), have trouble imagining rhythm based solely on differences of duration in sequences of elements. But the general theory of rhythm shows that an alternation of *short* and *long* is enough to create a sensation of rhythm. . . The essential features of Vedic and ancient Greek verse are thus: free positioning of the accent and the use of rhythm based on sequences of long and short syllables. These features are the consequence of the phonetic structure of the languages in the Vedic and ancient Greek groups, and this structure was inherited from Indoeuropean. (quoted in Emmanuel 1926: 110)

Emmanuel's comment on this passage is:

At the time when this structure changed by the transformation of the pitch accent into stress in Greek (and Latin), a revolution took place, not only in the metrics of poetry, but in all rhythmics, including music and dance, as well as speech. (ibid.: 110–11)

Emmanuel's comparison of ancient and modern rhythmics provides a suitable conclusion to this backward glance at history, in which we have sketched the changing conceptions of rhythm:

Ancient art derived all its rhythmics from the 'lengths' of syllables in speech. By a very simple transposition (since all ancient music involved song), these lengths were converted into the primary factors in a small number of standard rhythmic figures. Multiplication of the chronos prōtos (equivalent to the shortest sung syllable). . . produced a wide variety of extremely supple rhythms. . .

Modern art proceeds in opposite fashion and creates its rhythmic figures by division and subdivision of a long value. . . While ancient art enjoys combining, enlarging, switching, and 'modulating' the primary elements of rhythm, modern art is content with uniform series. It has submitted itself without argument to the tyranny of the bar. . . Rich ancient, and poor modern rhythmics are associated with two different kinds of language. One existed in ancient times and had an entirely melodic, stressless accent and supple, unconstrained syllable flow, which could be rhythmised as desired. The other includes the 'percussive' modern languages where the use of primary and secondary stress partitions speech into binary and ternary groups of syllables. These have overstepped their bounds and spread into instrumental music, where they impose divisions of no more than two and three.   (1928: I, 7–8)

2   Towards a precise terminology

2.1   INTRODUCTION

Our study of African rhythm and discovery of what we believe to be its basic features suggest there is a common denominator which can provide a link between African rhythm and the principles underlying the kind of rhythm practiced in the West. A critical examination of Western terminology has revealed a number of inherent contradictions but has also shown where they come from. We have seen that they are connected with the development of the idea of rhythm in the West. A short history of this development has helped us to understand this more clearly. We have found that, in Emmanuel's words, 'the development of rhythmics is related to the development of language' (1926: 111).

We have seen that the Indoeuropean languages which gave rise to Vedic poetry and later to Greek poetry had *pitch accents* and no stress. Their versification, the 'verbal rhythmics' which 'stylises the rhythm of language' (Emmanuel 1926: 106) and is therefore an intermediate stage between the unmeasured flow of speech and strictly proportional musical rhythm, was based only on the quantitative contrast of long and short syllables and not on dynamic intensity.

We should here recall that most African languages are *tone languages* and also have no stress. In such languages (cf. Book I, 2.2.5), the *pitch* of a syllable is a distinctive feature; the same syllable spoken on different pitches can change the meaning of the word containing it. *Tones* are to these languages as *pitch accent* was to Indoeuropean languages. In either one, stress may have an expressive role, but is unrelated to phonology, i.e., does not distinguish the meaning of words.

This gives us some insight into why *Indoeuropean rhythmics and African rhythmics, which are free of the linguistic constraints of a stress accent and therefore of accentual patterns, are satisfied to arrange values into feet and metres in one case, and into rhythmic patterns in the other.*

The idea of a stress pattern first appeared in the West as a consequence of the shift from a pitch accent to a stress accent in Greek and Latin (Emmanuel 1926: 110). Metrics, whose only task had previously been to 'gauge long and short syllables and arrange them into groups' (Emmanuel 1928: 113), then had to make allowance for a regular distribution of the stress accent as well, given the constraints it imposed on the rhyme. When the term 'metre' was introduced into musicological vocabulary, it thus entailed the idea of regularly repeated accents.

We have seen that the ambiguous use of the term 'metre' (which has in turn given rise to the notion of measure) is at the heart of most of the confusions in the field of rhythm. The resulting contradictory interpretations all involve the use of terms in too wide a sense, with ill-defined limits. To provide an accurate description of rhythmic systems which make no use of the notion of measure and the associated feature of the 'strong beat', we will therefore have to develop a precise and univocal vocabulary, i.e., one in which the meanings of two terms never overlap. This is exactly what we will try to do in the following pages. We will propose a set of definitions for the terms already assigned to it and its derivate. In versification, for example, metre implies an arrangement of long and short syllables, while in music it assumes accentual ranking. purely technical scope of our own discussion.

2.2   PROPOSED DEFINITIONS

2.2.1   Metre, *tactus*, beat, pulse

In *measured* music, these terms all denote one element in a sequence of regularly spaced, i.e., temporally equidistant reference points, which divide the musical continuum up into equal units and also act as a standard of measurement for all the durations in the music. The choice of the right word to denote such a unit is clearly a difficult one. Etymologically and semantically, *metre* would seem to be the most appropriate term, as it comes from the Greek *metron* and the Latin *metrum*: the *metron* is the unit indicated by the metronome (or *metron-nomos*), the device for measuring or controlling time. We will however be obliged to renounce the use of this term in order to avoid the possibility of confusion with any of the other meanings already assigned to it and its derivate. In versification, for example, metre implies an arrangement of long and short syllables, while in music it assumes accentual ranking.

Tactus is a term closely associated with the music of a specific period of Western history, namely, Medieval and Renaissance polyphony. It will therefore be preferable to set this term aside as well.

'Beat' is more neutral (and a French equivalent, *battue*, can be found). But the term is undesirable insofar as it involves the idea of materialisation by a bodily motion, since this is not to be found in African musical practice.

The best French term to express the idea is *temps*; however, the expression *'temps musical'* has a number of different meanings, some of which are connected with philosophy and perceptual psychology, and should therefore be excluded from the purely technical scope of our own discussion.

We will therefore fall back on the term 'pulse' or 'pulsation', which suggests the idea of temporal units such as those produced by the action of a metronome. By *pulsation* we mean the isochronous, neutral, constant, intrinsic reference unit which determines tempo. To take this definition piece by piece:

- *isochronous*, i.e., repeated at regular intervals
- *neutral* insofar as there is no difference between one pulsation and another: the idea of an arrangement of beats at a higher level is excluded
- *constant* in being the only *invariable* element in the course of the piece
- *intrinsic*, i.e., inherent in the music itself and specific to each piece: this makes it always a relevant factor
- a *reference unit*, i.e., establishing a unit of time
- *determining tempo* by setting the internal flow of the music it underlies.

Pulsations are an uninterrupted sequence of reference points with respect to which rhythmic flow is organised. All the durations in a piece, *whether they appear as sounds or silences*, are defined in relationship to the pulsation. In terms of the temporal organisation of a polyphonic ensemble, the pulsation is also the common denominator for all the parts.

2.2.2   Rhythm

The pulsation as defined above is not rhythm. For there to be rhythm, sequences of auditive events must be characterised by contrasting features. This contrast may be created in three different ways: by *accents*, *tone colours*, or *durations*. In practice, however, these three parameters usually operate together (though in a wide variety of ways). The distinction is thus mainly theoretical and is made here for methodological reasons only. Its purpose is to allow a strict classification of the different kinds of rhythmic phenomena. We must therefore examine each of these parameters separately, from the sole point of view of the type of contrast it represents, i.e., in terms of its own relevance.

Accents: Contrast is obtained by means of an accentual mark which may be repeated regularly or irregularly. When there are no contrasts of tone colour or duration, accentuation is the only criterion for the determination of rhythm.

Tone colours: Contrast is created by the regular or irregular alternation of different tone colours. When there are no accentual marks or contrasting durations, tone colour is the only criterion for the determination of rhythm.

Durations: Contrast results from successions of unequal values. In the absence of accentuation or differences in tone colour, contrasting durations are the only criterion for the determination of rhythm.

All the possible ways of producing rhythm can be summed up in nine cases. In fig. 1 we list these cases, but once again remind the reader that this inventory is applicable only to measured music.

Fig. 1

Type a   Identical durations with regular accentuation

Type b   Identical durations with irregular accentuation

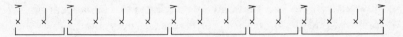

Type c   Identical durations with no accentuation but *regular* alternation of tone colour

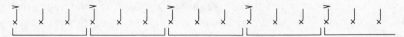

Type d   Identical durations with no accentuation but *irregular* alternation of tone colour

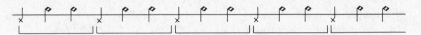

Type e   Differing durations with regular accentuation

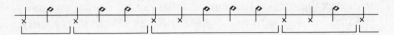

Type f   Differing durations with irregular accentuation

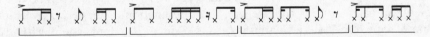

Type g   Differing durations with no accentuation but *regular* alternation of tone colour

Type h   Differing durations with no accentuation but *irregular* alternation of tone colour

Type i   Differing durations *with neither accentuation nor change of tone colour*

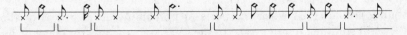
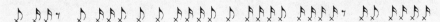

Types (a) and (b) are cited mainly for the purpose of theoretical exhaustiveness. They are rarely used systematically outside, perhaps, children's game songs (type (a)) or some American 'repetitive music' (types (a) and (b)). Types (c) and (d), however, are often found in traditional African music, particularly in polyrhythmic ensembles. Types (e) and (f) are the most frequent ones. They can be used both simultaneously and in succession. Type (e) is the one most commonly found in Western music of the classical period. Type (f) is current both in *ars nova* polyphony and in modern works such as those of Stravinsky. Types (g) and (h) are frequently used by African percussion groups. In type (i), the only rhythm-producing factor is duration. If all the values were equal, we would simply have the elementary pulsation. Unlike type (a), (b), (e), and (f), which can all be found to varying extents in Western cultured or folk music, type (i) is characteristic of ancient Greek music and the rhythm of some types of African music.

We must, however, emphasise that any of these types can appear *in succession* in a piece of monody, and *simultaneously* in the case of polyphony.

2.2.3 'Metrics'

If we accept the preceding characterisation of the possible types of rhythm, it becomes clear that 'metre' is nothing but the first of the nine in our list (type (a): identical durations with regular accentuation). *What is called metre in music is thus the simplest form of rhythmic expression.* In other words, musical metre has no independent status. Ignorance of this fact is the root of the many confusions between metre and rhythm.

Generally speaking, rhythm operates at two different levels in regularly accented music, whether monodic or polyphonic: the first derives from the distribution of beats into a given number of similar reference frames (or *measures*), which are defined by the regular repetition of an accented beat (type (a) rhythm); the second is determined by the durations of sounds and silences. The conjunction of these two levels results in rhythm of type (e). Western rhythm is thus two-sided. Rhythmic complexity is directly proportional to the extent of offsetting and ambiguity between the two levels.

The measure is always a temporal matrix and a reference unit. To draw an analogy, the measure is to the organisation of time as the *cantus firmus* (in the strict sense) is to the organisation of the other parts in polyphony. The *cantus firmus* is the basic part, expressed in long and often equal values. It stands at a lower level of organisation than the parts it supports and provides them with a *melodic* reference. In the same way, the measure as the basic level of rhythmic organisation provides a *temporal* reference for the musical durations.

It might be objected that accents and attacks do not usually coincide in heavily syncopated music. The durations are thereby freed from the framework of the measure and depend only on the second level of rhythmic organisation. If, then, the measure is really a part of rhythm, it should remain audible as rhythm itself does. The reply to this reasoning is that, even when the parts in polyphony are deprived of the *cantus firmus*, they still continue to refer to it. In the same way, the measure may be inaudible, but is nonetheless still taken as the temporal reference of the musical durations.

2.2.4   Heterometric and polymetric; heterorhythmic and polyrhythmic

The terms 'heterometric' and 'polymetric' are not differentiated by many writers. In order to establish a distinction, let us remark that, in current terminology, the prefix *poly-* assumes the simultaneous occurrence of several different events of the same type, as in *poly*phony, *poly*rhythm. Its use should therefore be restricted to phenomena of this kind. *Polymetric* should thus be used to refer to the *simultaneous* operation of different accentual patterns in different parts of polyphony.

Concomitantly, the prefix *hetero-* should be reserved for the temporal *succession* of different events of the same type and, in multipart music, for the *simultaneous* occurrence of the same event in each one. Thus, *heterometric* would describe a change of measure in monody; and in polyphony, a *joint* change of measure *in all the parts*. Types (b) and (f) defined above would thus be rhythmically heterometric.

In musicological literature, however, the confusion which reigns between the notions 'heterometric' and 'heterorhythmic', and between 'polymetric' and 'polyrhythmic', is at least as great as the confusion between *metre* and *rhythm*. The following assertion taken from the article 'Polymetrik' in *Riemann Musiklexikon* (1967: III, 739) is proof of this: 'No clear Distinction between the concepts of polyrhythmics and polymetrics has yet been made.'

If what is called metre is really rhythm, there can be no poly*metrics*. Whenever different patterns of accent are superposed in the same work, we have reached an elementary stage of *polyrhythm*. Consequently, whenever the durations are unequal in any melodic line (as happens in almost all works), the only term that can properly apply is *heterorhythmic*. Likewise, what is called homophonic music, i.e., music where all the parts move in identical rhythmic fashion, also belongs to the domain of heterorhythmics.

In the final analysis, the term 'polymetric' is only applicable to a very special kind of phenomenon. If we take 'metre' in its primary sense of *metrum* (the metre being the temporal reference unit), 'polymetric' would describe the simultaneous unfolding of several parts in a single work at different tempos *so as not to be reducible to a single metrum*. This happens in some modern music, such as some of Charles Ives's works, Elliott Carter's *Symphony*, B. A. Zimmermann's opera *Die Soldaten*, and Pierre Boulez's *Rituel*. Being polymetric in the strict sense, these works can only be performed with several simultaneous conductors.

We have said that, when the parts in a single work have different simultaneous rhythmic organisations, the situation is polyrhythmic, even if only elementarily so. In this sense, 'polyrhythmic' is the opposite of 'homophonic', which implies similar rhythmic articulations in every part (cf. Book II, 1.2.5). Some writers nevertheless reserve the term 'polyrhythmic' for a specific procedure called 'cross-rhythm', involving the conjunction of different independent but interlocked rhythmic figures (cf. Book II, 1.4.4). These figures cannot thus be related to each other through breakdown or amalgamation. The ethnomusicologists of African music often use the term 'polyrhythmic' in this sense.

Let us now turn to an examination of the principles underlying the temporal organisation of African music.

3   African rhythmics

3.1   ON MUSIC BASED ON THE *TACTUS*

African cross-rhythm is extremely complex, and is characterised essentially by the permanent sense of tension it creates: different interwoven rhythmic figures are repeated cyclically and uninterruptedly. The interlocked structure may involve irregular accentuation as well, making it extremely difficult for even the trained listener to analyse it by ear. This is what Apel (1970: 214) calls 'conflicting rhythmic patterns'.

No matter how complex it may be, however, African rhythm always has a simple ultimate reference: the pulsation as defined above, whose function is similar to that of the Medieval *tactus*. African practice thus resembles the practice in use in the West during the Middle Ages and the Renaissance, when the temporal organisation of music was based solely on this neutral, unmarked, intrinsic element.

Let us recall that the *tactus* as mere unit of duration had the sole function of providing the performers with equidistant reference points. As Schünemann says, that is why 'in olden times, the person beating time could only specify the tempo, not accentuation. . . He beat regularly with upward and downward motions of the hand like a metronome' (1913: 54). Given the strictly *metric* (in the primary sense of the term) nature of this governing principle, Auda says, 'In the thirteenth as in the sixteenth century, the laws of metric measure and rhythmic measure were the same' (1965: 141).

The *tactus* made it possible to obtain a direct coordination of the durations in all the parts of a polyphonic work without recourse to an intermediate level in the hierarchy: 'Until about the seventeenth century, there were no two-, three-, or four-beat measures, only a succession of *tactus* corresponding more or less to what we call a "beat" today' (Chailley 1967: 102). The measure as an intermediate hierarchical level is also absent from traditional African music. The pulsation is the only temporal reference the musicians have. It enables them both to develop their own parts and to interweave them with the others. It also constitutes the basic structural element of the periods, insofar as each one is composed of a given number of equal units of time (cf. Book I, 3.3.3).

The African musician thus proceeds neither by splitting, as in Western musical practice, nor by conjunction, as in the ancient Greek metric system. He neither divides a basic unit (such as a measure) up into a given number of beats, nor starts with a chronos prōtos of minimal duration, of which larger groups are multiples. This is one of the basic premises required for understanding African rhythm.

Dauer (1966: 445) showed he was aware of this when he wrote that African polyrhythm is based on a 'regulating pulse' (*Steuerungspuls*), a notion equivalent to what previous writers had called a 'metronomic sense' or 'beat': 'This "beat" usually has nothing to do with the real audible rhythmic or melodic products, but nevertheless constitutes the common, perceptible (*empfindungsmässig*) substratum which incorporates them all.'

These rhythmic and melodic figures are nearly always cyclic formulae. There is no intermediate level between the regulating pulsation and the temporal organisation of the figure as a whole. These structural features are not unrelated to the way a musician learns to play his instrument, as the Ghanaian musicologist Nketia remarks: 'The African learns to play rhythms in patterns' (1963: 10). This means that the African child perceives rhythmic figures as totalities. This learning process is comparable to learning to read by the whole-word method in our own civilisation of the written word. This method, instead of being based on juxtaposition of letters and syllables, proceeds by recognition of words as wholes. This is similar to what the African child does when he apprehends each rhythmic formula *as a whole* without breaking it down into its constituents. This basic point prevents the use of terms like 'additive' and 'divisive' rhythms, which some investigators have used to describe African rhythmics.

The Cameroonian ethnomusicologist Belinga (1965: 18) also disputes the application of Western notions to the transcription of durations in African music. He wonders why measures should be used to write traditional songs, since no such accentual framework is used in Africa: 'What do we do with the classical notions of strong and weak beats? In African music, only one thing matters: the periodic repetition of a single rhythmic cell.'

This remark leads us to examine the use made of one last term in the vocabulary of rhythm, *syncopation*. Let us recall what syncopation is. Rousseau (1768: 459) defines it as 'the extension of a sound begun on the weak beat onto the strong beat'. Amy, writing in the *Encyclopédie de la Musique* (1961: III, 762), says that syncopation is 'a rhythmic feature consisting of the presence of an accented element on a weak beat and its extension on to a strong beat'.

It is thus evident that there can be no syncopation in a musical system which makes no use of the contrast between strong and weak beats. In fact, Amy recognises this and adds: 'The idea of syncopation is inseparable from the theory of accentuation, which covers all periods of so-called measured music. It is associated with the distinction between *strong* (and half-strong) beats and *weak* beats within the measure.'

Rousseau (1768: 459) also notes that 'any syncopated note is off beat [à contretemps], and any sequence of syncopated notes is an off beat progression'. Rousseau rightly avoids saying that any off beat note is syncopated.

Once the two notions have been distinguished, an off beat note can be defined as starting on the second half (or any other part except the attack) of a beat. In other words, *any note which is attacked so as not to coincide with the attack of the beat* is 'off beat'.

As we have seen, syncopation requires that an off beat note extend on to part of the following beat, *specifically, the strong part*. Consequently, in music which has no strong beats, the word "syncopation" cannot be used to describe the extension of a contra-tempo note on to the following beat. In African rhythm, for example, notes which are attacked so as not to coincide with the pulsation are often accented more than others which do. The term 'syncopation' is not appropriate to describe this phenomenon. In current musicological terminology, however, there is no suitable term to describe the extension of off beat note onto the next beat, when the latter cannot be called 'strong', although this is quite frequently found in the field of African music. A new terminology will thus be required to cover the rhythmic phenomena of music with no regular accentuation.

Kolinski's (1973: 498–500) proposals will serve this purpose. He distinguishes *commetric* and *contrametric* rhythmic organisations. In the former, the figures and accents generally coincide with the metric (in the sense of *metrum*) pulsation; in the latter, they conflict with it. This contrast makes it possible to provide a rhythmically relevant description of a piece of music, as soon as the position of the pulsation has been determined. In these terms, black African music is clearly more contrametric than commetric.

Let us note that these notions can also be properly applied to Renaissance polyphony. Much of this music, where accents are offset with respect to the *tactus* for the main purpose of making certain words stand out from the text, can be described as contrametric. All the same, however complex the rhythm of a piece may be, its durations never fail to refer to the *tactus* as a regular reference unit.

To conclude this, we may say that

- if by *heterometric* we mean that there is an irregular succession of accentual matrices
- if by *polymetric* we mean that there is a simultaneous progression of several parts based on different accentual matrices and
- if we accept that music which is not subject to the regular repetition of accents does exist,

it follows that *neither heterometric nor polymetric rhythm can be found in music which makes no use of the notions of strong and weak beats*. This is precisely the case of most traditional African music.

3.2   ON APPLYING WESTERN *SOLFÈGE* TO AFRICAN MUSIC

It should now be much clearer why we have been so critical of researchers who use transcriptions which submit African music to the conventions of the Western *solfège*. The use of a method of writing suited only to cultured Western music, and an ignorance of the principles of temporal organisation of the music to be transcribed, can only result in distortions. Moreover, the writing conventions in question are not only arbitrary; they are also ambiguous. While bars only set off quantities, the indication of measure also entails a specific kind of distribution of accents.

The unit of time taken as a reference is thus not the same in a 6/8 measure, for example, as in a 3/4 measure, although both contain equal quantities. In the former, the reference unit equals half the measure (♩.), but only a third (♩) in the latter, and this entails two different kinds of accentuation.

We must again return to Medieval times to discover the origin of this ambiguity. According to *Science de la Musique* (1976: II, 923), the semibreve was used to represent a measured value as early as the beginning of the thirteenth century: 'In the fifteenth and sixteenth centuries, it became the basic measured value in the system. . . In the seventeenth century, it became the modern semibreve.'

Danhauser (1929: 82), however, writes in the section entitled 'On the use of numbers to indicate measure' of his famous handbook for conservatory students: 'Measure is indicated by two numbers in the form of a fraction *taking the semibreve as unity* [italics added].' But since the semibreve is divisible without remainder by two, but not by three,

Western notation has had to make use of two types of measure: 'simple' and 'compound'; and this is the crux of the question. Danhauser says that 'in simple measures, the *bottom number*, or denominator, indicates the duration of a beat', while 'in compound measures, the *bottom number* indicates the duration of a third of a beat'.

Science de la Musique (1976: II, 606) explains it in this way:

In the former, the denominator indicates the duration of a beat, and the numerator, the number of beats per measure; in the latter, the denominator indicates a third of a beat, and the numerator, three times the number of beats per measure. . . For example, 3/4 indicates a simple measure of three crotchets, corresponding to 9/8 in compound time (9 quavers arranged as three dotted crotchets).

This means that in one case the reference unit is explicit and derives from the *division* of the measure, while in the other, the reference unit is implicit but can be determined by *summing* its constituent values. A 3/4 measure would thus be *divisive*, while a 9/8 measure would be *additive*.

In the final analysis, this contradiction is inherent in our system of notation. As Chailley (1967: 102) says, 'Let us have the courage to admit that our method of numbering measures is a masterpiece of absurdity. It cannot be logically defended,. . . and its only explanation is to be found. . . in the historical stages of its derivation.'

Western music has made do with this method as best it could. But when a system of this kind is forced on African music, the result can only be nonsense. Numerous investigators have fallen victim to this difficulty. Finding it impossible to conceive of irregular accentuation outside an accentual framework, they have ended up treating every accented note as the first beat in a measure, i.e., as a 'strong beat'. By trying to marry irregular accentuation and the systematic distribution of accents characteristic of each type of measure, they have found themselves with a continuous succession of changes of measure.

To take a monodic example, we find Brandel (1961: 74) noting the fifteen quavers in a fragment of a Mangbetu choral song from the former Belgian Congo as a sequence of five measures marked 3/8, 5/16, 6/16, 7/16, and 3/8, respectively. Transcriptions of more complex music are even more arbitrary. Let us recall that Jones (1959: II, 11–40), for example, distributes the *Ewe Nyayito* dance melody from Ghana into alternating 3/8, 2/4, 6/8, 1/4, 3/4, 7/8, and even 1/8 measures. The seven percussion parts for this dance are marked as follows: the double bell is marked 12/8 (with 6/8 indicated in brackets); the first drum is assigned 12/8, while the claps are noted in 6/4. Then comes the master drummer's part, where 5/8, 3/8, 2/4, 5/4, 6/8, 3/4, and 1/4 are in permanent alternation. Two of the three remaining drums are marked 6/8, followed first by 3/8 and then by 4/8; the third remains in 3/8.

Another example is a *sanza* piece from South Africa, which Brandel (1970: 19) transcribes by the simultaneous use of two different metric systems: the right-hand part is notated in 2/4 and the left-hand one in 6/8, *although the value of the quaver is the same for each*. The result is that the bars on the two staffs only coincide every twelve quavers.

If we were to treat the snare drum part in Ravel's *Bolero* in the same way, i.e., if we were to note what the right hand and the left hand play on two different staffs, and if we put a bar in front of every accent, without distinction of hand, we would certainly 'discover' a polymetric relationship between them. But we know very well that the drummer apprehends this persistent figure as a repetitive overall pattern and not as the result of interconnecting two metric systems!

We would be even more unwise to suppose that two different pulsations can be conjoined in a single piece of traditional African music. Kubik (1964b: 152) nevertheless affirms just this. He suggests that, in Akadinda music for two xylophones, each musician feels himself to be playing in time, and his partner off beat (cf. Book II, 2.3.3). We could not conceivably accept Kubik's statement that 'In several forms of African instrumental music, the musicians can refer to two, three, or even four, ongoing pulsations' (1969: 57). His comments in the *Encyclopedia Britannica* are equally surprising: 'A basic characteristic of interlocking is the absence of a common guide-pulse to be taken as reference point by all players. . . The musicians in a group relate their parts to individual reference pulses, which can stand in various relations to each other' (1974: 247).

If this were true, we would have polymetric music in the sense defined above, i.e., a conjunction of different temporal reference units. Since, as we know, the musicians Kubik mentions have no outside coordinator, how do they manage to keep together?

Brandel's error derives from the fact that she was unaware of the principle of equidistant pulsations underlying African rhythmic organisation, and therefore treated the figures based on combinations of binary and ternary values as 'additive, irregular-pulsed rhythms' (1961: 73).

While it is true that African rhythmic patterns frequently display internal asymmetries, this does not prevent them from making constant reference to a *strictly regular pulsation*; as we have said, they have neither an additive nor a divisive structure. Though there are many examples, we will restrict ourselves to the ones already mentioned, involving investigators whose work is frequently quoted in the specialised literature.

Let us return once again to Jones, whose transcription of a complex polyrhythmic example we have mentioned above. The second volume of Jones (1959) is given over entirely to scores, almost all of which are noted in polymetric form superposing different measures whose strong beats do not coincide. This is all the more surprising in that he states several times in the first volume that there is no regular accentuation in the music he is dealing with. In his table summarising the general features of African music, he thus says, 'The claps or other time-background impart no accent whatever to the song' (Jones 1959: I, 49). This idea is one of the leitmotifs in Jones's work, from his earliest publications onwards. There is, however, another, contradictory one concerning the simultaneity of 'main beats'. Many authors have not noticed this contradiction and have accepted the second point without asking themselves whether it was justified in view of the first. This is probably one reason why there has been such an abundance of transcriptions in polymetric form.

Well before Jones began his own research, Béclard d'Harcourt (in Joyeux 1924: 173), who probably had no other contact with African music outside the cylinder recordings brought back from Upper Guinea by Dr Joyeux, remarked with respect to an extremely complex piece of music for six xylophones that 'rhythmic offsetting is produced simply by shifting the accents, but the quantities remain the same'. This insight is to be applauded; it is unfortunate that no reference whatever has been made to it in specialised publications. In fact, very few investigators have looked at rhythm in this way, although Estreicher, Kubik, and Dauer are exceptions.

In a study of Bororo Fulani rhythm, Estreicher remarks that 'the basic formula does not seem to impose any pattern of accentuation. . . The Bororo take advantage of this to insert accents in freely chosen positions. These accents are intentional and clearly marked' (1964: 188).

Kubik clearly recognised the inadequacy of the measure for noting African rhythm. For this reason, he places a figure indicating the total number of minimal values in the whole pattern at the top of some of his transcriptions. He calls this number a *Summationsmeter*, i.e., the sum number of metric units (Kubik 1961, 1964a, 1974).

Dauer (1966), following Kubik, used the same method, which is, in our opinion, the only one that respects the specific nature of African rhythmics and frees it from the arbitrary imposition of the measure. It enables the reader to follow the score easily without obscuring the periodic structure of the music. This suggests another analogy between traditional African music and a form of Western medieval music, the isorhythmic motet. Both are based on the principle of *isoperiodicity*. According to Apel (1959: 143), in the fourteenth century, 'a composer writing an isorhythmic motet would, first of all, have to count the number of notes contained in the Gregorian melody or melisma which he selects as the basis of his work.' Likewise, the ethnomusicologist should start his analysis of traditional African music by counting the number of units (pulsations or minimal values) in the period.

3.3   CONCLUSION

In most traditional African music, time is organised according to the following principles:

(1)   A strictly periodic structure (isoperiodicity) is set up by the repetition of identical or similar musical material, i.e., with or without variations

(2)   The isochronous pulsation is the basic structural element of the period. Whether the figures it contains are binary or ternary, or a combination of these, the period is defined by the *invariant* number of pulsations which constitutes its temporal framework

(3)   There are no regular accentual matrices. The pulsations or beats on which the period is based all have the same status. There is thus no intermediate level (measure, "strong" beats) between the pulsation and the period

(4)   The pulsation is not necessarily materialised.

It is easy to confirm that these principles exist. It will suffice to ask a member of a given culture to superpose hand-claps on a piece of music from that culture. Whether the experiment involves one or more informants, at brief or longer intervals, we have found that the results are always the same:

– the beat is isochronous and perfectly regular; the beats always fall at the same points in the melodic and/or rhythmic material contained in the period
– concomitantly, however this material may be distributed, it always reappears after exactly the same number of beats.

These essential principles of all measured Central African music, both monodic and polyphonic, also seem to govern most measured music throughout sub-Saharan Africa.

Bachelard (1950, 1963: 127–8) says that the basic temporal principle of rhythm is *bringing back a form*: 'A feature is rhythmic if it is brought back. . . When rhythm brings back a form, it often brings back energy.' Bachelard may have the key to why music and dance are so important in all social and religious activities in traditional Africa, and to why the rhythmic factor is so prevalent in the organisation of musical structures, when he says, 'Rhythm is really the only way of taming and preserving all forms of energy. It lies at the foundation of vital and psychic dynamics.'

Book VI

Structural principles and their application

1   Typology

In Book I, we have shown that traditional Central African music consists essentially of the strictly periodic repetition of similar material, with variations. Polyphonic music is naturally no exception to this principle. The overall structure of Central African polyphony of whatever type can be defined as an *ostinato with variations*. This definition is wide enough to cover all the observed melodic and rhythmic variety of this music, and still remain the shortest and most concise way of describing its cyclical nature. To avoid confusion, a clear distinction must be made between the 'tools' involved in producing this polyphony and the musical *techniques* employed.

The *tools* are the human voice and the musical instruments, used individually or in combination. These tools may vary not only from one ethnic group to another, but even within a single population, according to the type of repertory, which will itself be linked to a specific social function. The *techniques* are the structured ways in which these tools are actually used to produce polyphony.

Years of field work have convinced me that the techniques involved in the production of Central African polyphonic and polyrhythmic structures are few in number.

From a purely systematic, but still abstract, point of view, all polyphony and polyrhythmics in this region can be classified into four types:

(1) strict polyrhythmics
(2) polyphony produced by hocket
(3) polyphony produced by melodic instruments
(4) vocal polyphony

These are the basic elements, but the musical reality is more complex and requires further discussion. This is because all of these types, with the exception of hocket polyphony, which works differently, can be combined in various ways. We may recall (see Book I, 2.1) some of the obstacles facing anyone trying to classify African cultural phenomena, particularly the fact that elements which one would be inclined to place in mutually exclusive categories defined by distinctive features may turn out to combine in practice. This might suggest that a more suitable taxonomy could be set up using categories from the musicians' own cultures. Unfortunately, however, this procedure is unsuitable to our ends. This is because traditional African taxonomies, while adequate from a social and/or religious perspective, throw no light whatsoever on the systematic structure of the *musical techniques* employed. But our aim here is precisely to discover these techniques and describe them from a purely musical standpoint, yet still give a faithful representation of how they appear in practice. Once we have described and analysed the various types of polyphony and polyrhythms, we will therefore return to this practical dimension. For the time being, however, we will limit ourselves to the problem of characterisation and definition. The typology presented below is thus intended to capture the forms of musical organisation involved in the polyrhythms and polyphony of this part of Africa.

1.1   STRICT POLYRHYTHMICS

By *strict* polyrhythmics, we understand the superposition of two or more rhythmic figures, each of which is so articulated that its constituent elements (accents, tone colour, and attacks) are interspersed among those of the others so as to create an interwoven effect. All of these figures share a common temporal reference unit. Their periods may be of different lengths but will stand in simple numerical ratios such as 1:2, 1:3, 2:3, 3:4 and so on. Polyrhythmics is *strict* when produced by *nonmelodic* percussion instruments. The melodic parameter, i.e., the use of relative pitch heights on a scale, is thus neutralised.

The combinational formulae resulting from the superposition of different rhythmic figures constitute polyrhythmic 'blocks' which act as substructures to arrangements of other parts, such as monody or vocal parts at parallel intervals (with or without supporting melodic instruments), vocal counterpoint, or 'mixed' polyphony resulting from the combination of vocal and instrumental music.

1.2   HOCKET POLYPHONY

Hocket polyphony is based on the interweaving, interlocking and overlapping of several rhythmic figures which are *tiered on different pitch heights* in a fully defined scalar system. In Central Africa, such polyphony is generally obtained from several wind instruments (horns or whistles), each of which can only produce a single note. These instruments are played in groups ranging in number from five to twenty. Each of them is assigned one of the notes on the same anhemitonic pentatonic scale. Melody is thus obtained only from the ensemble; the individual instruments merely perform rhythmic figures *confined to a given pitch*. The assignment of pitch heights to rhythmic figures places the hocket technique on the very boundary between strict polyrhythmics and polyphony.

1.3   POLYPHONY PRODUCED BY MELODIC INSTRUMENTS

Some melodic instruments, i.e., instruments producing pitches on a specific scale, are played two-handed to produce melodically and rhythmically different parts simultaneously. The superposition of these parts yields a polyphonic lattice. This class contains instruments which are themselves polyphonic (*sanzas*, harps, and xylophones, in Central Africa). Their basic function is to provide a melodic and rhythmic framework for (generally monodic) vocal music. They may be employed singly (as when monody is accompanied by *one* xylophone), or in pairs of the same kind (e.g., accompaniment by *two* xylophones or *two sanzas*). The music produced in this way may also be supported by a strictly polyrhythmic block.

1.4   VOCAL POLYPHONY

This term refers to the superposition of two or more melodically divergent lines with different rhythmic articulations. In Central Africa, only the pygmies use this kind of polyphony. In its most frequent form, it is provided with polyrhythmic support by percussion instruments. In some circumstances, however, the percussion part is limited to simple isochronous hand-claps. In others, the vocal polyphony is enriched by a *strict* (invariant) *ostinato* performed by two whistles. In rare instances, it is performed *a cappella*.

Our study of all available sound archives, including both material recorded by other investigators since the end of the Second World War, and the documents we have ourselves collected over the last twenty years, leads us to believe that the four types defined above suffice for the classification of all the techniques used to produce poly-rhythmic and polyphonic music in the Central African Republic.

It may seem surprising that this classification should begin with the technique which may rightly be judged most complex, namely, *strict polyrhythmics*. This order has been chosen for methodological reasons: not only is this the most widespread and the most characteristic technique in the region; but, even more importantly, its fundamental principles are to be found in the other three types as well. Thus, most music performed by intrinsically polyphonic instruments involves relations of a poly-rhythmic type between the parts played by each of the performer's hands. It is moreover rare to find such an instrument being played without the support of at least one percus-sion instrument, in such a way that a polyrhythmic relationship exists between the two. This suggests that, if one can grasp the principles governing strict polyrhythmics, one will then find it easier to assimilate the ways in which the melodic instrumental and vocal types of polyphony are organised.

We have already remarked that the polyrhythmic technique is not intended for independent use; rather, it is used to provide support for melodic instruments. The same is true of the intrinsically melodic instruments, whose purpose is, as we have seen, to provide a melodic and rhythmic framework for *vocal* music. A vocal melody, either monodic or at parallel intervals, is thus superposed on practically all music performed by instruments. This is because, in the African tradition, musical instruments, whether intrinsically rhythmic or melodic, and however complex a musical lattice they may produce, have the primary function of providing a foundation and a framework for vocal music. Culturally speaking, the *song* remains foremost because its words transmit a verbal message. That is why purely instrumental music is so rare in this region.

Of the four techniques listed above, only the second, hocket polyphony, constitutes an independent class, and this independence is only relative. Thus, while horn and whistle ensembles do not make direct use of vocal music, all the pieces in their reperto-ries are immediately derived from traditional songs and are in fact orchestral versions of them. The remaining three techniques combine in practice to yield two categories, each involving strict polyrhythmics: in one, it is associated with music produced by intrinsi-cally polyphonic instruments; and in the other, with vocal polyphony. The justification for these distinctions of type will become fully apparent in the final chapter of this Book. Once we have discussed and analysed the techniques separately, we will look at them again in combination. The truncated examples taken out of context in the chapter on strict polyrhythmics will then reappear as the polyrhythmic blocks used to support the melodies produced by intrinsically polyphonic instruments. It will then be pos-sible to form an overall idea of the music as it appears in the concrete reality of traditional practice.

2   Analytical notions

The analysis of any cultural phenomenon is reductive by definition. This follows from the fact that, in the terms of Gilles-Gaston Granger (1967: 2), 'any attempt to understand any facet of man must start with a reduction of our experience to a set of correlative marks'. On this principle, if we want an adequate description of how Central African polyphonies operate as *systems*, we must find a suitable set of correlative marks, and say why we consider them to be basic. A further need will be to examine the various facets and levels in our data where we find these marks at work.

The first step in our analysis will be to reduce this music to writing by transcription. This involves a set of preliminary operations enabling pitch (degrees on a scale) to be discriminated, and temporal organisation (metrics and rhythmics) to be grasped. It will therefore also be necessary to give a principled explanation of the scores appearing in the remainder of this volume.

The main purpose of the present chapter is to provide an explicit statement, and in so doing to justify the choice, of the criteria we apply to the analysis of Central African types of polyphony and polyrhythmics. Two important questions must, however, be dealt with beforehand. The first concerns all types of Central African music, while the second relates only to music of the polyphonic type.

Can the term *mode* be applied to the arrangement of strictly pentatonic melodic material?

Can the notion of *harmony* be applied to the vertical structures engendered by this same material?

The importance of the answers we provide to these questions for our choice of analytical criteria and our results is immediately evident.

2.1   ARE CENTRAL AFRICAN PENTATONIC SYSTEMS MODES?

A musical scale may be defined as a closed set of pitches lying within an octave. When these pitches are arranged in ascending or descending order, each one constitutes a degree of the scale. This definition clearly excludes the possibility of establishing a hierarchy among the degrees, all of which are equally available for the creation of melody. The intervals separating the degrees are, however, generally unequal, so that their distribution confers a characteristic 'profile' on each arrangement, i.e., on each type of scale.

With a few very rare exceptions, all Central African music uses an anhemitonic pentatonic system based on a *succession* of two kinds of intervals: full tones and minor thirds. There are five possible kinds of scalar organisation in such a system, deriving from the five possible successions of these two intervals. Constantin Brăiloiu (1953) calls them 'pentatonic modes'. They are listed below.

I	G–A–B–D–E
II	A–B–D–E–G
III	B–D–E–G–A
IV	D–E–G–A–B
V	E–G–A–B–D

The different pentatonic modes are thus merely inversions of one another. While the degrees of the system themselves do not change, each inversion modifies the internal arrangement by altering the order of succession of the intervals. Thus, the G–A–B *pycnon* occupies the three lowest degrees in mode I, the three highest degrees in mode IV, and the middle degrees in mode V, while in modes II and III, it is split apart. The process of inversion thus confers a unique configuration and character on each pentatonic arrangement.

It thus seems that the pentatonic types are more than mere scales. Does this mean they can be accounted *modes*?

In order to reply to this question, we must determine whether, and if so, to what extent, any music which makes use of these pentatonic arrangements fits the definition of what is generally considered to be *modal* music. To do this, we will have to decide what features are characteristic of the object designated as a 'mode', as scholars are far from agreement on the meanings ascribed to this term.

This uncertainty is captured in the title of Jacques Chailley's (1960) work, *L'imbroglio des modes*, where he tries to introduce some order into the historical and geographical factors involved in the use of this term. His conclusion is that 'the notion of "mode" is not a UNIQUE one, applicable at all times and places', and therefore, 'it can only be defined in relation to the age and place where it is observed' (Chailley 1960: 9). He remarks that the generally accepted notion of mode

implicitly involves the following ideas:
   (a)   the choice of a standard octave as a fundamental unit;
   (b)   a tonic, which constitutes the first sound on the standard octave;
   (c)   the hierarchical harmonic organisation of the remaining degrees with respect to the tonic, as dominant, and so forth;
   (d)   the functional identity of all sounds reproducing any of the sounds of the standard octave on any octave whatsoever;
   (e)   the irrelevance of absolute pitch, compass, the individual octave, and the melodic idioms used.   (Chailley 1960: 5)

Now while Central African music fits some of these criteria (e.g., the choice of a standard octave, the functional identity of a sound irrespective of the octave where it appears, and the irrelevance to absolute pitch), it fails the others. It is therefore not amenable to classification in any of the four types of mode distinguished by Chailley (1960: 5–7).

Insofar as Central African pentatonic systems are more than mere scales, but do not have all the properties of modes, they must be assigned to an intermediate position between these two concepts. They may thus be defined as what Trân Van Khê (1968, XI: 152) has called 'modal scales': 'The modal scale is a necessary, *but not a sufficient* [italics added] element for defining the notion of mode'.

It therefore seems wise to use either this term or the term *pentatonic type* for referring to Central African pentatonic systems, insofar as both signify an intermediate entity between scale and mode.

2.2   Vertical organisation

All pieces of Central African polyphony rely on the regular repetition of identical, or at least similar, vertical combinations at certain positions in their fundamental period. These positions constitute reference points which coordinate the coherent movement of the various melodic parts. The content of each reference point is thus an element in a systematic organisational plan. This observation inevitably raises the question of how the underlying principles of such a vertical organisation can be ascertained.

Since Central African pentatonic systems make no use of the half-tone interval, any notion of a univocal centre of tonal attraction, as this term is understood in harmony, is foreign to them. Consequently, the only way to establish a hierarchy among the degrees forming an anhemitonic pentatonic scale would be to use *melodic* criteria, insofar as these degrees engender a set of vertical intervals of equal importance.

In Central African polyphony, one can in fact find clusters of all the combinations of intervals allowed by the scale, namely,

- octaves,
- fifths and (by inversion) fourths,
- major seconds and minor sevenths,
- major thirds and minor sixths,
- minor thirds and major sixths.

The number of sounds included in vertical combinations varies with the number and type of performing instruments: while there are no more than two in *sanza* music, it is not unusual to find four in xylophone music. In the limiting case, it can happen that the five sounds of the scale are simultaneously emitted as a cluster. This particular type of verticality can easily be explained by referring each sound comprising a 'chord' or sound cluster to its own melodic axis. It then becomes clear that the vertical configurations are the (partly fortuitous) consequence of the *horizontal conception* of *melodic counterpoint*.

In Central African instrumental polyphony, melodic counterpoint is achieved by *simultaneously stating* the various segments which make up a vocal monody, all of which fit a single periodic mould. These segments are thus stacked one above the other rather than being arranged sequentially. Such superposition is only possible, however, by virtue of the principle of the equality of the degrees which form the anhemitonic pentatonic system. These conditions imply that a piece can only be identified if the constituent elements of each of its segments scrupulously preserve their positions with respect to one another within the period.

Moreover, insofar as the words of a song must remain intelligible, this kind of counterpoint is inapplicable to vocal music, which would become impossible to follow. That is why melodic counterpoint is found only in the instrumental formula which accompanies the vocal part. Each song is associated with a polyphonic formula whose melodic and rhythmic components are so arranged as to allow the melodic material contained in the entire set of segments to be stated *simultaneously*. The instrumental formula of a song is thus to the ear what a transcription of it in the form of a synoptic table would be to the eye.

Melodic and rhythmic variations can, however, affect the instrumental formula, just as they can appear in the song the formula supports and summarises. These variations engender a large variety of vertical combinations, or *con-sonances*, in the etymological sense of the word. Seen against this background, vertical combinations take on two different but complementary functions, one of them *structural*, and the other *ornamental*.

We have already remarked that specific vertical combinations in each formula act as temporal reference points by virtue of their regular repetition at a given position in the periodic cycle. These combinations are the points at which several superposed melodic lines meet. They are usually based on octaves, fifths, and fourths, precisely the intervals which make up sections 1–4 of Chailley's resonance table (1960: 35), and this is certainly no accident. We may therefore assume that they take on a structural function.

All other *con-sonances* can be viewed in the same way as the result of conjunctions of different melodies, but unlike the regularly repeated ones, their content (and at times even their position) is an *arbitrary* consequence of the numerous melodic and, particularly, rhythmic variations allowed in the various realisations of the formula.

Con-sonances of this type seem intended to provide *colour*, over and above the *melodic* nature of their constituent elements. This is a natural consequence of the fact that musicians tend to make full use of their available resources to enrich and variegate the texture of sound when performing cyclic (or repetitive) music.

In the aspect of simultaneity, the desired effects of colour can be achieved by the use of infrequent combinations of certain intervals, and their inversions. Colour is quite often associated with the rhythmic interweaving of different parts, whereby it can also engender both "oblique" phenomena, such as anticipations and suspensions, and horizontal phenomena, such as drones and broken or ornamented pedal points.

This brief survey of the principles underlying the vertical organisation of Central African polyphonic music leads us to the conclusion that the absence of a genuine (i.e., harmony-generating) bass part, eliminates the notion of "harmony" itself, and that what we observe as polyphony is a product of techniques of melodic counterpoint. Any coherent analysis of this music must keep these facts in mind.

2.3   ANALYSIS

The transcriptions and analyses which appear in the following chapters stem from a careful examination of a group of representative pieces of all types of polyphony. Their purpose is to determine the rules which govern the functioning of each type, and to bring out their shared structural principles.

Our formal analysis will consist of a set of operations establishing the fundamental *principles* of the analysis itself; the functional or distinctive *parameters* to which these principles apply; and the distribution of these parameters with respect to analytical *levels* and *facets*.

If these procedures are to be reproduced, they must be made explicit. We must therefore now examine how they work.

2.3.1   Principles

Repetition and *commutation* are the two functional criteria by which music can be segmented into functional units. As both have been discussed at length in Book IV, it will suffice to review them briefly here.

Any musical discourse with an underlying code is based on what Nicolas Ruwet (1972: 134) calls a 'syntax of equivalences'. This notion applies particularly well to cyclic music, whose principle is the repetition of the same musical material, with variations. Thus, when several similar sequences stated on a horizontal (i.e., temporal, or syntagmatic) axis are projected onto a vertical (or paradigmatic) axis, units can be defined on various levels.

The set of all the members of a single paradigm constitutes a formal class, which may be called an *equivalence class*, assuming there is a cultural judgement of identity. This is to say that, when the units so defined are assigned the same cultural value, they can be taken to be *qualitatively* identical. Insofar as they are identical, they are also interchangeable, i.e., *commutable*. We may recall that, by *commutation*, we mean both the operation of substituting any member of a given paradigm for another, and the principle according to which this operation can be carried out. This principle operates at different levels. The members of a paradigm are both similar and dissimilar, in that they have at least one common feature, and one distinguishing feature whereby they differ. The *positions* occupied by the distinguishing features in such a system are *points of substitution*. But the terms located at a given point of substitution in turn constitute an equivalence class. This explains both the existence of the principle of variation in orally transmitted isoperiodic music, and the coherence of its application.

It must, however, be stressed that, in Ruwet's words, 'the various units may stand in any sort of equivalence relation' (1972: 134), i.e. that these relations may depend on different parameters. This means that the criteria of repetition and commutation must be applied first to each of the distinctive parameters separately, and then to combinations of them, in order to determine what the units are and how they are concatenated. Whenever two or more parameters lead to the same result, the coherence of the segmentation is corroborated.

2.3.2   Parameters

The parameters which are necessary and sufficient for the description of any polyphonic or polyrhythmic piece of Central African music may be classified under four headings: *scalar organisation*, *time structure*, *simultaneity*, and *tone colour*. Since three of these are equally relevant to the description of monodic music in the same region, it must immediately be pointed out that their constituent elements function in a partially or entirely different way in a polyphonic context.

There are two facets to *scalar organisation*: one is the type of pentatonic system employed, and the other is the range covered by this system. Generally speaking, the range is much wider in polyphonic music. The pentatonic type, and the range of the scale are relevant to melodic analysis by virtue of the configurations they engender.

The *time structure* depends on three parameters: the *periodicity*, the *pulsation*, and the *minimal operational value*.

In Central African music, the *periodicity* constitutes the basis of temporal organisation. Each period is characterised by an equal number of isochronous *pulsations*, which are therefore essential for defining the boundaries of the period. The polyphonic and polyrhythmic music of this region is so structured that its component parts are usually assigned different periodicities, which nevertheless always stand in simple ratios to one another (cf. *infra*, Strict polyrhythmics). Under these conditions, the pulsation becomes more than a mere marker. It takes on the role of temporal reference unit, a common regulator which synchronises all the parts and consequently co-ordinates the superposition of their periods.

The rhythmic organisation of a piece is based on an underlying pulsation which may be submitted to either a binary or a ternary type of subdivision. The shortest distinctive duration resulting from this segmentation will be called a *minimal operational value*. All durations which are not identical with this value are necessarily multiples of it. That is why the minimal operational value is an indispensable parameter for describing rhythmic, and a fortiori, polyrhythmic structures.

Phenomena of *simultaneity* can be apprehended by means of two parameters: *vertical organisation* and *counterpoint*.

The significance of *vertical organisation* is evident from the regular repetition of specific vertical combinations at identical predetermined positions in the period.

In Central African music, *counterpoint* appears in two forms: one *combining melody and rhythm*, and the other being *rhythmic alone*.

We have said that melodic counterpoint is characterised by the coherent super-position of two or more melodic lines, while strict polyrhythmics appears as the *interweaving* of several differently articulated rhythmic figures. This means that each of these types must initially be treated separately. In actual music, however, the two techniques are quite frequently found in a 'symbiotic' relationship, since the formulae produced by intrinsically melodic polyphonic instruments are provided with strict polyrhythmic support by two or more percussion instruments.

Tone colour is somewhat different from the other parameters. If one confines oneself to a single piece, or to a set of pieces from the same repertory, tone colour will be redundant and nondistinctive. In traditional Central African societies, there are a fixed number of musical categories, and these are indissociably linked to specific social and/or religious circumstances. Each category consists of a repertory containing a widely varying number of pieces, which can be performed only by a specific instrumental ensemble. Since the pieces in any category all require the same set of instruments, it is evidently impossible to distinguish them on the basis of tone colour. On the other hand, tone colour is essential to the differentiation of the categories themselves, and from this point of view, is in fact the most immediately evident distinctive feature.

2.3.3   Levels

We have seen that musical analysis necessarily involves the definition of formal classes, called equivalence classes. We must now use the criteria by which these classes are defined for the different types of Central African polyphony in order to determine

(1) what facets show equivalences and (2) how they are ordered hierarchically, for this will enable us to set the upper and lower limits to our analytical framework.

Traditional Central African music is submitted to a coherent hierarchical organisation, such that each of its levels is comprised of a set of equivalence classes with respect to the next higher level. Thus, if one takes as the domain of observation the entire musical heritage of this geocultural area, i.e., the set of all the musical heritages pertaining to all the ethnic groups living there, the heritage of each group constitutes a member of a single equivalence class.

We have also seen that the musical heritage of each ethnic community can, in turn, be ordered into functional categories which are indissociable from social and cultural circumstances. The set of all the pieces in any given category constitutes a repertory, which can, as we have said, be distinguished on the basis of tone colour from all the other repertories current within the community. Such a repertory is thus, in turn, an equivalence class in being unlike all the other musical categories pertaining to the same group. The distinctiveness of the repertories is reinforced by certain structural features of the music itself, primarily, the nature of the rhythmic or polyrhythmic substructure which supports the melodic instruments. The criteria of tone colour and rhythm tend to converge at this level: thus, the same name is usually applied to both the category itself and its particular characteristic rhythmic formula. On occasion, however, a repertory may be subdivided into two 'families', which differ precisely with respect to their rhythmic organisation. In such a case, each 'family' may be defined as an equivalence class distinct from the other on a hierarchical level which is intermediate between the level defined with respect to the repertories and the level of each of the pieces they contain. The pieces in a given category may have one or more other common structural features, aside from their rhythmic substructure, such as their modal scale, periodicity, subdivision of the pulsation, articulation of rhythmic material, order of entry of the various instruments, introductive and cadential formulae, tempo, or of course, polyphonic techniques. The features which are common to the pieces in a given category are thus *constants*, and those which differ are *variables*. The former provide *strictly musical criteria* confirming the coherence of the vernacular taxonomy, which is usually *symbolic* in nature. Therefore, any repertory can be described by means of these criteria, which can be discovered by the careful examination of each piece in terms of the parameters we heve named, at all the structural levels which have been identified by means of the principles of repetition and commutation. If one limits one's domain of observation to the forms of polyphonic music alone, it becomes apparent that they are organised into a similar and equally coherent hierarchy, which is likewise based on branching equivalence classes.

Three techniques are involved in the elaboration of instrumental polyphony: counterpoint, hocket, and strict polyrhythmics. Each constitutes a distinct equivalence class on this level. Next, each technique implies the use of several different instruments. In the Central African Republic, for example, counterpoint is found in music for the xylophone, the *sanza*, and the harp. With respect to technique, all *sanza* music thus constitutes an equivalence class distinct from the music associated with the other two kinds of instrument. We also know that the vernacular taxonomy of each ethnic group assigns the music for each instrumental ensemble or polyphonic instrument to a separate category. Here again, all the pieces assembled in such a category constitute an equivalence class. We thus find ourselves back on the level of the *individual piece of music*, which is comprised in turn of various equivalence classes. We have reached this point by a different route, but by respecting the internal logic of the system.

The classes in a piece of monodic music can, as we have seen, be treated as units, and horizontally juxtaposed so as to give rise to a relatively simple form. The structure of polyphonic music, which consists precisely of the superposition of several simultaneously stated and differently articulated sequences, is, on the other hand, complex and, in the strict sense, multidimensional. A polyphonic piece thus consists of a set of modules of different size which can be juxtaposed and superposed in a coherently ordered way, as it were like building blocks, so as to coincide with the overall periodicity. With only rare exceptions, a structure of this kind includes two sorts of elements displaying different types of organisation: on the one hand, there is a polyrhythmic formula which is *common to the entire repertory*, and is performed by percussion instruments; on the other, there is a polyphonic formula which is *characteristic of the individual piece*, and is performed by one or two melodic instruments.

The first stage in the formal analysis of a structure of this kind thus requires that the segmentation procedures described above be applied firstly, to each constituent part in each of the two components, so that its fundamental units can be established; secondly, to all the combinations which can be obtained by the superposition of the melodic parts among themselves, and the polyrhythmic parts among themselves, so that combinational units of each kind can be discovered; and finally, to the overall level conjoining polyphony and polyrhythmics, so that the maximal combinational units of the structure can be ascertained.

Two points remain to be examined before we conclude this section: the first involves precisely the discovery of these maximal units, while the second concerns the lowest and finest level of descriptive analysis.

When the cyclic structure of a piece involves the superposition of periods which stand in ratios of 2:3 or 3:4, the time interval separating occurrences of the point at which all periods coincide may be longer than the periods of either the polyphonic formula or its polyrhythmic substructure. This interval, which we will call a *macroperiod* (see Strict polyrhythmics, 3.1.3.4), must be used to determine the highest organisational level of the piece. At the same time, the smallest formal class which can be established as an equivalence class by reference to a cultural judgement of identity will be used to define the *minimal operative unit*. When this level has been reached, formal analysis has no further sense. Once these minimal units (a sort of musical morpheme) have been defined, the application of the same procedures in a reverse order should allow us to produce objects which are structurally similar to the ones we started with.

2.3.4   Representation by model

In Book IV, 'Description and Analysis' (2.2.4), we showed how models can be useful in confirming the results of analysis. We may recall that a *model* provides an integral, but simplified, representation of its object. It identifies and individualises this object by condensing it into a set of distinctive features and no others. For our present purposes, the model we are seeking is the *minimal realisation* of a musical entity, i.e., an ultimate reference and reduction to its essentials, which can still be identified by the cultural heirs of a musical tradition.

The model for polyphonic and/or polyrhythmic music includes three levels: the level of the individual component parts; the intermediate level, which provides the reference for both the purely polyphonic combination, and the strictly polyrhythmic formula, the latter being, as we have seen, common to a given repertory, or at least, to one of the 'families' comprising it; and the level of the entire musical edifice, obtained by the conjunction of all the parts.

It is interesting to note that, for pedagogical reasons, some repertories are assigned more than one model, i.e., there is a progressive series of three or four models. These models may be described as 'embedded', in the sense that each represents a level of increasingly difficult instrumental technique (see Book VI, 5.3 on the *sanza*). Progressive or 'embedded' models are of particular interest in that they allow us to observe, as it were through a series of superposed transparencies, the inherent nature of the structural features of the piece and, thereby, to verify its structural coherence over and above its individual realisations.

Models for orally transmitted music may be obtained either by *materialisation* or by *deduction*. The first method is, of course, simpler and, by far, more reliable. Musicians in communities where models are customary are usually able to provide a concrete realisation of the condensed form which constitutes the reference for a given piece, or for a given level of difficulty of that piece. These are *immanent* or *concrete* models. In cases where this method cannot apply, a representation can only be obtained by a sequence of formal deductions yielding a *theoretical* model.

The real situation in Central African music is such that the *behaviour* of models varies with the repertory. A model may thus be *manifest* (or *materialised*), *sporadic* (or *eclipsed*), or *implicit*.

When the model is *manifest* or *materialised*, it is realised without a single variation, in accordance with the principle of repetition alone. Whatever its rhythmic, or melodic-rhythmic, nature, a model of this type will behave like a strict *ostinato*. As its name suggests, a *sporadic* or *eclipsed* model differs from a manifest one in that it is only *discontinuously* materialised. It may be manifest at the start, and then partially or entirely disappear in the course of the performance; or it may be absent at the beginning of the piece, appear later on, and then remain through part or the whole of the remainder of the performance.

Finally, an *implicit* model is never straightforward, and remains, as it were, veiled by its own variations.

2.4   PRINCIPLES OF NOTATION

All the scores contained in this work have been transcribed by ear from tape recordings. We first listened to the pieces and their component parts several times, and then made our transcriptions from the recording played at reduced speed. We then checked these transcriptions against the recording at normal speed.

We must keep in mind that these transcriptions were not made so that the pieces could be performed from them. They are simply a visual representation designed to help in understanding the musical reality; as such, they are an indispensable tool for thorough analysis. We are therefore dealing with a *descriptive* notation.

The parameters which are necessary and sufficient for describing both the structure and the content of Central African polyphony and polyrhythmics are the ways in which they organise *pitches* into scales, and *durations* into rhythmic values and periodicity.

2.4.1   Pitches

All Central African music makes use of the anhemitonic pentatonic scale, which, as we have seen, can be organised in five ways, each involving a specific distribution of intervals. These distributions are all inversions of one another.

Constantin Brăiloiu's (1953) proposal for the definition of the pentatonic 'modes' was based on the position occupied in each by the *pycnon*. This criterion is perfectly valid, provided the intervals comprising the scale (particularly, the intervals of the *pycnon*) are, if not tempered, at least easily perceptible. This is not always the case in the types of music we are dealing with here. In Central African instrumental music, there is, in fact, a considerable margin of tolerance between two conjunct degrees, which may approach the interval of a semitone.

The arrangement of the degrees of the scale assigned to a given instrument may thus be interpreted in different ways, without thereby altering the pentatonic nature of the ensemble. This is why it is often extremely difficult to determine the precise modal scale of an instrument from how it is tuned, for the intervals of the *pycnon* which characterise the scale are themselves ambiguous. Curiously, this difficulty is even most pronounced in the case of instruments whose tuning cannot be adjusted, such as the xylophone.

Thus, in the case of a scale which, taken as a whole, could be perceived as composed of G–A–B–D–E, the B may sound much too high and seem more like a lowered C. But this new interpretation would be equivalent to shifting the position of the *pycnon* from the lower to the upper degrees of the scale, and thereby changing the pentatonic type. This ambiguity in instrumental tuning seems to be intentional, for such a margin of tolerance is precisely what allows the instrument to accompany songs belonging to both the G–A–*B*–D–E and G–A–*C*–D–E types without having to be retuned (or even replaced, in the case of an instrument with fixed tuning). Paradoxical as it may seem, the scale configuration of the instrumental substructure can therefore only be accurately identified from the *vocal* music for which it provides the framework; for the margin of tolerance between degrees is much smaller for vocal melodies than for the accompanying instrument. That is why, whenever we encounter this difficulty (which arises in music for xylophone, harp, and *sanza*), we shift the ambiguous degrees to the pitches which are closest to the ones in the vocal part(s), as these are clearly the proper constituents of the scale.

Thus, when two criteria belong to different domains (e.g., voice and instrument), and one is *ambiguous*, it can be clarified by checking it against the other concomitant, but *univocal*, one.

To make our scores easier to read and compare, we have avoided sharpening and flattening and have written all our pieces without a key signature. This decision is justifiable in the light of the fact that the notion of absolute pitch is entirely foreign to the traditional musicians, and therefore irrelevant.

2.4.2   Durations

All durations, whether sounds or rests, can be represented by the conventional signs of ordinary musical notation. There being no 'measure' to define a regular accentual matrix, the only metric reference unit is the pulsation; a readable notation therefore requires that each duration extending over two or more pulsations or 'beats' (e.g., ♩.) be rewritten with ties (♩♩♩). Moreover, the strong contrametric tendency of the music we are studying means that sounds will often be attacked on the offbeat and spread into the following pulsation: the use of a large number of ties thus becomes inevitable if a faithful representation is to be provided.

Transcribing durations gives rise to a dilemma involving a choice between two types of notation: *rhythmic* or *metric*. The former would represent each duration *by a single sign*, independently of whether it crosses from one pulsation to another. This would make it easier to visualise the constituent elements of a rhythmic figure, but would have the disadvantage of, as it were, 'desynchronising,' and thereby obscuring a vertical reading.

In metric notation, on the other hand, rhythmic values are represented with respect to an isochronous reference unit, the pulsation. While this type of notation requires the use of a large number of ties, it has the advantage of being familiar and of facilitating synchronous reading of superposed parts. This is why all the scores appearing hereafter are transcribed in metric notation. Rhythmic notation will, however, be used in numerous examples to illustrate certain principles of rhythmic organisation. Both will sometimes be used, superposed as in Ex. 1, to point up the antinomic relationship between rhythm and meter.

Ex. 1

The omission of *bars* (and concomitantly, of time signatures) from the scores reflects the absence of a regular contrast between strong and weak beats, the notion of measure being irrelevant.

The *periodicity* of a piece is defined on the basis of identical numbers of pulsations. The beginning of each cycle is marked by a Γ above the top staff in the score, and by a heavy vertical line drawn *across* the staffs. The appearance of a number n within the sign (i.e., Γn) indicates the nth repetition of the period.

Thin lines indicate the onset of the *pulsation*. They are intended to facilitate synchronous reading of the superposed parts and *imply no accentuation*.

The subdivision of the pulsation provides the criterion for determining *how the temporal reference unit is to be notated*: when the pulsation contains two or four minimal operational values, it will be notated ♪ or ♩, respectively. When the subdivision is ternary, the temporal reference unit will be notated ♩. . Pulsations having five minimal values will be notated either ♪. ♪ or ♪♪., according to how they are distributed.

Lastly, the *metronomic motion* of each piece is marked at the top of the score.

3   Strict polyrhythmics

3.1   PERIODICITY AND THE FUNDAMENTAL CHARACTERISTICS OF RHYTHM

Strict polyrhythmics consists of an ordered and coherent superposition of different rhythmic events. We must therefore carefully examine how its component elements are organised before we approach the concept itself.

3.1.1   Pure rhythmics

A clear initial distinction must be made between the rhythmic phenomena found in music where relative pitches form a scalar system (i.e., *melodic* music); and in music where the melodic parameter is neutralised, leaving only pure rhythmics. We wish to deal here with the latter case.

Pure rhythmics can be based on *accentuation*, on *changing tone colour*, or simply on *contrasting durations*. Pure rhythm can be produced in Africa, as elsewhere, by various sorts of musical instruments (in the main classifiable as idiophones or membranophones); however, parts of the human body may also be used, as for example, when people stamp their feet on the ground, clap their hands, and so on. Pure rhythmics is frequently not incompatible with the perception of melodic sequences resulting from the simultaneous use of diverse pitches and tone colours. There is, however, no immanent (i.e., *cultural*) basis for interpreting such sequences as melodic entities, because their constituent elements are not integrated into a *preconceived* system of relative pitch.

3.1.2   Fundamental characteristics

If one listens carefully to a Central African percussion ensemble, one will quickly perceive the fundamental characteristics prevailing in the rhythmics of this region:

- regular, *stable movement*, free of accelerando, rallentando, or rubato; the music is measured and contains strictly proportional durations.
- *strict periodicity*, evident from the predominance of uninterrupted repetitive formulae in which similar material reappears at regular intervals of time;
- formulae which are not completely identical; the repetitive system allows a certain degree of *variability*;
- simultaneous instrumental parts which are not arranged in exact vertical order with respect to one another, but rather are skewed according to a *principle of interweaving* of individual rhythms;
- absence of a temporal reference matrix based on the regular alternation of an accented sound with one or more unaccented sounds; the *notions of measure* and *strong beat* which are intrinsic to such a framework are dispensed with.

The interweaving of accents and tone colours, combined with the lack of a regular accentual framework, as a reference, creates in the listener a feeling of uncertainty, an impression of *ambiguity* regarding the articulation of the period. This feeling can be likened to what one experiences in a train, when one catches the regular rhythm of the sound of the wheels on the tracks, and then suddenly gets the impression that the period has shifted: what originally seemed like the 'strong beat', marking the return of the temporal cycle, turns into the weak beat, and vice versa. The same kind of phenomenon occurs if one listens for some time to the binary ticktock of clockwork. The accent one originally attributed to the 'tick' (TICK-tock) seems suddenly to shift on to the 'tock', and one hears TOCK-tick. Even greater ambiguity can result from a ternary period. Thus, an unaccented figure with two sounds of equal value and a rest of the same duration can be perceived in three different ways, as ♩ ♩ 𝄾 , 𝄾 ♩ ♩ , or 𝄾 𝄾 ♩ ┆ ♩.

In none of these cases, however, has the periodic cycle undergone the slightest modification; the only change has been in one's perception of the thing, in the *Gestalt* which the mind imposes on invariant data. The regularity of the objective sound is precisely what gives rise to the feeling of uncertainty and makes a variety of interpretations possible.

3.1.3   Periodicity

Definition: 'The period is a *temporal loop based on the "repetition of similar events at similar intervals"*' (Moles 1968).

All forms of music in the Central African Republic are constructed according to a principle of periodicity. We will now examine the organisational levels of this principle.

3.1.3.1   The period

The period provides a temporal framework for rhythmic events. It is invariably composed of whole numbers. These numbers are usually even, i.e., divisible by two (2, 4, 6, 8, 12, etc.). This means that the structure of the period is symmetric. The constituents of this structure are pulsations.

3.1.3.2   The pulsation

The pulsation is an isochronous reference unit used *by a given culture* for the measurement of time. It consists of a regular sequence of reference points in relation to which rhythmic events are ordered. Moreover, in polyrhythmic music, the pulsation is the common denominator, from the standpoint of temporal organisation, for all the parts in a piece. It is therefore the basic unit of time with respect to which all durations are defined.

The pulsation is, however, only rarely given material existence in this region of Central Africa. While it can *always* be given the material form of handclaps, it is nevertheless usually *implicit*.

3.1.3.3   The minimal operational values

The pulsation can be subdivided in three different ways: *binary* when it is split into two or four equal parts; *ternary* when it is split into three or, rarely, six equal values; *composite* when it is split, in a combination of the two preceding ways, into five equal values. The notation will then be ♩ ♪ = ♫♫♫ , or ♪. ♪ = ♫♫♪ , or ♪ ♪. = ♫ ♫♫ , as the case requires.

The *minimal operational value* is the smallest *relevant* duration obtained after subdivision; all other durations are multiples of this value. The period is thus equal to the total number of these values. A period a based on twelve pulsations will then contain thirty-six operational values in the case of ternary, and twenty-four (or forty-eight) in the case of binary, subdivision of the pulsation. It will become clearer hereafter how important the form of subdivision of the pulsation is for understanding Central African rhythmic organisation.

Metrically speaking, the period can thus be broken down on two lower levels, into the *pulsation* and the *operational values* it contains. We must remember that, characteristically, this organisation involves *no intermediate level* between the period itself and the pulsation, consisting of a regular accentual system, i.e., the 'measure' with its characteristic strong beat, as found in Western music. Consequently, *the 'beats' comprising the period all have equal status.*

3.1.3.4   On diverse periodicities

The preceding sections have dealt with the *metric* organisation of the period as a temporal framework for rhythmic events. In African music, however, several rhythmic events are usually found to occur simultaneously. This is what we call *polyrhythmics*, to which we will turn shortly. The important point for the time being is to note that the superposed rhythmic figures in a polyrhythmic context are of varying lengths, yet always stand in simple ratios, such as 2:1, 3:1, 3:2, 4:2, and multiples thereof. In metric terms, this means that different periodic forms are to be superposed. It will therefore be necessary henceforth to use the plural form "period," or more precisely, *periodicities*. We will also require four new terms: *amplification, macroperiod, long cycle*, and *quasiperiodicity*, which we will now proceed to define.

Amplification   By *amplification*, we mean the technique of *sporadically* developing the rhythmic material contained in a period over some multiple of it (usually two or three). For example, a period with four pulsations may be transformed into a short series of cycles of eight, twelve, or sixteen pulsations.

Macroperiod   A *macroperiod* is the cycle obtained when periods of different lengths are superposed, *and each individually is shorter*. This happens, for example, when two or more periods stand in a ratio of 2:3 and/or 3:4. The macroperiod then provides the only point at which *all the periods will coincide* (see Fig. 1).

Long cycles   These are cyclical, i.e., *regular*, sequences which are far longer than not only the longest period, but also the macroperiod. Long cycles mainly involve dancers,

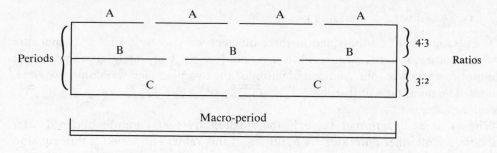

Fig. 1

who often participate in the elaboration of rhythm by means of sound-producing adjuncts such as rattles, jingles, and pellet bells, attached to parts of their body (arms, legs, ankles). The dancer can thereby turn himself into a rhythmic instrument for as long as he continues to dance.

Quasiperiodicity   Abraham Moles defines quasiperiodicity as 'variation of the delay with which [events] are repeated'. Quasiperiodicity may be said to exist 'when the period of repetition of a recognisable event is not constant, but relatively irregular' (Moles 1983). This definition applies particularly well to certain phenomena observable in Central African rhythmics, where perfectly recognisable figures reappear *with irregular frequency*.

Before concluding this section, we will have to say a few words concerning *tempo*. The tempo is inseparable from, and determined by, the basic structural element of periodicity and temporal unit of reference, the pulsation. The tempo expresses the *inner movement* of music. We have already seen that the movement of Central African music is extremely regular. We have confirmed this by comparing recordings made of the same pieces (performed, moreover, by the same musicians) over a period of more than ten years. In every case, metronomic measurements showed negligible fluctuations of tempo from one performance to another, even when several years apart. Thus, for a piece with ♩ as the metronomic unit of reference, the tempo will vary by no more than 148 to 156.

These observations bear out the remarkably intuitive suggestion made more than twenty years ago by André Souris (1961), that 'it may be assumed that civilisations having no written tradition are capable of absolute precision in orally transmitting the tempo of highly structured music'. Furthermore they support the more recent observations of David Epstein (1981), who describes this peculiar ability to preserve a temporal reference unit in a kind of bodily memory, as 'a highly accurate biological clock mechanism'.

3.2   RHYTHMIC ORGANISATION

We have hitherto been examining the metric aspects of the phenomenon of periodicity at various levels, i.e., we have been considering periodicity as a framework of temporal reference. We will now turn to the rhythmic organisation of the period, i.e., to the way in which rhythmic events are arranged within it. More precisely, we will describe their articulation, or division into cells and configurations, and define the underlying principles of this division. This means that we will now be dealing with rhythmic *figures*.

A *rhythmic figure* consists of an *ostinato*, which may be either strict or varying, and always (except in the case of figures composed of a single pulsation) contains an *even* number of equidistant pulsations.

3.2.1   The constituent features of rhythmic figures

Rhythmic figures are characterised by clusters of features drawn from different categories or orders. There are, in fact, five such categories, viz., the types of *mark*, *durations*, *morphology*, *metricity*, and *structure*. A cluster of distinctive features is ordered in such a way that it will contain one and only one feature from each category. This means that a cluster of five features will be necessary and sufficient for the description of any of the rhythmic figures we will be dealing with below.

3.2.1.1   Marks

A sequence of percussions can only be called a rhythmic figure if certain of its components are in some way marked. There are three kinds of mark: *accentuation, change of tone colour*, and *alternation of durations*.

The importance of the latter lies in the fact that rhythmic sequences with neither accentuation nor change of tone colour are frequently found in the music of Central Africa. Figures and their constituent configurations, if any, must then be defined by the arrangements resulting from alternating durations alone.

Marks are indispensable for the segmentation of rhythmic figures. Recurrent accents, changes of tone colour, or (failing these) contrasting durations can all provide a basis for the proper segmentation of figures into their constituent parts (cells and configurations). A sequence of *at least two sounds* is required for us to speak of a cell or a configuration. A single isolated percussion may thus never be treated as a constituent element of a rhythmic figure. Assuming that configurations and cells may be determined by one of the marks, we must now find a solution to the subtle problem of *setting limits to rests* and assigning them to one configuration rather than another. For the sake of convenience, we have decided to adopt the following procedure: seeing that it is extremely difficult to determine precisely when silence *begins*, i.e., the exact instant when the resonance of a preceding percussion has died out, we may as well combine the value of the rest with that of the preceding sound, and *treat the former as an acoustic extension of the latter*. We can accept this expedient, because experience shows that it has no bearing on the segmentation of the figure. It in no way affects the behaviour of the sound following the rest, since the time interval separating two sounds, *which in fact is the significant feature*, remains the same, whether or not there is an intervening moment of silence.

A figure giving the apparent acoustic effect of:

Ex. 2

may thus be notated:

Ex. 3

‖: ♪ ♩ ♪ ♪ ♪♪♪ ♩ ♪ ♪ ♪ :‖

Accentuation

Segmentation depends in this case on *recurring accents*, i.e., on the time interval separating two accented sounds within a given figure (ex. 4).

Ex. 4

Needless to say, a figure containing only one accent cannot be segmented on this basis. In such case, we must turn to another type of mark. On the other hand, a figure of this kind may contain *two or more consecutive accent-bearing sounds*. Since a configuration may not be comprised of a single sound, common sense suggests that we should take only the *first accent in the sequence* as relevant. The following configuration will be bounded by the first accented sound to be *preceded by at least one unaccented sound*. The following figure;

Ex. 5

‖: ♪̆ ♪̆. ♪♪ ♪̆ ♪̆ ♪̆. ♪♪ ♪̆. ♪♪ :‖

may be segmented thus:

Ex. 6

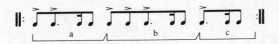

Changing tone colour

Figures without accentuation, but marked by *contrasting tone colours*, may be segmented on the basis of this factor. Cells and configurations will then be defined by the *recurrence of at least one sound whose tone colour differs from that of the preceding sound*. When a figure contains only one percussion individuated by its tone colour, this type of mark is inapplicable. It can only operate when *at least two sounds* contrast with all the others with respect to tone colour.

Tone colour can be changed in at least three ways:

1. *Sequences* of percussions *with identical tone colour* may alternate. This alternation then provides a basis for segmentation, and each sequence is treated as a cell, as in ex. 7.

Ex. 7

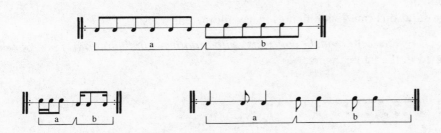

2. *Individual sounds* may alternate with one or more sounds having *the contrasting tone colour*. In this case, cells and configurations are bounded by the recurring *individual* sounds, as in ex. 8.

Ex. 8

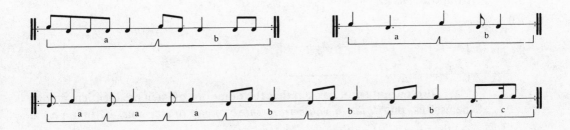

3. The third technique is a combination of the preceding two: sequences of sounds with the same tone colour are juxtaposed with figures defined by the presence of an individual sound alternating with one or more sounds in the contrasting tone colour. In such a case, every sequence of percussions which *contains a contrast of tone colours* acts as a constituent of the figure (see ex. 9).

Ex. 9

Alternating durations

When the sounds in a rhythmic figure have no accents and do not contrast in tone colour, segmentation is only possible with respect to alternating durations, i.e., on the basis of how the values resemble or differ from each other, and how they are grouped together.

Alternating durations can divide figures in seven different ways:

1. A given cell, *which contrasts with another configuration*, may be repeated in the figure, as in:

Ex. 10

2. Two or more *different cells* may *recur*, as in:

Ex. 11

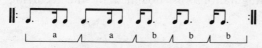

3. Two configurations, *one of which is based on identical durations*, may be juxtaposed, as in:

Ex. 12

4. Two or more groups such that the durations of each are identical among themselves, but *differ in value from those of the others*, may be juxtaposed, as in:

Ex. 13

5. A figure may contain configurations based on *similar groups*, i.e., groups which can be defined by *at least one common characteristic*, as in:

Ex. 14

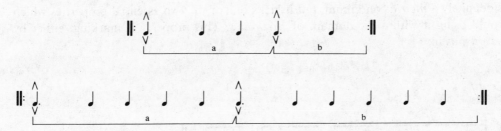

6. A single configuration may be repeated in such a way that *its position with respect to the pulsation differs at each recurrence* (cf. *infra*, Uniform morphology).

7. Two or more configurations of types other than those described above may be juxtaposed in such a way that the figure can be segmented into two parts of equal size, as in ex. 15.

Ex. 15

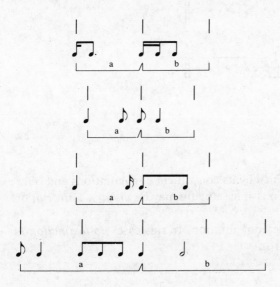

3.2.1.2 Durations

The durations comprising a rhythmic figure may be *equal* or *unequal*. While this remark may seem trivial, it has a bearing on the important, and often still confused problem of drawing a precise boundary between metrics and rhythmics. A sequence of equal values with no accentuation or difference in tone color, such as:

Ex. 16

is definitely a *metric* continuum, but it lacks one of the two essential properties which would bring it within the domain of *rhythmics*. This property is marking, either by *accents*, as in:

Ex. 17

or by a difference in tone colour, as in:

Ex. 18

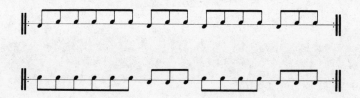

3.2.1.3 Morphology

The shape of a rhythmic figure is determined by its constituent configurations and cells. Three types of internal arrangement are possible: a figure may be *unitary, uniform,* or *multiform.*

It is *unitary* when it contains only one configuration. In this case, *no distinction is possible between cell and figure* (see ex. 19).

Ex. 19

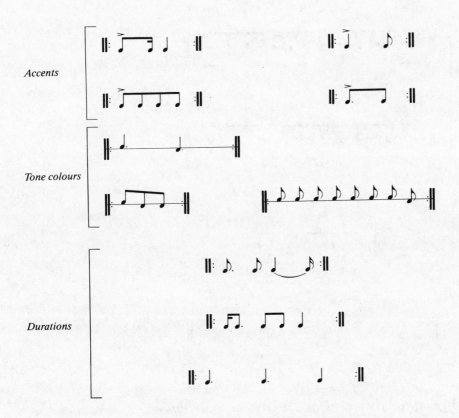

Accents

Tone colours

Durations

A figure is *uniform* when it is based on the repetition of a single configuration or cell, *whose position with respect to the pulsation varies at each recurrence.* This condition is the only feature which distinguishes a uniform from a unitary figure (see ex. 20).

Ex. 20

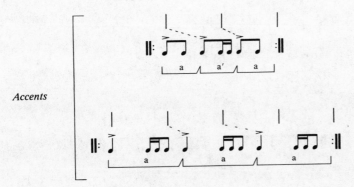

Accents

Ex. 20 (cont.)

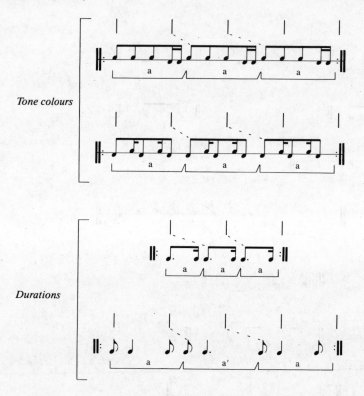

A figure is *multiform* when it includes *two or more different configurations*, as in ex. 21.

Ex. 21

Ex. 21 (cont.)

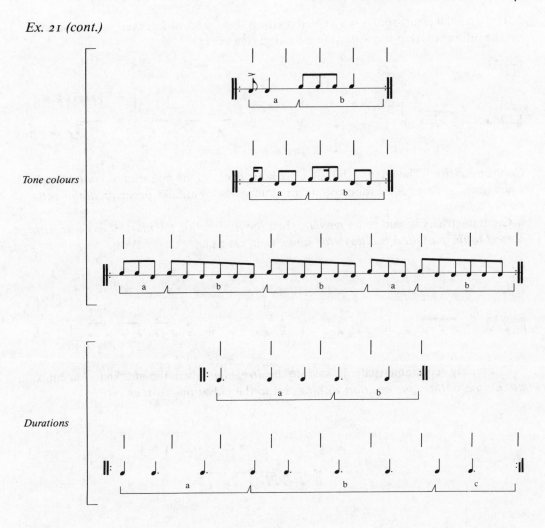

Tone colours

Durations

3.2.1.4   *Relation to time, or metricity*

There are five ways of defining the relationship of a rhythmic figure to the pulsation.
The relationship may be either *commetric* or *contrametric* (Kolinski 1973), and either
regularly or *irregularly* so, in each case. It may, however, also be *mixed*.

Commetricity   A figure has a *commetric* organisation when the accents, the changes
of tone colour, or (failing these) the attacks tend to coincide with the pulsations.

Commetricity is *regular* if *all* the accents, or *more than half* the changes of tone
colour or attacks fall on the pulsation; *no offbeat sound overlaps the following pulsa-*
tion (see ex. 22).

Ex. 22

It is irregular if any sound is accented on the offbeat; and/or *less than half* the sounds on the offbeat overlap the following pulsation (see ex. 23).

Ex. 23

Contrametricity The relationship of a rhythmic figure to the pulsation is *contrametric* when accents, changes of tone colour, or (failing these) attacks occur *predominantly on the offbeat*.

Contrametricity is said to be *regular* when *the position of the marked element with respect to the pulsation is always the same*, as in ex. 24.

Ex. 24

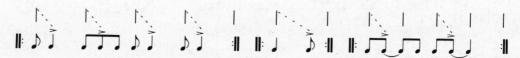

Conversely, contrametricity is said to be *irregular* when the marked element is *not always in the same position* with respect to the pulsation, as in ex. 25.

Ex. 25

Accents

Tone colours

Durations

The relationship to the pulsation is *mixed* when *commetric and contrametric elements are present in equal numbers* in a rhythmic figure (ex. 26).

Ex. 26

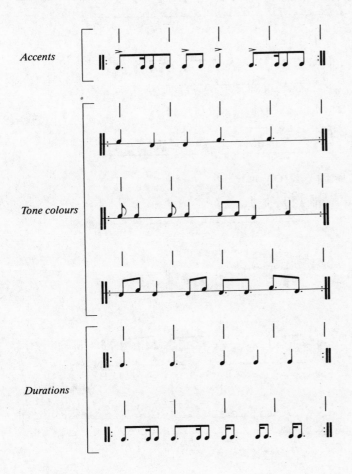

Accents

Tone colours

Durations

3.2.1.5 Structure

The structure of a rhythmic figure may be *symmetric, asymmetric,* or (more rarely) what we may call *indivisible*. Asymmetric structures alone may be either *regular* or *irregular*.

A figure is *symmetric* when it can be divided into *two equal parts* with respect to the position of at least two *noncontiguous* accents, changes of tone colour, or attacks (see ex. 27).

Ex. 27

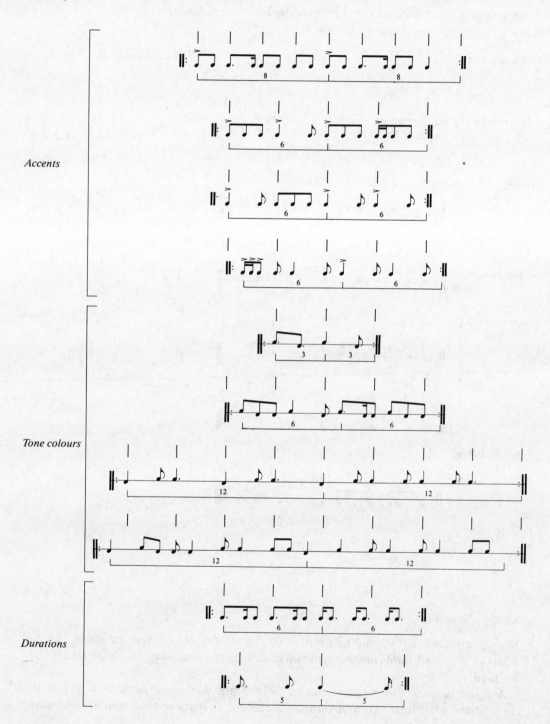

Accents

Tone colours

Durations

When the structure is *asymmetric*, the position of the accents, alternating tone colours, or attacks *will not allow a segmentation of this kind*.

Asymmetry is *regular* when the position of the marks is such that the cycle can be split into *any number of equal parts other than two and multiples thereof*, as, for example, in ex. 28.

Ex. 28

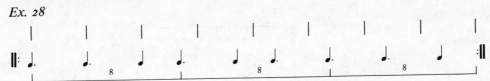

In Central Africa, regular asymmetry is usually based on the repetition of a single cell or configuration, whose position with respect to the pulsation is shifted each time it recurs in the rhythmic figure. This shifting comes about as a result of a difference in the arithmetic progressions of rhythm and metre. This, in fact, is the principle of the *hemiola* (see ex. 29).

Ex. 29

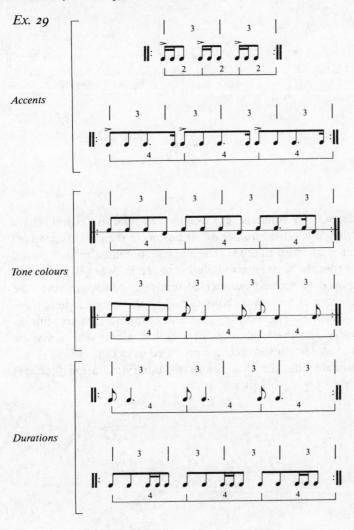

Asymmetry is *irregular* when the figure contains two or more configurations which *cannot be segmented into equal parts* (ex. 30):

Ex. 30

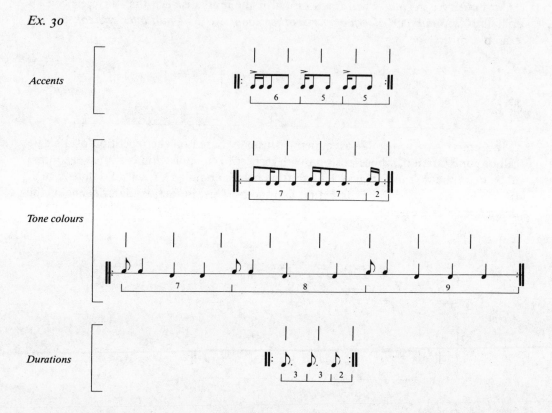

One particular form of asymmetry which is very frequently found in Central Africa may be called *rhythmic oddity*. When the *number of pulsations* in the periods involved is divided by two, the result is an *even* number. The figures contained in this period are nevertheless so arranged that the segmentation *closest to the middle* will invariably yield two parts, each composed of an *odd* number of minimal values, wherever the dividing line is placed. These figures are always constructed by the irregular juxtaposition of binary and ternary quantities. The resulting rhythmic combinations are remarkable for both their complexity and their subtlety. They follow a rule which may be expressed as 'half − 1/half + 1'. A few illustrations are provided in exx. 31–36.

The figure with eight minimal values (i.e., containing two binary pulsations) (ex. 31) is articulated as follows: $3/3.2 = 3/5 = 4 - 1/4 + 1$.

Ex. 31

A figure with a period containing twelve operational values arranged into four ternary pulsations (ex. 32) may be segmented into 5/3.4 = 5/7 = 6 − 1/6 + 1,

Ex. 32

or into 3.2/3.2.2 = 5/7 = 6 − 1/6 + 1, as in ex. 33.

Ex. 33

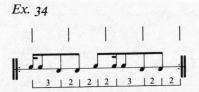

A figure with four pulsations subdivided into sixteen minimal values (ex. 34) has the following arrangement: 3.2.2/2.3.2.2 = 7/9 = 8 − 1/8 + 1.

Ex. 34

Finally, a cycle of eight pulsations divided into twenty-four operational values may be arranged as 3.2.2.2.2/3.2.2.2.2.2 = 11/13 = 12 − 1/12 + 1 as in ex. 35,

Ex. 35

or equally well, as 2.3.3.3/2.3.3.2.3 = 11/13 = 12 − 1/12 + 1, as in ex. 36.

Ex. 36

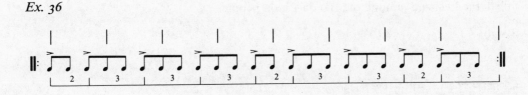

The technique of *rhythmic oddity* is based on the principle of *progressively inserting binary quantities into configurations bounded by ternary quantities*. This is clear from the paradigmatic representation of how this principle applies:

Cycle of 8 minimal values	3.	3. 2.
Cycle of 12 minimal values	3. 2	3. 2.2
Cycle of 16 minimal values	3. 2.2	3. 2.2.2
Cycle of 24 minimal values	3. 2.2.2	3. 2.2.2.2

The figure shown in ex. 36, however, applies an *inversion* of this principle, by inserting ternary quantities in configurations bounded by binary values. The twenty-four constituent minimal values are articulated thus:

$$\boxed{2.}\,3.3.3.\quad\boxed{2.}\,3.3.\quad\boxed{2.}\,3.$$

Finally, a structure is called *indivisible* if (1) the figure contains a single accent, or a single sound differing from all the others by its tone colour and (2) it contains only one duration, as in ex. 37; the case is quite rare but may occur in a polyrhythmic context.

Ex. 37

While unitary figures are indivisible when they contain only one accent, figures marked by contrasting tone colour may be unitary but nevertheless divisible: for example, the figure in ex. 38, which is comprised of two sounds with differing tone colour, is unitary, but its symmetric structure makes it divisible.

Ex. 38

3.2.2 How rhythmic features combine

We have seen that rhythmic figures are defined by a cluster of features. There are seventeen features in all, distributed into five different categories. Since a cluster may include only one feature from each category, it follows that five features are necessary and sufficient for the description of any rhythmic figure.

Let us consider a few examples. The figure in ex. 39, which is played by the drum called 'the husband' among the Banda-Linda people:

Ex. 39

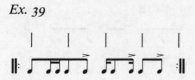

may be described as follows. It is marked by *accents*, it contains *unequal* durations, and it is *multiform* and *irregularly contrametric*, but *symmetric*.

The figure in ex. 40, played by the drum called 'the mother', is superposed on ex. 39.

Ex. 40

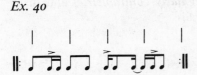

It has all the features of ex. 39 but one: its structure is *irregularly asymmetric*.

We now turn to the figures played by two double bells, which support a repertory of songs accompanied on the harp among the Ngbaka people. One of these, shown in ex. 41, is marked by *changing tone colour* and contains *unequal* durations; its

Ex. 41

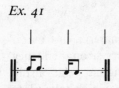

morphology is *uniform*, it has a *mixed* relationship to the pulsation, and its structure is *symmetric*. The other, shown in ex. 42, bears the *same mark* and likewise contains

Ex. 42

unequal durations; however, its articulation is *multiform*, its relationship to the pulsation is *irregularly contrametric*, and its structure is *irregularly asymmetric*.

Now that we can list the features which characterise a rhythmic figure, we can set up a typology. When *identical features* recur in different figures, we can place these figures in the same category.

The figures in ex. 43 are thus constructed with exactly the same systematic musical

Ex. 43

features: they are marked by *attacks*, they contain *unequal durations*, their morphology is *multiform*, their relationship to the pulsation is *irregularly contrametric*, and their structure is *irregularly asymmetric*. The same is true of the two figures in ex. 44. Both are marked by *accents* and have *unequal durations*, their articulation is *multiform*, their relationship to the pulsation is *regularly contrametric*, and their structure is *symmetric*.

Ex. 44

To conclude this examination of the ways of organising rhythmic material in Central Africa, we may say that the most striking property of rhythm is a very strong tendency towards contrametricity, which gives rise to a permanently conflictual relationship between the *metric structure* of the period and the *rhythmic events* which take place within it.

3.2.3   Realisations, variations, and models

The rhythmic figures utilised in the Central African Republic usually appear in polyrhythmic combinations. They are based on a principle of repetition involving a specific periodicity, and behave as rhythmic *ostinati*, which may or may not allow variations. This means that every figure is performed with reference to an underlying *model*, which may or may not be materialised.

Central African rhythmic figures fall into six types with respect to how they are realised:

(1) invariant figures, or strict *ostinati*
(2) figures which can be realised in different ways, but will not admit variations *in the course of any given performance*
(3) varying figures with a period of fixed length
(4) figures which vary by *amplification of the period*
(5) long cycles
(6) quasiperiodic figures

We will examine each of these types in succession.

3.2.3.1   *Invariant figures, or strict* ostinati

This type includes, first of all, the 'microfigures', which are composed of a single pulsation, as in:

Ex. 45

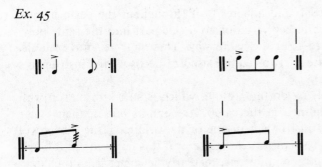

Strict *ostinati* are also found in certain repertories for private performance. A singer of 'thinking songs' among the Gbaya people will thus have a friend perform the figure in ex. 46 while he accompanies himself on the *sanza*.

Ex. 46

This figure will be constantly repeated without the slightest change. Likewise, in one Ngbaka repertory accompanied on the ten-string harp (*ngòmbí*), the four figures in ex. 47 are paired off according to the type of song, and performed uninterruptedly with no variation whatsoever.

Ex. 47

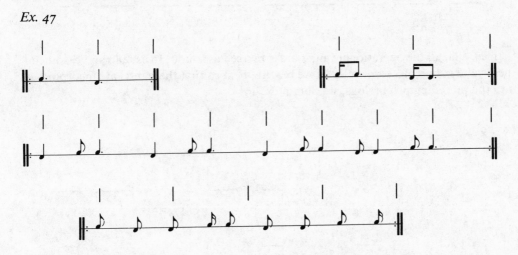

Strict *ostinati* can thus be said to realise their model without change.

3.2.3.2 *Variation-free performances*

Figures which can be materialised in different ways will sometimes be performed without variation. The musician consciously or unconsciously selects one of the variations from the range at his disposal, and adheres to it throughout the performance. At another time, he may choose another variation to fit his part into the same poly-rhythmic ensemble, and adhere to it in the same way. This happens, for example, among the Aka people in the case of two figures, used respectively for instruments called the *mò.kóngò* and the *dì.kétò*.

The *mò.kóngò* is a tree trunk lying on the ground, which is struck in unison with wooden sticks by all the available men in the camp. As soon as one of them starts playing the figure assigned to this instrument in one of its variations, the others will join in *with the same realisation*. The constituent features of this figure are as follows: it is accented, multiform, irregularly contrametric, regularly asymmetric, and charac-terised by rhythmic oddity. Its durations may be equal or unequal, depending on the realisation, but the durations of the model are unequal. We have observed three variations of the *mò.kóngò* figure, shown in ex. 48.

Ex. 48

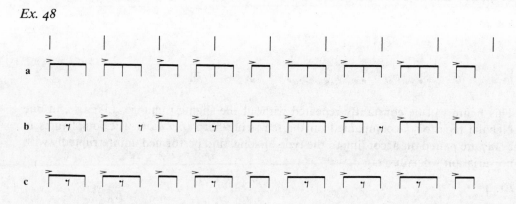

In ex. 48a, all the operational values are expressed as sound. In ex. 48b and c, some of these values are replaced by rests. If we rewrite them so that these rests are incorporated into the preceding percussions, we obtain ex. 49.

Ex. 49

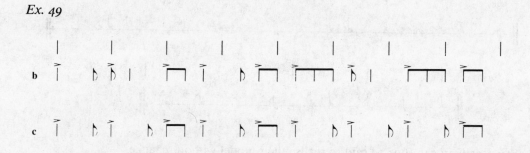

Two constants appear in each of the three versions: (1) the position of the accents is unchanged; and (2) the groups based on binary quantities do not change. This is why the Aka people themselves consider the three realisations to be *kà-mótì*, which literally means 'only one', i.e., they are equivalent, *assigned the same value*.

The ternary groups, on the other hand, can be materialised in two different ways, as either ♩ ♪ or ♪♩ , within the same realisation (ex. 49b). The possible arrangements of the ternary elements would thus theorectically allow an additional realisation, as shown in ex. 50.

Ex. 50

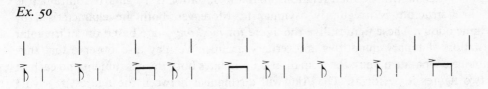

The figure is clearly individuated by the position of the accents. Since the Aka consider that changes in any other position do not affect the identity of the figure, they should, at least in theory, be able to recognise it when reduced to its accented percussions alone.

In order to verify this hypothesis, we performed the following experiment on several occasions. We played a sort of riddle game, which consisted of asking a group of several Aka musicians to identify various rhythmic figures taken from different repertories, which we produced by clapping our hands. One of these figures was:

Ex. 51

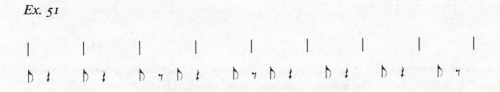

While the Aka never actually play the figure in this way, ex. 51 is in fact its model; and they recognised it every time, without the slightest hesitation, as the figure for *mò.kóngò*.

Now if we reduce a figure containing *irregularly spaced* accents to nothing but the sounds bearing this mark, we have in fact abolished the contrast between accented and unaccented sounds, as all the sounds remaining in the figure now have the same dynamic profile. It would therefore not seem unreasonable to consider this *theoretical* version, which contains all the distinctive features of the figure and only these, as the *abstract pattern* underlying the realisations in ex. 48, as well as any others we may not have recorded.

Unlike the figure for *mò.kóngò*, the ones performed by striking together two strips of iron (*dì.kétò*) are not marked by accents. As the tone colour does not change, they are marked by attacks alone. The strips produce two different rhythmic figures of unequal length: one has eight ternary pulsations and the other, four. The latter is used with only one sort of music, called *bòndó*, which is connected with the ritual of divination which precedes the departure of large group hunting expeditions. The former, however, is a sort of "wandering" rhythm; it can be found as part of several polyrhythmic combinations which provide support to six categories of music: *ngbòlù, mò.kóndí, yómbè, mò.nzòlì*, *mò.mbénzélé*, and *zòbòkò*, each of which has a specific social, or social and religious function.

Despite this difference in length and function, the two figures have exactly the same constituent features. Both are marked by attacks, their durations are unequal, their morphology is multiform, their relationship to the pulsation is irregularly contrametric, and their structure is irregularly asymmetric. Moreover, both are characterised by rhythmic oddity. These figures, like the figure for *mò.kóngò*, are based on an irregular alternation of binary quantities and ternary groups. We may also observe that they do not have separate names: the term *dì.kétò* designates both the instrument and each of the two figures it performs. The Aka will distinguish between the figures by saying simply 'the *dì.kétò* for *bòndó*' or 'the *dì.kétò* for *mò.mbénzélé*'.

The longer of the two is always realised in the following manner:

Ex. 52

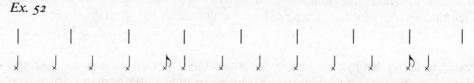

The *abstract* pattern for this figure should then be:

Ex. 53

Let us now examine the other figure performed by the iron strips to support *bòndó* music. We have recorded the five realisations, shown in ex. 54.

Ex. 54

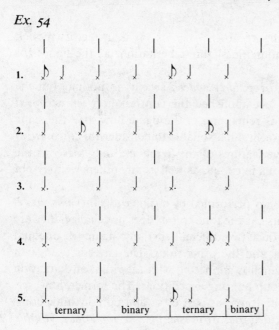

Four more versions of this figure are theoretically possible on the basis of different alternations of the ternary groups and binary quantities (ex. 55).

Ex. 55

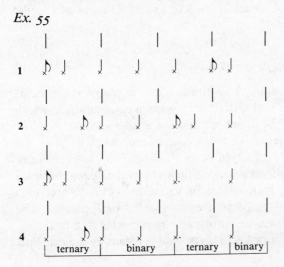

The model can be obtained by merging the ternary values (ex. 56).

Ex. 56

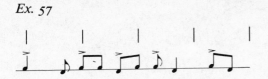

The accuracy of this model is confirmed by the figure played on the drum called 'the mother' (*ngúé*) in *bòndó* music (ex. 57).

Ex. 57

Although this figure is marked by accents, it is actually obtained simply by splitting the one played by the iron strips. In ex. 58 we place ex. 56 above ex. 57, which we have rewritten so as to eliminate the unaccented percussions.

Ex. 58

This shows that the accented sounds of the drum (which individuate the figure) and the percussions in the model for the *dì.kétɔ* figure coincide exactly. The realisations of the two figures are thus derived from identical models, except that one of them is accented while the other is not.

3.2.3.3 *Varying figures with unchanging periodicity*

This is the most frequently used technique. A rhythmic figure is assigned a specific periodicity, and may contain one or more cells, defined by a given configuration, which occupy fixed positions within the period. A figure may allow a greater or lesser number of variations according to its musical category or to the ethnic group using it. Thus, the Aka pygmies, whose musical creativity is displayed primarily in their vocal polyphony, make use of only a very small number of variations in their rhythmics. Each musician knows a certain number of admissible realisations, or variations (with respect to a model), for each figure, and uses them as he pleases during his performance. The contents of the cells are thus interchangeable, provided the musician respects their *position* within the figure and their configuration. This is what is meant by the principle of *commutation*.

All the realisations respect these two rules and are therefore considered *equivalent* from the cultural standpoint of those acquainted with the tradition. There is no more to the *internal* syntax of rhythmic figures than this.

In ex. 59, we show the variations with respect to the model (boxed in ex. 59a), performed during a single performance by the drum called *èyī.nɔ̀* 'the mother', for the Banda-Linda *àgā-tɔ́rúmɔ̄* ritual. The configurations are difined by accents, whose position can be seen not to vary.

Ex. 59

Ex. 59 (cont.)

Not only do marks bounding configurations remain invariant, but even one of the cells comprising the figure is often kept constant, as can be seen from exx. 60 and 61, both of which are assigned to the drum called 'the husband'.

The figure in ex. 60 is part of the dance music called *gàzà*, which is performed during

Ex. 60

the male initiation rites among the Banda-Dakpa people, by two wooden drums known as *lēngā*. Ex. 61 is part of the *àgā-tɔ́rúmɔ̄* ritual music, performed by an ensemble of three drums among the Banda-Linda people.

The highly structured way in which the constituent elements of these figures are arranged follows naturally from the overall organisation of the polyrhythmic ensembles in which they are inserted. The general principle is that the part assigned to the musician with the most experience (generally played on the drum called 'the mother') can freely develop rhythmic material outside the strictly periodic framework by either amplification or quasiperiodicity. The term *improvisation* is not inappropriate here. That is why the African soloist, like the jazz musician (or more aptly, the jazz musician, like the African soloist), must have solid points of temporal reference. These reference points are provided by the other drummers in the form of figures which scrupulously respect the periodicity (or periodicities) of the piece being performed.

The limitation of variation in the other parts is thus required to enable the master drummer to give free rein to his imagination. This is why the first half of the figures transcribed in exx. 60 and 61 is so stable, while the part reproduced in ex. 59, played by the 'mother' drum, allows variations in every position, even if they do not abound.

Ex. 61

The same is true of the 'mother' drum (*gúrú*) in the Zande *kpóníngbó* dance music; ex. 62 lists the realisations observed in a single performance. The need for temporal reference points will become clearer when we examine what variations produced by the techniques of amplification and quasiperiodicity look like.

Ex. 62

Ex. 62 (cont.)

We have already mentioned that the Aka pygmies make little use of variations in their polyrhythmics. Certain figures assigned to the 'mother' drum (*ngúé*) have only two realisations, e.g., in *yómbè* music, shown in ex. 63. Others, such as the *ngúé* part in the *ngbòlù* dance, shown in ex. 64, and the part played by the 'child' drum (*è.ndòmbà*), for both the *mò.nzòlì* and the *mò.mbénzélé* dances, transcribed in ex. 65, have three realisations.

Ex. 63

Ex. 64

Ex. 65

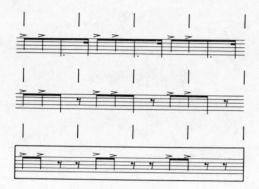

The 'mother' drum parts for both *mò.nzòlì* and *bòndó* each have five realisations. In *mò.nzòlì*, as in *ngbòlù* and *yómbè*, the model may be realised without change,

Ex. 66

while in *bòndó* (ex. 67), it must be obtained by 'abstraction', i.e., by merger of the ternary groups, as we have seen in ex. 58; it is, in fact, rarely realised in this bare form. Only *mò.mbénzélé* (ex. 68) has as many as six realisations, including the model.

Ex. 67

Ex. 68

The wealth of examples given above all concur to show that, however the figures represented may be realised, their marks (their accents, in this case) remain unchanged in every instance. This is precisely what individuates them, i.e., makes them distinguishable and identifiable.

The mark is also essential to the apprehension of the syntactic organisation of rhythmic figures: while this organisation is clearly apparent at the level of the figure itself, it cannot generally be said to be rule-governed at the next higher level, consisting of the sequences resulting from the concatenation of various realisations of the same figure. In certain cases, however, a preference can be observed for one type of sequence rather than another; and at times, the sequences will remain relatively constant. It may thus happen that a given realisation systematically precedes some other one in a given piece; but this is the exception rather than the rule.

Generally speaking, we may say that the syntax of the concatenation of the various materialisations of a rhythmic figure is free and unforeseeable, and the affirmations of our informants support this. The musician alone chooses the sequences he wants to play according to his state of mind at the time. Thus, a sequence of certain variations may be repeated several times in the course of a single performance, while others are completely omitted. This degree of freedom in forming concatenations is easily explained from the fact that, as we have already shown, all realisations are considered to be identical from the standpoint of the traditional musician. The significant aspect for him is the uninterrupted performance of the figure as such, which is superposed on other figures in a given synchronic relationship so as to create and preserve the coherence of the polyrhythmic ensemble. The purpose of the variations is to avoid monotony; they have no intrinsic value in themselves. We have consistently tried to find a syntactic regularity at a higher level, but have never succeeded; this is what our informants had led us to expect.

3.2.3.4 Variation by amplification

We may recall that the technique of *amplification* consists of *sporadically* developing the rhythmic material of a figure over some multiple of its initial period. This technique is usually employed by the master drummer in a polyrhythmic ensemble. At times, the second drum in a three-drum ensemble may be given the latitude to perform a few amplifications of modest length, if the first drum provides an *ostinato* with little or no variation to mark the periodicity unequivocally. This is the case with the Banda-Linda ensemble which performs for the *àgā-tɔ́rúmɔ̄* ritual. The second drum (*kàmíngà*) produces two types of amplification, one doubling, and the other tripling the original period: see ex. 69 (e) and (f). To the right of each realisation is the number of times it occurs in a single performance. This shows how sparingly the technique is used. We may further remark that amplification works 'backwards', i.e., the contents of the initial figure always appears at the end of the amplification.

Ex. 69

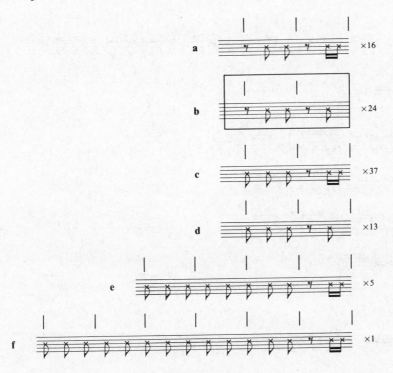

The situation is entirely different when the master drummer takes over the technique. We have thus observed eighteen realisations of the initial figure:

Ex. 70   bounded by the ending

Ex. 71

in the 'mother' drum part for the Banda-Dakpa *gàzà* dance. Eleven of these were amplifications ranging from two to four times the initial period. Twenty-one of fifty-eight occurrences of the figure remain within the initial period of two pulsations, while thirty-seven (i.e., nearly two-thirds) are amplifications. Thirty-one are *double* amplifications (over four pulsations), which might be called 'standard'; three are triple amplifications (over six pulsations), and three are quadruple (over eight pulsations), as shown in ex. 72. We will see below (3.2.3.5) that the technique of amplification can also be employed on a larger scale in connection with quasiperiodicity.

Ex. 72

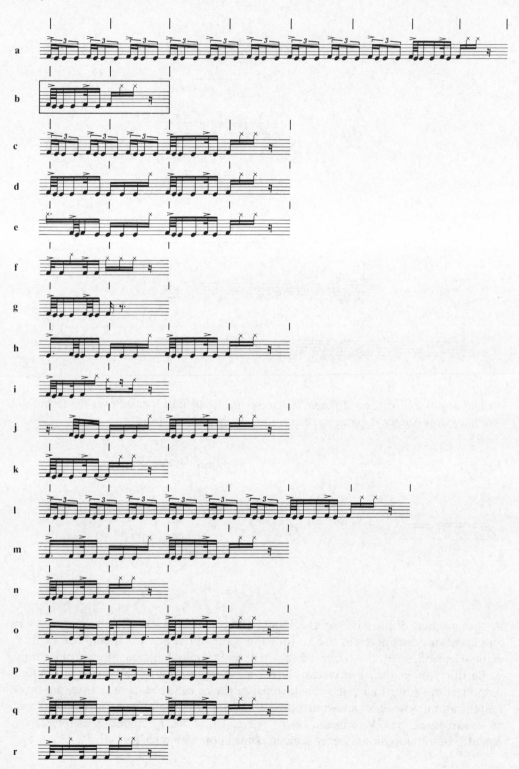

3.2.3.5 Long cycles and macroperiods

Long cycles are rhythmic sequences of regular periodicity, which are far longer than any other superposed period. This phenomenon can be encountered in the Sabanga dance repertory, *ngbàkè*.

The music for the *ngbàkè* dance requires the following ensemble: (1) a singer who accompanies himself on the xylophone (2) a pair of bells with internal clappers, a pair of pellet bells, and a small drum, which play in rhythmic unison (3) a large drum (4) bunches of jingles worn by a group of dancers around their ankles: they produce rhythmic sequences matching the dance steps. These sequences take the form of what we call *long cycles*.

The *ngbàkè* repertory includes three musically different pieces. The choreography for two of them (*yāfēmálè* and *āgōā*), is similar. Their dance sequences have an identical periodicity of twenty pulsations. The periodicity of the songs is different, however. In *āgōā*, the cycle for the melody and its xylophone accompaniment covers four pulsations. Five song cycles are thus necessary to cover one dance cycle, i.e., the ratio between the two is 5:1. *yāfēmálè* provides an example of a more complex relationship. The period of the song contains six pulsations, and the dance cycle twenty, so that they will only coincide again after sixty pulsations. Ten periods of the song will thus be required for three periods of the dance sequence. Since both of the superposed cycles are shorter than this, their relationship can be said to engender a huge *macroperiod*.

The period of twenty pulsations can be divided into segments, with the actual rhythmic figure in the centre. This 'heart' of the sequence is subject to variation, but is preceded by sets of steps which are practically invariable.

The version of *yāfēmálè* in ex. 73 contains fourteen different realisations for eighteen occurrences of the figure.

Ex. 73

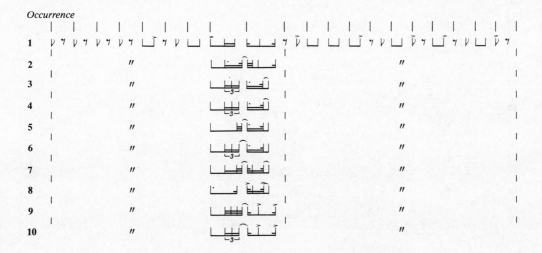

Ex. 73 (cont.)

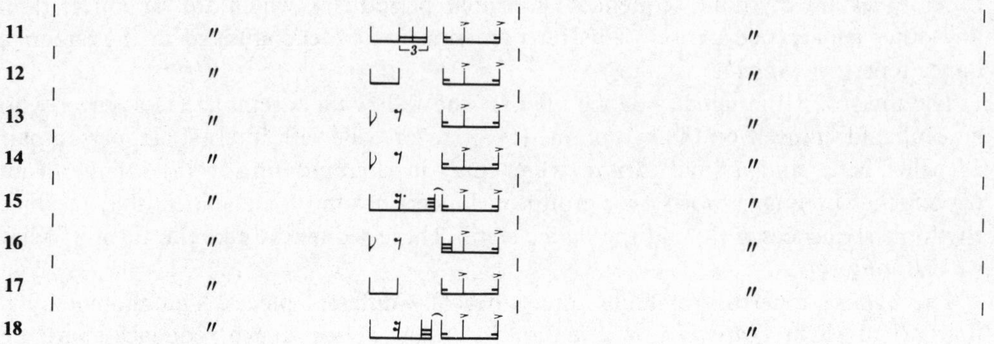

11   "

12   "

13   "

14   "

15   "

16   "

17   "

18   "

The version of *āgōā* in ex. 74 contains twelve different realisations for nineteen occurrences of the figure.

While the two dances have only one realisation in common,

Ex. 74

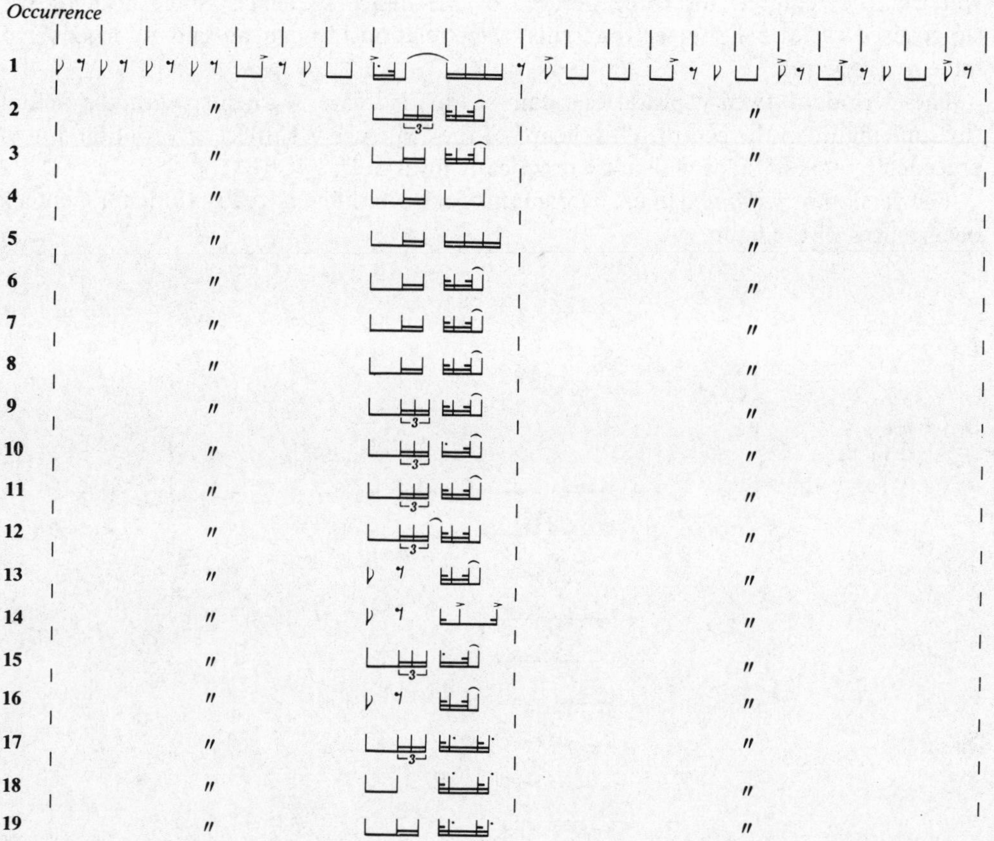

Occurrence

1

2   "

3   "

4   "

5   "

6   "

7   "

8   "

9   "

10   "

11   "

12   "

13   "

14   "

15   "

16   "

17   "

18   "

19   "

Ex. 75

the comparison of *all* their observed variations clearly shows that their rhythmic material is identical, i.e., that all their figures are derived from the same model.

3.2.3.6 *Quasiperiodicity*

Quasiperiodicity exists when the interval separating recognisable (i.e., identical or similar) rhythmic events is relatively irregular rather than constant. Quasiperiodic sequences constitute the only case in Central African polyphony and polyrhythmics where *no rational relationship* can be established between the musical substance of a given part and that of the others.

The *bàdá* dance, which also belongs to the Sabanga *ngbàkè* repertory, but is temporally organised in a different way from *yáfēmálè* and *āgōā*, provides a particularly good illustration of the technique of quasiperiodicity. Unlike its companion pieces, whose rhythmic material is subject to a wide variety of realisations, *bàdá* contains just one figure, which is repeated with only minute variations; only one (the fourth) of the eleven occurrences of the figure in the version shown in ex. 76 differs from the others by being abbreviated. In this dance, the principle of variation does not affect the rhythmic content of the figure, but rather the interval separating its occurrences.

Quasiperiodicity is usually, if not always, produced by dancers. The Dakpa *gàzà kōfē* repertory, which is used for the male initiation rites, includes two dances which are intended to be stylised representations of animals. The dance steps in each figure imitate these animals, viz. the squirrel (*bàdá*), the *oiseau mange-mil* (*ngùrùà*), and the white-coated monkey (*ngùyà*).

A brief description of the choreography of these dances will help in understanding the principles of their quasiperiodicity. The dancers move in a circle around the leader in a basic pattern of two steps to each pulsation. This part of the dance lasts between two and ten pulsations. The leader then cries, '*dɔ̄ngɔ̄ pèndèrè*', meaning more or less 'show how well you can dance', and after an *even* number of pulsations varying from four to ten, he calls out the name of the animal to be imitated by the next figure. He then cries, "*jéî*", which is an equivalent for 'let's go' borrowed from Mbororo Fulani. This call is the signal for the execution of a specific figure, which always begins two pulsations later. The periodicity of everything which precedes these last two pulsations is thus irregular. Moreover, the figures themselves vary in length: some are repeated one or more times in succession, and may last anywhere from two to twenty pulsations. The quasiperiodic cycle is comprised of the sequence of all the phases we have just described.

The two pieces from the repertory of the young *gàzà* initiates are entitled *bāmàrā gàzà* 'the lion of the gaza' (an allusion to the courage the initiate must show during the

Ex. 76

ritual ordeals), and *āyá.mɔ̄, mɔ̄ wú òyò* 'my brother, I am suffering' (a reference to another aspect of the initiation).

Tables 1 and 2 show how the quasiperiodicity is organised in each of these dances. They give the order of occurrence of the various sequences, the number of pulsations in each of their component phases, and the total length of each sequence. Paradigmatic transcriptions of the same dances are in exx. 77 and 78.

Table 1 Bāmàrā gàzà

Occurrence	Step	'Dɔ̄ngɔ̄'	Call	'Jei'	Figure	Total pulsations
1	10	6	4	2	10	32
2	–	–	4	2	10	16
3	–	–	2	2	10	14
4	–	4	4	2	16	26
5	–	–	–	–	18	18
6	2	6	4	2	8	22
7	–	–	–	–	11	11
8	–	4	4	2	16	26

Table 2 Āyá.mɔ̄, mɔ̄ wú òyò

Occurrence	Step	'Dɔ̄ngɔ̄'	Call	'Jei'	Figure	Total pulsations
1	8	10	12	2	10	42
2	–	–	10	2	10	22
3	6	10	6	2	6	30
4	–	–	–	2	10	12
5	6	8	4	2	6	26
6	–	–	–	2	2	4
7	5	6	8	2	8	29
8	–	–	–	2	2	4
9	2	8	6	2	20	38

A comparison of the paradigm in exx. 77 and 78 shows that they contain the same rhythmic material. They differ only in the arrangement and number of repetitions of the figures.

Our final illustration of variations definable in terms of quasiperiodicity is provided by the part performed by the master drummer for the two dances, *yáʃēmálè* and *āgōā*, from the Sabanga *ngbàkè* repertory. Their choreographic paradigm has already been transcribed in ex. 73 and ex. 74. The musician gives a virtuoso performance as he applies the technique of amplification to the rudimentary rhythmic theme, and breaks

Ex. 77 Bāmàrā gàzà: transcription

Ex. 78 Āyà.mẽ, mẽ wú òyò: transcription

out of the periodic framework, without sacrificing the recognisability of the original cell. The rhythmic material in these two pieces is identical. The basic cell is comprised of the extremely simple (and furthermore, regularly commetric) figure:

Ex. 79

This figure is bounded by an ending of three semiquavers, the first of which coincides with the pulsation, followed by a semiquaver rest. The drummer will amplify this figure up to twenty-six times its original size. At times, he will alternate it with transitional sequences based on the repetition of elements of a metric rather than a rhythmic nature, and thereby free himself from the constraints of periodicity. He thus proceeds similarly to the dancers in their choreographic movements. We here witness a bursting of the amplification technique, as true *development* takes over. We may profitably compare the simplicity of the initial elements, seven semiquavers and a semiquaver rest, with the richness of the combinations obtained by varying the groupings. The drummer takes advantage of the simple commetric structure of the initial theme, not only to change the durations but also to modify the accentuation: a single cell may be repeated several times in succession with a shift in some of its accents.

The part of the *gàsà* ('large') drum for the *yāfēmálè* dance is inventoried in ex. 80. The inventory of the part played by the same drum for the *āgōā* dance is shown in ex. 81. In order to give a general idea of the resources available to the musician as he works up his variations, we combine these two versions in exx. 80 and 81, and list in ex. 82 all the realisations contained in the first pulse of the initial figure.

3.3   Polyrhythmics

3.3.1   Definition and general characteristics

Polyrhythmics consists of the superposition of two or more rhythmic figures, each articulated in such a way that its constituent configurations (as determined by accentuation, changing tone colour, or alternating durations) will mesh with those of the remaining figures, and create an effect of perpetual interweaving. All the figures have a common temporal reference unit, the pulsation, and their periods, though differing in length, nevertheless stand in simple ratios, such as 1:2, 1:3, 2:3, 3:4, and so forth.

The superposed configurations are always performed at a fast tempo. The result is a state of permanent tension created by the antagonistic relationship among the figures. This antagonism appears simultaneously in two forms. We have already observed that each figure, taken individually, is in conflict with the temporal organisation of the period, i.e., its metric structure. In addition to this conflict between *rhythmic elements and metric elements*, there is a further conflict in the polyrhythmic situation between individual *sets of rhythmic elements*, i.e., between the contents of the individual figures.

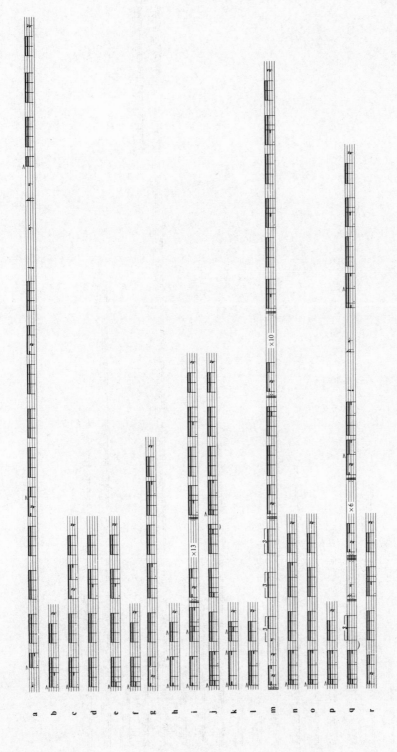

Ex. 80

Ex. 80 (cont.)

Ex. 81

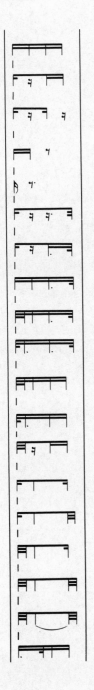

Ex. 82

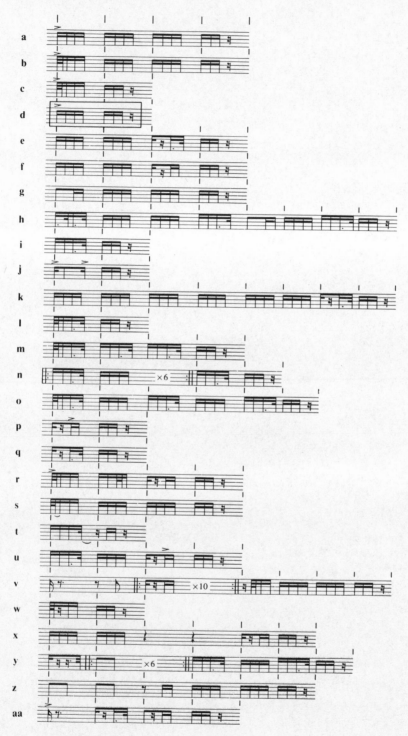

Ex. 82 (cont.)

When we carefully examine the kinds of music and musical techniques found in a traditional Central African society, we will see that its musicians make use of only a finite number of characteristic polyrhythmic constructions, which form a *closed* corpus of formulae associated with specific circumstances. These formulae are *distinctive* in that they contrast with one another with respect to their function, name, and of course, musical content. A corpus of this kind will rarely contain more than about ten formulae. For example, the Aka pygmies have no more than seven (*bòndó, ngbɔlù, mò.kóndí, yómbè, mò.nzòlì, mò.mbénzélé,* and *zɔbɔkɔ*), all of which have been discussed above.

3.3.2   Methodological principles

The simultaneous performance of different rhythmic figures engenders a polyrhythmic *block* or *formula*. Since each figure has its own period, but all the periods stand in simple ratios, the period of a polyrhythmic formula will always be the period of *the longest figure*. Since the marks defining the different figures occupy *specific positions* within them, we must find an easy way to locate them with respect to the entire poly-rhythmic combination. To do this, we must determine the total number of positions in the formula, which will be the number of minimal operational values it contains. For example, we will say that a polyrhythmic block whose longest figure contains eight ternary pulsations has a total of twenty-four *positions*.

The next step is to list all the marked positions in the formula, *independently of which figures the marks define*. This will tell us (1) the positions where the marks from several, or even all, the figures in the block coincide and (2) the positions where, on the contrary, the marks come from only one of the figures and are therefore inter-woven so as to *stand out alone* from the mass of the entire formula. The way in which marks are distributed and interact in the different parts of a polyrhythmic block is precisely what individuates this block and makes it intelligible (see 3.3.5 below).

Our approach to the analysis of polyrhythmic combinations can thus be summarised in three steps:

(1)   count the total number of positions
(2)   locate all the marked positions, independently of which figure the marks are taken from
(3)   locate, on the one hand, the *coincident* marks taken from several or all the parts, and on the other, the positions marked by a *single part* so as to stand out from the whole.

3.3.3   Forms of interweaving

Central African polyrhythmics is based on interwoven parts. We must now examine how the principle of interweaving works.

Interweaving takes one of two forms in a polyrhythmic ensemble: it is either *strict* or *partial*: it will be said to be *strict* when the marked positions in the various figures *never coincide*; it will be said to be *partial* when some marks in the superposed figures coincide, while others diverge.

These definitions apply to the model alone. In practice, it will often happen that variations in an accented part will give rise to transitory points of coincidence with marks from other parts.

3.3.3.1   Strict interweaving

It is extremely rare for all the parts of a polyrhythmic block to be strictly interwoven, i.e. for there to be no coincidence among the marks of different figures. We have recorded only one example, in the *gàzà* dance performed during the Dakpa male initiation rites, where there is strict polyrhythmic interweaving of the figures produced by two wooden slit drums (*lēngā*). The formula is comprised of two pulsations with binary subdivisions into eight operational values, and therefore has sixteen positions. Accents occupy six of these, three (at positions 7, 12, and 15) from the first drum ('the husband'), and three (at positions 3, 9, and 14) from the 'mother' drum. The two drums are thus strictly interwoven, as is clear from the transcription in ex. 83 and the diagram of the interweaving in ex. 84, where the long vertical lines indicate the pulsation.

Ex. 83

Ex. 84

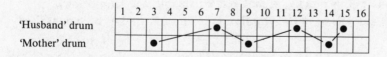

The rhythm of the dancers' ankle jingles (already examined separately above) adds counterpoint in the form of quasiperiodic sequences. While these are not actually strictly interwoven with the drum figures, the negligible number of exceptions does not affect the principle. In a version of this dance containing 1200 accented positions, the marks from the jingles coincide with those from one drum only thirty-six times, and are always strictly interwoven with those of the other drum. Only three of every hundred accents from all the parts combined are thus not interwoven.

Strict interweaving between *one of the parts and all the others* is less infrequent in some ensembles. The Banda-Linda *àgā tɔ́rúmɔ̄* music is a case in point. The figure produced by the dancer's ankle jingles contains a binary division of the pulsation, and crosses the superposed figures played by three drums, whose compositely divided pulsation contains binary and ternary minimal values, as shown in ex. 85:

Ex. 85

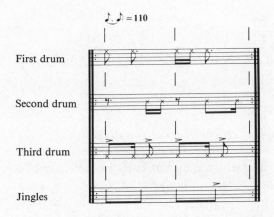

The interweaving is practically perfect, as the marks in the dancer's figure mostly fall offbeat on the second quaver. In a version of this piece containing 508 accented positions, 436 of which are in the third drum part (the other two drums do not use accentuation), and 96 in the jingles part, only 24, i.e. less than 5%, are common to both.

The most frequent form of strict interweaving is between two specific parts in a polyrhythmic block composed of a larger number. As examples, we will discuss two four-part polyrhythmic pieces performed by the Aka Pygmies. The first is taken from the *yómbè* dance, and refers to the parts played by the 'child' drum, *è.ndòmbà* (which is struck with the bare hands) and a pair of hard wooden sticks, *dì.kpàkpà*, (which are used to strike the sides of the drum with regular ternary accentuation). We may remark in passing that the Aka musicians generally perform three different rhythmic figures on a single two-headed skin drum lying on the ground: the *è.ndòmbà* part is played on the narrower end, and the *ngúé* ('mother') part on the wider end. The two drummers straddle the drum, sitting with their backs turned. The *dì.kpàkpà* player crouches between them facing the drum, and strikes the barrel in the middle.

The two interwoven figures in *yómbè* have the same configuration. The only difference is in the position of their marks with respect to the pulsation. The interweaving is thus not only strict but regular, as the diagram in ex. 86 shows:

Ex. 86

In the second example, the *mò.nzòlì* dance, strict interweaving occurs between the *dì.kpàkpà* part, which is always the same, no matter what combination it appears in, and the 'mother' drum part. The strict interweaving is irregular in this case (ex. 87):

Ex. 87

3.3.3.2 Partial interweaving

Partial interweaving is much more widespread. Some marked positions in each part are interwoven with marks from the other parts, while other positions are simultaneously occupied by anything from two to the entire number of parts in the ensemble. The greater frequency of partial interweaving is easily accounted for. Given how short the superposed figures are, the more there are of them, the greater will be the total number of marks. The result is an overall reduction of strict interweaving and a corresponding increase in partial interweaving. For example, if two of the three figures in a given polyrhythmic piece are strictly interwoven, each is likely to be only partially interwoven with the third. This is precisely what we find in the *mò.nzòlì* dance (ex. 88) when we add the 'child' drum (*è.ndòmbà*) to the strictly interwoven 'mother' drum and *dì.kpàkpà* parts already examined in ex. 87.

Ex. 88

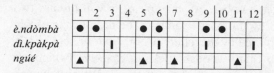

We see in ex. 88 that *nguè* and *è.ndòmbà* have a common accent in the first and fifth positions, while the *è.ndòmbà* and *dì.kpàkpà* accents coincide in the sixth and ninth positions. The coincidences thus occur in pairs, and there is not a single accent in the whole ensemble which is common to all three parts. Accents thus fall on ten of the twelve positions in the *mò.nzòlì* formula. There is strict interweaving at six of these points, but the other four are occupied by pairs of accents from two parts. This example shows that the combination of three rhythmic figures yields two-tiered polyrhythmics, and that strict interweaving remains predominant despite the coincidences on certain accentual positions.

Let us now turn to the partial interweaving of accents in *two-part* polyrhythmics. We may take as our first illustration the Zande *kpóníngbó* dance music, which is provided with a substructure by a drum (*gúrú*) and a pair of pellet bells (*nzɔ̀rɔ̀*):

Ex. 89

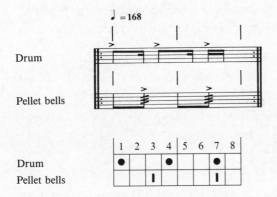

Four of the eight positions in this formula are occupied by accents, but only one of these (position 7) is common to the two parts. The other three are interwoven.

Another example is provided by the Aka *ngbɔlù* dance. Partial interweaving exists between the 'mother' drum (*ngúé*) and *dì.kpàkpà* parts. The two figures combined have twelve positions, seven of which are occupied by accents. Two (positions 3 and 9) are common to the two parts, while five are interwoven:

Ex. 90

	1	2	3	4	5	6	7	8	9	10	11	12
dì.kpàkpà			∎		∎				∎			∎
ngúé	▲		▲		▲				▲		▲	

In the Aka *bòndó* dance, the *è.ndòmbà*, *ngúé*, and *dì.kpàkpà* accents coincide. They stand in rhythmic counterpoint to the rattle (*mà.nzènzè*) accents, in a figure which has the rare feature of being regularly commetric (see ex. 91).

Ex. 91

	1	2	3	4	5	6	7	8	9	10	11	12
è.ndòmba, ngúé, dì.kpàkpà	●			●		●		●			●	
ma.nzènzè	□			□			□			□		

Seven of the twelve positions in the *bòndó* formula are accented. Two (1 and 4) are common to the two parts, while the other five are interwoven.

We will now provide four examples of partial accent interweaving in three-part polyrhythmic pieces, all drawn from Aka pygmy music. The first two are *yómbè* and *mò.nzòlì*.

Yómbè has nine accented positions, none of which is common to the three parts. *È.ndòmbà* and *dì.kpàkpà* are completely interwoven. *È.ndòmbà* and *ngué* have four accented positions (2, 5, 8, and 11) in common, while *dì.kpàkpà* and *ngué* have only one (position 6). Four strictly interwoven accents stand out from the whole, three provided by *dì.kpàkpà* (positions 3, 9, and 12), and one by *ngué* (position 7): as ex. 92 shows.

Ex. 92

	1	2	3	4	5	6	7	8	9	10	11	12
è.ndòmbà		●			●			●			●	
dì.kpàkpà			|			|			|			|
ngúé		▲			▲	▲	▲		▲			

In *mò.nzòlì* as in *yómbè*, none of the ten accented positions is common to the three parts. As we have shown in ex. 87, the *dì.kpàkpà* and *ngué* accents are strictly interwoven. *È.ndòmbà* and *dì.kpàkpà* have two coincident accents (at positions 6 and 9), as do *è.ndòmbà* and *ngué* (at positions 1 and 5). There are six single accents which stand out from the whole:

Ex. 93

	1	2	3	4	5	6	7	8	9	10	11	12
è.ndòmbà	●	●			●	●			●	●		
dì.kpàkpà			|			|			|			|
ngúé	▲				▲		▲			▲		

In *mò.mbénzélé*, the three drum parts furnish accents at seventeen points when superposed. Four (positions 6, 9, 18, and 21) are common to the three parts. Four more positions (3, 12, 15, and 24) are coincidently accented by *dì.kpàkpà* and *ngué*, and three others (1, 2, and 5), by *è.ndòmbà* and *ngué*. There are six interwoven single accents, one (position 4) provided by *ngué*, and five (positions 10, 13, 14, 17, and 22) by *è.ndòmbà* as in ex. 94:

Ex. 94

	1	2	3	4	5	6	7	8	9	10	11	12	13	14	15	16	17	18	19	20	21	22	23	24
è.ndòmbà	●	●			●	●			●	●			●	●			●	●			●	●		
dì.kpàkpà			|			|			|			|			|			|			|			|
ngúé	▲	▲	▲	▲	▲	▲			▲			▲			▲			▲			▲			▲

Finally, *mò.kóndí* has twenty-four positions, nineteen of which are accented. Two (positions 1 and 22) are common to the three parts, six (positions 4, 9, 10, 13, 16, and 21) are common to *è.ndòmbà* and *ngúé*, two (positions 8 and 17) to *dì.kpàkpà* and *ngúé*, and two (positions 6 and 19) to *è.ndòmbà* and *dì.kpàkpà*. There are single accents at seven positions (3, 5, 7, 11, 14, 18, and 20), as is clear from ex. 95:

Ex. 95

	1	2	3	4	5	6	7	8	9	10	11	12	13	14	15	16	17	18	19	20	21	22	23	24
è.ndòmbà	●			●		●	●		●	●			●			●			●	●		●		
dì.kpàkpà	|		|			|		|			|			|			|		|			|		
ngúé	▲			▲	▲			▲	▲	▲			▲			▲	▲			▲	▲	▲		

We now turn to partial interweaving in *unaccented* figures. There are two cases to be considered: figures with *changing tone colour*, and figures with *alternating durations*.

Rhythmic figures marked by *changing tone colour* are usually included in ensembles whose other parts have accents, i.e., combinations based on this mark alone are extremely rare. We have recorded two cases, one of which is not, properly speaking, polyrhythmic. The latter involves two pairs of double bells (*kpòlò*) which provide the rhythmic support for the Ngbaka 'harp songs', a repertoire of privately performed pieces which are always accompanied by a ten-string harp (*ngòmbí*). This repertory contains two 'families' of songs which differ both in their periodic framework and in the way they subdivide the pulsation (the subdivision is ternary in one family and binary in the other). There is a *kpòlò* formula (which is always played in the same way without the slightest modification) corresponding to each family.

The first of these formulae, together with a diagram of the interweaving, is shown in ex. 96 (the difference in tone colours produced by a single instrument is indicated by $\overline{}$ $\underline{}$).

Ex. 96

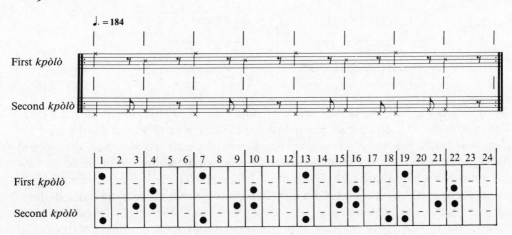

	1	2	3	4	5	6	7	8	9	10	11	12	13	14	15	16	17	18	19	20	21	22	23	24
First *kpòlò*	●		●				●		●				●		●				●		●			
Second *kpòlò*	●		●	●			●		●	●			●		●	●			●		●	●		

This formula is based on eight pulsations with ternary subdivisions, and contains two regularly commetric figures. All the percussions of the first double bell are located on the pulsation, and eight of the thirteen percussions of the second coincide with those of the first. The two *kpòlò* thus produce coinciding sounds on all the pulsations in the period, and the first has not a single interwoven percussion. Four of the other five sounds produced by the second double bell are regularly distributed on the third minimal value of every other pulse. The fifth is an exception and, in fact, a variant of the formula in ex. 97, which is the opening cell of the formula in ex. 96. Ex. 96, however is not polyrhythmic.

Ex. 97

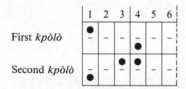

The second formula in ex. 98 is quite a different case. Thirteen of the sixteen positions in this combination are struck, but only four are common to the two instruments.

Ex. 98

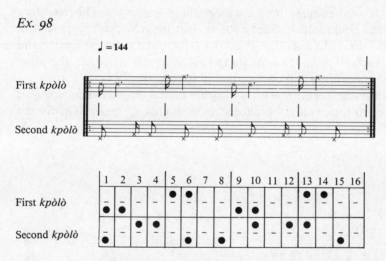

We can also see that the *combination of tone colours* is different in each of these four positions. The other nine percussions are interwoven. The first *kpòlò* provides four irregularly spaced percussions with alternating tone colour, and the second provides five with the same characteristics. We may also note that the rhythmic content differs within each pulsation of the combined formula. The first contains four percussions; the other three pulsations have only three, but the tone colours are ordered differently in each. The simultaneous presence of these two characteristics, diversity of tone colour and variety of position, is precisely what makes this formula polyrhythmic.

The interweaving of figures marked by *alternating durations* is quite rare. Such figures are always combined with at least one other accented figure. This is the case, for example, with two of the drum parts (*àkɔ.nɔ̀* and *kàmíngà*) in the Banda-Linda *àgā-tɔ́-rúmɔ̄* (see above, 3.2.3.3), which are combined with a third (*èyī.nɔ̀*) marked by accents:

Ex. 99

	1	2	3	4	5	6	7	8	9	10
First drum	●		●			●		●	●	
Second drum				●	●			●		●

As ex. 99 shows, the subdivision of the pulsation is composite, i.e., contains five minimal operational values. The formula is comprised of two pulsations and thus has ten positions, eight of which are occupied by attacks. The two drum parts are almost strictly interwoven, as the instruments are struck simultaneously at only one position (8). The attacks cross each other at the other seven.

3.3.3.3 Interweaving of accented and unaccented figures

Now that we have described the techniques of rhythmic interweaving separately for each type of mark, we may consider how the marks mix in polyrhythmic combinations. In other words, we have still to examine how rhythmic figures marked by accents are interwoven with those distinguished by attacks alone.

We will begin with the full formula for the *àgā-tɔ́rúmɔ̄* music, in ex. 100. A careful analysis of this formula gives us much information:

Ex. 100

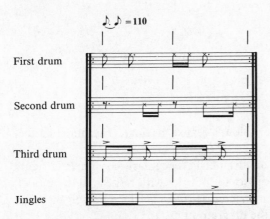

(1) There is a two-tiered periodicity, characterised by a ratio of 1:2, as the figures produced by the first two drums and the jingles employ a cycle containing two pulsations, while the third drum uses only one.

(2) In the drum parts, the pulsation contains five minimal values arranged in binary *and* ternary groups, while the division of the jingles part is perfectly binary.

(3) Rhythmic interweaving occurs simultaneously in two forms: between the two unaccented parts, on the one hand, and between the accented parts, on the other, and the formula as a whole conjoins them.

(4) The three drums are struck simultaneously at some positions (1, 3, 4, 6, and 8); their parts are therefore partially interwoven.

(5) Since the jingles figure is based on a *binary* division of the pulsation, it follows that its accent will not coincide with *any* of the percussions contained in the drum parts; the interweaving between jingles and drums is therefore *strict*.

(6) The first drum figure regularly juxtaposes quantities of two and three, which antagonise with the arrangement of the accents of the third drum in equally regular sequences of three and two, while the second drum *alternates* these two arrangements; the distribution is thus different in each of the two pulsations in the second drum figure: the first has a three-and-two arrangement, and the second, a two-and-three arrangement.

The Aka people systematically combine one unaccented figure with others marked by accents in their polyrhythmic music. The unaccented figure is always produced by striking together two iron strips (*dì.kétↄ*). Let us recall that *dì.kétↄ* has a choice of two figures, each with the same constituent features, but differing in length: one has four, and the other has eight pulsations, with ternary subdivisions, making totals of twelve and twenty-four operational values. The shorter figure is used only for *bòndó* music. This piece requires five instruments, *è.ndòmbà*, *dì.kpàkpà*, *ngúé*, *dì.kétↄ*, and a rattle, *mà.nzènzè*, to produce only two-part polyrhythmics. *È.ndòmbà*, *dì.kpàkpà*, *ngúé*, and *dì.kétↄ* all perform a figure based on the same model shown in ex. 101.

Ex. 101

This case, where four instrumental tone colours realise a single rhythmic model, is unique in Aka music.

Dì.kétↄ, which performs an irregularly contrametric, irregularly asymmetric figure characterised by rhythmic oddity, introduces some splitting with respect to the model. This part contrasts with the regularly commetric rattle (*mà.nzènzè*). The polyrhythmic formula in ex. 102 can be summarised by the diagram in ex. 103.

When we allow for the splitting in *dì.kétↄ*, we find the formula has nine marked positions, two of them (1 and 4) common and the other seven interwoven.

We have already remarked that Aka polyrhythmics comprises only seven combinations in all. Each is used in a given category of music, which is connected with a specific social (or social and religious) situation.

Ex. 102

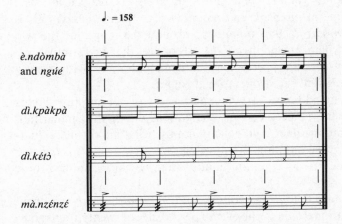

Ex. 103

	1	2	3	4	5	6	7	8	9	10	11	12
First part	●		●	●		●		●	●		●	
Second part	I			I			I			I		

(1) *Bòndó*, which we have just examined, is the music used in the rites which precede the departure of certain collective hunting expeditions.

(2) *Ngbòlù* used to provide the musical support for a divining rite, but the polyrhythmic formula and the songs included in this category are now performed for mere amusement.

(3) *Mò.kóndí* is the music for a ritual dance held to consecrate a new campsite; the spirits of the ancestors are invoked and asked to assure the prosperity of the new site by plentiful childbirths and successful hunts.

(4) *Yómbè* music is not linked to any specific ritual occasion; it is performed for the festivities following the capture of large game, or to welcome people arriving from another campsite, or again for mere amusement; *yómbè* is also allowed among the dances performed during the mourning periods after funerals.

(5) *Mò.nzòlì* music is played and sung on several consecutive evenings after an elephant has been killed.

(6) *Mò.mbénzélé* is a dance performed on two occasions: at funerals and during the festivities following the return of a successful hunting party.

(7) *Zòbòkò* music accompanies a rite of divination by fire which precedes the departures of the large collective hunting expeditions, which may last several weeks, or even months.

We will first examine these formulae individually, and compare them afterwards. This is for two separate reasons. Firstly, a small number of components are economically used to create a large variety of music. Some of the parts, i.e., some of the figures included in these combinations, 'wander' and show up in several categories. The *è.ndòmbà* part is thus the same in *mò.nzòlì* and *mò.mbénzélé*, the *dì.kpàkpà* part is identical in *ngbɔlù*, *yómbè*, *mò.nzòlì*, and *mò.mbénzélé*, and the longer of the two *dì.kétɔ* figures appears everywhere except in *bòndó*. Secondly, the six formulae excluding *bòndó* are defined by the same periodicity of eight pulsations with ternary subdivisions, and thus all have twenty-four operational values.

This combination of an identical metric structure and a sort of 'all-purpose' figures raises the basic question of how pieces can be recognised. Given the similarities, how is immediate identification possible? And concomitantly, what are the individuating features? We will reply to these questions by showing that each formula is capable of retaining its individuality despite its common points, after we have examined these formulae separately.

In three of the six combinations (*ngbɔlù*, *yómbè*, and *mò.nzòlì*) where the drum parts employ only twelve operational values, the overall periodicity of twenty-four values is dictated by the *dì.kétɔ figure*.

The *ngbɔlù* formula superposes three periodicities: *dì.kétɔ* with twenty-four, *ngúé* with twelve, and *dì.kpàkpà* with three. The ratio is thus 1:2 between *dì.kétɔ* and *ngúé*, 1:4 between *ngúé* and *dì.kpàkpà*, and 1:8 between *dì.kétɔ* and *dì.kpàkpà* (see the transcription in ex. 104). In terms of interweaving, twenty positions are marked, as shown in ex. 105.

Ex. 104

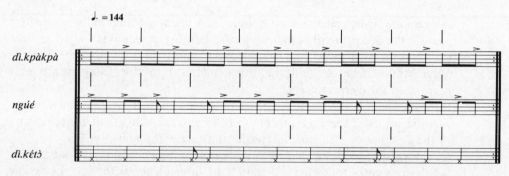

Ex. 105

	1	2	3	4	5	6	7	8	9	10	11	12	13	14	15	16	17	18	19	20	21	22	23	24
dì.kpàkpà			I			I			I			I			I			I			I			I
ngúé	▲		▲		▲				▲			▲		▲		▲		▲			▲		▲	
dì.kétɔ	*		*		*		*	*		*			*		*		*	*		*		*		

     – two marks (at positions 3 and 21) are common to the three figures

     – two marks (at positions 9 and 15) are common to *ngúé* and *dì.kpàkpà*

     – three marks (at positions 1, 5, and 23) are common to *ngúé* and *dì.kétɔ*

     – two marks (at positions 12 and 18) are common to *dì.kpàkpà* and *dì.kétɔ*

       – eleven marks are provided by a single part,
           three by *ngúé* at positions 11, 13, and 17,
           two by *dì.kpàkpà* at positions 6 and 24, and
           six by *dì.kétò* at positions 7, 8, 10, 14, 16, and 19.

Mò.kóndí has four parts in all, one of them being *è.ndòmbà*. The *è.ndòmbà* and *ngúé* parts are of the same length. The *dì.kpàkpà* part, on the contrary, covers the entire cycle. All the parts in the formula thus stand in the simple ratio of 1:2, as the transcription in ex. 106 shows.

The diagram in ex. 107 shows that *mò.kóndí* has twenty-one marked positions:

Ex. 106

Ex. 107

       – one (the first) is common to the four parts
       – nine (positions 4, 6, 8, 10, 16, 17, 19, 21, and 22) are common to three parts
       – four (positions 3, 9, 13, and 14) are common to two parts
       – seven (positions 5, 7, 11, 12, 18, 20, and 23) contain the marks of single
           instruments.

We may note that the nine positions common to three parts provide four different combinations of tone colour (compare positions 4, 6, 8, and 22). The four positions common to two parts yield two combinations (see positions 3 and 13). The single marks are distributed as follows:

- two are from *è.ndòmbà* (at positions 7 and 18)
- one is from *dì.kpàkpà* (at position 11)
- two are from *ngúé* (at positions 5 and 20)
- two are from *dì.kɔ́tɔ̀* (at positions 12 and 23).

The *yómbè* dance constitutes a rare and interesting case of ambiguity between two parts, *è.ndòmbà* and *dì.kpàkpà*. Both are morphologically identical, having three operational values, the first of which is accented. They differ only in the position of their accents. In *è.ndòmbà*, the accent falls on the second value of the pulsation, and coincides with most of the *ngúé* accents. It is systematically crossed by the accent produced on the third value of the pulsation by *dì.kpàkpà* striking the side of the drum. Both figures are, however, regularly contrametric:

Ex. 108

Ex. 109

	1	2	3	4	5	6	7	8	9	10	11	12	13	14	15	16	17	18	19	20	21	22	23	24
è.ndòmbà		●			●			●			●			●			●			●			●	
dì.kpàkpà			❙			❙			❙			❙			❙			❙			❙			❙
ngúé		▲			▲	▲	▲	▲				▲			▲			▲	▲	▲	▲			▲
dì.kétɔ̀	*		*		*		*		*	*		*		*		*		*		*		*	*	

Yómbè has a three-tiered periodicity with twenty-four, twelve, and three operational values. The parts stand in the same ratios as for *ngbɔ̀lù*. Twenty-two of the twenty-four positions are marked, so that almost all the available positions are used:

- three parts have five marked positions in common (5, 14, 18, 20, and 23)
- two parts have nine in common (2, 3, 6, 7, 8, 9, 11, 12, and 17)
- eight single marks are interwoven (at positions 1, 10, 15, 16, 19, 21, 22, and 24), four of them (1, 10, 16, and 22) produced by *dì.kétɔ̀*.

Mò.nzòlì and *mò.mbénzélé* have the same *è.ndòmbà* part. Its figure is a *hemiola* obtained by forming three groups of four operational values. This arrangement contrasts with the four groups of three values in the *dì.kpàkpà* figure for the same categories.

Ex. 110

The appearance of figures displaying this particular type of 3:4 ratio is a natural consequence of the fact that all Aka music (with the exception of a single category, *kólí*) is based on a ternary division of the pulsation, and that their rhythm are systematically provided with a periodic organisation into either four or eight pulsations. Periods of this size *invariably* contain either twelve or twenty-four operational values, both of which numbers have the property of being *divisible by both two and three*. A considerable number of rhythmic figures (such as *ngúé* in *bòndó*, *dì.kpàkpà* in *mò.kóndí*, and *dì.kétò* in every category) are based on the horizontal *juxtaposition* of configurations obtained with groups of *both* binary *and* ternary values. But with periods of twelve or twenty-four values, such configurations can also be vertically *superposed*. This would be impossible for any combination based on *either* binary *or* ternary values alone, and the vertical hemiola may be said to sum up this type of relationship.

The exceptional nature of *kólí* (where the pulsation receives a binary subdivision) can be accounted for by its social function. This category contains a single piece of the same name, a mourning song sung by the entire community after the body has been prepared for burial. It is performed solely *a cappella* without even the isochronous handclaps which the Aka will readily adapt to any other repertory. *Kólí* is thus set entirely apart from the rest of the Aka musical heritage by its binary organisation and by the absence of any rhythmic, or even metric support.

We now complete our analysis with the examination of *mò.nzòlì* and *mò.mbénzélé*. The *dì.kpàkpà* and *dì.kétò* parts are common to these two dances, like the *è.ndòmbà* part just now mentioned. The differing *ngúé* parts are thus the only means of distinguishing them. Since both of these parts have the same periodicity, the ratios in *mò.nzòlì* and *mò.mbénzélé* are as follows: 1:2 between *dì.kétò* and the *è.ndòmbà* and *ngúé* parts, 1:4 between the latter and *dì.kpàkpà*, and 1:8 between *dì.kpàkpà* and *dì.kétò*.

The formula for *mò.nzòlì*, followed by the diagram of its interwoven marks, appears in ex. 111.

Ex. 111

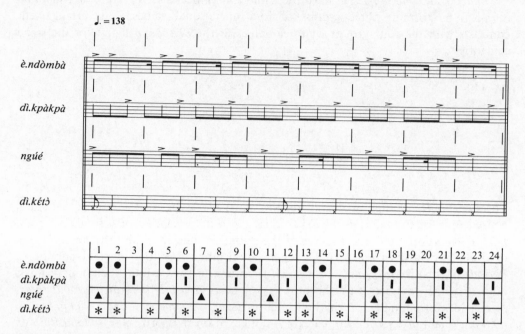

Here as in *yómbè*, twenty-two of the twenty-four positions are marked:

- the marks of all four parts never coincide
- five marks are common to three parts (at positions 1, 6, 13, 17, and 21)
- nine marks are common to two parts (at positions 2, 5, 9, 10, 12, 15, 18, 19, and 23)
- eight single marks stand out (at positions 3, 4, 7, 8, 11, 14, 22, and 24).

Let us now look at polyrhythmic combination for *mò.mbénzélé*:

Ex. 112

Ex. *112 (cont.)*

	1	2	3	4	5	6	7	8	9	10	11	12	13	14	15	16	17	18	19	20	21	22	23	24
è.ndòmbà	●	●			●	●			●	●			●	●			●	●			●	●		
dì.kpàkpà			I			I			I			I			I			I			I			I
nguè	▲	▲	▲	▲	▲	▲			▲			▲			▲			▲			▲			▲
dì.kétò	*		*		*		*		*		*		*	*		*		*		*		*		*

Of the twenty-one marked positions in *mò.mbénzélé*,

- two (9 and 18) are common to all four parts
- six (1, 3, 5, 6, 21, and 24) are common to three parts
- six (2, 12, 13, 14, 15, and 22) are common to two parts
- seven (4, 7, 10, 11, 16, 17, and 20) stand out alone.

Polyrhythmic complexity depends on more than just the number of parts. It is equally dependent, if not more so, on their internal organisation. The greater the ambiguity (contrametricity, asymmetry, and particularly, rhythmic oddity) intrinsic to the superposed rhythmic features, the more complex will be the polyrhythmics resulting from their conjunction. The following set of examples is an eloquent illustration of this assertion. The polyrhythmic substructure for the *zɔbɔkɔ* rite involves only two figures, which moreover have identical periodicity. Both have been examined above (see 3. 2.1.5).

One is *mò.kóngò*, shown in ex. 113.

Ex. 113

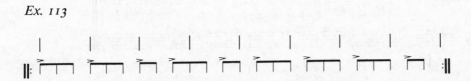

It is played by several men who crouch alongside a tree trunk lying on the ground, and strike it in unison with hard wooden sticks. The other is the 'wandering' figure of *dì.kètò*. Before we discuss the way in which these figures are superposed, we may usefully recall their constituent features.

Mò.kóngò is marked by *accents*, *dì.kétò* by *attacks*. The percussions in *mò.kóngò* are all of *equal* duration, while those of *dì.kétò* are *unequal*. Both have a *multiform* morphology, an *irregularly contrametric* relationship to the pulsation, and an *asymmetric* structure. The *asymmetry* in *mò.kóngò* is *regular*, however, while it is *irregular* in *dì.kétò*. Let us now analyse these observations.

Two of these five features are common, and three are different. Both figures are based on the juxtaposition of binary and ternary quantities. In *mò.kóngò*, the ternary quantities are placed in the interval separating three *isolated* binary units. The opposite happens in *dì.kétò*: binary quantities are inserted between two *isolated* ternary elements. This insertion of binary quantities filling up the space between the two ternary islands is precisely what makes it possible to divide the figure into two segments composed respectively of eleven and thirteen minimal values. Since the period has a total of twenty-four values, we see that *dì.kétɔ* is not only asymmetric, but also obeys the rule of rhythmic oddity, 'half − 1/half + 1'.

Mò.kóngò also follows this rule, but unlike *dì.kétɔ*, its asymmetry is regular. It can indeed be divided into three equal parts, each containing eight minimal values: 3.3.2/3.2.3/3.3.2. These three segments make use of only two cells, one of which (3.3.2) is repeated twice. But while the two occurrences of this cell are rhythmically identical, metrically, they are not, as the cell's position is shifted with respect to the pulsation (ex. 114).

Ex. 114

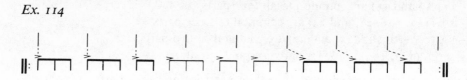

We now superpose the two figures below to obtain the formula for *zɔbɔkɔ*.

Ex. 115

The vertical analysis of this formula reveals a two-tiered articulation. On the first level, the cycle is divided into two asymmetric 'hemistichs' (marked A and B in ex. 116) containing thirteen and eleven minimal values.

Ex. 116

This segmentation reveals the second level of articulation. Each component 'hemistich' can be divided into two segments of unequal length: six plus seven values for A, and six plus five for B. There is therefore a regularity in the two 'hemistichs', in that the first segment is even (and moreover contains an equal number of values), while the second is odd. A careful examination of the formula furthermore reveals that the binary and ternary groups in each figure are generally superposed so as to conflict. With the exception of the binary–ternary–binary sequence common to the two instruments at positions 7, 9, and 12, there is strict antagonism, as ex. 117 shows: every time one of the figures has ternary quantities, the other uses a binary organisation.

Ex. 117

Three techniques are thus used in combining the two figures. Each appears in a different unit at the second level of articulation: (1) 'Hemiola'-like interweaving in the first and third segments, where two ternary groups in *mò.kóngò* are superposed on three binary groups in *dì.kétò*; (2) rhythmic identity in the second segment, where the percussions of *dì.kétò* coincide with the accents of *mò.kóngò*; (3) finally, rhythmic interweaving in the fourth segment, brought about by reversal of the arrangements, so that a ternary-binary sequence in *mò.kóngò* will match a binary-ternary sequence in *dì.kétò*.

Each 'hemistich' is thus subdivided into two units, a–b in A, and a–c in B, as in ex. 118.

Ex. 118

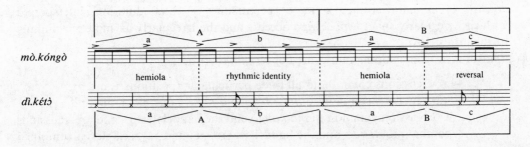

If we now count groups of each type in each figure, we will find that the total number of values in the *binary* configurations in one will equal the total number of values in the *ternary* figures in the other, as the table below shows:

mò.kóngò	dì.kétɔ
six ternary groups	nine binary groups
6×3=18	9×2=18
three binary groups	two ternary groups
3×2=6	2×3=6

The polyrhythmic character of this piece is based on the interweaving of certain *mò.kóngò* accents with certain *dì.kétɔ* attacks. Isochronous handclaps added to the whole materialise the pulsation *in this particular case*. The period contains eight pulsations. Nine accents are produced by *mò.kóngò*, three of which are commetric and thus coincide with the pulsation. The other six are irregularly contrametric. Five of the attacks in *dì.kétɔ* are commetric, but the remaining eight are irregularly contrametric. All the commetric accents in *mò.kóngò* do not, however, coincide with the commetric attacks in *dì.kétɔ*. It is clear from the formula that the commetric accents and attacks coincide only twice, on the first and third pulsations. Elsewhere, they are interwoven. The effect of interweaving the quite different qualities of sound produced by these two instruments is to thwart the regularity of the handclaps. The pulsations which do not coincide with a *mò.kóngò* accent or a *dì.kétɔ* attack may even be said to acquire a real rhythmic function, insofar as they are materialised by handclaps, which are themselves *interwoven* with these accents and attacks. The interaction of these three types of sound may thus be envisaged as *three-part* interwoven polyrhythmics, with a *mò.kóngò* accent at position 17, three *dì.kétɔ* percussions at positions 3, 5, and 18, and two irregularly spaced handclaps at positions 13 and 19, all standing out, as represented by the diagram in ex. 119.

Ex. 119

	1	2	3	4	5	6	7	8	9	10	11	12	13	14	15	16	17	18	19	20	21	22	23	24
mò.kóngò																	■							
Hand claps													‖						‖					
dì.kétɔ			◆		◆													◆						

The three tone colours stand out well from the mass of the formula, which, we repeat, consists of an uninterrupted series of percussions of equal duration, interspersed with the irregularly spaced *mò.kóngò* accents and the irregularly asymmetric clinking of the iron strips.

Insofar as the remaining marks are concerned, there are:

- 2 percussions common to all three participants (positions 1 and 7),
- 5 percussions common to *mò.kóngò* and *dì.kétɔ* (9, 12, 14, 20, and 23),
- 1 percussion common to *mò.kóngò* and the handclaps (4), and 3 percussions common to *dì.kétɔ* and the handclaps (10, 16, and 22), i.e., eleven combined percussions in all.

This number, taken together with the six isolated percussions, makes a total of seventeen rhythmic events for a cycle with twenty-four minimal values. Seven different sound combinations are thus created with only three tone colours, as ex. 120 shows.

Ex. 120

1	2	3	4	5	6	7	8	9	10	11	12	13	14	15	16	17	18	19	20	21	22	23	24

Now the interaction of all these events takes place at a tempo of ♩ = 160. This means that the entire cycle containing them hardly lasts four seconds.

To conclude, we may say that the superposition of two figures of equal length, standing in an irregularly contrametric relationship to the pulsation each of which irregularly juxtaposes binary and ternary configurations in differing arrangements, engenders a polyrhythmic web of remarkable subtlety when considered in the light of the small number of component elements involved.

The last six formulae have shown us that, while the figure assigned to *dì.kétò* is always the same, it is differently positioned in each category, i.e., the way in which its points of attack are interwoven differs in each case. We must therefore now ask ourselves how this one figure can be fitted into six different combinations.

Several parameters are responsible for this capability:

(1)   the *periodicity* of *dì.kétò* always stands in a simple ratio to that of the other figures in the same formula.

(2)   the *pulsation is divided in the same way* in every polyrhythmic combination: the subdivision is systematically ternary, so that the minimal values of *dì.kétò* will always match those of the other figures, whatever their source (the heads or sides of the drum, or *mò.kóngò*, the tree trunk).

(3)   *dì.kétò* always has the same *relationship to the pulsation*: it contains a sequence of two asymmetric cells, the first comprised of eleven minimal values including four binary configurations, and the second, of thirteen, including five binary configurations; each of these cells is bounded by the ternary configuration, ♪♩ ; metrically speaking, each of these configurations always stands in the same relationship to the pulsation: in one occurrence, *the quaver coincides with the pulsation* (♪♩), and in the other, *the following crotchet* (♪♩). This simple shift in position from one configuration to the other is enough to create and maintain rhythmic ambiguity in the relationship of *dí.kétò* to the remaining figures, both individually and as a whole.

The way *dì.kétò* meshes with the superposed figures in each polyrhythmic combination remains as constant as the position of its constituents with respect to the pulsation. This is to say that it interlocks in a specific and invariant way with each of the formulae containing it. The comparative table in ex. 121 shows the exact position *dì.kétò* occupies in each of the six polyrhythmic ensembles, according to our transcription of their cycles.

Ex. 121

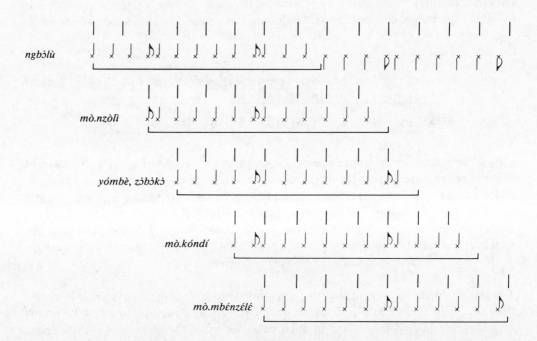

The *dì.kétò* figure works like a mould:

- in *mò.nzòlì*, it is shifted two pulsations to the right with respect to *ngbòlù*
- in *yómbè* and *zòbòkò*, it is shifted another pulsation with respect to *mò.nzòlì*
- in *mò.kóndí*, it is shifted a further two pulsations with respect to the latter
- and in *mò.mbénzélé*, it is shifted a final pulsation with respect to *mò.kóndí*

Not the slightest change is thus discernible in the internal organisation of *dì.kétò*, however it may interlock with the other figures. The only difference is in the point at which it meshes with the other parts in each category.

3.3.4   Variations

The degree of variation in a polyrhythmic formula is evidently dependent on the amount of variation in its constituent parts, which may range from absolute invariability through the forms of *ostinato* with variations and amplification, to free improvisation beyond the constraints of periodicity. Everything points, however, to the idea that the degree of variability in Central African polyrhythmic combinations is far from fortuitous, but rather is coherently related to the musical characteristics of the types of music they support. Variability in a polyrhythmic substructure may thus be said to be inversely proportional to that observed in the superposed melodic material. For example, the polyrhythmic support provided by the two double bells in the Ngbaka 'harp songs', where the vocal soloist introduces incessant variations in the melodic theme, is itself invariable.

On the other hand, in the Sabanga *ngbàkè* repertory, a repetitive melody is linked with a xylophone part composed of very short and minimally varied periods. The big drum, however, plays nearly free improvisation, while the dancers superpose long and varied cycles on the short voice and xylophone periods. Similarly, the Banda-Dakpa *gàzà* music involves a vocal part accompanied by two xylophones with markedly repetitive material. The master drummer, on the other hand, makes use of the technique of amplification, while the dancers perform on a quasiperiodic basis. Again, limited variation in the melodic parts corresponds to considerable variability in the polyrhythmic support. Conversely, the Aka pygmies, whose polyphonic vocal music abounds in variations, use very little in their polyrhythmics. The purpose of their percussion instruments is to preserve a strict periodicity providing clear points of temporal reference to the member of the group who take part in the singing.

How are variations put into practice? All the possible realisations of a given rhythmic figure are culturally speaking identical, so that the order in which they are repeated is almost always random. A figure with several realisations can thus just as well be indefinitely repeated in a given form as appear successively in every one of its admissible forms. In other words, with only rare exceptions, the order in which the realisations of a given figure are concatenated is optional. This in turn means that no syntactic constraints apply. Any realisation of a given part in a polyrhythmic ensemble can thus be superposed on any realisation of any other part, *provided the conditions of interweaving, as defined by the position of the marks within the period, are respected.*

Anyone who knows and scrupulously observes these very simple grammatical rules can produce a number of combinations which is directly proportional to the inventory of variations characteristic of each of their component parts. This is in fact how Central African musicians themselves go about creating their highly diversified polyrhythmic combinations.

If the reader himself wishes to use the transcriptions of invariant figures and the paradigmatic representations of variable ones, as presented below, to construct polyrhythmic formulae, assuming he understands and respects the rules of this grammar, he may do so. His combinations should be perfectly acceptable to bearers of the tradition, if he has made no change in the position of the various elements.

The paradigms for the three drum parts in the Banda-Linda *àgā-tɔ́rúmɔ̄* ritual music are shown below. Letters are used to designate each realisation.

Ex. 122

Ex. 122 (cont.)

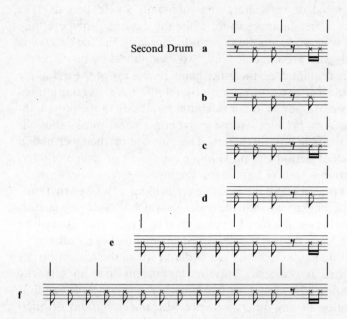

Ex. 122 (cont.)

There is only one syntactic constraint in this music: in the second drum part, the amplification (e) is always preceded by (b), and may be followed by (b), (c), or (d), while (f) is always preceded and followed by (b). Thus, by superposing (a) of drum 1 with (b) of drum 2, and (d) *and* (h) of drum 3 (since the period of the third drum stands in a 2:1 ratio with the others, its figures are only half as long), we may obtain the combination in given in ex. 123.

Ex. 123

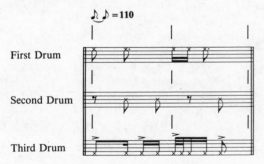

Aka polyrhythmic constructions offer more limited choice. In *yómbè* music, only one (*ngúé*) of the four parts has two possible realisations:

Ex. 124

This formula therefore has the smallest possible degree of variability.

Ngbɔlù, with three possible ngúé realisations (ex. 125), is only slightly richer. The other two figures (è.ndòmbà and dì.kpàkpà) are invariable:

Ex. 125

Mò.nzòlì contains four figures, three of which (è.ndòmbà, dì.kpàkpà, and dì.kɛtɔ) are fixed. We have recorded five realisations of the ngúé part (ex. 126).

Ex. 126

We have also observed three realisations for the è.ndòmbà figure (which is common to mò.nzòlì and mò.mbénzélé), but *only one is used in the course of a single performance.* The ngúé part stands in a 2:1 ratio to dì.kétɔ, a 1:4 ratio to dì.kpàkpà, and a 1:1 ratio to è.ndòmbà. To obtain one of the admissible polyrhythmic combinations for mò.nzòlì (ex. 127), we must therefore superpose on dì.kétɔ two ngúé realisations (here ex. 126 (a) and (d)), two repetitions of the è.ndòmbà figure, and eight of the dì.kpàkpà figure:

Ex. 127

The *ngúé* part in *mò.mbénzélé* (ex. 128) has the largest observed number of realisations (six):

Ex. 128

Its period stands in a 1:1 ratio to *dì.kétò*; we thus need only superpose two successive instances of one of the three possible *è.ndòmbà* figures, and again, eight repetitions of the *dì.kpàkpà* cell.

3.3.5   Formal recognition: how polyrhythmic combinations are identified

Polyrhythmic music is perceived as a whole. The listener hears an aggregate of sound consisting of a specific combination of tone colours, with individual marks, or groups of marks, standing out at various positions. Each tradition in Central Africa has its own finite set of such combinations, one for each category of music with its own social, or social and religious function within the community.

The fact that these combinations can be perceptually distinguished raises the problem of how complex sound forms can be recognised. To illustrate this point, we will turn again to the polyrhythmic heritage of the Aka pygmies. Our corpus contains seven formulae, which we have already analysed individually. One question has a particular relevance in a case such as this, where all the combinations have certain features in common:

(1)   the subdivision of the pulsation is always ternary
(2)   six of the seven formulae have the same length
(3)   certain figures recur within these six:
    the *dì.kétò* figure is common to all six
    an identical *dì.kpàkpà* figure is found in four (*ngbòlù*, *mò.nzòlì*, *mò.mbénzélé*, and *yómbè*)
    an *è.ndòmbà* figure is common to two (*mò.nzòlì* and *mò.mbénzélé*)
    the *mò.kóngò* figure in *zòbòkò* can also be found in *mò.kóndí*, where it is played on the side of the drum.

How can a listener, within or outside the Aka community, distinguish among these combinations when so many identical figures are seen to recur?

The ability to discriminate is founded on two criteria, the *accentuation* and the *diversity of tone colour*, which operate concurrently. With respect to accentuation, the 'mother' drum (*ngúé*) figure is different in each formula. Even if *è.ndòmbà* plays an identical figure in two differnt formulae, the resulting rhythmic combination will be *different* in each one by virtue of the accentuation of the two drum parts. To this we may add the effect of the difference in tone colours. While the accents of *è.ndòmbà* and *ngúé* can easily be confused, the ones produced on the sides of the drum are clearly distinguishable by their nonreverberant colour. The clear, sharp sounds of *dì.kétò* are even more distinct. Each formula thus has, on the one hand, different ways of merging tone colours (e.g., by having drum accents coincide with those of *dì.kpàkpà* and/or *dì.kétò*), and on the other, different instances where the characteristic tone colour of each part stands out alone.

Formulae may thus be distinguished on the basis of the perception of either how the different tone colours are *superposed* in certain positions, or how they are *juxtaposed* within the cycle. These two ways of looking at the matter are simply two aspects of a single object, something like the positive and the negative of a single photographic image.

We will now test the validity of these affirmations. Two of the seven formulae in Aka polyrhythmic music (*bòndó* and *zòbòkò*) are easily disposed of: *bòndó* is radically different in being much shorter than the others and having a specific *dì.kétò* figure. The periodicity of *zòbòkò* is the same as that of the other formulae, but is easily distinguished by the absence of a drum part and the presence of the quite characteristic tone colour of *mò.kóngò*, the tree trunk struck with sticks, which is used only for this formula. The superposition of *dì.kétɔ* and *mò.kóngò* produces a very distinctive sound combination with respect to the rest of the corpus. We must now compare the other five combinations from the standpoint of both the *superposition* and the *juxtaposition* of their diverse tone colours.

We first present a synoptic representation of the rhythmic content of each formula (ex. 129).

Ex. 129

The following five synoptic diagrams display, for each formula, the successive parts (*dì.kpàkpà*, *ngúé*, *è.ndòmbà*, *dì.kétɔ*) plotted against a grid of 24 pulses (numbered 1–24, grouped in threes). Tone colours are marked with the symbols: ● (*è.ndòmbà*), I (*dì.kpàkpà*), ▲ (*ngúé*), * (*dì.kétɔ*).

ngbɔlù

part	1	2	3	4	5	6	7	8	9	10	11	12	13	14	15	16	17	18	19	20	21	22	23	24
dì.kpàkpà		I			I			I			I			I			I			I			I	
ngúé	▲		▲		▲				▲		▲		▲		▲		▲					▲		▲
dì.kétɔ	*		*		*			*	*		*		*		*		*		*	*		*		*

mò.kóndí

part	1	2	3	4	5	6	7	8	9	10	11	12	13	14	15	16	17	18	19	20	21	22	23	24
è.ndòmbà	●				●		●	●		●	●			●			●		●	●		●	●	
dì.kpàkpà	I		I			I		I			I			I			I		I			I		
ngúé	▲				▲	▲				▲	▲	▲		▲			▲	▲			▲	▲	▲	
dì.kétɔ	*		*	*		*		*		*		*		*		*	*		*		*		*	

yómbè

part	1	2	3	4	5	6	7	8	9	10	11	12	13	14	15	16	17	18	19	20	21	22	23	24
è.ndòmbà		●			●			●			●			●			●			●			●	
dì.kpàkpà			I			I			I			I			I			I			I			I
ngúé		▲		▲	▲	▲	▲		▲			▲			▲	▲	▲	▲			▲			
dì.kétɔ	*		*		*		*	*		*		*		*		*		*		*		*	*	

mò.nzòlì

part	1	2	3	4	5	6	7	8	9	10	11	12	13	14	15	16	17	18	19	20	21	22	23	24
è.ndòmbà	●	●			●	●		●		●			●	●			●	●			●	●		
dì.kpàkpà			I			I			I			I			I			I			I			I
ngúé	▲			▲		▲			▲		▲			▲		▲			▲			▲		
dì.kétɔ	*	*		*		*		*			*	*		*		*		*		*		*		

mò.mbénzélé

part	1	2	3	4	5	6	7	8	9	10	11	12	13	14	15	16	17	18	19	20	21	22	23	24
è.ndòmbà	●	●					●	●		●	●		●	●		●	●			●	●			
dì.kpàkpà					I				I			I			I			I			I			I
ngúé	▲	▲	▲	▲	▲	▲		▲			▲			▲			▲			▲			▲	
dì.kétɔ	*		*		*		*		*		*		*	*		*		*		*		*		*

The synoptic table in ex. 130 shows each formula in the form of two superposed diagrams. The upper one represents its characteristic *combinations of tone colours*, and the lower one, its particular way of *juxtaposing individual tone colours*. A letter designating the instrument responsible for the tone colour is placed at the positions where the marks appear (see key). This table shows clearly that tone colours are both *superposed* and *juxtaposed* in ways that differ considerably from formula to formula.

Ex. 130

ngbòlù

Upper row:
1		3		5	6	7	8	9	10	11	12	13	14	15	16	17	18	19		21		23	24
H I		S H I		H I				S H			S I			S H			S I			S H I		H I	

Lower row:
| S I I | | I H | | H I | | I H | | I | | | | | | | | | | | | | S |

mò.kóndí

1		3	4	5	6	7	8	9	10	11	12	13	14		16	17	18	19	20	21	22	23
S H I		S I		H I		S H I		S H I			H I			S I			S H H I	S H I		H H I		S H I

Lower row:
| H | | H | | H | | S I H | | | | | | | | H | | H | | | | I |

yómbè

1	2	3		5	6	7	8	9	10	11	12		14	15	16	17	18	19	20	21	22	23	24
		S H I		S H H I			S I		S I				H I			S H I		H I			H I

Lower row:
| I H | | | | | | | H | | I H | | | | S I H | | H | | S I | | S |

mò.nzòlì

1	2	3	4	5	6	7	8	9	10	11	12	13	14	15		17	18	19		21	22	23	24
H I	H I				S H I			S H I		S I		H I		S I		S H H I	S H I		H I			

Lower row:
| S I H | | H I | | | H | | | H | | | | | | | | | | | H | | S |

mò.mbénzélé

1	2	3	4	5	6	7		9	10	11	12	13	14	15	16	17	18		20	21	22		24
H I		S H I		H H I			S H I		S H H H I				S H I			S H H I			S H I	

Lower row:
| H | | H | | I | | H I | | | | I H | | | I | | |

H for the drum *heads*
S for the *sides* of the drum
I for the *iron strips*

It follows that each is characterised by its own sort of organisation, and therefore has an identity all its own.

The polyrhythmic substructure in traditional Central African music may be described as a sort of *braid* whose strands are fixed, both individually and with respect to one another. This 'braid' is what someone who listens to a polyrhythmic combination takes in as a whole. Are we then entitled to separate out its component elements, as we have thus far, when their real existence can only be simultaneous?

We believe these strands had to be unravelled, before we could understand how such musical constructions are put together, and what kind of rules govern the arrangement of their texture. To this the present chapter has been addressed.

4 Polyrhythmics as a way to polyphony: Hocket

Definition

Polyphony by way of polyrhythmics, or hocket, is created by the interweaving, over-lapping, and interlocking of several rhythmic figures *located on different pitch levels* in a specific scalar system.

General characteristics

In Subsaharan Africa, the hocket technique is utilised by ensembles of wind instruments. All the instruments in the ensemble are invariably of the same type (horns or whistles), but of different size. Their pitches are assigned according to a predetermined scale. The number of instruments in the ensemble may vary from five to twenty. Each emits a single pitch chosen from among the degrees of the scale. The factor of melody thus only comes into play *at the level of the whole ensemble*, as each individual instrument is confined to performing a *rhythmic* figure, which is *inseparable from a predetermined pitch level*.

Each musician is assigned his own rhythmic figure for each of the pieces in the repertory of the ensemble. In some cases, this figure allows variations. The fact that these figures are meshed and *tiered at different fixed pitches within a predetermined scale* results in a very strict type of hocket which stands *precisely at the boundary between strict polyrhythmics and polyphony*. This is an extremely widespread technique in Africa, which can be found in the west (Cameroon), centre (Congo, Zaïre, Central African Republic), east/northeast (Kenya, Uganda, Ethiopia), and south (South Africa).

In the Central African Republic, only the Dakpa and Linda peoples, who belong to the wider Banda ethnic group, seem to use this kind of hocket. Specific repertories employing it are provided for horn ensembles in both communities. While the principle governing this particular kind of multipart music is the same in each case, both the repertories and the morphology of the instruments differ noticeably, as the communities perpetuate, in this as in other ways, their own particular ancestral tradition.

We will here be discussing the Banda-Linda ensembles alone. This group is comprised of some 27,000 people who inhabit a savannah region in the heart of the Central African Republic. The Linda horn ensembles include ten to eighteen such instruments (*āngɔ̄*), and a pair of pellet bells (*ɔ́ngbí*).

Predominantly melodic music intended for exclusively instrumental performance (i.e., which is not used to support a vocal performance or in which no singing takes place) is rare in the Central African Republic, as in the whole of Central Africa. The Banda-Linda horn ensembles nevertheless fall into this category. We will see below, however, that the music they perform, while exclusively instrumental, is linked in close and subtle ways to traditional Banda-Linda vocal music. *Measured* vocal and/or instrumental music which does not include supporting or accompanying dances among its functions is rarer still. But this is precisely the case with this repertory, whose only purpose is to provide pleasure for its performers and audience.

This chapter will be based on the careful study of one Banda-Linda horn ensemble (the local ensemble in the small town of Ippy), and an exhaustive analysis of its repertory, which is comprised of twelve pieces. Our purposes here are:

> (1)   to reveal the underlying coherence governing the organisation of ensembles using the hocket technique, i.e., to show *the musical significance of the instrumental distribution*
>
> (2)   to describe the constraints imposed on the musical material by the organological nature of the instruments
>
> (3)   to determine the musical principles governing the use of the technique, viz.,
> - the formal structure of the pieces,
> - the functioning of the individual parts: their figures, reference points, and variations,
> - how the parts mesh together,
> - the characteristic polyrhythmic combination for each piece,
> - the relationship between pieces and their models,
> - the construction of models for the entire repertory,
> - to clarify the relationship between this particular type of polyphony and the vocal music it derives from,
> - and finally, to throw light on various aspects of the relationship between code and message, *as the bearers of the tradition themselves perceive and materialise it.*

4.2   THE ORGANISATION OF BANDA-LINDA HORN ORCHESTRAS

The principles of the musical organisation of Linda horn orchestras are closely dependent on the organological nature of the instruments. Instrumental constraints have a direct effect on how this hocket music is elaborated. Moreover, when one looks carefully at how these orchestras are organised, one sees that the musical data are intrinsically linked to another set of extramusical data of a symbolic nature. This means that we can check our analysis of the musical principles governing the repertory of the horn orchestras by comparing related cultural data with the strictly musical data. We will find that these convergent criteria from different facets are all required to establish the coherence of the system. That is why it will be inadvisable to separate these aspects in the following discussion.

The Linda horn ensembles are closely linked with the male adolescent initiation rites. The youths are thus taught to play the instruments, and learn the repertory, during their initiatory retreat.

The orchestras include from ten to eighteen horns of different sizes, varying in length from 30 to 170 centimetres. The material these instruments are made from, the way they are manufactured and played, and their musical potentialities are all interdependent. The six horns with the highest pitch are made from the horns of various species of antelope. They are side-blown *transverse* horns. They also have a pitch-modifying hole (*ōgōrō āngɔ̄* lit. 'hole of horn') formed by cutting off the tip of the horn. The next ten instruments in decreasing order of pitch are made by hollowing out roots of the ōpō tree, which are naturally funnel-shaped. Their mouthhole is at the tip, but is chamfered so that the same playing position as for the transverse horns will be required. The peculiar 'oblique' design of this type of instrument satisfies both acoustic and visual requirements. The row of musicians can thus not only hear one another better, but also watch one another. The latter will be seen (see 4.3.2.2) to affect the way variations are realised. Finally, the instruments with the lowest pitch are hollowed out of papaw-tree trunks. Their mouthhole is located at the tip, and they are therefore *end-blown*.

The repertory for *āngɔ̄* ensembles includes from ten to fifteen pieces, *each of which corresponds to one of the community's traditional songs*. The Banda-Linda people use an anhemitonic pentatonic scale. This is evident from the pitches of their xylophone keys. But *precisely these keys are used to provide reference pitches for the manufacture of the horns*. The latter must therefore have the same scalar system. Whatever the tolerances the musicians may be ready to allow in performance, this reference to the xylophone scale shows that the music for the Banda-Linda horn orchestras must be based on a pentatonic system.

The playing technique has one essential feature: as a general rule, *each instrument will emit no more than one sound*. Nevertheless, the pitch-modifying hole on the six highest-pitched horns enables them to produce another note, which should be the next higher conjunct degree on the pentatonic scale. This 'embellishing note', whose interval with respect to the base sound may fluctuate, is used only for embroideries, appoggiature, and trills. The musical material in the pieces in the repertory is distributed in such a way that each horn is assigned a rhythmic figure tiered on a given pitch, with an extremely strict periodicity. Each musician thus has his own figure and a set of variations for each piece.

The horns are designed to produce intervals of a minor third, two major seconds, and a minor third *in descending order*. The Linda orchestra converts this arrangement into the degrees G–E–D–C–A. This pentatonic system is duplicated as many times as the available instruments allow. The pieces in the repertory are organised in accordance with this order, with the instruments coming in one after another from the highest- to the lowest-pitched. This is why the musicians stand in a curved row, in the same descending order, with the highest-pitched horn, which plays the first phrase, on the far right, and the lowest-pitched, on the far left. The pellet bell musician stands at the middle of the curve, and a bit behind it. The 'master of the horns' (*ɔ̀ndè*) stands opposite the musicians, facing them. He is the man who has learned all the parts in all the pieces, and then taught them one by one to the musicians. In some ways, he acts as a conductor, by giving a hand signal to begin, telling each of the musicians when to come in, and telling them when to end the piece. At the same time, he supervises the way the performance is going, and joins in himself if he thinks it necessary. For example, when a performer is not sure of his rhythm, the *ǝndè* comes over to him and mimics the way he should be playing. If the result does not satisfy him, he will take the instrument away and give the less skilled player a demonstration. He will then give back the horn, wait a moment to see that he has been understood, and finally return to his place.

The instruments come in one after another in descending order. Each musician, with the obvious exception of the first horn, will thus initiate his own part with reference to the part played by the immediately preceding one (whose note is located on the next higher conjunct degree of the pentatonic scale). Each musician needs quick reflexes and great rhythmic precision to handle both the subtle and complex polyrhythmics resulting from the interlocked figures and the invariably fast tempo of the pieces (in one, $\flat = 192$). The slightest miscalculation of the point of entry by any player would be likely to throw off all those who come in later. That is why the second horn will not come in until the first horn's figure is perfectly well established, and the third will wait until the combined rhythmic effect of the first two instruments has become entirely stable before he begins. The time interval between one entry and the next diminishes thereafter, as the remaining horns, and the pellet bells (which mark the pulsation) come in.

The pieces for horn orchestras do not last long in comparison with other types of music found in this area. They generally take about three to six minutes. Four successive stages can be distinguished in the performance: (1) A responsive introductory formula consisting of a few notes played initially by the first horn, and punctuated twice by a sort of cluster of long held notes from the remaining instruments. (2) This is immediately followed by the entries of all the instruments, one after another, in an *invariable* descending order from the highest- to the lowest-pitched. The piece actually begins and establishes itself during this stage. (3) The third stage is the most important one. As soon as the lowest-pitched horn has come in, the ensemble gets down to work and starts producing variations in every part. The musicians with the antelope-horn instruments perform embroideries, embellishing notes, and trills, while held notes predominate in the lowest register. The musicians with the oblique instruments turn from side to side to start up musical dialogues with their closest neighbours, as they break in on, reply to, and pretend to parody one another. This part will last as long as the *ǝndè* likes. (4) To end the piece, the *ǝndè* signals the first horn to start the coda formula, which is exactly the same as the introductory one, or simply cuts the piece off with a motion of his hand.

The introductions and codas are identical not just for each piece, but for all the pieces in the repertory. They therefore have no distinctive function at the level of the individual piece. No listener can identify the piece the orchestra is playing until the instruments begin to superpose their individual rhythmic figures so as to engender the characteristic combination for a given piece. That is why introductions and codas are in fact optional, and one, the other, or even both are often omitted in actual performances.

Each piece has the same name as a particular song. When the orchestra play their *exclusively instrumental* music, Linda people immediately recognise the song at its source. The scalar material is thus the same for the entire repertory, but each piece in it makes use of different melodic material.

All instruments separated by octave intervals are assigned the same rhythmic figure in a given piece. This means that the musical structure of each piece is based on a set of only five conjunct instruments arranged in the already mentioned descending G–E–D–C–A order. All other instruments reproduce this original set. This shows that the Linda people are fully aware of this musical organization. This is furthermore clear from the names given to each horn: *all the instruments separated by octave intervals bear the same name*. Whatever their register, the instruments playing G are called *tété*; the ones playing E, *tā*; the ones playing D, *hā*; the ones playing C, *tútûlé*; and the ones playing A, *bòngó*.

Furthermore, each pentatonic system of five instruments in a given register, starting from the highest-pitched horn, constitutes a 'family' with a special name. The first group of five on the highest register is thus called *tūwúlē* or *tūtūwúlē*; the second, *ngbānjā*; the third, *āgā*, and the fourth, *yāvīrī*.

Tūwúlē is an onomatopoetic term for the embroidered figures played by the antelope-horn instruments using their embellishing note, as in ex. 1.

Ex. 1

tù-wu-lē

Ngbānjā designates a kind of file or rasp, for as the Linda people say, 'The rasp makes a loud noise'. When someone speaks in a loud voice, they say, 'He has a voice like a *ngbānjā*'. This register is the easiest to play in.

Āgā designates a kind of fish. The master of the horns says no one remembers any longer why this register is so called ('All the elders who knew are now dead').

Finally, *yāvīrī* is the word for 'heavy rain, storm, thunder'. The table in ex. 2 summarises the structure of an eighteen-horn orchestra.

Ex. 2

		Name of instruments and their notes				
		tété	tā	hā	tútûlé	bòngó
"Family"	Register	G	E	D	C	A
tūwúlē	𝄞	H. 1	H. 2	H. 3	H. 4	H. 5
ngbānjā	𝄞	H. 6	H. 7	H. 8	H. 9	H. 10
āgā	𝄢	H. 11	H. 12	H. 13	H. 14	H. 15
yāvīrī	𝄢	H. 16	H. 17	H. 18	/	/

The columns are the degrees of the pentatonic scale; the rows show the octaves defining 'families' of instruments with the same names. H = horn.

We can now see why the Linda horn ensembles do not contain a fixed number of instruments. The structure of each piece is entirely determined by the parts assigned to the initial group of five horns (*tūwúlē*) located at specific intervals on the pentatonic scale, as described above. As soon as the first horn in the second group comes in, the original system is duplicated without affecting the structure of the piece. That is why many orchestras will make do with ten instruments covering a range of two octaves. This includes the two highest-pitched 'families', *tūwúlē* and *ngbānjā*. Obviously, the more instruments there are, the larger the range will be; variations will likewise become more plentiful, and the lattice of the musical construction will be more closely knit. The multiplication of the number of octaves is nevertheless not indispensable from the standpoint of the self-sufficiency of the musical system employed, and the Linda musicians are quite aware of this.

The material, musical, and symbolic aspects of the organisation of Linda horn ensembles reveal an underlying coherence when distinctive features *from several different facets* are jointly considered.

> (1)   Octaves are distinctively identified, as instruments separated by this interval bear the same name.
>
> (2)   The way musical material is arranged within each piece is distinctively identified, as the instruments separated by an octave interval perform the same figures.
>
> (3)   The scalar system is distinctively identified, as the instruments on each degree have a different name.
>
> (4)   Finally, the relationships between organology and symbolic notions (represented by instrument names), and between the arrangement of the instruments and the organisation of the musical material itself are also distinctively identified.

These features provide mutual confirmation insofar as they all point to the same conclusions. We may thus assume that two instruments are 'missing' from an eighteen-horn orchestra to make up four complete octaves. According to the Linda musicians, the ideal orchestra would indeed be composed of four complete 'families'. They say, however, that it is hard to find tree trunks long enough to make horns capable of producing the two lowest sounds. When trees of adequate size cannot be found, they will make do with an orchestra of no more than sixteen, or even ten horns. The number of horns is no longer relevant, once the required minimum has been reached. A five-horn ensemble would already be sufficient to reproduce the intrinsic content of the musical material for each piece.

The highest-pitched instruments can never be done away with. The 'missing' instruments must be the lowest in pitch, *never intermediate.* We may recall that every piece in this repertory is played with the instruments coming in one after another, starting from the highest-pitched. Each musician refers his own part to the one played by the immediately preceding instrument. *If any link were missing, this chain would be broken.* We thus have another distinctive feature which is relevant to both orchestral organisation and the constraints imposed by the music itself. There may be any number of horns greater than five, but they must stand in an uninterrupted succession starting from the one with the highest pitch.

We see that several features are required to describe such orchestras, and that they are mutually corroborative. Distinctiveness operates in many aspects, e.g., from a *functional* standpoint, the horns are only played in public at the conclusion of male initiation rites; consequently, if we find an orchestra in the village, we know these rites have recently come to an end. We have seen that the makeup of the orchestra, its *infrastructure*, is also marked by convergent distinctive features. *The symbolic names can be paired with the functions of the horns within the musical structure, since all the instruments separated by an octave have the same name and the same rhythmic figure. Furthermore, any 'family' of five instruments located within the framework of a single octave is theoretically sufficient to reproduce the musical system governing the full orchestra.* It is thus possible to infer *the name and function* of a horn from the figure it plays; and conversely, given the name of a horn, we can determine what figure it will perform in any given piece in the repertory.

4.3   THE STRUCTURE OF THE MUSIC FOR BANDA-LINDA HORN ORCHESTRAS

We will examine two points in this part: firstly, the musical technique of instrumental hocket, and secondly, how it relates to its sources in vocal music.

Firstly, we will try to describe how the individual parts work, how they mesh with one another, and what polyphonic combinations characterise each piece. We will see that a given piece may exist in many versions which are never entirely identical because of all the possible variations, but that beyond these individual performances there is a highly simplified structural entity, or *model*, which may be said to underlie them.

Secondly, we will look at the vocal background to the repertory. We hope to reply to what we believe is a fundamental question in this social and cultural context viz., how could such elaborate and complex instrumental music be developed, or *composed* in the narrow sense, i.e., put together, combined, realised, in a society whose music is essentially vocal, and monodic or homophonous at that. We will see that ultimately, when we look beyond the polyphonic technique, the monodic and/or homophonous principle does seem to prevail among those members of the community who use and perform this music.

4.3.1   Instrumental hocket

The repertory of the Ippy horn orchestra, which we are about to analyse, is comprised of twelve piece. They are all alike in their strict periodicity: in each one, the musical material is spread over a cycle of unchanging length. Pellet bells are struck together to materialise its pulsation. The cycle is always short, lasting hardly a few seconds. The entire 'message', i.e., the piece's basic musical material, is present in each recurrence of the cycle. The piece consists of the uninterrupted repetition of *diverse realisations* of the rhythmic figures assigned to each instrument. In other words, the figures are performed in a large number of variations. Each horn is assigned a figure which fits the periodic framework and can be materialised in several ways. All these variations derive from a single simplified motif which provides each musician with the ultimate reference, or *model*, for his part.

Individual variations are of major importance here because the motifs are so short, and could quickly become boring for both performers and listeners. That is why the musicians themselves say that pieces which do not easily lend themselves to variation are not included in the repertory.

The figures become *discrete units* by being repeated with regular periodicity. Their structure is not, however, such as to allow them to be segmented in any relevant way. Each figure is indivisible, and therefore equivalent to a *cell*. When one examines the different realisations of a given part, one realises that they are all variants of a single model.

There are furthermore no constraints on how realisations of a given figure are to be concatenated. The variations derived from a given model thus follow each other in an indeterminate order. This means that the pieces in the repertory have *only one level of syntactic articulation*, the level of their period. The analytical method we will apply to them may therefore be based on the principle of the *recurrence* of figures within this periodic framework, and by way of consequence, on the principle of the *commutability* of their contents. We will thereby be able to divide up the contents of each part as we observe it on the *horizontal, or syntagmatic axis*, as in ex. 3, and assemble the resulting units into *equivalence classes on the vertical, or paradigmatic axis*, as in ex. 4.

Ex. 3

The same method of analysis can be applied to the examination of the combinations engendered by the superposition of the various constituent cells in each piece. We will therefore make extensive use of paradigmatic analysis throughout this section. We will find it useful: (1) for identifying the models underlying the pieces, (2) for showing how the model and its realisations are related, and (3) for shedding light on the relationship bewteen *vocal* music and *instrumental* hocket.

Ex. 4

4.3.1.1 *From the realisations to the instrumental model*

We will now set out the principles governing the type of instrumental hocket we have in view: we will show, on the one hand, how the individual parts operate, how they mesh, and what polyrhythmic combinations they produce; and on the other, how the realisations of a given piece are related to their underlying model.

Ex. 5

Ex. 5 (cont.)

Ex. 5 (cont.)

Ex. 5 (cont.)

Ex. 5 (cont.)

Ex. 5 (cont.)

Ex. 5 (cont.)

Ex. 5 (cont.)

To this end, we will first submit the initial piece in the repertory, *Ndòròjé bāléndōrɔ*, to careful analysis by a sort of 'X ray'. We will take a realisation of this piece and note the following points:

(1)   the contents of each instrumental part
(2)   the set of all the variations in each one
(3)   the combinations of the parts taken in pairs (the first horn with the second, the second with the third, and so forth); this will allow us to account for the characteristic 'mosaic' effect produced by each combination. We will find, for example, that the configuration produced by combining the second and third horns differs considerably from the one obtained by interlocking the second and the first, despite the fact that one part is held constant.
(4)   the 'cumulative' combinations, i.e., those obtained by combining the first three horns, then adding the fourth, and finally the fifth to complete the pentatonic system
(5)   the ways of establishing a model for the piece
(6)   the immanence of the instrumental model in any realisation.

We will then submit another piece to a similar analysis. This will be *Āméyā*, which is second in the order of presentation. Our purpose will be to show that the individuality of each piece in the repertory does not conflict with the fact that their structural features and operational rules are identical in every way.

It will be sufficient for our purposes to present only the *model* forms for the remaining ten pieces. Section 4.3.2 of this chapter, dealing with the relationship between the hocket technique and its vocal source music, will describe in detail how realisations are obtained from these models.

Now let us return to *Ndòròjé bāléndōrɔ*. The orchestra which recorded our version contained eighteen instruments. In ex. 5 (p. 316), the reader will find the beginning of the *score* for this piece, as an illustration of how it is constructed, and particularly, of how the instruments come in one after another in descending order.

In exx. 6 to 23, the parts for each horn, from the highest- to the lowest-pitched, are shown separately in paradigmatic form. The members of each paradigm are preceded by a number indicating their order of occurrence in the score.

A second set of paradigms showing the inventory of the variations in this version is presented in exx. 24 to 41.

They will enable us to see that:

(1)   in each part, the musical material is organised into identical periods
(2)   each part can be analysed into units which are in fact a variety of realisations of a single rhythmic cell. They are, in the felicitous terminology of Jean-Jacques Nattiez (1975: 264), 'paradigmatic themes', i.e., 'a set of criteria which provide the basis for associating units on a given axis of equivalence'
(3)   the embellishing note which the first six horns are capable of producing is never directly attacked, i.e., it is always preceded by the basic note
(4)   finally, the figures the horns perform *have no accents whatsoever*.

Ex. 6 Horn 1: tété

Ex. 7 Horn 2: tā

Ex. 8 Horn 3: hā

Ex. 9 Horn 4: tútûlé

Ex. 10 Horn 5: bòngó

Ex. 11 Horn 6: tété

Ex. 12 Horn 7: tā

Ex. 13 Horn 8: hā

Ex. 14 Horn 9: tútûlé

Ex. 15 Horn 10: bɔ̀ngɔ́

Ex. 16 Horn 11: tété

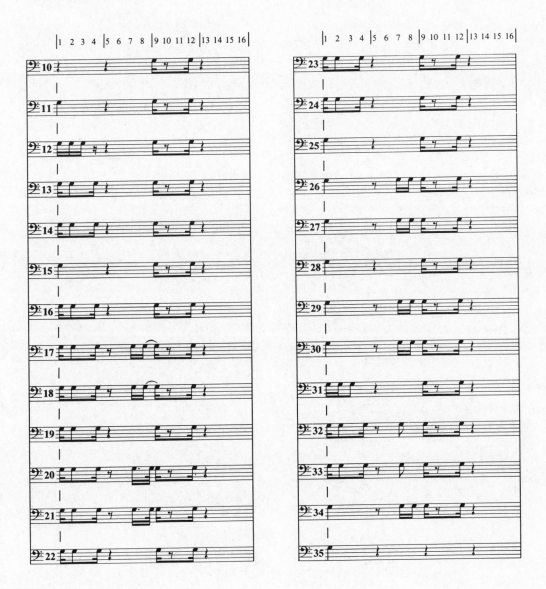

Ex. 17 Horn 12: tā

Ex. 18 Horn 13: hā

The lowest-pitched instruments are harder to play than the others because of their large mouthhole. That is why some values tend to be merged into long held notes. This is particularly visible in the fourteenth, seventeenth, and eighteenth horn parts.

Ex. 19 Horn 14: tútûlé

Ex. 20 Horn 15: bɔ̀ngɔ́

Ex. 21 Horn 16: tété

Ex. 22 Horn 17: tā

Ex. 23 Horn 18: hā

The extent of variation in each part, as listed in exx. 24 to 41, depends primarily on the creativity of the individual musician. Each one has his own personal stock of whatever size, on which he draws at will.

Note: The number which precedes each combination indicates its *first occurrence* in the score.

Ex. 24 Horn 1: tété

Ex. 25 Horn 2: tā

Ex. 26 Horn 3: hā

Ex. 27 Horn 4: tútûlé

Ex. 29 Horn 6: tété

Ex. 28 Horn 5: bòngó

Ex. 30 Horn 7: tā

Ex. 31 Horn 8: hā

Ex. 32 Horn 9: túlûlé

Ex. 33 Horn 10: bɔ̀ngɔ́

Ex. 35 Horn 12: tā

Ex. 34 Horn 11: tété

Ex. 36 Horn 13: hā

Ex. 37 Horn 14: tútûlé

Ex. 38 Horn 15: bɔ̀ngɔ́

Ex. 40 Horn 17: tā

Ex. 41 Horn 18: hā

Ex. 39 Horn 16: tété

We have already seen that the instruments at octave intervals bear the same name and are assigned the same paradigmatic theme. This means that the figures performed by, for example, all the horns called *tété*, whatever 'family' they happen to belong to, are *assigned the same value* in any given piece. We may therefore assemble all the realisations performed by the four *tété* horns in our orchestra into a single paradigm. Our transcriptions show that each part taken individually has a relatively simple structure. But the complexity of hocket music is directly proportional to the number of superposed parts. If we pair off the instruments in the order in which they come in, i.e.,

horns 1 and 2

2 and 3

3 and 4

4 and 5,

and so forth, we will be able to observe how conjunct parts are interwoven. We will thus obtain an eloquent illustration of how the Linda horn orchestras apply the hocket principle. It is in fact clear from the simplest combinations, involving only two instruments, how individual variations are used to attenuate the monotony which would inevitably result from the unbroken repetition of a cell of extremely brief duration.

When the variations contributed in random order by each instrument are superposed, a considerable number of melodic and rhythmic combinations result. Any variation in one of the parts will suffice to change the melodic and rhythmic formula obtained by combining them. Examples 42 to 58 show how diverse the results of these pairings can be.

Note: The number which precedes each combination indicates its position in the score.

Ex. 42 Horns 1 and 2: tété – tā

Ex. 43 Horns 2 and 3: tā – hā

Ex. 44 Horns 3 and 4: hā – tútûlé

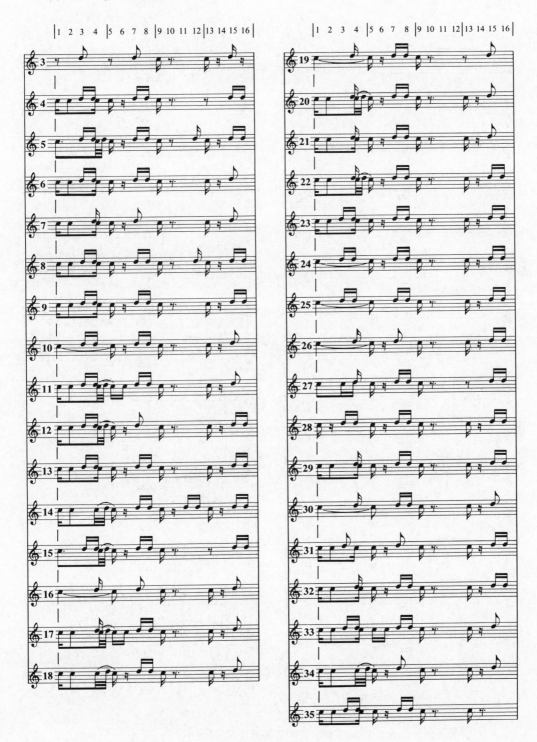

Ex. 45 Horns 4 and 5: tútûlé – bòngó

Ex. 46 Horns 5 and 6: bɔ̀ngɔ́ – tété

Ex. 47 Horns 6 and 7: tété – tā

Ex. 48 Horns 7 and 8: tā – hā

Ex. 49 Horns 8 and 9: hā – tútûlé

Ex. 50 Horns 9 and 10: tútûlé – bòngó

Ex. 51 Horns 10 and 11: bòngó – tété

Ex. 52 Horns 11 and 12: tété – tā

Ex. 53 Horns 12 and 13: tā – hā

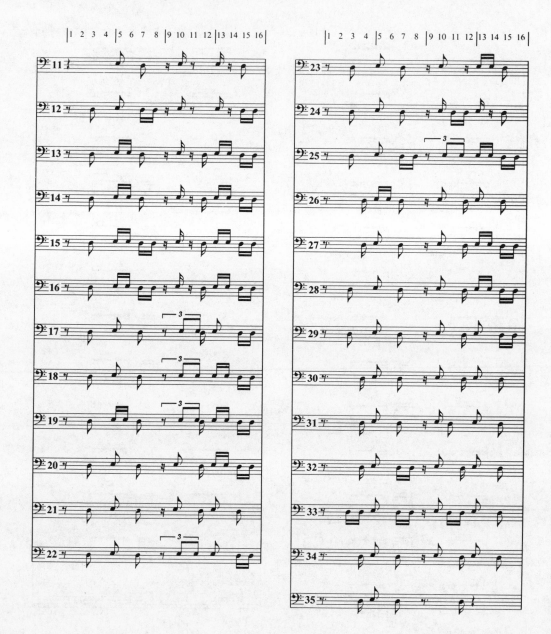

Ex. 54 Horns 13 and 14: hā – tútûlé

Ex. 55 Horns 14 and 15: tútûlé – bòngó

Ex. 56 Horns 15 and 16: bɔ̀ngɔ́ – tété

Ex. 57 Horns 16 and 17: tété – tā

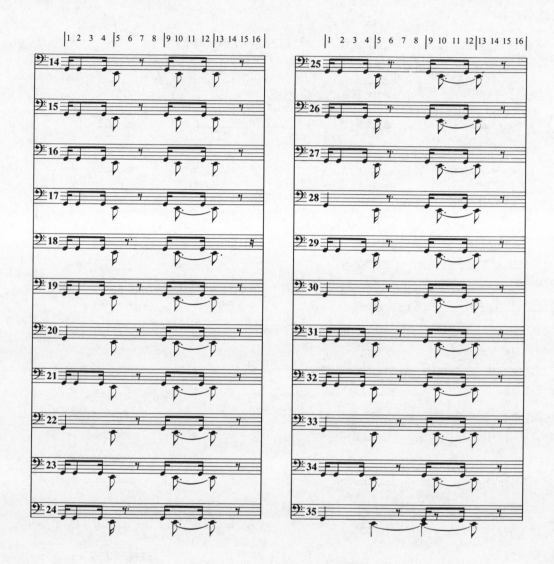

Ex. 58 Horns 17 and 18: tā – hā

The polyrhythmics become more complex as the number of parts increases. The combination obtained by superposing the first three horns is shown in ex. 59. What happens with the first four is shown in ex. 60.

Ex. 59

Note: The number preceding each combination indicates its position in the score.

Ex. 60

The full hocket combination is achieved with the addition of the fifth horn. Each group of five successive instruments (starting with a *tété* horn) is characterised by practically all the features which go to make up the hocket technique:

    (1)   the pitch relationships among the instruments
    (2)   the rhythmic cells assigned to each part
    (3)   their paradigmatic theme
    (4)   the way they are interlocked with one another
    (5)   the resulting melodic and rhythmic combinations (see ex. 61).

Ex. 61

The 'families' differ in only one feature, their *register*, i.e., their compass within the overall range of the orchestra. We therefore see (1) that each pentatonic series is a sort of microcosm of the whole, in that it contains all the constituent properties within the framework of a single octave and (2) that the assignment of the same figures to the instruments separated by an octave means that the 'families' are variants of one another insofar as they have an *equivalent* musical content. We will have further proof of this below when we see how the model shows through the various realisations.

Now that we have seen in detail how the hocket technique is put into practice in one of the pieces in the repertory, we must find an answer to the following question: what do the musicians use as a reference? In other words, what minimal realisations do they start from to produce their variations? What structural pattern, what implicit or explicit *model* furnishes the framework for this complex musical construction resulting from a plethora of variations, gives it cohesion, and individuates it?

If we could extract the models from the individual parts, we would only need to combine them to obtain the composite model representing the meshing of all the piece's component parts. How then can these models be given material form?

It took me some time to achieve this aim. Since all instruments at octave intervals are assigned the same rhythmic figure, I started with an experiment whose purpose was to restrict the production of variations as far as possible. I did this by changing the instruments' order of entry. I asked all the *tété* horn players, i.e., the first in each group, to play their figure *simultaneously*. My hypothesis was that the musicians would react to the artificiality of these conditions, and the lack of the reference provided to each horn (except the highest-pitched one) by the immediately higher part, by cautiously avoiding multiple variations and limiting themselves to the essentials. The minimal formula for the entire piece could then be synthetically reconstituted in five entries instead of eighteen, by combining the recording obtained in this way with similar ones for all the horns playing *tā*, *hā*, *tútûlé*, and finally *bɔ̀ngɔ́* parts. We were thus able to obtain a much more simplified, and of course more 'anaemic' version than a spontaneous performance, where the framework of the piece nevertheless remained discernible. The instruments in each set of the same name did not, however, play exactly the same figure. Minor variants remained, such as the splitting of some values.

The master of the horns was both curious and surprised that I should proceed in this way. It occurred to me to ask him whether the boys learning to play the horns during their initiatory retreat were not taught first to play simpler figures than the ones performed by more experienced musicians. I thus learned that there is a highly simplified figure for each of the five basic horn parts in each piece of the repertory, which is used for purely didactic purposes. This figure is *minimal* in the sense that nothing more may be removed from it without destroying the structure, and thereby the identity of the piece. This bare figure furthermore has a name; it is called *àkɔ́.nɔ̀* which literally means 'the husband, the male'. Now the Banda-Linda use the same term to designate the *ultimate reference* or simplest realisation of *each of the constituent parts of any musical entity*. Any vocal melody, any rhythmic formula played by percussion instruments, any xylophone part will thus have its own *àkɔ́.nɔ̀*. Not only do we have a *model* here, i.e., a fundamental organisational principle to which every realisation of every constituent part in a given piece refers; but moreover, this model is clearly conceptualised by the Linda people themselves. Consequently all I had to do to discover the models for the twelve pieces in the repertory was to ask the musicians in any one of the 'families' to play the *àkɔ́.nɔ̀* for their instruments, piece by piece, under the supervision of the *ɔ̀ndè*, and to repeat it several times with no variation. We asked the *ngbānjā* group to do this, as their instruments are the easiest to play and give the clearest sound.

We had to try several times, for the musicians, had a deeply ingrained habit of introducing variations, and were quite unaccustomed to uniform repetitions of a single rhythmic cell over a certain length of time without the slightest change. Once they got the idea, however, we were able to record all the pieces in the corpus without a hitch.

I now needed to check whether we had obtained the right models in this way. I hypothesised that a composite polyphonic model for each piece must contain all the features required to distinguish it from all the others. Consequently, Linda people, who know their own musical heritage, should be able to identify the versions obtained by our method. We therefore took our recordings to a neighbouring village, played them for a group of about fifteen people, and asked them whether they recognised them. They were immediately identified, although there were some objections to the reduced size of the ensemble and to the flatness caused by the absence of variations.

The model for *Ndɔ̀rɔ̀jé bāléndōrɔ̄* is shown in ex. 62. (The numbers placed above a model indicate the positions of its constituent sounds.) We need only compare ex. 62

Ex. 62

with any realisation of this piece to see clearly that it represents a condensation of all the distinctive features. All the musical features contained in the model are thus present in each realisation beneath the multiplicity of variations.

The compact representation of the model on a single staff, as in ex. 63, provides an illustration of how the *principle of the economical use* of musical elements, is applied:

Ex. 63

(1)   the formula is based on a cycle of four pulsations; the durations of the sounds in this cycle include no more than a crotchet, twelve quavers, and two semiquavers

(2)   no degree on the pentatonic scale has a total duration exceeding the value of a dotted crotchet

(3)   there are only two sorts of 'con-sonance' (i.e., *simultaneity*), both fifths (C–G and A–E, the latter being used twice).

Ex. 64 shows how the model is immanent in each 'family' and remains transparent in all the derived realisations; we have circled the sounds which are part of the model, and separated the different 'families' by horizontal lines.

Ex. 64

Ex. 64 (cont.)

We will now use a similar procedure to analyse another piece, *Āméyā*. Let us remember that our purpose is to show that all the pieces in the repertory have the same structural features, and work in ways which are wholly identical. Let us first turn

Ex. 65

our attention to the beginning of the score in ex. 65. We will see that the instruments come in in exactly the same order as in *Ndɔ̀rɔ̀jé bāléndōrɔ̄*.

Ex. 65 (cont.)

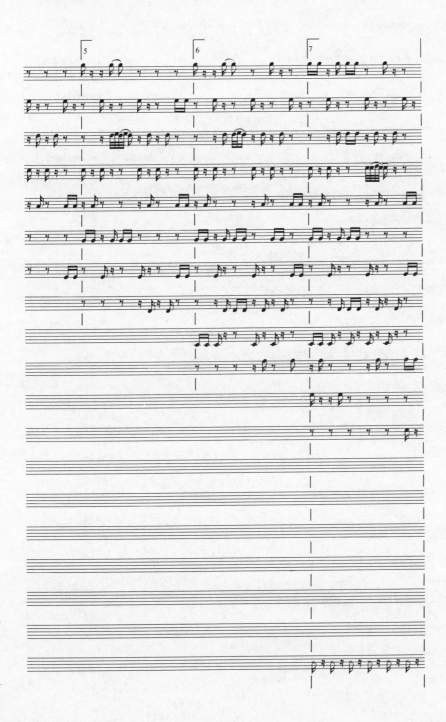

Ex. 65 (cont.)

Ex. 65 (cont.)

Ex. 65 (cont.)

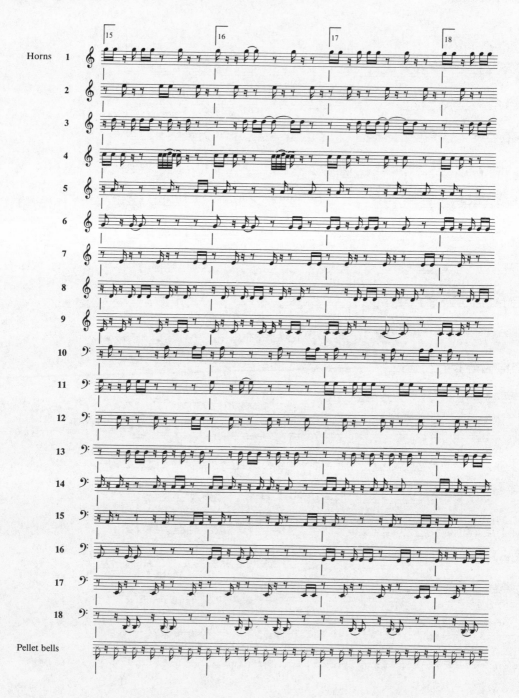

Ex. 65 (cont.)

Ex. 65 (cont.)

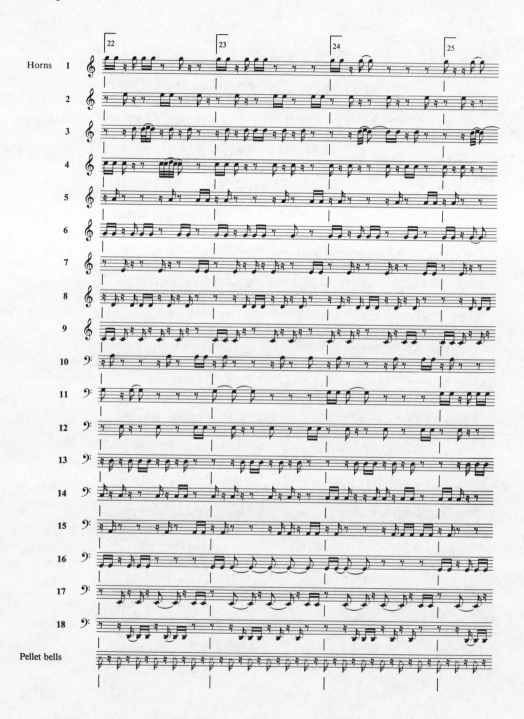

Ex. 65 (cont.)

Ex. 65 (cont.)

The paradigms for each of the horn parts in ex. 65 are shown in exx. 66 to 83.

Ex. 66 Horn 1: tété

Ex. 67 Horn 2: tā

Ex. 68 Horn 3: hā

385

Ex. 69 Horn 4: tútûlé

Ex. 70 Horn 5: bɔ̀ngɔ́

Ex. 71 Horn 6: tété

Ex. 72 Horn 7: tā

Ex. 73 Horn 8: hā

Ex. 74 Horn 9: tútûlé

Ex. 75 Horn 10: bɔ̀ngɔ́

Ex. 76 Horn 11: tété

Ex. 77 Horn 12: tā

Ex. 78 Horn 13: hā

Ex. 79 Horn 14: tútûlé

Ex. 80 Horn 15: bòngó

Ex. 81 Horn 16: tété

Ex. 82 Horn 17: tā

Ex. 83 Horn 18: hā

The parts are constructed in the same way as in the first piece we analysed, with short sounds (except for a few instances in the case of the lower-pitched instruments) separated by intervals of silence. In ex. 84 to 101, we now show the *inventory of variations* for each instrument.

Ex. 84 Horn 1: tété

Ex. 86 Horn 3: hā

Ex. 85 Horn 2: tā

Ex. 88 Horn 5: bòngó

Ex. 87 Horn 4: tútûlé

Ex. 89 Horn 6: tété

Ex. 90 Horn 7: tā

Ex. 92 Horn 9: tútûlé

Ex. 91 Horn 8: hā

Ex. 93 Horn 10: bòngó

Ex. 95 Horn 12: tā

Ex. 94 Horn 11: tété

Ex. 96 Horn 13: hā

Ex. 97 Horn 14: tútûlé   *Ex. 98 Horn 15: bɔ̀ngɔ́*

Ex. 99 Horn 16: tété

Ex. 100 Horn 17: tā

Ex. 101 Horn 18: hā

The combinations obtained by pairing off neighbouring parts by order of entry are shown in exx. 102–118.

Ex. 102 Horns 1 and 2: tété – tā

Ex. 103 Horns 2 and 3: tā – hā

Ex. 104 Horns 3 and 4: hā – tútûlé

Ex. 105 Horns 4 and 5: tútûlé – bòngó

Ex. 106 Horns 5 and 6: bòngó – tété

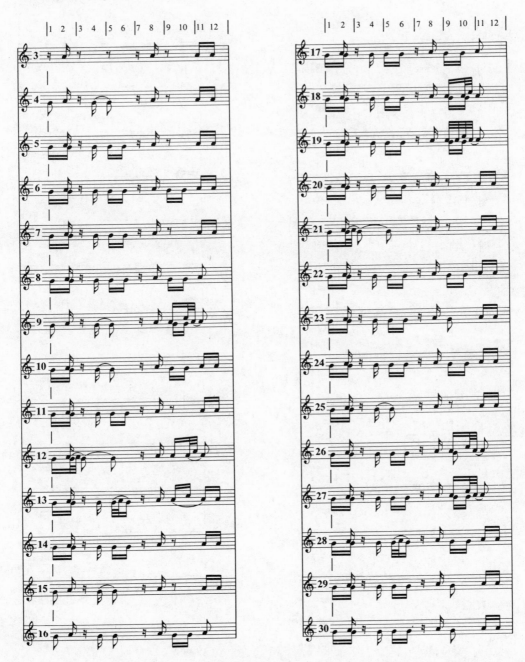

Ex. 107 Horns 6 and 7: tété – tā

Ex. 108 Horns 7 and 8: tā – hā

Ex. 109 Horns 8 and 9: hā – tútûlé

Ex. 110 Horns 9 and 10: tútûlé – bɔ̀ngɔ́

Ex. 111 Horns 10 and 11: bɔ̀ngɔ́ – tété

Ex. 112 Horns 11 and 12: tété – tā

Ex. 113 Horns 12 and 13: tā – hā

Ex. 114 Horns 13 and 14: hā – tútûlé

Ex. 115 Horns 14 and 15: tútûlé – tété

Ex. 116 Horns 15 and 16: tété – tā

Ex. 117 Horns 16 and 17: tā – hā

Ex. 118 Horns 17 and 18: hā – tútûlé

The combinations of the three highest-pitched horns may be represented as in ex. 119.

Ex. 119

A few combinations of the first four horns are shown in ex. 120.

Ex. 120

The addition of the fifth horn completes the hocket structure characteristic of this piece, as shown in ex. 121.

Ex. 121

The parts in *Āméyā* are clearly interwoven and interlocked in the same ways as in *Ndàràjé bāléndōrɔ̄*.

The *àkɔ̄.nɔ̀* for *Āméyā*, i.e., the structural form providing the basis for all realisations, is given in ex. 122.

Ex. 122

When we compress the model onto a single staff, as in ex. 123 we can again see what economical use is made of the musical material:

Ex. 123

(1) the formula relies on a cycle of six pulsations, whose sounds have no durations other than quavers and semiquavers

(2) no degree on the scale has a total duration exceeding five semiquavers

(3) there are only three sorts of con-sonance: a fourth (D–G), a major third (C–E), and a fifth (A–E).

As in the case of the preceding piece, the model is present in every realisation, see ex. 124.

Ex. 124

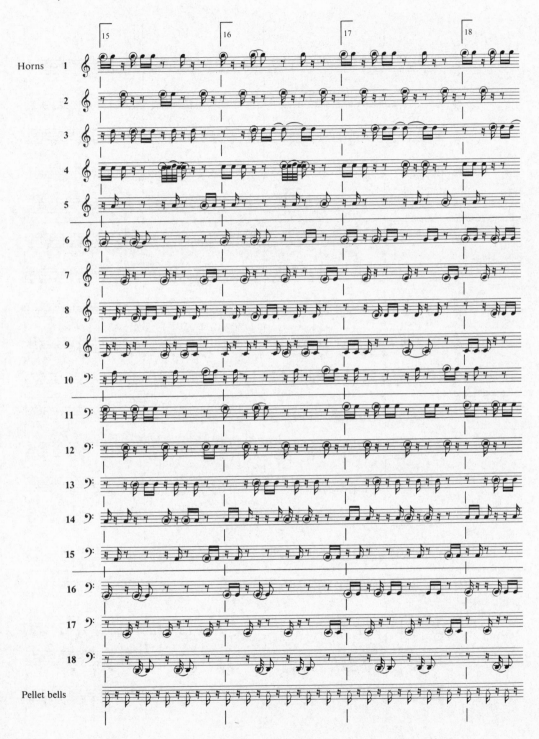

Ex. 124 (cont.)

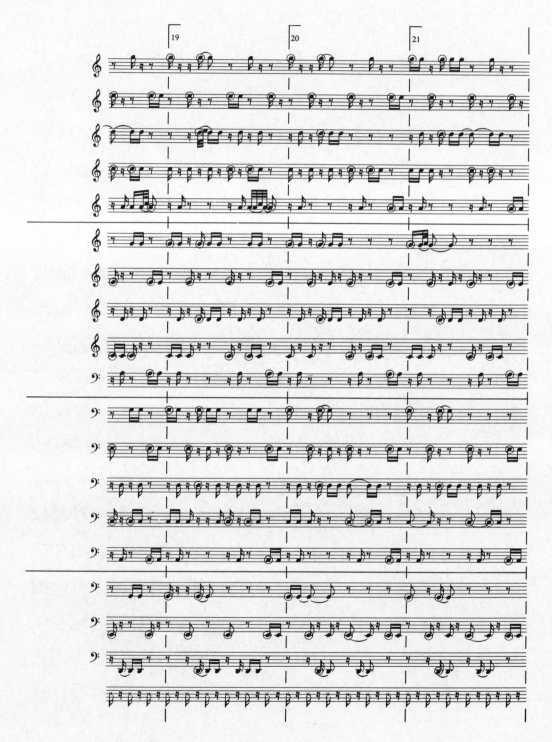

In exx. 125 to 134, we now present the *models* for the ten remaining pieces in the repertory, in order to show that the structural features are indeed identical throughout.

Ex. 125 Piece 3: Kāndā bàlē bɔ̀zɔ́ dùārɔ̀

This piece has a period of four pulsations with a ternary subdivision yielding twelve operational values and as many positions. There are attacks at seven positions in the model, three of which (1, 4, and 7) coincide with the pulsation. The other four are offbeat: there are two attacks on the second semiquaver of a pulsation (positions 2 and 11), and two on the third (positios 6 and 9). This piece is therefore *irregularly contrametric*. The only instances of *con-sonance*, or *simultaneity*, are two intervals of a fifth (C–G at position 1, and A–E at position 9).

Ex. 126 Piece 4: Àmbōrōrō mátɔ́ kūmù kàgà

Piece 4 has a period of four pulsations with a binary subdivision yielding sixteen minimal operational values. There are attacks on constituents of the model at eight positions, four on the pulsation (positions 1, 5, 9, and 13) and four offbeat (positions 7, 10, 12, and 15). The metricity of this piece is therefore *mixed*. The instances of simultaneity are just three intervals of a fifth (C–G at positions 1 and 12, and A–E at position 13).

Ex. 127 Piece 5: Èbɔ́nā kā cémà tò

Piece 5 has a cycle consisting of four ternary pulsations, subdivided into twelve minimal values. From the metric organisation of the phrases of the song from which this piece is derived (and which determines the structure of the model), we can tell that the model begins and ends on the offbeat. It has seven constituents, two coinciding with the pulsation (positions 4 and 12), and five on the offbeat (positions 1, 3, 6, 9, and 14). This piece is therefore characterised by a markedly *irregular contrametricity*. The instances of simultaneity are as follows: a fourth (D–G at position 6), a major second (D–E at position 9), and two fifths (C–G at position 12 and A–E at position 14).

Ex. 128 Piece 6: ?ē jī kīlīngbī nà yīndà tōrō tówò

Piece 6, with a period of six binary pulsations and twenty-four minimal values, is the longest in the repertory. The constituents of its model are nevertheless attacked at no more than eight positions, five of which coincide with pulsations. This piece therefore has a *contrametric* relationship to the pulsation. The con-sonances are two fourths (D–G at positions 1 and 13), two fifths (C–G at position 3, and A–E at position 6), a major second (D–E at position 17), and a major third (C–E at position 21).

Ex. 129 Piece 7: Gànjà kɔ̄ngɔ̄ ngɔ́ tànjē tā ángēmbá

Piece 7 has a period comprised of four ternary pulsations yielding twelve minimal values. There are six constituents in the model: three are on the pulsation and three are offbeat. The metricity is thus *mixed*. From the metric organisation of the phrases of the song for this piece, we can tell that the model begins on the semiquaver preceding the pulsation. The simultaneities are two fifths (C–G at position 1 and A–E at position 11) and a fourth (A–D at position 10).

Ex. 130 Piece 8: Árɔ́ dɔ́ kɔ̄tí yē

Piece 8, with three ternary pulsations and nine minimal values, is the shortest in the repertory. The position of three of the six characteristic sounds in its model coincide with the pulsation; its metricity is thus *mixed*. The con-sonances are two fourths (A–D at positions 1 and 9), a fifth (C–G at position 2), and a minor seventh (A–G at position 4).

Ex. 131 Piece 9: Kùzū wōtɔ̄ kɔ̀ wó yālú.kūmù

This piece has a period of six ternary pulsations, i.e., eighteen minimal values. The constituents of the model are found at eight positions (1, 5, 7, 9, 11, 13, 15, and 17), *all of them uneven*, only three of which coincide with the pulsation. The antagonism between the ternary *metric organisation* and the binary *rhythmic structure* of this piece invest it with a markedly *irregular contrametricity* of a *hemiolic type*. There are simultaneities of two fourths (D–G at position 1, A–D at position 13), two fifths (A–E at positions 9 and 17), and a major third (C–E at position 11).

Ex. 132 Piece 10: Ā gànjà ngbéngā mándá kɔ̄vɔ̀kpá

Ex. 133 Piece 11: ɘ̀njē zá ɘ́ngbí kɔ̄wà mùnjú tɘ̀ àmbɘ̀nɘ̀

The models for pieces 10 and 11 have the following properties in common: a cycle of four ternary pulsations containing twelve minimal values, and six constituents. They differ (1) in their metricity, the former being *contrametric*, while the latter has a *mixed* relationship to the pulsation; (2) in the positions of their constituent sounds, the distribution being:

in piece 10, but

in piece 11; (3) in the occurrences and types of con-sonances: in piece 10 there are two fifths (C–G at position 1, A–E at position 10), a minor seventh (A–G at position 3), and a fourth (A–D at position 8); while in piece 11 we note two fifths, each repeated twice (C–G at positions 1 and 7, and A–E at positions 4 and 9).

Ex. 134 Piece 12: Dángá.yē

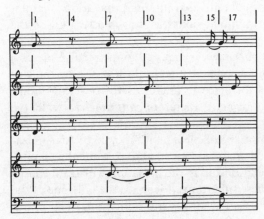

The period in piece 12 has six ternary pulsations, i.e., eighteen minimal values. The constituents of the model are found in seven positions, five of which coincide with pulsations. The piece is thus markedly *commetric*. The simultaneities are two fourths (D–G at position 1, A–D at position 13), two fifths (C–G at position 7, A–E at position 17), a major third (C–E at position 10), and a minor seventh (A–G at position 15).

4.3.1.2 *Formal recognition: how pieces are identified*

Looking at the full set of models for the repertory of a Banda-Linda horn orchestra, one can see that the scale material is strictly identical throughout. We have already mentioned that a single formula is used to introduce and conclude all the pieces, and that the order in which the instruments come in, from the highest- to the lowest-pitched, is invariable. It is also clear that the hocket technique remains unchanged throughout the repertory, with each instrument playing only a single sound. Given all these constant factors, one may rightly wonder what set of criteria, or cluster of features, enables the listener, whether Banda-Linda or foreigner, to distinguish among these pieces.

Four features are involved, some of which are mutually exclusive, while others combine: these are *periodicity*, the *type of subdivision of the pulsation*, the *relationship to the pulsation*, and of course, the *melodic and rhythmic configuration of the material*. To keep our discussion clear, let us deal with these features individually.

The first distinction relates to the *periodicity*, i.e., to the number of pulsations in the characteristic formula for each piece. Four of the twelve pieces in the repertory (2, 6, 9, and 12) thus have a cycle of six pulsations, seven (1, 3, 4, 5, 7, 10, and 11) have four, and a single piece (8) has only three. From this point of view, the pieces can be placed in three categories according to whether they have six, four, or three underlying pulsations. Piece 8, which is the only member of the third of these categories, can thus be easily recognised.

The *subdivision of the pulsation* into *binary* or *ternary* values is a factor in distinguishing among the remaining eleven pieces. Two (2 and 6) of the four pieces with six pulsations are binary, while the other two (9 and 12) are ternary. The two binary pieces can be easily identified because the pulsation, which is materialised by the pellet bells, is differently subdivided: in piece 2, it contains two minimal operational values, but four in piece 6. The former, with twelve minimal values, is thus in a 1:2 ratio to the latter, with twenty-four.

The third feature, the *relationship to the pulsation*, is required to distinguish pieces 9 and 12. The constituent elements of piece 9 are located at eight positions, only three of which coincide with pulsations. The model for piece 12 makes use of seven positions, five of which coincide with pulsations. The former is therefore *contrametric*, while the latter is *commetric*.

Let us now look at the last category comprised of pieces with a cycle of four pulsations. It contains seven pieces, three of which are binary (1, 4, and 5), while the remaining four (3, 7, 10, and 11) are ternary. The relationship to the pulsation will again enable us to distinguish the pieces within each of these subgroups. Piece 4 is the only one of the three binary ones to have mixed metricity. Pieces 1 and 5 are both contrametric, but in differing degrees. In the model for piece 1, there are five offbeat attacks, and four on the pulsation; while in piece 5, only two of the seven attacks coincide with pulsations, the other five being offbeat. Furthermore, the metric organisation of the phrases of the song, which determines how the instrumental model is organised, make the model begin on the semiquaver following the pulsation, rather than on the pulsation itself. This feature alone is sufficient to distinguish piece 5 from piece 1, which begins on the pulsation.

We are now left with pieces 3, 7, 10, and 11, which are based on a cycle of four ternary pulsations containing twelve minimal values. Two of these (pieces 3 and 10) are contrametric, while the other two (pieces 7 and 11) are mixed. While the latter are identical with respect to the number of commetric and contrametric elements in their models, they nevertheless differ on one point: piece 11 starts on the pulsation, while the metric organisation of the phrases of the song from which piece 7 derives, situates its beginning on the semiquaver preceding the pulsation.

Finally, to distinguish between pieces 3 and 10, we must turn to the last feature, the *configuration of the rhythmic and melodic material.* Let us compare the positions occupied by the constituents in their models:

| Piece 3 | 1 | 2 | | 4 | | 6 | 7 | | 9 | | 11 | |
| Piece 10 | 1 | | 3 | | | 6 | | 8 | | 10 | | 12 |

We can see that, even without reference to the pitches of the sounds appearing in each of the positions, the criterion of rhythmic organisation alone provides an easy way of distinguishing the two. They have in common only two (1 and 6) of the eleven positions occupied in the two models. Five of the nine remaining positions (2, 4, 7, 9, and 11) appear only in piece 3, and the other four (3, 8, 10, and 12), only in piece 10.

In this repertory, the hocket principle is applied in the strictest possible way. Since each instrument is limited to the production of a single sound, the combinations of horn parts are obtained essentially by *interweaving.*

When we look at the entire set of models, we can see that the paired instrumental parts (1 and 2, 2 and 3, 3 and 4, 4 and 5, and 1 and 5, the latter being the reversal of 5 and 6) are *strictly* interwoven (i.e., *there are no simultaneous attacks*) in fifty-nine out of sixty cases, the only exception being the combination of 1 and 5 in piece 8.

In eight out of twelve pieces, the horn combinations 1-2-3 and 3-4-5 are also strictly interwoven, and in nine, the 2-3-4 combination. This is a measure of how widely the principle is applied.

Ex. 135 summarises the ways in which strict interweaving of the horn parts is arranged in each of the models. The reader will observe that absolutely identical arrangements are used in pieces 1, 3, 4, 5, and 11, on the one hand, and 2 and 6 on the other. Thus, despite the extremely brief formal framework of three to six pulsations, and despite all the similarities mentioned above, the internal logic of this repertory is such that its component pieces cannot be mistaken for one another. This is a fact which is easily confirmed by on-site observation. A few seconds at the beginning will suffice for any listener acquainted with traditional Banda-Linda songs accurately to recognise any piece being performed by a horn orchestra.

Ex. 135

Horns↓ Pieces→	1	2	3	4	5	6	7	8	9	10	11	12
1–2	+	+	+	+	+	+	+	+	+	+	+	+
2–3	+	+	+	+	+	+	+	+	+	+	+	+
3–4	+	+	+	+	+	+	+	+	+	+	+	+
4–5	+	+	+	+	+	+	+	+	+	+	+	+
1–5 (=5–6)	+	+	+	+	+	+	+		+	+	+	+
1–3	+		+	+	+		+	+		+	+	
2–4	+		+	+	+		+	+		+	+	+
3–5	+	+	+	+	+	+					+	
1–4		+				+			+			
2–5							+	+				+
1–2–3	+		+	+	+		+	+		+	+	
2–3–4	+		+	+	+		+	+		+	+	+
3–4–5	+	+	+	+	+	+			+		+	
1–2–4												
2–3–5												
2–4–5							+	+				+
1–3–5	+		+	+	+		+				+	
1–2–5							+					+
1–4–5		+				+			+			

4.3.1.3 *From the instrumental model to its realisations*

Our investigation has taken us from the realisation of each of the pieces in the repertory of a Banda-Linda horn orchestra to the identification of their underlying models. We must now prove that these models have operational force. To do so, we will proceed in the opposite way, i.e., from the model, we will try to engender realisations which are similar to the ones which led us to it in the first place. The diagram below is thus a schematic representation of our bidirectional method:

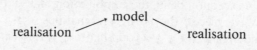

If the realisations on either side of the model have the same structural features, we will have proof of the inherent relationships between the messages and their underlying code, and thereby, of the coherence of the entire system.

It is important to realise that this route from the code back to the messages, just like our previous transtion from the messages to the code, involves no abstract speculation. The messages obtained in this way are neither artifacts nor imitations nor simulations. Just as before, the material we observe is produced by the Linda musicians themselves.

The method was to ask the same five members of the *ngbānjā* 'family' who provided the models to listen to this skeletal framework through headphones and to flesh it out, i.e., to ornament it with variations just as they would do in a normal performance.

I suggested to the musicians that they build progressively on the model and enrich it with an ever greater number of variations. This bidirectional procedure leading from the message to the code (from praxis to theory), and then from the code back to the message, is thus left entirely in the hands of the musicians themselves.

In exx. 136, 137, and 138, I present extracts from transcriptions of the realisations *obtained from the models* of the first three pieces in the repertory, which are the clear favourites of the Ippy orchestra. The model itself precedes each transcription.

Ex. 136 Ndə̀rə̀jé bāléndōrɔ̄

Ex. 136 (cont.)

Ex. 136 (cont.)

Ex. 136 (cont.)

Ex. 136 (cont.)

Ex. 136 (cont.)

Ex. 137 Āméyā

Ex. 137 (cont.)

Ex. 137 (cont.)

Ex. 137 (cont.)

When ex. 136 and ex. 137 are compared point by point with ex. 5 and ex. 65, respectively, no doubt can remain as to the identical nature of the musical material leading to and derived from the model.

The model for the third piece, *Kāndā bàlē bɔzɔ́ dùārɔ*, and the realisation obtained from it, are shown in ex. 138.

Ex. 138 Kāndā bàlē bɔ̀zɔ́ dùārə̀

Ex. 138 (cont.)

Ex. 138 (cont.)

Ex. 138 (cont.)

Ex. 138 (cont.)

An examination of exs. 136–138 clearly reveals how similar their structural features are, and to what extent they operate in the same way. They can thus only be assumed to be governed by a single set of principles. If we accept this inference, we may consider ourselves dispensed from reproducing the realisations of the remaining pieces in the repertory.

4.3.2   The relationship between instrumental hocket and vocal music

We have already stated that the Banda-Linda people derive all the pieces in their horn orchestra repertory from their vocal music. Now all Banda-Linda songs are of a monodic and/or homophonic nature. The only forms of polyphonic music they use are instrumental, and for the most part performed on the xylophone, which always accompanies vocal music.

When we confront the strictly instrumental music of the horn orchestras, we are naturally inclined to wonder, first of all, why the Linda people use anything like the hocket technique; and secondly, how the pieces played by the horn orchestras are related to the songs with the same titles. We also want to know how the songs are adapted to a technique of this kind, i.e., how a melody sung in unison or at parallel intervals can be treated or transformed so as to give rise to instrumental hocket of such a complex type. We may also wonder how the Linda listener approaches such music: does he hear it vertically, horizontally, or diagonally?

The practice of the musicians themselves poses another question: what are the horn players trying to do as they perform their figures on their single-note instruments? Is it their intention to create a vertical superposition of the parts, i.e., a sort of rhythmic counterpoint, or are they each contributing their individual sound to reconstitute segments of the original melody of the piece?

We must now find answers to all of these questions. To do so, we will use a bi-directional procedure comparable to the back-and-forth method we have used previously: this time, from instrumental hocket to vocal music, and from vocal music back to hocket.

4.3.2.1 From instrumental hocket to vocal music

All the pieces for horns have a title; each title is that of a song known to the community. Simply listening to a piece will not, however, be enough to enable a foreigner to the culture to grasp how the orchestral music matches the song of the same name, and this is what we want to discover. We therefore asked the members of the orchestra to *sing* each of the pieces in chorus. But being accustomed to hocket performances, they sang more of a vocal imitation of their orchestral instrumental technique than a traditional version of the song itself. Each musician would thus sing one or two notes in the form of short staccato cries and brief pauses. While melodic motifs did appear here and there, the relationship between the instrumental and vocal music was in no way clarified.

It then occurred to me that this relationship might be better brought out if I asked the master of the horns to superpose the song on the instrumental version. I then recorded each piece in the repertory in the form of a vocal solo over a prerecorded orchestral version. A certain resemblance began to appear: the length of each melodic phrase was exactly equal to the *period* of the instrumental formula, and certain elements of the vocal part were arranged so as to coincide with certain melodic combinations produced by instrumental hocket. Since the orchestral latticework was so complex, I tried a further step, and had the melody performed by a vocal soloist superposed on the bare version of each piece, the instrumental model. The match became even more evident with the elimination of instrumental variations. Nevertheless, there were so many variations *in the vocal part*, usually resulting from changes in the words, that it was still impossible to determine what reference points were used, i.e., the nature and number of the fundamental melodic phrases giving rise to the vocal variations. For example, we noted around one hundred phrases for *Ndə̀rə̀jé bāléndōrɔ̄*, some of which were similar, but almost none identical.

I then thought we might superpose a *humming* soloist on the preceding recording of the instrumental model plus the song with words. I thereby hoped to reduce the number of variations by the elimination of text. However, the hummed version in no way affected the number of melodic variations, although the attacks became sharper, and the rhythmic relationships clearer. The match between vocal and instrumental configurations also became more patent. The arrangements of the vocal material and the greatly compressed instrumental material of the model form were now nearly identical.

Although the songs were initially monodic or homophonic, the two soloists whose voices were superposed on the instrumental model did not sing in unison, or even at parallel intervals. Individual performances of songs allow considerable verbal improvisation and leave the singer entirely free to choose any sequence of the various segments of the melody, each of which covers a full period. These periods are, as we have said, of the same length as the periods of the instrumental formula for the given piece. The differences in the simultaneous statements of the two singers would then have to be attributed to the freedom of commutation affecting the phrases in the vocal part.

The second soloist, singing without words, was thus in no way constrained in formulating his version of the song (i.e., in ordering his own segments) by what the preceding singer had done. He was obliged only to respect the framework of the period and the arrangement of the melodic elements within it.

The inevitable result of this superposition was a polyphonic relationship between the two vocal parts. Since any phrase could be found in a vertical relationship to any other, the polyphony was, so to speak, of a fortuitous nature. Each melodic phrase was, however, always superposed in a coherent way on the melodic and rhythmic combination contained in the instrumental model form.

This observation led me to the following hypothesis: *the sounds comprising the melody must be assigned to the instruments with the same pitch as those sounds.* An undesirable consequence of this conjecture is, however, that, if the song is based on the repetition of a single melodic phrase, the con-sonances included in the instrumental model become purposeless. If, on the other hand, the song is composed of several melodic phrases, how can they all be assembled in a single instrumental combination? The latter possibility can only be envisaged if the instrumental model is designed to condense all the potentialities of the material contained in the melody, i.e., the set of melodic phrases which support the original words, prior to the elaboration of any individual variations. Now while these melodic segments almost always appear in the different versions of the singers, they are dispersed and thereby disguised. How then can we identify them? We needed the *àkɔ.nə̀*, the model for each of the songs which had been adapted for orchestral use. But the vocal *àkɔ.nə̀* for each song contains only a single phrase, both verbally and melodically speaking; and the melody of this vocal model can in fact be clearly discerned in the corresponding instrumental *àkɔ.nə*. How then are we to explain the presence in the instrumental models of the other sounds *which do not appear in this one phrase*? The answer is that, unlike instrumental music where the model includes *all* the material, what is called the *àkɔ.nə* for songs in fact constitutes no more than an *incipit*, and not a 'standard version'. A complete form of the latter will contain several phrases, one melodic segment for each original set of words. This full set of *key phrases* is what the singers take as their reference in elaborating both textual improvisations and the associated melodic variations.

The number of key phrases in the songs adapted for horns varies from two to four. They are invariably present in the instrumental model, although *in schematic form*. Most of their constituent sounds are distributed among the various instruments at the proper positions.

The first song, for example, has three key phrases, shown in ex. 139a (in all transcriptions of key phrases, phrase A is always the *àkɔ.nə̀*). Ex. 139b shows how they can be found 'diagonally' in the instrumental model.

We can see that certain sounds in certain positions are common to two phrases (for example, the C at positions 1 and 9 is common to phrases B and C). This procedure of *agglutination* works by virtue of the principle of the *commutability of key phrases*, which applies within an invariant periodic framework.

The applicability of this principle leads, however, to another important question: what factors and rules are involved in the creation of instrumental variations? To reply, we will first have to find out how variations work in *vocal* performances: see 4.3.2.2, where we have said they are essentially the result of textual improvisation. Linda is a

Ex. 139a

Ex. 139b

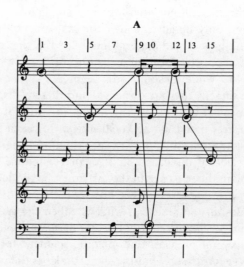

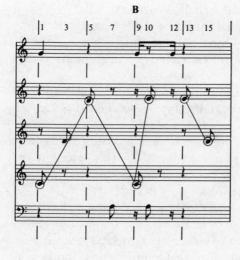

tone language, and any change in the words with respect to the original text of a musical phrase will almost automatically affect its melodic profile. As long as the number of syllables remains unchanged, only the melody will vary. But when the singer adds or removes syllables (and this is the most common case), the rhythmic organisation of the phrase will also be subject to variation. If the singers limited themselves to these procedures alone, it would be relatively simple to *infer which implicit key phrase was acting as the reference for each type of variation,* to *reconstruct the key phrases* from which the variations are derived by noting the similar elements, and thereby to *determine how many key phrases are used for each song.*

In practice, however, the singers combine these procedures with an additional one, which involves *arbitrarily juxtaposing fragments from different key phrases in a single melodic phrase.* This is another case of commutation at a lower level. We have already spoken of the commutability of key phrases among themselves; we now find that melodic segments of a given phrase are also commutable, provided they occupy the

Ex. 140

same position within the period. Thus, if a song has three key phrases, A, B, and C, each of which contains two fragments (A1-A2, B1-B2, C1-C2), A1 may commute either with B1 or with C1, A2 with B2 or C2, B1 with C1, and B2 with C2. A few of these microcommutations in the key phrases of *Ndɔràjé bāléndōrɔ̄*, which appear in the version sung by the master of the horns, are shown in ex. 140. Each phrase may thus include fragments drawn from any of the song's key phrases, including of course the one designated as *àkɔ̄.nɔ̀*. Richness in variations is thus directly proportional to the singer's imaginativeness, which he demonstrates by instantaneous improvisation of words, and spontaneous choice among a stock of paradigrmatic sets of melodic fragments. A good singer will introduce considerable variation into his melodic units rather than repeating himself. That is why I was able to record nearly a hundred different phrases for a single piece, each having a certain number of fragments in common with others.

At the time, however, I did not know that there was a 'standard version' of the song, or how its fragments were related. Only after I had discovered the key phrases for the songs did I realise that the variations in the vocal versions worked as 'wandering segments'. We will shortly see (in 4.3.2.2.) that the vocal variations have a considerable bearing on the variations performed by the horn players in the instrumental pieces of the same name.

To conclude this section, and to provide further illustration of how the principle of commutation works, I present transcriptions of the second and third pieces in the repertory, *Āméyā* and *Kāndā bàlē bɔ̀zɔ́ dùārɔ̀*. The respective key phrases are given in exx. 141a and 142a, the instrumental models in exx. 141b and 142b, and the vocal versions in exx. 141c and 142c.

Ex. 141 Āméyā

(a) Key phrases

(b) Instrumental model

Ex. 141 (cont.)

(c) Vocal version

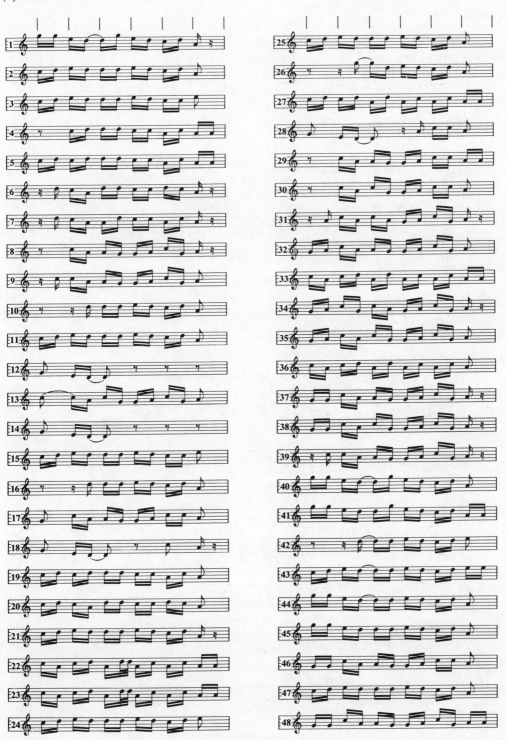

Ex. 142 Kāndā bàlē bòzó dùārɔ̀

(a) Key phrases

(b) Instrumental model

Ex. 142 (cont.)

(c) Vocal version

Ex. 142 (cont.)

4.3.2.2 From vocal music to instrumental hocket

The melodic and rhythmic material contained in the full set of key phrases for each song reappears in schematic form in the instrumental model. The melody is there distributed among the instruments according to their pitch, and the rhythmic material is placed at the proper positions in the cycle. It should thus now be theoretically possible to reconstitute the instrumental model for each song on the basis of its key phrases alone. Let us check this hypothesis using the fourth piece in the repertory of the Ippy orchestra, called *Āmbōrōrō mátɔ́ kūmù kàgà*. We will then compare our construct with the model materialised by the musicians in the orchestra. The key phrases for this piece are shown in ex. 143. If we distribute all of the material in ex. 143 among the instruments of the *ngbānjā* group, we get the combination in ex. 144.

Ex. 143

Ex. 144

Now when we compare this *theoretical* model with the *material* I was given for the same piece, we find that the latter has been pruned a bit. It does not contain *each and every one* of the sounds, nor all the rhythmic values in the key phrases. It is rather more like a 'distillation' which retains only what is essential to preserve the identity of the piece. It is thus a *minimal* formula.

The behaviour of the instrumental model is only logical, in view of the fact that, as a didactic tool, its main purpose is simplification. We may recall that the instrumental model is obtained by superposing the minimal cells for the five instruments in any given 'family', which the initiates learn during their retreat. When, however, we look at the synthetic instrumental version obtained by superposition of recordings of all the instruments with the same name (which are tuned in octaves), we find that the key phrases of the corresponding song are taken over in nearly every detail. Now it should be remembered that the reason why I made these recordings of octave sets was to get a better idea of the structure of the piece so that we could see how it resembled the instrumental model. When, much later on, I got the actual *àk5.nɔ̀*, I found that the combinations obtained by forming octave sets were too 'rich' and full. When compared with the material contained in the set of vocal key phrases, however, these pairings turn out to be nearly an exact instrumental reproduction, a sort of *simultaneous* replica.

In exx. 145 to 156, I now present the transcription of the key phrases, the octave sets, and the instrumental model for each of the pieces in the repertory, for purposes of comparison.

Ex. 145 Piece 1: Ndòròjé bālandōrɔ̄

(a) Key phrases

(b) Octave sets

(c) Instrumental model

Ex. 146 Piece 2: Āméyā

(a) Key phrases

(b) Octave sets

(c) Instrumental model

Ex. 147 Piece 3: Kāndā bàlē bɔ̀zɔ́ dùārɔ̀

(a) Key phrases

(b) Octave sets

(c) Instrumental model

Ex. 148 Piece 4: Āmbōrōrō mátɔ́ kūmù kàgà

(a) Key phrases

(b) Octave sets

(c) Instrumental model

Ex. 149 Piece 5: Èbónā kā cémà tò

(a) Key phrases

(b) Octave sets

(c) Instrumental model

Ex. 150 Piece 6: ʔē jī kīlīngbī nà yīndà tōrō tówò

(a) Key phrases

(b) Octave sets

(c) Instrumental model

Ex. 151 Piece 7: Gànjà kɔ̄ngɔ̄ ngɔ́ tànjē tà ángēmbá

(a) Key phrases

(b) Octave sets

(c) Instrumental model

Ex. 152 Piece 8: Árɔ́ dɔ́ kɔ̄tí yē

(a) Key phrases

(b) Octave sets

(c) Instrumental model

Ex. 153 Piece 9: Kùzū wōtɔ̄ kə̀ wó yālúkūmù

(a) Key phrases

(b) Octave sets

(c) Instrumental model

Ex. 154 Piece 10: Ā gànjà ngbéngā mándá kɔ̄vòkpá

(a) Key phrases

(b) Octave sets

(c) Instrumental model

Ex. 155 Piece 11: ə̀njē zá ə́ngbɨ́ kāwà mùnjú tə̀ àmbànə̀

(a) Key phrases

(b) Octave sets

(c) Instrumental model

Ex. 156 Piece 12: Dángáyē

(a) Key phrases

(b) Octave sets

(c) Instrumental model

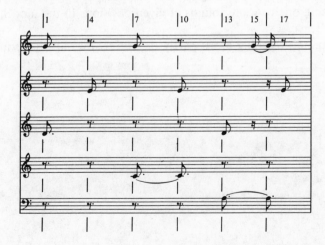

We might say that the materialisation of a piece by the synthetic procedure of forming octave sets lies midway between the instrumental model of the piece (i.e., its minimal reference) and any one realisation. This is easy to see from the analysis of the first three pieces above (*Ndə̀rə̀jé bāléndōrə̄*, *Āméyā*, and *Kāndā bàlē bə̀zə́ dùārə̀*).

The gap between the model (or the model-like version obtained by forming octave sets) and the ordinary realisations can be attributed simply to the variations introduced by the musicians. Before we can understand how these variations are realised, and what they take as a reference, we must take time to examine how they are related, first of all, to the instrumental model, and then to the vocal music.

Let us begin by looking at the techniques by which variations are produced. These are *splitting*, *merger*, *omission*, *extension*, *anticipation*, *transmutation*, and *insertion*.

Splitting consists of dividing up the total duration of a given sound into shorter values, as in ex. 157.

Ex. 157

Merger is the reverse process, consisting of amalgamating the values of conjunct sounds, as in ex. 158.

Ex. 158

Omission consists of replacing one or more sounds at given positions in the model, or even the entire model, by silence.

Extension occurs when a sound preceding a rest partly or entirely overlaps it, as in ex. 159.

Ex. 159

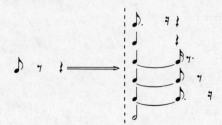

Anticipation involves slightly overlapping the rest which precedes an attack, as in ex. 160.

Ex. 160

Transmutation consists of transforming binary into ternary elements, and vice versa, as in ex. 161.

Ex. 161

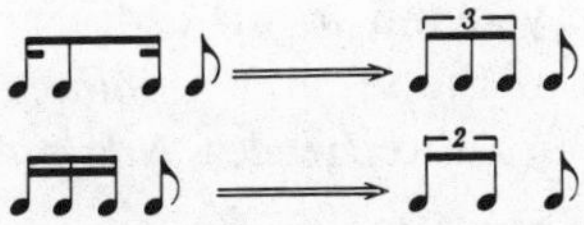

Insertion consists of introducing additional sounds at the positions assigned to rests, as in ex. 162.

Ex. 162

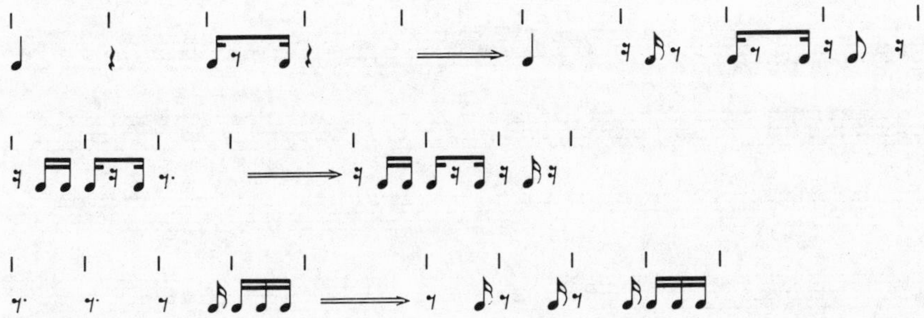

These seven techniques are the only ones available to the musicians for the production of variations. They can be combined: splitting does not exclude anticipation, insertion of additional sounds, omission by elision, or transmutation.

Let us now turn to the relationships between variations in the horn parts and the vocal music from which the pieces are derived. We have already said that vocal variations affect the variations performed by the orchestral musicians. How then are the latter created? And what is the musician trying to achieve as he plays them?

The sum of the orchestral variations is always equivalent to a 'diagonal' reading of a potential melodic phrase in the song of the same name. It is as if the musicians' inner ear started by suggesting a melodic phrase from the song (a phrase they can only partly reproduce), and they then tried to materialise it by involving their immediate neighbours to the right and to the left. By constantly repeating a given variation, the musicians seem to manage to transmit their intentions to their neighbours and get them to combine their sounds to reconstruct the phrase which a given musician has in mind at the time. When one watches the bodily movements of the musicians during a horn performance, and sees how they swing their torso from side to side and signal to each other with their heads, one finds this hypothesis even more convincing. We can now see how important it is that the musicians be able to maintain visual contact among themselves. Otherwise, it would be impossible to perform in this way. Using this contact, any musician can take the initiative and try to get the others to follow.

Given what we have just had to say about the effect of vocal variations on the variations performed by the horn players, if we give them a specific song in the Linda repertory, they should be able to recreate an appropriate orchestral version of it. I thus tried to confirm this new hypothesis by asking the *tété* horn player in the *ngbānjā* group to listen to a recording of a solo vocal version of each song, and to superpose his own part upon it. We then successively added the remaining instruments in the 'family', *tā*, *hā*, *tútûlé*, and *bɔ̀ngɔ́*. This experiment gave a conclusive result: the instrumental version obtained in this way was similar in every detail to an ordinary realisation. Proof of this can be found in the transcriptions of the versions *obtained from the vocal version* (shown on the uppermost staff) of the first three pieces, *Ndɔ̀rɔ̀jé bāléndōrɔ̄*, *Āméyā*, and *Kāndā bàlē bɔ̀zɔ́ dùārɔ̀*, as shown in exs. 163-165.

Ex. 163 Piece 1: Ndɔ̀rɔjé bāléndōrɔ̄

Ex. 163 (cont.)

Ex. 163 (cont.)

Ex. 163 (cont.)

Ex. 163 (cont.)

Ex. 163 (cont.)

Ex. 164 Piece 2: Āméyā

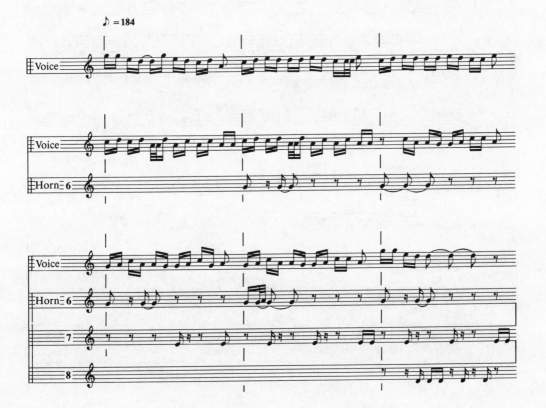

Ex. 164 (cont.)

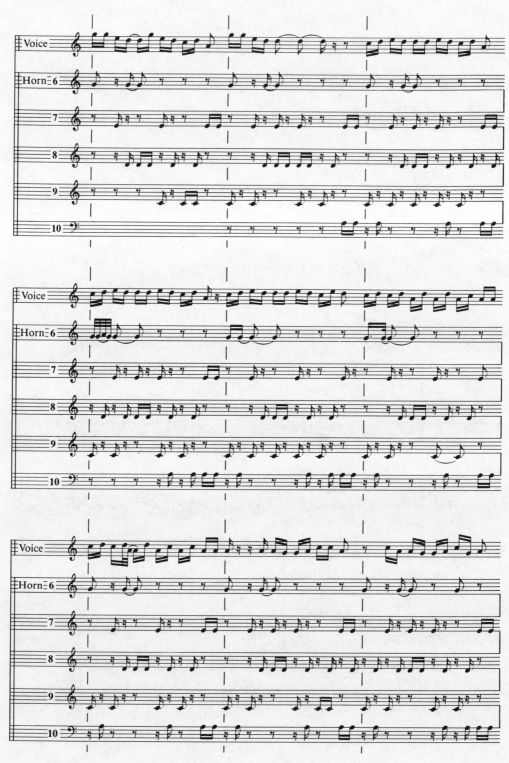

Ex. 164 (cont.)

Ex. 164 (cont.)

Ex. 165 Piece 3: Kāndā bàle bɔ̀zɔ́ dùārɔ̀

Ex. 165 (cont.)

Ex. 165 (cont.)

Ex. 165 (cont.)

Ex. 165 (cont.)

The instrumental variations obtained from a vocal version of the piece of the same name are thus clearly quite similar to any version the orchestra could have performed without *material* reference to vocal music. We may recall that my investigations began with the recording of the repertory of orchestral music, for which I later obtained the underlying instrumental models. I then went even further back, to the songs themselves from which the hocket music is derived. We have now come back down to our starting point.

The preceding discussion shows that, if we have the key phrases and a vocal version of any song which can be adapted for horns, we can construct both a model-like orchestral version (which should be quite similar to the version obtained by forming octave sets) and a simulated realisation which the Banda-Linda people themselves are quite likely to accept as genuine.

To end this section, which has taken us from vocal music back to instrumental hocket, I will now give the key phrases, the theoretical models, the model-like versions obtained by forming octave sets, and fairly long extracts of vocal versions of the remaining nine pieces in the repertory (exx. 166–172).

This set of examples begins with the fourth piece, *Àmbōrōrō mátɔ́ kūmù kàgà* (ex. 166).

Ex. 166 Piece 4: Àmbōrōrō mátɔ́ kūmù kàgà

(a) Key phrases

Ex. 166 (cont.)

(b) Theoretical model

(c) Octave sets

Ex. 166 (cont.)

(d) Vocal version (fragment)

Ex. 167 Piece 5: Èbɔ́nā kā cémà tò

(a) Key phrases

(b) Theoretical model

(c) Octave sets

Ex. 167 (cont.)

(d) Vocal version (fragment)

Ex. 168 Piece 6: ?ē jī kīlīngbī nà yīndà tōrō tówò

(a) Key phrases

(b) Theoretical model

(c) Octave sets

Ex. 168 (cont.)

(d) Vocal version (fragment)

Ex. 169 Piece 7: Gànjà kɔ̄ngɔ̄ ngɔ́ tànjē tà ángēmbá

(a) Key phrases

(b) Theoretical model

(c) Octave sets

(d) Vocal version (fragment)

Ex. 170 Piece 8: Árɔ́ dɔ́ kɔ̄tí yē

(a) Key phrases

(b) Theoretical model

(c) Octave sets

(d) Vocal version

Ex. 171 Piece 9: Kùzū wōtɔ́ kɜ̀ wó yālúkūmù

(a) Key phrases

(b) Theoretical model

(c) Octave sets

Ex. 171 (cont.)

(d) Vocal version (fragment)

Ex. 172 Piece 10: A gànjà ngbéngā mándá kɔ̄vòkpá

(a) Key phrases

(d) Vocal version

(b) Theoretical model

(c) Octave sets

Ex. 173 Piece 11: ə̀njē zá ə́ngbí kāwà mùnjú tə̄ āmbānə̀

(a) Key phrases

(d) Vocal version (fragment)

(b) Theoretical model

(c) Octave sets

Ex. 174 Piece 12: Dángáyē

(a) Key phrases

(b) Theoretical model

(c) Octave sets

Ex. 174 (cont.)
(d) Vocal version

In this chapter, I have analysed a technique whereby polyphony is produced by the use of polyrhythmics. This technique has been exemplified by the repertory of a horn orchestra of Banda-Linda origin in the Central African Republic. I hope to have brought out the underlying coherence in the internal organisation of orchestras using this technique, the nature of the musical principles behind it, and the intrinsic relationships connecting this kind of instrumental hocket with an essentially linear type of vocal music.

With the *active* help of the Linda musicians, I have been able to establish the theoretical principles at the base of their hocket technique, and see how they go about adapting traditional songs to the constraints it imposes. I have been able to check these principles by a bidirectional methodology which proceeds from conventional performances of the pieces in the repertory to their underlying models, and then back again from the models to 'new' performances.

Before concluding this chapter, I must insist, first of all, on the *ingeniousness of the technique*, i.e., on the particularly economical use made of musical resources, and secondly, on the peculiar underlying idea from which it derives.

Linda hocket music involves simply a pentatonic scale, each of whose degrees are assigned to a different instrument. Five different rhythmic figures, each at a different pitch level, can thus be produced within the framework of a predetermined periodicity. These figures are subject to variation. The component parts may be duplicated as the number of available instruments permits. The range is thereby considerably increased, and may reach nearly four octaves. At the same time, individual variations proliferate so as to create the densest possible musical lattice. It is as if this very complexity were intended to compensate for the simplicity of the linear vocal music at its source.

Banda-Linda instrumental hocket works on a polyrhythmic principle involving the *interweaving of several rhythmic figures*. Since these figures are produced simultaneously at different pitch levels, they can be used to reconstruct *melodio phrases* and create counterpoint. This type of hocket therefore lies on the *borderline between strict polyrhythmics*, as we have defined it, and *polyphony*.

Seeing, however, that the Banda-Linda people have a predominantly linear, i.e., monodic or homophonic, conception of music, it is more than probable that the pieces performed by the horn orchestras are not intended to be heard vertically in the strict sense. Just as the musicians attempt to produce melodic phrases, so it would seem that the listener tries to extract certain melodic motifs from the complexity of the musical texture, and combines them in whatever way he pleases. He is therefore an *active* listener, for he is constantly obliged to pick out the sounds in the vertical agglomeration which can be put together to reproduce the melodic phrase he wants to hear. If this is the case, the Banda-Linda people do not in fact perceive their music either vertically or horizontally, but rather *diagonally*.

Paradoxical as it may seem, this music should, despite its polyphonic nature, be deemed the 'accidental' result of a basically *melodic* intention.

5 Polyphony produced by melodic instruments

5.1 DEFINITION AND GENERAL CHARACTERISTICS

Definition

By *polyphonic instruments*, we mean instruments *designed* for *melodic* music, i.e., provided with pitch levels from a predetermined scale, and played in such a way that the musician's hands *simultaneously* perform two parts which *differ* in both melody and rhythm.

General characteristics

The three polyphonic instruments found in the Central African Republic are the xylophone, the *sanza*, and the harp. They are only rarely used independently, their primary function being to provide support for a song which is *invariably sung by the musician himself*, but may also involve a response from a choir, or simply from a partner. This instrumental support does several things. It defines the periodic and modal framework for the song, and in so doing, furnishes a set of metric, rhythmic, and melodic reference points. The regularity of the invariant periodicity and the stability of the reference points help the musician to develop a nearly automatic motor behaviour, which frees his mind from attention to manual activity. When he has reached this stage, he can devote his attention entirely to melodic and verbal improvisation in his song. Far from confining itself to an organisational function, the instrumental formula provides a sort of 'launching pad' for the musician's inspiration by suggesting melodic associations.

Functionally speaking, the xylophone may be set apart from the harp and the *sanza*, as it is used primarily to accompany group dances. Accordingly, it is habitually a part of larger ensembles, including percussion instruments (particularly drums). The harp and the *sanza*, however, are used on more intimate occasions, althouth this is not incompatible with the adjunction of one or more percussion instruments, such as double bells or rhythm sticks.

To keep our discussion clear, we will consider the music of each of these instruments out of context. We will reinsert them later on, when we come to the chapter on the conjunction of polyphony and polyrhythmics.

We may separate the instruments in the same way from the standpoint of polyphonic technique: xylophone music is close to being homophonic, while *sanza* and harp music are more clearly contrapuntal. Let us remember that, if the words of African songs are to remain intelligible, they must respect the tones of the language they are sung in.

All music involving several voices must therefore move in parallel intervals. Counter-point may only appear in instrumental music.

In music (even homophonic music) produced by polyphonic instruments, no hierar-chical relationship is established between the parts assigned to each of the musician's hands. No melodic line predominates. These instruments are used mainly to accompany vocal music, where improvisation is more widespread, both with respect to the inven-tion of verbal expression, and to the ways in which different melodic expressions are arranged. When singing is going on, the level of variation in the instrumental music is thus usually extremely low, at times nil. In the latter case, we will see that the in-strumental realisation is actually nothing but the materialisation of the model. On the other hand, instrumental variations will abound during interludes without song, which can be as many and as long as the musician desires. Four techniques are used to produce variations in this music: (a) *splitting* or *merger*, which involve subdividing or com-bining durations, (b) *insertion* of additional melodic elements in one or more parts, as in ex. 1, (c) *rhythmic offsetting* of sounds in one part, resulting in phenomena of *anticipation* or, which bring about the rhythmic interweaving of the two parts (see ex. 2) and (d) *commutation*, whereby one vertical combination replaces another at given positions in the periodic cycle, as in ex. 3.

Ex. 1

Ex. 2

Ex. 3

These techniques may be combined in practice, and it is not unusual to find all of them, not just in any one realisation of a given piece, but even in the realisation of a single formula. In pieces involving instrumental variations, the formula will allow a large number of commutations, to the extent that its realisations look like the result of a sort of 'patchwork', or *centonisation*, based on the concatenation of a large number of micro-elements, each of which fits into an invariable predetermined position in the temporal matrix, as shown in ex. 4.

Ex. 4

In this chapter, we will examine successively the music for the xylophone, the *sanza*, and the harp. The xylophones show a wide variety of material forms, musical range, layout, and playing technique. We will analyse seven xylophones pieces belonging to four different ethnic groups. The examples of *sanza* music all come from one population group, and all the harp music from another. Three pieces will be taken as representative of the repertories for each of these instruments.

A diagram of each type of instrument will be provided to show how it is laid out, and how the sounds are distributed between the musician's hands.

The transcription of an extract of each piece will be provided prior to analysis. In the case of pieces with an instrumental formula allowing variations, the beginning of at least one of its realisations will be presented. The length of this extract will be proportional to the number of variations contained in the version considered. When the instrumental formula of a piece is repeated with no variations whatsoever, we will merely furnish the transcription of its model.

Each piece transcribed will be subjected to a detailed analysis of its constituent features, which can be arranged under the following three headings: organisation of pulsation and pitch, formal structure, and commutation techniques.

The *organisation of pulsation and pitch* covers the periodicity, type of subdivision of the pulsation into minimal operational values, scalar arrangement of the sounds, and range covered by the instrumental formula.

The *formal structure* deals with the way the musical material can be divided up into units. This segmentation is based on the principle of the recurrence of one, or the convergence of several of the following parameters: sequence of vertical combinations and/or chords, motifs or melodic configurations, and rhythmic figures and cells.

The third heading includes the *commutation procedures* which can be discovered in each of the component parts of each piece. Paradigmatic tables will be used to show the variations in each part, and the extent to which both rhythmic and melodic commutation are allowed.

5.2   THE XYLOPHONES

The xylophones found in the Central African Republic belong to one of three types: the socalled 'leg' xylophone, the pit xylophone (of a variant which is laid across banana-tree trunks), and the portable xylophone.

We need make only passing reference to the first and most rudimentary type. It is composed of no more than a few wooden slats (usually three) which the seated musician lays across his thighs, and strikes with two wooden sticks. This instrument is a sort of musical toy, and has no other purpose than the amusement of the user, and perhaps a few onlookers.

The pit xylophone seems to be used only by the Zande people, who inhabit the easternmost part of the country. It is part of a specific orchestral ensemble, and provides support for a particular type of choreography. It is played by two musicians at the same time.

The portable xylophone is by far the most widespread, and is used by most of the country's ethnic groups. It has a part in almost every social and cultural event involving musical ensembles; it is in fact the main instrument, the nucleus as it were, in such ensembles. It is also used to accompany dances for mere amusement. Some ethnic groups set up ensembles in which two portable xylophones perform together.

The last two types, the *pit* xylophone and the *portable* xylophone, will be discussed here in that order. The use of the pit xylophone will be illustrated by a piece of Zande *kpóníngbó* music. The music for portable xylophone will be represented by three pieces from the Sabanga *ngbàkè* dance repertory, and by a piece connected with the Banda-Linda *āméyā* cult of twin worship. Finally, the music for two portable xylophones will be discussed with respect to two pieces from the Banda-Dakpa repertory for *gàzà* initiates.

5.2.1 The pit xylophone

The pit xylophone is assembled whenever it is needed. Among the Zande people, the instrument is composed of twelve keys which are laid in parallel fashion across two banana-tree trunks. A rectangular hole dug in the ground acts as a resonator. The keys are not attached to the tree trunks, but are held in place by small pegs driven vertically into them.

The *kpóníngbó* is played by two musicians. They squat side by side and divide up the keyboard between them. Each has a thick wooden stick in each hand, with which he strikes the instrument. The same name is used to designate the instrument and a type of dance it is used to accompany.

The diagram in ex. 5 shows how the *kpóníngbó* keyboard is laid out. The instru-

Ex. 5

ment has a range of two octaves plus a major second. The keyboard is divided between the two xylophonists. The higher register is assigned to one (musician 1), and the lower register to the other (musician 2). The latter is assigned five keys, and the former seven. However, the high G is hardly ever struck, and the adjoining F never is, so that musician 1 is also essentially required to play only five keys.

We may remark that, whatever their ethnic origin, Central African xylophonists generally play an *odd* number of keys. These keys are nevertheless distributed in *symmetric* and *equal* fashion between the player's hands. Thus, the centre key is always struck *alternately* by the two hands. This allows each hand to play three.

The keys of the *kpóníngbó* are thus distributed as shown in ex. 6.

Ex. 6

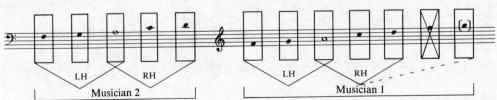

The first few pages of a piece of *kpóníngbó* music are transcribed in ex. 7.

Ex. 7

Ex. 7 (cont.)

Ex. 7 (cont.)

The instrumental formula for this piece has a period of eight pulsations. The subdivision of these pulsations is binary, and the minimal operational value is the semiquaver. The scale is of the F–G–A–C–D type. As we have said, the total range covers two octaves and a second, which is unusually wide for this region. The part played by musician 2 can be seen to copy the part of musician 1 at the interval of an octave (with the exception of sporadic divergence on the fourth pulsation). Melodically speaking (and hence, in terms of vertical combinations), the piece has only two component parts. The two copied parts have therefore been eliminated from the representation in ex. 9 of the sequence of con-sonances in the instrumental formula.

We have numbered vertical combinations so that they and their concatenations will be easier to recognise. This numbering system must not, of course, be confused with classical harmonic notation. The number beneath each combination thus indicates only the kind of interval(s) it includes:

2   indicates a second (always major)
3M   indicates a major third
3m   indicates a minor third
4   indicates a fourth
5   indicates a fifth
6M   indicates a major sixth
6m   indicates a minor sixth
7   indicates a seventh (always minor)
8   indicates an octave.

Intervals exceeding an octave are indicated by the number designating their true nature, followed by an indication of the real interval in parentheses. A ninth, for example, will be marked 2 (9).

Combinations of two or more intervals are indicated by superposed figures. A fourth surmounted by a ninth will thus be written as in ex. 8:

Ex. 8

The numbers which appear *above* the staffs indicate the pulsations, which are separated by vertical lines. The exact position of any vertical combination, or chord, in the period can thereby be precisely determined.

The con-sonances in this piece are represented in ex. 9 (the divergency on the fourth pulsation appears in brackets on a separate staff).

Ex. 9

The vertical organisation of the formula is comprised of fifths, fourths, and a major third. Given the absence of melodic variations (outside of the one divergency already mentioned), this representation may reasonably be taken to constitute the model for the piece, insofar as vertical combinations are concerned. Since there are no regular concatenations to which we might apply the principle of repetition, we may take it to be the maximal and minimal statement, in 'harmonic' terms, of the content of the piece.

The principle of repetition can, however, be applied to the rhythmic structure. Here we note that the durations are distributed in practically the same way in the first and fifth pulsations, and again in the fourth and eighth pulsations, in the parts of all four hands. The recurrence of similar rhythmic events at different positions enables us to divide the rhythmic formula into two symmetric units, A and B, each of which is defined by its beginning and end. These units cover pulsations 1 to 4 and 5 to 8, respectively. The accuracy of this segmentation, based on all the parts, is supported by the fact that the rhythmic figure performed by each of the two lefthand parts on pulsations 5 to 8 is an exact repetition of what they play on pulsations 1 to 4.

Let us now look at an inventory of the variations in each part, i.e., for each of the four hands separately. These inventories appear in paradigmatic representation in exx. 10–11. (The reader should remember that the number preceding each variation indicates the *first* occurrence of that variation in the score.)

Ex. 10 Musician 1

Right hand

Ex. 10 (cont.)

Left hand

Ex. 11 Musician 2

Right hand

Left hand

We can see from these inventories:

> (1) that certain positions in the cycle are more subject to variation than others
> (2) that the degree of variation is considerably higher in the righthand than in the lefthand parts
> (3) that these variations are practically all rhythmic in nature.

How are variations produced? We have already said that, when instrumental formulae are subject to variation, their realisations result from a process of *centonisation* yielding a concatenation of a variable number of micro-elements. This observation requires some clarification. The inventories of the variations in each part clearly show that several positions within the mould of the instrumental formula are *substitution points*, since the elements appearing there can commute with one another. This means that any element in a given position can be juxtaposed to any element in a neighbouring one. This is true of every component part in every piece. The centonisation technique accordingly gives rise to an extremely large number of different combinations, and considerably multiplies the overall possibilities of diversifying music based on the periodic repetition of similar material.

In both the piece transcribed in ex. 7 and all subsequent pieces, we treat the *content of each pulsation*, i.e., all the events occurring in the interval between the start of one pulsation and the start of the next, as a substitution point. There is a certain amount of arbitrariness in this decision, for some commutations involve only a portion of a pulsation, while others overlap into the following one. This is why it is important to stress that our only purpose is to give the clearest possible description of how the process of centonisation works in practice. Let us also recall that a substitution point is not a syntactic unit. We have already seen that the minimal statement in the Zande piece in ex. 7 covers four pulsations.

The ways in which the principle of commutation applies will be represented in table form, with each table illustrating the potentialities of a given part in the piece in this regard. These tables should not, however, be taken as an exhaustive catalogue of possible substitutions and concatenations. We will see later that the number of commutable elements at any substitution point is usually proportional to the number of versions we have recorded of the same piece.

In the tables below, each substitution point has a number above it which corresponds to the order of the pulsations in the period. The substitution points are furthermore separated by spaces, and their contents are arranged quincuncially so that the possible concatentations can be more easily visualised. The terms of these microparadigms are designated by two numbers: the first refers to the position they occupy, and the second to their order in the inventory for this position.

The table of possible commutations in the righthand part of musician 1 is shown in ex. 12.

Ex. 12

According to what we have just said, the musician could produce realisations which are not found in our version, by simply recombining the elements appearing in ex. 12, for he is entirely free at all times in his choice of the element which is to appear in the next substitution point (only positions 1 and 7 in this part allow no commutation). The realisation could thus just as well be 1.1/2.2/3.1/4.1/5.2/6.1/7.1/8.1 as 1.1/2.1/3.2/4.2/5.1/6.2/7.1/8.2 or any one of many more.

The substitution points where some elements overlap the pulsation, i.e., which involve tying together two or more pulsations, are presented in schematic form below the tables for the parts where the overlapping takes place. Since we are dealing with *rhythmic* commutations alone, only the sequence of durational values is shown (the numbers above the configurations indicate their position in the period).

The inventory of *ties* in the righthand part of musician 1 is shown in ex. 13.

Ex. 13

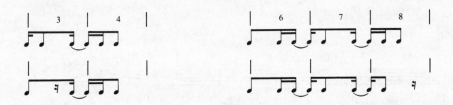

When there is no commutation in any of several juxtaposed pulsations, or when a commutation systematically affects two or more neighbouring pulsations, no space is left between them. Both of these situations occur in the lefthand part of musician 1 (positions 1 to 5 are in the first case, and 7 and 8 in the second).

The table of commutations for this part is shown in ex. 14, and the ties are given in ex. 15.

Ex. 14

Ex. 15

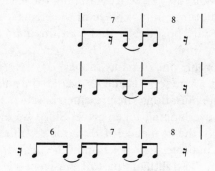

Positions 1 to 3, and 5, in the righthand part of musician 2 do not allow commutation in our version (see ex. 16).

Ex. 16

The ties in this part affect positions 3-4, 7-8, and 6-7-8, as shown in ex. 17.

Ex. 17

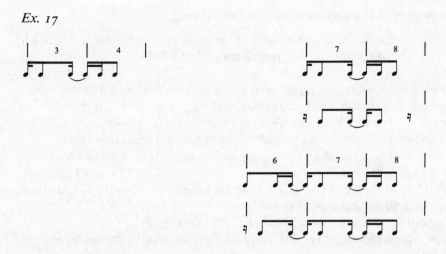

The lefthand part contains only a single substitution point, on the seventh pulsation (see ex. 18), and two possible ties, on pulsations 7–8, as in ex. 19.

Ex. 18

Ex. 19

5.2.2   The portable xylophone with multiple resonators

In this sort of instrument, the keyboard and the resonators are attached to a wooden frame. This frame is comprised of two crosspieces held in parallel position by a strong arched branch.

The keys (the number of which varies from group to group) are tied perpendicularly to the crosspieces. A gourd is attached beneath each key to act as a resonator. Its size is carefully calculated to match the dimensions of the key. A small hole is cut in the side of the resonators and covered with a thin membrane to obtain a *mirliton* effect.

The portable xylophone is held in playing position by a strap running around the musician's neck. It is attached to the ends of the crosspiece farthest from his body. He rests the middle of the curved branch against his stomach, so that the slightly tilted keyboard will be held far enough away for him to play it comfortably. The keys are struck with wooden sticks fitted with a ball of rubber at the end.

We will now discuss the music for one, and then for two portable xylophones.

5.2.2.1   *Music for one portable xylophone*

To illustrate this music, we will take three pieces from a choreographic repertory employed by the Sabanga people, and a Banda-Linda piece connected with twin worship (*Āméyā*). We may recall that the latter has been adapted for the Linda horn orchestra, in a version which has already been subjected to a detailed analysis in the preceding chapter on instrumental hocket. We will now examine the xylophone version of the same piece.

The Banda-Linda *kálángbá* and the Sabanga *mānzā* are like the portable xylophones of many other ethnic groups in having ten keys which in theory comprise a double pentatonic system. Unlike the pit xylophone, where the pitch levels are regularly ordered on the keyboard, the keys for each octave interval are paired up. Practically speaking, the ten-key xylophone works as if it were using a single pentatonic scale, with degrees composed of octave intervals. This interpretation is supported by both the playing technique and the keyboard layout (shown in ex. 20). The musician thus holds *two sticks* in each hand, and strikes the pairs of neighbouring keys simultaneously. This naturally reinforces the sonority of the individual keys.

Ex. 20

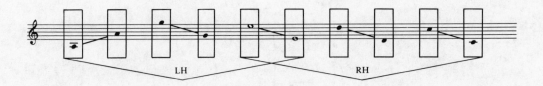

The keyboard is divided equally between the two hands, and the double key in the middle is struck alternately by each. We can see from ex. 20 that the keys are so arranged that the lowest sound is at the far left of the keyboard, next to the highest sound, and that from there on, the sounds are arranged in descending order towards the right.

This arrangement may look strange at first, but is in fact intended to economise hand movements over the keyboard. This feature is common to all the portable xylophones in the region, whatever the number of keys.

The first part of the score for *Āméyā* is shown in ex. 22. Since all the degrees on the scale are double, we have omitted the upper octave from our transcription for the sake of greater simplicity.

This piece is based on the repetition of a period containing six pulsations (noted as quavers). The subdivision is binary, and the minimal operational value is the semiquaver.

The pentatonic scale is of the A–C–D–E–G type. The real range (i.e., excluding the second octave) covers a seventh.

There are several variations in the sequence of vertical combinations. The most frequent intervals and concatenations are shown on the top staff in ex. 21. The variations appear in brackets on the lower staffs. The con-sonances which are not subject to commutation are noted as semibreves.

Ex. 21

Ex. 22 Āméyā

Ex. 22 (cont.)

Fourths and fifths are the predominant combinations, but con-sonances of thirds, and occasionally a second, may be inserted.

On the basis of the recurrence of the concatenation in ex. 23 and the concomitant

Ex. 23

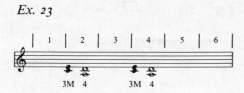

rhythmic figure, shown in ex. 24, the instrumental formula can be divided into two

Ex. 24

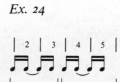

segments of unequal length, represented in ex. 25.

Ex. 25

Segmentation into such brief units is not, however, likely to be significant. We will therefore take ex. 25 to be both the minimal and the maximal statement of the formula for this piece.

The variations in ex. 22 are inventoried in ex. 26.

Ex. 26
Right hand

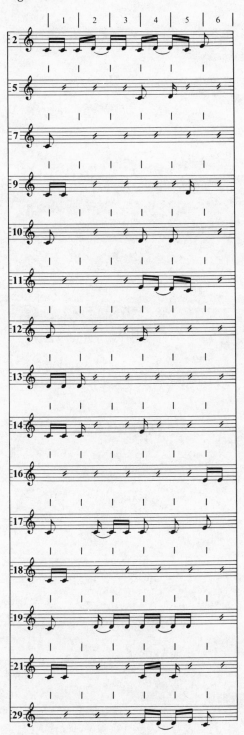

Left hand

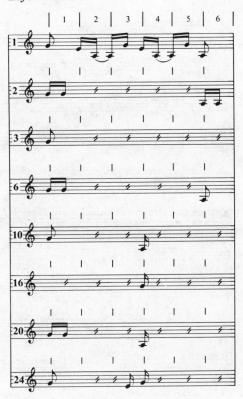

A comparison of the inventories in ex. 26 shows that the righthand part has a much higher degree of variation. The same conclusion may be drawn from the table of commutations in ex. 27.

Ex. 27

Right hand

Left hand

Ties which connect commutable elements in neighbouring pulsations are found in the same positions for each hand, see ex. 28.

Ex. 28

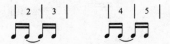

The Sabanga xylophone (*mānzā*) is exactly like the Linda *kálángbá* with the exception of the arrangement of the intervals. The keyboard layout and the way the keys are assigned to the musician's hands are shown in ex. 29.

Ex. 29

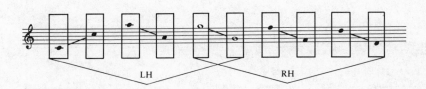

The real range of the instrument is a major sixth. Sabanga xylophone music will now be illustrated by three pieces from the *ngbàkè* dance repertory. All were performed by the same musician.

The beginning of the first of these pieces, *Yáʃēmálè* ('Initiated woman'), is shown in ex. 30. This piece has a period of six pulsations with binary subdivision, making the semiquaver the minimal operational value. The pentatonic scale is of the C–D–F–G–A type. The concatenation of vertical combinations is quite stable and shows no variation whatsoever.

Ex. 30 Yāfēmálè

Ex. 30 (cont.)

Ex. 30 (cont.)

Ex. 30 (cont.)

The realisation shown in ex. 31 is therefore the materialisation of the model in this

Ex. 31

respect. This model is essentially based on a sequence of fifths and fourths. The changes in con-sonance occur according to a regular rhythmic pattern of three repetitions of two quavers and a crotchet. There are thus grounds for segmenting the formula into three units, each comprised of two pulsations: 1–2/3–4/5–6. Since there is no melodic variation, the only variations in this version arise from changes in durations, as the inventory for the two parts in ex. 32 shows.

Ex. 32

Right hand

Ex. 32 (cont.)

Left hand

The tables of commutations in ex. 33 show us the rhythmic resources of each part.

Ex. 33
Right hand

Left hand

The second piece in this repertory is called *Āgōā* ('Buffalo'). We have recorded two very similar versions; the beginning of one of them is shown in ex. 34.

Ex. 34 Āgōā

Ex. 34 (cont.)

Ex. 34 (cont.)

Ex. 34 (cont.)

The period in this piece contains four pulsations. The subdivision of the pulsation is binary, as in the case of *Yáſēmálè*, and the semiquaver is the minimal operational value. This piece has a peculiar characteristic. The left hand plays a figure which remains essentially unchanged, although enriched with numerous variations; but the right hand makes use of two different motifs of equal length, which alternate freely and unpredictably. The first motif is thus used from the beginning of the transcription in ex. 34 up to and including the sixth repetition of the formula. It is then replaced by the second motif from the seventh to the fifteenth, and again from the twenty-fifth to the thirty-second repetition. We must thus provide two schematic representations (in ex. 35) of the con-sonances, one for each of these motifs. For easier comparison, we place them one above the other. The con-sonances which are the same in both versions are noted as semibreves.

Ex. 35

These schemes are repeated in ex. 36 with their variations, of which the first contains only one. It should be noted that only one of the sounds in each variation differs with respect to the vertical combinations represented in the scheme itself.

Ex. 36

Ex. 36 (cont.)

Second scheme

The motif for the right hand involves repeating the same figure twice, as shown in ex. 37. At the beginning of the piece, each of these repetitions is set against a different

Ex. 37

left hand configuration, as in ex. 38. Thereafter, from the fifteenth occurrence of the

Ex. 38

formula on, the second configuration replaces the first, and is repeated in the same way to produce the realisation in ex. 39. The formula for this piece can thus be segmented into two symmetric units on the basis of the articulation of the lefthand part.

Ex. 39

Let us now examine the inventory of variations in each part, as shown in ex. 40. The inventory for the righthand part contains two paradigms, one for the first motif and one for the second. Each paradigm is furthermore divided into two parts: the upper part shows the variations in the version transcribed in ex. 34, while the lower one shows those *additional* variations which are to be observed in the second version.

Ex. 40

Right hand

Motif 1

Motif 2

Ex. 40 (cont.)

The tables of commutations include the variations observed in both versions. Two tables are required for the right hand, and one for each motif (exx. 41 and 42). Ex. 42

Ex. 41 Right hand: motif 1

shows that the two elements comprising the second righthand motif, ▚▚▚ and ▚▚ , can appear equally well in any position. This means that they are concatenated in a perfectly indeterminate way. The inventory of rhythmic ties for the left hand alone is shown in ex. 44.

Ex. 42 Right hand: motif 2

Ex. 43 Left hand

Ex. 44

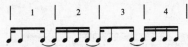

The last piece we will examine from the *ngbàkè* repertory is called *Bàdá* ('Squirrel'). We have three different versions of this piece. We give the first part of our transcriptions of each of them in exx. 45–7.

The second version is performed without the slightest variation. It will therefore suffice to present only the first few occurrences of the instrumental formula in ex. 46.

Ex. 45 Version 1

Ex. 45 (cont.)

Ex. 45 (cont.)

Ex. 46 Version 2

The first page of our transcription of the third version is shown in ex. 47.

Ex. 47 Version 3

Ex. 47 (cont.)

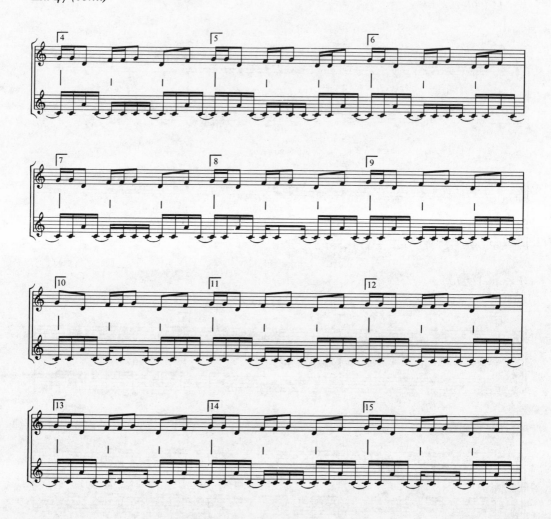

Bàdá makes use of a periodicity of three pulsations. A binary subdivision is used, as in *Yāfēmálè* and *Āgōā*, so that the minimal operational value is the semiquaver. The scale is of the C–D–F–G–A type. Generally speaking, the sequence of con-sonances is identical in all three versions. There is only one variation, which is found in the first version. The schematic representations for the three versions are shown in ex. 48.

Ex. 48

Version 1

Ex. 48 (cont.)

Version 2

Version 3

The three versions are merged in ex. 49.

Ex. 49

We can see in ex. 50 that the same concatenation of vertical combinations is repeated twice:

Ex. 50

The position of the second repetition is, however, metrically offset with respect to the first. This divergency is clear from the distribution of the durations (all of equal value), creating ambiguity in rhythmic perception. With no beats or accents, the formula in ex. 51 could just as well be perceived as in ex. 52.

Ex. 51

Ex. 52

This is precisely what we might call 'hemiolic ambiguity'.

We can see from comparing the three versions that there are more variations in the lefthand than in the righthand part. We also note that the musician favours one particular figure for the realisation of the lefthand part in each version. Thus, once the figure is firmly established in the first version, from the fourth occurrence on, it can practically be described as a drone of quavers on C, as in ex. 53. In the second version,

Ex. 53

each group of two quavers is partially split and converted into a strict *ostinato*, which is repeated in the same form throughout the realisation (ex. 54). In the third and final

Ex. 54

version, the values are offset, and there is systematic overlapping of the pulsation. The resulting anticipations and suspensions cause a perpetual rhythmic interweaving of the two parts (ex. 55).

Ex. 55

We now turn to the inventory of variations. There is only one additional variation in the second version with respect to the first for the righthand part, and none in the third (ex. 56).

Ex. 56 Right hand

The lefthand part, shown in ex. 57, displays great diversity in the organisation of its durations, and provides an eloquent example of how many rhythmic variations can be produced within a quite limited periodic framework, by making use of nothing more than a binary subdivision of the pulsation. The second version contains only one variation, and the third, two.

Ex. 57 Left hand
Version 1

Version 2

Version 3

When we count the variations which appear in several versions of the same piece, we quickly reject the idea that they may be unlimited in number. On the contrary, it becomes clear that there is a sort of stock of limited size. The impression of diversity that we get when we listen to this music can be attributed far more to the possibilities of the commutation technique, which creates a wealth of different combinations from a set of micro-elements, than to the number of variations itself.

The tables of the commutations observed in *Bàdá* are shown in exx. 58 and 59. The elements from all three versions are combined:

Ex. 58 Right hand

The lefthand part allows no less than fourteen variations on the first pulsation, nine on the second, and ten on the last.

Ex. 59 Left hand

In this piece too, the only ties (listed in ex. 60) are in the lefthand part.

Ex. 60

5.2.2.2   *Music for two portable xylophones*

The music for two xylophones will be illustrated by two pieces from the Banda-Dakpa *gàzà* dance repertory, which is associated with their male initiation rites. There are no particular differences in the polyphonic techniques employed in music for two, as compared with music for a single xylophone. We do, however, find a somewhat wider range, extending to a full octave, and a denser texture, resulting from the production of chords containing three or four sounds, whereas a single instrument can only produce two. The Dakpa xylophone has five keys, which the musician strikes with a stick in each hand.

The registers of the two *kálángbá*, rather than being exact copies at octave intervals, are offset by one degree on their common pentatonic scale.

The keys of the first and higher-pitched of the two xylophones (*àkɔ́.kálángbá* 'husband xylophone') thus play F-G-A-C-D, while those of the second and lower-pitched (*èyī.kálángbá* 'mother xylophone') play D-F-G-A-C. The instruments thus have four sounds in common, and a fifth which is different, viz., the one which completes the octave (low D and high D). The keys are arranged in the same way as in portable xylophones for individual use. The lowest sound is always on the far left, and the highest immediately to its right. The remaining three are then placed in regularly descending order. The assignment of keys to the musician's hands also remains unchanged. The middle key is always struck alternately.

The keyboard of the first xylophone is represented in ex. 61. It has a range of a sixth. The keyboard of the second, shown in ex. 62, covers a seventh.

Ex. 61

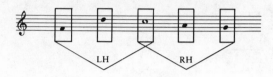

Ex. 62

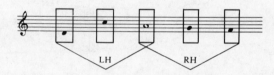

The structural features underlying the two pieces we are about to analyse are quite identical in all respects: temporal organisation, arrangement of rhythmic figures, and concatenation of chords. For easier comparison, we will present the opening pages of our transcriptions of both pieces together.

The first is called *Bāmàrā gàzà* ('*Gàzà* lion'), and is shown in ex. 63.

Ex. 63: Bāmàrā gàzà ('*Gaza* Lion')

Ex. 63 (cont.)

Ex. 63 (cont.)

Ex. 63 (cont.)

The second piece in this repertory is called *Āyá.mə̄, mə̄ wú òyò* and is shown in ex. 64.

Ex. 64 Āyá.mə̄, mə̄ wú òyò (My brothers, I suffer)

Ex. 64 (cont.)

Ex. 64 (cont.)

Ex. 64 (cont.)

An examination of exx. 63 and 64 will prompt the following observations: both pieces have a period of six pulsations. The subdivision of the odd pulsations (1, 3, and 5) is binary, but the even pulsations (2, 4, and 6) make systematic use of two dotted semiquavers (each equivalent to three demisemiquavers) and a semiquaver. The rhythmic structure of the even pulsations is thus based on the juxtaposition of two ternary values and one binary value (3 + 3 + 2), except in the first piece, where these values are sometimes permuted in the righthand part of the first xylophonist into a 3 + 2 + 3 order. Whatever the order of concatenation, however, the sum of these values (eight) is divisible into neither two nor three equal parts. Consequently, these pieces display a regular rhythmic alternation of a pulsation whose content can be subdivided into equal durations, with another whose content cannot. The rhythmic structure of the formulae for these two pieces thus consists of a threefold repetition of the figure shown in ex. 65:

Ex. 65

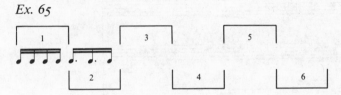

This arrangement is quite stable, so that variations affect pitch more than rhythm, as the inventories of variations for each hand, presented in exx. 66–73, show.

Ex. 66 Piece 1

Ex. 66 (cont.)

Ex. 66 (cont.)

Xylophone 2

Right hand

Ex. 66 (cont.)

Left hand

Ex. 67 Piece 2

Ex. 67 (cont.)

Xylophone 2

Right hand

Ex. 67 (cont.)

Left hand

One can see from these inventories that the rhythm is almost perfectly stable on the second, fourth, and last pulsations in the formula. The tables of commutations are presented in exx. 68 and 69.

Ex. 68

Xylophone 2

Right hand

Left hand

Ex. 69 Piece 2

Xylophone 1

Right hand

Left hand

Ex. 69 (cont.)

Right hand

Xylophone 2

Ex. 69 (cont.)

Left hand

It can be seen that the *melodic* character of the variations in these two pieces is more pronounced than in the preceding examples, particularly in the lefthand parts of the second xylophonist. These pitch changes result in a large variety of vertical combinations in identical positions. Some of these include as many as four of the five sounds making up the scale, in sorts of 'harmonic clusters'. On the other hand, a small number of other positions display consonances and chords of *invariant* groups of two or three sounds to which no other sound can be added. These positions are therefore the reference points in the vertical structure of these pieces, and are indicated in ex. 70 by the use of square notes.

Ex. 70

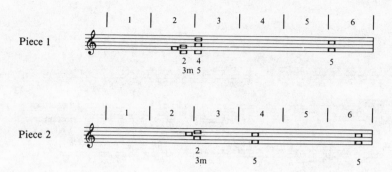

In the other chords, a distinction must be made between those sounds which appear in every one of the realisations (indicated by rhombic notes), and those which are frequently, but not always, present (indicated by semibreves). The schematic representations in ex. 71 thus show which constituents of the vertical combinations are stable in these two pieces. These stable sounds are quite likely to be included in the real 'harmonic' models.

Ex. 71

It is easy to see how the two representations in ex. 71 differ with respect to both the content of the chords and their positions within the cycle (which is of identical length, and moreover, is rhythmically segmented in the same way). From the instrumental standpoint alone (i.e., without regard to the melody of the song which is associated with these formulae), the two pieces can be distinguished on the combined basis of these two features (the essential constituents of the chords, and the positions in which the chords appear).

Let us now see how variations are brought about by examining a few of them in exx. 72 and 73. We place the boxed schematic representation of each piece in the middle, for easier reading.

Ex. 72

Piece 1

Ex. 72 (cont.)

We can see that variations are created in two ways: (1) Additional sounds (notes as crotchets) may be conjoined to any of the chords except those with square notes. This happens in both pieces. (2) *Different* con-sonances and/or chords may be inserted in the predetermined rhythmic figure, in place of those which would be *repetitions of the preceding vertical combination.*

We can construct the formulae in ex. 73 for these pieces, on the basis of the frequency

Ex. 73

of the various chords and their concatenations. These formulae, which should not be confused with models insofar as they have not been materialised as such by the traditional musicians themselves, represent what we might call a standard realisation of each piece.

5.3   THE *SANZA*

The *sanza* is an invention peculiar to Africa, and is certainly the most widely used instrument in all the Subsaharan part of the continent. It consists of a set of plucked lamellae.

We will be discussing the *sanza* music of the Gbaya people, taken from a repertory for private performance containing a melancholy sort of songs called *gìmá tà-mɔ̀*, literally 'thinking songs'. These are played and sung by the same musician.

The Gbaya instrument resembles the ones used by many other ethnic groups in the Central African Republic. It consists of a set of metal lamellae of unequal length, each producing a different sound. The number of these lamellae will vary considerably from one musician to another. The lamellae are attached to a trapezoidal wooden box resonator with a sound hole, by means of two crosspieces which act as bridges. The flexible end of the lamellae is slightly raised, and can be set in vibration by the thumbs. The other fingers are used to hold the instrument. To obtain increased sonority, the musician may place his instrument within a hollow hemispherical gourd which acts as an amplifier. This accessory is kept in place by a strap around the musician's neck. The first two pieces we will discuss are played on a seven-lamella instrument, and the third on an eleven-lamella instrument.

In an important work on this repertory, Vincent Dehoux (1986) has recently shown that 'thinking songs' are divided into two 'families', *Nàá Yàngà* ('mother of Yanga') and *Piéré* (from the French name, Pierre), which may be distinguished on the basis of their temporal organisation. All 'thinking songs' are based on a period of eight pulsations. In the *Nàá Yàngà* 'family', each pulsation receives a *ternary* subdivision into minimal operational values, while in the *Piéré* 'family', the subdivision is *binary*. As a result, the songs in the *Nàá Yàngà* category have twenty-four minimal values, and those in *Piéré* (where each pulsation is divided in four) have thirty-two. In the same way, the two rhythm sticks (*gàdà*) used to support this repertory have two different figures, each of which is intrinsically connected with the temporal structure of one of the 'families'. We thus have a fine example of a cultural classification which, though expressed in metaphorical terms, rests on purely musical criteria, viz., *the metric and rhythmic organisation of the pieces*. Dehoux's 1986 work will enable us to see the relationships between realisations and models in this repertory, at several levels.

The first two pieces we will discuss belong to the *Nàá Yàngà* category. This is in fact the title of the first, from which the 'family' takes its name. The second is called '*Sàlò*' ('The single man').

The layout of the seven-lamella sanza on which these pieces were performed is shown in ex. 74. Several remarks are required on this example. (1) The range (a ninth) is considerably wider than the range of portable xylophones. The number of possible vertical combinations is therefore much greater (twelve instead of eight). (2) Unlike the xylophones, where the middle key is struck alternately by the musician's right and left

Ex. 74

hands, no *sanza* lamella is common to both thumbs. The right thumb plucks four, and the left thumb three. (3) The way the degrees of the scale are distributed on the keyboard is quite different from the distributions for the pit and portable xylophones, and is surprising at first sight. In fact, as in the preceding cases, the arrangement is economical in that it keeps the distance of thumb movements to a minimum. The most frequently played lamellae are thus grouped around the medial axis of the keyboard.

We have recorded two versions of *Nàá Yàngà*, both by the same musician. The beginning of the first of these is shown in ex. 75. The scale for this piece is of the

Ex. 75 Nàá Yàngà

Ex. 75 (cont.)

Ex. 75 (cont.)

C–D–E–G–A type. The range is a ninth, as we have said. The octave, followed by the fourth and the third, appears as the most frequent vertical combination. Sporadic seconds and minor sevenths appear in the variations. There is, however, not a single fifth. The stable positions are indicated by semibreves in ex. 76.

Ex. 76

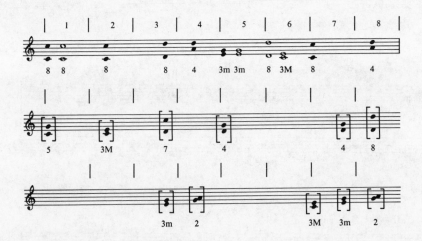

The formula for *Nàá Yàngà* can be divided into two symmetric units, A and B, which include pulsations 1–4 and 5–8, respectively. This division is based on the application of the principle of repetition to *metre*, *rhythm*, and *melody*, as all three parametres are convergent.

Metre: All the attacks in the parts for both hands are offbeat, with the exception of the first and the fifth pulsations.

Rhythm: Each segment nearly always ends with the same configuration in both parts (♪♪♩); in the other positions, the rhythms tend to be interwoven.

Melody: Segments A and B for the left thumb differ only in their initial sound.

These two segments are thus discrete units, as is evident when they are shown paradigmatically in ex. 77. The distinguishing note is shown as a minim. The instrumental formula for *Nàá Yàngà* may thus be segmented as in ex. 78.

Ex. 77

Ex. 78

The inventory of variations in ex. 79 includes those observed in both of our recorded versions. It shows that (1) the right hand has many more variations than the left, (2) the number of variations is considerably increased by the inclusion of the second version, unlike what we observed in the case of the xylophones and (3) the variations are essentially rhythmic in nature.

Ex. 79

Ex. 79 (cont.)

The table of commutations, including the variations appearing in the second version, is shown in ex. 80. There is a huge inventory of rhythmic ties (ex. 81). This is a result of the contrametric nature of the piece, to which we will shortly return.

Ex. 80

Right hand

Left hand

Ex. 81

Right hand

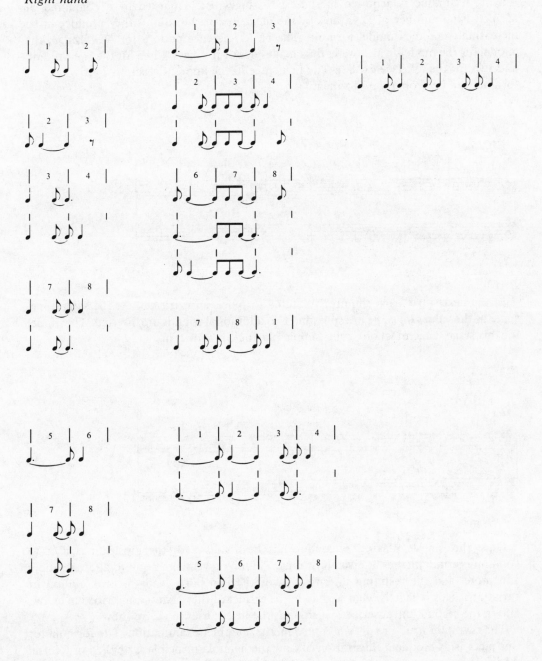

Vincent Dehoux's (1986) work on 'thinking songs' shows us that the notion of model in this repertory is intimately connected with the process of learning to play the *sanza*. Playing technique is acquired in successive stages, each marked by a command of an increasing number of keys, and by the inclusion of the sounds they produce in an increasingly complex model formula. The basic reference pattern for *Nàá Yàngà*, the 'model for the models', as it were, thus makes use of five keys, three for the right thumb and two for the left (see ex. 82). The first stage in the apprenticeship is over when this formula can be properly performed.

Ex. 82

In the next stage, each thumb is required to pluck an extra key. At the same time, some of the values in ex. 82 are split, and two additional sounds are inserted. The model for this stage, which Dehoux calls 'simple playing', is shown in ex. 83.

Ex. 83

Once the 'simple playing' technique has been mastered, the musician is able to commute certain pitches at given positions. Thumb movements begin to alternate more and more, and the resulting interweaving of the two parts leads to proliferation of variations. This is exactly what we find in the extract of the version transcribed in ex. 75, and in the second untranscribed version, as the inventories in ex. 79 show.

The rhythmic structure of *Nàá Yàngà* merits lengthier examination. The formula for this piece is an eloquent illustration of how the hemiola principle is applied in Central Africa. Let us return to the minimal formula, or *pattern*, for this piece – see ex. 82. If we replace our notation of the metric organisation with a rhythmic notation (which symbolises the duration of each sound by a single sign), we can rewrite ex. 82 as ex. 84. This type of representation shows that the formula is based on six equal dura-

Ex. 84

tions, each composed of four operational values, which means the total can be divided by two or by four. The *rhythmic structure* of the piece is thus basically *binary*. This can easily be seen when the lefthand realisations are examined individually. The *metric organisation* (eight pulsations subdivided into three minimal values) is, however, unquestionably *ternary*. The two are thus in a ratio of 6:8 (or 3:4). This is one of the ratios characteristic of *vertical* hemiola as it appears in many types of Central African music.

Let us now examine the second piece from the repertory of 'thinking songs'. It is called *Sàlò* ('The single man') and belongs, like the preceding one, to the *Nàá Yàngà* category. Again, we have two versions; the beginning of the first is transcribed in ex. 85.

Ex. 85 Sàlò

Ex. 85 (cont.)

Ex. 85 (cont.)

The periodicity, the way the pulsation is subdivided, the pentatonic scale, and the range are, of course, identical to those of the preceding piece. The vertical frame is composed essentially of fourths and octaves, with some ninths, sevenths, and seconds inserted. A minor third is also found in the variations. There are no fifths, just as in *Nàá Yàngà*. The most frequent concatenations, and the main variations are schematically represented in ex. 86.

Ex. 86

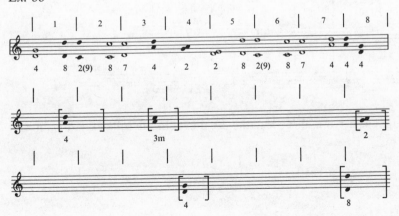

Unlike most of the pieces for polyphonic instruments we have examined so far, some concatenations of vertical combinations are repeated in *Sàlò*. The paradigmatic representation in ex. 87 shows the recurrent con-sonances (notated as semibreves).

Ex. 87

The schematic representation of combinations is thus symmetrically structured, particularly in view of the fact that the D–G interval on the eighth pulsation often commutes with G–A. From the rhythmic standpoint, the formula can be shown to be divisible into two units, A and B, covering pulsations 1–4 and 5–8, respectively, by the repetition in the righthand part of a four-pulsation cell (ex. 88). The same is true of the lefthand

Ex. 88

figure when it is not broken by rests. Moreover, the same rhythmic cell generally takes on the same melodic configuration.

The two lefthand segments are paradigmatically represented (with B under A) in ex. 89, in two forms: all sounds are present in the realisation on the left, but the D appearing in the first and fifth pulsations is replaced by a rest on the right.

Ex. 89

This piece therefore has a symmetric structure, as shown in the following diagram:

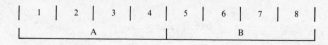

The inventory of righthand variations in ex. 90 has two parts: the upper one shows the variations in the version partially transcribed in ex. 85; the lower one shows new variations observed in the second version. The latter contains no new variations of the lefthand part. The table of commutations is in ex. 91.

Ex. 90

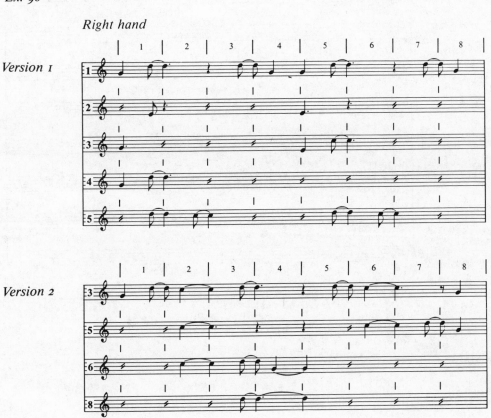

Ex. 90 (cont.)

Left hand

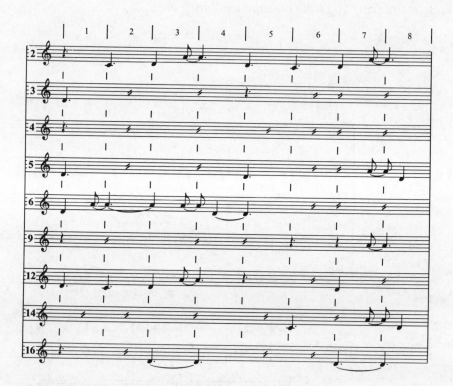

Ex. 91

Right hand

Left hand

There are many ties, just as in *Nàá Yàngà*. The inventory in ex. 92 shows that they may cover the entire period. As in *Nàá Yàngà*, this abundance may be attributed to

Ex. 92

Right hand

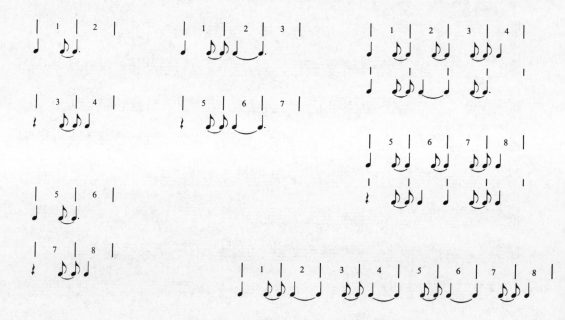

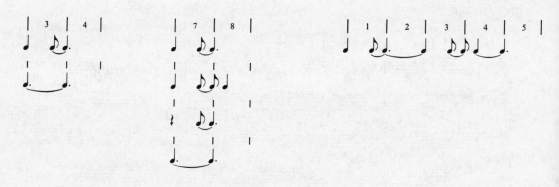

Left hand

the markedly contrametric way in which the durations are arranged. The minimal
formula providing the 'model for the models' of all realisations of this piece is shown
in ex. 93. We must recall that it is played on only five keys, three plucked by the right

Ex. 93

thumb, and two by the left. At the following stage of 'simple playing', each thumb
plucks an extra key (four for the right thumb and three for the left). Some durations are
split by the insertion of additional sounds, rests are invaded, and some righthand
attacks are offset, as the model in ex. 94 shows. When this stage has been reached,

Ex. 94

the apprentice musician starts to work on what the Gbaya call *dúbɔ̀léè* playing (from
the French *doublé*). 'Double playing' involves almost complete rhythmic interweaving,
so that the thumbs will never pluck two keys at the same time. There is no difference
between 'double playing' and 'simple playing' for the right hand. The interweaving effect
is obtained solely by offsetting some of the lefthand attacks. The 'double playing' model
for *Sàlò* is given in metric notation in ex. 95 and in rhythmic notation in ex. 96.

Ex. 95

Ex. 96

The final piece in this repertory is *Piéré*, from which the name of the second category is taken. We may recall that the latter is distinguished by employing a *binary* sub-division of its temporal reference unit. *Piéré* is played on a *sanza* with eleven lamellae. Their arrangement on the keyboard and assignment to the musician's thumbs are shown in ex. 97. The left thumb plucks six keys, and the right thumb five. The range of the instrument covers two octaves. The pentatonic scale is of the G–A–C–D–E type.

Ex. 97

A transcription of one realisation of *Piéré* appears in ex. 99. The formula for this piece can be segmented on the basis of the repetition of characteristic identical melodic and rhythmic configurations in the parts for each hand. For a *given* realisation of the formula, pulsations 1 to 3 and 4 to 6 in the lefthand part always contain the same material. The simplest representation is given in ex. 98. The first three pulsations can

Ex. 98

Ex. 99 Piéré

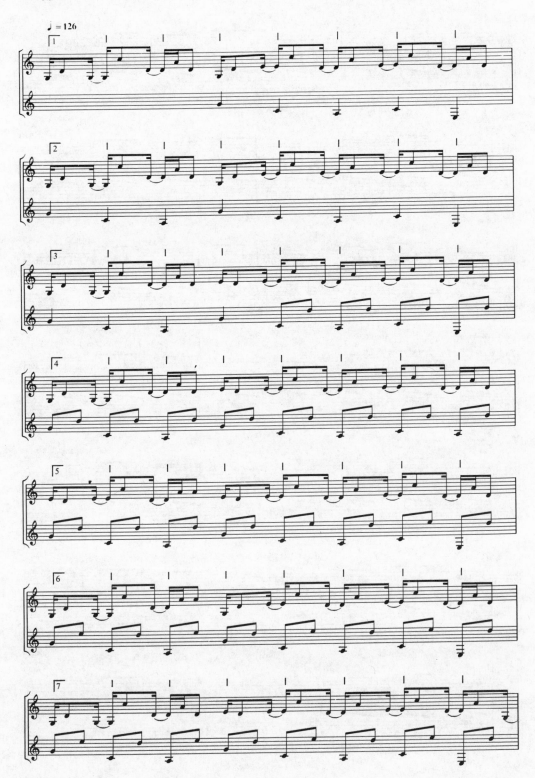

Ex. 99 (cont.)

Ex. 99 (cont.)

be treated as a unit on the basis of the way their contents resemble the material in pulsations 4, 5 and 6. It would then seem logical to treat the latter three as another unit, equivalent to the first three. But what will we do with the two pulsations left over? Should they be treated as a separate unit, and if so, on what basis? The answer is provided by the righthand part, where the beginnings of the first and fourth pulsations

are marked by the same sequence, 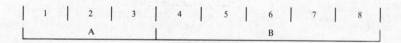, while the second and third pulsations,

like the seventh and eighth, are marked by the concatenation, . These

two features, at the beginning and the end of the segments indicate that the formula is based on two asymmetric units, one covering the first three pulsations, and the other the following five. The structure is then as shown in the following diagram:

	1	2	3	4	5	6	7	8	
	A				B				

The accuracy of this segmentation is confirmed by the fact that the only two points where both hands coincide (i.e., where both thumbs strike a key *simultaneously*) are located at the beginning of the first and the fourth pulsations. These two points are furthermore the only ones where the interval of an octave can appear. The asymmetric structure of this formula, with three pulsations on one side and five on the other, constitutes another example of the principle of contrast between external symmetry and internal asymmetry, applying the 'half − 1, half + 1' rule stated in Chapter 3 (on strict polyrhythmics). Here, however, the principle applies, not at the level of the grouping of minimal operational values, but at the level of the overall structure of the instrumental formula.

The inventory in ex. 100 shows more variations in the righthand than in the lefthand part, just as in the preceding pieces from the 'thinking song' repertory.

Ex. 100

Right hand

Ex. 100 (cont.)

Ex. 101 gives the table of commutations, and the inventory of ties in the two parts is given in ex. 102.

Ex. 101
Right hand

Left hand

The four types of ties in the righthand part (ex. 102) are very long; one of them covers

Ex. 102
Right hand

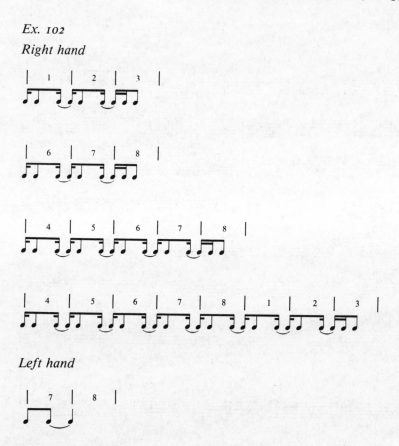

Left hand

the entire period. On the contrary, there is only one sporadically occurring tie for the left hand, involving just two pulsations. This is because the latter part is based on two kinds of values (notated ♩ and ♪) in a simple 2:1 ratio, which coincide with the pulsations and create a binary subdivision. The righthand part, however, works by *insertion*, and fills in the positions left 'empty' by the other hand. That is how the musician obtains rhythmic interweaving resulting in almost perpetual crossing of minimal operational values (exceptions are found in the second half of the third pulsation, and at times, in the same part of the eighth as well). This is shown in ex. 103, where the durations are notated separately and without stems, for the sake of clarity.

Ex. 103

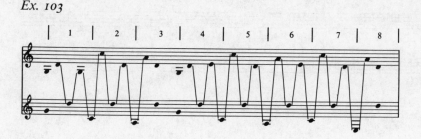

There are four stages in the apprenticeship to the eleven-key *sanza*, and the pieces have models of increasing difficulty at each one. The pattern for *Piéré* (i.e., the minimal formula by which the piece can be identified, and which lies at the base of both the other three models and all possible realisations) is materialised be seven keys, four for the left thumb and three for the right. Its rhythmic structure is perfectly commetric and extremely simple (see ex. 104).

Ex. 104

The vertical combinations, shown in ex. 105, consist of two octaves, two fourths, two major thirds, and a minor seventh.

Ex. 105

The lefthand part remains unaffected at the next stage, but the righthand part undergoes major changes. It adds two extra keys, whose sounds (A and C) are inserted on the offbeat, and at the same time, rhythmically offsets two of the three sounds (D and E) included in the pattern. The model for this type of 'simple playing' is shown in ex. 106.

Ex. 106

These changes create anticipations in the positions indicated by the heavy numbers in ex. 107.

Ex. 107

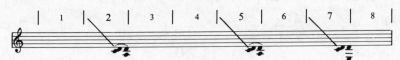

In the third stage, 'double playing', the righthand part is changed by the reduction of all the durations containing three minimal values to binary durations (pulsations 1, 3, and 8). The technique of anticipation initiated in the preceding stage thereby becomes systematic. When the high D key is added to the lefthand part, this sound can be inserted in the figure in regular alternation. The highest-pitched sound, D, thereby provides a pedal point (see ex. 108).

Ex. 108

At this stage, the right hand has reached its optimal level of production. The next and final stage of the learning process involves only the left hand. This part is now enriched by the addition of the eleventh key, which produces the high E. This E will henceforth replace the neighbouring D every other time. The regular alternation of these two keys produces a sort of ornamented pedal point in the higher register (see ex. 109). This

Ex. 109

ornamented pedal point is strictly interwoven with the melody in the lower register (but still produced by both hands), giving rise to the truly contrapuntal relationship shown in ex. 110.

Ex. 110

Each of the models described above is subject to variations, the diversity of which is, of course, proportional to the number of keys and rhythmic combinations available at each stage. Furthermore, the musician is free to switch from one style of playing to another as he gains mastery of the successive stages. This is, in fact, what the musician does in the version transcribed in ex. 99. During the first two repetitions of the formula and the first half of the third, his lefthand adheres to the pattern, while his right hand realises the model of the third stage ('double playing'), with some variations. Starting at the second half of the third occurrence of the formula, his left hand too refers to the 'double playing' model (with pedal point on D). Beginning at the sixth repetition, he moves to the model for the final stage (with ornamented D–E pedal point), then returns to the preceding stage at the ninth repetition, and again shifts to the most elaborate model at the thirteenth. We thus see not only how configurations of varying degrees of complexity can be juxtaposed and superposed, but also the wide variety of combinations made available to the musician by his freedom to realise the models for different levels simultaneously. All these techniques combine with the 'classic' kinds of variation to create remarkable diversity in an instrumental formula, the essence of which is the regular repetition of the same material.

Vincent Dehoux's (1986) discovery of the existence of several models of increasing difficulty for each piece in the repertory of 'thinking songs' is interesting from two points of view. It shows us that precise and coherent didactic principles underlie the process of learning to play a traditional instrument, and it provides an excellent example of how originally homophonic material can be progressively transformed into perfectly contrapuntal music.

5.4   THE HARP

Two kinds of harps are found in the Central African Republic. The most widespread type is called *kùndì* in many languages, and is a small arched instrument, generally with five strings (see Kubik 1964a). The other is more elaborate and is used only by the Ngbaka people. It is a large arched ten-string harp called *ngòmbí*, and it is the one we will be discussing here.

This instrument is composed of a boat-shaped body cut from a tree trunk and covered with an animal skin, which is stretched tight and tied securely. It has two holes to form the soundboard. The body often has a sculpted knob at the top, resembling a human head. A slightly arched wooden neck forms an angle of about 120° with the soundboard. The strings are parallel and of unequal length. They are stretched obliquely between the body and the neck, where they are fixed by pegs which are used to adjust tension. These strings used to be made of plant fibres, but are now generally nylon.

The musician plays in a seated position and holds the instrument vertically. Its bottom rests lightly against his right arm and leg. The highest-pitched strings, which are closest to his body, are plucked by his right hand, and the lowest-pitched ones by his left. The degrees of the scale are laid out in regular order from the highest- to the lowest-pitched. The *ngòmbí* has a double pentatonic scale of the G–A–B–D–E type. The range of the instrument covers an octave and a major sixth. The diagram in ex. 111 shows how the strings are assigned to the musician's hands.

Ex. 111

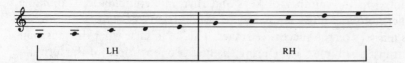

The repertory of *sī-bè-ngòmbí*, 'ngòmbí songs', will be illustrated by the instrumental formulae for three pieces. Unlike xylophone and *sanza* music, the degree of variation in *ngòmbí* music is almost nil. The repetitions of the instrumental formula in a given performance are thus nothing but materialisations of its model.

The first piece in this repertory, *Zè zè zè kūlū.sè* 'Spirit of the ancestors', is associated with ancestor worship. It can be played in either of two different and mutually exclusive styles, neither of which allows variation. The simplest form of this piece (and its model) is shown in ex. 112. We may note the simplicity of vertical organisation and

Ex. 112

the homophonic nature of this formula. The right hand expresses sequentially what the left hand plays simultaneously, i.e., the former breaks up the vertical combinations of the latter, and reproduces them on the melodic axis.

This formula is based on a period of eight pulsations with ternary subdivision.

The characteristic con-sonances are fifths, fourths, and octaves, as shown in ex. 113.

Ex. 113

Let us now look at the second way of realising the formula, shown in ex. 114. We can

Ex. 114

see that there is no change in the lefthand part with respect to the model in ex. 112. Furthermore, the change which occurs in the righthand part affects neither the pitches nor, strictly speaking, the rhythm. It is in fact of a *metric* nature, and consists of systematically delaying the durations of all sounds by one minimal value ($\flat$). This is clear from the comparison of the rhythmic notation of this part (form 2 in ex. 115) with its

Ex. 115

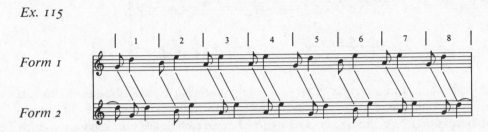

model (form 1). This metric offsetting gives rise to constant rhythmic interweaving and perpetual crisscrossing of the two parts, as they no longer have any common point of attack. This interweaving also creates a number of 'harmonic' suspensions. The consonances 'tilt', i.e., the vertical combinations become 'oblique'. This is an excellent example of how homophonic music can be made contrapuntal, simply by an offset of one minimal value.

The formula for this piece can be divided into two units on the basis of both the vertical and the horizontal organisation, which simply reflect each other. The principle of repetition, applied to the righthand part, shows that pulsations 1 to 3 and 5 to 7 contain the same melodic sequence. The formula can thus be divided into two perfectly symmetrical melodic units on the basis of the divergency of the contents of pulsations 4 (A–E) and 8 (G–D). This is clear from the paradigmatic representation in ex. 116.

Ex. 116

The next piece, *Kódà* ('Twins'), is associated with the rites celebrated on the occasion of the birth of twins. It has a period of eight pulsations, each subdivided into four minimal values.

The formula for this piece can be performed in only one way, equivalent to the model. The only commutation allowed involves a single sound with a duration of one minimal value, on the last semiquaver in the fourth pulsation of the righthand part (see ex. 117).

Ex. 117

The schematic representation of vertical combinations in ex. 118 is similar to the one for the preceding piece, with the addition of a minor third. The sequences of vertical combinations in *Kódà* display alternate use of the two techniques used separately in the two forms of *Zè zè zè kūlū.sè*, i.e., homophony and 'oblique harmony'. Several anticipations and a suspension (marked by the symbols ○ and △, respectively) result.

Ex. 118

Formally speaking, the piece is based on twice-repeated sequences with identical rhythmic articulation (pulsations 1 to 4 and 5 to 8) in each hand, but different melodic content and concatenations of con-sonances. The two parts are represented paradigmatically in ex. 119.

Ex. 119

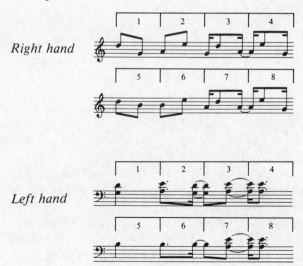

Right hand

Left hand

Vertically considered, the initial sounds in the first two pulsations are attacked simultaneously by both hands. The formula may thus be segmented into two symmetric units, A and B, which are distinguished by their melodic configurations and the concatenation of their con-sonances, as shown in:

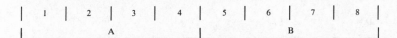

Using a decidedly formalist approach, we could divide each of these units into two cells, *a* and *b*, on the basis of a difference in rhythmic articulation, as shown in ex. 120. We do not, however, feel that this second segmentation is significant.

Ex. 120

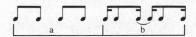

We must now give our attention to the rhythmic organisation of the lefthand part. We will find it helpful to eliminate the melodic parameter and retain only the articulation of the durations. We then replace the *metric* notation in ex. 121:

Ex. 121

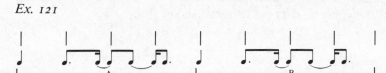

with the *rhythmic* transcription in ex. 122:

Ex. 122

It thus becomes clear that each of the units obtained by segmentation contains five durations, the first consisting of four minimal values, and the other four of three each. This makes a total of sixteen minimal values for four pulsations. Setting aside the first duration, whose total value coincides with that of the pulsation, we see that the other four durations are assigned to only three pulsations. We thus have another example of the hemiola principle (in a 4:3 ratio), this time in a binary metric framework. And, once again, there is no way of dividing the rhythmic figure comprising each of the units into two equal parts: however we try, we will invariably come out with either 7+9 or 9+7 minimal values. We thus encounter once more the principle of external symmetry and internal asymmetry by rhythmic oddity, in accordance with the 'half +1/half −1' rule.

Three melodic lines emerge from the combination of the two hands. A sequence based on the G–A–B pycnon in the middle register, shown in ex. 123, and an ornamented D–E pedal point with a recurrent symmetric structure in the upper register, represented in ex. 124, are superposed to the lefthand part (partly in parallel fifths).

Ex. 123

Ex. 124

There are thus three ways to approach listening to this piece, one vertical, one 'oblique', and one horizontal. The listener can, of course, 'switch perception' and change freely from one approach to another in the course of the performance.

The third piece, *Yòkí-ō*, is connected with a Ngbaka institution called the *yòlè*. This is a ceremony which makes official the choice of a partner for marriage.

The instrumental formula for this piece will not allow any variation whatsoever. It is therefore consistently repeated in its model form, shown in ex. 125.

Ex. 125

With the exception of a period based on a cycle of twelve pulsations, *Yòkí-ō* has the same structural features as the preceding piece: (1) The pulsation has a binary subdivision into four minimal values. (2) The schematic representation of the vertical combinations contains only fifths and fourths. (3) Homophony and 'oblique harmony' alternate; the latter creates effects of anticipation.

The formula can be divided into three segments of equal size, each containing four pulsations (1 to 4, 5 to 8, and 9 to 12). The accuracy of this segmentation is confirmed by the convergence of rhythmic and melodic criteria. The rhythmic structure of the three segments is perfectly analogous; and with respect to melody, not only is the material in pulsations 9 to 12 of the righthand part an exact repetition of pulsations 1 to 4, but the cell in pulsations 5 and 6 is also identical to the one in the first two pulsations of the other two segments. The only difference is thus in the contents of pulsations 7 and 8. All this is evident from the paradigmatic representation of this part in ex. 126.

Ex. 126

These three segments could thus be interpreted as consisting of two four-pulsation units, A and B, arranged in an A–B–A sequence. If, however, we try to apply this interpretation to the lefthand part, we will find that none of the three segments constitutes an identical reproduction of any other. While similar, segments 1 and 3 differ in their first pulsation. The middle segment is set clearly apart by a movement in parallel fifths. The paradigm for the lefthand part is shown in ex. 127. Since this piece is com-

Ex. 127

prised of unvarying repetitions of the model, we must make allowance for such differences, no matter how minor they may seem. That is why the formula for *Yòkí-ō* should be taken as composed of three units of equal size, A, B, and C, or less formalistically, A, B, and A', as shown in ex. 128. The parts are rhythmically articulated in exactly

Ex. 128

the same way as in the preceding piece. The effects of rhythmic interweaving are thus the same in *Yòkí-ō* as in *Kódà*. Periodicity aside (twelve pulsations here against eight in the preceding piece), what distinguishes these pieces is, on the one hand, their concatenations of vertical combinations, and on the other, the configurations of their melodic lines in each register. The way the intervals are arranged in the righthand part is different in each piece. The absence of the B note in *Yòkí-ō* thus changes the G–A–B pycnon, found the middle register in *Kódà*, into an ornamented G–A pedal point, which interlocks with the D–E pedal point on the upper register. Two nearly strictly interwoven ornamented pedal points can thus be heard above the *ostinato* with variations, provided by the lefthand part (and copied in the middle segment at the interval of a fifth). The structure of these pedal points is, however, different: the upper one on D–E gives rise to a ryhthmic figure which is spread over four pulsations and repeated three times, while the middle one displays an asymmetric organisation, as shown in ex. 129.

Ex. 129

In the Central African Republic, polyphonic instruments are intended primarily to accompany vocal music. The singer and instrumental musician are furthermore always one and the same person. In some cases, polyphonic instruments may be included in a larger ensemble, which invariably contains percussion instruments as well. To keep our discussion clear, we have taken them out of context in this chapter.

All pieces for polyphonic instruments are based on a formula, i.e., a temporal mould, which is fitted into a periodic cycle defined by a given number of pulsations.

The primary melodic, rhythmic, and con-sonantic elements of each formula are arranged to provide a set of reference points. The three types of elements are furthermore often interrelated.

Each formula has an underlying model, which may be repeated unchanged throughout the performance, or more commonly, with variations.

The variations may affect durations, pitches, and vertical combinations, separately or simultaneously. The techniques for the production of variations include splitting and merging durations, rhythmic offsetting, and commutation, any of which may be combined. Commutation will take place at specific points in the cycle, called substitution points. By the principle of commutation, the content of any substitution point (and consequently, the elements of the concatenation appearing in any two sucessive points) may be changed. This process of centonisation creates a large number of possible combinations and thereby allows considerable diversification of the realisations of any given formula.

Music for polyphonic instruments makes use of both homophony and counterpoint. The homophonic nature may predominate (as in the case of xylophone music), the two procedures may alternate, or the formula may be entirely contrapuntal (as occurs in both *sanza* and harp music). We have seen that counterpoint results from rhythmic offsetting in one of the component parts. This offsetting brings about the rhythmic interweaving of the two parts. We are thus led back to essentially polyrhythmic principles, here applied to melodic instruments.

6   The association of polyphony and polyrhythmics

6.1   GENERAL CHARACTERISTICS

Strict polyrhythmics and polyphony produced by melodic instruments have thus far been examined separately and out of context so as to give us a better view of how each works. In the musical practice of this part of Africa, however, the polyphony produced by melodic instruments always rests on a rhythmic or polyrhythmic substructure. We must therefore now consider the principles which govern the conjunction of these two components within a musical construction. We will do so by returning to the pieces which we have examined in partial form in the preceding chapters.

We may recall that the polyphony performed by melodic instruments itself acts as a support and a modal, periodic, and metric framework for *vocal* music.

There are several ways of performing such vocal music:

(1)   It may be performed entirely by a soloist
(2)   It may be performed by a soloist, backed by a choir, although the choral part may on occasion be assigned to a single person
(3)   It may be performed responsorially in two parts, the first of which is sung by the soloist and may display variations, and the second of which is an invariant response sung by the choir.

In every case, the solo part is sung by the instrumental musician himself or, in the case of music performed with two melodic instruments, by one of the two musicians (usually the most experienced one). While the solo part is subject to variation, the response by the choir or any individual singer remains unchanged. It acts as an extremely stable, if not perfectly strict melodic and rhythmic *ostinato*. The musical material in the vocal parts is condensed in the formula for the melodic instrument, and scarcely enriches the polyphonic texture in any way. The melodic structure of the realisations of the vocal solo is based on the existence of specific positions where the sounds do not change. These may be called *pivot notes*, since they serve as reference points on both the horizontal and the vertical axes.

A sort of dialogue between the voice and the supporting instrument is often set up in the course of a performance. We may find an instrumental variation suggesting a melodic idea in the vocal part, or equally well, the reverse. The singer/instrumentalist will also often interweave the durations of the sounds in the two parts so as to give them an additional polyrhythmic dimension.

At times, in the vocal parts, the words seem more important than the melody; without them, the song would be meaningless. This can often be convincingly seen from audience reaction. There is, however, always an intimate link between the vocal part and the instrumental formula, insofar as the latter is a condensation of the former. Putting it differently, we might say that the solo part behaves like an uninterrupted sequence of 'variations without a theme', but is nevertheless always constructed with reference to the 'lattice' provided by the instrumental formula.

The purpose of this chapter is to give a structural description of how strict polyrhythmics, polyphony produced by melodic instruments, and the superposed vocal part are combined into a single construction.

Central African music is based on the repetition of the same material with variations, within a strict periodic framework. It will therefore be unnecessary to reproduce the scores presented in preceding chapters. It will be sufficient for our purposes to summarise the organisation of any piece by citing a single periodic cycle, i.e., its model or one of its realisations.

This is also why we have not thought it worthwhile to reproduce the entire vocal solo part in the following transcriptions. Several realisations of this part are presented *in paradigmatic form* above the instrumental combination so as to give some idea of the kind of commutations it allows.

The representation of each piece will thus be comprised of the following elements, starting from the *bottom*:

(1) The rhythmic or polyrhythmic mould, in model form, which is characteristic of the repertory (or 'family' within the repertory) to which the piece belongs

(2) Above the mould, we place the specific polyphonic instrumental formula for the piece; this will consist of either one of its most common realisations, or its model

(3) At the very top, we give several realisations of the vocal solo in paradigmatic form, so as to show the extent of variation in the song

(4) The vocal *ostinato* is shown between the song paradigm and the polyphonic formula.

Each piece will be subjected to a formal analysis involving the following points:

(1) The structure of each of its components (vocal solo and choral part,

instrumental formula, rhythmic or polyrhythmic mould), and if necessary, their internal organisation, i.e., their segmentation

(2)   The relationship between among the melodic elements in the vocal parts and the instrumental formula

(3)   The relationship between these two components and the rhythmic or polyrhythmic mould, i.e., the nature of their overall interaction

(4)   The periodic relationships among all the component parts in the piece.

A variety of periodicities are superposed in all the pieces in which polyphony and polyrhythmics are associated. This means that their overall structure involves several levels of temporal organisation.

If we make an exception of the dancers, who produce rhythmic sequences of irregular duration (i.e., quasiperiodic sequences) with body instruments such as jingles on their ankles, these periodicities will always stand in simple ratios, no matter how many of them there are. The levels of periodicity will here be determined with respect to the longest *melodic* sequence to be found in the given piece.

Our analyses will be followed by diagrams summarising these relationships.

The pieces discussed in this chapter are ordered, for the sake of clarity, by increasing complexity. This complexity depends directly on the number of percussion parts which are combined with the polyphonic formula to fill out the musical latticework.

We will first consider music in which *only one instrument* furnishes a strict percussion part (viz., the Gbaya 'thinking songs'). We will then proceed to music in which the polyrhythmic substructure is based on *two interwoven rhythmic parts* (examples from Zande and Ngbaka music), and finally to music containing *three different rhythmic parts* (the Sabanga *ngbàkè* and Banda-Dakpa *gàzà* dance music). In the last case, we will encounter the techniques of amplification and quasiperiodicity.

6.2   INSTRUMENTAL POLYPHONY WITH A RHYTHMIC SUBSTRUCTURE

This category will be illustrated by the Gbaya 'thinking song' repertory, where the percussion part is provided simply by two rhythm sticks (*gàdà*) being struck together. We may recall that the 'thinking song' repertory contains two 'families', *Nàá Yàngà* and *Píéré*, which differ in the way the pulsation is subdivided: into three minimal operational values in the former, and four in the latter. The *gàdà* figure will therefore also differ according to which 'family' the song it accompanies belongs to.

The first two pieces we will examine are *Nàá Yàngà* and *Sàlò*, which belong to the first 'family'; and the third is *Píéré*, which belongs to the second. All three have three component elements: the *sanza* formula, the *gàdà* figure, and a vocal part with no response.

The condensed transcription for *Nàá Yàngà* appears in ex. 1.

The paradigmatic table for the song cycle contains eight different realisations. The sanza formula is the one used for 'simple playing'. The *gàdà* part is presented in two superposed notations, one *metric* and the other *rhythmic*. It should be emphasised that there is no accentuation whatsoever in these parts.

The vocal part furnishes a good illustration of the relationships between reference points and substitution points. We may note the absolute stability of the C on pulsations 1 and 2, compared with pulsation 3, where it may commute with G; with posi-

Ex. 1

tion 6, where it commutes with E; and with position 7, where it commutes with G *and* E. G may furthermore commute with D on pulsation 5, and D in turn may commute with A on pulsation 4. The substitution points, and the commutations at these points, will be seen practically to match the schematic representation of the vertical combinations in the *sanza* formula for this piece, which has already been analysed in an earlier chapter (3. The *sanza*). The relationship between the song and this formula is now evident.

We can see that many other realisations can be engendered from the eight units in this paradigm by 'diagonal' combination, provided the reference and substitution points are respected. The same is true of the instrumental parts to be discussed in this chapter.

The song cycle cannot be segmented by reference to the criterion of repetition. The maximal and minimal statement of this part is therefore comprised of eight pulsations.

The instrumental formula, however, can be divided into two rhythmic units, A (pulsations 1 to 4) and B (pulsations 5 to 8).

The *gàdà* figure has four pulsations. It must therefore be performed twice to match the period of the song and the *sanza*. It is worth repeating that the *gàdà* figure is produced simply by striking the sticks together, and involves no change of tone-colour.

The temporal structure of this piece is comprised of two levels standing in a 2: 1 ratio:

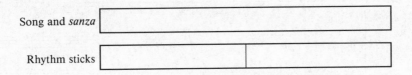

Fig. 1

There is only limited interweaving of the song part and the *sanza* formula, produced by the splitting of some durations in the former. The most concise form of the instrumental formula (the pattern) is much more noticeably interwoven with the *gàdà* figure. Only one of the five attacks in the latter coincides with a *sanza* attack. This is clear from the example in *rhythmic* transcription in ex. 2 where both hands in the *sanza* part are shown on the same staff.

Ex. 2

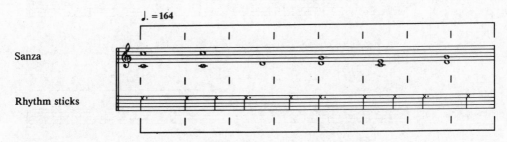

The condensed transcription of *Sàlò*, the second piece in the same 'family', appears in ex. 3.

Ex. 3 Sàlò

The song part in ex. 3 has nine realisations. The pivot notes are D on pulsations 3 and 7, E on pulsation 5, and C on pulsation 6. D commutes with C on pulsation 2, with G on pulsation 1, and with A and G on pulsation 4.

The *sanza* formula is for 'double playing', and is more complex than in the preceding example. The two parts are strictly interwoven, so that the hands never attack simultaneously.

The instrumental formula may be vertically compared with the substitution points in the song to see how the principle of commutation applies and what possibilities it provides for the musician.

Sàlò is structurally similar to *Nàá Yàngà* in every respect.

(1)   The song period cannot be segmented.

(2)   The *sanza* period contains two symmetric units, A (pulsations 1 to 4) and B (pulsations 5 to 8).

(3)   The *gàdà* figure is the same, so that the temporal structure is again as shown in fig. 1.

Only the *gàdà 'incipit'* differs in being offset by one pulsation, as shown in ex. 4.

Ex. 4

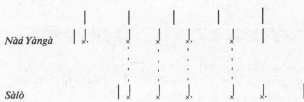

The pattern for the sanza formula and the *gàdà* part are almost strictly interwoven in *Sàlò*. Only one of the ten *gàdà* attacks in the two cycles required to match a sanza period coincides with an attack in the latter (see ex. 5).

Ex. 5

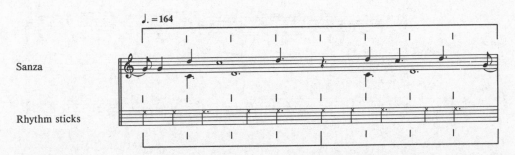

The final 'thinking song' piece is *Piéré*, which belongs to the 'family' of the same name. Like the preceding pieces, it has a cycle of eight pulsations, but they receive a *binary* subdivision, so that the minimal operational value is the semiquaver.

A condensed transcription of this piece is shown in ex. 6.

Ex. 6

The reference points in the vocal part are quite stable on pulsations 2 (C), 5 (E), 6 (A), 7 (E), and 8 (D). The substitution points are located on pulsations 3 (where D commutes with A) and 4 (where D commutes with G).

Once again, the content of the vocal-part paradigm can be compared with the *sanza* formula to obtain clear proof that the latter condenses all the potentialities of the former.

The *sanza* formula is realised according to the 'double playing' technique. The regular sequence of quavers played by one hand is interspersed with those played by the other, resulting in a nearly perpetual movement of semiquavers.

The thumbs come together on the first semiquaver in pulsations 1 and 4, each time at the interval of an octave. These two criteria (simultaneity and octave interval) enable us to segment the formula into two asymmetric units (A and B), consisting of the first *three* and the last *five* pulsations. We could segment the song cycle in the same way, but this would be of no further help to us.

The *gàdà* figure containing four pulsations is superposed on this asymmetric structure. It must therefore again be stated twice in order to match the period of the sanza formula.

This yields an overall periodic structure with the rhythmic counterpoint shown in ex. 7, between the pattern of the sanza formula and the *gàdà* figure. We can see how

Ex. 7

the *external symmetry* of the *gàdà* figure thwarts the *internal asymmetry* of the *sanza* formula. A closer look shows that the *gàdà* figure also has an internal asymmetry: there is no way of arranging its sixteen minimal operational values into 8+8. Only 7+9 or 9+7 is possible. If we rewrite the representation in ex. 7 on the basis of these values, we obtain the proportions shown in fig. 2.

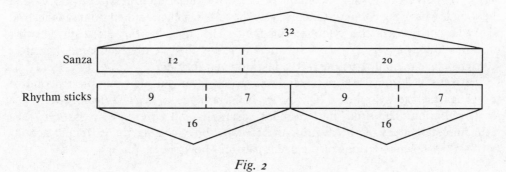

Fig. 2

The principle of rhythmic oddity in its 'half −1/half +1' form (see Book VI, 3.2.1.5) is thus exemplified at the levels of both the overall period and the *gàdà* figure.

This interweaving of two asymmetric and entirely unaccented structures of different length helps to create a feeling of ambiguity with respect to the pulsation, and to sustain a permanent state of tension.

The overall structure of *Pîéré* employs two types of periodicity in the 2:1 ratio shown in fig. 1.

6.3   INSTRUMENTAL POLYPHONY WITH A POLYRHYTHMIC SUBSTRUCTURE

6.3.1   Two-part polyrhythmic substructures

This category is represented firstly by a Zande *kpóníngbó* dance piece performed by a drum, a pair of pellet bells, and a pit xylophone, and secondly by three Ngbaka 'harp songs' which have a polyrhythmic substructure provided by two double bells.

The condensed transcription of the *kpóníngbó* piece is shown in ex. 8.

This piece has the following component parts:

- a solo song part with no response
- the pit xylophone formula, performed by two musicians squatting side by side
- the figure for the single-head skin drum (*gúrú*)
- the pellet bells (*nzɔ̀rɔ̀*), which are struck together.

The pit xylophone formula and the melodic cycle have the same period of eight pulsations with a binary subdivision, and the semiquaver as minimal value.

The *rhythmic* structure of the instrumental formula is identical for all four hands on pulsations 1 and 5, and again on 4 and 8. The formula may thereby be divided into two symmetric units, A and B, which are marked off by their first and last pulsations. This segmentation can also be seen in the song part, though less clearly.

The vocal part has the unusual feature of containing no position where the sound never changes. Every position is therefore a substitution point. The degree of stability does, however, vary. The reference points for the movement of the song part are in fact the positions which allow *only two sounds* to commute (provided we set passing and auxiliary notes aside). G thus commutes with D on pulsations 1 and 3, G commutes with C on pulsations 6, and A commutes with F on pulsation 8. It will be noticed that the sounds which can commute are precisely the ones which are stated simultaneously at the same positions in the xylophone formula. The same is nearly true in the other positions (pulsations 2, 4, 5, and 7), where the song melody diverges somewhat more from the con-sonantal structure of the instrumental formula.

The pellet bell and drum periods are superposed on the eight-pulsation period of the song and the xylophone. The pellet bells produce a strict *ostinato* covering a single pulsation. The drum part contains variations and covers two pulsations. The eight minimal values of the drum figure contain three irregularly distributed accents (3+3+2). A few realisations of the drum part are shown in ex. 9.

Ex. 8

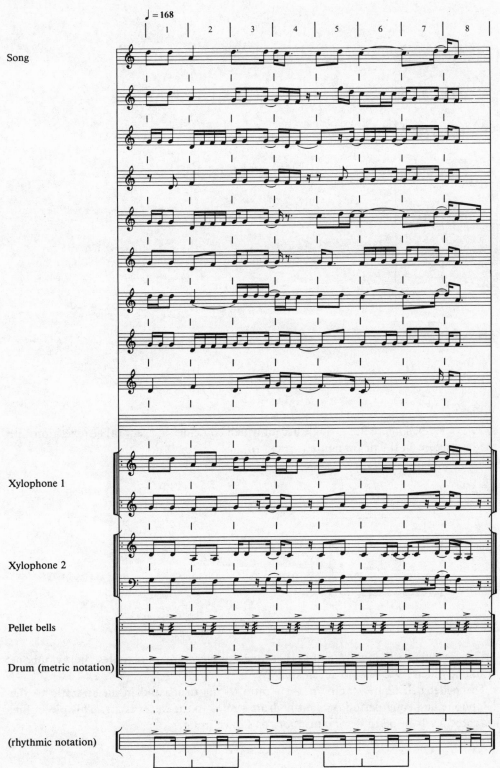

Ex. 9

The pellet bell figure has a single accent which coincides in every other repetition with the last accent in the drum figure (see ex. 10).

Ex. 10

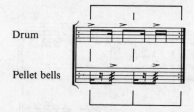

The formula resulting from this rhythmic counterpoint punctuates the xylophone formula, which itself has no accents.

The pellet bell figure stands in a 2:1 ratio to the drum and in an 8:1 ratio to the xylophone and song period, while the drum's ratio to the latter is 4:1. This piece thus has three levels of periodic organisation, as shown in fig. 3.

Song and xylophone							

Drum				

Pellet bells								

Fig. 3

All three Ngbaka 'harp songs' belong to a single repertory, and have the same components:

> the song itself, divided between a soloist and a choir
> the harp formula
> the figures for each of two double bells.

There is no variation in either the harp formula or the double-bell figures in these pieces. They are thus strict *ostinati*, and materialisations of their respective instrumental models.

We must note that the double-bell figures are defined by a distribution of their rhythmic configurations over two pitch levels, the actual interval being of no significance. Their articulation is thus based on a tone-colour contrast. Finally, we may remark that none of the three components contains any accentuation.

The first harp song we will discuss is *Zè zè zè kūlū sè*, as transcribed in ex. 11.

Both the harp formula and the vocal part contain eight pulsations with ternary subdivision.

The vocal solo and the choral part are partially superposed. The solo part has twelve realisations and only one real pivot note (A in pulsation 7). The rest is all substitution points. D may thus commute with G on pulsation 1; G with B (with D as an auxiliary note) on pulsations 2; E with A (with G as an auxiliary note) on pulsations 3 and 4; G with B on pulsation 6, and with both G and D on pulsation 5.

The harp formula for this piece can be realised in two ways, one homophonic and the other contrapuntal. The musician will not, however, switch from one to the other in the course of a performance. The contrapuntal version, which the Ngbaka harpists prefer, is shown in ex. 11.

The content of pulsations 1 to 3 and 5 to 7 is identical in this formula, whichever way it is realised. The differences appear in pulsations 4 and 8. This distribution of the musical content allows segmentation into two parts, A and B, containing pulsations 1 to 4 and 5 to 8 respectively.

Let us now turn to the two double bells. The figure for the first bell consists of the repetition of a single perfectly commetric cell every two pulsations. The figure for the second one is also commetric but has the same length as the harp and song cycle. It can be cut into three segments comprised of two units. The first unit, A, covers two pulsations and is repeated twice. It is followed by the second, B, which covers four pulsations. This figure is thus articulated as shown in fig. 4.

Ex. 11 Zè zè zè kūlūsè

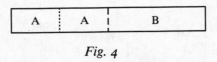

Fig. 4

Since the two double-bell figures are commetric, there can be no polyrhythmic relationship between them. We will see below that just the opposite is true of the other pieces in this same repertory.

The structure of *Zè zè zè kūlūsè* contains two types of periodicity: the first is common to the song, the harp formula, and the second double bell, and covers the entire cycle. The second is assigned to the first double bell, and stands in a 4:1 ratio with the others, as shown in fig. 5.

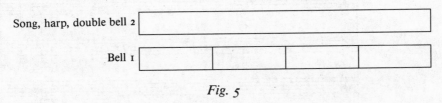

Fig. 5

The other two pieces in this repertory, *Kódà* and *Yòkí-ō*, differ from *Zè zè zè kūlūsè* in that their pulsations have a *binary* subdivision, with the semiquaver as the minimal operational value. Their double bell parts are furthermore polyrhythmically combined in an identical way.

Kódà has a period of eight pulsations. The song is comprised of a solo part, for which we provide eight realisations, and a response which slightly overlaps the solo. This piece is transcribed in ex. 12.

The solo part consists only of a brief intervention, mainly on pulsations 6, 7, and 8 (with anticipations at times on pulsation 5), and only sporadically on pulsations 3 and 4. The rest of the cycle is assigned to the response.

The pivot notes in this part are D (in the middle of pulsation 7), A (pulsation 8), and occasionally E (pulsation 4).

The vocal parts can be divided into two parts on the basis of the rests separating individual statements. These parts are symmetric in the response (pulsations 1 to 4 and 5 to 8), but asymmetric in the solo (pulsations 3 to 5 make up one, and pulsations 6, 7, 8, 1 and 2 the other).

The harp formula has been analysed in the preceding chapter, and the double-bell formula has been discussed in Chapter 3 (Strict polyrhythmics). We will therefore limit ourselves here to an examination of how these two components are combined at the level of overall structure.

The rhythmic articulation of the harp formula is the same on pulsations 1 to 4 and 5 to 8, although the melodic configurations are different. The formula may thus be divided into two symmetric units, A and B.

The first double bell has a symmetric figure based on repetitions of a single rhythmic cell ♫. ; however, each repetition is on a different pitch, as in

Ex. 12 Kódà

This figure therefore contains two pulsations and must be performed four times to match the longer cycle of the harp and song.

The second double-bell figure contains four pulsations, and must be played twice to equal a harp period. While this figure is externally symmetric, its internal articulation is characterised by rhythmic oddity. However we divide it, we will always come out with seven minimal values on one side and nine on the other (see fig. 6). We thus have a new case of our 'half +1/half −1' rule.

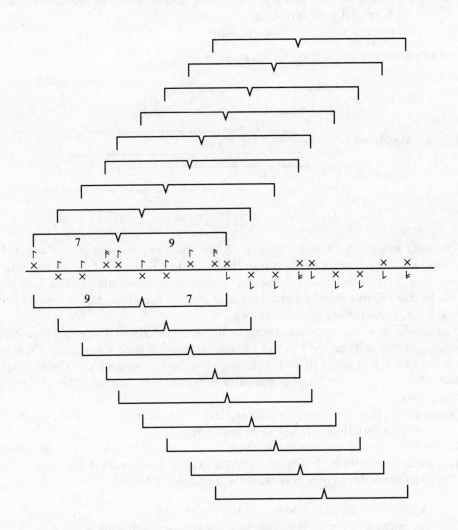

Fig. 6

Rhythmic counterpoint results from the contrast between this asymmetric arrangement and the symmetric figure of the first bell. In the absence of any accentuation, this leads to ambiguity in the perception of metre. The melodic counterpoint created by the two parts in the harp formula (which is also accentless) is then superposed on this purely rhythmic type of counterpoint.

The ratios in the periodic organisation of *Kódà* are thus:

2:1 between the first bell and the second, and between the second bell and the harp and song formulae

4:1 between the first bell and the harp.

These ratios are summarised by the diagram in fig. 7.

Fig. 7

The only structural difference between *Kódà* and the last piece in this set, *Yòkí-ō*, is the periodicity of twelve pulsations in the latter. In *Kódà*, the rhythmic organisation of the harp formula was based on two repetitions of a combination lasting four pulsations. In *Yòkí-ō*, the polyrhythmic mould is exactly the same, but is repeated three times, as the transcription in ex. 13 shows.

The soloist and the response alternate in the vocal parts. Each of these can be divided into two units on the basis of the rests separating their statements. These units are pulsations 1 to 4 and 5 to 12 for the response; and pulsations 3 to the first half of pulsation 6, and the second half of pulsation 6 to pulsation 2 of the following cycle, for the solo part.

We may note how the solo part remains stable on pulsations 10 to 12, where there is practically no variation in the D–A–D sequence.

In one position (the last semiquaver in pulsation 3 and the first one in pulsation 4), D may commute with low A. On pulsations 6 to 9, it may commute with G.

Yòkí-ō contains three types of periodicity. Their ratios are:

2:1 between the first double bell and the second

3:1 between the second double bell and the harp and song cycle

6:1 between the first double bell and the harp and song cycle.

Ex. 13 Yòkí–ō

These relationships are summarised in the diagram in fig. 8.

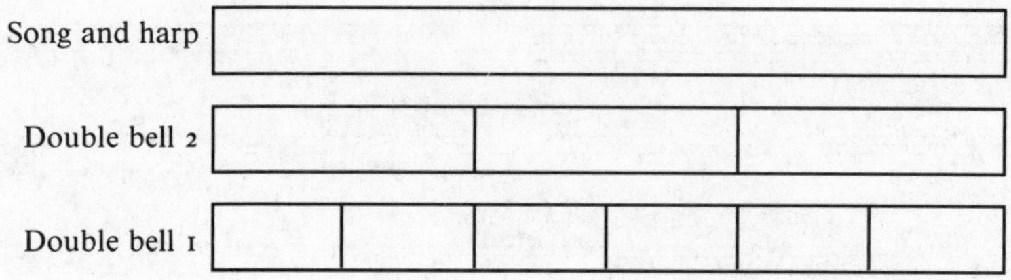

Fig. 8

6.3.2   Three-part polyrhythmic substructures

The effect of an increase in the number of strict percussion parts is not only to augment polyrhythmic interweaving but also to foster the use of techniques leading to more complex periodic (and hence structural) relationships. In the remaining pieces in this chapter, we will thus see the principles of amplification, macroperiodicity and quasiperiodicity coming into play, and at times combining. We will again follow an order of increasing complexity, and deal first with amplification, then see how it combines with macroperiodicity, and finally, with quasiperiodicity.

These three cases are illustrated by three pieces from the Sabanga *ngbàkè* repertory. The component elements of the pieces in this repertory are:

(1)   a solo vocal part
(2)   the xylophone formula
(3)   a percussion section comprised of five different instruments:

   two iron bells with an internal clapper (*àmànà kōlō*, literally 'mouth of *kōlō*, *kōlō* being an onomatopoetic representation of the sound of the instrument), which are held one in each hand and shaken alternately,
   a pair of iron pellet bells (*ɔ́ngbí*)
   a large single-head skin drum (*ngàsà*)
   a small drum of the same type (*āyā ngàsà*, 'child of *ngàsà*')
   bunches of jingles (*āzámbà*) made from nut shells, which are attached to the ankles of about ten dancers.

These five instruments produce only three parts, because the bells, pellet bells, and small drum always play the same cell, i.e., they are, rhythmically speaking, in unison.

The first *ngbàkè* piece we will examine is *Āgōā*, a transcription of which appears in ex. 14.

Ex. 14 Āgōā

The period used by both the song and the xylophone contains four pulsations whose subdivision is binary. The minimal operational value is the semiquaver.

The variations in the song phrase are illustrated by nine realisations. The reference points in this short cycle are located on the first pulsation (G) and on the second halves of pulsations 3 and 4 (C and A respectively).

This phrase forms a single unit and cannot be segmented. As we have seen in the preceding chapter, however, the instrumental formula can be divided into two symmetric units, each covering two pulsations, on the basis of the articulation of the lefthand part.

Before we examine how these two components are related to the polyrhythmic substructure, we should recall how we defined *amplification*: amplification consists of the sporadic development of the rhythmic material in a figure over some multiple of its original period.

In this piece, and throughout the *ngbàkè* repertory, the two bells, the pellet bells, and the small drum perform a one-pulsation cell without interruption. This cell may therefore be described as a strict *ostinato*. It has the special property of containing an internal subdivision into *five* minimal values in a 3 + 2 arrangement, in contrast to all the other parts, which can be subdivided on a binary basis. Consequently, if the time value of the crotchet is set metronomically at 116 for the song, the xylophone, the large drum, and the jingles, whose pulsations have a binary subdivision, the same value may be assigned to a dotted quaver tied to a quaver for the remaining three instruments, although these two symbolisations must be taken as having exactly equivalent durations.

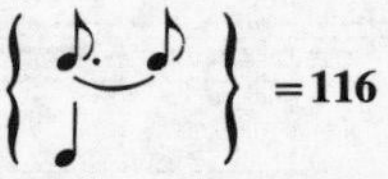

$$\left\{ \begin{array}{c} \text{♪. ♪} \\ \text{♩} \end{array} \right\} = 116$$

The basic figure for the large drum is binary and covers two pulsations. It is defined by its final three semiquavers (the first of which coincides with the pulsation) and the following semiquaver rest:

Both here and in *Yāfēmálè*, this figure can be amplified up to twenty-six times its original size, as demonstrated in ex. 15.

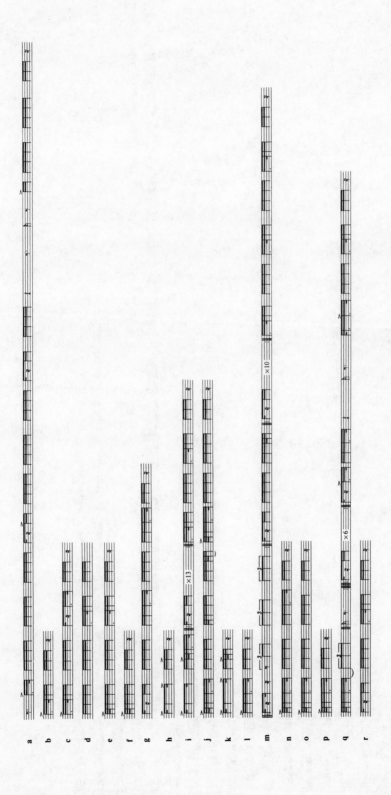

Ex. 15 Āgōā: amplification

Ex. 15 (cont.)

The dance steps trace a regular choreographic movement, which is transformed into rhythm by the jingles on the dancers' ankles. There are twenty pulsations in the choreographic sequence, this being the longest cycle in the piece. Since the xylophone cycle has four pulsations, it will have to be repeated five times to bring the dancers and the instrument to the beginning of their cycles at the same time. This is illustrated in ex. 16, where the dancers' figure is placed *beneath* the xylophone formula, and is broken down into five matching, vertically numbered sections. The 'nucleus' of the dance figure covers two pulsations and alternates between the following two realisations.

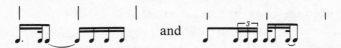

It is invariably placed on the last pulsation *of a xylophone cycle*, and the first pulsation of the following one. This position corresponds, with the same regularity, to pulsations 8 and 9 *of its own cycle*, as indicated by the horizontal numbering in ex. 16.

Ex. 16

The structure of this piece thus contains four types of periodicity, viz.,

a single pulsation for the bells, pellet bells, and small drum,
two pulsations for the large drum,
four pulsations for the xylophone and song, and
twenty pulsations for the jingles.

These are related in the following ratios (see the diagram in fig. 9):

2:1 between the bells, pellet bells, and small drum and the large drum, and
   between the latter and the xylophone,
5:1 between the xylophone and the jingles,
10:1 between the large drum and the jingles,
20:1 between the bells, pellet bells, and small drum and the jingles.

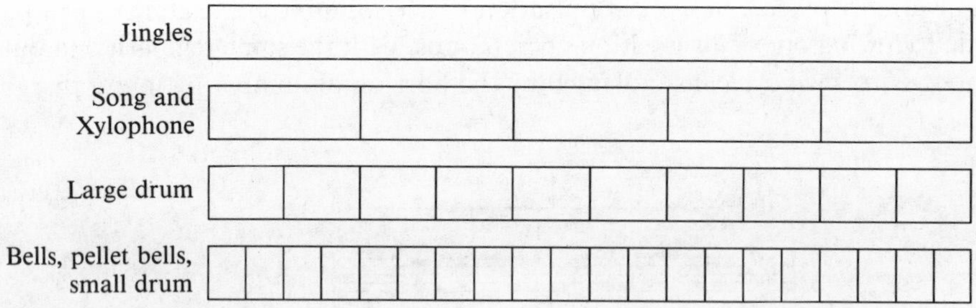

Fig. 9

The score for *Yáfēmálè* appears in schematic representation in ex. 17.

We reproduce eleven realisations of the song, which has only one real pivot note (A on the fourth pulsation), as the predominant D in the second pulsation may nevertheless commute at times with A. G commutes with C on the first pulsation, with D on the sixth, and with A and D on the second quaver in the third. Lastly, C and F commute on the second quaver of the fifth pulsation.

As in *Āgōā*, the vocal phrase is a single block. It has the same length (six pulsations) as the xylophone formula, which itself could be divided into three units of two pulsations each on the basis of the threefold repetition of a single rhythmic mould. No such division of its vertical melodic organisation is, however, possible.

This piece has the same percussion parts as the preceding one. The xylophone formula has six pulsations instead of four as before, but since both are even numbers, this has no effect on the relationship between this formula and those percussion instrument figures of which it is a multiple.

The case with the jingles, which have the same twenty-pulsation cycle as in *Āgōā*, is entirely different, for the smallest number divisible by both six and twenty is sixty. When these two parts are combined, we get what we have called a *macroperiod*, i.e., the result of superposing two or more periodicities, all of which are individually shorter. The macroperiod is then their smallest common multiple.

Ex. 17 Yāʃēmálè

Thus, in the present instance, ten repetitions of the xylophone cycle and three of the dance figure are required to bring them back to their initial relationship. Only then will we again find the nucleus of the dance figure, on pulsations 8 and 9 of its own cycle, in the same position with respect to the xylophone figure. This is shown in ex. 18, where the jingles figure is again placed beneath the xylophone formula and broken down against it.

Ex. 18

Xylophone cycle

Jingles cycle

The structure of this piece thus involves the following ratios:

2:1 between the bells, pellet bells, and small drum and the basic large drum cell,

3:1 between the large drum and the xylophone and song cycle,

6:1 between the bells, pellet bells, and small drum and the xylophone and song cycle,

10:1 between the large drum and the jingles,

20:1 between the bells, pellet bells, and small drum and the jingles,

10:3 between the xylophone and song period and the jingles period.

Thus, while the longest period within the piece has twenty pulsations, the macro-period giving cohesion to the full set of superposed periods has sixty, as shown in fig. 10.

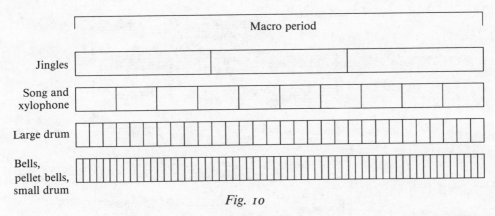

Fig. 10

The third and final piece in the *ngbàkè* repertory is *Bàdá*. There are three different versions of the xylophone formula because of variations in the *lefthand* part. We *superpose* these versions in ex. 19 in order to clarify the position of certain sounds in the song with respect to this formula. We can see that A is almost entirely absent from the first version, but present in the other two, though in neighbouring positions, i.e., *offset by a semiquaver with respect to each other*.

Unlike all the other pieces discussed thus far, the song period (six pulsations) is twice as long as the xylophone formula, which has only three. The melodic content of the second half of the song phrase is therefore forced to respect constraints imposed by the arrangement of the material in the instrumental formula.

The reference points are located on the first quaver of the second pulsation (F), and on the second quaver of the fourth (C). C has a predominant function in this song, as it commutes with every other degree of the scale:

with G on the second quaver of the second pulsation, the first quaver of the fourth, and the second quaver of the fifth

with D on the first quaver in the third and sixth pulsations

with F on the first quaver of the fifth pulsation

with A on the second quaver of the sixth pulsation

with F *and* A on the second quaver of the third pulsation.

We can see that the sounds which appear in a given position in the song are found in the same positions in one version or another of the instrumental formula.

Ex. 19 Bàdá

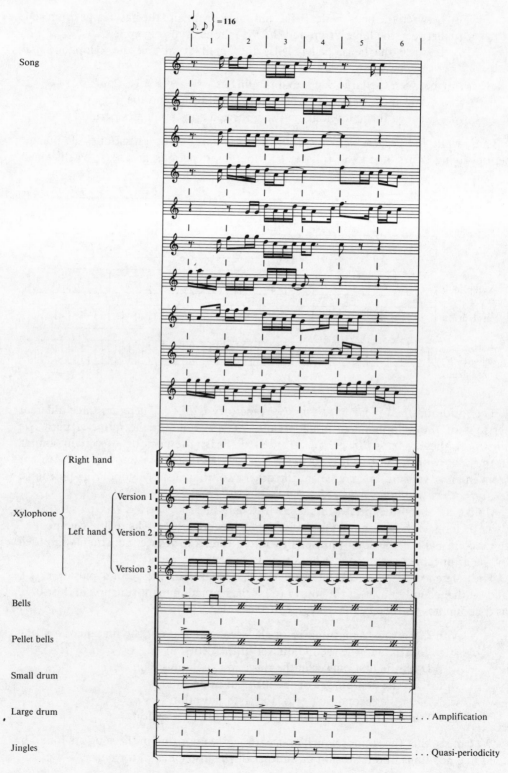

The bells, the pellet bells, and the two drums perform the same figures as in the preceding pieces. The basic drum cell covers two pulsations, and the xylophone cell, three; they meet again only after two xylophone and three drum cycles. This superposition does not, however, result in a macroperiod, because the vocal part has a period of the same length.

We do, however, encounter the phenomenon of quasiperiodicity in the dancers' rhythmic part. Let us recall that quasiperiodicity occurs when the temporal interval separating the occurrence of identical or similar (and hence recognisable) rhythmic phenomena is relatively irregular rather than constant.

This is precisely what we find in the dance sequences in *Bàdá*. Rhythmic motifs derived from the same model reappear only at *irregular* intervals. In other words, the location of the nucleus of the sequence produced by the dancers with their ankle jingles, with respect to the temporal organisation of the other parts in the piece, is irrelevant and *fortuitous*. The jingles part in *Bàdá* has already been transcribed in the chapter on strict polyrhythmics (§2.3.6, where the technique of quasiperiodicity is presented in detail).

The ratios of the strictly periodic parts in this piece are thus as follows:

2:1 between the xylophone formula and the song,
3:1 between the basic large drum cell and the song, and between the bells, pellet bells, and small drum and the xylophone formula,
6:1 between the bells, pellet bells, and small drum and the song,
3:2 between the large drum and the xylophone formula.

These ratios are summarised by the diagram in fig. 11.

Fig. 11

The last two pieces we will examine belong to the *gàzà kōfē* dance repertory, which is associated with the Banda-Dakpa male initiation rites. Both have not only identical component parts, but the same structural features as well.

The component parts are these:

a vocal solo and a choral part
two xylophones
two slit drums (*lēngā*), and ankle jingles.

Insofar as the structure of the two pieces is concerned:

(1)   The periodicity of the song and the two xylophone formulae contains six pulsations with binary subdivision.

(2)   The *rhythmic* organisation of the formulae for the two xylophones consists of a threefold regular alternation between a pulsation whose durations can be symmetrically subdivided: ♩♪ , ♫♪ , and ♫♫ and another asymmetrically arranged pulsation based on groups of 3+3+2 or 3+2+3: ♫.♪. , ♪.♫. .

(3)   Both the xylophone formula and the song are unaccented.

(4)   The drum parts use the same rhythmic figures in both pieces.

(5)   The choreography is the same, and the rhythmic sequences produced by the dancers' ankle jingles are therefore also similar.

The condensed score for the first of these pieces, *Bāmàrā gàzà*, is shown in ex. 20.

There are few variations in the solo voice phrase. It starts one pulsation later than the xylophone formula and covers four pulsations. The complementary choral part starts on the last pulsation of the xylophone formula and continues until the solo begins again in the following cycle; it also includes isolated intervention, a single G on the third pulsation.

The song cycle is thus divided into two parts, with the soloist taking up four pulsations, and the choir two.

The predominant sounds in the vocal solo are C (pulsation 2), D (pulsation 3, where it creates an interval of a fifth with the choir's G), and again C (pulsation 5).

We now turn to the relationship between the song and the xylophone formula in the second piece in the repertory, *Āyá mɔ̄, mɔ̄ wú òyò*, as shown in ex. 21.

This song has a strict responsorial form and is symmetrically distributed between the soloist, who begins on the second half of the period (pulsation 4), and the choir, which replies on the first part of the following cycle.

We will now conclude by examining the overall structure common to these two pieces.

The xylophone formulae can be segmented into three units of two pulsations each on the basis of their rhythmic organisation into three repetitions of a single mould.

The part assigned to the smaller of the two drums, *àkɔ̄.lēngā* 'the 'husband' or 'male' *lēngā*' is no more than a strict *ostinato* comprised of two pulsations. It is marked by two irregularly placed offbeat accents.

The *èyī.lēngā* ('mother' *lēngā*') part is also based on a two-pulsation theme, and is marked by three accents, only one of which is located on the pulsation. These accents are strictly interwoven with those of the smaller drum (cf. Book VI, 3.3.3.1).

The invariant *ostinato* produced by the latter provides the reference for variations by the master drummer on the 'mother' drum, whose initial theme is developed by amplification to between two and four times its original length. (cf. Book VI, 3.2.3.4, where an example of this drum part is provided).

As in the Sabanga *ngbàkè* dance, the jingles part displays quasiperiodicity, resulting from the variety of choreographic configurations executed by the dancers, each representing a different animal. These figures, whose length varies with the animal being imitated, are interspersed with regular 'interludes' in which each pulsation contains

Ex. 20 Bāmàrā gàzà

Ex. 21 *Āyá mɔ̄, mɔ̄ wú ɔ̀yɔ̀*

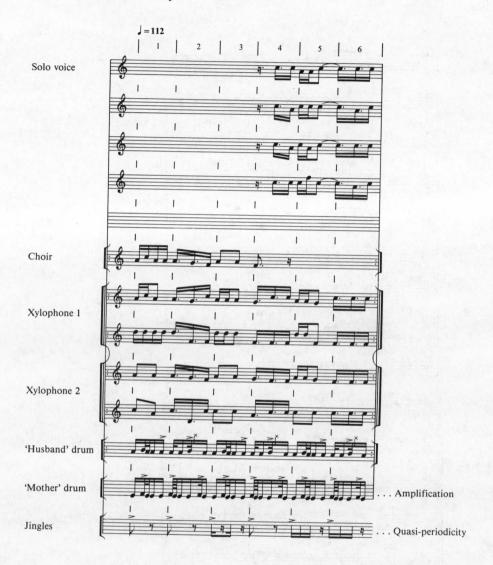

two steps, at least one of which must fall on the pulsation. This 'base movement' itself, which separates the imitations in the dance, has no predetermined periodicity. That is why the performance must be synchronised by the dance leader, who makes three coded calls preceding the execution of each figure, the last of which is exactly two pulsations prior to the start of the announced figure, i.e., the imitation of a given animal by the dancers' bodily motions and by the rhythm of their ankle jingles (cf. Book VI, 3.2.3.6, where the jingles parts for these two dances are transcribed).

Quasiperiodicity is thus engendered by the alternation of these animal imitations with the base movement, none of these elements being governed by a strict periodicity.

In this chapter, we have looked at how the music of Central Africa is organised concretely when its polyrhythmic and polyphonic components are combined, and appear with the song they support.

It has not been our purpose to describe in detail how each piece works (this was the task of the preceding chapter), but rather to shed light on their overall design, in every significant facet and at every observable level. We should now understand how the song, the polyphony produced by the melodic instruments, and the strict polyrhythmics are related an interact.

We have seen that none of the *polyphonic* formulae we have discussed is accented at all. The same is true of some percussion parts, e.g., the Gbaya rhythm sticks and the Ngbaka double bells, but in others (in Zande, Sabanga, and Dakpa music), all rhythmic figures contain accents.

There are thus two types of counterpoint between the *polyrhythmic* and *polyphonic* components, according to whether they are interwoven without accents, or whether the accents in the polyrhythmic mould impose an extraneous articulation on the formula for the melodic instrument, which may thus have the morphology of its own content perceptually altered, as it were, by 'contagion'.

All parts, with the exception of those which are materialised in their model form, have a variety of realisations, i.e., are subject to variation.

Variations are allowed only in the solo vocal part in the Ngbaka 'harp songs', but in all the other repertories we have examined, *only one part is required to maintain a strict ostinato*, i.e., all the others may vary.

Variation, which may be defined in this context as *diversity in the presentation of a single theme*, is governed by the principle of commutation, which allows certain elements to be substituted for others at given positions in the period. This principle has a fundamental role insofar as it makes up for the lack of genuine development by allowing continually different and often unforeseeable realisations. That is why Central African music creates the effect of a "sound kaleidoscope", despite its strictly determined structure.

The coherence of the overall musical construction is evident from the ratios obtaining between the various parts. These ratios are *always* simple, even when the technique of amplification is used, or a relationship of macroperiodicity is established.

Sequences of a quasiperiodic type constitute the only case in these kinds of music where the musical content of any part displays *no rational relationship* to the others. While this technique is apparently entirely free (though produced only by body instruments such as jingles), it is nevertheless subject to the *metric* organisation of the piece.

The kinds of music we have been discussing in this chapter involve, firstly, the association of several tone colours, provided by the human voice, melodic instruments, and various sorts of percussion instruments, and secondly, the conjunction of strict polyrhythmics and melodic counterpoint. The latter results from two-handed playing by the musician, and itself has a polyrhythmic character.

No common rhythmic arrangement is produced when polyphony and strict poly-rhythmics are combined. On the contrary, the fact that each component part retains its own rhythmic articulation results in an even closer overall polyrhythmic texture.

The multipart music found in this part of Africa thus displays two levels of counter-point between two superposed polyrhythmic structures. The first includes the percussion parts alone, and involves only rhythm and tone colour. The second is melodic, with rhythm articulated over predetermined pitch levels. Polyrhythmic principles are thus omnipresent.

If the reader has followed all we have said thus far, he or she should now be able, by referring to the two preceding chapters, to reconstruct realisations of any piece, or by exploiting the possibility of commuting elements, produce 'new' versions which traditional musicians are likely to find acceptable.

Conclusion

Ethnomusicology, which strictly speaking is the study of ethnic music, and *musical anthropology*, which is primarily concerned with the role music plays in a given society and the way it interacts with the surrounding cultural context, are often treated as synonyms. This situation is doubtless a consequence of the rapid development of a young discipline.

The reader is now aware that our own perspective is specifically ethnomusicological: our purpose is to study certain musical techniques which are practised in societies that are generally made the subject of ethnological description.

Our initial objective was to discover the principles, or the underlying theory, governing polyphonic and polyrhythmic forms of music in a specific geocultural region. But a valid theory must be supported by the convergence of data gathered by observation and confirmed by experience, with pertinent statements regarding musical practice elicited from the traditional musicians themselves. We are therefore logically required to sustain a constant dialogue between 'objective' and cultural data, or equivalently, between the ways in which the traditional musician and the researcher understand the same object.

As we understand it, the proper task of ethnomusicology is to study the principles governing all forms of ethnic music within their cultural context, i.e., in the area where people actually use them, and where light can be thrown on them from within.

I

This work has both descriptive and methodological aims. We would have been unable to decipher and transcribe Central African polyphony if we had not developed a suitable and previously non-existent methodological tool. That is why we have felt obliged to give a precise description of this tool and describe in detail how it is to be used.

The musical corpus providing the basis for this work was collected over a relatively short space of time spanning some ten years. We were thus aiming at strictly synchronic descriptive analysis; we wanted to be able to describe specific kinds of musical technique found at a given place and time, or more exactly, over a period short enough to guarantee that they would undergo no significant structural change.

Nevertheless, as one gains greater understanding of the mechanisms involved in a *hic et nunc* cultural activity, one tends to find that its underlying principles extend beyond, often far beyond, the particular case, not only spatially, with respect to neighbouring cultures, but temporally as well. One is thus led step by step from one's initial synchronic approach to questions relating to phenomena of a historical nature. By, as it were, 'working backwards' in this way, one may be able to get a view of these phenomena which is rarely sought by historians.

Once we have understood the polyphonic and polyrhythmic techniques which are current today in the Central African Republic, we can in fact prove that some of them, described in reliable historical documents, were already in use in other parts of Africa at the end of the fifteenth century. It is therefore likely that they are actually much older.

This historical aside is in no way intended to provide any explanation of how these techniques were diffused and became current over an enormous area which today comprises nearly all of Subsaharan Africa.

Our empirical observation of numerous types of polyphonic practice in the field quickly led us to the conclusion that, despite their complexity, they all had some common underlying principles, and that several different techniques were being brought *simultaneously* into play. We therefore thought it would be best to start by classifying these techniques.

Our next step was to inventory all the features and rules characterising the behaviour of each technique. Such a list provides the only means of specifying what distinguishes any given technique or type from any other.

The existence of rules implies the existence of *systematic relationships* among elements. Insofar as different types combine to form a single structure, they are rarely independent. We are thus dealing with a system whose components are themselves systems, or subsystems.

Our typology of techniques was established on the basis of their characteristic structural features, with little regard for the criterion of ethnic origin.

Two kinds of systematic parameters must be considered: those which are common to all kinds of music, and those which only come into play in a polyphonic situation. The former category includes phonology, morphology, and syntax. We may recall that we use the term phonology in a wide sense, covering all the constituent elements which act as discrete units, *at whatever level*, viz., the scales and the sounds comprising them, and the periods and their underlying metricity. Morphology deals with the ways in which the musical content is arranged. Musical discourse can thereby be segmented into distinctive units. Finally, syntax describes how these units are concatenated.

The parameters specific to polyphonic music are vertical organisation, the way the superposed parts are fitted together and interlocked, the principles governing the simultaneous movement of different periodicities, and the combinations of tone colour resulting from the use of different kinds of instruments.

The *structural features* consist of the specific ways in which certain parameters systematically combine in given social and musical circumstances, i.e., in a repertory with a stylistic unity, which is culturally (and hence intrinsically) linked to a specific social function.

The fact that such a repertory is always locally classified as a separate musical *category* by the bearers of the tradition shows they have a clear notion of the nature of a musical system.

The method I have developed and applied to deciphering and transcribing orally transmitted polyphonic and polyrhythmic music is based on the use of *rerecording* techniques in the field. We can thereby isolate each part in a polyphonic and/or polyrhythmic whole without desynchronising it with respect to the others. This method also has the useful property of doing away with the longstanding dichotomy between analysis and synthesis, by establishing a continuous back-and-forth movement between the two poles.

It consists of a set of operations whereby the musical construction is taken apart, or broken down, by extracting and setting up a model for each constituent part, and then synthetically reconstructed. All the steps in this process are performed by the traditional musicians themselves. The establishment of models in this way has nothing to do with the construction of artefacts on the basis of deductive speculation: the models obtained experimentally *are materialised in the form of recordings*.

We have already described how we apply the rerecording method, and what its potentialities are. One of its most desirable effects is that it does a great deal to foster communication with the musicians and the elders. Somewhat paradoxically, the experimental conditions under which the music is treated as if it were in the process of construction elicit many quite important spontaneous comments from the musicians, comments which would rarely be obtained in the course of ordinary investigative procedures, or even of informal conversation. These are direct reactions to the music itself, responding to mistakes or to unusual displays of creativity, and are instructive not only with regard to the ways in which this music is conceived and practised, but also with respect to how the people who use it perceive it.

The results obtained by means of this method have now been presented in the form of transcriptions and analyses.

We have also shown:

(1)   That despite its experimental nature, this method can be applied without undermining the spirit of the music. This will be evident to anyone who reads the scores while listening to ordinary recordings of the same pieces.

(2)   That our procedure is anthropologically valid, insofar as the traditional musicians participate willingly, unhesitatingly, and even with pleasure, and moreover, give ultimate approval to the musical syntheses.

(3)   That precisely because of its experimental nature, this method provides easier access to the models which lie behind the multiplicity of realisations of any one musical entity, and act as a reference for each performance.

We have been continually alert to the dangers of ethnocentrism, whereby thought-categories and classificatory procedures from the researcher's own culture are projected on to the activities of a different culture and their practitioners. We have taken every possible precaution to avoid this by constantly relying on the musicians' own initiative in every phase of the rerecording process. We have already indicated that we thereby hoped to come to grasp basic musical principles *in the same way as they were conceived and perceived by the people who are their traditional heirs*. With this in view, we have intentionally confined ourselves to coordination rather than incitement.

We have checked many times in the course of collecting individual polyphonic parts and playing them back, sometimes several years later, to make sure that we had not become lost in gratuitous speculation, by seeking the approval of those who had been directly or indirectly involved in our research. We have invariably obtained the most concrete sort of proof that every document we have collected, whether completely out of context or as a partial or fragmentary representation of a piece of music, was acceptable and accepted in this form as culturally relevant and genuine within an age-old musical tradition and practice.

With such confirmation, we could confidently proceed to the subsequent stages of our task, in which we would receive no assistance, namely, working up the transcriptions which we had been unable to prepare and check in the field, and completing our analyses. The reader will have noticed that these analyses are intended primarily to describe as clearly and as precisely as possible how these types of music are constructed with respect to their components, their articulation, and their structural levels, rather than to provide a tiresome or superfluous hermeneutic structure to accompany each piece (or to be more precise, each of the many possible realisations of the same piece). For there is something beyond the various ways in which any given piece can be realised, something by virtue of which they can in fact be considered to be a single musical entity, and identified as such. This is the *model*, which, while often implicit, nevertheless is always there as a reference for each musician, every time he performs.

There is no use in inventorying realisations if the model can be discerned in every one of them. The important thing is rather to reveal the relationships which exist between the model and the realisations derived from it, or in other words, the type and extent of variations it will allow. The number of realisations (or variations) in two performances, or even in a single one, would seem more than sufficient to illustrate this point.

Our every effort throughout this work has been directed at bringing into focus this ultimate reference which constitutes the quintessence of each piece. At every stage in this process, we have tried to explain why we proceeded as we have.

II

The types of music we have been examining display a striking contrast between their apparent complexity and the small number of elements from which they are constructed: a strict periodicity yielding cyclic forms, and an anhemitonic pentatonic scale giving rise to sets of superposed melodic structures whose lengths are related in strictly proportional ratios, these are the only conceptual factors involved in Central African forms of polyphony.

We have seen that, without a leading note and a harmony-generating bass part, their verticality was not strictly speaking a form of harmony. Vertical conjunctions are rather the meeting points of several simultaneous melodic lines. The resulting consonances, some of which are fortuitous, are intended to enrich the musical texture by creating a colouring effect.

The essence of this polyphony thus lies in the rhythmic independence of the parts. This is what makes the different melodic lines perceptible, and therefore what leads to the formation of polyphonic perception. That is why we can describe it as being an *application of polyrhythmics to the 'melos'*, or *a melodic form of polyrhythmics*.

The Central African forms of polyphony are thus the exact opposite of Western polyphony, particularly the *organum*, which had a melodic origin and was invested with rhythm primarily because words had to be fitted to the music. In Central Africa, rhythm was at the source, and is still the quintessence and ultimate result. We might therefore say that, just as the vertical conjunctions are intended to colour the melodic texture, it is frequently the case that the primary function of the melody itself is to colour the rhythmic texture.

Central African music thus comes into its own in the richness, complexity, and subtlety of its polyrhythmic constructions. The most important point is to realise that this music, which is perceptually polyphonic, is actually polyrhythmic in essence.

The geographical location of the Central African Republic in the heart of the continent, and the diversity of its more than one hundred ethnic groups, make this country an ideal place to study African forms of polyphony. Other research at various points in West Africa (Ghana in particular), East Africa, and Southern Africa (e.g., in Zimbabwe and in the Kalahari Desert in the Republic of South Africa) shows that the basic principles governing both strict polyrhythmic and hocket techniques are no different from those in the Central African Republic. This view receives support from published recorded documents obtained in countries as far from each another as the Ivory Coast and Tanzania, Nigeria and Sudan, Senegal and Uganda, and Angola and Ethiopia.

We may surmise that a strong similarity also exists in other principles governing certain characteristic contrapuntal techniques applied to melodic instruments such as the *sanza* and the harp, which have not yet received systematic study outside the Central African Republic.

Though my initial intention was to confine myself to describing the systematic structure of the polyphonic and polyrhythmic music found in a limited geocultural region, I have in fact encountered techniques which have been reported elsewhere in forms governed by the same principles. One thus finds that this research may have a much wider scope than expected, and apply in unforeseen ways.

I would therefore be pleased if the present research could stimulate musicological interest in types of polyphonic music current in other parts of Africa, this being still the most poorly explored field in all of ethnomusicology.

The principles underlying African polyphony and polyrhythmics testify admirably to the ingeniousness of their inventors and of the people who still make use of them today. For many outsiders, however, 'African music' still means no more than a stereo-type with half-clothed perspiring men beating wildly on drums and other percussion instruments in supposedly 'improvised' fashion. This pejorative 'tom-tom' image implies some sort of entirely spontaneous music with no rational organisation. I would hope to help correct this attitude by showing how coherent and complex this music actually is; by formulating its rules and underlying theory; by reporting how it is conceived and classified in the terminology of the native language; by making clear how much creativity and subtlety it involves; and by describing how various musical categories are intrinsically related to social and cultural circumstances. I hope thereby to have made a contribution in some way to fostering greater recognition of the value of the culture of the Others through increased interest, more equitable appraisal, and better understanding.

No less importantly, this is also one way, and perhaps not the worst way, of combat-ting the blind discrimination of racism.

Bibliography

Adler, Guido, 1908, Über Heterophonie, *Jahrbuch der Musikbibliothek Peters XV*, Leipzig, pp. 17–27

Apel, Willi, 1947, *Harvard Dictionary of Music*, Cambridge (Mass.), Harvard University Press, x–833pp.

    1970, *Harvard Dictionary of Music* (Second edition, revised and enlarged. . .), London, Heinemann Educational Books, xvii–935pp.

    1959, Remarks about the Isorhythmic Motet, *L'Ars Nova, Recueil d'études sur la musique du XIVe siècle. Les Colloques de Wégimont II, 1955*, Paris, 'Les Belles Lettres', Bibliothèque de la Faculté de Philosophie et Lettres de l'Université de Liège, Fasc. CXLIX, pp. 139–48

Arom, Simha, 1969, Essai d'une notation des monodies à des fins d'analyse, *Revue de Musicologie LV/2*, pp. 172–216

    1973, Une méthode pour la transcription des polyphonies et polyrythmies de tradition orale, *Revue de Musicologie LIX/2*, pp. 165–90

    1974, De la chasse au piège considérée comme une liturgie, *The World of Music XVI/4*, pp. 3–19

    1976, The Use of Play-back Techniques in the Study of Oral Polyphonies, *Ethnomusicology XX/3*, pp. 483–519

    1982, Nouvelles perspectives dans la transcription des musiques de tradition orale, *Revue de Musicologie LXVIII/1–2*, special issue: André Schaeffner, pp. 198–212

    1984, Structuration du temps dans les musiques d'Afrique Centrale: périodicité, mètre, rythmique et polyrythmie, *Revue de Musicologie LXX/1*, pp. 5–36

Aubry, Pierre, 1909, *Trouvères et Troubadours*, Paris, Félix Alcan, 223pp.

Auda, Antoine, 1965, *Théorie et pratique du tactus; transcription et exécution de la musique antérieure aux environs de 1650*, Brussels, Oeuvres de Don Bosco, 176pp.

Augier, Pierre, 1971, La polyrythmie dans les musiques du Sahara, *Lybica XIX* (Algiers), pp. 217–33

Augustin (Saint), *La musique, De musica libri sex*. Text of the Benedictine edition. Introduction, translation and notes by Guy Fianert and F.-J. Thonnard, Bruges, Desclée, De Brouwer et Cie., 1947, Oeuvres de Saint Augustin, 1ère série: *Opuscules, VII, Dialogues philosophiques* (Bibliothèque Augustinienne), 546pp.

Bachelard, Gaston, 1950, *La dialectique de la durée*, Paris, Presses Universitaires de France (Bibl. de Philosophie Contemporaine), new edn 1963, xi–150pp.

Bahuchet, Serge (ed.), 1979, *Pygmées de Centrafrique. Ethnologie, histoire et linguistique*, Paris, SELAF (Bibliothèque 73–74, Etudes pygmées III), 175pp.

Ballantine, Christopher, 1965, The Polyrhythmic Foundation of Tswana Pipe Melody, *African Music III/4*, pp. 52–67

Béclard-d'Harcourt, Marguerite, 1924, Notes relatives à la transcription des phonogrammes, *in* Joyeux Ch., Étude sur quelques manifestations musicales observées en Haute-Guinée Française, *Revue d'Ethnographie et des Traditions Populaires V/18*, pp. 173–202

Belinga, M.S. Eno, 1965, *Littérature et musique populaires en Afrique Noire*, Paris, Ed. Cujas, 258pp.

Benary, Peter, 1973, *Rhythmik und Metrik. Eine praktische Einleitung*, Cologne, Musikverlag Hans Gerig, (Theoretica 7), 112pp.

Blacking, John, 1957, *The Role of Music amongst the Venda of the Northern Transvaal*, Johannesburg, International Library of African Music

1971, Deep and Surface Structure in Venda Music, *Yearbook of the International Folk Music Council* III, pp. 91–108

Bosman, Guillaume, 1705, *Voyage de Guinée, contenant une Description nouvelle et très exacte de cette côte. . .*, Utrecht, Antoine Schouten, 520pp.

Bowdich, Thomas Edward, 1819, *Mission from Cape Coast to Ashantee*, London, John Murray, viii–512pp.

Brăiloiu, Constantin, 1931, Esquisse d'une méthode de folklore musical, *Revue de Musicologie* XII/1, pp. 1–35

1949, Le folklore musical, *Musica aeterna* (Zurich, M.S. Metz), pp. 277–332

1953, Sur une mélodie russe, *Musique russe, Etudes réunies par Pierre Souvtchinsky*, Vol. II, Paris, P.U.F. (Bibliothèque Internationale de Musicologie), pp. 329–91

1959a, Musicologie et ethnomusicologie aujourd'hui, *Bericht über den Siebenten Internationalen Musikwissenschaftlichen Kongress Köln 1958*, Kassel, Bärenreiter-Verlag, pp. 17–29

1959b, Réflexions sur la créativité musicale collective, *Diogène* 25 (Paris, Gallimard), pp. 83–93

1969, *Oeuvres II, traduit et préfacé par Emilia Comicel*, Bucharest, Edition musicale de l'Union des Compositeurs de la Rép. Soc. de Roumanie, 236pp.

1973, *Problèmes d'ethnomusicologie, textes réunis et préfacés par Gilbert Rouget*, Geneva, Minkoff Reprint, 236pp.

Brandel, Rose, 1952, Music of the Giants and the Pygmies of the Belgian Congo, *Journal of the American Musicological Society* V/1, pp. 16–28

1961, *The Music of Central Africa. An Ethnomusicological Study*, The Hague, Martinus Nijhoff, 272pp.

1965, Polyphony in African Music, *The Commonwealth of Music in Honour of Curt Sachs* (G. Reese and R. Brandel eds.), New York, the Free Press, London, Collier-Macmillan Ltd., pp. 26–44

1970, Africa, *Harvard Dictionary of Music*, 2nd edn, pp. 17–24

Bright, William, 1971, Points de contacts entre langage et musique, *Musique en Jeu* V, pp. 67–74

Burchell, William, 1822–24, *Travels in the Interior of Southern Africa*, London, Batchworth, 1953, Vol. II, 473pp.

Caillois, Roger, 1974, La réponse de M. Roger Caillois, *in* Sous la coupole: l'Académie Française a reçu M. Lévi-Strauss, *Le Monde*, 28 June, pp. 21–2

Chailley, Jacques, 1951, *La musique médiévale*, Paris, Ed. du Coudrier, 167pp.

1955, *Formation et transformations du langage musical. I. Echelles*, Paris, Centre de Documentation Universitaire, 214pp.

1959, Essai sur les structures mélodiques, *Revue de Musicologie* XLIV, pp. 139–75

1960, *L'imbroglio des modes*, Paris, Alphonse Leduc, 92pp.

1961, *40 000 ans de musique. L'homme à la découverte de la musique*, Paris, Plon, 326pp.

1963, Intervention suivant l'exposé de M. Barkechli 'Les échelles régulières du cycle des quintes. . .', pp. 174–82, and Synthèse et conclusions, pp. 293–9, *La résonance dans les échelles musicales, Paris 9–14 mai 1960, Etudes réunies et présentées par Edith Weber*, Paris, Editions du CNRS, Colloques Internationaux du CNRS, Sciences Humaines, 403pp.

1964a, Comment entendre la musique populaire, *Journal of the International Folk Music Council* XVI, pp. 47–9

1964b, Ethnomusicologie et harmonie classique, *Les Colloques de Wégimont IV, 1958–1960, Ethnomusicologie III*, Paris, 'Les Belles Lettres', Bibliothèque de la Faculté de Philosophie et Lettres de l'Université de Liège, Fasc. CLXXII, pp. 249–69

1967, *La musique et le signe*, Lausanne, Les Editions Rencontre, 128pp.

Cloarec-Heiss, France, 1972, *Le verbe banda. Etudes du syntagme verbal dans une langue oubanguienne de République Centrafricaine*, Paris, SELAF (Tradition Orale 3), 136pp.

Cloarec-Heiss, France and Thomas, Jacqueline M.C., 1978, *L'aka, langue bantoue des Pygmées de Mongoumba (Centrafrique): Introduction à l'étude linguistique. Phonologie*, Paris, SELAF (Tradition Orale 28, Etudes Pygmées II), 204pp.

Collaer, Paul, 1954, Notes sur la musique d'Afrique Centrale, *Problèmes d'Afrique Centrale* XXVI, pp. 267–71

Cooper, Grosvenor and Meyer, Leonard B., 1960, *The Rhythmic Structure of Music*, Chicago, the University of Chicago Press, ix–212pp.

Coussemaker, Edmond de, 1852, *Histoire de l'harmonie au moyen-âge*, Paris, V. Didron, xiii–374pp.

Dapper, Olfert, 1696, *Description de l'Afrique, contenant les noms, la situation & les confins de toutes ses parties. . ., les moeurs, coûtumes, la langue. . .*, Amsterdam, W. Waesberge, Bloom & van Someren, iv–534pp.

Dauer, A.M., 1966, Afrikanische Musik und völkerkundlicher Tonfilm. Ein Beitrag zur Methodik der Transkription, *Research Film* V/5, pp. 439–56

   1969, Research films in ethnomusicology: Aims and Achievements, *Yearbook of the International Folk Music Council*, I, pp. 226–31

Dehoux, Vincent, 1986, *Les 'chants à penser' des Gbaya (Centrafrique)*, Paris, SELAF (Ethnomusicologie II), 219pp.

Éboué, Félix, 1933, *Les peuples de l'Oubangui-Chari. Essai d'ethnographie, de linguistique et d'économie sociale*, Paris, Publications du Comité de l'Afrique Française, 104pp.

Eco, Umberto, 1972, *La structure absente. Introduction à la recherche sémiotique*, (trans. from Italian by Uccio Esposito-Torrigiani), Paris, Mercure de France, 447pp.

Emmanuel, Maurice, 1921, Grèce (Art gréco-romain), *Encyclopédie de la Musique et Dictionnaire du Conservatoire* (Lavignac), first part: *Histoire de la Musique, Antiquité-Moyen-Age*, Paris, Delagrave, vol. 1, pp. 337–537.

   1926, Le rythme d'Euripide à Debussy, *Compte rendu du 1er Congrès du Rythme tenu à Genève du 16 au 18 août 1926* (A. Pfrimmer ed.), Geneva, pp. 103–146.

   1928, *Histoire de la langue musicale*, vol. 1: *Antiquité-Moyen-Age*, Paris, H. Laurens, 332pp.

Enc. Fasquelle, 1958–1961, *Encyclopédie de la Musique* (François Michel ed.), Paris, Fasquelle, 3 vols.

England, Nicholas M., 1967, Bushman Counterpoint, *Journal of the International Folk Music Council* XIX, pp. 58–66

Epstein, David, 1981, A Cross-Cultural Study of Musical Tempo, Paper presented to the Working Group on *Biological Aspects of Aesthetics*, Bad-Homburg, Werner-Reimers-Stiftung

Estreicher, Zygmunt, 1957, Une technique de transcription de la musique exotique (Expériences pratiques), *Bibliothèques et Musées de la Ville de Neuchâtel (Rapport), 1956*, Neuchâtel, pp. 67–92

   1964, Le rythme des Peuls Bororo, *Les Colloques de Wégimont IV, 1958–1960, Ethnomusicologie III*, Paris, 'Les Belles Lettres', Bibliothèque de la Faculté de Philosophie et Lettres de l'Université de Liège, Fasc. CLXXII, pp. 185–228

Gardin, Jean-Claude, 1974, *Les analyses de discours*, Neuchâtel, Delachaux et Niestlé (Zethos), 178pp.

Gide, André, 1927, *Voyage au Congo. Carnets de route*, Paris, Gallimard, 86th edn, 246pp.

   1928, *Le retour du Tchad. Carnets de route*, Paris, Gallimard, 57th edn, 252pp.

Golberry, Sylvain Meinrad Xavier de, 1802 [An X], *Fragmens d'un voyage en Afrique: fait pendant les années 1785, 1786 et 1787, dans les contrées occidentales de ce continent, comprises entre le Cap Blanc de Barbarie. . .et le Cap de Palmes. . .*, Paris, 2 vols.

Granger, Gilles-Gaston, 1965, Objets, structure et signification, *Revue Internationale de Philosophie* LXXIII/3, pp. 251–90

1967, *Pensée formelle et sciences de l'homme*, Paris, Aubier-Montaigne, (Analyse et raisons), 226pp.

Grimaud, Yvette, 1957, (with Gilbert Rouget), *Note sur la musique des Bochiman comparée à celle des Pygmées Babinga, d'après les enregistrements de la Mission Marshall au Kalahari (1954) et de la Mission Ogooué-Congo (1946) publiés sur Disque Microsillon LD9*, Cambridge (USA) et Paris, Peabody Museum, Harvard Museum et Musée de l'Homme, French and English text, 20+VII p.

1963, Les polysystèmes des musiques de tradition orale peuvent-ils être intégrés à la résonance?, *La résonance dans les échelles musicales, Paris 9–14 mai 1960, Études réunies et présentées par Édith Weber*, Paris, Éditions du CNRS, Colloques Internationaux du CNRS, Sciences Humaines, pp. 237–48.

1964, Étude analytique de la danse 'Choma' des Bochiman !Kung (Polyrythmie), *Les Colloques de Wégimont IV, 1958-1960, Ethnomusicologie III*, Paris, 'Les Belles Lettres', Bibliothèque de la Faculté de Philosophie et Lettres de Liège, Fasc. CLXXII. pp. 171–83.

Guattini, le R.P. Michel-Ange and Carli, le R.P. Denis de, 1680, *Relation curieuse et nouvelle d'un voyage de Congo: fait és années 1666 & 1667*, Lyon, Amaulry, viii–296pp.

Günther, Robert, 1964, *Musik in Rwanda. Ein Beitrag zur Musikethnologie Zentral-Afrikas*, Tervuren, MRCB, Annales, Série in-8°, Sciences Humaines 50, 129pp.+68pp. of transcriptions

Haardt, Georges-Marie and Audouin-Dubreuil, Louis, 1927, *La croisière noire. Expédition Citroën Centre-Afrique*, Paris, Plon, vii–262pp.

Harrison, Frank, 1973, *Time, Place and Music: An Anthology of Ethnomusicological Observation c. 1500 to c. 1800*, Amsterdam, Frits Knuf, 221pp.

Herzfeld, Friedrich, 1974, *Ullstein Lexikon der Musik*, Frankfurt, Berlin, Vienna, Ullstein Verlag, 631pp.

Herzog, George, 1949, Canon in West African Xylophone Melodies, *Journal of the American Musicological Society* II/3, pp. 196–7

1957, Music at the Fifth International Congress of Anthropological and Ethnological Sciences, *Journal of the International Folk Music Council* IX, pp. 71–3

Hood, Mantle, 1963, Musical Significance, *Ethnomusicology* VII/3, pp. 187–92

1971, *The Ethnomusicologist*, New York, McGraw-Hill, XII+386pp.

Hornbostel, Erich M. von, 1909, Ueber Mehrstimmigkeit in der aussereuropäischen Musik, *Bericht über den Dritten Kongress der Internationalen Musikgesellschaft, Wien, 25-29 Mai 1909*, Wien, Artaria, pp. 298–303

1928, African Negro Music, *Africa, Journal of the International Institute of African Languages and Culture* I/1, pp. 30–62

Hornburg, Friedrich, 1950, Phonographierte Afrikanische Mehrstimmigkeit, *Die Musikforschung* III/2, pp. 120–42+musical transcriptions, pp. 161–76

Jakobson, Roman, 1932, Musicologie et linguistique, rev. in *Musique en Jeu* V, pp. 57–9

1963, *Essais de linguistique générale*, Paris, Ed. de Minuit, 255pp.

1973, *Essais de linguistique générale, II. Rapports internes et externes du langage*, Paris, Ed. de Minuit (Arguments), 317pp.

Jones, A.M., 1934, African Drumming. A study of the combination of rhythms in African Music, *Bantu Studies* VIII/1, pp. 1–16

1937, The Study of African Musical Rhythms, *Bantu Studies* XI, pp. 295–319

1954, African Rhythm, *Africa, Journal of the International African Institute* XXIV, pp. 26–47

1958a, *African Music in Northern Rhodesia and some other places*, Livingstone, The Rhodes-Livingstone Museum, 80pp.

1958b, On Transcribing African Music, *African Music* II/1, pp. 11-14

1959, *Studies in African Music*, London, Oxford University Press, 2 vols.

Jones, A.M. and Kombe, L., 1952, *The Icila Dance Old Style. A Study in African Music and Dance of the Lala Tribe of Northern Rhodesia*, Cape Town, Longmans, Green and Co. for African Music Society, 49pp.

Joyeux, Charles, 1910, Notes sur quelques manifestations musicales observées en Haute-Guinée, *La Revue Musicale* X/2, pp. 49-58

1924, Etude sur quelques manifestations musicales observées en Haute-Guinée Française, *Revue d'Ethnographie et des Traditions populaires* V/18, pp. 170-212

Junod, Henri A., 1936, *Moeurs et coutumes des Bantous. La vie d'une tribu sud-africaine*, Paris, Payot, 2 vols.

Kalck, Pierre, 1974, *Histoire de la République Centrafricaine des origines préhistoriques à nos jours*, Paris, Berger-Levrault (Mondes d'Outre-Mer), 341pp.

Kirby, Percival R., 1930, A Study of Negro Harmony, *The Musical Quarterly* XVI/3, pp. 404-30

1933, The Reed-Flutes Ensembles of South Africa: A study in South African Native Music, *Journal of the Royal Anthropological Institute of Great Britain and Ireland* LXIII, pp. 313-88

1934, *The Musical Instruments of the Native Races of South Africa*, London, Oxford University Press, 285pp.

1949, Bantu, *M.G.G.*, vol. I, pp. 1219-28

Koetting, James, 1970, Analysis and Notation of West African drum ensemble music, *Selected Reports*, vol. I/3, Los Angeles, University of California, pp. 116-46

Kolb, Peter, 1719, *Caput Bonae Spei hodiernum, das ist: vollständige Beschreibung des africanischen Vorgebürges der Guten Hofnung,. . .was die eigenen Einwohner, die Hottentoten, vor seltsame Sitten und Gebraüche haben. . .*, Nürnberg, bey P.C. Monath, 846pp.

Kolbe, Pierre, 1741, *Description du Cap de Bonne-Espérance: Où l'on trouve tout ce qui concerne l'histoire naturelle du pays; La religion, les moeurs & les usages des Hottentots; et l'établissement des Hollandais. Tirée des Mémoires de Mr. Pierre Kolbe, Maître ès Arts, Dressés pendant un séjour de dix Années dans cette Colonie, où il avoit été envoyé pour faire des Observations Astronomiques & Physiques*, Tome Premier. A Amsterdam, chez Jean Catuffe, xx-370pp.

Kolinski, Mieczyslaw, 1960, Compte rendu de A.M. Jones: Studies in African Music, *The Musical Quarterly*, XVI/1, pp. 105-10

1973, A Cross-Cultural Approach to Metro-Rhythmic Patterns, *Ethnomusicology* XVII/3, pp. 494-506

Kubik, Gerhard, 1961, Musikgestaltung in Afrika, *Neues Afrika* V, pp. 195-200

1962, Oral Notation on some West and Central African Time-Line Patterns, *Review of Ethnology* III/22 (Vienna), pp. 169-76

1964a, Harp Music of the Azande and Related Peoples in the Central African Republic (Part I - Horizontal Harp Playing), *African Music* III/3, pp. 37-76

1964b, Xylophone Playing in Southern Uganda, *The Journal of the Royal Anthropological Institute* 94/2, pp. 138-59

1965, Transcription of Mangwilo Xylophone Music from Film Strips, *African Music* III/4, pp. 35-51

1967 (with Maurice Djenda), Music in the Central African Republic, *Afrika* VIII/1, pp. 44-8

1968, *Mehrstimmigkeit und Tonsysteme in Zentral- und Ostafrika. Bemerkungen zu den eigenen, im Phonogrammarchiv der Oesterreichischen Akademie der Wissenschaften archivierten Expeditionsaufnahmen*, Vienna, Böhlaus, Oesterreichische Akademie der Wissenschaften (Sitzungberichte), 65pp.

1969, Transmission et transcription des éléments de musique instrumental africaine, *Bulletin of the International Committee on Urgent Anthropological and Ethnological Research* XI, pp. 47–61

1974, Contributor to: 'African Peoples, Arts of' III 'African Music' *Encyclopaedia Britannica*, 15th edn, London

Kunst, Jaap, 1950, *Métrique, rythmique, musique à plusieurs voix* (Ethnomusicologica I), Leiden, E.J. Brill, 47pp.

Labat, Jean-Baptiste (Père), 1728, *Nouvelle relation de l'Afrique occidentale contenant une description exacte de Senegal & des Païs situés entre le Cap-Blanc & la Riviere de Serrelionne. . .*, Paris, G. Cavelier, 5 vols.

1730, *Voyage du Chevalier des Marchais en Guinée, isles voisines, et en Cayenne, Fait en 1725, 1726 & 1727. . .*, Paris, Saugran l'ainé, 4 vols.

1732, *Relation historique de l'Ethiopie occidentale, contenant la description des royaumes de Congo, Angolle et Matamba. . ., traduite de l'italien. . .et augmentée de plusieurs relations portugaises des meilleurs auteurs. . .*, Paris, C.J.B. Delespine le fils, 5 vols.

Lajtha, Laszlö, 1956, A propos de l'"intonation fausse' dans la musique populaire, *Les Colloques de Wégimont, Cercle International d'Études Ethnomusicologiques*, Brussels, Elsevier, pp. 145–53

Larousse de la Musique, (Norbert Dufourcq ed.), 1957, Paris, Larousse, 2 vols., 627+644pp.

Leng, Ladislav, 1959, Technische Probleme bei der Schallaufzeichnung mehrstimmiger Volksmusik, *Studia instrumentorum musicae popularis 1, Bericht über die 2. Internationale Arbeitstagung der Study Group on Folk Musical Instruments des International Folk Music Council in Brno, 1967* (Erich Stockmann ed.), Stockholm, Musikhistoriska Museets Skrifter 3, Musikhistoriska Museet, pp. 171–5

Lévi-Strauss, Claude, 1960, La structure et la forme, *Cahiers de l'Institut de sciences économiques*, 1960, XCIX, pp. 3–36

1964, *Le cru et le cuit* (Mythologiques I), Paris, Plon 402pp.

List, George, 1963, The musical significance of transcription, *Ethnomusicology* VII/3, pp. 193–7

1974, The reliability of transcription, *Ethnomusicology* XVII/3, pp. 353–77

Lomax, Alan, 1959, Folksong style, *American Anthropologist*, LXI/6, pp. 927–54

1968, *Folk Song Style and Culture* (with contributions by the Cantometrics Staff and with the editorial assistance of Edwin E. Erikson), Washington D.C., American Association for the Advancement of Science (Publication No. 88), xiii–363pp.

Mache, François-Bernard, 1971, Méthodes linguistiques et musicologie, *Musique en Jeu* V, pp. 75–91

Malm, William P., 1972, On the meaning and invention of the term "disphony", *Ethnomusicology* XVI/2, pp. 247–9

Maquet, Jean-Noël, 1954, La musique chez les Bapende, *Problèmes d'Afrique Centrale*, XXVI/4, pp. 299–315

1956, La musique chez les Pende et les Tshokwe, *Les Colloques de Wégimont, Cercle International d'Études Ethnomusicologiques*, Brussels, Elsevier, pp. 169–87.

Marcel-Dubois, Claudie, 1965, Le tempo dans les musiques de tradition orale, *Fontes Artis Musicae* XII/2–3, pp. 204–6

Meillet, Antoine, 1937, *Introduction à l'étude comparative des langues indo-européennes*, Paris, Hachette, 8th edn, xiv–516pp.

Merriam, Alan P., 1959, Characteristics of African Music, *Journal of the International Folk Music Council* XI, pp. 13–18

1962, The African idiom in music, *Journal of American Foklore* LXXV/2, pp. 120–30

1964, *The Anthropology of Music*, Evanston, Northwestern University Press, xi–358pp.

Mersenne, Marin, 1636, *Harmonie universelle*, Paris, Vol. II, *Livre Cinquième*, Facsimilé edn, 1963, Paris, Éditions du CNRS, 442pp.

M.G.G., 1949–1979, *Die Musik in Geschichte und Gegenwart*. . ., XVI vols.

Moles, Abraham A., 1983, Concept of Rhythm Periodicity and Time Series in Musical Aesthetics, paper presented to the Working Group on *Biological Aspects of Aesthetics*, Bad-Homburg, Werner-Reimers-Stiftung

Molino, Jean, 1975, Fait musical et sémiologie de la musique, *Musique en Jeu* XVII, pp. 37–62

Morelet, Arthur, 1864, *Journal du voyage de Vasco da Gama en 1497* (translated from Portuguese by Arthur Morelet, corresponding member of the Academie of Sciences of Lisbon), Lyon, Imprimerie de Louis Perrin, xxx–140pp.

Nattiez, Jean-Jacques, 1975, *Fondements d'une sémiologie de la musique*, Paris, Union Générale d'Editions (10/18), 448pp.

Nettl, Bruno, 1956, *Music in Primitive Culture*, Cambridge (Mass.), Harvard University Press, 182pp.

1964, *Theory and Method in Ethnomusicology*, New York & London, Collier-Macmillan Publishers, 306pp.

1971, De quelques méthodes linguistiques appliquées à l'analyse musicale, *Musique en Jeu* V, pp. 61–6

Nketia, J.H. Kwabenia, 1962, The Hocket-Technique in African Music, *Journal of the International Folk Music Council* XIV, pp. 44–52

1963, *Folk Songs of Ghana*, Legon, University of Ghana, 205pp.

1972, Les langages musicaux de l'Afrique Subsaharienne. Etude comparative, *La musique africaine. Réunion de Yaoundé (Cameroun), 23–30 février 1970, organisée par l'UNESCO. La Revue Musicale* 288–289, pp. 7–42

1975, *The Music of Africa*, London, Victor Gollancz, viii–278pp.

Pantaleoni, Hewitt, 1972, The three Principles of Timing in Anlo Dancing Drumming, *African Music* V/2, pp. 50–7

Park, Mungo, 1800 [An VIII], *Voyage dans l'intérieur de l'Afrique, fait en 1795, 1796 et 1797 . . .*, Paris, Dentu et Casteret, 2 vols.

Pepper, Herbert, 1950, Musique Centre Africaine, *Afrique Équatoriale Française*, Paris, Encyclopédie Coloniale et Maritime, pp. 553–72

Pike, Kenneth, 1954–1955, *Language in Relation to a Unified Theory of the Structure of Human Behaviour*, Glendale (Calif.), Summer Institute of Linguistics, 2 vols.

Reinhard, Kurt, 1968, *Einführung in die Musikethnologie*, Wolfenbüttel und Zurich, Möseler, 119pp.

Ricks, Robert, 1969, Russian Horn Bands, *The Musical Quarterly* LV/3, pp. 364–72

Riemann, Hugo, 1931, *Dictionnaire de Musique*, Paris, Payot, 2 vols.

Riemann Musiklexikon, 1967, vol. 3: *Sachteil*, Mainz, Schott, 1087pp.

Rouget, Gilbert, 1956, A propos de la forme dans les musiques de tradition orale, *Les Colloques de Wégimont. Cercle International d'Études Ethnomusicologiques*, Brussels, Elsevier, pp. 132–44

1959, *Musique pygmée de la Haute-Sangha* (record sleeve) Paris, BAM LD 325

1961a, La musique en Afrique Noire, *Enc. Fasquelle*, vol. III, p. 939–40

1961b, Un chromatisme africain, *L'Homme. Revue Française d'Anthropologie* I/3, pp. 1–15

Roulet, Eddy, 1974, *Linguistique et comportement humain. L'analyse tagmémique de Pike*, Neuchâtel, Delachaux et Niestlé, 139pp.

Roulon, Paulette, 1976, Litanie et expressivité: la litanie en pays gbaya (RCA), *Journal de Psychologie Normale et Pathologique* III–IV, pp. 379–90

Rousseau, Jean-Jacques, 1768, *Dictionnaire de la Musique*, Paris, chez la veuve Duchesne, 547pp.

Ruwet, Nicolas, 1966, Méthodes d'analyse en musicologie, *Revue Belge de Musicologie* XX, pp. 65–90, rev. 1972 in *Langage, musique, poésie*, Paris, Ed. du Seuil (Poétique), pp. 100–34

Rycroft, David, 1967, Nguni Vocal Polyphony, *Journal of the International Folk Musik Council* XIX, pp. 88–103

Sachs, Curt, 1953, *Rhythm and Tempo. A Study in Music History*, New York, W.W. Norton, 391pp.

1962, *The Wellsprings of Music*, Amsterdam, Martinus Nijhoff, 228pp.

1964, *Reallexikon der Musikinstrumente*, Hildesheim, Georg Olms Verlagbuchhandlung (Olms Paperback Band 3), 442pp.

Saussure, Ferdinand de, 1916, *Cours de linguistique générale*, rev. 1971, Paris, Payot, 331pp.

Schaeffner, André, 1936, *Origine des instruments de musique. Introduction ethnologique à l'histoire de la musique instrumentale*, Paris, Payot, 405pp.

1950, La découverte de la musique noire, *Le Monde Noir*, Présence Africaine, special issue VIII–IX, pp. 205–18

1951, *Les Kissi, une société noire et ses instruments de musique*, Paris, Hermann & Cie (L'Homme 2), 86pp.

Schmidt-Wrenger, Barbara, 1975, *Musique des Tshokwe du Zaïre*, (record sleeve), Coll. "Enregistrements de musique africaine édités par le Musée Royal de l'Afrique Centrale, Tervuren", n° 11, 81 pp.

Schneider, Marius, 1934, *Geschichte der Mehrstimmigkeit. Erster Teil: Die Naturvölker*, Berlin, Julius Bard Verlag, 107+47pp.

1951, Ist die vokale Mehrstimmigkeit eine Schöpfung der Altrassen? *Acta Musicologica* XXIII/1–3, pp. 40–50

1957, Primitive Music, *The New Oxford History of Music*, vol. 1: *Ancient and Oriental Music*, London, Oxford University Press, pp. 1–82

1963, Présence ou absence de la constante de quarte, de quinte, d'octave et de tierce. Son rôle structurel dans la consonance polyphonique primitive, *La résonance dans les échelles musicales, Paris 9–14 mai 1960, Études réunies et présentées par Édith Weber*, Paris, Éditions du CNRS, Colloques Internationaux du CNRS, Sciences Humaines, pp. 150–8.

Schünemann, Georg, 1913, *Geschichte des Dirigierens*, Leipzig, Breitkopf & Härtel, ix–359pp.

Schweinfurth, George, 1875, *Au coeur de l'Afrique 1868–1871. . .*, Paris, Hachette, 2 vols.

Science de la Musique: Formes, Technique, Instruments, 1976 (M. Honegger ed.), Paris, Bordas, 2 vols.

Seeger, Charles, 1958, Prescriptive and Descriptive Music Writing, *Musical Quarterly* XLIV/2, pp. 184–95

Seeger, Horst, 1966, *Musiklexikon in Zwei Bänden*, Leipzig, VEB, Deutscher Verlag für Musik, 2 vols.

Senghor, Léopold Sédar, 1958, *Liberté 1. Négritude et humanisme*, Paris, Éd. du Seuil, rev. 1964, 444pp.

Springer, George P., 1971, Le langage et la musique: parallélisme et divergences, *Musique en Jeu* V, pp. 31–43

Strasbaugh, Lamar Gene, 1973, Two Lullabies from the Babinga Babenzele Pygmies. Transcriptions, analysis and commentary, *Mitteilungen der Deutschen Gesellschaft für Musik des Orients* XI, pp. 79–101

Tiby, Ottavio, 1960, La musique des civilisations gréco-latines, *Histoire de la Musique. I. Des origines à Jean-Sébastien Bach*, Roland-Manuel ed., Paris, Gallimard (La Pléiade), pp. 377–449

Tiersot, Julien, 1922, La musique chez les Nègres d'Afrique, *Encyclopédie de la Musique et Dictionnaire du Conservatoire* (Lavignac). first part: *Histoire de la Musique*, vol. 5, Paris, Delagrave, pp. 3197–225

Thomas, Jacqueline M.C., 1970, (with Simha Arom and Marcel Mavode), *Contes, proverbes, devinettes ou énigmes, chants et prières ngbaka-ma'bo (République Centrafricaine)*, Paris, Klincksieck (Langues et Littératures d'Afrique Noire VI), 908pp.

Thomas, Jacqueline, M.C., and Bachuchet, Serge (eds.), 1983, *Encyclopédie des Pygmées Aka. Techniques, langage et société des chasseurs-cueilleurs de la forêt centrafricaine (Sud-Centrafrique et Nord-Congo)*, I. *Les Pygmées Aka. Introduction à l'Encyclopédie*, fasc. 1 Paris, SELAF (Tradition Orale 50, Études Pygmées IV), 135pp.

Tracey, Hugh, 1958, Towards an Assessment of African Scales, *African Music* II/1, pp 10-20

Trân văn Khé, 1968, Modes musicaux, *Encyclopedia Universalis*, Paris, vol. 11, pp. 148-53

Wachsmann, Klaus P., 1953, *Tribal Crafts of Uganda. Part Two: The Sound Instruments*, London, Oxford University Press, xxi-422pp.

Waterman, Richard Alan, 1952, African Influence on the Music of the Americas, *Acculturation in the Americas. Proceeding and Selected Papers of the XXIXth International Congress of Americanists* (Sol Tax ed.), Chicago, University of Chicago Press, pp. 207-18

Wegner, Max, 1956, Griechenland. A. Antike. B. Griechische Instrumente und Musikbräuche, *M.G.G.* vol. V, pp. 865-81

Wiora, Walter, 1963a, Le point de vue des musicologues, *La résonance dans les échelles musicales, Paris, 9-14 mai 1960, Études réunies et présentées par Édith Weber*, Paris, Éditions du CNRS, Colloques Internationaux du CNRS, Sciences Humaines, pp. 38-42

1963b, Présence ou absence de la constante de quarte, de quinte et d'octave. Son rôle structurel dans l'ethnomusicologie primitive, *La résonance dans les échelles musicales*. . . (see above)